THINKING ABOUT SOCIETY: THEORY AND PRACTICE

BOSTON STUDIES IN THE PHILOSOPHY OF SCIENCE

EDITED BY ROBERT S. COHEN AND MARX W. WARTOFSKY

VOLUME 93

I. C. JARVIE

Professor of Philosophy at York University, Toronto

THINKING
ABOUT SOCIETY:
THEORY
AND PRACTICE

D. REIDEL PUBLISHING COMPANY

A MEMBER OF THE KLUWER ACADEMIC PUBLISHERS GROUP

DORDRECHT / BOSTON / LANCASTER / TOKYO

Library of Congress Cataloging in Publication Data

Jarvie, I. C. (Ian Charles), 1937–
    Thinking about society.

    (Boston studies in the philosophy of science ; v. 93)
    Bibliography: p.
    Includes indexes.
        1.   Social sciences—Philosophy.   2.   Social sciences—
Methodology.   3.   Sociology—Philosophy.   4.   Anthropology—
Philosophy.   I.   Title.   II.   Series.
Q174.B67 vol. 93 [H61]   001'.01 s   85–24420
ISBN 90–277–2068–1   [300'.1]

Published by D. Reidel Publishing Company,
P.O. Box 17, 3300 AA Dordrecht, Holland.

Sold and distributed in the U.S.A. and Canada
by Kluwer Academic Publishers,
190 Old Derby Street, Hingham, MA 02043, U.S.A.

In all other countries, sold and distributed
by Kluwer Academic Publishers Group,
P.O. Box 322, 3300 AH Dordrecht, Holland.

Printed in The Netherlands

For
MAX

TABLE OF CONTENTS

EDITORIAL PREFACE

I. C. Jarvie was trained as a social anthropologist in the center of British social anthropology — the London School of Economics, where Bronislaw Malinowski was the object of ancestor worship. Jarvie's doctorate was in philosophy, however, under the guidance of Karl Popper and John Watkins. He changed his department not as a defector but as a rebel, attempting to exorcize the ancestral spirit. He criticized the method of participant observation not as useless but as not comprehensive: it is neither necessary nor sufficient for the making of certain contributions to anthropology; rather, it all depends on the problem-situation. And so Jarvie remained an anthropologist at heart, who, in addition to some studies in rather conventional anthropological or sociological molds, also studied the tribe of social scientists, but also critically examining their problems — especially their overall, rather philosophical problems, but not always so: a few of the studies included in this volume exemplify his work on specific issues, whether of technology, or architecture, or nationalism in the academy, or moviemaking, or even movies exhibiting excessive sex and violence. These studies attract his attention both on account of their own merit and on account of their need for new and powerful research tools, such as those which he has forged in his own intellectual workshop over the last two decades.

The hallmark of Jarvie is just this: his patient readiness to comprehend the social settings which give rise to a problem, as well as that which that problem addresses. He thereby achieved two results distinctly his own. First, by patiently examining extant and erroneous views — whether extant solutions to given problems or extant background presuppositions with which they are currently approached — Jarvie attempts to list all the assets of the errors he wishes eliminated and all the functions they fulfill, well or not-so-well, so that it becomes clear what is required of any substitute for the old error. Second, by a careful situational analysis of social change he managed to explain such change as the results of changes of every ingredient of the situation — the total changing physical or social circumstances — by the changing views and values of the people involved, as well as by the changing degrees of rationality of the actors who initiate or institute the changes; and he applies situational analysis, further, to explain the changes in views, values, and rationality. He has thus met the complaint, quite traditional and quite well-known, that situational analysis cannot cope with social change, whose explanation is said to require the *ad hoc* introduction of extra factors into the situational analysis (such as the rise of charismatic leaders).

Since Jarvie is the author of a goodly number of powerful monographs, we stress that this volume avoids both repetition and the inclusion of odds and ends: it presents the best of Jarvie to illustrate his research methods. His rules are deceptively simple and quite well-known: pin-point a problem, describe it and its background explicitly and clearly, discuss extant solutions, their strengths and weaknesses, and the significance of all this to the people thus studied. The examples of Jarvie's own researches are therefore enlightening in that they show that this simple advice is not usually heeded, and hardly ever all the way. His ability to follow his rules, and to explain changes of values as well as social change, characterizes him as a critical and imaginative social research investigator as well as a distinguished social philosopher.

September 1985   JOSEPH AGASSI
                                                                    ROBERT S. COHEN

INTRODUCTION

There is a standard formula for writing about the philosophy of the social sciences. Starting from a philosophical position, such as logical empiricism, or, more narrowly, a recent "result" of that doctrine, an attempt is made to apply it to the social sciences generally. Where application is specific the example will frequently be a commonsense one: why did x kill y, why did x cross the road, etc. By means of this formula it is easy to show that: the social sciences closely resemble the natural sciences; the social sciences are nothing like the natural sciences, and all positions in between. It is notable that the formula is the same whether the writing is by a social scientist seeking enlightenment by dabbling in the philosophical literature, or a philosopher condescending to help out social scientists by sharing current results in his 'field.'

The dry and abstract quality of such formulaic philosophy of the social sciences is not the worst of its faults. The worst fault is that such philosophy of the social sciences is an exercise in futile intellectual ingenuity. Futile because the exercise is directed to no good purpose; it solves no problem. Ingenuity thus very quickly spends itself on the pursuit of trivial detail through formulae; or on windy if not murky language. Both results are metaphysical in the bad sense, the sense in which nothing is being said.

Although my trade is philosophy, it would be unfair of me to suggest that the worst sinners in the use of this formula are philosophers. For every philosopher with no problem more serious than extending the hegemony of doctrines to which he is partial, there are social scientists eagerly casting around in philosophy looking for the latest "results" to appropriate to castigate their colleagues. An often noted feature of philosophy ensures such searches are fruitful. Philosophy is subject to frequent radicalist revolutions which declare all previous work superseded; there is thus an endlessly renewed supply of "results" to keep philosophers and social scientists going with new variants of the formula. Recent examples are logical empiricism, Hermeneutics, Marxism, epistemological anarchism, methodology of scientific research programmes.

The use of the formula in search of intellectual power over others calls for no special comment. The slide over into sterile kinds of metaphysics does.

Why should philosophising about the social sciences be prone to generate metaphysics? The answer is, I conjecture, that society itself and all the things we study as part of it are abstract objects. The group, the tribe, the institution, the role, the class, the structure, the collectivity, the social relations, all of these 'things' are very abstract sorts of things. Mostly they cannot be seen, heard, tasted, touched, or smelled. They are, as I argued in *Concepts and Society* (1972), abstractions devised to organise and explain the phenomena of human life. One of the reasons, perhaps, for recurrent positivist spasms is the tendency of our abstractions to take on a life of their own, to preoccupy us, to distract us from the real world problems to solve which they were devised.

If my own efforts in philosophy of the social sciences differ in any global way from the formula style it stems from the effort to retain contact with concrete things and the problems to which they gave rise. Thus my concern has been less with applying Popper's philosophical "results" to the social sciences, than with using his philosophy to try to solve problems of social thought.

The papers assembled in this book, which have appeared over the course of some twenty years, fall into two groups. First, a group that grapples with the claim that there are special methodological and conceptual features of the social sciences (Part I); second, a group that applies ideas from the social sciences, mainly functionalist ideas, to specific problems in social life (Part II). This placement of methodology before substance misrepresents my view of their order of priority. It is problems of explanation of society that stimulate fruitful methodological and conceptual discussion, in my view, and such discussion should interleave rather than precede work on those problems. Yet in the ordering of a book such as this, placing the more abstract methodological and philosophical chapters first feels right, looks more 'logical'. So the arrangement is a concession to the standard view rejected in the book itself.

Not only is this standard view rejected here, its rejection is followed through in my own career. By avocation a social scientist since my mid-teens, first in economics, economic history and geography, later in social anthropology, the turn to philosophy developed late out of dissatisfaction with the prevailing mode of explanation in social anthropology. This immensely fruitful and powerful social science, rightly regarded as second only to economics, was powered by the structural-functional tradition created by Bronislaw Malinowski and A. R. Radcliffe-Brown. Because of its claim to power and frutifulness, the merits and limitations of this tradition were hotly debated among teachers and fellow-students at the London School of Economics (and wherever there was a strong outpost of the tradition). While I accepted the strong claim for the superior status of social anthropology it was always with a sense that it could be still stronger and more fuitful if certain weaknesses were overcome. One weakness identified by Gellner was the explanation of social change, one identified by Popper was the use of a pseudo-empirical inductive method. A comprehensive attempt to expose and correct these weaknesses was made in my book *The Revolution in Anthropology* (1964), which attached all its methodological strictures to the study of a single problem of social change: cargo cults. A genuine problem of social explanation was to be clarified and moved nearer to solution with the help of philosophy.

This project at the intersection of anthropology and philosophy had an unintended consequence: it showed the need to discuss the philosophy and anthropology of anthropology (Gellner's parallel project of studying the philosophy and anthropology of philosophy was an inspiration). One problem which kept recurring concerned the relation of anthropology to empirical observation, to fieldwork. Inductive solutions face quite insuperable logical difficulties, so all attempts to base the empirical method on induction were bound to fail. Disappointment at the failure of induction to yield progress might, I thought, tempt anthropologists to abandon the empirical tradition unless an alternative could be worked out. Popper's alternative model of empiricism could explain the relation of anthropology to fieldwork as one of falsifiability. Despite my efforts in this direction, the prediction about abandoning the empirical tradition came true with the rise of a "symbolic anthropology" that espouses relativism and repudiates truth and rationality along with empirical science. The rise of symbolic anthropology could be explained philosophically; it was a turn towards the irrational brought about by disappointed expectations of the empirical method. One way of combatting it was to expose its philosophical errors. To allow disappointment to push one into repudiation of a goal is irrational; to assume induction is the only empirical method is a logical mistake; to embrace the irrational on the rebound is effectively to embrace nothing at all. Several papers in this volume take up these themes. Diagnosing errors was only part of the task I set myself; clearly symbolic anthropology was more than reactive; it also had positive appeal. Anthropologists were not alone in being seduced by irrationalist philosophy. Symbolic anthropologists were interested in the conceptual character of society, the way society is constituted by its member's conceptions of it. Mentality, thus, was to be found in the collective — not quite as

Durkheim envisaged it, but not without debt to him. Such rationality as there was in this I endeavoured to sift out in *Concepts and Society* (1972). Without denying that symbolic interpretations are good fun (anything but good *clean* fun!), they were clearly an abnegation of the traditional rationalist interest in explaining things. A standard anthropological challenge, namely, why do *those* people symbolise *that* in just *those* ways, was one they could to meet. To carry further the developing project of explicating a non-inductive explanatory anthropology it seemed appropriate to elaborate on what a social science should be like: the logical role of its empirical base, its objectivity, its ethics, the nature of the entities it postulates and the conclusions about human diversity it supports. These are the subjects of Chapters 1 through 5 and recur elsewhere throughout the volume. The touchstone of all my more general reflections was close analysis of the case of social anthropology, arguing for its non-inductivist origins (Chapter 6), its non-inductive method (Chapter 7), the logic of its functionalist explanations (Chapter 8), its objectivity (Chapter 9), its moral self-deception (Chapter 10), its scientific character (Chapter 11 and 12), and against its tendency to irrationalism and symbolism (Chapters 12 through 16).

Moving beyond these philosophical concerns to apply the emerging ideas to genuine social questions produces in Part II two chapters on the creation and criticism of art (Chapters 17 and 18), four on the position of technology in society (Chapters 19 through 22), and three on issues of social control: the nation (Chapter 23), the movies (Chapter 24) and studies of media sex and violence and efforts to control them (Chapter 25).

ACKNOWLEDGEMENTS

To my former graduate assistant, Noam Ziv, warm thanks for conceiving of the project of this volume, for making the initial selection of pieces, and for arranging for it to be published. The final selection and arrangement differs slightly from his. Individuals and institutions are thanked in footnotes where appropriate, editors and journals in a separate list at the end. Almost every line in the book was gone over at one time or another by my colleague Joseph Agassi, to whom I am indebted for this and much else. One day, it would be nice to think, the book may catch the interest of my son Max, to whom, therefore, it is dedicated.

Toronto, December 1984

PART I

PROBLEMS AND THEORIES IN THE
SOCIAL SCIENCES

CHAPTER 1

The Notion of a Social Science

As a philosopher of the social sciences, addressing a symposium on recent approaches to the social sciences, I reflexively ask, what is it about the social sciences that leads them again and again to reflect upon themselves, that has even given rise to specialists in such self-reflection, for example myself, and frequent invitations to them to renew and restate their inquiry? My answer to this question is that the social sciences are haunted by the example of the natural sciences, and the philosopher of the social sciences is an exorcist, a specialist in getting rid of ghosts, who performs an exorcism ceremony consisting of reflections on the state of the art. However ironic this sounds, it is seriously meant. In the course of today's exorcism ceremony I hope to invoke some exciting recent work in the philosophy of the social sciences, work which helps me at least to combat and dispel the haunting effect of the natural sciences. Such recent work is important less because it devises new positions and more because it breaks down some old polarities and distinctions, one of the most pernicious of which is the very demarcation between the natural and the social. To stop the haunting it is necessary to show that the ghostly phenomena are perfectly understandable, unmysterious events in this world.

My paper advances through several distinct stages. To begin with, I want to back up my claim that we in the social sciences are haunted by the example of the natural sciences. Following that I shall sketch various observable reactions to that haunting. Only then shall I be in a position to attempt my exorcism. This will consist in various arguments that criticize the usual distinction between the natural and the social sciences. Instead, I suggest we should view the scientific enterprise as a unified whole, and hence draw any distinction between what is natural and what is social *within* the unified enterprise of science. The differences, if any, between the natural and the social then become a subject of empirical investigation, rather than an *a priori* or metaphysical demarcation between two sorts of sciences, natural and social.

Moving between methodological, metaphysical, and quasi-historical arguments, the paper may not always strike you as decisive. So be it. To add what plausibility I can I shall also endeavour to show how what are conventionally thought of as the natural and the social constantly intermingle, and that the distinction between them, if any, has as a matter of fact to be worked out in any science as it goes along.

I

Haunted by Natural Science

Throughout the modern era all of man's cognitive efforts have been undertaken in the dominating shadow of the success of the natural sciences—in a situation somewhat similar to that in which some scholars claim Greek thinkers laboured under the shadow of the success of mathematics.[1] By almost any criterion you cared to set up, physics, chemistry and biology were in their turn successful: by criteria of practical applicability, predictive power, simplicity, abstraction, mechanization, explanation of the puzzling, whatever. Accepting for the sake of the argument the received view of the Middle Ages as a time of social, political and cognitive stagnation; and also the received view of the sixteenth and subsequent centuries as ones of great social, political and cognitive change; we cannot but notice the vast number of books, pamphlets and broadsheets that appeared in the post-Medieval period. It was a time of religious, social and political upheaval, that was expressed in these writings, writings to which much of contemporary political science, economics, anthropology, psychology and sociology can be traced back. Despite these roots into the fairly distant past, it is often said that our cognitive endeavours in the social field are feeble compared to those in the natural sciences. Sometimes, in a spirit of charity, an exception to this generalization is made for economics. Otherwise, the social sciences are often declared to fall short of the natural sciences by the same criteria of success: practical applicability, predictive power, simplicity, abstraction, mechanization, explanation of the puzzling, etc. Above all, by the criterion of cumulative progress, it is held that the social sciences compare poorly to the natural sciences.[2] More *natural* phenomena are explainable today than was the case in 1578; it is at least arguable whether more *social* phenomena are explainable today than in 1578. To offer the excuse that these subjects are new is scarcely credible, since their problems and therefore speculation on their problems has to be as old as speculation of any kind. To explain their poor performance by their youth may be to put the cart before the horse. They appear not to be mature, but since they have longevity we cannot infer to their youth.

Several responses to this perceived state of affairs are possible, and each of them has from time to time been adopted. One is to endeavour to build social sciences that meet some or all of the criteria for success mentioned above. This is *naturalism*. It accepts that the criteria for success in natural science are applicable *pari passu* to the social sciences. Another response is to question the appropriateness of these criteria for success and hence of the use of the natural sciences as a model for the social sciences. *This is anti-naturalism*. A third response is very radical: to suggest that the way the social is studied, albeit fragmentary as yet, might be taken as a model for the natural sciences, rather than *vice versa*. Different criteria of success may be invoked; indeed, treating success as a virtue may be questioned. Science is a human activity, perhaps, and should be judged as such, not be encouraged to be a cold and mechanical calculation. If I were a punster I would call this holding up of the social as a model for the study of the natural—parallelling naturalism—socialism. However, that word having been preempted for other purposes, I will choose *humanism*.

I have started with the historical situation created for social studies by the existence of developed natural sciences. That is supposed to be the situation of the modern period, even if it is not the situation of the ancient period. But this way of talking of things presupposes, implicitly if not explicitly, an unproblematic demarcation between the natural world and the social world, and hence between studies of the natural and studies of the social.[3] Notice that naturalism, anti-naturalism and humanism all accept that there are natural studies and there are human studies. Whether one should ape the other, as naturalism and humanism maintain, or they should go their separate ways—as anti-naturalism maintains, it is acknowledged that they are separate and distinct. This is an assumption in common that I shall challenge. For the moment it is enough to notice it and to stress its

philosophical and historical importance. Its key component is
that although the study of nature is an endeavour undertaken by
human beings, it is not just another social activity. It has an
autonomy and separateness all its own.

When Copernicus, Kepler, Galileo and Newton worked on
celestial and terrestrial mechanics, they did not bother to suit their
findings to harmonize with such social factors as public opinion,
morality, taboo, status and power.[4] On the contrary, they urged
the autonomy of the scientific enterprise whatever offence it gave
to its sponsors or the authorities. The received views they opposed
usually meshed neatly into the existing social fabric, and they
could hardly fail to be aware of the repercussions their ideas might
have on that delicate material were they to be taken seriously.
Pious men, on the whole, by no means social outcasts, if they were
accused of upsetting the social order their ultimate defence was
that the social order was one thing and the order of nature (the
facts) was another thing.[5] The attempt to establish this demarcation was a cognitive break of the greatest magnitude: science and
the scientists were held to get their authority not from the powers
that be in the society they inhabited, but in some way directly from
nature itself.[6]

The result was an incredible success. As Bacon had forecast, if
science made a radical break with the past and asserted its
autonomy from all worldly authorities, and trusted only to every
man's innate talent for inquiry, it would flourish.[7] Within a
generation of Bacon's death, Newton had appeared with an
achievement that dwarfs most others in the intellectual history of
mankind.[8] This triumph for the mechanization of the world
picture[9] even moved some philosophers to argue for the mechanization of man. My point, however, is to note that no Newton
appeared to dominate the study of society, despite the greatness of
those who dabbled in the social sciences such as Plato, Aristotle,
St. Augustine, Hobbes, Locke, Mandeville, Smith, Comte,
Tocqueville, Mill, Marx, etc.

II
The Demarcation Between Natural and Social

Ironically, the process I might call the secularization of cognition was reinforced by means of ingenious theological argu-

ments to the effect that scientific investigation was legitimate because it was a carrying out of God's will. God has made the natural world and man as a part of that world, and he has endowed us with the God-like capacity to study and understand his creation. This study of creation should of course include man and his works, including his social life. But somewhere along the line this argument wouldn't quite go through; social life is intractably separate from the rest of creation. I don't know whether the reason for this is the introduction of the factor of free will, thus demarcating man and his works in some decisive way from the rest of natural creation, or whether it goes back to the distinction we find so clearly in Ancient Greece between nature, what is given, and convention, what man has wrought. Those thinkers who tried to assimilate man and social studies to the general study of God's creation were often not believers in God at all, such as La Mettrie, who wrote *L'Homme Machine*, and Comte, who saw sociology, the natural science of society, as the queen of the sciences, and moreover a queen who would give birth to a new nature-worshipping religion.

The distinction between nature and convention, on which I shall concentrate, seems roughly to be this. What is natural is what cannot be otherwise, what is ruled by natural law. All creation is subject to this rule. Natural law, however, does not prescribe for all situations. There is leeway, there are contingencies. In particular, men can manipulate certain things themselves. This is the realm of convention, things that are thus and so only because men have made them so, and, where they want them to be different, they can be.

If you like, then, I can trace back the notion of a social science as something distinct from a natural science to the view that the social or conventional is something metaphysically distinct from nature in general. I cannot today give a scholarly history of this distinction. Clearly, it is controversial. Some naturalists want to repudiate it and suggest that natural laws govern all phenomena, that there will one day be a social physics, that we are simply rather behindhand in developing it. This argument is hard to sustain, for it is almost certainly going to have to fall back on some special qualities of the social as opposed to the natural in order to explain the relative backwardness of social studies, yet that is the very distinction it seeks to overcome.

In his important recent book *Legitimation of Belief* Ernest
Gellner has stressed the other side. He maintains that once upon a
time all cognition was social, as it still is in many less developed
societies, including less developed sub-societies within our society. His view is that as far as cognitive success is concerned most of
these world views were much of a muchness: while some may have
been marginally better than others at gaining power over nature,
the gap between them and the scientific world picture is enormous. On these pre-scientific views everything is in our terms
conventional: the world picture saturates all explanations of
events which, if not the product of human volition and action, are
then the product of animate forces like witchcraft and magic, or
capricious spirits like gods. Withal, there are no iron laws of
nature detached from the manipulations of the social world. The
great breakthrough, or ditch as Gellner calls it, is between this
antediluvian view, and the view that the natural world is rational,
non-magical, non-enchanted, non-manipulable, is the way it is
without reference to human social arrangements, wishes, values,
religious beliefs and practices, power structures, hopes, or what
have you. So long as man took himself and his miracles and magic
as the measure for all things he did not get very far; indeed it was
easy to lose ground. The Middle Ages might have had less
knowledge than the Greeks. Social conditions immediately before
the scientific and industrial revolutions may have been worse
than in Neanderthal times. A major shift in cognitive outlook was
needed. Instead of the meaningless proliferation of rival attempts
at understanding by rival social systems, crossing the big ditch
enables mankind to cooperate and make progress in his cognitive
endeavours. Once the assimilation of nature to convention was
broken, that made possible the scientific revolution, the industrial revolution it in turn made possible, and the immense
progress in the growth of wealth, power, human longevity and so
on which make us hesitate any longer to deny that we are better off
than our Neanderthal ancestors.

Gellner's vision that it is our achievement of a concept of nature
beyond our control, yet rationally intelligible, that makes possible the enormous improvement of cognition and of life, is one I
fully accept. What, I now ask, are its consequences for the social
sciences? They are, so far as I can see, innocuous enough. It
follows from Gellner's view that the demarcation between what is

under human control and what is not is of the greatest importance, and that studying the emergence and consequences of the
great transition is a central problem.[10] The line between nature
and convention is not a given.

Also of late there have been a number of writers called the socio-
biologists who have presented other arguments for attacking the
distinction between nature and convention. It is an obvious
enough line of thought. Mankind is part of natural creation; has,
for long, evolved under the control of natural forces; and may still
be far more their creature than his delusions about free will, moral
autonomy, God-given capacity to understand and control nature
would allow. Great play is made with the fact that our final
physiological form seems to have been fixed when our mode of
livelihood was as roaming bands of hunters and gatherers. How
far this argument is to be taken depends on the specific individual
thinker you look at. For my purposes, all I need is to stress how the
drift of the position is again to emphasize that far more of social
life can be explained by reference to natural conditions than was
thought by those inclined to separate nature and society sharply.[11]

Without associating myself with the socio-biologists' project in
general, I do want to go along with them in their downplaying of
the gap between the natural and the social. Yet I also want to
accept Gellner's crucial point about the great difference the
discovery of non-anthropomorphic nature made. Perhaps what I
really want to quarrel with is the metaphysical separation of
nature and convention. By this I mean a sharp demarcation
between the two settled on before scientific inquiry begins: The
idea that the phenomena of the world can be unproblematically
classified into natural and social, natural or conventional. My
general philosophical position is that the identification of
phenomena is a product of our theories and that *a fortiori* the
classification of the phenomena identified is also under the
control of our theories. These issues are not prior to theory.

To signal what I shall be arguing for requires me to say this.
There is indeed only one scientific enterprise: science is a unity.[12]
However, the problems we face, and the theories we devise to solve
them, from time to time lead us to make distinctions such as that
between nature and convention. Our views on these distinctions
change from time to time just as do our theories. Perhaps the line
between the natural and the conventional is itself conventional,

i.e. not laid down in advance, not itself natural, but a function of our intellectual and practical interests. As we pursue these, we from time to time find it convenient to note how some aspect of the natural world is not amenable to this or that theory or practice. We then assign it to some special category, social or whatever, and explore it separately. For a very long time now we have concentrated our theoretical endeavours on what we call the natural world, i.e. those aspects of nature we found most readily assimilable to abstract and general laws. Social, political and economic matters have been dealt with on a practical rather than a theoretical level. Yet all the laws of physics, chemistry and biology are of course obeyed by human beings, indeed some of what it has become possible for societies to accomplish has been possible only because of that understanding of the natural constraints on man which enables him to turn them to his advantage.

For example, it was once thought to be impossible for men to fly; or impossible for them to fly outside the atmosphere; or impossible to fly to the moon; or impossible to fly to the sun. Where the line of possibility would be drawn now is moot. Most likely we would say it is impossible to fly to the sun, but how near we can get, like how near to absolute zero, how near to the speed of light, how far we can shave away at the time it takes to run a mile, these are not absolute given values. The limits nature places on us are yet to be mapped.

III
Responses in Detail

I will put a little flesh on that sketch of my own view later in this paper. For now, I want to contrast it with the various other approaches to the problem of the feebleness of social science vis-à-vis natural science. Let me do this with an eye on the social science I know and appreciate most, anthropology. The three responses I mentioned earlier, naturalism, anti-naturalism, and radicalistic humanism, have all played over anthropology. Theoreticians as various as the structural-functionalist Radcliffe-Brown and the cultural materialist Leslie White have offered the naturalistic programme of 'a natural science of society.'[13] Their conception of natural science was a positivistic one, and hence they searched for a data base, for a method, and for fundamental categories of cognitive organization. The data base was to be empirical facts about human social and cultural life collected by direct contact in the field with the societies and cultures concerned, the method was to generalize these field findings in the inductive direction, and the fundamental categories were left in dispute. White wanted a holistic science of culture; Radcliffe-Brown wanted a holistic, structuralist science of society. An anti-naturalist backlash was to be expected.

Around 1950 the late great British anthropologist E. E. Evans-Pritchard, later to be dubbed Sir Edward by his Queen, rose up against this well-established scientism and argued that social studies, concerned as they were with the life of man, should take as their model the humanities, and especially history.[14] He poured scorn on the scientific pretensions of the positivists, especially Durkheim (presumably a stalking-horse for his then still-living predecessor Radcliffe-Brown) for seeking a science of society yet not being able to produce a single example of a law of anthropology.[15] He hinted that social studies dealt in meanings as much as fact, but he continued to endorse intense field study as the only method of coming to grips with the true meaning of social events. It was an irony to see one of the most gifted contributors to theoretical social anthropology arguing that his subject was not a science after all. Underlying his arguments seemed to lurk a deep respect for human autonomy; the idea that it was presumptuous for social scientists to reduce and explain human behaviour on the model of inanimate nature. From the provenance of a later lecture one could deduce that there were religious convictions underpinning these views.[16]

As to radicalist humanism, of late, some social scientists have turned the tables completely and argued that the human sciences have much to teach the natural sciences. Gellner has suggested that this is part of a general anti-scientific revolt, a rejection of the cold, mechanical and comfortless world picture offered by natural science, and an attempt to re-enchant the world and make it warm, cosy and human once again. This line of attack is not the exclusive property of one school or group, it is widely diffused. Although few go so far as to want to re-enchant physics and chemistry, to bring in gods, spirits, magic, ESP or human volition, there is an impulse of that kind at work. Strength is drawn from what can only be described as the de-bunking of science by social studies of science. From Robert Merton[17] to Thomas Kuhn,[18] all unwittingly at first, social studies of science have demystified it; have said scientists dazzle us with their tricks, but, like stage musicians, they are really no more than extremely skilled ordinary human beings, organized in understandable, even standard ways, with all the characteristics and foibles of any social group. The triumphs of science are to a considerable extent attributable to that organization. The most radical proponents of this view go so far as to suggest that what the social organization of science does is to construct reality, thus making the study and mastery of it something of a foregone conclusion. The reality it copes with is only *a* reality, not the reality; there is on this view, sometimes called 'the radical programme in the sociology of science,' no such thing as reality as such.[19]

What are the positions of the naturalists, anti-naturalists and radical humanists on the question of the demarcation between nature and convention? The radical humanists are close to assimilating everything to convention. This move is surprisingly simple. What man does is convention, what man knows is part of what man does, therefore what man knows is convention(al). A total cognitive relativism is inescapable, and often imperturbably embraced. The anti-naturalists want to preserve the soul of man and his works from assimilation to the rest of nature. Nature as portrayed in science they see as cold, deterministic, amoral, aspiritual, irreligious. But man groups himself into society for warmth and support, to gain control over hostile nature, and characteristically develops morality, spirituality and religion. Comforting as this view is, its consequences for social studies are rather grave. The project of man gaining a general understanding of himself and his works in order, among other things, to improve his life in society is set back. If history is to be the model of the social sciences, one can only gloomily recall Hegel's apothegm: the only thing we learn from history is that no one ever learns from history.[20]

In continuing to press the project of sciences of society, united with rather than hauntedly separate from natural sciences, I would offer as their aim that of learning from experience in a systematic, progressive and hence transmittable manner: quantitative where appropriate, qualitative where called for. What I would like to do is rehabilitate the naturalism of Radcliffe-Brown and White, while jettisoning its positivist and inductivist baggage. What I like about the approach is that it neither ends up in a relativism of unassessable conventions, nor does it have to rely on an uneasy metaphysical demarcation between cold, mechanical, push-pull nature and warm, organic, spiritual man. What it does, rather, is to investigate the limits of nature and map the extent of convention *as part of its scientific approach*. Bronislaw Malinowski, for example, tried to link basic human biological needs with diverse arrays of social conventions; the diversity, he argued, was simplified if one saw each variation as simply a grace-note on the themes of food, shelter, defence and reproduction.

In criticism of this, Radcliffe-Brown stressed its triviality, since, by definition, societies that did not satisfy the basic human biological needs of their members would not have any humans around with needs to satisfy, still less with social institutions to explain. In place of Malinowski's biological explanation of society Radcliffe-Brown argued for a subtler and more shaded picture. Of course, he did not deny that all social systems are devices for coping with the basic problems involved in human survival. Perhaps, however, man was not free to devise any old social conventions he pleased. Certainly, such social conventions as were observable by anthropologists and reported in historical documents revealed a very wide diversity; but closer scrutiny of the evidence revealed certain themes and patterns widely separated by time and place that might portend there were constraints on human social ingenuity, rules or even principles that had to be followed for social arrangements to work. Within the conventional, then, there might be inescapable patterns and connections. This subtle blending of nature understood as what could not be otherwise because ruled by law, with convention understood as what man can alter, but not to his heart's content, strikes me as a model for the human sciences. Man is, to be trite, part of nature. It can be argued that he is unique in having the capacity to grasp nature, to turn its inexorabilities to his own uses, and to discover within it degrees of freedom and of necessity, and to adapt his actions accordingly. Social scientists, then, in making a commitment to the metaphysics of determinism, or materialism, or relativism are preempting their own task and choices, they are even foreclosing issues that are part of their empirical work. If Radcliffe-Brown is right that there are limited degrees of freedom in the patterning of kinship systems, e.g., we learn something important about our own options and about other societies. His hypothesis already bore fruit in the form of enlightening studies of puzzling matters in Homer and the Old Testament.[21]

So much for anthropology. What of other social sciences? A few inconclusive words about some of the other social sciences is all I dare venture before an audience as distinguished as this one. A great economist like Keynes is great, one might argue, because he altered the lines between nature and convention, between what is given and what can be manipulated. In particular, he repudiated the view that the business cycle was an inevitability which just had to be let run its course. Psychologists and political scientists who adopt behaviourism as an article of faith avoid, I would have thought, the main task, namely offering theories about minds and politics respectively, theories which contain ideas about the line between nature and convention. In the end, the problem of drawing the line between nature and convention in the case of the human mind may be one of the deepest in human intellectual inquiry, so difficult that it provokes men to despair or to mysticism. In their recent book on the body-mind problem, one of the key interfaces of the control of nature and the limits of human autonomy, Eccles and Popper confess that the problem may be inherently insoluble.

> The problem of the relation between our bodies and our minds, and especially of the link between brain structures and processes on the one hand and mental dispositions and events on the other is an exceedingly difficult one. Without pretending to be able to foresee future developments, both the authors of this book think it improbable that the problem will ever be solved, in the sense that we shall really understand this relation. We think that no more can be expected than to make a little progress here or there.[22]

Progress will consist of chipping away at a block of ignorance so vast that we can no more expect to live to see it as a finished sculpture than we can expect to see a three-minute mile just because runners keep on trimming fractions of a second off the present record.

IV
Conclusion

To sum up, then, the notion of a social science that I have tried to formulate here is one which does not stand in awe of, or attempt to ape, the natural sciences. Rather it is one that accepts the methodological unity of science because of the metaphysical unity of the world. Science is simply critical inquiry, into whatever problems interest us, with empirical tests as its cutting edge. A fundamental problem that interests us is that of drawing the line between what cannot be otherwise (nature) and what can be otherwise (convention). What cannot be otherwise constrains what can be. Men believe that they straddle this line both as individuals and as social beings. As man tries to live in harmony with nature, so the social sciences need to live in harmony with, even symbiotically with, the natural sciences. This concludes the exorcism.

Notes

[1]See K. R. Popper, 'The Nature of Philosophical Problems and their Roots in Science,' *British Journal for the Philosophy of Science*, 3, 1952, 124-56; reprinted in *Conjectures and Refutations*, London 1963, chapter 2.

[2]There are even those who maintain that there is no social science at all, the whole thing is merely a pretentious redescription of the application of common sense to the affairs of man. See A. R. Louch, *Explanation and Human Action*, Berkeley and Los Angeles 1966. For a vigorous critique see Ernest Gellner, 'A Wittgensteinian Philosophy of (or Against) the Social Sciences,' *Philosophy of the Social Sciences*, 5, 1975, 173-99.

[3]See chapter 5, 'Nature and Convention,' of K. R. Popper, *The Open Society and Its Enemies*, London 1945 et seq. Also, G. H. Von Wright, 'What is Humanism?' The Lindley Lecture, University of Kansas 1977; and J. Agassi, *Towards a Rational Philosophical Anthropology*, The Hague 1977.

[4]This viewpoint is forcefully urged by Ernest Gellner in his pathbreaking *Legitimation of Belief* (Cambridge 1974):

> In a traditional belief-system, cognition, the discovery of endorsement of beliefs, is an event in the world, and this means the social and moral world. Hence they are subject to the same kinds of obligations and sanctions as are other kinds of conduct. . . . Man the knower is not alienated from the citizen and the moral being. At this point, it is . . . hard not to suppose that in one sense the traditional outlooks are correct: we do not believe that our cognitive activities are *really* extra-territorial, are qualitatively distinct from the rest of our lives. Nevertheless, as Kant pointed

out, we assume (contrary to all consistency) that such extra-territoriality does in fact obtain, and our attributions of 'objective validity' to our own thinking hinges on this odd assumption. (P. 166)

[5]One thinks of the beautiful story, whether apocryphal or not, of Galileo under the greatest pressure to recant and admit error, murmuring of the earth, 'and yet it moves.'

[6]Cf. Ernest Gellner, 'The Pure Enquirer,' in *Spectacles and Predicaments*, Cambridge 1979; and P. K. Feyerabend, *Against Method*, London 1975, p. 46.

[7]Francis Bacon, *Novum Organum*, London 1620, Aph. CXI-XCIII, CXXII.

[8]Alexander Pope wrote:

Nature and Nature's laws lay hid in night:
God said, Let Newton be! and all was light.

[9]See E. J. Dijksterhuis, *The Mechanization of the World Picture*, Oxford 1961.

[10]See his *Thought and Change*, London 1964.

[11]E. O. Wilson, *Sociobiology*, Cambridge 1975; for criticism see Michael Ruse, *Sociobiology: Sense or Nonsense*, Boston 1979.

[12]J. Agassi, *Science in Flux*, Dordrecht 1975, chap. 18.

[13]A. R. Radcliffe-Brown, *A Natural Science of Society*, Glencoe 1957; Leslie A. White, *The Science of Culture*, New York 1949.

[14]E. E. Evans-Pritchard, 'Social Anthropology: Past and Present,' *Man, 50*, 118-24; also in his *Essays in Social Anthropology*, London 1962.

[15]Op. cit., p. 20 in *Essays*.

[16]E. E. Evans-Pritchard, 'Religion and the Anthropologists,' The Aquinas Lecture, 1959, *Essays in Social Anthropology*, London 1962.

[17]Robert K. Merton, 'The Sociology of Science: An Episodic Memoir,' in Robert K. Merton and Jerry Gaston, eds., *The Sociology of Science in Europe*, Carbondale 1977.

[18]Thomas Kuhn, *The Structure of Scientific Revolutions*, Chicago 1962.

[19]Especially those who might be called the Edinburgh Relativists, grouped around the journal *Social Studies of Science*. See John Law, 'Is Epistemology Redundant? A Sociological View,' *Philosophy of the Social Sciences, 5*, 1975, 317-37; John Dean, 'Empiricism and Relativism—A Re-Appraisal of Two Key Concepts in the Social Sciences,' *Philosophy of the Social Sciences, 8*, 1978, 281-88; Barry Barnes, *Scientific Knowledge and Sociological Theory*, London 1974; David Bloor, *Knowledge and Social Imagery*, London 1976. Some criticisms are offered by Roger Trigg in 'The Sociology of Knowledge,' *Philosophy of the Social Sciences, 8*, 1978, 289-98.

[20]G. W. F. Hegel, Introduction to *Philosophy of History*: 'What experience and history teach is this—that people and governments never have learned anything from history, or acted on principles deduced from it.'

[21]For Homer see M. I. Finley, *The World of Odysseus*, London 1956 and S. C. Humphreys, *Anthropology and the Greeks*, London 1978; for the Old Testament, see Isaac Schapera, 'The Sin of Cain,' *Journal of the Royal Anthropological Institute, 85*, 1955, 33-43.

[22]Sir John Eccles and Sir Karl Popper, *The Self and Its Brain*, New York 1977.

CHAPTER 2

Social Perception and Social Change[1]

How do we ever come to perceive society in such a way that a need for social change makes itself apparent? This is an odd question. It assumes that dissatisfaction, not satisfaction, with society is what needs explaining. The reasoning behind this is very simple. Assume that our perception of the physical world is heavily influenced by our preconceptions and expectations, and these in turn are heavily influenced by our early education and primary socialization. When we turn from the physical world to consider the social world the following transpires. Whereas the way the *physical* world is is *not* a function of the way we perceive it to be; the way the *social* world is, I shall argue, *is* heavily influenced by the way we perceive it to be, which in turn is heavily influenced by our early education and primary socialization.

How then do we ever come to perceive society in such a way that a need for social change is apparent? That is, how are we able to break out of the (mental, social?) set with which we perceive the world the way we do, and induced in us by education and primary socialization, and perceive instead a world that falls short of what we would like it to be, and which thus becomes a candidate for change and improvement?

It should be clear from my formulation that this problem is a replay of one of the classical philosophical problems of epistemology, namely, do we perceive the world as it is or merely as it seems? This is known as the problem of appearance and reality. I find its sociological version attractive both as a philosophical difficulty with practical consequences, and because these consequences bear on a central problem of social studies: the explanation of social change. On a solution to the problem of appearance and reality turns the possibility of a social science, on which turns the possibility of arguing the need for reform of the way things are. We seem to want to conduct such arguments even though the way things are, is, as we have seen, heavily dependent on how we see them, and even though, despite this dependence, the way things are proves in fact very difficult to change.

The argument of the paper proceeds as follows: first, the thesis that there is an acute dependence of the way things are in society on the way we see them will be discussed (I). It will be maintained that, despite the dependence, the way we see things and the way they are, or what we

J. Theory Soc. Behaviour **11**, 3. *Printed in Great Britain*

might call "social reality", are distinct, so a realistic social science is possible (II). Moreover, it is possible for us to appraise that social reality and find it wanting (III). And finally this puzzling ability of ours to break out of socialization will be explained with the help of Popper's doctrine of the third world and it will be argued that our struggles to draw objective maps of society provide a basic impulse towards social change (IV).

I The Dependence of the Way Things Are on the Way We See Them

In his classical discussions of the social sciences Popper characterizes their basic assumption as the rationality principle: many social events occur because people undertake purposive or goal-directed action in pursuit of certain aims, and within a physically and socially defined *situation*. Not all social events are explicable as so intended, however, for example, traffic accidents, the system of social classes, or the Great Depression. These sorts of events are the more intellectually interesting because it is not obvious how they have come about. Popper suggests explaining them as unintended repercussions through the institutional network of society of actions directed at other goals than the event being explained.

Explanation by means of the rationality principle Popper calls explanation by reconstructing the logic of the situation facing the actor; the other he calls explanation by tracing the unintended consequences of human actions. Logic of the situation is an ideal-typical method. The idea is to explain actions by constructing a model of the situation the actor saw himself in, and by seeking to identify the aim he was attempting to realize. It is important then to model both the *situation as the actor sees it* and *the situation as it (really?) is*, for often the very tension between the two will result in the most interesting of the unintended consequences.

A simple illustration would be the answer to the question, "why is that man crossing the road?" Let us suppose his movements were agitated and erratic and the traffic was dense and dangerous. The answer might be that he had run out of cigarettes, was desperate for more, and was in the process of getting as quickly as possible to the nearest source of supply, namely a store on the other side of the road. We accept the explanation because it does explain what he did, no contrary facts are known, and the malleability of the social and physical situation confronting the actor is such that it allows him to achieve his aim with normal effort. His actions had both intended and unintended consequences – he was able to do his work better afterwards, he took the opportunity to leer at the female store clerk, the cigarette company's profits were increased marginally, as were the government's tax revenues, and so on. Unintentionally he may have missed an important phone call while he was out, caught a chill by being in too much of a hurry to dress warmly, severely shaken up a driver who had to brake sharply to avoid that crazy, jay-walking, idiot, etc. (As to increasing his chances of getting lung cancer which he certainly didn't intend to do, but which, since he knew of the danger, was hardly *un*intentional, we may need to discriminate further between wanted and unwanted consequences, as well as known and unknown.)[2]

Any genuinely problematic social situation – such as our cigarette buyer being injured by a car – is problematic precisely in the ways it differs from this simple example, namely, in that the participants' aims are not sufficient to explain what happened, there is no guaranteed fit between the situation as it is (accident-prone) and the situation as the actor sees it (shortest route to cigarettes); and the distinction between what is to be explained as goal-directed action and what is to be explained as unintended consequences is *not* clear. The attempts people make to explain serious social, political, and historical problems like racialism, poverty, student unrest, Vietnam, the causes of the second world war, and so on, are fraught with debate over what is the situation, what is to be explained and how, i.e., which events stem from goal-directed actions, which are unintended consequences, etc.

Doubtless it could be objected that since by my own argument what I have called the *situation as it (really) is* is nothing of the sort, but no more than the *situation as the investigator sees it*, such investigation is not science. If this argument held, physical science would not be science either, since all we ever have is the world as the investigator sees it, to the best of his ability. But the objection is not thus fully answered. Rather it points towards an interesting subjectivism in the notion of the logic of the situation which shows itself in the following manner. An actor will act to achieve his aim on the basis of his information about – if you like his perception of – the situation he is confronting. A typical example would be the attempts the High Command makes to get information in a war zone. Usually they have a staff to piece together such information as is available from field commanders and intelligence into a coherent picture, and it is on that picture that the High Command bases its decisions. Without a veridical picture of the situation as it really is the decisions are likely to be poor ones.

This is vividly shown in cases of invasion and surprise attack. Let us look at two examples from World War II. The Germans failed to respond adequately to the allied invasion of Normandy because they were convinced it was a feint which was going to be followed by the "real thing" in the Straits of Dover. One may be tempted to explain this by lack of information – after all the Germans had long ago lost air supremacy. Yet the invasion was an event the Germans had been steeling themselves for for months and were poised to defeat on the beaches. In fact, only fixed ideas in OKW and Berlin can explain the failure to "read off" from the information that was pouring in something approximating what was happening.

Whereas, then, physical science describes the world and rectifies its descriptions, social science describes the world and rectifies it, and the world is that of people who describe the world and rectify. Indeed, social science often centers around just such rectification. Consider the Pearl Harbour disaster and attempts to rectify both the descriptions and explanations of it given by the historian and the military. All traditional views on it may have to be scrapped in view of Roberta Wohlsetter's excellent book *Pearl Harbour Warning and Decision* (Stanford, 1962). She convincingly shows there that the cause of the disaster was not too little information in the hands of the military and intelligence communities (or negligence, conspiracy or stupidity), but far too much, coupled with totally inadequate theoretical frameworks for sifting it. This lack in turn was due to organizational blocks which prevented adequate theoretical information filtering down to the level at which key intelligence appraisals were made.[3] But the general question arises, in trying to rectify descriptions of the rectifiers, is there ever enough information to get a veridical description, does one ever know what is really going on? Can what is really going on be separated out from people's reconstruction of it? Will the tendency for the historians of each successive generation to reevaluate and rewrite history as they now see it not persist? Is the state of affairs we naively designate as "what really happens" perhaps a function both of what happened and how we interpret it?

As if this were not complicated enough, the historical and the military descriptions are not separable. How the Americans acted in Honolulu, how Hitler and von Runstedt reacted behind the Atlantic Wall, we all agree, was obviously a function of how they saw the situation. In particular, we agree, the situation immediately subsequent to the attacks, was a product partly of how (as we see it) things were, and partly of how things seemed – the decisions being based on the latter, and *not* the former. Now, once it is conceded (and it usually is) that decisions have been predicated on how things have *seemed* at the time, one obvious corollary follows: how things *are* subsequently to a decision cannot be explained without reference to how they seemed prior to that decision. All this is obvious; in anthropology it is reflected in a basic distinction drummed into every student: the distinction between how things *are* (or are observed by the anthropologist) and how people *say* they are to the anthropologist.

Yet a second corollary, which is also obvious, is not uncontroversial, and it is a thesis of the present paper: reality, the situation as it really is in the social world, is a joint product of how things are, how the actors see them, and how we act; social reality therefore has a conceptual component, is to an extent formed by and thus dependent on our concepts or ideas of it.

Peter Winch has given a twist to this discussion which generalizes it in a manner useful to our argument. He argues that our concepts or conceptions of things enter into our actions in an essential way: they guide and control how we act. Thus, if we want to understand why people act as they do, we need closely to study their conceptual system as well as their behaviour – indeed the latter is not intelligible *action* without the interpretation provided by the former. So far so good.

However, Winch's argument leads him to a conclusion I find curious. Concepts like surprise attack or invasion, to use our examples, are – according to Popper – abstract objects, hypostatizations, theoretical constructs we use to interpret our experience – to explain our experience. Winch will not have this. Such entities are, for him, not constructed objects but concepts on the basis of which I act in the way that I do. My behaviour, he says, is *informed* by these concepts, not *explained* by them, and this is different from the physical world where the falling of the apple is not informed by the concept of gravity, but is explained by the theory of gravity. What Winch says does not really contradict Popper, it adds something. It draws our attention to the fact that concepts, or, as I should prefer to say, ideas, play a role in shaping and informing the social world that they do not in the physical world. This means that the advantages of simplification conferred on the social sciences by the rationality principle – the assumption that human action can be explained by attributing to it rationality or purpose – is almost immediately lost by this interference factor of concepts with reality. The social situation confronted by an actor is shaped and defined both by his actions and by the ideas on which he based his actions. Thus by both thought and action he is constantly shaping and reshaping the actual and perceived situation.[4]

(Parenthetically, I would like to suggest that this may help explain some of the difficulty of making predictions in the social sciences. How a man acts will depend on how he sees things. We, the scientists, often find that the way he acted is our only clue as to how he saw the situation. Thus we cannot know in advance how he will see the situation, what weight he will give the information, so we are unable to predict his behaviour. This applies to the actor, too; he may not know how the situation will seem to him until he confronts it and thus be unable to predict his own behaviour. So in a sense only retrodiction once all the information is in is possible in many situations in the social sciences. However, to the extent that the individual, his situation, and the range of factors bearing on him can be *typified*, highly successful large-scale prediction can be successful. We rely on this everyday in social living – the electricity supply will continue, the buses and trains will run, the letters arrive, etc.)

II The Independence of the Way Things Are From the Way We See Them

In all this what seems to get lost is the possibility of objectively discussing the way things really are, and with this is also lost the idea of truth on which the very idea of a social *science* turns. Nothing could be further from my aim than to lose sight of truth. We cannot blink the complications of the social sciences, but unless we can maintain some notion of a social world independent of how we see it there can be no social science at all. I see no reason why we can not be realists despite the foregoing arguments. Society was here before us and doubtless will be when we are gone, so I see no reason not to say it is "there" independently of any and all of us. Moreover, if we can ever show that we (as actors or investigators) have been mistaken about society, its independence of us is decisively established. The importance of this is that not all explanations in the social sciences concern themselves solely with explaining how people act by how they see things. Indeed, as I have noted, Popper along with Mill, Marx, Weber, etc., maintains that most of the problems of the social sciences are located rather in the category of the unintended consequences of our actions. Now these are far less straightforwardly an outcome of the way we see things. Our initial and subsequent actions may be influenced by our ideas. But the repercussions of those actions take place regardless of our ideas on the subject if the social matrix in which they are embedded is independent of us. Each person who rushes to the bank does so to avoid the consequences of a bank run. The run which results is the reverse of what anyone wanted to bring about, yet it nevertheless happened. Now certainly a bank run is in Popper's sense an abstraction, an interpretation of concrete miseries like locked bank doors, long queues outside, panic, etc. It is nonetheless a real entity and a perceived entity. Dr. Johnson invented the unjustly maligned kick-test of reality – kick a stone and if it hurts it is real. Popper, who proclaims himself a naive realist (very naive, he sometimes adds) adds to Dr. Johnson's test the notion of kicking back as a test of reality. A bank run has a fearful kickback. If you shout "nonsense" or "you are nothing but a pack of cards'' at the judge then find yourself in gaol, the reality of the legal abstraction "contempt of court" is brought sharply home to you by this kickback. Groups, traditions, institutions, societies exemplify their reality when they kick back. They are the fixed points in the social situation within which all action takes place, there whether they seem to be there or not.

Having suggested the distinction between the situation and how the situation seems can be retained, we can return to the notion of the logic of the situation and make an objective rather than a subjective interpretation of it. For, as well as the way we see things, or how the investigator sees things, there is the way they are. Without this latter notion we cannot explain the outcome of the actions taken or the possibility that the explanation is mistaken. Supposing a general orders an advance believing there are no troops to oppose him. The explanation of the subsequent decimation of his army must take account of the fact that he ran into a well camouflaged, well-dug-in, and very powerful opposing force. Even so, the explanatory account may fail to explain the decimation because the investigator did not ask why the general did not beat a hasty retreat. The investigator may mistakenly have assumed failure to retreat was a matter of choice, when in fact it transpires later it was due to poor training and co-ordination. Again, an account of what happens to someone who invests in a shaky company believing it to be sound has to take into account the *fact* of the shakiness. In some cases, of course, the fact of the matter is acutely dependent on belief. The value of money, for example. Money is a useful fiction which is able to continue because no one chooses to challenge it seriously. If once they do, a wheelbarrow full of notes is not enough to buy a loaf of bread.

III Appraising the Way Things Are

How we look upon this social reality which can kick back is not something worked out from first principles, nor is it a question of our correctly or incorrectly seeing what is "there" – in some naive sense. More than anything else, we are taught through custom and language a manner of seeing common to the section of society we are being socialized by. Yet, remarkably, although we are there being shown how to cope with society, how to get along with it, we end up of necessity unwilling to do just that – get along with it the way it is. This must mean that our socialization techniques, our induction of children into adjusting to society, are imperfect. But imperfection in itself would not be an explanation of our capacity for critical appraisal of what we are supposed to have been being taught to accept. The imperfections of the process could be quite random. Such random failure of socialization would simply produce misfits and rebels who are not necessarily in favour of social change at all – if they can exploit the statuses of misfit and rebel they may be anything but.

Must it not be that socialization fails in some systematic, and perhaps even intentional, manner? It produces soild citizens *and* critics, very often in the same person. What is the explanation of this? How do we produce people who see the way things really are to the extent that they can survive well enough, but can also pass unfavourable judgement on this state of affairs and even act to try to change it? Where do the standards come from against which the reality is being judged? The answer of course is and must be: the socialization process. Somehow or other the socialization process is not a brainwash, it is a process that endows people with the capacity to be critical of the society it is serving, that allows them to develop values by which they find the society that has socialized them wanting. Perhaps a graphic demonstration of this was the unrest on American campuses a decade ago. Society was being criticized and attacked with weapons it provided. Not only had student radicals absorbed their radicalism with their liberal middle class mother's milk courtesy of Dr. Spock, they had been offered positive reinforcements throughout their short lives to give vent to it. The logic of the situation demanded that when they entered the universities, among the most morally and politically radical institutions around, they should excoriate them as falling short of their merciless ideals of purity and goodness.

This pattern of radicalism was, however, seriously deviant. While socialization allows for its own reform and improvement as part of the wider society, it breaks down when it looses radicals on the world. For radicalism is a force of destruction and chaos, not critical assessment and improvement. The naiveté of all radicalisms – epistemological no less than social – is staggering, since radicalism like any other doctrine is a product of the society it was learnt in. It has no meaning outside the matrix of the society that spawned it. Ironical when it demands destruction of that society, i.e. suicide. Popper has said in an epistemological context, *à propos* of Bacon and Descartes' radical view that knowledge must begin by wiping the mind clean and beginning anew: if we begin where Adam began there is no reason to think we could get any further than Adam. Of social radicalism one can add that it is self-defeating and irrational. It is self-defeating in that a consistent radicalism which wants a complete break with the traditions and ideas of the past must break with itself. It is irrational in that it urges us to plunge into new and unknown territory where, since we learn from experience, from our mistakes, and since we have not been there before and can have no experience of it and therefore know nothing of it, we can be expected to make many mistakes, big and small. Then, whatever we do will have to be modified to correct the mistakes we discover through experience. Then, either the pure radical will demand it all be wiped out again as a failure (it was not perfect but had to be modified), or they will allow that after all the much despised piecemeal method of trial and error, cautious and boring though it is, is the only rational one, indeed the only one. These arguments explain not only the naiveté of radicalism, but its impossibility: no society ever has or ever will be totally transformed because radicals do not really want to break with themselves or to plunge into a totally new and uncharted darkness, and even if they did, they could not.

Radicalism may be naive and destructive and thus a failure of socialization, but on the other hand, someone who has been socialized to the extent that he finds society not open to criticism at all is a failure of socialization in another way. Socialization is the transmission of certain information which will enable one to get along in the world. But part of the ability to get along in the world is the ability to learn – this is presupposed in the ability to adapt. Someone who cannot learn, cannot criticize what is, does not recognize mistakes, cannot learn from experience, is decisively handicapped. How do we manage to develop values which allow us to evaluate the society which taught us these values? Values may be carried and taught by a large society, but they cannot simply endorse that society otherwise they would not be usable as standards to judge it by. As soon as we learn, in socialization, standards by which to judge our society, we have transcended that society in a decisive way. Successful socialization must be a self-transcending process – a properly prepared adult is one who can look back on the process of preparation itself and evaluate it. But if what is taught in socialization – the value of being critical and the values to be critical with – transcend the society they are transmitted by, in what realm are they? This brings us at last to the third world.

IV The Impulse Towards Change and Reform

In two already classical papers Popper expounds the view that,

the world consists of at least three ontological categories; or, as I shall say, there are three worlds; the first is the physical world or the world of physical states; the second is the mental world or the world of mental states; and the third is the world of intelligibles, or of *ideas in the objective sense*; it is the world of possible objects of thought. ('Objective Mind', p.26)

He notes that the first two worlds can interact, and so can the last two;

but the first and third can interact only through the meditation of the second.

Popper's claim when applied to the social suggests that society, social structure, institutions, traditions, groups, as well as values, ideas and so on, are all objective entities *of the third world*. Both the actors and the social scientists try to give second world descriptions (statements – preferably true) of these third world entities and their relationships one to another. These attempts constitute activity in the second world of thought and belief, and in the first world of physical actions and behaviour. (Such *second* world cogitation may have been brought about by a *third* world conflict such as whether there is a logical inconsistency in a mathematical system, or, a clash between the way the social world is and the way our third world values tell us it should be.) Whether or not an event in the physical world is a socially significant *action* is a question of interpretation at the level of the second world, but which is an attempt to capture a truth of the third world.

(Before further exploring Popper's idea an intriguing consequence of it may be worth noting. The third world contains all intelligibles or objects of knowledge, so truth and consistency, social organization, etc., are third world "things". Moreover, a very interesting third world entity is clearly the self. Persons are hardly physical or mental entities, yet they are objects of knowledge, so where else can we locate them?)

Let us now try to see how Popper's third world can resolve the basic problem of our paper: how is it possible to perceive society in such a way that the need for social change is apparent?

When we choose and act we are subject to two sets of constraints; on the one hand hard reality: our physical surroundings and bodily limitations; on the other hand soft reality: our putative knowledge, our morals, fears, neuroses, imagination, etc. Between hard and soft, further constraining us, canalizing all we do – the frame of reference, so to speak – is the social world made up of other people, institutions, groups, friendships, relatives, etc. These are neither hard nor soft, but a bit of both. How are we to characterize this simultaneous intangibility (our five senses give us no direct access to, say, the institution of marriage or to the social structure in which it is embedded), and manifest effectiveness of social entities (so effective that the debate over the paramountcy of nature or nurture seems endless?) On the one hand social entities are, like mental states, intangible; like friendliness and goodwill they may come out of nothing and fade into nothing. On the other hand, they are like physical states, they react strongly to our probes: when, as an exercise, one *acts* as though a brick wall is not there, one may suffer severe consequences, and the same is true of many social institutions, from table manners to taxes.

What I am suggesting is that while social entities are wholly neither in the physical world nor the mental world, they are nevertheless real; their reality is partly mental, partly physical, but mainly third world and *sui generis*. The problem of just how real social entities are is usually, and quite naturally, studied within the matrix of a general theory of reality. This is what I have done in adopting Popper's third world doctrine. Philosophers hitherto have usually contrasted the real world with the (delusive) world of appearance. Naive realists deny this contrast (albeit implicitly, of course), holding that the world is just as it seems. Phenomenalists hold that the world is constructed by us out of the phenomena which impinge on our senses. Idealists fantasize that the world is a mental projection either by us (psychological idealism or solipsism), or by the Absolute (sociological idealism); materialists fantasize that mentality is an aspect of the material brain. All of these positions, and their variations, can be found knocking around among the casual remarks gathered together in textbooks of the social sciences under titles like "the nature of society". Strangely enough, when almost any philosophical position on the real is applied to social entities a short circuit takes place, since the viability and reality of social entities turns to such an extent on what people take them to be, their appearance. This means that all monisms when applied to social entities are self-refuting because a full account of the behaviour of these entities has to include the mental and social and physical repercussions and hence feedback in worlds other than that permitted by the monism. (I take it that the social monist is not denying the physical or mental worlds, merely trying to reduce the social to one or the other). This argument is embarrassingly sweeping; perhaps one should give seriously entertained doctrines more of a hearing. Mentalist monism about social entities is no more serious than solipsism, so let us instead give serious discussion to a materialist monism, perhaps the most prevalent position in the philosophy of the social sciences today, namely, the positivist-phenomenalist doctrines of behaviourism. This doctrine comes to assuage the frustration felt by sociologists and psychologists when forced to state their problems using notions like "mind", "thought" and "social institution". Are not these entities at the very best inferred rather than directly perceived? How can vague, subjective notions of this kind undergird "hard science?" Why not stop inferring and work only with raw observations?

A special complication, however, appears when behaviourism is applied to the social. To a very considerable extent social entities depend on what people think they are, upon ideas. Not wholly and completely, however. Hayek (1955) goes further than Winch and distinguishes two levels here: the ideas we have about society and the **ideas we have** without which society could not work. Some "ideas. . . .are *constitutive* of the phenomena we want to explain. . . .a condition of the existence of 'wholes'. . . .which will exist irrespective of the concepts which people have formed about these wholes'' (pp.36-7). The example he gives are the ideas people have that make them produce goods and sell them. These ideas may be quite different from their ideas about the market or the economy in which they are participating. Decisions to produce and sell are necessary to constitute a market, but notions *about* markets are not. Markets are social entities that can be the results of human actions but not of human design. So our behaviour may constitute a market without our perceiving it as a market. The actions which together constitute a market, however, are not automatic. They do draw on certain expectations and ideas of what is possible. These unreflective expectations about how the world will react if we produce goods are what shape our actions and thus the world as it is. These expectations involve entities we can only infer. Since social entities are not directly perceived, but rather "inferred", our actions taken in regard of them are already predicated on inference.

So the behaviourist, by forswearing inferences (why else deny mentality?), can neither identify social entities as such, nor understand why people act, because inference has been intrinsically involved in both. Thus, if we mistakenly infer from a news broadcast that a race riot has started and we roam the streets attacking those of the race to which we do not belong, then the net effect is not greatly different from what it would have been had the news broadcast been accurate in the first place. The explanation of the race riot, however, would be somewhat different in the two cases – in one it would be an unintended consequence of the news broadcast. We could sum this up in the slogan: society is what society does.

The behaviourist has an answer to this. Skinner says, society is what people do, where "do" includes "say". This does not bridge the gap from saying "There is riot in the street" to rioting in the street. Yet riot sometimes makes people report riot and vice versa. With that I leave monistic ontologies of the social and try to develop Popper's more liberal ontology.

People living in a society have to find their way around it, both to accomplish what they want and to avoid what they do not want. We might say that to do this they construct in their minds if they are laymen, in books if they are social scientists, a conceptual map of society and its features, of their own location among them, of the possible paths which will lead them to their goals, and of the hazards that confront them. The maps are in a way softer than geographic maps – like dream maps they create the terrain they are mapping. Yet in a way this is a harder reality: geographical maps are never real but sometimes reflect real terrains, yet social maps *are* terrains to be studied and mapped by other people. The difficulty the view I am outlining immediately faces is that everyone will be seen as having his own map, a product of his personal interpretation and selective perception, and drawn to his personal projection. Are we, then, confronted with a chaos of subjective maps and no way of getting at the reality that is supposed to being mapped?[5] I think not, and I would back this with two arguments: 1) the fact that individuals' maps are to some extent – but not fully – co-ordinated with each other (this is the basis of social action); 2) the fact that on occasion – but not always – individuals can test for the truth or falsity of their maps. 1) is a precondition of description and communication about society and hence of purposeful social action. The fact that people can describe, discuss, and argue about the features of their social world, and then act in concord, constitutes an on-going process of intersubjectively comparing and co-ordinating their maps. 2) even without explicit co-ordination with others, people can act, observe the outcome, and learn; in other words try to co-ordinate their maps not only with each other but with the world. This process is only a special case of the co-ordination and interaction described in 1), because *in the social world all action is interaction*. We can reasonably argue, then, that the possibility exists that our maps bear some relation of verisimilitude to what they are supposed to be maps of. The fact that that which the maps try to map (society and others' maps of society) is in a continual state of change, makes the process of checking and revising our maps of paramount importance. (Indeed, one might even try to relate the rise of these self-conscious and explicit attempts to map society and its workings which we call the social sciences to the increasingly diverse, abstract, massive and complicated nature of the social world.) It is a process we begin as soon as we attempt to grasp and come to terms with the world as infants. We acquire our initial maps during primary socialization within the nuclear family, but the process does not stop there – or, if it does, sociopathy may result. As we attempt to come to terms with social realities outside the nuclear family, in school and job (secondary socialization), our perspective on the social world constantly shifts. We are always having to redraw our internal maps as we go along. Some people do this less than others. If a map has hitherto been a perfectly satisfactory guide, one will not easily jettison it. Yet we value schooling and travel because among other things they broaden the mind – to wit, alter our perspective on things, and especially on the social world.[6]

One's mental map of the social world, I have suggested, is largely concerned with other people's mental maps. The mental map is also one on which it locates itself and, inasmuch as one does identify with one's mental map, it locates one's self; in this way it contributes to one's identification of self and thus one's internalized sense of reality. Consequently, the failure of actions guided by the map can seem threatening and ego-bruising. This can lead not to learning, but to the attempt to coerce society to bring it into line with one's maps. Freud argued that children and certain neurotics suffer from the belief that they can work their will on the disobedient world. The dictator leading the army, or the exultant revolutionary, are both fantasizing that the world is theirs to command. Fear of ego-bruising can also result in overeagerness to learn and adapt, resulting in severe loss of identity and individuality. Armies and other total institutions sometimes deliberately make use of this reaction in order to remould people to their purposes. [7]

The social scientist would appear to be in the awkward position of trying to stand outside the point of view of any one individual and drawing maps of society which only show features on which there is some general agreement, where people's maps overlap. But this account will not suffice. The social sciences also attempt to reveal "hidden" realities behind the appearances, to show counter-intuitive connections, to point out phenomena like poverty in rich countries which may hardly have intruded into the consciousness of anyone other than the poor themselves, or to show feud as a cohesive force between tribes. Assuming some of these things are discoveries by individual social scientists, the maps they will be proferring will be as idiosyncratic as those of any individual. Yet, somehow, superior scientific status is being claimed for them, and with the short-circuiting result that they soon are mapped by (incorporated into the maps of) many others and thus enter the public domain, become a factor influencing action, etc.

Here we are coming up against another weakness of the map metaphor. It is somewhat instrumentalist: maps are usually drawn to serve a purpose, to be useful. Doubtless this is the biological reason why we try to acquire knowledge: because it will be useful in the struggle to survive. The sciences, however, go beyond this, and seek to judge our ideas by whether they are true or false. [8] In the social sciences too, we aspire to truth even beyond its manifest utility. Usefulness is not unconnected with truth and falsity. Clearly, grossly false maps will not be useful. Nevertheless, we can navigate around cities with sketch maps, which are for many purposes misleading (false), and some people may get through life with the equivalent of sketch maps of the social world. But just as no map is useful for all purposes, no social map can correctly represent the whole truth about the social world. The set of all possible useful maps of either the social or the physical world is infinite. And so the search for the perfect map is a dream, an essentialist wild goose chase.

Essentialism leads to an arbitrary and uncritical metaphysics. The dream that there is a perfect map is epistemic essentialism. Dreaming after it is harmless; believing you have it is not. One's principal objection to epistemic essentialism is that there are no criteria for knowing that we have penetrated to the essence. In the absence of criteria, the logical thing to do is declare all claims on the essence tentative. This will avoid the danger of arbitrary and uncritical metaphysics. This danger may explain why Popper, who is far from an essentialist, so strongly endorses the value of keeping practical aims uppermost in the social sciences. Having a practical check on our mapping operations, our search for the perfect map, is better than having no check at all, especially when the thing we are trying to map in the social sciences is so elusive. This elusiveness of social reality is at the heart of what is being argued in this paper: the conceptual nature of social reality: the location of social reality in the third world, a world the features of which are constantly changing as they interact with physical states through the mediation of mental states. However, it needs to be said that not all societies and social entities in this third world are equally difficult to map. Some are smaller and changing less than others. One of the big differences between the societies that are as a rule studied by anthropologists, and those taken as the province of the sociologists, is the greater difficulty of constructing accurate maps of the latter. One of the beauties of small-scale, largely face-to-face societies, is the close co-ordination of the component individuals' social worlds or maps. Kinship network, political system, co-operative agriculture, rights and duties, role performance, all are closely defined and co-ordinated by constant exchange and intercourse. This may be what gives these societies their strength and endurance until their world-map is shaken by contact with another and cognitively more powerful one.

Interaction between ideas and mental states is stronger in our large-scale and abstract society, where only very small sub-groups are aware of each other and what is going on; where total communication and therefore total co-ordination of maps of society is impossible; much of the dynamic of the society arises from clashes and tensions between these discrepant maps. There are two levels of lack of co-ordination: there is lack of co-ordination between the maps of different people and between people's maps and the world as it is. Yet the so-called "world as it is" is a product of people acting on the basis of their maps, discrepant or not.

The short-circuiting of their interaction is, indeed, particularly strong in the case of discrepancies just because people try to sort out the discrepancies on both levels. They try to co-ordinate their maps of what it is like out there by communicating about them, discussing them, refuting, refining, and replacing them. They also try to bring their maps into line with the way the world is. Every action we take is a probe into the social environment, and from the feedback is gained certain information relevant to the map. But we go further than this. We overtly try to persuade other people to bring their maps into line with ours. (This may not be the most efficient way to approximate the reality mapped; but in view of ego-involvement it is perfectly understandable). The other people may be quite content with their understanding but we may take it on ourselves to rouse them from that state with new revelations and map projections which they are encouraged to adopt. This persuasion may be gentle, or it may be violent, done in a critical spirit, or done in the heretic-exterminating frenzy of the religious fanatic. We also may take similar attitudes towards the world out there. We may gently probe it and try to refine our ideas about it, we may also assault it violently in order to try to force it to come into line with our ideas of how it should be, even if it isn't.

So much for what is going on, for the changeability yet objectivity of social entities, for the separation of social entities from mental and/or physical states, and for the interplay of the three, especially in modern abstract society. How is all this relevant to the problem of social change? This constant struggle, this pushing and pulling between competitive maps, this attempt by people to persuade others that things are not quite the way they think, their direct attempts to see that things do not remain the way they are, provide much of the motive force for change in a modern, large, pluralistic society. As Berger and Luckmann rightly stress,[9] it is the failure of perfect socialization that makes this possible. Were children perfectly socialized so that they all internalized the same accurate map of their society and its working then their adopting a critical attitude either to change or to learning about society would be very difficult to conceive. Happily, no society socializes its young perfectly, and the bigger and more complex the society the less is this feasible anyway. So that there is no problem in the fact that large modern societies have wide discrepancies between the maps of their members, rather is that the secret of their success.

It should however be admitted that pluralism of this kind imposes a great deal of strain on the individual. The adaptive purpose of human knowledge seems to have a lot to do with expectation, and hence control of, or at least defense against, the environment. Constantly disappointed expectations, repeated failures of defense, can produce anxiety and poor function of the organism. While a plural society is not necessarily one that is threatening directly, its diversity, unpredictability, and liability to change can produce strained reaction in many people. Their survival may not be threatened, but they sometimes act as though it is. This dysfunctional strain is only the other side of the coin of the strain towards improvement and changed engendered in a similar way.

NOTES

[1] Read to the Philosophy Club at Carleton University, Ottawa, November 7, 1961, and to the Boston Colloquium in the Philosophy of Science, November 13, 1969. Some of the material in section IV overlaps with that in chapter 6 of my (1972). As always, Joseph Agassi was generous with his help.

[2] These distinctions are discussed on pp. 220-221 of my (1964).

[3] "The job of collecting data is intimately bound up with the job of evaluating it. A sensitive collector knows what sounds to select out of a background of noise, and his presentation of the significant sounds is in itself a major first step in evaluation. For perception is an activity. Data are not given; they are taken. Moreover, the job of lifting signals out of a confusion of noise is an activity that is very much aided by hypotheses and by a background of knowledge much wider than the technical information we have considered so far. Such a background might have included awareness of the state of U.S. secret negotiations with the Japanese and of the actions that might be taken in response to Japanese moves. Theater Intelligence, however, was denied knowledge of both the negotiations and the diplomatic plans". (Wohlsetter, p. 70)

[4] These remarks are also true if for "situation" is substituted "self" – *mutatis mutandis*.

[5] Marvin Harris (1964) faces this question on p. 169 and declares that the fact that cultural things in their knowable states are partially a creation of the observer does not conflict with materialism. He does this only at the immense cost of insisting that "'thinking', wishing, yearning, believing, and praying cannot alter the environment". If we are to believe J. M. Cameron (*New York Review of Books, November 6, 1969*), Marx takes up this question in his *Theses on Feuerback*. But in thesis two Marx dismisses our present question as scholastic and harps there and elsewhere on grasping and proving through practice, revolutionary practice. This is connected with his idea that society is not an object "out there" confronting human consciousness, because human consciousness itself is a social product. This seems like a *non-sequitur*. Just because one entity or state of affairs is the product of another does not mean that the produced thing cannot become an object to what produced it and then have feedback (think of mother-child relations). Human social relations may indeed be what underlies society, language, the sense of self and even consciousness. Nevertheless, in the world as it is experienced, society, language, etc., are outside self influencing it, yet amenable to influence by it also.

[6] This could be the ontogenetic recapitulation of which history is the phylogenetic counterpart.

[7] See "The Moral Career of the Mental Patient" in Goffman (1961).

[8] Compare Simmel, (1959, p.310).

[9] In their important (1966).

REFERENCES

BERGER, P. and LUCKMANN, T., 1966 *The Social Construction of Reality*, New York.

GOFFMAN, Erving 1961 *Asylums*, Glencoe: Free Press

HARRIS, Marvin 1964 *The Nature of Cultural Things*, New York.

HAYEK, F. A., 1955 *The Counter Revolution of Science*, Glencoe: Free Press

JARVIE, I. C., 1964 *The Revolution in Anthropology*, London: Routledge

—— 1972 *Concepts and Society*, London: Routledge

POPPER, K. R., 1968a 'Epistemology Without a Knowing Subject', in *Proceedings of the Third International Congress for Logic, Methodology and Philosophy of Science*, ed. B. van Rootselaar and J. F. Staal, Amsterdam, pp. 333-73; also as ch. 3 of Popper 1972.

—— 1968b 'On the Theory of the Objective Mind', *Akten des XIV. Internationalen Kongress für Philosophie*, Vienna, pp. 25-53; also as ch. 4 of Popper 1972.

—— 1972 *Objective Knowledge*, Oxford: O.U.P.

SIMMEL, Georg 1959 *Essays on Sociology, Philosophy and Aesthetics*, New York

WOHLSETTER, Roberta 1962 *Pearl Harbor, Warning and Decision*, Stanford: Stanford U.P.

CHAPTER 3

REALISM AND THE SUPPOSED POVERTY OF SOCIOLOGICAL THEORIES[1]

For all the Idols of the Mind or Profession regnant today the worst is that which Bacon
might have placed among his Idols of the Theatre: the belief, first, that there really is
something properly called theory in sociology, and second, that the aim of all sociological research should be that of adding to or advancing theory. It is a truth we should
never tire of repeating that no genuinely good and seminal work in the history of sociology was written or conceived as a means of advancing theory − grand or small. Each has
been written in response to a single, compelling intellectual problem or challenge provided by the immediate intellectual environment. William James did not err in labelling
as "tender minded" all systems-builders, whether religious or law, and placing under
"tough minded" those who welcome and deal with life in its actual concreteness.

Robert Nisbet, *Sociology as an Art Form*, New York: O. U. P. 1976, p. 20

My title may be misleading. This paper will argue that contemporary sociological theories are not impoverished. On the contrary, it is my observation
that contemporary sociological theories are rich and diverse.[2] There are
abroad Marxists, functionalists, structuralists, phenomenologists, symbolic
interactionists, ethnomethodologists, conflict theorists, labelling theorists,
critical theorists, and so on. That they battle and proliferate strikes this
philosopher of the social sciences as healthy, fruitful and exciting.[3] As an
editor, I never know what is going to flop into my in-tray next. In addition,
there are certain maverick figures who are doing incredibly illuminating
thinking at the theoretical level, especially Edward Shils, Raymond Aron,
Ernest Gellner and Erving Goffman.[4] So, much of my space will be given
over to explaining how such richness can be denigrated and the claim of
theoretical poverty made.

Poverty, like health or wealth, is a comparative concept, a question of
relative deprivation.[5] If the state of theoretical sociology appears to some
to be impoverished, it must be being measured against certain expectations;
in trying to show that it is anything but impoverished I shall need to expose
and criticise those expectations and try to replace them with more defensible
ones.

Expectations of sociology have run pretty high. Auguste Comte, our
revered High Priest, placed sociology at the top of the hierarchy of the
sciences; the king, as it were, to mathematics, which is commonly called
'the queen of the sciences.'[6] As befits the top science, it has been expected

35

R. S. Cohen and M. W. Wartofsky (eds.), Epistemology, Methodology and the Social
Sciences, 107−121.
Copyright © 1983 D. Reidel Publishing Company.

that sociology would explain and predict human action with a precision and depth comparable to theories in the natural sciences, especially physics. It is significant that less mathematical, less abstract and less precise natural sciences such as geology and biology were not taken as exemplary. Indeed, such is the prestige of physics that biology and geology themselves labour under its shadow. By the standards of physics we are all weighed in the balance and found wanting.

There are at least two very good physical reasons why it is inappropriate for other sciences to take physics as an exemplar. The first is *abstraction*. Physics is the most general natural science, its domain is the entire range of phenomena in the natural world. Everything obeys the laws of physics. Because of this scope, physics operates on a very general and abstract level. Or, rather, we describe it this way because, as physical systems, we human beings are of middling size. The very large galactic systems and the very small molecular and atomic systems are literally invisible to us unaided, yet we believe that many of what physicists call the most fundamental of physical processes take place in those ranges. The physics of those phenomena appear somewhat remote from our own, quotidian level.

The second reason why physics should not automatically be taken as an exemplar for other sciences is *isolation*. When physics is admired for the precision and depth of its theories, what is usually being thought of is not its treatment of heat and light, or sound and electricity; it is, I suggest, mechanics in general and celestial mechanics in particular. Nuclear physics is too arcane for most of us; whereas predicting sunsets, sunrises, comets and eclipses is both spectacular and accessible. Unfortunately, even within physics, there is something unique about celestial mechanics. For purposes of calculation, the solar system can be treated as a physically isolated system, i.e. one on which the effect of outside forces is negligible. Such a system is wonderful to work with but, to say the least, not very common in the known world. In particular, no such isolated systems exist in the social world. We may, for heuristic purposes, attempt to treat social systems in isolation to see if that bears any fruit. The most successful example of this clearly being the case of economics. While that discipline is impressively elegant, precise and algebraic, there is much debate about the testability and applicability of its results.[7]

From these arguments I wish to draw the following conclusion: we should guard against excessive expectations of the social sciences. To expand: we cannot expect the abstraction, precision and hence mathematicisation so familiar in physics; we also cannot expect the depth, in the sense of the revelation of unsuspected hidden processes that totally govern us; and, finally, we cannot expect anything like the degree of consensus that is to be found in the natural sciences. There is quarrel, party and confusion there too, but there is bound to be more in the social sciences. For one thing, every man cannot but operate with mental models of the social world and hence is a social scientist and knows himself to be such; every man cannot but operate with mental models of the physical world and hence is a physicist also, but does not know himself as such. Hence we might expect greater diversity of opinion and more vigorous debate in the social than in the natural sciences. Another reason for this might be the very direct connection between views on how social life works and views on how social life should be. There is no problem of how nature should be, in physics; nature is as nature is. It is different with society. People are as interested in how things should be in society as in how they are; perhaps more interested.[8]

So, while the social sciences may not be able to be so abstract, precise, surprising and convergent as the natural sciences, there is every reason to expect they will be theoretically rich and vigorously debated.

Let us not go too far in lowering our scientific expectations. Although social systems are neither as general nor as isolated as the solar system, and indeed despite their being among the more complex systems known in the natural world, and despite their complex patterns of interaction with each other and with the so-called environment, they nevertheless have order and coherence. Remarkably, human beings are highly predictable, as demographers and actuaries will attest. The shock of recognition when we read the brilliant — albeit atheoretical — observations of Erving Goffman, or Harold Garfinkel and his students, derives from this predictability. Every time we go to the bus-stop or the airport without phoning ahead we display our confidence that most of the time our fellow humans are predictable, and hence that man-machine systems are predictable also.

How can this be so? How can the uniquely complex human being, strongly interacting with his environment, nevertheless be highly predictable? Clearly, there is *some* means of coordination, some means of simplifying and regulating interaction. In my view the means of coordination is the capacity of the human mind to model all the elements of its environment, not excluding itself. We build, I argue, models of how the world seems to us, models we then use to guide us in acting to achieve our aims.[9] Indeed aims themselves are models of a sort, since they involve envisaging or modelling a future state of affairs. But if millions of heterogeneous human beings were busily modelling their environment there is not the slightest *a priori* reason to suppose that they would come up with anything other than a bewildering chaos of variations. What coordinates our model-building efforts? Two obvious factors: structural similarities in human beings connected with their very capacity to model themselves;[10] and reality. The notion of reality, nature and its objects given, as they are, independent of the perceptions of men, is not just a metaphysical postulate: it is an essential ingredient of the success of life in society. Ontological realism is not an assumption we can blithely dispense with.[11] It undergirds our essential coordination and the fundamental rationality of our model-building. Supposing, as we do, that our models are models of something, namely a unitary and relatively unchanging world, we act to modify and improve them, to, as we say, 'get it right.' Our inclination to do this stems from the very obvious point that if we act on mistaken information, i.e. incorrect models, we are unlikely to achieve our aims. If, in coming to deliver this paper, I was misinformed about the date, time or venue, its accomplishment would be threatened. To say to my hosts that 'sociology is not concerned with a "pre-given" universe of objects, but with one which is constituted or produced by the active doings of subjects'[12] would be a poor excuse. Indeed, we might reflect on the very fact that accomplishment of my talk is facilitated by the calibration of time and space into days, months, hours, streets, buildings and rooms, yet that calibration is clearly a social construction, a set of conventions widely accepted around the world. The conventionality of our calibration does not infect its objects: and yet, time and space, and the entities that can be plotted on those coordinates, are to a certain extent pre-given. Languages, those other widely diffused conventional systems, are even more remarkable, since they not only accomplish the task of coordination, but they even permit discussion of the possibility that there is now a world to coordinate our discussions of and actions in.[13]

There will be those who contend that what I have described as reality, what is really there, to speak naively, is simply the general consensus of opinion. This looks tempting. However, it confuses a test of reality, i.e. what most people think it is, with reality itself, i.e. what it in fact is. It is obvious that if what were actually the case were the same as what a majority thought was the case, then there could never be any rational change of views, especially of the kind we call correcting. Yet this happens all the time: the majority has to revise its opinion because of the arguments often enough of a single hold-out against orthodoxy. In the end, what is persuasive, what is the strongest argument there is, is that the hold-out is correct about the world.

What I am saying is that our capacity to explain and predict what is happening in society, to do sociology, can be traced back to our model-building activity, to our all being ur-sociologists. We need to be sociologists of no little skill to function effectively in society. Goffman has shown how even the mad must build a coherent and model-able social system within the 'total institution.'[14] The fundamental problem of and for the psychotic is that his model of himself and also of his surroundings is so discrepant that his behaviour is inexplicable and unpredictable on ordinary modelling assumptions. To pretend that he is possessed of deep insight is to elevate honest disagreement into bad philosophy. The madman has succeeded in being classified as such because the models on which he acts are at variance not just with the way others model, but also with the way the world truly is.[15] A less fanciful model will make it easier for the madman to accomplish his aims, and less liable to classification as someone irresponsible.

Madness is an example of a social phenomenon that challenges the common-sense sociological models of everyday folk. Acting on those models we would reassure the paranoiac that not everyone is against him, attempt to cheer up the depressive with some bromide. But these moves fail, can even make things worse. We had to wait until Freud came along and began the work of building a whole sub-field of sociology called psychology before we could reconstruct the modelling that might be going on. Freud showed us how mad behaviour becomes explicable and hence predictable if you infer that the person has and therefore inhabits a different model of the world than the rest of us. In particular, the models of persons and the structure of the nuclear family and of the self are often what is most seriously warped, albeit in an effort at self-defense. Equipped with this insight we can de-mystify madness.

Much the same happened in the creation of anthropology. Parochial or ethnocentric models of other people's social behaviour, including speech, yielded little of explanatory and predictive power when applied to the exoticism of preliterate tribesmen. Indeed, in early contact situations aboriginals were described as living in a confused, chaotic, and savage manner, possibly incapable of coherent speech. This is a wonderful example of projecting the problems and bafflement of the investigator onto his subjects. Again, new and much more sophisticated models had to be built, incorporating the modelling assumptions of the aboriginals. These models constitute the corpus of theory of social and cultural anthropology.[16]

Were I out to be really provocative, I could suggest that economics is the name given to the model-set that treats the wealth system to the extent that it can be analytically separated from the other systems in society, and that political science is the name for the somewhat less successful set of models that attempt to isolate the power system. Each is a branch of sociology.

Turning aside from such reckless attempts to be provocative, let me turn back to the idea that the explicability and predictability of social life stems from our innate capacity to be sociologists, i.e. to model ourselves, others and the system in which we all interact. This would give rise, one might naturally expect, to a great wealth of sociological theorising at the popular and at the professional levels. Whence then the charge that there is a poverty of sociological theorising? The cry comes partly from uninformed outsiders who just don't know enough to be taken seriously; and partly from sociologists and their kin. It is the latter I want to diagnose. There are those locked into rigid theories from which they cannot be budged; there are those so elusive no one can tell whether they operate with theories or not, still less what those theories might be; and there are still others who are explicitly atheoretical and/or antitheoretical. All three categories can, I believe, be explained together: they are reactions to what is seen as the failure of sociological theory. As I have already argued, such reactions are overreactions based on excessive expectations. Towards the end of this paper I shall try to show how more modest expectations, combined with an acceptance of refutation as a learning experience, can defuse these over-reactions. In the meantime, I postulate that all three types of theoretical inadequacy stem from disappointment.

Characteristically, when a cherished view is decisively refuted, four different kinds of reaction can be observed. There is the reaction of stubbornly holding on to the cherished view, this I shall call dogmatism. There is the reaction of modifying the cherished view towards vagueness and hence irrefutability, this I shall call mysticism. There is the reaction of despair: if this cherished view can succumb then all views must succumb, so what is the use; this I shall call *scepticism*. And finally there is the uncommon reaction of saying that the refutation at least has taught us something, and this I call *critical rationalism*.

Work on millennial religious cults provides crisp illustration of these reactions. Failure of the end of the world to arrive on schedule has the following effects. Some cultists drop out and become sceptical of this religion or all religions; some cultists go right on believing as before, perhaps slightly altering the prophecy; some seek hidden meaning in the messages and prophecies; and almost none simply conclude that, well, now we know that the world is not going to end.[17] A remarkably similar spectrum of reactions could be observed in the United States as the Watergate scandal unfolded. What was disclosed was a challenge to believers in Richard Nixon and to believers in the integrity of the office of President. The rational reaction that Richard Nixon was shown once more to be a scoundrel and that nothing magical in the office of Chief of State prevented its seizure and misuse by unsuitable persons, was not only relatively rare in the welter of dogmatism, mysticism and scepticism (the latter sometimes diguised as cynicism), but was in some quarters actually ridiculed as naive.

My suggestion is that sociologists have been disappointed with the performance of sociology and that their disappointment is a function of their excessive expectations. That we have had the good fortune in the past to model society with some little success should not delude us into thinking that we know it all. Then, if we do come a cropper, we need not dogmatically pretend nothing happened; mystically proclaim that events surpass ordinary understanding; or sceptically declare that the quest to understand is hopeless.

Instead, we can try to learn from experience. The rise of sociology in the modern world can be seen as a case of society learning from the hard knocks of experience. Learning from experience consists in learning that something we thought we knew, some mental model of the world that hitherto served us well, is false, i.e. no longer explains what is happening. Our policy in the face of this discovery obviously should be to find out how extensive the failure is and to see whether a new model can be developed to fit these new cases and the old ones, or whether models will have to be proliferated, or what not.

Before the rise of modern science, I would maintain, all societies operated under comprehensive world-views that explained and predicted what happened in society and also, conveniently, explained failures to explain and predict. A new situation was created with the rise of modern science and its world-view, or should I perhaps say, its opposition to comprehensive, all-explaining world views. Science is less a world-view on the same level as its magical and religious predecessors, and more a meta-level doctrine about how we should proceed, namely, by casting models, theories or world-views, and then tempering them on the anvil of recalcitrant experience.

The rise of sociology is a specialisation of this general process relative to the modelling of society. The triumph of the mechanical world-view of science and its embodiment in industrialisation and industrial society presents a fundamental challenge to all traditional models of society. No longer do official religions or hierarchies sufficiently assist displaced industrial man to model society. The rise of sociology is the rise of a group of specialists to help in the formulation of social models that can cope with change and learning from experience in the same way that natural science has. Not all sociologists will accept this description. I would nevertheless maintain it to be a correct account of one function of the institutuion of which they are part. The folk sociology of ordinary people having proved inadequate, we must beware of allowing the folk sociology of sociologists to replace it. Folk sociology is that received from the tradition and trying to preserve it. Culture clash, social change, industrialisation, catastrophe should neither be simply ignored, nor glibly reconciled with tradition. The life of man has taken a decisive new turn in the last three hundred years, and sociology's job is to try to understand it.

Despite the obviousness of this commission, sociologists are prone to over-optimism and hence to over-reaction to failure. The fundamental failure is not to have been able to perfect society. The optimism engendered by the social and intellectual liberation that began in Europe roughly in the fifteenth, sixteenth and seventeenth centuries was enormous. The optimism for the future that underlies the American and French revolutions and much social and philosophical thought in the eighteenth and nineteenth centuries is there for all to see. Yet many sociologists seem disappointed; neither society nor sociology has turned out as over-optimistic expectations allowed.

Let me flesh this out a little by looking briefly at four founding fathers of sociology, their problems, their aims and their eventual failures, and let me argue that it is from these intellectual failures that we learn, and hence that the name 'failures' may be a misnomer.

Alexis de Tocqueville was intrigued by the problem of how this new phenomenon, democratic society, could maintain social order without the institutions and rules of aristocratic society. Karl Marx struggled to understand how Adam Smith's arguments that minimally regulated capitalism would result in the greatest possible wealth for nations, failed to predict the exploitative poverty and degradation of large masses of people. Max Weber tried to show that there was a connection between religion and the rise of capitalism and hence that Marx's materialism was false; and he also argued that order in modern society rested on a new kind of legal-technical rationality, embodied in industry and bureaucracy. Emile Durkheim was puzzled by social regularities, by the constancy of suicide rates and by man's capacity to classify.

One would not call these problems of these great sociologists negligible

— a science with four Galileos hardly needs to doff its hat to its sisters. Yet the charge of theoretical poverty is still laid; sociology does not come up to scratch. What, however, is scratch? My suggestion is that scratch has been thought of as perfect understanding leading to perfection of society.[18] Even as I write this down it seems absurd. But I know of no other explanation. Because sociology does not yet have the truth, and because we need the truth to set us free, sociology is decried even by its own. Marx, although explicitly denouncing utopianism, nevertheless vaguely hinted at society coming to a kind of perfect resolution as sociological knowledge (he called it 'class consciousness') became widely diffused and led to appropriate action. For this reason, Marx's intellectual influence has been somewhat baleful.

When a social scientist offers to try to solve a problem, let us say unemployment, it is sloppy logic and bad faith to treat him like the Pied Piper and, when he has finished, say, 'yes, but what about the inflation?' An inventory of the social and intellectual problems that have been eliminated, reduced, minimized in industrial society would be an extensive one. The success of sociological reflection should, I would argue, be measured against that, not against what remains to be done.

Yet, it is my conjecture that it is precisely against the inventory of what remains to be done that sociology is tested and found wanting by those who declare it to be theoretically impoverished. Democratic society may have ensured that the privilege, snobbery, inequality and lack of social mobility of aristocratic society were overcome. To now charge that democracy is not without its faults, that some of these things have re-emerged in new form, together with imperialism, militarism, racialism, etc., is to hark after an unreasonable perfection. It is also to forget that Tocqueville foresaw some of it. Marx and Methodism, it is said in England, produced the welfare state and all the hopes that attached to it. Alas, those hopes were dashed, for the welfare state not only had social problems, but it even has some that survive from the previous state of affairs. Weber's ideas of the connection between religion and economic organization, and on the necessary growth of the bureaucratic mode of organization continue to hold up. To castigate Durkheim's explanation of order and cohesion by pointing to the conformity and privatisation of affluent society is to mistake new or modified problems for old, to fail to give credit to theoretical sociological thinking where it is due.

The logical name for the fallacy we see at work here is shifting your ground. It is one of the most pervasive fallacies and also one of the most difficult to detect. Why does it happen? Why should there be a denigration of sociological thought when the achievements are so considerable? The answer by now should be fairly obvious: dissatisfaction stems precisely from success. In sociology we call it the revolution of rising expectations; that is, it is when conditions are getting better that revolutions come about. It seems as though in hopelessly oppressed conditions discontent is contained, inarticulate. Only when a small improvement raises hope for further improvement, and when that improvement is felt to be too slow, only then does discontent and rebellion break through. How ironical then that sociologists implement their own theory: they participate in the process of getting some improvements in society and this makes them find the remaining unrelieved conditions intolerable. Under the influence of sociologists and their cohorts in the other social sciences our society has fought the war to end all wars, the war on poverty, for the establishment of the right to work, for the four freedoms, for desegregation, equitable immigration, and so on. Alas, a small lesson from epistemology might help here: the successful solution to a problem always leads to the appearance of new problems and a revision of the schedule of urgency with regard to still unsolved ones.

Indeed, problems breed like nuclear reactions. When P is solved by S, S itself will have components (entities and relationships) $E_1 \ldots E_n$ and $R_1 \ldots R_n$: and each of these components can in its turn yield a new problem-cluster. If I explain the splitting of the atom by a model that says an atom is not an indivisible basic entity, but in fact a complex made up of three entities, protons, electrons and neutrons, the problems now arise as to what the exact details are of their spatial arrangement, their energy and other characteristics, what kinds of forces hold them in place and so on. The whole process reminds one of medicine. A disease like diphtheria ravages children. An antidote is found, but then some react badly to the antidote, whether it be immunising serum, drug therapy or hospital treatment. Next thing you know there are hospital and drug-induced diseases, etc. Only by keeping the original aims in mind is it possible to avoid scepticism in the face of this failure of disease to disappear, physics to reach a resting place, society to be free of problems.

Given then that sociologists may have been disappointed by their own subject, we can now analyse their reactions in greater detail utilising the three characteristic reactions to refutation discussed earlier. All three view a refutation as a failure, a defeat. As I shall try to show, only by reversing this and seeing refutation as a success, as a clear growth in our knowledge, can these reactions be avoided.

Reaction one: *dogmatism*. The despair of dogmatism lurks in some of the most radical sociological theories, such as Marxism and behaviourism. Despite repeated refutation of these theories in detail, they still have many stubborn adherents. This is helped by the fact that both are highly pro-grammatic theories, that is, theories that promise that a great deal more will be forthcoming. What has not yet been forthcoming can hardly be refuted. It is also part of the appeal of these theories that they embody a total world-view and world-views do not, indeed cannot, get straightforwardly refuted.[19]

Reaction two: *mysticism*. We are familiar with the mystical reaction in religion, especially when internal contradictions are exposed and devotees seek refuge in the ineffable. The most popular language in which to express mysticism in the social sciences is Hegelian. Hegel has been described even by his own followers as scarcely intelligible, but a lot of it is quite impres-sive-sounding. We find mystical Hegelian talk among some Marxist social scientists, many phenomenological social scientists, among critical theorists, and in the group influenced by Alan Blum. Some critics contend that nothing is being said; others that banalities are disguised in high-sounding language; still others that there are unplumbable depths of confusion involved. My explanation, that they are reacting to the disappointment of refutation by making their doctrine immune to it, strikes me as the best reconstruction.

Reaction three: *Scepticism*. Scepticism about the very possibility of sociological theory is far and away the most common of the three reactions today. As representatives of this scepticism I shall instance analytic philoso-phy, atheoretical empiricism, ethnomethodology and the sociology of knowl-edge. Let me expatiate a little on each.

Analytical philosophy took a sociological turn with the advent of Wittgenstein. Although, so far as we know, he knew no social science what-soever, he did try to ground the study of concepts and categories into the matrix of social life to which they belong. It was from reflection on how language is used to mean that he came to his famous conclusion that the meaning is the use and the use involves studying the forms of life in which the language is embedded. But then Wittgenstein's disciples neatly reversed the equation and argued that studying social life is studying meaning, studying meaning is studying concepts and rules, and that studying concepts and rules is an *a priori* activity reserved to philosophers.[20] A science of society is not possible because the events in society are meaningful in a way that events in brute nature are not. Quantification, precision, explanation, prediction, all these become category mistakes. With minor variations this line of argument has been pushed by Peter Winch, A. R. Louch and Keith Dixon.[21]

Atheoretical empiricism is a less articulate position, as it denies that any convincing rationale is possible for collecting data. Just doing the survey, tabulating the results are difficult to justify with the bald assertion that the author finds them interesting. And the inductivist defense that only when we have enough data classified and tabulated will we be ready to generalise, i.e. theorise, has worn a little thin, even without the by now well-known existence of knock-down arguments against it.[22]

Ethnomethodology, in its curious way, also eshews theory for observation: it adopts the premise that society is constituted by those in it, and that their rules and practices are what sustain the social order. Whereas I have contended that people are theoretical sociologists, ethnomethodology emphasises the indisputable fact that they are practical sociologists, too. There is also a convergence with analytic philosophy in that both give pride of place to concepts and rules employed by the social actors (or members), rather than the artificial and imposed categories of the sociologist.[23]

Finally, the extreme and articulate scepticism of the sociology of knowledge as developed by Berger and Luckmann and some of their even more radical followers. Their radicalism consists not in delimiting the possibilities for theorizing in the social sciences, as analytic philosophers, atheoretical empiricists and ethnomethodologists do, but rather in arguing that sociology shows that a theoretical science of society is impossible because a theoretical science of anything is impossible. The so-called real world itself is held to be a social construction and the activity of scientific investigation of it is merely a disguised projection of sociological necessity. The world seems the way it does to us because of the conceptual spectacles we take from our social conditoning. Any science with pretensions to depict the world as it really is, is naive. For a subject to connive in this way in its own self-destruction is a radical scepticism indeed.[24]

There is a fourth reaction to refutation which diffuses the disappointment and which I recommend, namely, allow refutation to teach you: i.e. learn from experience. If a favourite theory flounders on a nasty, recalcitrant fact, comfort yourself with the thought that that step backward for you may be a giant step forward for mankind. But I am getting too sententious. Such a policy of critical rationality is psychologically hard to adhere to, and yet is characteristic of what we call the scientific attitude. It is a pity that it is not more often consciously given a chance. Social theory is constantly subject to the test of being implemented by politicians in programmes of social reform. Because politicians embrace ideologies, and because for some unknown reason they never want to admit to making mistakes, the results of these tests are rarely discussed critically and rationally. Reform is almost never implemented with a clear understanding that if such and such is achieved that will be success, if it is not achieved, that will be failure.[25]

Although the attitude to sociological theorising is rarely what it could be, I nevertheless want to declare the state of the art rather healthy. My point would be that although poor philosophies and methodologies can perhaps inhibit the growth of knowledge, the logical force of the problems and the facts themselves seems to be enough to prevent our endeavours grinding to a halt. This cannot be allowed to conduce us into a complacent tolerance of poor philosophies. An especially poor philosophy I wish to chastise is what might be called the consensus model of science; it is opposed to the dispute or debate model that I espouse. Talcott Parsons, who died recently, was a man who did much for sociology, but who also did it great harm with his fantastic thesis that all previous sociologies could be lined up in a kind of convergence towards agreed scientific findings.[26] Another and perhaps even more baneful convergence model has hung over us since 1962, when Thomas Kuhn published his magnum opus.[27] In that work we are told that the squabbles and debates in the social sciences are precisely what mark them off from (and as inferior to) the natural sciences. On the awesome authority of his expertise as an historian of celestial mechanics, Kuhn claims that real natural scientists do not quarrel about fundamentals, do not argue and debate, but quietly get on with the business-as-usual of puzzle-solving. Kuhn is a good sociological observer, and has impeccable scientific credentials.[28] Yet his view should be contested. Some bemused sociologists have happily convinced themselves that our competing theoretical systems and schools of thought are really paradigms, under the auspices of which puzzle-solving can be carried out.[29] This will not go through: Kuhn thinks multi-paradigm situations are rare, and are a sign a discipline hasn't settled down yet to scientific work. Better to consider the possibility that sociology refutes Kuhn, making one re-examine his claims about sciences as authoritarian in structure and routinised in activity. When we do this, examples are to be found everywhere of quite fundamental debate, and plenty of scientific schools where dissent not consensus is encouraged.[30] Perhaps the philosophy of the social sciences takes its most urgent problems less from the struggles of living science and more from the need to defend such honest toil from the bad advice of philosophical amateurs. In doing so, the philosopher can offer philosophical, not scientific, advice. Any science concerned about theoretical poverty could best initiate a debate about it — this is the rational policy — despair is never the rational option.

NOTES

[1] This paper was written while I was on sabbatical leave from York University and an Associate of the Center for Humanities, University of Southern California, in receipt of research monies from the Canadian Humanities and Social Science Research Council (no. 451–790154). I am grateful to those institutions. It was read in the lecture series 'Philosophy and Sociology: Confrontation and Rapprochement', University of Dayton, October 9, 1979, and to the Department of Sociology Colloquium, UCLA, November 7, 1979.

[2] See John C. McKinney and Edward A. Tiryakian (eds.), *Theoretical Sociology, Perspectives and Developments* (Appleton Century Crofts, New York, 1970).

[3] I must qualify this generalization by reference to the work of one of my students, Jean E. Saindon. In his Ph. D. dissertation he reports that there is much smoke and very little fire in the running debates between empiricist and idealist (or interpretative) sociology. See his 'Epistemological Dogma in Sociological Thought', Ph. D. Dissertation (York University, Toronto, 1979).

[4] Edward Shils, *The Intellectuals and the Powers* (University of Chicago Press, Chicago, 1972); and *Center and Periphery* (University of Chicago Press, Chicago, 1975). Raymond Aron, *Main Currents in Sociological Thought* (Basic Books, New York, 1965); *Eighteen Lectures on Industrial Society* (Weidenfeld and Nicholson, London, 1967). Ernest Gellner, *Thought and Change* (University of Chicago Press, Chicago, 1964); *Legitimation of Belief* (Cambridge University Press, Cambridge, 1975); *Spectacles and Predicaments* (Cambridge University Press, Cambridge, 1979); *Muslim Society* (Cambridge University Press, Cambridge, 1981); Erving Goffman, *Frame Analysis* (Harvard University Press, Cambridge, Mass., 1974).

[5] W. G. Runciman, *Relative Deprivation and Social Justice* (Routledge and Kegan Paul, London, 1966).

[6] The dynastic marriage has not been consummated in sociology as it has, e.g. in economics and geography. That should not be a matter of concern, as I shall argue below.

[7] G. C. Archibald, 'Method and Appraisal in Economics', *Philosophy of the Social Sciences* 9 (1979), 305–316.

[8] See my 'Nationalism and The Social Sciences', *Canadian Journal of Sociology* 1 (1976), 515–528.

[9] This thesis is argued in detail in my *Concepts and Society* (Routledge and Kegan Paul, London, 1972).

[10] I do not need a Chomskian innate capacity to learn language (as per his *Cartesian Linguistics* (Harper and Row, New York, 1966), all I need is a disposition to survive in the environment and hence to 'develop' tools that aid that quest.

[11] See my 'Cultural Relativism Again', *Philosophy of the Social Sciences* 5 (1975), 343–353.

[12] This is Rule A, One, of Anthony Giddens' *New Rules of Sociological Method*, (Basic Books New York, 1976), p. 160. The original is in italics.

[13] Whether the position can even be affirmed without self-contradiction, I leave for another occasion. See also *Concepts and Society*, note 9 above, chapter 5.

[14] Erving Goffman, *Asylums* (Doubleday Anchor, New York, 1961).

[15] *Pace* Laing and Szasz.

[16] I argued this at length in *The Revolution in Anthropology* (Humanities Press, New York, 1964; Regnery, Chicago, 1968); and *The Story of Social Anthropology*, (McGraw-Hill, New York, 1972).

[17] Leon Festinger, H. W. Riecken and Stanley Schacter, *When Prophecy Fails* (University of Minnesota Press, Minneapolis, 1956). See also *The Revolution in Anthropology*, note 16 above, and Bryan Wilson, *Magic and the Millennium* (London, 1973).

[18] Barbara Goodwin, *Social Science and Utopia* (The Harvester Press, Brighton, 1978).

[19] See K. R. Popper, *Conjectures and Refutations* (Routledge and Kegan Paul, London, 1963), chapter 1.

[20] See Ernest Gellner, *Cause and Meaning in the Social Sciences* (Routledge and Kegan Paul, London, 1973), chapter 4.

[21] Peter Winch, *The Idea of a Social Science* (Routledge and Kegan Paul, London, 1958); A. R. Louch, *Explanation and Human Action* (University of California Press, Berkeley and Los Angeles, 1966); Keith Dixon, *Sociological Theory* (Routledge and Kegan Paul, London and Boston, 1973).

[22] Classically set out by K. R. Popper in *The Logic of Scientific Discovery* (Basic Books, New York, 1959).

[23] Harold Garfinkel, *Studies in Ethnomethodology* (Prentice-Hall, Englewood Cliffs, 1967).

[24] This seems to me to happen to the radical programme in the sociology of knowledge. See *Philosophy of the Social Sciences* 11 (1981), 173–243.

[25] Consider the disappointment over Headstart that led Moynihan to propose "benign neglect"; over crime and penal problems that led to 'labelling theory'; over Project Camelot that led to suspicion of all academic connections to government and so on.

[26] Talcott Parsons, *The Structure of Social Action* (Free Press, Glencoe (Ill.), 1937). See also B. Berelson and G. Steiner, *Human Behaviour: An Inventory of Findings* (Harcourt Brace, New York, 1964).

[27] *The Structure of Scientific Revolutions* (University of Chicago Press, Chicago, 1962).

[28] His credentials are scrutinised in Robert Merton, 'The Sociology of Science, An Episodic Memoir', in Robert Merton and Jerry Gaston (eds.), *The Sociology of Science in Europe* (Southern Illinois University Press, Carbondale and Edwardsville, 1977). Some of my comments are to be found in 'Laudan's Problematic Progress and the Social Sciences', *Philosophy of the Social Sciences* 9 (1979), 484–97 and my review of Kuhn's essays, *The Essential Tension*, in *Queen's Quarterly* 87 (1980), 65–8.

[29] Especially Robert Friedrichs, *A Sociology of Sociology* (Free Press, New York, 1970).

[30] J. Agassi, 'Scientific Schools and their Success' in his *Science and Society*, (D. Reidel, Dordrecht, 1981).

CHAPTER 4

Rationality and relativism [1]

ABSTRACT

Relativism is easily confused with tolerance and hence with rational scepticism. Absolutism is easily confused with sure conviction and hence with irrational fanaticism. But cognitive relativism, by denying absolute truth even as a regulative idea, evacuates the possibility of criticism, and hence the project of co-operative, progressive, learning from experience. All this is permitted by weak absolutism which is also able crisply to define the notions of relative truth and of toleration. Hence it is a better framework for the cognitive work of the anthropologist since it assimilates every community of knowers to the model of the community of science, be they primitive peoples or sophisticated anthropologists. Evans-Pritchard on the Azande, Turnbull on the Ik, and Gellner on *Legitimation of Belief* are discussed.

Anthropological liberalism

Nothing can teach us a better lesson in this matter of ultimate importance than the habit of mind which allows us to treat the beliefs and values of another man from his point of view . . . The Science of Man, in its most refined and deepest version should lead us to such knowledge and to tolerance and generosity, based on the understanding of other men's point of view. (Bronislaw Malinowski, *Argonauts of the Western Pacific*, London 1922, p. 518)

Science as an absolute achievement

Primitive peoples have answers to all the important questions, which is, strictly speaking, omniscience . . .. From the standpoint of the achievement of civilization intellectually, omniscience is one of the greatest obstacles to the achievement of a civilized mind. The achievement of pure, uncontaminated, unadulterated

The British Journal of Sociology   *Volume 34*   *Number 1*   *March 1983*
© R.K.P. 1983 0007 1315/83/3401-0044 $1.50

ignorance by science, the insistence upon not-knowing when we do not know, and the defending of this ignorance with vigor and determination, is what characterizes the modern civilized mind and distinguishes it from all its predecessors. (Leslie A. White with Beth Dillingham, *The Concept of Culture*, Minneapolis 1973, p. 67)

I   PRELIMINARIES

If, as the Enlightenment taught us, all mankind is one;[2] and if, as Aristotle suggested, our unity is rooted in our rationality;[3] and if, as some anthropologists argue, we must assume that men everywhere are more or less equally rational;[4] can we still avoid the relativist conclusion that whatever men do, think, and believe is of more or less equal value? To put it another way, does the doctrine of the rational unity of mankind force on us the view that cultures, customs and ideas cannot be subjected to comparative assessment? My answer is, no. Indeed, if the unity of mankind is a consequence of man's rationality, and if man's rationality exemplifies itself best in the activities of criticizing, evaluating and learning about cultures, customs, and ideas, then relativism, by placing limits on what such activity can achieve, clashes with the unity of mankind. The deep error behind relativism, I shall suggest, is a passive and individualistic view of human rationality, rather than an actively critical and social one.

This paper builds on previous work that tried to diagnose the appeal of relativism, arguing that it draws strength from seeming to be merely the corollary of a consistent liberalism.[5] Despite its respectable auspices, relativism has these objectionable consequences: namely, that by limiting critical assessment of human works it disarms us, dehumanises us, leaves us unable to enter into communicative interaction; that is to say, unable to criticize cross-culturally, cross-sub-culturally, cross-individually; ultimately, relativism leaves no room for criticism at all.[6] In other words, behind relativism nihilism looms.

In the present paper I concentrate on rationality and on the clash between rationality and relativism. A further reason, I suspect, why people get stuck in, and hence with, relativism, is that they think the only alternative to it is what I shall call 'strong absolutism'.

Strong absolutism is the view that there are only absolute truths. Weak absolutism allows that there are degrees of truth as well as absolute truth, and the former is defined as approximation to the latter. If $2 \times 2 = 4$ is absolutely true, then $2 \times 2 = 3\frac{1}{2}$ is more true than $2 \times 2 = 2\frac{1}{2}$. That the earth circles the sun is a degree closer to the absolute truth written in the book of nature than is the idea that the sun circles the earth. Absolutism and relativism are best seen as contraries, not contradictories, so that while they cannot be true together, they can be false together and space for a middle ground remains.

TABLE I

RELATIVISM	1 All truths are relative	I No absolute (i.e. non-relative) truths exist
WEAK ABSOLUTISM	2 Some non-relative truths exist	II Some absolute truths exist
STRONG ABSOLUTISM	3 No truths are relative	III All truths are absolute

Ignoring problems of formulation in Table I and the possible play that can be made with the word 'truths', consider now what relativism amounts to. Relativism is the position that all assessments are assessments relative to some standard or other, and standards derive from cultures. The attempt to assess without regard to cultural context and, particularly, the attempt to assess cognitive statements on some transcendental scale of truth, is futile. No assessment can escape the web of culture and hence all assessment is culturally relative. This position is captured in its positive and negative forms in the statements numbered Arabic 1 and Roman I. Absolutism in its weak form is the position that there are absolute, i.e. non-culturally-relative, truths. This is formulated in Arabic 2 and Roman II. Absolutism in its strong form is the position that the only truths there are are absolute, and this is captured by Arabic 3 and Roman III: if something is a truth it is true for all times and places; there are no 'local', partial or relative truths; $2 \times 2 = 3\frac{1}{2}$ and $2 \times 2 = 2\frac{1}{2}$ are alike in being not-truths, i.e. falsehoods. However, strong absolutism is very strong and one need not be surprised if absolutists equivocate between the strong and the weak poles. Hence one can also understand the relativist's tendency to collapse absolutism towards its stronger pole.

My purpose is to argue for weak absolutism by showing a connection between it and the rationality involved in learning about the world, when we subject our experience of cultures, customs and ideas to criticism and assessment. Relativism allows comparison but disallows assessment. Unexpectedly, strong absolutism gets in trouble over assessment. There are three options: the strong absolutist either possesses all the truths there are, or some, or none. If he possesses them all new candidates need not be assessed, merely *mechanically* compared to the set of truths and either found to be identical to one or more of them or else to be not a truth. If he possesses some of the truths but not all the relativist may argue these are true only relative to the full set, hence not absolute, hence incorrectly assessed. If he possesses none of the truths that there are, his claim that there are any is in doubt and assessment becomes a problem. Since I believe neither that my culture or I has a monopoly of truth, nor that all cognitive efforts are on a par, I opt for weak absolutism as formulated in Arabic 2 and Roman II, where it is assumed for the sake of argument that there is something to be rational about, namely the search for truth, the goal of solving problems, and the task of assessing candidates.

This weak absolutism seems to me a presupposition of a quite commonsense theory of rationality, one that says we can learn from (culturally bound) experience about a world-structure that is not itself culturally bound, but, rather, bounds cultures. Rationality is displayed in the application of reason to tasks, and that knowledge of how to achieve tasks is more effective than ignorance and hence our rationality is displayed in adopting the strategy that maximizes the growth of knowledge. The strategy which does that, and which typifies science, hitherto mankind's best effort at cognition, is, I believe, trial and error: offering solutions to problems and then doing our level best to assess them by criticism and improve them in its light.

Psychologistic theories of rationality locate this strategy in the mind-set of the inquiring individual, who should cultivate detachment, objectivity, respect for evidence, devotion to truth.[7] Trial and error can be adopted as an attitude of mind but this is neither necessary nor sufficient. Trial and error can be translated into a set of social arrangements, institutions that are open and tolerant, and which foster and reward original criticism as well as original theories and which discriminate between culpable, careless or interesting errors and interesting, challenging or creative errors.[8] Growth of knowledge is fostered not by the mind-set of the individual inquirers but by the institutional setting in which they operate. To build scientific organizations that maximize criticism and yet which tolerate diversity of opinion is a miniature of the general social task which is to improve societies in the matters of tolerance, criticism and, so, rationality.

Thus the general idea of promoting rationality becomes indistinguishable from the project of a critical, tolerant and undogmatic search for intellectual and social progress. Under such social arrangements individuals can fall short of the ideal of disinterestedness while yet sustaining the institutional project. Both strong absolutists and relativists cannot help backing in towards the psychologistic reading of rationality as a mind set: strong absolutists are either in possession of truths or are sceptical of the possibility of their acquisition and so hardly need concern themselves with the arrangements for acquiring more; relativists hold there are no truths to be found. Strong absolutists shy away from this social model of rationality because they are uncritical of, and dogmatic about, what they know: there is no progress beyond the dogmatically known truth, be that positive doctrine or sceptical doubt, therefore no need of a social organization that encourages both tolerance and criticism in the hope of progress towards enlightenment. Relativists by contrast might seem open-minded and tolerant (although not progressive since they allow no general or absolute measure of progress), but they also fall into dogmatism and intolerance. Relativism in effect tells one that, to use a recently fashionable formulation, 'anything goes'. This may sound tolerant, but it is not tolerant of picking and choosing, and especially of that picking and choosing we call criticism and assessment of cultures, customs and ideas (including the idea 'anything goes'). Nevertheless, so long as their philosophical views are ignored, individuals holding strong absolutist or relativist outlooks can be effective inside an organization designed by weak absolutists to pursue knowledge — they are inimical to it only if they take control and set policy, e.g. to disband; so long as they function as sources of ideas and criticism they can help rather than hinder the rational pursuit of knowledge.

My argument does not I hope turn on an idiosyncratic redefinition of rationality. I am operating with a widely held and so innocuous definition of it: rationality as the application of reason to tasks, effective action to achieve goals. The most effective action is that based on knowledge not ignorance, hence the highest form of rationality is action taken to increase rationality, i.e. to increase knowledge. Socrates argues that the most promising recipe for increasing knowledge is dialectical interaction, open and critical debate. What I am trying to do is translate that notion of open and critical debate into a general, social, form, as a philosophical alternative to relativism for anthropologists. Never mind whether rationality is an observable characteristic of the human species some or all of the time, whether it is a temperament or a talent; focus instead on it as a social and political programme: rationality then becomes the aim of building a society that fosters rationality, i.e. that is open, tolerant and yet critical, since that is the best means known for maximizing the growth of our at best partial knowledge. I call it a programme in order to stress that it is not necessary to assume our society has fulfilled the programme in order to criticize other societies; yet it is possible to discuss to what extent different societies are committed to and have succeeded in realizing the programme. A rational society, that is, does not require perfectly rational men; only those who want to improve their rationality. This is similar to the situation in epistemology: criticism does not presuppose that the critic of the incorrect answer knows the correct answer; and not having the correct answer does not prevent discussion and evaluation of what answers are available.

I shall divide the rest of my argument into three sections. The next section argues that there is a strong association between rationality and science, but that the identification of science with rational thinking, or with empirical investigation is mistaken. Rather, the rationality of science is better seen as the product of institutional arrangements designed to improve upon our ignorance, to make knowledge grow and to progress, to institutionalize open-mindedness and criticism. Such an analysis of the rationality of science will allow us to make sense of the attribution of a higher degree of rationality to science, and a lower degree to other systems of ideas, without falling into nineteenth century ethnocentrism. It will also provide a benchmark for the assessment of cultures and customs on this cognitive sector.

The subsequent section, centres on the argument (among the many arguments that can be deployed against a relativistic devaluation of the rationality of science, perhaps it is the most powerful) that relativism ends up denying the possibility of rational or critical interaction between diverse peoples, and hence the possibility of learning from each other, and hence of learning at all.[9]

The concluding section, will present the ideal of the rational and moral unity of mankind as manifesting itself in important ways in critical discussion and learning, and that it guides our attempt to steer —albeit somewhat gingerly — between the Scylla of strong absolutism aπd the Charybdis of relativism.

II   RATIONALITY

Rationality in its most general sense means something like man's capacity for applying reason to tasks, i.e. for reasoning. It is customary to take science as somehow the epitome of these efforts. Or, rather, we usually think of cognition, the acquisition of knowledge, as the purest manifestation of rationality, and science as the purest form of cognition. There are two ways in which science is customarily held up as the exemplar of rationality, one (S_1) emphasizes what it is, the other (S_2) what it is not:

(S_1) one is that science is critical, practical and above all progressive
        rather than

(S_2) vague, mysterious and superstitious like pseudo-science and
        pre-science.

One hundred years ago anthropological opinion closely identified science with rationality and concluded that because so-called primitive peoples lacked science, they also lacked rationality. A later and less extreme position was to grant that what primitive societies did have, namely *pseudo*-scientific and *pre*-scientific cognition, was *some* sort of rationality, but to declare it deficient. It is no longer fashionable to attribute zero or limited rationality to primitive peoples. Instead, we often encounter a two-sided argument that goes, since all social systems, including primitive ones, can be seen to embody some sort of rationality, i.e. applying reason to tasks, maybe all man's attempts at cognition are equally rational, and maybe it is ethnocentric to take science as exemplary of rationality, rather than canoe building, kinship systems, mystical beliefs, binary oppositions and the rest. This is an astonishing move. Both the positive and negative characterizations of science are rejected and rationality is attributed to non-progressive but adequate technology (e.g. canoe building) and sophisticated systems of pseudo-science (e.g. Azande witchcraft).

Clearly this is a new mapping of science and rationality. It is as though we were to declare that in our society gardener's rules of thumb and popular beliefs in astrology were not to be assessed against the standards of rationality displayed by science but by their own implicit standards of rationality. This is relativism: their standards of rationality render them rational; our standards do not apply to them but to us.

I shall confront this argument later. In this section I want to investigate the decay of the strong and self-confident identification of rationality with science. This happened, I conjecture, because of problems discovered by the debate on the question of why primitive people's cognitive efforts lacked scientific rationality. As a starting point let me pick out *the theory of primitive thinking*: the idea that early man just couldn't ratiocinate, possibly because he was still childlike, in that his passions dominated his thought processes. This drew on a further theory, the theory that man is bifurcated into two sides or temperaments, reason and the passions. A passion is something either lacking in logic (Lévy-Bruhl), or lacking in empirical observation (Tylor).

Lucien Lévy-Bruhl considered that primitive thinking was 'pre-logical' — for him, logic was the measure of rationality.[10] Tylor and his follower Frazer thought science not logic was the measure of rationality, and that the basis of science was empirical investigation. Lévy-Bruhl saw pre-logical thinking as mystical or participatory thinking; such would always be with us, he said, if with diminished importance; and this diminution of the role of the pre-logical he saw as progress. Tylor and Frazer, by contrast, saw empirical investigation and its product, science, as the progressive force that would sooner or later vanquish superstition and other forms of unreason altogether. It was a subtle consequence of their view that magic was less irrational than religion because it was a primitive and misguided but rectifiable form of empirical investigation, whereas religion was purely metaphysical and thus not rectifiable although also misguided.

Ironically enough, it was philosophers, of all people, who discovered the decisive arguments which refute both identifications, namely of rational science with logical thinking, and of rational science with empirical thinking. The argument about logical thinking has two parts: first, that logic cannot generate science; second, that thinking is neither logical nor illogical, and anyway, it too need not generate science. The argument about logic goes back at least as far as Sir Francis Bacon in the early seventeenth century. He cited the well-known fact that a syllogism does no more than rearrange the information given in the premises, it does not add anything new. But science appears to grow and progress, and to gain *new* knowledge. So, its methods and hence its rationality, cannot be identified with logic.[11] In the later nineteenth century, several logicians, but especially Husserl and Frege, suggested the second part of the argument against logical thinking, when they showed that logic is not the study of correct thought processes at all, but the non-psychological study of correct patterns of argument, and hence is no more about mentality than is mathematics.

> We deny that the theoretical discipline of pure logic, in the independent separateness proper to it, has any concern with mental facts, or with laws that might be styled 'psychological'. We saw that the laws of pure logic, e.g. the primitive 'laws of thought', or the syllogistic formulae, totally lose their basic sense, if one tries to interpret them as psychological.[12]

This result was generalized by Popper, who argued that logic was a necessary but by no means a sufficient condition for the rationality of science, which so far from being attributable to how people think, was rather attributable to how they created social conventions that maximize rational criticism.[13]

As to Tylor and Frazer's identification of the rationality of science with its empirical character, it was David Hume, a great 'rationalist' if you will forgive the pun, who discovered two difficulties with it. His first point was that science is about causes, what causes what, what explains what; whereas empiricism is about facts, what can be empirically observed; you can never, Hume observed, observe a cause. But then, he asks, how do we get from empirical facts to non-empirical causes? We can see things but not causes.[14] If we try to define a causal relationship empirically as the regular succession of one observed event followed by another (constant conjunction, to use his idiom), Hume makes the second point of asking how an observation can tell us that such a regular pattern will continue? Well, you might say, the pattern has always been observed to be like that, so why shouldn't we expect it to continue? Ah, says Hume, that begs the question, which is, how can we use the observed pattern to argue that the not-yet-observed pattern will continue?[15]

Hume found his own arguments depressing, because he believed in a world of causes; a world without causes would violate the pinciple of sufficient reason and hence not be, for him, rational. He had found an argument he did not know what to do with.[16]

Interestingly enough, the first glimmerings of a solution to the dilemma thus created for early anthropologists by pesky philosophers of whose work they were doubtless unaware can be found in later anthropology, apparently reached by an independent route. I have in mind the late Professor Sir Edward Evans-Pritchard's classic monograph, *Witchcraft, Oracles and Magic Among the Azande* of 1937, where he shows clearly that Zande magicians think as logically as we do, and also, that Azande can be empirical and critical and yet, they have no science. The work is widely discussed because it describes an African society permeated by witchcraft, whose under-lying principles are immune to refutation and yet seemingly function well. Although not himself believing in witchcraft, Evans-Pritchard found it perfectly possible to regulate his daily life with its help. He tries to show that there is something about the social organization in which their world view is embedded that makes it different from the social organization that supports science. They have, he notes, answers to every critical doubt concerning principles, whether logical inconsistency or factual refutation. Moreover, the answers to, and more so the acceptance of, specific doubts reinforce the system as a whole. The system, then, fits the empirical world in the sense that it never clashes with the empirical world. Hence it never changes in a rational way. The awful possibility, which you and I, and Evans-Pritchard entertain with some equanimity, that there are no witches, that things can be otherwise explained, just does not arise. Yet the Azande are rational by all measures except possession of science.

My own most intensive studies in anthropology have been in similar material, namely cargo cults.

Cargo cults are messianic religions, primarily of Melanesia, which expect the consummation of their religious efforts in the form of a return of the spirits of the dead, bringing with them a mass-ive shipment of European consumer durables (hence 'cargo') to be distributed to the natives. Goods on the list include jeeps, aeroplanes, canned food, tobacco, radios, guns, etc. Anything, indeed, natives in Melanesia might have seen Europeans using and might have coveted. Cargo cults are thus exceptionally exotic phenomena cloaking as they do, hardware-store aspirations in a religious form.[17]

Here were people whose cults seemed irrational and bizarre, although the rest of their social behaviour seemed straightforward enough. Moreover, the cults made very daring predictions which were falsified: spirits and cargo did not arrive. It is possible that, like the Azande, cargo cultists have a multiplicity of *ad hoc* argumentative devices to explain away failures of prediction.[18] Failure often reinforces the faith of those involved. The cargo cultists' explanations of how cargo is to be obtained never get beyond the groove of magic and ritual. This cannot be explained by any failure of thought (logic), nor of methodology (e.g. empirical investigations). It is clearly and solely explicable by utilizing Evans-Pritchard's idea that a world view is both a doctrine and a social organization, so that rectification of world view and of social organization go together. Most of mankind live in societies where the social world and, for want of a better word, the intellectual world are part and parcel of each other. The unique breakthrough of science is to de-socialize that world, to attempt to create institutions that can support and coexist with widely differing world views, indeed, social institutions that can embody the possibility of constantly changing the fundamentals of the world view, including world views which demand changes in the social organization.

The debate has moved then from attributing science to a special kind of thinking (logical versus pre-logical), or a special method (empirical versus metaphysical) to rather a special kind of social arrangement wherein reason has been applied to the task of applying reason to tasks. Rationality within a given society can be measured by the standards of the society, thus finding the behaviour of the Azande witch, the Melanesian cargo cultist and the Canadian space scientist to be more or less on a par in their several societies. The further question of the rationality of the standards of the society themselves is not so smoothly and harmlessly disposed of.[19] For one thing, the questions get especially urgently pressed in regard to science and technology because they cross so many social and cultural boundaries that their rationality seems to be detachable from the society of origin. This portability of their rationality raises the question of the rationality of non-portable rationality. To the seeming paradox of this reflexive move I shall return when discussing Gellner's ideas.

III   RELATIVISM

Relativism can take and has taken various forms: cultural, ethical and epistemological.[20] Roughly, it is the doctrine that there is no absolute truth, whether in cultures, ethics, or cognition. This means either that there is no truth known to us, and hence all attempts to capture it are equal, since there is no way to judge between cultures and their efforts; or it means that truth is whatever is declared true *by a system*, that systems of culture, ethics or knowledge have their own differing means of appraisal, but there is no super-systemic means of appraising these means of appraisal.

Anthropologists, I propose, fall into relativism for two main reasons: one very noble, and one logical. The noble reason is basically a respect for the views of others, a respect for the subjects of anthropological inquiry, their society, their culture, their ideas. This is mirrored by an embarrassment with the patronizing attitude of early observers. The problem with this view is the same problem as arises with liberal tolerance in general: where do you draw the line? To answer, 'I won't draw the line' is unreasonable, so that, not surprisingly, it does get drawn. As the tolerant society cannot tolerate the murderer, the tolerant anthropologist cannot tolerate the society that beheads and eats anthropologists. So, the argument becomes one of line-drawing. Turnbull, in a fascinating book called *The Mountain People*, suggested that among the Ik of Uganda he had run into his limits of tolerance. He claims to have found a society almost literally depraved by starvation, and consequently better off disbanded and dispersed than allowed to continue.[21] Frederick Barth, another well-known anthropologist, criticized Turnbull in a paper sub-titled 'Calling A Colleague to Account'. Barth took it upon himself to instruct Turnbull in the reprehensibility of his particular attempt to draw lines. Barth accused Turnbull of violating professional ethics. Barth thus drew his line.[22] Interestingly enough, Barth framed his attack in such a way that rational debate was hardly possible, since he denounced line drawing by drawing a line. Turnbull was understandably a bit nonplussed.[23] When we argue about line-drawing, we must be careful to be self-critical. In striving not to patronize our subjects directly we may end up patronizing both them and our colleagues.

The other argument from logic to relativism is due to Melville J. Herskovits and goes like this: 'Judgements are based on experience, and experience is interpreted by each individual in terms of his own enculturation.' In other words, we cannot break out of the enculturating screen: the system allows us to make judgments, but there is no breakthrough to the beyond where we can judge the system and hence its judgments. This argument, which is sometimes called the argument from ultimate presuppositions, or the argument from the framework, cuts very deep and has I believe also been defeated in philosophy, but that result is still controversial, so I shall merely mention it here.[25]

As I mentioned earlier, both of these arguments crystallize in a revulsion from strong absolutism. For 'strong absolutism' here we should read any self-confident system of ideas, whether the science-based arrogance of nineteenth century evolutionists, or the firmly held convictions of missionaries about pagan darkness and superstition, etc. Such strong absolutism seems intolerant and illiberal, and also ultimately dogmatic, since its tenets cannot themselves be justified. And indeed, I share this basic revulsion from strong absolutism. Ours is an age of uncertainty and scepticism, by contrast with the confident optimism of our Victorian ancestors, and we do not want a philosophical basis for anthropology that reassures us that all is right with our world and *we* happen to be on top of it.

On the other hand, relativism cannot function as a basis for anthropology because it leads to an omni-tolerant nihilism. What I want to espouse is a moderate intermediate position in which judgments can be made and discussed, and their basis in enculturation can be examined and discussed, and the rational status of science can be discussed. A weak or methodological absolutism.

Why is this important? Well, the rational and moral unity of mankind seems to enjoin us to communicate and learn from one another, inter-culturally as well as cross-culturally. Any argument which suggests that this cannot in principle succeed is suspect, since we so obviously do succeed. Cultures do modernize, and secularize; they do introduce the tender shoot of science and its rationality, and sometimes it flourishes. This being so, how come? For the answer I turn back to an anthropologist.

Evans-Pritchard is not a relativist. Here is a much discussed passage from his study of Azande witchcraft:

It is an inevitable conclusion from Zande descriptions of witchcraft that it is not an objective reality. The physiological condition which is said to be the seat of witchcraft, and which I believe to be nothing more than food passing through the small intestine, is an objective condition, but the qualities they attribute to it and the rest of their beliefs about it are mystical. Witches, as Azande conceive them, cannot exist.[26]

I find this passage quite unexceptionable; indeed, like much of the rest of the book, profound and laudable. Evans-Pritchard also shows how in Zande beliefs there is room for empiricism, for doubt and for defence. But his relativist critics raise the question: in invoking objective reality and the category of the mystical, in concluding that witches cannot exist, Evans-Pritchard is employing the concepts and categories of *his* culture to judge another. But what basis can he have for such an argument? Are not his concepts culture-bound and hence limited, hence inappropriate to Zande ones?

Perhaps the simplest answer to this relativist argument is to admit that perhaps it is a mistake to say there cannot be witches, but that need not deter one from advancing it as an hypothesis nevertheless. This simple solution is not so simple, but I shall not pursue its ramifications now. What relativists want is for Evans-Pritchard to say that the Azande have their concepts and hence their world, and that we have ours, and it is highly doubtful if any general comparisons can be made. We can explore, wonder at our difference, but there is no neutral standpoint or universe of discourse that will allow us to mediate between them.[27]

The way I would want to criticize this is to argue that were we to take this doctrine literally, other societies would become not objects of wonder and fascination, but of bafflement and incomprehension. It is precisely because accounts that seem rational to us can be given of what is going on in primitive society that anthropologists have been able to escape the old condescension, ethnocentrism, primitive mentality, etc. views of predecessors in anthropology. If, then, this can be done in general with other *societies*, why not do it with beliefs and cognition? Certainly, in the process we may distort or oversimplify the living texture of society, but that, after all, is always true, and over-simplification has its uses and advantages, as well as its drawbacks.

Evans-Pritchard offers us as close and sympathetic a rational reconstruction of an alien thought system as exists in the anthropological literature, so I hardly think his crisp judgments can be said to have yielded oversimplification. What I want to stress is that he is concerned less with the falseness of Azande views and more with the mutual support systems of ideas and social institutions. It is the social support mechanisms which undergird witchcraft, allay doubts, blunt scepticism. It is, perhaps, the interlocking of society and cognition that limits the rationality of the Azande. It is the unfusing of cognition from the social web that allows greater rationality. Here I will borrow from the British anthropologist and philosopher Ernest Gellner.[28]

IV   RATIONALITY AND RELATIVISM

Gellner first makes the paradoxical point that as a matter of fact for most of human history and for most of the contemporary world, relativism is as near as no matter true. That is to say, neolithic beliefs, Babylonian beliefs, medieval theology, alchemy, astrology, there is really nothing much to choose between them when it comes to rationality; pay your money and take your choice. Much the same is true today in the third world. Aboriginal Australian beliefs are not interestingly different as cognitive systems from South American Indian, or Azande. Where Gellner wants to deny relativism is at what he calls the big ditch, namely that gulf dividing societies with what might be described for want of a better word as traditional world views, from societies that are wholly or partly modernized and have science and technology as the centre of their cognitive system. This ditch, which is the boundary beyond which relativism cannot be allowed to go, is, he believes, rather hard to characterize. He manages, however, to pin it down to four crucial distinctions: denial of idiosyncratic norms, the cognitive division of labour, the question of entrenched clauses, and the diplomatic immunity of cognition.

By *idiosyncratic norms* Gellner characterizes a feature of traditional thought that science repudiates. Science aims to explain by means of publicly specifiable and repeatable structures such as mechanism, and not general myth or specific local phenomena. Hence scientific cognition is 'not, at the same time, the delineation of a moral or social order. On the contrary: the formal criteria they must satisfy, at the same time make them singularly ill-suited for the underpinning of moral expectations, of a status- and value-system. They tend to be "meaningless" and "morally blind".'[29]

Cognitive division of labour means for Gellner that in scientific cognition certain concepts do certain kinds of work, and other concepts other kinds. Contrast this with Lévy-Bruhl, who says, 'the dictum deduced from Hume's argument, that "anything may produce anything" might have served as a motto for primitive mentality'.[30] The key to the cognitive division of labour is not so much which concepts do which, but that there be a sensitivity to the division. Concepts which do explanatory work must be testable, public and repeatable; other kinds of concepts do other kinds of work (moral, religious etc.) and there must be no crossing over from one side to the other.

Gellner uses the phrase *entrenched cognitive clauses* to point out how many beliefs in a traditional thought system cannot be replaced or denied without significantly disturbing the total picture and the society's composure. He argues that scientific cognition strives constantly to reduce any entrenched clauses, anything we *have* to believe in order to go on, and indeed sometimes seems to embody the hope that that amount can be reduced to zero.

Finally, the *diplomatic immunity of cognition* brings us to the paradox of reflexivity I mentioned earlier. Let Gellner formulate and resolve it in his way:

In a traditional belief system, cognition, the discovery and the endorsement of beliefs, is an event *in* the world, and this means in the social and moral world. Hence they are subject to the same kinds of obligations and sanctions as are other kinds of conduct — indeed, when these ideas touch the entrenched clauses, they are quite especially subject to them. Man the knower is not alienated from the citizen and the moral being . . . we do not *really* believe that our cognitive activities are *really* extra-territorial, are qualitatively different from the rest of our lives. Nevertheless, as Kant pointed out, we assume that such extra-territoriality in fact obtains, and our attribution of 'objective validity' to our own thinking hinges on this odd assumption.

The social implications of this assumption are of course of the utmost importance. Here there is an interesting difference between Western liberal societies, where the officially endorsed entrenched clauses of the belief-system have an eroded status and importance . . . and thus facilitate the notion of autonomy, and those other societies which possess entrenched clauses that are still taken with some degree of seriousness, such as Marxism. The consequence of this is of course that in such societies the autonomy of cognition is only partial, and in so far as it exists . . . it generates painful strain.[31]

Whereas in our society,

Newtonian physics was revered by many thinkers as the very paradigm of well-established, permanent truth. It is interesting to note that when Newtonian physics was tumbled from this pedestal, virtually no tremors were noticed in the rest of the social fabric.[35]

In an old-fashioned manner of speaking, what Gellner is saying is that the notion of truth is a regulative idea, namely of assertions somehow corresponding to a given world or nature, a world or nature not under the control of, certainly not produced by, the social structure, and a relation of correspondence that either obtains or doesn't, again, regardless of the social structure, that this notion, fantastic as it may seem to relativists, lies behind the science, freedom and affluence of modern society.

Now this notion is implicit, I think, in all communication: it is the assumption that there is, in the last analysis, something to measure rationality against, goal-states either are or are not achieved: there are goal-states. Goal-directed action is the more rational the more thoroughly the information on which the action has been predicated is checked out. The best-checked information is, clearly, that which is correct. Action towards achieving that state is highly rational only if, in a regulative sense, there is that state to be achieved. To defuse the notion of Truth of its alarming metaphysical charge, one can employ the notion of error to be escaped: whatever the world *is* like, it is not like that.

Without some such fairly naive realism about the world and the objects in it, it is difficult to make sense of communication in general and of language in particular. This a relativist may admit but claim he captures naive realism within his relativism — indeed the naive realisms of diverse societies. He thus misses the point, which is that what is at issue is the naive realism that rules out relativism because peoples communicate on the supposition that they are communicating about something fixed and given. However different the categories and concepts of individuals and cultures, the remarkable fact remains that communication is achieved, and cultures learn from each other how to pursue their goals more rationally and how to be more rational in their choice of goals. If the social evolution of mankind is not to be dismissed, this conclusion is inescapable.

Let me, finally, sum up the situation as I see it. Our rationality leads us to take over from blind fate the problem of survival. Survival means food, water, sleep, shelter, reproduction, protection from enemies and disease. It means getting control over nature — preferably by getting to know nature better. Once this process has begun, other problems emerge: wealth, power, government, and even more abstract ones about pure knowledge. The newly emergent problems are tackled rationally, by cooperative communication and discussion. The moral unity of men shows itself in their selection and ranking of problems. Our rational unity shows itself in the friendly-hostile cooperative endeavour in which we undertake to solve them. That social order which encourages critical cooperation is the highest expression of our rationality and is what begets and sustains science. I do not for a moment delude myself that we ever get cognitive endeavours that are once and for all free of the web of society. Rationality shows itself in our building a self-improving social organization, not in the delusion that through it we escape social life.

NOTES

1. Read to an audience at Dartmouth College, 1.3.77 and to the anthropology departments at McGill University (17.3.77) and the University of Southern California (6.12.79), and to the Philosophy Colloquium of the University of Southern California (7.3.80).

2. This is the title of Lewis Hanke's book (De Kalb, Northern Illinois University Press, 1974) devoted to the disputation on this matter between Bartolomé de Las Casas and Juan Ginés de Sepulveda in 1550.

3. The closest Aristotle seems to come to saying this is at 1421 a 11.

4. They are, after all, survivors.

5. I.C. Jarvie, *The Revolution in Anthropology*, London, Routledge & Kegan Paul, 1964, ch. 1, §2; review of Schoek and Wiggins, *British Journal for the Philosophy of Science*, 15, 1964, pp. 151-8; *Concepts and Society*, London, Routledge & Kegan Paul, 1972, ch. 2; 'Epistle to the Anthropologists', *American Anthropologist*, 77, 1975, pp. 253-66, 'Cultural Relativism Again', *Philosophy of the Social Sciences*, 5, 1975, pp. 343-55; 'Nationalism and the Social Sciences', *Canadian Journal of Sociology*, 1, 1976, pp. 515-28.

6. See also my paper with J. Agassi, 'The Rationality of Dogmatism', in Th. Geraets (ed.), *Rationality Today*, Ottawa, University of Ottawa Press, 1979, pp. 353-62.

7. This list of ingredients is most

68 CHAPTER 4

clearly formulated in Sir Francis Bacon's works, *The Advancement of Learning*, London and *Novum Organum*, London, 1620.

8. See J. Agassi, *Towards an Historiography of Science, History and Theory*, Beiheft 2, 1963.

9. Since we learn only from interaction. When we do it alone it is by means of what might be called an 'inner dialogue' with a second self.

10. Lucien Lévy-Bruhl, *How Natives Think (Les Fonctions mentales dans les sociétiés inférièures)*, London, Allen, 1926.

11. Bacon, *Novum Organum*, op. cit. note 7, aphorisms xi–xiv.

12. Edmund Husserl, *Logical Investigations*, London, Routledge & Kegan Paul, 1970 (originally Halle 1913).

13. K.R. Popper, 'Towards a Rational Theory of Tradition', and 'Back to the Presocratics', both in *Conjectures and Refutations*, London, Routledge & Kegan Paul, 1963.

14. David Hume, *A Treatise of Human Nature*, London, 1738, Everyman Edition, vol. I, Book I, Part III, 'Of the Component Parts of Our Reasoning Concerning Cause and Effect'.

15. Ibid. 'Of the Inference from the Impression to the Idea'.

16. Ibid. Book I, Part IV. 'Conclusion of this Book'.

17. See my 'Theories of Cargo Cults: A Critical Analysis', *Oceania*, 34, 1963, pp. 1–31 and pp. 108–36; and *The Revolution in Anthropology*, op. cit., note 5, *passim*. The quotation is from my 'On the Explanation of Cargo Cults', *European Journal of Sociology*, 7, 1966, pp. 299–312.

18. See Edward Rice, *John Frum He Come*, Garden City, N.Y., Doubleday, 1974. Rice wavers between swallowing the cargo cult and re-interpreting it as a response to colonial oppression.

19. Compare on this point the distinction between strong and weak rationality made by J. Agassi and myself in our 'The Problem of the Rationality of Magic', *British Journal of Sociology*, 18, 1967, pp. 55–74.

20. See J. Tennekes, *Anthropology, Relativism and Method*, Assen, Van Gorcum, 1971.

21. Colin Turnbull, *The Mountain People*, New York, Simon & Schuster, 1972 and his second thoughts in *Current Anthropology*, 16, 1975, pp. 354–8.

22. Frederick Barth, 'On Responsibility and Humanity: Calling a Colleague to Account', *Current Anthropology*, 15, 1974, pp. 99–103.

23. Colin Turnbull, 'Reply', *Current Anthropology*, 15, 1974, p. 103.

24. Melville J. Herskovits, *Cultural Relativism*, New York, Random House, 1973, p. 15.

25. See K.R. Popper, 'Facts, Standards and Truth: A Further Criticism of Relativism', an Addendum to volume two of the fourth and subsequent editions of his *The Open Society and Its Enemies*, London, Routledge & Kegan Paul, 1962; and 'The Myth of the Framework' in Eugene Freeman (ed.), *The Abdication of Philosophy*, La Salle, Open Court, 1974.

26. E.E. Evans-Pritchard, *Witchcraft, Oracles and Magic Among the Azande*, 1937, p. 63.

27. Cp. Peter Winch, 'Understanding a Primitive Society', *American Philosophical Quarterly*, I, 1964, pp. 307–24: 'What Evans-Pritchard wants to be able to say is that the criteria applied in scientific experimentation constitute a true link between our ideas and an independent reality, whereas those characteristic of other systems of thought — in particular, magical methods of thought — do not. It is

evident that the expressions "true link" and "independent reality" in the previous sentence cannot themselves be explained by reference to the scientific universe of discourse, as this would beg the question. We have then to ask how, by reference to what established universe of discourse, the use of those expressions *is* to be explained; and it is clear that Evans-Pritchard has not answered this question.'

28. Ernest Gellner, *Legitimation of Belief*, Cambridge, C.U.P., 1974.
29. Ibid., p. 171.
30. Op. cit. note 10, above, p. 377.
31. E. Gellner, op. cit.
32. Ibid., pp. 180-1.

CHAPTER 5

Popper on the Difference between the Natural and the Social Sciences[0]

1. Introduction

Popper always told us to open a paper with a problem: I have two problems. The first is whether in the years that have elapsed since 1943–1944, when "The Poverty of Historicism" was originally published, there have emerged new arguments to challenge what Popper said about the differences between the natural and the social sciences. To address this problem I have to face a second one: just what, in that work and his other comments on the topic, did Popper consider the main differences between the natural and social sciences to be? Both problems are enmeshed in a sociological problem, that of the strange reception of Popper's ideas in general,[1] and the extraordinary sidestepping of *The Poverty of Historicism* in particular.

When I took my first course with Popper in 1955, the only book of his then available in English was *The Open Society and Its Enemies* of 1945. Popper had published many papers, but even at the London School of Economics (LSE) freshmen were not advised to read them. This may explain why when the famous paper "The Poverty of Historicism I, II and III" came out in book form in the autumn of 1957, it caused ripples. I remember the New Left (*première cru*) were particularly exercised by it, and prominent spokesmen like Charles Taylor and John Silber spoke at the LSE or wrote in *Universities and Left Review* about how reactionary/anti-Marxist it was, and how unjust to Marx, who was no historicist. The implication was that historicism was a straw man. One should have been warned by those stirrings: the book rubbed too many people in too many sore places to be other than buried as soon as possible. It has become an anticlassic: read but not praised; diffused but not read; influential but disparaged.[2] Even Popper slights the book in his autobiography as stodgily written and structurally flawed.[3]

The Poverty of Historicism deserves rediscovery. Together with Hayek's *The Counter-Revolution of Science* it is a major work on the philosophy of the social sciences, worthy to stand alongside Durkheim's *Rules of Sociological*

70

Method and Weber's *Methodology of the Social Sciences*. The book begins not with a problem but with a doctrine: historicism, that is, that there are historical laws of social development. The book is a relentless critique of all versions of historicism. Popper suggests that this doctrine is widely diffused in the intellectual atmosphere of our time—acknowledged and, more often than not, unacknowledged—and that it underpins totalitarianism. His critique is to the effect that it is a philosophy of the social replete with error, advocating a method of tackling social problems that will make things worse, not better. It is easy to see a parallel with Popper's 1934 classic *Logik der Forschung*,[4] which was a sustained critique of a philosophy and methodology of science (logical positivism) which he thought erroneous and unfruitful, especially for understanding the crisis in physics created by quantum theory and the pretensions of Marxist and Freudian pseudoscience. In *Logik der Forschung*, however, he does begin with a problem—what is scientific method, or, what distinguishes science from other kinds of inquiry—and he proceeds to a critique; whereas *The Poverty of Historicism* is structured as a broad attack on a doctrine (historicism) converging on a problem—what methods characterize the social sciences? Perhaps his dislike of *The Poverty of Historicism* is rooted in his considered preference for *problemstellung*. Although understandable, this is unfair: *The Poverty of Historicism* had to concentrate on criticism for two reasons. First, historicism was more prevalent and more socially pernicious than logical positivism. Second, Popper had less to say about the methods of the social sciences than about the methods of science generally. Indeed, a major thesis of his critique of historicism is that historicism exaggerates such differences as there are between the methods of science in general and the methods of the social sciences in particular.

2. Natural versus Social Sciences

The difficulty of writing about Popper's view of the differences between the natural and the social sciences, then, has partly to do with the structure of Popper's main work on them, *The Poverty of Historicism*. That work is divided into four parts: Part One sets out objections to the extension of the methods of the natural sciences to the social sciences; Part Two sets out some parallels between the methods of the natural sciences and the social sciences. Parts Three and Four look as though they are going to be criticisms, respectively, of Parts One and Two. But the parallel one hopes for is not quite there in the text. Each of the ten sections in Part One sets out an argument as to why the social sciences cannot proceed in the same manner as the natural sciences. A parallel structure would be ten sections in Part Three assessing these arguments. Instead (see table), there are only eight sections in Part Three, organized as follows: Sections 19 and 20 ("Practical Problems" and "The Technological Approach") state Popper's own views about the task of the social sciences. Then there are two sections on utopianism that speak more to some points raised in Part Two (15, 16 and 17) than to arguments in Part One. Sections 23 and 24 criticize holism as it is set out in Section 7. Section 25 criticizes Section 2, and Section 26 criticizes Section 1. The sections on novelty, complexity, inexactitude, and so on are not given a parallel section of criticism. Much the same is true of the structure of Parts Two and Four.

Organization of The Poverty of Historicism

Part I: The Anti-Naturalistic Doctrines of Historicism	Part III: Criticism of the Anti-Naturalistic Doctrines
1. Generalization. (see 26)	19. Practical Aims of this Criticism.
2. Experiment. (see 25)	20. The Technological Approach to Sociology.
3. Novelty.	21. Piecemeal versus Utopian Social Engineering. (see 15 and 17)
4. Complexity.	22. The Unholy Alliance with Utopianism. (see 16)
5. Inexactitude of Prediction.	23. Criticism of Holism. (see 7)
6. Objectivity and Valuation.	24. The Holistic Theory of Social Experiments.
7. Holism.	25. The Variability of Experimental Conditions. (see 2)
8. Intuitive Understanding.	26. Are Generalizations Confined to Periods? (see 1)
9. Quantitative Methods.	
10. Essentialism versus Nominalism.	

Part II: The Pro-Naturalistic Doctrines of Historicism	Part IV: Criticism of the Pro-Naturalistic Doctrines
11. Comparison with Astronomy. Long-Term Forecasts and Large-Scale Forecasts.	27. Is There a Law of Evolution? Laws and Trends. (see 14)
12. The Observational Basis.	28. The Method of Reduction. Causal Explanation. Prediction and Prophecy. (see 11)
13. Social Dynamics.	29. The Unity of Method. (see 12)
14. Historical Laws.	30. Theoretical and Historical Sciences. (see 14, 15, 16)
15. Historical Prophecy versus Social Engineering.	31. Situational Logic in History. Historical Interpretation.
16. The Theory of Historical Development.	32. The Institutional Theory of Progress. (see 6)
17. Interpreting versus Planning Social Change.	33. Conclusion. The Emotional Appeal of Historicism.
18. Conclusion of the Analysis.	

There are reasons for this failure to carry through a parallel structure. To begin with, Popper is not critical of all the arguments he attributes to the historicists—he hardly could be, seeing that some historicists are pro-naturalistic, some anti-naturalistic—and he attributes to each the best argument he can find. But, because he tries to separate exposition and assessment, Popper tells us only at times which argument is not objected to, or is objected to only if developed in certain ways; at times he is hard to follow, as when he endorses holism but denies that it is specific to the social sciences or absent from the natural sciences—giving some readers the impression that Popper is against holism. A second reason is that whenever possible Popper organizes his assessments around certain attempts to state his own views on the methodology of the theoretical social sciences (i.e., in 19, 20, 21, 29, 31, and 32); and since these sections are scattered among the critical sections, no symmetry of structure is possible.

Can we restructure *The Poverty of Historicism* on the same lines as *Logik der Forschung*? What problem does the work address? My suggestion is: what are the methods of the social sciences? How, if at all, do the methods of the social sciences differ from the methods of the natural sciences? How do the answers to these questions bear on (then) current social problems, including the war and postwar reconstruction? Concern with the last question animates the entire book, although more as a subtext (glimpsed in notes and asides) than on the surface. According to the "Historical Note," *The Poverty of Historicism* was worked out in the mid and late 1930s, as the great debate about ways of improving society deteriorated into hostilities between powers embodying philosophies of the social (communism, fascism, and social democracy). Popper is out to discredit the historicist prescriptions of totalitarianism, and also to distinguish them sharply from the piecemeal philosophy and method intrinsic to liberal democracy. His strongest argument is to demand with Kant that we discipline our dreams and speculations by reference to the concrete task of improving the condition of humanity (p. 56). There is a similar move in his general fallibilist philosophy. Already in his work on the natural sciences, *Logik der Forschung*, fallibilism leads him to emphasize the value of testing theory by experience in order to ensure that our speculations do not lose all contact with reality. He seems to think that loose speculation in the social sciences is especially reprehensible because of both the urgency of the problems social science should help solve and the devastation wreaked on humankind when ill-thought-out ideas are imposed wholesale. Hence the valuable discipline of both testing and application to practical aims is also a ready-made standard by which to appraise our ideas.

It should be noticed that practice is an added control, not the main target. Socially, Popper seems to believe in active intervention and in the possibility that such action will improve conditions. This makes him sound like an optimist, which he often describes himself as, both in social matters and in epistemological matters. Yet he fears that kind of optimism that makes us confident that we know what to do and hence precipitate. At other times he expresses amazement that we have fared so well socially and epistemologically. This is hardly a straightforward optimism. His philosophy centers on mistakes: we learn from them, so not only are we bound to make mistakes, if we did not make any we would cease to learn and improve. This too is not exactly optimism.

Similarly on the contrast activist/passivist. Popper certainly believes in actively fighting for justice and working at righting wrongs; but he also believes in leaving well alone, at least until one can show that one's remedies will not be worse than the disease.

At the time of writing *The Poverty of Historicism* (the 1930s) and *The Open Society and Its Enemies* (late 1930s and early 1940s) Popper was, with good reason, very pessimistic.[5] The possibility of civilization being destroyed was quite real. Furthermore, his fellow liberals accepted some of the false theories of human nature and human society that buttressed the doctrines behind fascism and communism. Totalitarians claimed that history supported them, while liberals claimed that history supported them too. Both appealed to the historical social sciences. The urgency of criticizing the philosophy of the social sciences that enabled totalitarians to claim scientific authority was in a sense much greater than with, say, chemistry. Real lives and suffering of concrete people were involved. Hence a kind of methodological pessimism and quietism permeates Popper's reflections on the methods of the social sciences, since we know so little and our interventions are apt to make things worse.[6]

It is my observation that these important cautions have gone almost unheeded, as witness the blithe radicalism in the academic atmosphere since the 1960s, with scarcely a passing thought for the actual alleviation of concrete suffering, still less for the danger of making things worse. Optimistic and activist social scientists are quite loath to discuss the failures of social reform and radical change, still less the possibility of a social science equivalent to iatrogenics.

Yet Popper is a staunch believer in the possibility of the theoretical social sciences, that is, in explanatory, empirically testable hypotheses about society. He acknowledges that there are difficulties with experiment, novelty, complexity, interests, and quantification, but these go to theory not method. He isolates only one phenomenon that makes a great methodological difference between the natural and the social sciences—the "Oedipus Effect" (later known by Merton's label "The Self-Fulfilling Prophecy"). This is an easy notion to grasp, but not an easy one to see the significance of. Oedipus's downfall was brought on by the very prophecy of it, since his father and later he too made efforts to prevent it, which efforts enabled it to come about. In general, the Oedipus Effect can be observed wherever the social scientist adds to the stock of information on which people predicate their actions. Notoriously, opinion polls can influence voters, although it is possible for this influence to go either way (with the winner or with the underdog), or one way for opposite reasons (with the winner or against the loser, or against the winner and for the underdog). Notoriously also, people act in a way that feeds inflation just because they expect inflation to continue.[7] All this is obvious enough; less obvious is Popper's contention that this Oedipus Effect makes a lot of methodological (and theoretical) difference. In particular it makes it hard to test and apply theories—unless they include the Oedipus Effect.

As for other suggestions about the differences between the natural and the social sciences, Popper's general position seems to be that there is a tendency to exaggerate difficulties into impossibilities. Certainly there are all sorts of differences involved in solving problems concerning our fellow human beings that are not involved in solving problems concerning nature in general. But: (a) often enough parallels are missed where they exist; (b) in the domain of the natural sciences, from the study of life at the macro level through to the study of inanimate matter at the micro level, most of the special difficulties involved in studying human beings are simulated; and (c) for every advantage physics has against the social sciences, an argument can be made for an advantage the social sciences have over physics. In particular, Popper argues, people's rationality makes it easier for us to understand why we behave the way we do than to understand why atoms and particles behave the way *they* do. By this reckoning, social science is on the whole easier than natural science.

Before I discuss some suggestions that have emerged since 1944 about other sorts of differences that may exist between the natural and the social sciences, and to assess their force, there are a few preliminary points to be made. These have to do with Popper's general attitude about the enterprise of sciences of society. Although Popper says that the natural sciences have been more successful than the social sciences, this is not a matter of principle.[8] Indeed, his most forceful negative remark in the Introduction to *The Poverty of Historicism* is to the effect that the social sciences have yet to find their Galileo. This is an odd remark, since clearly there are claimants, such as Adam Smith, Auguste Comte, Karl Marx, Emile Durkheim, Max Weber, J. M. Keynes, and so on. Doubly odd in view of the stress Popper lays here and later[9] on the rationality or zero principle that, he says, undergirds all of social science; it is the false but necessary assumption that we act rationally (to achieve given goals). Under this assumption Popper believes the work of the social sciences to consist mainly of two tasks: first, constructing models of social action that envisage people trying to reach goals under the constraints of their situation; second, tracing out the unintended consequences of the actions of many persons. The first he calls the logic of the situation or situational logic; the second, unintended consequences analysis. Following through these two tasks enables social scientists to reconstruct, explain, and predict human conduct.[10] The predictions can serve as both tests and applications. Building these models is rather low-level theoretical work, logically similar to applied science since it manipulates the initial conditions rather than the universal theories. All the classical social scientists achieved their results primarily by brilliant reconstructions of the initial conditions of the situation that make sense of actions within it.[11] Besides those mentioned above we could cite Plato, Bacon, de Tocqueville, Malinowski, Radcliffe-Brown, and Evans-Pritchard. Some of the most famous but zany sociological models are of this character too, such as those by Lenin, Wittfogel, Adorno, and Lévi-Strauss. Perhaps there are too many candidate Galileos. Perhaps a Galileo of initial conditions is an oxymoron.

It seems simple enough to say how a person intended to achieve a goal and acted accordingly. But conscious and intended action has unintended and sometimes uncontrollable consequences. The exciting new idea here is that from trivial and obvious hypotheses we can obtain far from trivial explanations and predictions. Hence, for example, a revolution that sees all power as evil and strives for total equality and participation will attempt an overthrow of the *ancien régime*, and under easily specifiable conditions. This is the obvious part. But take it a step further. There will then be a power vacuum: lots needing to be done but no one in a position to do it. Into such a vacuum someone might step, with the highest motives—someone who, then being resisted, may have to take drastic action against former comrades, now "enemies of the revolution." In the name of the abolition of the evil of power, power may be used to do evil. Hence the charge of triteness or triviality against the social sciences is a logical mistake, to wit, the view that corollaries to obvious hypotheses are obvious.[12] Much applied natural science takes its theories for granted and adds some obvious models to them, but just because the theories and models are obvious one cannot conclude that they will not be illuminating or powerful; to do so is to underrate the power of applied science no less than that of the social sciences.

Popper has a much stronger vested interest in the social sciences than he has in physics. Denying both the view that societies do not significantly change and the view that if societies change they do so in fixed and inevitable ways, Popper declares (on p. 51) that societies sometimes stagnate, sometimes change, and in surprising and unintended ways. This means he is pessimistic about his own situation, a refugee from Hitler's totalitarianism developing a philosophy that offers no comforting hope that it will not happen again. We cannot reliably predict the future; the only thing we can be sure of is that what happens will surprise us. The best we can do is concentrate on the problems that immediately confront us (at the end of the war these were the dangers posed by communist totalitarianism; these now include religious totalitarianism) and not naively hope for a time when we will not have to defend ourselves against such dangers.

Against this background understanding of Popper I want now to look at arguments that have appeared since *The Poverty of Historicism* was worked out. The social sciences have come a long way since 1944. My impression is that several arguments concerning the differences between the natural and the social sciences have gained currency since then. These were either not covered in *The Poverty of Historicism*, or not expressed in a manner suitable, or emphatic enough, for today. They however can be dealt with in a Popperian spirit, as I shall try to show. All these arguments are anti-naturalistic: few seem to be fighting for the cause of a natural science of society anymore. I am.

At the end of the essay I shall offer some observations on the reception of Popper's ideas in the intellectual world. Bartley says that if Popper is right, most philosophers and indeed a great many intellectuals waste their lives.[13] I suspect this implication is not lost on those who find confrontation with Popper's ideas too much to bear. What I shall call the arguments from meaningfulness, interests, and reflexivity are used as reasons for burying Popper's philosophy of the social. Hence, the discussion of these arguments can also help us to understand Popper's reception. Each of the arguments ramifies widely, and sometimes they are held together or in various combinations. I separate them out and reformulate them in order to present them in their strongest form.

3. The Argument from Meaningfulness

There is a widely bruited argument that some trace back to Max Weber and beyond, which surfaced in its most cited form (soon after *The Poverty of Historicism* appeared as a book) in Peter Winch's monograph *The Idea of a Social Science* (1958).[14] This is the argument from meaningfulness. It goes to show that the very phenomena presupposed by the natural sciences are intrinsically different from the phenomena of the social sciences. It is held that the phenomena of social life, such as an event or an action, are not pieces of nature, slices through a given flux of experience, but are rather intentional objects—something, that is, created by or decided upon by human beings. It is human beings, language-using creatures, who constitute significance out of the infinity of physical phenomena.[15] This process of attributing significance or meaning will differ from time to time, from culture to culture, and even from person to person. Hence there is in a strong sense nothing much "given" in the social world. Or, to put it differently, there is no external point of view from which to do social science. Social science requires one to enter or contact a social world, a social world that is constituted, defined, and sustained by the meaning-generating activities (or "work") of its members. To get a handle on these one must start from those meaning-generating activities and try to grasp the rules they embody. What happens will then "make sense."

So getting to know a society, even becoming aware that there is a society there, involves interaction with the human beings constituting it. The primary means we have of engaging in such interaction is through learning to use their language, not just in the naive sense of being able to ask them simple questions, but in the strong sense that we master their way of ordering the world into *their* social world—not *the* social world. This sort of inquiry is a conceptual inquiry, not unlike the sort of conceptual inquiry Wittgenstein urged that we undertake to come to terms with meaning in our own everyday world.[16] Quantitative methods, social evolution, comparison of societies, predictions, value-judgments, questionnaires, and indeed much of the apparatus of traditional social science becomes on this argument of questionable value. Perhaps the social anthropologist engaged in deep fieldwork comes closest to the Winchian ideal, but there are limits to what this data authorizes the anthropologist to say.[17]

Some philosophers have pursued this or similar lines of argument into a field curiously called "the philosophy of mind," where they concentrate on the problem of whether it is possible to characterize an action, that is, a socially meaningful event, in such a way as to distinguish it from an autonomic reflex.

Others take a slightly different tack. Society is, they maintain, the domain of humanity's meaningful or symbolic discourse. That is, in building for ourselves a common life we do not just enter into practical albeit meaningful interactions with nature and our fellow human beings. We also engage in all sorts of behavior and utterances that suggest that we seek to conjure an order out of chaos and threat. This order can be called the symbolic order. Too much has been written on this for it to be systematized and expounded simply. The range is from Lévi-Strauss's view that humans seem to want to order the universe in binary oppositions (though at times these are tertiary) through to latter-day Durkheimian views that humans produce and reproduce the order of social life in the order of symbols. Turner and Douglas in particular seem to believe that there is an autonomous order of discourse employing symbols that is internal to all social life.[18]

Yet another version of the argument from meaningfulness, and the last I shall expound on here, is due to Quine, and is often called his "radical translatability thesis." Roughly, this amounts to the claim that "manuals for translating one language into another can be set up in divergent ways, all compatible with the totality of speech dispositions, yet incompatible with each other."[19] So thick is the forest of symbols, so varying are the many nuances of meaning, that translation from one natural language to another is not possible without loss. Hence there is a sense in which what we are dealing with in the social sciences—ways of life—are somehow inherently impenetrable. We cannot understand without entering into them; but once we enter into them we cannot translate (communicate) what we find. We can only describe and redescribe and hint and hope that somehow or other something of what we want to get across does so.

Confronting these highly plausible arguments, I feel as must have the author of *The Poverty of Historicism*: wanting to criticize arguments I by no means totally reject. Indeed, I can eschew direct criticism altogether and concentrate on the implications drawn from these arguments, for it seems to me they make no difference at all to the project of sciences of society, so long as that project is not construed in a positivistic or essentialistic way. Suppose it is indeed the case that there are no data "given" to experience, no "externally" observable events, that there is a forest of symbolic meanings that cannot be captured in any possible translation. Why should this pose any special difficulty? Much the same can be said of the entities postulated by natural science: atoms, molecules, cells, plants, animals. Each of these entities is assumed because it is a useful device for coping with experience by the use of some theory or other in which we embed it. True, so long as the theory survives, we might claim that it describes the world as it is. This is not at all to say that our description is true, or even the best, although we hope it is; still less to deny that there are hosts of alternative ways the world can be described; it is to say either we have not worked those out as yet, or, if we have, we do not find them as adequate for our purposes.

The argument from meaningfulness similarly postulates "meaning" as entities or devices to help cope with experience and possibly to be descriptive of it. However, a true devotee of the meaningfulness argument will find this unsatisfactory. To this person, an atom or a stone is a thing; an action or an institution is of another order, a meaning. Such things as social scientists are interested in can only be "perceived" by meaning-generating and hence meaning-sensitive animals, language-using animals. Meanings are not postulated; they are. To this I can reply that it is essentialist, and it underestimates other animals. Essentialism I take to be the "naive" error of assuming there are essentially distinct natural things and natural kinds that present themselves to experience as such. This overlooks the point that however different stones and actions seem, it is not hard to conjure theories that stress similarities. The history of our changing theories of the world should warn us against identifying essences: what is, what is similar and different, are all matters that are functions of the theories we hold. As to the maligned lower animals, their environment is alive with possibilities and dangers, that is, forms of meaning. The slide from such lower forms of meaning to the higher levels made possible by human language involves differences of degree not kind.

There is a deeper and more sociological criticism of the argument from meaningfulness: if the phenomena of the social world to a considerable extent consist of the unintended consequences of human action, then the meaningfulness of the actions of human beings to themselves and the symbolism they see in their actions and consequences may well be irrelevant and uninteresting to the social scientist. It will depend upon the social scientist's formulation of the problems he or she intends to solve. Suppose a poor country has a religion and a value system that laud poverty and deprivation, and enjoins on people actions that are supposed to prevent anyone getting rich. Suppose as a social scientist I take it as my problem to explain the poverty of that country. One hypothesis might well be that the religion and value system are effect not cause. The cause of poverty I might trace back to a weak material-resources base, lack of capital, and poor economic organization—all categories not indigenous, hence not meaningful to the native people at all. So, whereas if asked why they are poor, they might say it is because they approve of it, *I* might say it is because of economic conditions and could not readily be changed even if they did not approve of it. Were a group to arise in the society that taught that poverty was evil and wealth good and set out to reform attitudes, it is my contention that this group would not make very much headway unless and until it dealt with the economic causes, that is, the unintended consequences of living where that society does and as it does.[20] Neither the society's new love of wealth nor my economic remedies might achieve prosperity, and that would show either that both "explanations" of poverty are false or that one or both had not been implemented effectively. This is not a notional example. One of the most pervasive social problems of today's world is that of relative deprivation; that is, of social and political discontent in societies that measure themselves against others: see a "meaning" in their condition only because they look beyond their own social experiences and stock of meanings. This is an unintended consequence of modernization and communication.

At heart, the argument from meaningfulness and its variations as to action, rules, symbols, and translation strike me as philosophers' arguments in the worst sense: they are purely skeptical, not produced in the attempt to advance any concrete scientific problem. Quine, for example, iterates this almost trivially true argument about translation. Yet doubtless he knows that people learn other languages all the time, that brilliant translators can be found standing next to world leaders, philosophical skepticism notwithstanding. Diplomats can and do quibble endlessly about interpreting a word in two-language versions of a treaty, yet treaties are signed and enforced all the time. No doubt Quine, like all of us, reads translations of books (about logic, e.g.) in languages he does not know. Translation is difficult, tends to be redone every generation or so, and nevertheless seems worthwhile. Communication is always bad, even between English speakers; any text seems susceptible to almost infinitely many interpretations; but these are not reason enough to throw up one's hands, to declare a science of society impossible or severely limited. We measure our endeavors against our aims, not against the implicit perfectionism of the skeptic. Social anthropology does not fail to give usable accounts of very strange societies and cultures because it does not give perfect accounts. Perfect translation is not a standard to judge ourselves by.

Bartley[21] has explained how any position can be harrassed by repeated challenge to justify the moves being made. Only by unfusing criticism from justificationism can one defeat this strategy. The positive challenge—which says that meaning is a realm unique to and not comparable with natural science—must be parried differently. Its essentialism, counterexamples, and lack of grasp of the problem-oriented nature of scientific inquiry have been brought out. The latter needs expansion.

Popper always has contended that the first question is, What is the problem? and the second is, What is the thesis or solution? If the scientific problem is to explain, say, how an Azande can be both a witch doctor and a specialist trained at the London School of Hygiene and Tropical Medicine, then to remark on the difficulty of translating one idiom to the other, to see one as symbolic discourse and the other as instrumental, to talk of rules of meaning, is totally unenlightening and no aid to action at all.[22] But to postulate, as Evans-Pritchard did, the idea that there is a strong connection between a system of ideas and a social organization, and that a social organization can have the unintended consequence not only of supporting but in a sense embodying a system of ideas, and can contain multiple and effective devices for sustaining that social organization and hence the associated system of ideas in the face of difficulties,[23] this makes headway, because it gives us an intelligible model for how a person can become "of two worlds"—in fact, of two social structures. Boldly, Winch tried to give a "meaning" account of Azande witchcraft, but one's main impression of a bulky literature of discussion is that no one could make out what he meant![24]

To sum up, then, the argument that there are, as it were, no data not impregnated with meaning in the social realm, no phenomena of social life there to constitute social science except what the actors, so to say, choose and sustain, has no force if one is not imprisoned in the positivist view that science starts from the observation of facts or the gathering of data. Such models of science assume that what science does is closely to study observable phenomena and to penetrate to the essence of things, or the most general laws governing things. But if one sees entities, *including the entities singled out and operated with by ordinary people*, as stemming from and sustainable only with theoretical systems (which have a sustaining dimension), and one tries to be critical of theoretical systems in terms of their capacity to solve the problem at hand, one springs this trap. This view does not divide the world into phenomena and noumena, with the one as a high road to the other, or with impassable barriers between them. It views the world as a unity in which we come across problems—contradictions between theories we hold, what they lead us to expect, and what we actually find. In grappling with these we clearly have to abandon either what we thought we found (difficult) or the theory with which we started (which may be hidden even to us). Either way, we shall set out to reconceptualize things, and no given conceptualization, whether past science, commonsense thinking, or symbolism, has any priority.

4. The Argument from Interests

I am not altogether sure that the argument from interests deserves to be treated as new, but even if it has variations that Popper did not deal with, I think his position can very easily cope with it. At first approximation the argument might go as follows. Human beings have a greater or more immediate interest in the outcome of social scientific investigations than they have in that of natural science investigations. Whether, for example, the atom can or cannot be split is an issue on which social classes, ethnic groups, nations, communities, or families are unlikely to divide. They do not feel threatened by the outcome. This is not to deny that within natural science there may not be partisan attitudes for or against the different possibilities. But this is not the same thing, because there the allegiances, let us say, over splitting the atom, are what define the group threatened, not the preexisting social groups such as class or nation siding with one side or the other. In the social sciences, however, the case seems different. If, for example, the problem under consideration is the causes of the Great Depression, it is quite on the cards that an economic theory will come along that pinpoints certain groups as inherently connected to the problem and hence as prime targets if things are to be rectified: a clear example would be Marx's views on the bourgeoisie, and the equally uncompromising views of Lord Keynes to the effect that what might be needed was the euthanasia of the rentier. In these circumstances it can clearly be seen why social groups have more than just a truth-interest in the outcome of social investigations. Hence it is possible that this interest-bias infects the investigators themselves, since they are recruited from groups in the society and move into other groupings and hence will have interests of their own to consider, and it may infect such things as the allocation of grants for research, the publication of books and articles, and so on.[25]

If we interpret this as an argument from bias, then Popper squashed it fairly straightforwardly when he argued in *Logik der Forschung* that natural scientists being socialized human beings are also subject to all sorts of bias. This, however, evades the suggestion of an intrinsic and direct connection between theories in the social sciences and interests in society at large. We may try to clarify this suggestion as follows. The problems that confront us in the social sciences are infected by interests because what we take to be intellectual problems are cases where society falls short of some expectation we have of it, say, for efficiency, for health care, for prosperity, for education, for freedom from want, fear, or exploitation. Sometimes it is said that humanity has an interest in its own emancipation from the chains of social forms and that social science is closely connected to that impulse. This means that the social sciences have, as it were, a built-in value orientation, a goal toward which they are dedicated in a way that the natural sciences are not. True enough, the old slogan "ye shall know the truth and the truth shall set ye free" is sometimes attached to natural science, but our understanding of it nowadays is more that first comes the search for truth, which is in some way detached from any human hopes and aspirations other than that of knowing the truth, and it may only be a pious hope that the truth shall set ye free. It is also on the cards that atom bombs, recombinant genetic engineering, cloning, and all sorts of other things may yield unrivaled powers for re-enslaving people in the manner suggested in works such as *Brave New World* or *1984.*

In criticism of this argument it is perhaps best to begin with the question of whether the scientific quest, both natural and social, has any intrinsic connection with human aspirations and emancipation. There are these tags, and I think there is little doubt that historically the social sciences grow out of the emancipatory impulse. But then natural science grows out of the impulse to master rather than to be subservient to nature, that is, the impulse to technology; and look at the bad press that impulse has been getting lately.[26] Be all that as it may, origins are irrelevant to functions. It seems to me that these practical orientations were all very well for a primitive beginning but that very shortly an exciting new philosophical idea took over their guidance. This is the theory that the most effective way to achieve such goals as emancipation or practical applicability is always, in the long run, to search for the truth. This notion of truth was itself an incredibly imaginative idea: conceiving of the world as a whole being in a certain state in and of itself. We are invited to take a God's-eye view. The godlike view may be the most important contribution of religious thinking to the intellectual evolution of humankind. We try to think of science as capturing the state of things as they are regardless of how we believe them to be or would like them to be; we try to read what is written in the book of nature. The excitement of the idea has to do with the argument also that although in the short run all sorts of ideas and devices may do the immediate trick, if they contain mistakes and misapprehensions in the long run they will not work. Hence we force ourselves to seek out the way things are as the most effective way of achieving our aims. Freedom is, as it were, firstly the recognition of necessity, of what cannot possibly be otherwise.[27]

This brings me to the second main answer to the argument from interests: that it fails to see the quest for truth in science as a social project. To give an analogy: Every modern state takes account of the fact that government office provides opportunities for corruption. What is enacted are certain guidelines about conflict of interest, certain rules of disclosure, and penalties for culprits. In the sciences also we know that the individuals who do science are prone to preference, conscious and unconscious, that they come from social groups and educational backgrounds that infect their thinking in ways beyond imagining, and so the question is, What do we do about these facts? The answer is, we laud the ideology of truth; we also train scientists in the dangers of bias and preference and urge them to be alert to it; but those are only the minor moves. The major move we make is to situate the pursuit of knowledge in social institutions. I question Wittgenstein's view that there can be no private language, but he would have been right if he had said there is no private knowledge.[28] Knowledge has to be communicable in language, whether ordinary or technical; it has to be subject to certain kinds of public check, and hence it can be generated only in social institutions such as schools, universities, laboratories, conferences, colloquia, seminars, lectures, journals, newsletters, and so on. The function of these forums is often mistakenly thought to be that of communication, that is, informing one another about results, what has been discovered. This is a manifest function that conceals the much more important latent function of ensuring public cooperation of both formal friendliness and aggressive criticism in the work of finding things out. Papers are heard and attacked; lectures are discussed; articles are refereed; results are taken away and scrutinized elsewhere for flaws of reasoning, calculation, interpretation, and repeatability. As a matter of fact, scientists do not go around constantly re-running each other's experiments. But this is by no means unknown. When important work in the field smells fishy, it may be redone, and woe betide anyone whose results cannot be replicated in other labs.

Just as the social institutions constructed to guard us against corruption do not do a perfect job by any means, and just as they need not only constant and vigilant implementation but also constant scrutiny and revision, so in the social matrix of knowledge is there a permanent injunction on everyone to keep alert and also to devise new ways to foster cooperation and information in the hope of exposing error, bias, interest, and incompetence in the name of truth.

This leaves us with the sixty-four-thousand-dollar question: will the search for truth in the social sciences facilitate emancipation? Efforts have been made to discourage research into some topics, such as the relation of intelligence to inheritance,[29] for fear that the truth might be other than we would wish it to be. My view is that one has to take a hard and consistent line on this: the truth is the most effective means of achieving aims in the long run, and that includes truths about society. If we discover unpalatable things, we shall have incentive either to refute them or to face them as moral choices without deceiving ourselves. The dangers of technology are easy to exaggerate, but it is obviously true that the more we know, the more power we have. There is no godlike possibility of censorship or denial of free inquiry without the danger of greater abuse.

To sum up on interests, then, there is no reason to suspect that they vitiate the project of a social science more or less modeled on the natural sciences. The permeation of interests may be more intricate, but the social organization needed to check and correct such interests is the same. As to the hidden subtext that there is an intrinsic connection between emancipation and knowledge: "emancipation" here is a political term, opposed to exploitation, domination, and so on. While conceding the historical connection, we ask, What of the allegedly intrinsic connection? The answer is that the argument is empty and rhetorical. No one claims to be against emancipation—Hitler and Stalin, as much as Abraham Lincoln. So the charge has to become one of latent function, of being against emancipation even while apparently being for it. Popper, for example, in criticizing Marx and extolling the virtues of bourgeois democracy is said to be making himself a lackey of capitalism and hence an enemy of the workers. Such latent functionalist arguments can easily be turned around, as when Adorno and Marcuse became frightened by the student anger they had a hand in arousing, knowing not what they had wrought, inviting the suggestion that much "emancipatory" interest in social science (like the classic Frankfurt School) is latently a conspiracy to reduce the degree of freedom already enjoyed in bourgeois society.[30] One could go on reflexively to show that the argument that Popper is fostering reaction is itself reactionary. And so on.

5. The Argument from Reflexivity

It is possible to regard this argument as a stronger form of the argument from interests and also as a stronger form of the argument from the sociology of knowledge. In shortest form it seems to go like this. The natural sciences are not natural; they are social constructions. As has been admitted in the social description of the pursuit of truth, the social sciences are social too, so the social sciences are in the odd position of having to give an account of social processes and social causation that, if comprehensive, must include the processes and causation of the social sciences themselves. Hence the social sciences have to explain and predict themselves, and this looks at first blush like a paradox. It was this paradox that probably led Mannheim to back away and argue that the intellects that pursued science, especially natural science, were in some way detached from their interests and hence need not be explained away. No one has found this satisfactory.[31]

Of late we have seen the first attempt not to back away from it emanating, with great irony, from Edinburgh, where the Science Studies Unit and its journal *Social Studies of Science*, together with a few sympathetic scholars, have yielded up "the strong programme in the sociology of knowledge." This carries through the argument that sciences are social institutions. Believing that the notions of reality, nature, and truth are social constructs along with the sciences that employ them; and also believing, in a watered-down Marxist way, that the fundamental social pressures are the material ones of making a living and class interest; the adherents of the "strong programme" try to show that natural science and mathematics are social products not just in the sense of being social institutions but also in the sense that their content, the ideas themselves, have a suspiciously convenient fit with the material interests of, or pressures on, a scientist or scientific community at any one time.[32]

This way of putting things certainly undercuts two of Popper's main arguments against the sociology of knowledge: namely, the anomalous position of Mannheim's free-floating intellectuals, and the failure of sociologists of knowledge to study the actual social processes in which scientific knowledge comes into being.[33] Neither Popper nor I, though, would want to accept the conclusion that scientific ideas can be explained by social factors, any more than can social ideas. This is not to say that the social situation of the time may not have great significance in the development of science, particularly with regard to the formulation or recognition of the problem and even more so with regard to the urgency assigned to it. There can be little doubt, for example, that competition between nations nowadays plays a significant part in the development of science both in that certain problems will be taken more seriously if it is known that a rival country is working on them (the space race, high-energy accelerators, etc.), and also in that the formulation of the problems will owe something to that fact. And the possible technological significance of scientific work lurks much nearer the foreground than one would like to admit.

That said, is there any need to concede more to the strong program? Basically not. My suggestion here would be that there is no difference between the natural and the social sciences. If one must reflexively explain itself, so should the other. But neither does so. The strong program remains a program. A program in the end is proved in execution, like a pudding in the eating. The strong program has yet to come forward with a plausible theory that links social circumstances and the production of ideas in a causal chain: interesting parallels, striking insights, and so on are not enough. In what way does the brain of the scientist get organized by the social pressures? Let's leave it there.[34]

Another variation of the reflexivity argument comes to us from the criticism of natural science that stems from Kuhn. Kuhn thought paradigms and eschewing the discussion of foundational issues demarcated the natural sciences from the social sciences. In the hands of social scientists that argument got twisted a bit. Some held that the social sciences were not paradigm-less but multi-paradigm, or that they had paradigms Kuhn did not notice. More than that, they turned the argument back on the natural sciences. You see, the natural sciences are demystified, they said. The scientists have feet of clay; they are dogmatic, authoritarian, stubborn, and change comes only as they die off. So far from there being a clean demarcation between the two, we social scientists now see the natural sciences as being much like the social sciences—a big mess. They are diverse in structure; made up of many schools and parties; more prone to revolutionary upheavals than to orderly incremental growth; and moreover there is so little continuity between the science as it stands before and after the revolution that a real question arises as to whether it can be thought to be dealing with the same world.[35]

To everyone's surprise, Popper called Kuhn his best critic[36] (a slight to Agassi and Bartley), and so perhaps these arguments and their twist deserve serious thought. The most striking thing about Kuhn's view is his endorsement of the practices whose ethnography he does. Why, though, have the social sciences not got the authoritarian, dogmatic, revolutionary, and puzzle-solving features that Kuhn sees as characterizing natural science? Here my point would be simple: Kuhn equates the present structure of science as he has experienced it with the natural and correct way of organizing science. What he finds in the social sciences—endless debate about fundamentals, many warring parties, diverse strategies—can plausibly be argued to be a healthy state of affairs. There is the case of the social sciences in the Soviet Union until recently as a contrasting instance of paradigm-dominated puzzle-solving yielding no results.[37] Perhaps it would be enough to say that the growth of science has a great deal to do with the belief that science feeds technology and that technology feeds economic growth, affluence, and comfort. As a result, and also partly as a result of competition between nations, science has been secularized, institutionalized, bureaucratized, and routinized. These results pull against the spirit of diversity and criticism that Popper among others has taken to characterize science. Natural science as Kuhn describes it ("post critical," as his forerunner Polanyi termed it) might well be thought of as in an unnatural and unhealthy state where dogmatism and relativism and pragmatism rule the day. To the extent that the social sciences try to ape the natural sciences as Kuhn pictures them, the social sciences are heading for their own disaster. But perhaps because of the clear connections with concrete problems of human interest in the social sciences we need not fear that things can ever deteriorate to the extent that they have in natural science. What will happen in natural science is not difficult to predict. It is possible that the next great revolutions in physics may come close together: either this will disillusion scientists and the general public, or science will split open because there will be attempts to suppress the revolutions within science.

6. The Problem of Popper's Reception

Let us now look at the reception of Popper's ideas as a sociological problem and contrast the accounts given by the meaning, interests, and reflexivity approaches with those yielded by the problem-oriented unintended consequences approach. As mentioned before, Popper's is a radical and challenging philosophy, that from the time of the publication of *The Open Society and Its Enemies* has often put him in the public eye. Yet as late as the 1950s he was in philosophy and the social sciences neglected and vilified, alluded to but excluded from the curriculum. Throughout his career Popper never had an academic status commensurate with the importance of his ideas or with his post-retirement standing; he never occupied a named or endowed chair; he never headed or taught permanently at one of the distinguished philosophical schools of the English-speaking world; he had very few research students; he wielded very little political influence in philosophy; and he was little read and poorly understood. These are all sociological problems that have been put down to personality ("a difficult man"),[38] to the vagaries of exile (New Zealand

1937–1945), or to the ascendancy of a rival Viennese philosopher and his doctrines (Wittgenstein).[39]

The meaning explanation usually given for the odd lack of seriousness with which Popper was taken was that he was not a professional: that is, his philosophy was one of large claims and broad pictures rather than of careful and scrupulous attention to detail. The generation that founded *Analysis* had no idea what to do with a living systematic philosopher. There are many discussion articles, once his major works begin to appear, that purport to show that some simple contradiction or ambiguity vitiates his philosophy.[40] The rules and meaning of philosophy had become those of a community that took its ancestors to be Wittgenstein and Austin, its methods to be theirs, and its social organization to be the Oxford tutorial.[41] Popper ignored these rules of the community and on occasion denounced them. Hence only fragments of his work could be discussed, namely, those that somehow were socially meaningful. These tended to be not the overall ideas, but technical treatments of aspects of them.

Plausible though it is, this explanation has false premises. By any standards of meticulous professionalism, Popper's *Logik der Forschung* was outstanding, more so than the rambling, aphoristic, and piecemeal work of Wittgenstein and Austin, whose professionalism was more in their followers than themselves. *The Open Society and Its Enemies* was not commented on by the professionals, even though its footnotes contain a range of professionally argued philosophical essays on such topics as the influence of mathematics on Greek thought, the Socratic problem, Wittgenstein's *Tractatus*, and so on. Hence the meaning-philosophers' insinuation that Popper was "unprofessional" had elements of self-deception: not only was Popper thoroughly professional when required, his theory and practice showed meaning philosophy to be uninteresting. This is why he was excluded from the community.

From this I want to draw an unintended consequence explanation. Popper always sought to communicate with other philosophers, but he underestimated the neurotic element there would be in the reception of his highly boat-rocking ideas. A rationalist expecting rational response, his ideas had the unintended consequence that people found them a threat and dealt with them by foisting interpretations on them, trying to pigeonhole Popper as part of some wider entity that was thought to be under control—as, for example, debates internal to logical positivism, a doctrine thought to have been superseded by Wittgenstein. Carnap abetted this tactic.[42] The other interpretation was to dismiss him as some sort of renegade or crank, talented, perhaps, but flawed (insufficiently professional?). Hence consign his contribution to marginal status at the edge of the professional debate. Teaching philosophy in that den of social scientists, the LSE, might almost seem a penance Wittgenstein could have devised. The mistake was to not silence him. From that base Popper was able to struggle for and eventually get some sort of hearing.

It is not altogether clear to me what an "interests" explanation of Popper's neglect and subsequent acceptance would be like. Certainly, at the time he first became known, after the publication of *The Open Society and Its Enemies* in London in 1945, his warnings about how easy it is in politics to make things worse when trying to make them better went against the attitudes of the men in power—Mr. Attlee's first Labour administration. If Popper was a philosopher serving the interests of the bourgeoisie, then he was publishing at a time when the bourgeoisie was in retreat before socialism. Later, in the 1950s, the bourgeois party, the Conservatives, came to power, but Popper's star still did not rise. Furthermore, in 1950 *The Open Society* was published in the United States, and there was no notable rush to lionize Popper.

Strangely enough, it was Germany, a land whose language and culture he had repudiated, that first began to discover him as a major philosophical theorist of social democracy and a major philosopher of science. By the time the baby-revolutionaries appeared at Berkeley, Berlin, Paris, and London, Popper was sufficiently prominent a figure to be identified as the enemy.

A more plausible explanation might be this. As a war work, Popper's *The Open Society* appeared too late—after the war was over. As a discussion of postwar political problems, it appeared a little too early—before, that is to say, the romantic haze around Stalin's Russia had dissolved, before disillusion with socialism and dirigisme emerged, before the successful restoration of democracy in Germany, Austria, and Japan had succeeded. By the time those things happened, Popper himself had moved on to other philosophical interests that would keep him out of the limelight until after 1959, when *Logik der Forschung* appeared in English.

We look then to Popper's problems (the intellectual roots of totalitarianism, right and left), the unintended consequences of the timing of publication, and the vagaries of world events. Precisely because his major work in English was in political theory, and because he had chosen to bury major philosophical essays in the footnotes rather than publish them separately, he labored under the self-created disadvantage of seeming to be primarily a political philosopher, then, later, primarily a philosopher of science, rather than a philosopher, *tout court*. By and large the power and kudos in philosophy in the English-speaking world go to those thought to be "pure" philosophers.

Popper's ideas can be applied to their own reception. He portrays science and the way it works in a manner that allows his own contributions a place: open-minded and critical, even of its presuppositions. To accuse him of a naive subject/object positivism that exempts his own work is seriously to misread. But science, social science, and philosophy are not in a perfect state by any means; if they were, Popper's life-project of debating the methods of science would have been unnecessary. So to an extent Popper is a victim of the system he is trying to reform and improve. Fashion, snobbery, academic prestige, eroded traditions of learning, irrationalism, dogmatism, conservatism, and feelings of threat are some of the many reasons why Popper's own reception has not been as enlightened as a "literal" reading of his philosophy (as a description of the way things are in science) would lead one to expect. This is the objective component of his gossip description as a difficult man. Had he been received as his philosophy recommends, his work might have seemed redundant. But instead, his philosophy of science that views it as in a permanent state of revolution also serves to explain his reception: all change creates vested interests that resist further change, so there is a systemic need for anti-establishment figures. With his philosophy of criticism, Popper fitted this role beautifully, but his exclusion from the centers of power and influence delayed his acting it out.

7. Conclusion

The status of a classic is always ambiguous. We all are supposed to have learned from it, but it is easy to forget it; if it warns us against strong temptations, to the extent that we are tempted, we ignore it. What is clear from the foregoing discussion is that the arguments on the differences between the natural and the social sciences that fill the literature that has appeared in the postwar period have not superseded *The Poverty of Historicism*—yet that book is all too often slighted.[43] Popper's thought generally was slighted until the 1970s: there is a whole generation emerging that begins its approach to him with *Conjectures and Refutations* (1963) and works forward, not backward. This exacerbates the misunderstandings that feed the slighting, because much of Popper's later work is commentary on, correction of, and extensions to, his earlier work. He is a thinker with strong lines in his *oeuvre* that are better followed from start to finish. Garbled Popper is easier to slight than understood Popper.

However, the logic of the situation regarding the problem of Popper's reception is clear. In addition to the probems that faced Popper as he wrote, we have to take into account the context of problems, meanings, symbols, interests, and reflexivity in which *The Poverty of Historicism* was received. Its cool and searching arguments hurt disappointed Marxists. Positivism is so pervasive a philosophy that Popper's total repudiation of it sometimes cannot be grasped even when it is stated bluntly. His whole view of method, namely the attempt to suggest and improve methodological guidelines for the conduct of inquiry, is bound to seem to some as attempts to restrict freedom. Popper put into the book version a dedication to the victims of historicism that appeared to say that the people the book criticized had something to do with the crimes of totalitarianism. To the closet totalitarians of the left and the right, of which the academic community is full, this was very offensive and guilt-making. To those used to talking in a language different from Popper's, let us say Hegelian, or

Marxist, or Wittgensteinian, the book was almost untranslatable, especially as it contains uncompromising attacks on those languages, explicit and implicit. In his footnotes to Hayek and economics and in what I have called his social pessimism or skepticism—namely, the refusal to daydream about the ideal society, the urgent demand to concentrate on present evils coupled with the implication that that is not enough because the well-laid plans of mice and men, and so on—Popper was seen as someone with interests (status quo capitalism); as having symbolic meaning in trying to impose the inhuman values of natural science; of lacking interest in emancipation; and so on. One might say that Popper took on or made too many enemies for his expectation of rational debate about the issues to flourish. Instead, what happened to him and has continued to happen is that he is read, he is unread, he diffuses into the atmosphere in garbled form, but that one way or another the agenda that he set out gets discussed—not well, not clearly, not ideally. That should not surprise those of us who take our cue from his ideas. The world has grave defects, and every attempt to improve them is itself fraught with endless new possibilities for making things worse and making new things go wrong. Only by standing back a little from the hurly-burly can one develop a position that resists despair. From that position one can say that there is much to be gained from very close and thoughtful study of Popper's ideas on the relation between the natural and the social sciences; that much of the literature supposedly devoted to this question does not assist matters; but that things are not as bad as they were. Popper has I think succeeded in making historicists self-conscious and defensive, since people are now alert to them and armed with strong arguments from him; similarly, because of *Logik der Forschung*, inductivism is no longer an uncritically assumed philosophy.[44] But in the meantime Popper's reputation has vaulted to one of great eminence with the general intellectual public even if not with the professional philosophers; while, for many, natural science has become an ogre, somehow connected with environmental depredation, military expenditure, and Vietnam, and Popper gets vilified as one of the ogre's henchmen. There seem to be no gains without losses; are those unintended consequences?

NOTES

0. Parts of this essay were read to the Philosophy Department, Claremont Graduate School, Claremont, California, April 22, 1980. I wish to thank my questioners and also Joseph Agassi.
1. Popper's "Replies to My Critics," in *The Philosophy of Karl Popper*, ed. P. A. Schilpp

(LaSalle, Ill.: Open Court, 1974), concentrates on the ideational content of the Popper legend. As we shall see, however, the logic of the situation of new ideas has a sociological dimension that can help explain the frustrating misunderstanding and misrepresentation from which Popper has suffered.

2. Sociological hypothesis: those who deceive themselves into believing they have given up a doctrine will be particularly withering and dismissive of criticism of that doctrine. Compare the reaction of fellow-traveling historicists to Popper with that of fellow-traveling language philosophers to Gellner, not to mention fellow-traveling justificationists to Bartley, fellow-traveling inductivists to Popper again, and so on.

3. "*The Poverty of Historicism* is, I think, one of my stodgiest pieces of writing. Besides, after I had written the ten sections which form the first chapter, my whole plan broke down." Popper, "Intellectual Autobiography," in *The Philosophy of Karl Popper*, ed. Schilpp, p. 90.

4. Translated into English and published in late 1959 as *The Logic of Scientific Discovery* (New York: Basic Books).

5. In the 1950 "Preface" to the revised edition of *The Open Society and Its Enemies*, and on p. 91 of the "Autobiography," Popper writes of the mood of gloom in which that book was written, perhaps fearing the war would be lost by the Allies, a mood that apparently lifted only after his first visit to the United States.

6. Stalinists use the specious justification of Lenin that you cannot make an omelet without breaking eggs. Breaking human heads and bodies does not yield a pleasant-tasting dish. Alexander Solzhenitsyn's *The Gulag Archipelago* (New York: Harper & Row, 1973–1978) systematically shows how in virtually every respect conditions were worse in Lenin's and Stalin's Russia than under the czars.

7. Excellent examples of the latter were given in an article, "Many Benefit as Inflation Goes Higher," by Martin Baron, *Los Angeles Times*, March 13, 1980, pp. 1ff.

8. Thus he is not allied with those who attack the social sciences because of pretentiousness, such as Pitrim Sorokin, C. Wright Mills, A. R. Louch, and Stanislav Andreski. It should be noted that Popper had second thoughts about the Oedipus Effect, as he recalls in the "Autobiography," pp. 96–97.

9. See *The Poverty of Historicism*, secs. 29 and 31, and his "La rationalité et le statut du principe de rationalité," in *Les fondéments philosophiques des systemes economicaus*, ed. Emil M. Claassen (Paris: Payot, 1967), pp. 142–150.

10. I have expanded on this in *Concepts and Society* (London: Routledge & Kegan Paul, 1972), esp. chap. 1.

11. A bold extension of the method to explain fashion and style is attempted by E. H. Gombrich in "The Logic of Vanity Fair," in *The Philosophy of Karl Popper*, ed. Schilpp, pp. 925–957, a paper generously praised by Popper in his "Replies."

12. See Alan Musgrave, "Impersonal Knowledge: A Criticism of Subjectivism in Epistemology" (Ph.D. diss., University of London, 1969); and J. Agassi, *Science in Flux* (Dordrecht: Reidel, 1975), chap. 6.

13. W. W. Bartley, III, "The Philosophy of Karl Popper: Part I: Biology and Evolutionary Epistemology," *Philosophia* 6 (1976): 463–494. [See also his essay in the present volume—Ed.]

14. It appeared too soon after to be read as a reply to *The Poverty of Historicism*, and it criticizes Popper on matters (such as social engineering and the unity of method) treated fully only in *The Open Society and Its Enemies*. Winch's teacher was Rush Rhees, author of a denunciation of *The Open Society and Its Enemies*, namely, "Social Engineering," *Mind* 56 (1947): 317–331.

15. The argument is also fully discussed by F. A. Hayek in *The Counter-Revolution of Science* (Glencoe, Ill.: The Free Press, 1955) (originally in *Economica*, 1942–1944).

16. Wittgenstein's reflections on Frazer, recently published as a slim volume (*Remarks on Frazer's Golden Bough* [Atlantic Highlands, N.J.: Humanities, 1979]), are fascinating. Winch hints at all this in his elusive and allusive paper in *The Philosophy of Karl Popper*, ed. Schilpp. The example he gives is understanding the "force" of the reasons Sorel offered for supporting the General Strike: "the force of these 'reasons' could be understood only by someone who was familiar with the particular character of the movement within which it was offered" (p. 903) (the anarchosyndicalist movement). Winch's statement (on the same page) that "to understand such situations, we have to understand the peculiar character of these institutions and people's participation in them . . . a kind of understanding quite different from anything that Popper gives

an account of," is something of an understatement. For although Popper's logic of the situation reconstructs understanding, it does so in a critical spirit, seeking typicalities as well as peculiarities in the situation, governed by the problem at hand, not treating any position as privileged, and so denying any special understanding to the participants.

17. Namely, Winch's castigation of Evans-Pritchard in "Understanding a Primitive Society," *American Philosophical Quarterly* 1 (1964): 307–324, and the immense literature of debate this has generated, which can be tracked through the *Philosopher's Index*, and the widely scattered writings of Robin Horton, Ernest Gellner, Steven Lukes, Martin Hollis, John Skorupski, and myself.

18. V. Turner, *The Forest of Symbols* (Ithaca, N.Y.: Cornell University Press, 1967); Mary Douglas, *Purity and Danger* (London: Routledge & Kegan Paul, 1965), *Natural Symbols* (London: Routledge & Kegan Paul, 1970), *Implicit Meanings* (London: Routledge & Kegan Paul, 1975). More recently, see Edmund Leach, *Culture and Communication* (Santa Monica, Calif.: Goodyear, 1979). Agassi and I have offered transcendental criticism of this position in "The Problem of the Rationality of Magic" and "Magic and Rationality Again," both in *British Journal of Sociology* 18 (1967): 55–74, and 24 (1973): 236–245. Severe criticism is already to be found in Walter Kaufmann, *Critique of Religion and Philosophy* (New York: Harper & Row, 1958).

19. W. V. O. Quine, *Word and Object* (Cambridge, Mass.: MIT Press, 1960), p. 27. For a useful guide to Quine's view (no straightforward matter), see Christopher Hookway, "Indeterminacy and Translation," in *Action and Interpretation*, ed. Christopher Hookway and Philip Pettit (Cambridge: Cambridge University Press, 1978).

20. This would generate some obvious criticisms of the views of Max Weber, *The Protestant Ethic and the Spirit of Capitalism* (London: Allen and Unwin, 1930), and R. H. Tawney, *Religion and the Rise of Capitalism* (New York: Harcourt Brace, 1924/1926).

21. Bartley, *The Retreat to Commitment* (New York: Knopf, 1962); "Rationality versus the Theory of Rationality," in *The Critical Approach to Science and Philosophy*, ed. M. Bunge (New York: Free Press, 1964).

22. See the papers by Agassi and myself, "Problem of the Rationality" and "Magic and Rationality," and the work of J. H. M. Beattie to which we refer there.

23. E. E. Evans-Pritchard, *Witchcraft, Oracles and Magic among the Azande* (Oxford: Oxford University Press, 1937).

24. See the literature indicated in note 17.

25. I have had to reconstruct wholly the argument from interests, since I find much of the literature obfuscating and unquotable. Recently, P. K. Feyerabend has espoused it: see *Against Method* (London: New Left Books, 1975).

26. Francis Bacon bluntly declared the aim of science to be power over nature, in *Novum Organum*, and added that truth was the best means to power. He also alluded to God's promise to Noah of domination over nature as a warrant.

27. On what could not possibly be otherwise, see my "The Notion of a Social Science," in *Recent Approaches to the Social Sciences*, ed. H. K. Betz (Calgary: Calgary University Press, 1980), esp. sec. 3.

28. The private language argument is essentialist, turning on what language is and does, or must minimally be or do. If we refuse to place such stress on the words "language" and "private," then the talk of the San Diego twins Gracie and Ginny (see Jean-Pierre Gorin's documentary film *Poto and Cabengo*, 1979), speaking in tongues, and even Wittgenstein's own coded (and now, we understand, deciphered) notebooks, can be treated as private languages.

29. Arthur Jensen, *Bias in Mental Testing* (London: Methuen, 1980).

30. Consider the argument in R. P. Wolff and H. Marcuse, *A Critique of Pure Tolerance* (Boston: Beacon, 1970), where tolerance of freedom and democracy is to be restricted because they are vulnerable to fascism.

31. I have discussed Mannheim in *Concepts and Society*, chap. 5.

32. The principal literature is cited at p. 495, note 29, in *Philosophy of the Social Sciences* 9 (1979).

33. An entire literature on this topic has grown out of the work of Robert K. Merton and is now being added to by the Edinburgh group and some ethnomethodologists, for example, such recent volumes as Roy Wallis, ed., *On the Margins of Science* (London: University of Keele, 1979);

Bruno Latour and S. W. Woolgar, *Laboratory Life* (Beverly Hills, Calif.: Sage, 1979); and Barry Barnes and Steve Shapin, eds., *Natural Order* (Beverly Hills, Calif.: Sage, 1979).

34. L. Laudan offers some further criticism in "Views of Progress: Separating the Pilgrims from the Rakes," *Philosophy of the Social Sciences* 10 (1980): 273–286.

35. This reading of Thomas Kuhn, *The Structure of Scientific Revolutions* (Chicago: University of Chicago Press, 1962), is developed in my "Laudan's Problematic Progress and the Social Sciences," *Philosophy of the Social Sciences* 9 (1979): 484–497; and my review of Kuhn's *The Essential Tension*, in *Queen's Quarterly* 87 (1980): 65–68.

36. In his "Normal Science and Its Dangers," in *Criticism and the Growth of Knowledge*, ed. I. Lakatos and A. Musgrave (Cambridge: Cambridge University Press, 1970), Popper writes: "Professor Kuhn's criticism of my views about science is the most interesting one I have so far come across" (p. 51).

37. Recent more healthy trends in Soviet anthropology are chronicled by Ernest Gellner in the conference volume *Soviet and Western Anthropology* (London, 1980), and his papers, "State before Class, the Soviet Treatment of African Feudalism," *European Journal of Sociology* 18 (1977): 299–322, and "Soviets against Wittfogel," forthcoming.

38. See Section 1 of Bartley's "Popperian Harvest" in the present volume.

39. D. F. Pears argues in his *Bertrand Russell and the British Tradition in Philosophy* (London: Collins, 1967) that after early Russell the torch of British empiricism passes to Wittgenstein and his followers.

40. Examples are: John Canfield and Keith Lehrer, "A Note on Prediction and Deduction," *Philosophy of Science* 28 (1961): 204–208; R. H. Vincent, "The Paradox of Ideal Evidence," *Philosophical Review* 71 (1962): 497–503; A. Grünbaum, "The Falsifiability of Scientific Theories," *Mind* 73 (1964): 434–436; after 1967 further examples can be found through the *Philosopher's Index*.

41. In this respect I fully endorse the sociological discussion in Ernest Gellner's *Words and Things* (London: Gollancz, 1959; Routledge, 1979).

42. Carnap's "Testability and Meaning" included Popper as one of the gang in a manner that somewhat pleased Popper at the time (see his comments in "The Demarcation between Science and Metaphysics," in *Conjectures and Refutations* [London: Routledge & Kegan Paul, 1963], p. 255; and pp. 968ff. of "Replies") but that obscured his very deep differences with the Vienna Circle and thwarted his subsequent efforts to dissociate himself from their concerns. (See the whole discussion of this in secs. 2 and 3 of "Replies.")

43. Important exceptions are P. D. Shaw, "Popper, Historicism, and the Remaking of Society," *Philosophy of the Social Sciences* 1 (1971): 299–308; John Passmore, "*The Poverty of Historicism* Revisited," *History and Theory*, vol. 14, *Essays on Historicism*, pp. 30–47; Peter Urbach, "Is Any of Popper's Arguments against Historicism Valid?" *British Journal for the Philosophy of Science* 29 (1978): 117–130.

44. Astonishingly, there is a recent counterexample in the *British Journal for the Philosophy of Science*, a journal Popper helped found, and which has long been known as a forum for his ideas and those of his followers. See Mark Wilson, "Maxwell's Condition—Goodman's Problem," *British Journal for the Philosophy of Science* 30 (1979): 107–123.

CHAPTER 6

THE EMERGENCE OF SOCIAL ANTHROPOLOGY FROM PHILOSOPHY *

In a way, almost every "subject-matter" now taught in the groves of academe has "emerged" from philosophy, if only because the Greek notion of philosophy was comprehensive. However, when Aristotle came to summarize the knowledge of the Greek world he wrote a *Politics* but did not write a *Sociology* or an *Anthropology*. This is puzzling, as it is not hard to show that his teacher Plato was a very sophisticated sociological thinker.[1] This being the case, should sociology and social anthropology be dated from Plato, or even from Herodotus? All such questions are an elaborate form of game—with rules, outcomes and pay-offs to suit the players. It certainly seems to me a preferable game to that in which the antecedents of sociology are traced to Comte because he coined the *word*.

One might try the following idea. *Sociology* separated out from politics and political economy as, in the post-medieval era, men set out to theorize about the nature of society and government in the course of the political turmoils of the time. The English Revolution led to much profound reflection on the nature of society and political authority. Problems concerning the wisdom of the economic policy of mercantilism galvanized Adam Smith, who was in a center of political and social thought at Edinburgh. The ghastly conditions of England after the industrial revolution led to the cogitations of Marx. Together, these influences formed sociology.[2] *Anthropology,* on the other hand, is the study of diverse forms of social life and a primary factor in its inception must be the development of *awareness* of these diverse social forms.[3] 'Awareness' must be interpreted as stronger than 'vaguely aware of'. I doubt if there is a society in the world, not excluding remote and allegedly isolated Pacific Island societies, which was unaware in some vague way that it had neighbours who ordered

---

* J. W. Burrow, *Evolution and Society* (Cambridge University Press, 1966).

95

their social arrangements somewhat differently. 'Awareness' is something going beyond this. It implies giving serious thought to the comparison with other ways of life and questioning of the reasons for, advantages of, and even moral value of the ways in which we order our arrangements.[4]

In order for this sort of interest to develop, I would contend, some doctrine like the theory of the rational unity of mankind must be fashionable. The belief in the unity of mankind has to face challenges from the facts of man's physical, social and psychological diversity and show that diversity does not jeopardize the unity. This is why race is of interest, it is why Freud was so interested in anthropology, and it's what makes diverse social forms interesting—to see if they are counterexamples to the unity of mankind.[5] Such an idea of unity was entertained in Greece by Pericles but seems to have disappeared from the scene again until the post-medieval period, when we find it as one of the dominating ideas of the Enlightenment. (Whether Christ preached the unity of mankind is a contentious point.[6])

How in fact and in detail the notions of anthropology grew out of the Enlightenment is the subject of a fascinating new book by J. W. Burrow, *Evolution and Society*. But before coming to the story he has to tell I want to glance at another question, namely why we suddenly now are getting the beginnings of a serious attempt to see the history of the social sciences as part of the general history of ideas.

The problem of the dearth of studies of the history of anthropology and sociology is a sociological problem in itself. In the case of social anthropology I have elsewhere offered the explanation that the success of the subject after an apparently radical new start gave credence to the idea that history is of no explanatory value in social studies, and this generalization applies *a fortiori* to social science itself. In the case of sociology there is room for some dispute: Mauss, Becker, Barnes, Parsons, have all had their say. But again, a theory that the subject was new did much for its impact and spread. Close study of origins might dispel the sensation of newness and so was to be avoided. Besides all this, there is an interesting intellectual explanation for the neglect of the history of all the sciences by the scientists themselves. If one enquires of a physicist whether he studies the history of physics, more likely than not he will query the point of spending time learning about a lot of people's past mistakes. This view is so widespread that one searches hard to find the person who combines active scientific work with active interest in the history of science.

However, when a subject has been around for a while, and has had its measure of success, one would expect that its history would begin to intrigue scholars. The history of science has been going strong since the eighteenth century. It looks as though now the social sciences are slowly getting underway. (This does not show that they *are* new and only now mature enough to sustain research into their history; it shows that their practitioners *believe* this). In the last generation quite a few volumes on the history of sociology have appeared, and most recently Parsons, Shils and Neagle's *Theories of Society,* Aron's *Main Currents of Sociological Thought,* and Nisbet's *The Sociological Tradition.* In so far as sociology and anthropology share a common sphere of interest and a common tradition these studies are relevent to both. But to the extent that they diverge the paucity of material on anthropology itself is remarkable. What I shall principally discuss here is Burrow's book on the history of social anthropology in the nineteenth century which is a companion to Margaret Hodges' *Early Anthropology in the Seventeenth and Eighteenth Centuries,* the only other serious study that exists.

Now on the face of it, evolution would be a gift to the unity of mankind when that doctrine gets into difficulties. It allows all diversity to be explained away as stages, and leaves the potential unity and equality of mankind intact. Yet the adoption of evolution was much more complicated than that, as we shall see from studying Burrow's book. Burrow is a young historian of ideas trained at Cambridge and acknowledging Plumb and Kitson Clark as his mentors. He begins by discussing the distinction between rational and non-rational behaviour; by the latter he means ceremonial, reverential and status-ordered as opposed to manifestly "useful" conduct. In the study of primitive societies non-rational conduct is crucial because it is unfamiliar. Familiarity, in this case, breeding not contempt, but an inability to doubt something's rationality. Overcoming this inability is one of the main results of a good anthropological training.

Burrow begins his history with the lively discussions of social life conducted by the rationalists of the Enlightenment, and by the Scottish philosophers of common sense, with their emphasis on conjectural historical reconstruction. Then he comes to one of his problems. How is it that between the Scottish philosophers in the late eighteenth century— who look so promising as precursors—and the 1850's, there is a gap in social studies? This is his historical problem (The Historical Gap). His sociological problem is: how can we explain the hold doctrines of social evolution had over so many Victorian intellectuals (Evolutionism's Hold)? His thesis is that evolutionary social theory is largely "the outcome of a tension between English positivistic attitudes to science on the one hand and, on the other, a more profound reading of history, coming to a large extent from German romanticism, which made the older form of positivist social theory, philosophic radicalism, seem inadequate" (p. xv). A tension developed, then, which could only be released by some theory of social evolution.

These are the two problems articulated in the book. But his discussion answers a third problem which we can get at in the following way. To discuss The Historical Gap, Burrow begins with the conjectural history approach of the Scottish. Their attempts to provide rational reconstructions, or models of the history of mankind, were potentially good tools for sociology and anthropology. How then the gap? Firstly Burrow asserts that there was no gap, there was utilitarianism, and especially the works of Bentham and James Mill. These were, he argues, anti-historical and not sociological—much given to explaining human behaviour from postulated or intuited first principles. To those who cite in Bentham's and Mill's works places where historical examples, references to primitive contemporaries, and recognition of the difficulties created by these, Burrow says, acutely, "It is no defence, for example, of a sociological theory which lies under the imputation of being unable to account for social change, to say that the author is aware of the problem" (p. 32). More importantly, James Mill's *History of British India* does not aspire to "that sympathetic understanding which was beginning to be postulated as the goal of historical writing . . ." rather in it "the urbane tolerance and even qualified admiration of the eighteenth century for alien and barbaric cultures was giving way to censoriousness and denigration. More than ever, contemporary Europe was being taken as the measure of all excellence" (p. 43).

We see, then, that Burrow's book treats of a problem which is not stated in so many words. The eighteenth century's belief in the unity of mankind was not shaken by the explorers' discovery of the facts of human diversity (Captain Cook, etc.). *How came it, then, that Victorian intellectuals regressed to a belief in their own superiority and the relative inferiority of savages* (Victorian Regress)? The rise of evolutionist philosophies, Burrow's argument implies, explains this regression.

In the following uninterrupted summary of the story of evolutionism and society, which follows the order in which Burrow tells it, these three problems—The Historical Gap, Evolutionism's Hold, Victorian Regress—have been used to control the emphasis.

Though James Mill exhibits both some admiration for barbarians and adverse judgment upon their customs, based upon European standards, it is the latter attitude which is more significant for him. And so, we need not be surprised that Mill castigates Sir William Jones (an eighteenth-century peddler of the ideas of the wisdom of the East, and of cultural diffusion) for his sympathetic attitude to Hindu customary law. States of society were to be measured rather ". . . exactly in proportion as Utility is the object of every pursuit." Mill is also a conjectural historian and thus also the last descendant of the Scottish school. But Mill's contempt for non-Europeans hardly encouraged the comparative study of social institutions. Between 1770 and 1830 conjectural history declined; this is explained by impatience, i.e., in policy matters its tendency was to go slowly, not proceed radically to change and reform. John Stuart Mill, for example, allows democracy only to societies on the same level of what we would call 'development'. His philosophy of history—that we move forward in stages —is found irrelevant by those seeking the answers to current political questions, since what is good for one stage is not necessarily so for another stage. Thus adoption of Mill's outlook would prevent any radical appeal to a universal set of basic principles.

In the works of John Stuart Mill and Macaulay the explanation of human behavior from universal principles is attacked with arguments that show evidence of various influences, including that of continental "historical relativism"; that of the view that history should be less political and dynastic, more broad-based, more social; and also that of the belief in the unique character of historical periods. Macaulay claimed that explanation from universal principles was not empirical, i.e., not Baconian, and J. S. Mill confessed that he found these first principles, such as the desire for happiness, contingent, arbitrary and, finally, no reason to do things.

Meanwhile, geographical exploration was throwing up "apparently irrational types of social organization" (p. 75) in the world here and now, and administrators of colonies and the like, forced to cope with them, had to take them seriously. The utilitarians, however, dismissed irrationality, usually appealing to some such theory as Condorcet's of a priestly conspiracy to dominate and exploit people.

So much, then, for The Historical Gap, or the delay in arriving at the rudiments of social anthropology. These began to emerge in the third quarter of the nineteenth century. The National Association for the Promotion of Social Science was founded in 1857, the Anthropological Society of London in 1863. Mill's *System of Logic* with its sections on the social sciences had appeared first in 1843, and his and others' interest in

Comte stirred during the forties and fifties. Also in the third quarter, the major works of Spencer began to appear "A sterile and unrealistic a priorism, so the new orthodoxy ran, had been superseded by patient observation of social facts" (p. 82).

However, sociology still seemed to mean the laws of social development, i.e., the philosophy of history. Why was there no social statics, no really detailed mapping of institutions and structures? Comte and Mill at least showed themselves aware of the possibility. One reason for the lack was that fieldwork was difficult, expensive and undreamt of. And why were such social surveys as were done not related to sociological and anthropological theory? Spencer answered by saying that in sociology as in anatomy you need a physiology before you can have a pathology and that the aim of a pathology is not to adapt a physiology; that is to say, he thought we could ascertain objectively what produces happiness and unhappiness and then bring society into line.

Now, more positively, what problems did this historical sociology come to solve? Basically and above all the ethical problem of how to preserve the unity of mankind in the face of cultural and historical diversity —in other words, how to avoid relativism. Evolutionism did this (pp. 98-99). Religion no longer did so in a world of cataclysmic change. Perhaps also there was the problem of trying to tame the cataclysmic change by understanding it (p. 100).

But why did they try to explain society before exploring and mapping it? They hoped sociology would give a parallel mastery of the chaotic social world to match the mastery over the natural world supplied by natural science. To prove human life part of an ordered universe leads to an emphasis on how one state of society gives rise to another, i.e., on social change. This belief in the universal operation of natural causation is itself both the cause and effect of scientific success, notably in geology, paleontology, evolutionary biology, comparative philology, and prehistoric archaeology. Burrow says that social evolution owes more to geology and comparative philology than to biology. The geologist Lyell, like Darwin, freed the historical natural sciences from "finalism," "providentialism" or "catastrophism," as physics and chemistry were freed in the seventeenth century. Geology gave huge new time spans; ways of dating fossils by strata; and a relationship between this chronology and structural complexity, i.e., paleontology. Darwin placed man in nature, not outside it; allowed racial differences to be traced to environment, not to be ultimate; and propounded a theory of natural selection. Lastly, the geological time scale was applied to man in the late 1850's, overcoming initial resistance. From the rudimentary tools that were dug up it seemed that the ancestors of civilized man were as rude as contemporary savages. Therefore, contemporary differences might equal different stages on the approach road to the present. However, since social differences had no archaeological significance, it was difficult to date the stages: the tendency became to classify them intuitively by rationality (apparent) or complexity, and then assume: less complex or less rational equals earlier.

There are, however, some difficulties in the program. Evolutionary theory is a subspecies of positivism—universal wants and conditions of existence explain all. To explain all is to forgive all. This relativism threatens the "rational ethics" beloved of Victorian thinkers, and leads to an undifferentiated chaos. For if ends are irrational or random, how is it there is a social order at all? One solution is contract theory—society is a device, created and human. But neither coercion nor calculation of advantage explain society—much is dependent on habits and customs, i.e., the irrational element, and yet they seem to contribute to social order. The social contract saw this order as designed (or quasi-designed). There was also the theory of the natural identity of interests (Adam Smith out of Leibniz *et al.*). Evolution was a way of making the customs and habits rational in a new and objective sense of the word: such as were conducive to survival survived, others, with a few exceptions, called, strangely enough, survivals, did not. In summary at this point Burrow remarks that "Essentially it was the belief that the intelligent pursuit of clearly recognized ends was adequate as a key to understanding society that was breaking down in the mid-nineteenth century" (p. 105).

Anti-Evolutionists are still widely considered to have been anti-scientific, at least anti-empiricist, and fundamentalists, at least religiously biassed. Burrow corrects this impression. The serious resistance to Evolutionism was in the Anthropological Society of London; among its prominent members were medical men, who were reputed for their empiricism if not even godlessness (pp. 127-128). Its discussions centered around visible differences. Comparative anatomy had revealed structural differences between races and threatened the idea of the unity of mankind. The Anti-Evolutionism of the Anthropological Society indeed was racist—as between it and its opponents the question was, are our primitive contemporaries missing links, or degenerate freaks? (p. 131) It was a confused Society of the ultimate losers—for outside its confines, and despite its bitter opposition, Evolutionist anthropology was developing apace.

So much for Evolutionism's Hold. I shall conclude my presentation with a summary of Burrow's detailed study of several thinkers who occupy critical positions in the development of anthropology: Sir Henry Maine (1822-1888), Herbert Spencer (1820-1903) and Sir Edward Tylor (1832-1917).

Maine: Whatever view is taken of the early influences on Maine, his famous work *Ancient Law* was not Darwinian; although it was published in 1861, there is evidence that the ideas took form in 1853 under the combined influences of the German school of historical jurisprudence and comparative philology—and perhaps even Max Müller. Maine in that book tried "to trace the real, as opposed to the imaginary, or the arbitrarily assumed, history of the institutions of civilised men" (p. 154). His approach was historical, inductive and comparative.

Maine sharply distinguished barbarism and civilization and acknowledged that the latter had roots in the former. Governmental despotism is all right, he argues, if it is for the benefit of the barbarians. This was a convenient doctrine in the age of the empire. Maine had been in the government in India, and the question arises, did he take the Indians as models of intelligible conduct, or as barbarians? Neither. He was a comparative gradualist. Our language shows our kinship with India. India includes many Aryan institutions and customs "in a far earlier stage of growth and development than any which survived beyond its borders" (p. 161). He avoided comparisons beyond the Aryan pale as having nothing except common humanity to connect them with the Teutons and Celts. This forced him to assume that India was in a "frozen" state as opposed to progressive societies. Yet he allowed that some changes take place among other barbarians, why not among the Aryan Indians? He was trapped by his own injudicious mixture of evolutionism and diffusionism. Crudely, evolutionism in its strong form holds that man came down from the trees at one place or another and then evolved his customs and culture at different rates in different places. Diffusionism is the view that man learns and borrows from other men, and that culture may therefore have its origins in certain *creative centers.* Maine believed that Aryan customs diffused from India, but was then trapped by the argument that, if *we* Aryans have developed, what is to say the Indian Aryans have not developed too, and therefore may well not be in the stage they were when they exported us and the roots of our culture?

Burrow agrees that Maine's outlook was typically positivist in its assumption that there are general laws of development. Yet at times

Maine was more tentative than some. His theory says that in its infancy a society adopts those usages which are generally best-suited to promote its physical and moral well-being. Incapable of understanding this expediency, the multitude invent superstitious reasons for their permanence, and then wrongly extend them to other matters. The great exception for Maine was Rome, where customs were legislated into a code while they were still wholesome and well-suited to it. Maine went on to argue that a code of this sort does not guarantee progress, but he thought progress cannot ignore it.

Burrow argues that Maine's intellectualism, his whole picture of primitive man looking at his situation *qua* incompetent sociologist, led him to ignore irrational action and non-utilitarian conduct. Superstition is too easy a way to explain these. Moreover, Maine really was interested only in progress, and backward societies served only to illuminate this as a kind of "anti-environment," to adopt a McLuhanism, but were of little interest in themselves. His attitude to India was that above all British rule should strive not to block progress and give rigidity to native usages: this less out of respect for native usages than of hope for progress.

Spencer: Spencer embodied the nineteenth century tension "between the hope of constructing a social series developing according to ascertainable laws and the approach to societies as systems of complex functional relations" (p. 191). How to reconcile the doctrine of survivals and the abstract comparisons attendant of evolutionism, with the view of society as an organic functioning structure? The question looks difficult to us; the conjunction was entirely natural to Spencer. He believed that it was structures which evolved—they made functional modifications. Irrational superstitions were to be explained by their role in social evolution and not their role in social life (p. 198). What, then, are the mechanics of this social evolution? Spencer was an environmental determinist: physical factors, the nature of man, changes in his environment, influence of society on man, of other societies and culture, determine the social system he has. Religion is to be explained as produced by fear and a mistake; political authority is due to propitiation by the weak and acquisitiveness by the strong; the division of labor is to be explained by a rational appreciation of its advantages (p. 204).

Spencer's deterministic belief in the universality of natural causation and his desire to render scientific his radical political opinions both tended to favor evolutionism. The first suggests that "the universe and all things in it have reached their present forms through successive stages physically necessitated" (p. 206, Burrow quoting Spencer's autobiography). It is also an answer to teleology and special creation. But it led him to try to trace the causal chain back to physical factors, and in this quicksand his sociology expired. His belief in the uniformity of nature replaced God; and grasp of this uniformity was Enlightenment, even Grace (p. 212). Evolution, for Spencer, equals progress. He did not advocate throwing aside the state and taboos because of a rational perception of the laws of nature, or because of the ultimate identity of interests, or because coerced by a utilitarian legislator. Rather, he saw them as a product of the evolutionary process in which conflict and the protective influence of taboos and irrational practices have been major factors. Like Marx, he believed this conflict will cease. He was a bit Rousseau-ist, holding " the claims of society, the institutions—other than economic institutions—by which human energy is shaped and guided, as something essentially alien to the human personality, something from which it will ultimately liberate itself, and not as something without which men can be neither human nor individual in any way which we can understand" (pp. 225-226).

The predilection of evolutionists for recognizing the function of irrational practices only in other societies or, if in their own, as essentially transitory, might be explained as a means of having it both ways: being detached towards others and the past, yet denouncing our society's own evils.

In a way, Spencer is a digression from the story of anthropology; who reads him now? Burrow takes up the story again, examining three mainstream thinkers who, between them, got academic anthropology moving along: the two minor figures, Sir John Lubbock and J. F. McLennan, and Sir Edward Tylor.

Lubbock: Lubbock alone of the three came to evolutionary social theory from evolutionary biology and prehistoric archaeology. The apparent development of technology illustrated by archaeology stirred his interest in cultural evolution. He thought primitive peoples ought to be studied because of the empire, they are our ancestors, they illustrate many things fossilized in our culture, and they help us see the future.

McLennan: McLennan was a lawyer who seems to have been led by his research into studies of the origin of society. He believed the outline of the course of human progress can be traced back well before philology. In contrast to Maine who accepted the unity of the Aryans, if not the unity of mankind, McLennan regards "the ethnological differences of the several families of mankind as of little or no account compared with what they have in common" (quoted on p. 232).

Tylor: The advent of Tylor, the first professional anthropologist, could have been regarded as a disaster by a contemporary functionalist. Religion was to be explained by a hypothetical account of primitive psychology. Whereas McLennan explained marriage by capture as a *system* due to population pressure, female infanticide, exogamy and the prejudice against intermarriage, Tylor explained animism as due to fear and a mistake. Tylor, while he did not invent the idea of survivals, made survival-hunting a major anthropological activity—this promoted what Burrow calls an antiquarian rather than a sociological attitude. Tylor's first book was a travel book on his archaeological experiences in Mexico and displayed no interest in contemporary Mexico at all. He mainly discussed the centers *versus* separate evolution issue and came down for the latter. Believing in the unity of mankind, in a common human nature, and also believing in the association of ideas, Tylor was able to make animism seem a highly rational theory for men in a low state of knowledge. Archaeological developments, survivals, and the intelligibility of savage views buttressed his use of the evolutionary comparative method. When he wrote, "the science of culture is essentially a reformer's science" (quoted p. 254), he was arguing for moral and intellectual reform against the theologians and moralists who support survivals like the church. His *Primitive Culture* was an Enlightenment document: it attacked superstition, metaphysics, meaningless tradition, empty forms and ceremonies—all were shown to be once sensible but now relics.

Burrow ends his book with a few reflections on the development of evolutionary anthropology as he has reviewed it. As essential background, he says, we must take the general malaise and excitement caused by disturbances to orthodox faith and the revision of established views of the cosmos. The nineteenth century revival of radical politics involved acceptance of the conservative critique of the ignorance of those who ignored history, and of the over-confidence of those who overestimated the ability of man to mould society, or of the rationality of man. What transpired was simply a rewrite of the philosophy of history to a radical tune, i.e. progress. For tradition is replaced by the laws of social dynamics. But what about the equation "evolution=progress"? Does evolution promote the good, or is *it* good? This is a difficult issue to decide since arguments for one look like arguments for the other too. Spencer lauds development but then adds, because it increases pleasure. There is this constant vacillation in these

thinkers between describing development and prescribing development—
the attempt to deny that the sense the world makes, the value the world has,
must be extrinsic. Lovejoy labelled evolutionary biology the temporalization of the Great Chain of Being; similarly, Burrow christens social evolutionism the temporalization of natural law (p. 272). Hobhouse, a latter-day
evolutionist, tried only to show a correlation between 'better' and 'more
advanced'. Yet for Hobhouse sociology culminates in showing that what
has been ought to have been, and that what ought to be will be. The
future, sayeth Hobhouse, is not only law-governed, it is glorious (p. 273).

This is the gist of Burrow's story. The transition from evolutionism
to modern anthropology, viewed thus, seems patently all gain and no
loss. In my view, however, it was somewhat of a mixed blessing. Admittedly, excess and naiveté marred high evolutionism, and a critical reaction to it was no doubt to be expected. It is nevertheless sad to note that
it was killed by the revival of the drab and nasty little idea called
"relativism."

REFERENCES

[1] K. R. Popper, *The Open Society and Its Enemies* (Princeton, 1963), Ch. 4 and 5.
[2] H. Becker, and H. Barnes, *Social Thought From Lore to Science* (New York, 1961).
[3] E. E. Evans-Pritchard, *Social Anthropology* (Glencoe, Illinois, 1952).
[4] J. Swift, *Gulliver's Travels* (New York, 1961).
[5] I. C. Jarvie, *The Revolution in Anthropology* (New York, 1964), Ch. 1.
[6] A. Schweitzer, *The Quest for the Historical Jesus,* trans. by W. Montgomery (New York, 1950), Ch. XV.

CHAPTER 7

ON THEORIES OF FIELDWORK AND THE SCIENTIFIC
CHARACTER OF SOCIAL ANTHROPOLOGY*

The following intellectual as opposed to practical reasons for all anthropologists doing fieldwork are examined: fieldwork: (1) records dying societies, (2) corrects ethnocentric bias, (3) helps put customs in their true context, (4) helps get the "feel" of a place, (5) helps to get to understand a society from the inside, (6) enables appreciation of what translating one culture into terms of another involves, (7) makes one a changed man, (8) provides the observational, factual basis for generalizations. None of these is found sufficient to make fieldwork imperative for all anthropologists, although they are quite sufficient to allow that it is imperative for anthropology as a whole that field-work in some form by some people continue. In place of the view of fieldwork as an essential preparation for doing anthropology, an alternative role for it is explored: namely as a testing procedure. The implications of this—that the study of problems and the articulation of theories can usefully proceed prior to or even independently of fieldwork—are drawn out, and a new institution of selective fieldwork is proposed.

I

Theories of fieldwork explain why anthropologists do fieldwork. They are theories of method, since fieldwork is *a* method of doing anthropology (other methods include the arm-chair, the library, by proxy, the questionnaire, informants, and so on).[2] There are parallel theories to explain why natural scientists employ the empirical method, i.e. observation and experiment. All schools of anthropology emphasize that fieldwork stands at the center of the subject. Malinowski and Radcliffe-Brown, who thought anthropology was a science, placed the same emphasis on fieldwork as does Evans-Pritchard, who denies that it is a science. My concern is to pin down exactly what benefit anthropology and anthropologists derive from fieldwork.

The problem for theories of fieldwork to explain then is, "What is the importance of fieldwork to anthropology?" or, to put it another way, "why should *all* anthropologists do fieldwork?" This latter question should be carefully distinguished from, "why *do* all social anthropologists do fieldwork?", which will not be discussed. The reasons why anthropologists do fieldwork may be quite different from the reasons why they should do fieldwork. For one thing, the reasons why they do do fieldwork may be much more practical and less abstract than the reasons why they should do

* Received February 1966.

1 This paper, which has been somewhat abridged for the present publication, takes up and amplifies some points of my book [22]. It was read to the staff seminar of the Department of Anthropology, University of Manchester, in November 1964, and completed with the help of a research grant from the University of Hong Kong. It is a pleasure to thank Professors Joseph Agassi, K. O. L. Burridge, Max Gluckman and H. J. Lethbridge for helpful criticism.

2 The authoritative account of the standard fieldwork pattern is to be found in Evans-Pritchard [10], pp. 75-80.

fieldwork. Such practical reasons for doing fieldwork as the desire to pass into the anthropological profession, foot-looseness, or the desire to accumulate publications, are not my concern; I seek the intellectual support for fieldwork, quite apart from other supports for it—social, aesthetic, etc.

After discussing (in section II) the view that *all* anthropologists should do field-work and after showing (in section III) that the arguments support only the view that *some* should, I shall propose (in section IV) an alternative theory of fieldwork and of its conduct and discuss (in section V) how this increases the scope and flexibility of anthropological method. The discussion will refer to certain general problems of method in anthropology, and raise the question of its scientific charac-ter.[3] The view that will be developed is that *some* people should go into the field, and *some* should not, depending on preference and specialism. Ideally, perhaps, every anthropologist should have been into the field at least once; and every an-thropologist should have time for theoretical reflexion as well. The following facts, however, jeopardize realization of this ideal. Fieldwork takes a long time, and an even longer time to write up. When combined with an academic post anything between ten and twenty years may in the end be invested in one field area. At this stage of the development of anthropology the opportunity cost seems to be too great. The present compulsion which makes fieldwork the pre-condition of theoretical studies (and tends to put obstacles in the way of fieldworkers doing theoretical studies—the need to write-up, publish, teach) is open to question. It excludes from anthropology the person, for example, who prefers not to do fieldwork because he is urbanized—equally averse to the wilds of Nuerland or of Welsh villages, and per-haps also rather shy—or bed-ridden. There are bed-ridden physicists and biologists; why not anthropologists? It might be replied that shy or bed-ridden people are not suited to anthropology. This answer is mistaken: they may be unsuited to doing fieldwork; but an urbanized, shy, or sick person can be deeply interested in the problems of any field, anthropology included, and able to make a contribution to the advance of that field.

It should be stressed that the present paper is in no way an attack upon fieldwork. Rather the contrary. Anthropology is an empirical science, and a successful one at that; moreover it is fieldwork that makes anthropology an empirical science. Field-work, however, functions mainly as a testing procedure for whatever empirical theories are available for criticism. This is a vital role, but vital roles do not require

---

[3] It has been put to me that a better strategy would have been to compare two studies of a single society one of which involved fieldwork, and the other of which didn't. This objection misses the point, and amounts to the proposal to compare theoretical physics done by experi-mental physicists with theoretical physics done by one who makes no reference at all to any experiment. This bypasses the Einsteins who refer to experiments but seldom perform them, or the Newtons who explain all astronomical data without spending nights in observatories. *Any* serious study of a society will have references to *some* empirical work, whether by an-thropologist or traveller or missionary or government officer does not matter.

Incidentally, it might have been interesting to compare the unsophisticated fieldwork of missionaries and travellers with the sophisticated brand practised by anthropological profes-sionals. But this paper is not about why anthropologists think their fieldwork is better than untrained and casual observation. It is about the methodological role of fieldwork in social anthropology: this is a problem of the philosophy of science, not a problem of anthropologi-cal technique.

everybody's participation, and so it is not imperative that everyone should do field-work, much less that it should act (as it does now) as a means of demarcating 'real' anthropologists from the rest.

II

Why *should* social anthropologists do fieldwork? What is the methodological role of fieldwork in social anthropology? Why, in particular, should *all* social anthropologists be forced to do fieldwork? I turn to the various arguments which appear in the literature.

(1) Anthropologists should do fieldwork in order to record societies and ways of life that are dying out. This argument is incontestable, but carries no methodological force whatsoever. Societies are dying out and it would be nice to have them on record. But there is no need for *all* anthropologists to take part in this task, and it is clear that this kind of recording for posterity is a task that may not appeal to certain kinds of people at all. Underlying this argument, though, is an interesting view of the nature of anthropological science. This is that anthropology is a science like ornithology or lepidoptery which concentrates on the collection of specimens and their classification and sub-classification—it can be called 'comparative sociology'. On such a view, the more specimens one can collect the better: the broader-based are one's generalisations, the more exhaustive one's classificatory schemes.

Two weaknesses are to be found in the argument that fieldwork should be under-taken "for the record". One is that such fieldwork may be vitiated by being unavoid-ably done in terms of present categories. The other is that unless the fieldworker knows what he is looking for he may go off to a new society and then find it is a replica in all sociologically relevant matters of some well-documented society. These weaknesses do not tell against fieldwork; they rather indicate that if everyone spent all their time doing fieldwork they might be wasting time that could be better spent. A new instance which simply confirms current theories is of little scientific value: it doesn't lead to progress. If a new instance *appears* at first to refute a theory, but later turns out to confirm it, then it has really put the theory to test. Unless the new instance is a *prima facie* counterexample it does not, by overthrowing the previous explanation and forcing us to devise a new one, foster scientific progress. The his-torical record value of fieldwork is a by-product. Granted that recording is of some value, it is a sufficient reason for doing fieldwork, but since it may also be of no value, it can hardly be a necessary reason.

However, searching around a bit, there does seem to be a stronger justification for the collection of the facts on dying societies. It is this. If we make general state-ments about human societies it may happen that they do not apply to certain un-recorded or dead societies. Now this would be very serious, for even though such statements might well accord with all *known* facts about extant societies, they are still false; our theories in any field are always in danger from unknown and forgotten facts.[4] However, since we cannot anticipate what facts are going to be important in this way, it is wasteful to try to make huge catalogs since present categories are

---

[4] Nadel [32] quotes Huxley as speaking of beautiful hypotheses undermined by an 'ugly little fact' (p. 22).

likely to be revised; it is possibly better to regard the recording of such refutations as a by-product of research done for some other reason.[5]

So much for the usefulness of recording dying societies. Next in the array of arguments to be considered is a series connected with what fieldwork will do to a person or to his views—or to both—if he goes through it.

(2) Fieldwork will cure, or at least lessen, ethnocentric bias.[6] This argument can be re-stated in a number of different ways and subsections (3)-(7) are developments or more precise statements of it; here, however, we shall consider the problem created by bias *tout court*. Ethnocentric bias is the unarticulated assumption that the outlook and way of life of your own culture is 'normal' and every other pattern is deviant. Thus nineteenth century anthropologists felt compelled to explain matrilineal modes of descent, or the complicated marriage systems of certain Australian Aborigines as relics left over from previous (more normal?, more rational?) forms of social organization. Today's anthropologists argue that if one sees these 'oddities' functioning smoothly in their social context, one will conclude that they no more need explanation than the fact that the English have no lineages or clans. Fieldwork will not only cure crude views about 'savages', it will also expand one's horizons as to what variations there are in human society. After fieldwork one's reporting will be less infused with ethnocentric notions of what is normal, and one will not waste one's time explaining what needs no special explanation.[7] At this point an intriguing problem appears:

[5] The importance of what I am relegating to by-product status could lead to the argument from expediency, which I mention somewhat diffidently as it perhaps belongs among the sociological arguments laid aside in section I. It could be formulated like this: primitive societies are dying and vital factual information is disappearing and going to waste. Recorders are in short supply, how to increase their numbers? Answer: make recording-type fieldwork compulsory on all who want to be anthropologists. Sacrifice them, make them make their contribution, by-product or not.

There is a certain self-defeating character in this argument. If recording is really important, why should it be made compulsory? That it is made compulsory rather suggests that the *cognoscenti* believe: either that it is interesting but not vital, so people must be forced to do it; or, that it is really important but people are too stupid to see it and so must be forced. Neither alternative is a particularly attractive position to take up, which may be why the argument tends to be insinuated, rather than stated, in elite anthropological circles. The answer to it is not perhaps the obvious one, but rather that its imposition is inefficient. Willing workers work better than slaves; interested workers produce better work than bored ones. These are results attested by fieldwork. In a free society things get done faster and more effectively if people are allowed to exercise their choice and judgment. Those who value undirected, 'recording' fieldwork would get better and more interesting material by explaining their case to the newcomers and letting them do what they wish.

[6] For a recent statement of this view see Lienhardt [28] pp. 21ff.

[7] Oddities cease to be odd and only the general fact that human societies are diverse has to be explained. With the overthrow of evolutionism ('Societies are gradually improving according to a criterion something like survival of the fittest and their differences reflect their being at different stages') and diffusion ('Societies borrow from each other different things and to different degrees thus their differences stem from their differing permutations') it seems that there is no general explanation of the general fact of social diversity on offer except watered-down hodge-podges of evolutionalism and diffusionism.

Q. If you are not ethnocentric, should you be cured even though you are not sick?
A. Yes, because you can't *know* you are not sick otherwise.
Q. But when you are cured how do you know it?
A. Because you will cease even implicitly to treat your own society as the norm.
Q. But if you deny that your own culture is the norm, what then do you take as the norm?

One answer to this is to retreat into a 'normless' relativism; or, rather, a relativism in which every case is a norm. A different answer is put forward in my book ([22], pp. 216-224). We first compare the behavior and social contexts of other people with our own behavior and social context. Since we think we understand our own behavior it is divergencies from it that need explaining. We so to speak put ourselves in these other people's shoes, conjecture their aims, and try to derive their course of action from the hypothesis that they are acting rationally to attain those aims in that institutional set-up. We do not necessarily attribute to them our kind of aims, but we do explain by postulating that, other things being equal, they will adopt the most rational, most economical means of attaining their aims. This is a model by means of which we try to make rational sense of other people's societies, to show that their behavior is intelligible. In order to be able to use this procedure it is not required that you do-it-yourself; the anthropologist living in the society, the same anthropologist writing up his notes, the non-fieldworker trying to figure out some sociological problem,[8] or the historian trying to reconstruct the past, must use it.[9] In contrast to those who think we strive in sociology for a set of neutral descriptive concepts with which to describe any society, I believe we utilize this—ethnocentric, if you like—model of rational action, and we usually stop demanding further explanations at that point where the actions derivable from this model approximate to what happens. We proceed in this way largely because we know of no other way—comparing the unfamiliar with the familiar is the procedure for making sense of what people are doing. This is not to say that our first assumption, namely that we understand our own society, may not itself become problematic.[10]

Ethnocentric bias, then, is not in the nature of a curable disease, except in its most superficial and glaring manifestations—such as the discredited idea that 'savages are stupid'—and fieldwork is no antidote on this superficial level. You probably have to stop believing 'savages are stupid', or at least open your mind on the subject before it can seem worthwhile to do fieldwork. Plenty of civilized people have lived in

[8] Vide Carmichael [7], Finley [12], Goody and Watt [20], Leach [23], Schapera [40], Steiner [41], Uberoi [42], Worsley [44]. Neither Uberoi, Steiner, Finley or Carmichael did *any* fieldwork before they wrote: while Worsley, Schapera, Leach and Goody were writing about areas other than those of their experience.

[9] It is therefore especially odd to find it ridiculed as the Sherlock Holmes argument by Lienhardt [28] pp. 34 *ff*. His discussion is quite incoherent and confused. There is nothing wrong in principle with the Sherlock Holmes method ('what would I do if I were placed . . .'). What is wrong with such accounts is that Frazer etc. had some difficulty in seeing the whole situation they were trying to put themselves in. (In his recent *Politics, Law and Ritual in Tribal Society*, Gluckman recalls a conversation in which Radcliffe-Brown ridicules this as the if-I-were-a-horse argument [19] p. 2.).

[10] See further my [22], pp. 24-25. In a recent paper [43], Winch argues that only by seeing a society in its own terms can we properly talk about it.

contact with 'savages' for generations and still regard them as stupid. Hence field-work removes ethnocentric prejudice (sometimes) by means subtler than its advocates describe.

And to top it all, fieldwork can sometimes throw up its own ethnocentrism, a phenomenon that can be called 'double-ethnocentrism'. This is the situation where the anthropologist treats what goes on in primitive society x—which he happens to have studied—as normal. Dr. Leach in *Rethinking Anthropology*, comments that some anthropologists see all human society mirrored in the particular one they have studied: 'Malinowski . . . has so assimilated himself into the Trobriand situation that he is able to make the Trobriands a microcosm of the whole primitive world. And the same is true of his successors; for Firth, Primitive Man is a Tikopian, for Fortes, he is a citizen of Ghana ([25], p. 1.). This is somewhat rhetorical, but it alludes to a view close enough to the truth to warrant more serious discussion than it gets. I call it 'double-ethnocentrism'—the scientist coming to see the particular primitive society he has studied as typical of all society.

(3) Fieldwork, and only fieldwork, enables one to see the strange customs of others in their true context where they make sense. This is a good and valid point with only one snag; as authors like Gellner and Agassi have pointed out, it is mis-leading to say everything in a society makes sense. Strictly speaking there are mean-ingless oddities in any society, like certain ceremonial offices, and while it is salutary to resolve never to dismiss anything too easily as meaningless, it is just a mistake to think there are no oddities. A (presumably apocryphal) story is told of Mali-nowski trying to figure out the function of *lederhosen* slapping in Bavarian dancing; which seems like carrying the hunt for meaning further than is fruitful. Gellner has contended that there are even social institutions which function solely *because* they are meaningless; that sometimes meaninglessness is socially required ([17], passim).

Yet suppose that without a fieldwork-induced grasp of a social context one *would* be prone to error. Does it follow that all social anthropologists should do fieldwork? If so, should we force them on the strength of this view? To both questions the answer is 'no'. Its proneness to error is not a sufficient reason for discarding a method. To some extent all intellectual enterprise is prone to error. And the feeling that one should avoid avoidable error must be qualified by the division of labour. If the opportunity cost of fieldwork is high then it may aid scientific progress for some scholars to risk making errors of context by putting forward ideas freely and allowing others to criticise them. But the whole of this argument is too much of a concession. If contextualism is true then we cannot be in a position to judge the truth of contextualism, since that too is relative to a context; and so in employing it we use an extreme view, prone to error, in order to reduce proneness to error. This is a little question begging, which is sufficient reason to leave it and proceed.

(4) Fieldwork enables one to get the feel of a place, to avoid obvious errors, just as a novelist visits a place he writes about, or a court of enquiry visits the scene of an accident. This is connected with a similar argument, that the first job of a fieldworker is the mapping of the outlines of society, recording its principal structural features, before selecting specific problems in it for investigation. Both arguments seem to be entirely valid. But unless one or two fieldwork trips have the general effect of ensuring one avoids factual errors when one discusses societies one has not visited then all fieldwork does is to help one to avoid error on the particular societies

one has visited. The following three arguments suggest that the advocates of universal fieldwork do think the experience is generalizable.

(5) Fieldwork is the only way one can get to think like a member of another society; to understand them from the inside, so to say. In this quotation Beattie [5] combines arguments (4) and (5):

> For a Western anthropologist [fieldwork] . . . can be a vivid, almost traumatic experience. The fieldworker who spends a year or more of his life as a member of a group of hunters and gatherers in Borneo, or of a tribe of African peasants or pastoralists, lives in more intimate contact with the basic conditions of human existence than has been possible for generations in the modern world. Birth, illness and death, the daily effort to win food from the environment with the simplest equipment, the smell of the hot earth, the wind and the rain—the urgent, first-hand awareness of these things is something new and yet somehow familiar to the visitor from a city culture . . . the experience is an unforgettable one (pp. 82-3).

Ignoring the overtones of noble savagery in this passage (I can certainly imagine the experience being unforgettably horrible[11] and the anthropologist rushing back to a society where one is not forced to be preoccupied with nothing more than survival, birth, illness and death), it contains a clear suggestion that one can come to a deeper understanding of one's deprived brothers even after a single contact with them. Unless a single experience of this character were sufficient to enable one always to make the leap of understanding when discussing any society, the above quotation would not constitute a valid argument. And it is only generalizable, it seems, because primitive peoples are a homogeneous group in the sense that being all of them rather deprived they all live closer to basics, so that contact with one group is contact with them all.

This view that primitive peoples are a homogeneous group in my sense has been under attack for a long time. Frazer quotes Dr. Johnson as endorsing it:

> pointing to the three large volumes of Voyages to the South Seas which had just come out [he] said: "Who will read them through? A man had better work his way before the mast than read them through; they will be eaten by rats and mice before they are read through. There can be little entertainment in such books; one set of savages is like another ([14] p. 19).

Already in 1908 Frazer dismissed this lumping-together of all primitive peoples. Today it is doubly inaccurate since anthropologists do not confine their fieldwork to deprived peoples. Fieldwork in a Welsh village, among the sophisticated Chinese of Singapore, in the East End of London is commonplace, and hardly likely to bring one into contact with a society preoccupied with basics. So the argument that the peoples among whom fieldwork is done are sufficiently alike to make a single experience generalizable falls to pieces.

---

[11] On the severity: 'The water was scanty and foul, the cattle were dying of rinderpest, and the camps swarmed with flies', Evans-Pritchard [9], p. 12. The Nuer turned their backs on Evans-Pritchard, blocked his questions, scrutinized his most intimate actions; they live in smoke-filled huts and eat cheese fermented with bull's urine. Small wonder that he speaks of 'physical discomfort at all times' (p. 14) and, in [10], p. 81, of isolation and the ever-present danger of illness as among the main tribulations of the anthropologist.

Even were it generalizable, I would contend, as before, that it is not fieldwork that works the change, that makes one see primitive peoples as they really are rather than veiled by prejudice and misinformation. On the contrary, a prior decision to allow the evidence to speak is required—a state of mind in which one is prepared to try to come to see the world in their terms. The usual name for talent of this kind is 'imagination', and fieldwork certainly doesn't confer this, nor necessarily correct the lack of it; though, admittedly, experience enhances imagination, some very experienced people are less imaginative than others who have never left their hometown, e.g. Immanul Kant and Jules Verne. Also, anthropologists are not alone in needing imagination. The historian is expected to have what is called 'historical imagination'; why can't the anthropologist simply develop 'anthropological imagination'? Or is history seriously prone to error and unscientific because it does not use the time machine? Indeed, in the nineteenth century, anthropology received a boost because it was thought to be history's ersatz time machine (this is crystal clear in the passage where Frazer quotes Dr. Johnson: Frazer refers to primitive peoples as "living documents," "human archives"). But present-day primitive peoples cannot easily be assumed to be fossils. They may have developed through many stages, none of them similar, though some of them contemporary with, the stages our society went through. Whether they are fossils or not cannot be shown. To find out what our society was like even 100 years ago we must use critical imagination. If one is preoccupied with general sociological problems what is the objection to using this same faculty?

(6) Without having done fieldwork one cannot even understand what translating one culture into terms of another means. It is rather difficult to know exactly what this argument amounts to. It has an air of importance hanging around it. Perhaps it simply says that until one has done fieldwork and seen just how difficult cross-cultural communication is one cannot possibly appreciate the difficulties. The answer to this would be again that appreciating the difficulties is largely a matter of imagination: some people may require field experience and even more to do it; others may not. I don't want to minimize the point here. Certainly coming to terms with a totally alien culture is a different matter from, say, an Englishman learning to live in France. Hence, fieldwork is for certain sorts of people a good exercise which forces them to employ and develop their imaginations. But certainly the difference between France and the Trobriand Islands is a difference of degree rather than of kind;[12] some people would experience little difficulty in adjusting to either; some would find France easier but not a fundamentally different problem. It all turns on the kind of person and the degree of imaginative effort and flexibility he displays.

(7) The experience of fieldwork ((3)-(6)) makes one a changed man. Evans-Pritchard says

> What comes out of a study of primitive people derives not merely from intellectual impressions of native life but from its impact on the entire personality, on the observer as a total human being ([10], p. 82.)

I have never heard this argument fully worked out, but the idea—which already permeates the introduction to Malinowski's *Argonauts*—seems to be that fieldwork

---

[12] 'Certainly', because the difference between a difference of degree and a difference of kind is itself a difference of degree.

teaches one a proper scientific attitude as well as (or, which is the same as) a humility before the lives and societies of one's fellow creatures; that one will look, perhaps, on human society in a drastically new way, and that this will be reflected in a greater truthfulness in one's ideas. Now for this argument to gain methodological force it requires to be supplemented: one has to show (a) that the kind of man one is changed into is a desirable kind (from a scientific point of view), and (b) that fieldwork is the best and/or most economical way of bringing about the change. If we knew in what this new way of looking consisted, we might find out whether it can or cannot be attained simply by an effort of imagination; otherwise it may be difficult to know whether the change is desirable; consequently we might find it hard to give much emphasis to the argument. For, it should be recalled, the obvious suggestion that all the change consists in the elimination of ethnocentric bias—the ability to understand other societies, or translate other societies—has been previously shown to be defective.

It should be noted that the question discussed in this section is not whether field-work is desirable for the procuring of information: nobody denies that; the question is whether every one should do fieldwork, namely for his own good. The information can be procured by one and studied by another; the experience, it is claimed, cannot. Yet, when we confront these arguments from experience in detail, we find that they all seem to make one point—fieldwork prevents one from making factual mistakes. The first argument suggests that if we record dying societies we won't make so many false generalisations; the second argument says fieldwork will check the mistakes consequent on ethnocentrism; the third argument says fieldwork prevents mistakes consequent on not seeing things in their proper context; the fourth arguments says fieldwork will prevent simple errors of fact caused by not having been there and seen for oneself; the fifth argument says fieldwork will help avoid errors caused by not seeing things from the other chap's point of view; the sixth argument says fieldwork will prevent naive errors of cross-cultural communication; the seventh argument hints that the scientific work of the changed man will be better, which can mean—at least amongst other unuttered things—less prone to error, than that of the unchanged man.

Certainly, it is important in scientific work to test one's ideas for error; indeed it is important in any discourse whatsoever. But it is hardly convincing to paint error as a demon tempting us to go astray. After all, science progresses, and most of what we say is likely to be shown to be error sooner or later. We can aim to do our best, but we cannot aim to be perfect. Of course, if we could visit all societies, no doubt our rate of error would be reduced. The trouble is, it might be reduced to zero since there are many societies and life is short, and in trying to visit them all before committing oneself one might never get a chance to say anything. Even a weaker view that recommends that we simply try to visit, not all, but as many societies as we can results in the same: in effect they prevent the doing of anthropology.

Perhaps in recognition of this a still weaker thesis seems to be the unstated motto of some scholars. This thesis is that one should at least not write about societies one has no experience of. Predictably even this cuts down rather on one's possibilities. As a consequence, maybe, one comes across anthropological works bearing some bold and promising general title and finds that within a very short time the author has ended up discussing the one or two societies he has visited, and feeding us a few more pages from his voluminous field notes.[13] No danger of going wrong there!

The choice, then, seems to be between spending much of one's life at a task of limited scientific importance, or being paralysed from formulating any general theories at all, or both; or taking a more relaxed view of the danger of error. In a general way travel (like study) broadens the mind and should be encouraged. But why is there a widespread feeling that fieldwork is in some essential way different from such casual advice, why is it canonised as something scientific?

III

This brings us from the discussion of whether all social anthropologists should do fieldwork to the different problem of the methodological role of fieldwork in social anthropology. To deny that all social anthropologists must do fieldwork for their own good, is not to deny that fieldwork is good. Fieldwork is the main source of anthropological information and therefore obviously some anthropologists must do fieldwork if this supply is not to dry up. So the question arises concerning this or any other kind of information: 'What is the use of it?' We are long past the stage of collecting information for information's sake. We all know that there is only time for, and point in, collecting *some* information. Which some, though? Well, relevant information, interesting information, is what we want. So now we come to the question what information is interesting or relevant to social anthropology? What role does information play?

(8) This brings me to the central argument of this paper: fieldwork has the same functions as laboratory experiments in science, it is the observational, factual basis of scientific social anthropology. As Malinowski said in 1936 in his foreword to Firth ([13], p. xi), 'After all, science lives by inductive generalisation'. And it is the function of fieldwork to provide the factual material from which the inductive generalisations can be made. Facts are conceived of as meat, induction as a sausage-machine, and science as the product of pushing the one through the other. No conjectures, no imagination, no web of guesses in this conception of science—which, incidentally, is far more widespread than the frequent disavowals of it suggest. For all the attempts at hypothetico-deductive modifications we find it in Radcliffe-Brown,[14] Nadel,[15] and even in Beattie[16] and Lienhardt[17] who try hard to show they

---

[13] The following works all suggest sweeping scope, whereas they in fact confine themselves to one society or a closely related group of societies: Leach's "The Structural Implications of Matrilateral Cross-Cousin marriage" [26], Lienhardt's "On the Concept of Objectivity in Social Anthropology" [27] and Schapera's *Government and Politics in Tribal Society* [39]. In the latter work there is a preface which explains that the original lectures drew examples from all over the world, but that a more 'satisfactory' basis for generalization is to confine the printed version to four peoples of South Africa.

[14] Methodological connoisseurs are referred to [37] where, despite protestations of innocence, Radcliffe-Brown puts forward an appallingly sophisticated inductivist-essentialist view of the methods of science. He says "The method of science is one involving observation, classification, and generalisation, not as separate processes, but as parts of a single complex procedure" (p. 28) and then adds a little later "The first step in the development of any science is taxonomic" (p. 32) and proceeds to look for natural kinds of social systems.

[15] Nadel, too [32] hides behind lip-service to deductive science when he says that "Science starts with problems . . ." (p. 23). But he gives himself away by, e.g. seven uses of the word

have gone beyond it. They've certainly learned their methodological lessons, but they haven't yet managed to apply and work them out in anthropology. Again, the inductivist view is to be found, for example, at the back of the theory that field-workers should publish as many of the facts they have collected as possible, and with as little interpretation as possible so that *others* may come along and synthesize generalisations from them. Such a view is expressed in Dr. Leach's *Pul Eliya* [24] where he justifies what he acknowledges to be an overlong and unreadable[18] book with the argument that he wants to set down all the facts of the case; he also says that he has strived to present the evidence without doctoring it to suit his own interpretation, which anyway he needn't do because 'I claim that the evidence "speaks for itself".' ([24], p. 12). I have heard Professor Fortes' work on Tallensi kinship praised because it yielded Worsley's reinterpretation in economic terms [44], . . . and I have heard another well-known anthropologist denigrated because, it was said, he publishes only such facts as suit his interpretations, . . . Then, crime of crimes . . ., burns his original field notes.

This Baconian-inductivist theory of fieldwork was undoubtedly a case of totally wrong reasons being put forward to support an admirable procedure. Thinking that scientific social anthropology must be based on true observed facts, and perhaps accepting Bacon's view that only the pure mind could make true observations, anthropologists turned to fieldwork. Personal observation, learning the language, reporting observations and *then* doing anthropology was the pattern. Utilising other people's observations, especially those prejudiced by missionary or government ac-tivities, would be unreliable and unscientific. Utilising informants would involve failure to observe personally and to eliminate bias. Interpreters would interfere with the process of observation. Thus most previous ethnological data was useless, and only the cleansed could use the scientifically collected data. Here then is a well-developed theory of fieldwork which follows in many details Bacon's primitive theory of scientific method (including the slow ascent of the ladder of axioms, i.e. first of all generalisations confined to the tribes in one locality, then in one continent or subcontinent, and then the world).[19]

Neither fieldwork or anthropology will be in the slightest damaged by an attack on this justifying philosophy. To say that their present philosophy is false does not imply that they are false. After all, Bacon's methodology has been abandoned, with-

'synthesis' (pp. 25-27) in reference to 'data'. If I may quote a passage: 'Thus much . . . . . ethnographical data is still raw material [*sic*] . . . much still awaits that fuller synthesis which will alone lead to valid generalisations on primitive culture and society' (p. 27). (Inci-dentally, the original terminology is reversed by Nadel: Newton says in the penultimate para-graph of his *Opticks* ([33] p. 404) that the synthetic method is from cause to effect and it should be preceded by the analytic method from effect to cause by induction).

[16] At p. 85 of [5] Beattie asks us to imagine an anthropologist coming across correlations that are unexpected, such as between duration of marriage and occupational rating! Hypotheses to explain this unexpected marvel would then have to be framed.

[17] Lienhardt [28] resorts to the give-away phrase. . . . 'conclusion that may be drawn from this body of detailed information . . .' (p. 30).

[18] Leach [24], p. 12: 'The extra detail goes in at the cost of readability, but I cannot avoid that'.

[19] The theory is to be found in Schapera [38] with acknowledgements to Radcliffe-Brown.

out damage either to physical science or to its procedure of experiment and observation. Some reinterpretation may however be necessary.

This whole view, that the fieldworker collects facts, and that these facts are the 'basis' on which science is built, can be challenged from top to bottom. The alleged facts of ethnography are not in themselves unproblematic in that not only does the fieldworker select what he is interested in from the millions of events he could record, but also in that his actual recording of what he does record is permeated with his interpretation from the word go.[20] No wonder Dr. Leach thinks the evidence 'speaks for itself'![21] Let me explain. Take the reported fact that 'John got into his car and drove off'. In describing it I am isolating it from the continuous flow of time in which events take place, I am arbitrarily drawing two lines, and beginning my account after one and finishing it before the other. That is one piece of interpretation because I am assuming this isolating of a segment will not involve distortion. And in not describing it in a number of other ways I am also making an interpretation. I could have said 'A ghost disguising himself as John got into his motor car and drove away'. Or, 'John was swallowed by the monster which then ran off roaring its satisfaction'. Or, 'John by magic made a lump of metal into a horseless carriage'. Or any number of other versions. In reporting the event as 'John got into his car and drove off' I assume John was acting intentionally, that the car moved because of and not despite him, that it was John and not some simulation of John I saw, that it was an inanimate car, neutral rather than malevolent, mehanical rather than magical, into which he got. In short I presuppose a thoroughly western point of view.

What conclusion can be drawn from this reduction of a simple, seemingly unproblematic statement of fact to a sea of shifting sand? Not that everything is relative; but that what is to be taken as unproblematic depends on your framework; that all statements of fact are theoretical and conjectural to this or that degree; and that the naive idea that one can just collect facts is a chimera. What happens is that a fieldworker interprets everything he sees in terms of his assumptions. If he is a trained anthropologist, it is likely his assumptions will be that much more sophisticated and held that much more critically.[22] But not always. For instance, he may be less sophisticated because he believes in contextualism—the false doctrine discussed earlier that says everything in all social systems makes sense when it is seen in its proper context.

The logical successor to the naive view that science is simple generalization from pure facts is the view that science is the making of hypotheses and confirming them— a more sophisticated induction. This method is displayed if we study the main general problem which has preoccupied social anthropologists since the time of Malinowski and Radcliffe-Brown; namely the problem of making sense of social systems. Previous anthropologists had explained away puzzling features of savage

[20] Beattie [5] p. 41, makes this point but isn't able to push the argument home.

[21] This classically inductivist remark hardly suggests the author understands as well as he claims the point that facts do not manifest themselves independently of theories.

[22] In a recent review Gellner argues that social anthropology in fact "already contains in itself, implicitly, a set of questions and even hypotheses (often negative) which, if a researcher does his job at all competently, lead to results which are not merely fairly reliable, but above all usable for further comparative work". [18].

social life as a result of historical quirks. The new anthropologists believed all social systems made sense and their job was to display this and remove any sense of puzzlement. This is a huge task which can go on absorbing anthropological attention for a long time to come. And it is the basic and unquestionable reason for doing fieldwork: find a society which no-one has yet tried to make sense of, and make sense of it and *confirm* the hypothesis that all societies can be made sense of. But would we not all gladly consent to the proposition that all human societies can be made sense of? Is confirmation of the idea required? (Of course there arise the further questions of how much one is going to make sense of—the problem of oddities— and how much sense one is going to make of it (cf. (3) above); these questions are vexed and sorely neglected).

A third, and still more refined theory of fieldwork would be this. The anthropologist invents hypotheses then does fieldwork in order to confirm them, or to modify them and later confirm them. Such a view is to be found in Radcliffe-Brown's posthumous *A Natural Science of Society*. The feeling of methodological refinement is there; yet, surprisingly, this methodology leads to the same old blanket endorsement of fieldwork. This is because tacitly it is assumed the hypotheses will be generalizations; theories in a vacuum. This method too is inadequate because although the fieldwork is directed by the hypotheses, the hypotheses aren't directed by anything. What they should be directed by is problems.

IV

The theory of fieldwork I propose states that: (*a*) anthropology is the study of problems, which can be discovered by fieldwork or any other method. (*b*) the job of the anthropologist is to put forward explanatory theories which solve these problems; and (*c*) to criticize and test these theories as severely as he can by fieldwork or any other means. This theory of fieldwork assigns it the primary roles of providing problems and testing theories. These two roles are much the same: a problem arises when a theory or expectation is refuted; a test of a theory is an attempt to refute it. Problems arise when theories are refuted; fieldwork may be undertaken to seek refutations. I will now expand a little on (*a*), (*b*) and (*c*) before explaining the advantages this theory of fieldwork has over the inductivist one.

(*a*) It is convenient to identify a subject as the study of a cluster of problems. This explains overlap, and shifts of interest, since connections can usually be seen between any two problems. The traditional account of fieldwork concentrates on technique and on selecting an area, not on selecting a problem. This is most unfortunate, as practically no scholar manages to write a book that doesn't center on a problem. Most of the field monographs which are published concentrate on selected and problematical aspects of the societies concerned. Only books in series like *The Ethnographic Survey of Africa,* and *Case Studies in Cultural Anthropology* avoid problem-orientation altogether. To take some examples: Radcliffe-Brown's papers nearly all deal with one problem each: whether the importance given to the relationship between mother's brother and sister's son in certain societies is indicative of a matriarchal past; why in some societies people avoid their mothers-in-law; why in some societies particular objects get raised to the status of totem; why in some societies alternate generations have a 'joking relationship'; why in some societies kinship terms are extended beyond their exact biological denotation; why certain entities are taboo in certain societies; why in every society some social usages are sanctioned others not. Each of Malinowski's Trobriand books centres on a problem: *Argonauts of the Western Pacific* on the reason why Trobrianders go through the elaborate ritual exchange of sea shells and necklaces; *The Sexual Life of Savages* on how kinship organization and sexual mores completely different from ours can be as well-regulated a means of social organization as our own arrangements; *Coral Gardens and their Magic* on why Trobrianders who are adept at techniques like fishing and gardening bother to compound their efforts with magic. Evans-Pritchard's first book *Witchcraft, Oracles and Magic Among the Azande* explores the problem of how a well-ordered social life is possible when so much of it is guided by magic, oracles and witchcraft, all of which are known to be false; his second book *The Nuer* centres on how anarchy was avoided among the Nuer, who have no chiefs or central political authority and who ruthlessly pursue feuds with other groups of Nuer. These are classical writers, but the pattern has not changed. The problem of how different and often terribly complex kinship systems serve as efficient means of social organization; the problem of how tribes without centralized authority organize their affiars; the problem of how industrialization and urbanization effects the social organization of preindustrial peoples; the problem of how far religion is required to buttress rules of conduct; the problem of how primitive economic systems work; the problem of the administration of law and justice in societies without centralized political authority, or without written codes—all these and many others have had monographs devoted to them again and again. Since it is almost a necessity to write around a problem, perhaps the paucity of problems as between societies—rather than within societies—accounts for the relative lack of general studies. It strikes me that failure properly or explicitly enough to formulate problems within societies accounts for this. Because all problems are general, the search for special comparative problems is likely to be fruitless. All monographs are at least implicitly comparative.

One of the points I made in *The Revolution in Anthropology* was that anthropology used to contain rather more problems: in particular there used to be a much livelier interest in the development or evolution of societies, and the diffusion of customs and institutions. It is hard to doubt that societies did evolve (even if the story is apocryphal which Popper tells of the society in India which died out rather than change: it stuck to a belief, however inconvenient, the belief that life was sacred, including the life of tigers); similarly it would hardly be possible to study and understand the constitution of many present-day Commonwealth societies without taking into account the diffusion of ideas and institutions. Yet there is little about evolution or about diffusion in the current works of social anthropologists. They reject the valid questions 'how did societies evolve', 'how have institutions spread' along with the invalid question 'what hypothetical prior stage, or pattern of spread, can I use to explain this society?' Certainly, we are all entitled to be interested in what we are interested in and not interested in what we are not interested in: as a person interested in making sense of other people's social systems, *and* in the problems of evolution and of diffusion, I merely remark the impoverishment of social anthropology.[23]

---

[23] Lienhardt [28] maintains this exclusion of problems has been part of the development of the subject: "like other, more unambiguously scientific, subjects, social anthropology has devel-

(*b*) Once there are problems, of whatever kind, statements to be explained, the anthropologist can begin formulating theories to do this. Here I think fieldwork plays little or no part. How one dreams up theories is one's own business. The main thing is to be clear what kind of problem one is trying to solve. Building up 'comparative generalizations' is attempting to construct theories in a vacuum. The alternative is to work always and only in a problem-situation. This is the fundamental tenet of the hypothetico-deductive, as opposed to the inductive, method.

The construction of theories to explain problems means constructing theories from which the problematic statements can be deduced. Unless they can be so deduced the theory does not solve the problem it is intended to solve.

To sum up so far, then, the theory that fieldwork is the collecting of facts from which science will be synthesized can be strongly contested. First the so-called collecting is in fact biassed selecting; second the so-called facts are unproblematic only from certain points of view; third the idea that science is synthesized from facts is an inductivist myth. Science consists not so much of generalizations of facts, but of theories. Theories are explanatory—that is, they try to tell us why something happened. It is true their logical form is that of a universal or unrestricted generalization—but not all generalizations deserve to be accorded the status of explanatory theories. 'All live men have bodies' or 'All societies have politics' are important statements, but they explain very little. The main explanatory theory in social science is 'All men act rationally'.

This theory, which is false, has been turned into a methodological rule: try to explain human actions with a model of rational action. The strategy of such models is one devised by Weber and elaborated by Parsons and Popper. It consists in reconstructing the aims, beliefs and social circumstances confronting an individual and seeing if the actions deducible from such a reconstruction correspond to those we want to explain. It is described as a 'model' because, life being very complicated, it involves assumptions that may be untrue and even known to be untrue. For example we know that the assumption that capitalist entrepreneurs singlemindedly pursue the aim of maximising their profits is false. Nevertheless this has not hampered the development of economics.

The model consists of a set of statements, concerning aims, beliefs and circumstances and that the actor will act in these circumstances to realize this or that aim in the simplest and most economical manner possible. From this possibly quite large set of statements certain others will be deducible. Among these it is hoped those statements which were thought problematic in the first place will be included. If they are, or some approximations to them are, the model has explained them. Thus explanation in anthropology is deductive in character, however concealed that character may be.[24] A statement is explained if and only if it can be validly derived from a set of other statements. As an example, take the problem: why do people go

oped by dismissing altogether some questions that once seemed to be of central importance, and restating others in the light of increased factual knowledge and understanding". (p. 3). This is a moot point. If only pseudoproblems are dropped then this is progress; but if perfectly genuine problems are dismissed the only benefit can be that of concentrating one's energies.

[24] The vast literature begins with Popper [35], Hempel-Oppenheim [21], Popper [34] and is reviewed in Brown [6] and Bartley [2].

to the cinema? The statement we want to explain is 'People go to the cinema.' Conjecture: people go to the cinema because they believe they will be entertained there, and as free agents they can go: this is why people go to the cinema. This explanation appeals to the universal: (Major premiss) 'Everyone has the aim to be entertained.' Then, together with the minor premisses:

(P$_1$) The cinema is thought to be entertainment by everyone

(P$_2$) The cinema is available to everyone

and the general rule 'Everyone acts to attain their aims' we can derive the conclusion that 'People go to the cinema.' If we push the explanation further back, and discuss why people want to be entertained, or why they find the cinema entertaining we are shifting to different problems from the one we started with. Thus does the problem act as a check on our endeavors. Sticking to the original problem it is noticeable that if for any particular person either premiss (P$_1$) or premiss (P$_2$) is false, i.e. if someone either doesn't consider the cinema entertaining, or finds it not available because he has no money or is in prison, then we will have an explanation of why he does *not* go to the cinema.

Here is a slightly more sophisticated problem from the anthropology of Great Britain: why is a meal provided after a wedding, and why is it expected that the bride's family shall pay for it? Conjecture: the meal is provided and paid for by the bride's family because it is traditional and most people stick to tradition; they equate it with doing the thing (marriage) properly. This does not satisfy and we turn at once to a second problem, trying to focus on what is really puzzling. Why do people want to do things like marriage properly? Because in general people try to live up to community standards—unless they have specific objections to them or are in special circumstances—as the price of community acceptance and respect. We seem to be getting only truisms, so we shift to yet another problem. How has the wedding meal and the bride's family paying for it become part of the tradition of doing things properly? Conjecture: (a) the meal is a relic of a sacrificial feast, which was held to entreat the goodwill of the gods on the marriage; (b) the bride's parents footing the bill is a part of the dowry. As to (a) the only evidence I can think of is that alcoholic toasts may indicate pagan ancestry and such toasts are the center-piece of the wedding breakfast. But this 'pagan relic' explanation has no power to explain unless we add that some social customs survive more or less intact, some survive modified, and others disappear. Unless we can specify that all of a certain type of custom survives in a modified form, we cannot explain why only a relic of the sacrificial feast has survived instead of surviving intact or disappearing entirely. And only at this stage do we approach the interests of the modern anthropologist. He believes that examination of other features of the society will reveal a role for the wedding feast, and that this will explain its survival in modified form. As a Weberian I would approach it differently. Given that in general people accept custom, its survival does not have to be explained, it is a simple corollary of there having been no effective or acceptable criticism of the custom; what does have to be explained is the modifications. And these can be presented as macro-effects of individuals acting to attain their ends, given their beliefs and circumstances. Many beliefs and circumstances have changed which would affect sacrificial feasts to the gods. Christianity has replaced paganism, animal sacrifice has come to be regarded as cruel, and anyway Christianity does not require it. These new beliefs and their effects resulted in modification of the wedding feast.

(*b*) I have nothing to offer in support of (*b*), but the problem of why people pay dowry and why it has survived—again, modified—is as long and as involved as (*a*). Briefly: one should perhaps begin with the conjecture that the dowry is a payment for services rendered. The services rendered are that another family relieves the natal family of a mouth to feed in return for her fertility, or something like that. But then, why has it survived so long? Conjecture: women for a long time did not cease being an economic liability. Now that they *have* ceased, the dowry is rapidly dying out and so is the rigid custom of who pays for the feast.

As to theories about the role of foregatherings after weddings in strengthening social ties and such like, they are solutions to still other problems like 'What general social consequences does a wedding feast have?' etc.

(*c*) The institution of criticising such theories as have been put forward is perhaps a unique and distinguishing characteristic of the scientific tradition. Despite the force of logic, empirical criticism seems to carry the greatest impact. Thus science, which has institutionalized empirical criticism, is held in high esteem. There are four basic ways in which criticism checks theories in the hypothetico-deductive theory of science. First there is the check of whether the theory solves the problem it was intended to solve. Second there is the check whether the theory is consistent with itself; third whether it is consistent with other accepted theories—the 'framework' of present science; and fourth whether it is consistent with known statements of fact. All of these tests are important and all should be as severe as possible—to try to avoid error. As an example of a test, take the speculative explanation of the dowry as payment to get rid of female economic liabilities. It would be refuted if we could find a society with the institution of the dowry yet where women are not an economic liability. Or it would serve equally well if we could find a society where women were still liabilities but which did not have and never had had the dowry or anything similar.

V

Anthropologists, on the view advocated here, are those scientists who put forward testable conjectures intended to solve anthropological problems, or subproblems of these problems. One role of fieldwork is to provide the empirical criticism of these conjectures. It is a little odd to think of this criticism being collected before there are conjectures to be criticised, as the inductivists believe. This science of social anthropology would not, on this alternative view, be an accumulation of so-called ethnographic fact, but a set of problems and subproblems, and various tentative solutions to these problems and the empirical facts which clash with or conform to these solutions.

In this scheme the role of fieldwork is essential but not universal. Anthropologists can do it in the vague hope that they will discover problems. They can do it in order to test a theory or theories. Or they can do it in an orthodox manner simply to increase the stock of knowledge in present categories. Alternative methods of coming across problems are: reading and reflection. Alternative methods of testing theories are, in libraries, by informants, by third parties, by reflection and the construction of a model (as in economics, or war games).

The conclusion is forced on us that however useful fieldwork may be, it is a part of anthropology *qua* science that should not be forced on people. It is a desirable experience no doubt. It is equally desirable that all specialists in forensic medicine have Ll.D degrees. In both cases the opportunity cost is too high and division of labour is called for. Anthropology may be a moral education, but it is also a science that needs to progress. Fieldwork may be splendid, but specialization is forced on us by the lack of time to undertake all desirable activities. This point is trite, yet it is frequently overlooked.

But our revision of the theory of fieldwork also leads us to a much more flexible view of anthropological method. First of all the emphasis on the self-consistency of theories and systems of theories is strengthened. Secondly, fieldwork is not the only empirical method; informants, the armchair, etc. can be used freely if they are used critically from the point of view of logic and from the point of view of known facts. Thirdly, in so far as the orientation is shifted to problems, field expeditions can be mounted simply to test solutions to these problems and then be wound up when the answer is found. Such expeditions could be short or long, conducted singly or in groups. Fourthly, the guidance of problems not only allows greater precision it also introduces the factor of severity of testing. In a given society one can test an explanation by looking at aspects of it which one expects will refute it. Say one has the theory that kin-based societies and capitalist societies are incompatible, because kin obligations are bound to cut across considerations of efficiency and profitability. Then one could seek out nations with strong ramified kinship systems and capitalism, and also nepotism in capitalist societies. Beginning from the files one might expect to end up doing selective fieldwork. Similarly, if one had the theory that the social role of the British monarchy is mainly ritual, one could try to investigate areas where it is least ritual, like the selection of prime ministers and the signing of bills and see how much emphasis there is on ritual there, or one might investigate the sources of real power and see how much the monarchy enters into their considerations. And so on.

This theory of fieldwork in my view strengthens it by making it more flexible on methodological grounds and supplementing it with other techniques. In its place as the key to social anthropology are put problems. We begin and end with problems, because when a test is successful and a solution is refuted what do we have but another problem?

There is a certain danger in characterizing social anthropology as the study of problems anthropologists are concerned with: someone may then come up with: 'My problem is the search for correlations or common combinations of social institutions'. So it may be worth saying that 'problem' is here used rather carefully—a problem is generated when an expectation, a guess, a prediction, or a theory succumbs to criticism. Something one had expected to happen didn't, something one had thought one understood turned out differently, this creates a problem—a new theory is required. For example, Evans-Pritchard has pointed out [8] that Radcliffe-Brown's theory of attitudes to the mother's brother is both circular and refuted by Malinowski's Trobriand material; that his theory that the form taken by religion is determined by the social structure is refuted by the Bedouins, who have lineages but no ancestor worship; that his attempt to explain totemism by the theory that important objects tend to become the object of the ritual attitude is refuted by the Penan, who have no such attitude towards the vital sago palm (pp. 23-4). Lest I appear to approve of Evans-Pritchard's argument, I will add that the lecture I quote is in grave methodological error when it argues that universal theories have a tendency to become vacuous. What I cite the passage for is that here are three brand new problems—the Mother's Brother, the form of religion, and totem—all are made open again with the rebuttal of what Radcliffe-Brown said about them. Evans-Pritchard's view that we should give up hope because previous theories are false, is absurd. This is what fieldwork is for, to yield new, skull-cracking problems by knocking out old theories. It is, then, the ability of anthropological theories to be refuted by statements of empirical fact that gives social anthropology a true claim to scientific status. The special details of the particular procedure for gathering these test statements is irrelevant.

REFERENCES

[1] Agassi, J., "Methodological Individualism", British Journal of Sociology, vol. xi, pp. 244-270.

[2] Bartley, W. W., "Achilles, the Tortoise and Explanations in Science and History", British Journal for the Philosophy of Science, Vol. 13, 1962-3, pp. 15-33.

[3] Bartley, W. W., "Rationality versus the Theory of Rationality", in, The Critical Approach to Science and Philosophy, Essays in Honor of Karl Popper, edited by M. Bunge, Glencoe: The Free Press, 1964.

[4] Bartley, W. W., The Retreat to Commitment, New York: Alfred A. Knopf 1962.

[5] Beattie, J., Other Cultures, London: Cohen & West, 1964.

[6] Brown, R., Explanation in Social Science, Chicago: Aldine Publishing Co.

[7] Carmichael, J., The Death of Jesus, New York: Macmillan, 1962.

[8] Evans-Pritchard, E. E., "The Comparative Method in Social Anthropology", in The Position of Women in Primitive Societies and Other Essays, Glencoe: Free Press, 1965.

[9] Evans-Pritchard, E. E., The Nuer, London: Oxford University Press, 1940.

[10] Evans-Pritchard, E. E., Social Anthropology, London: Cohen & West, 1951.

[11] Evans-Pritchard, E. E., Witchcraft, Oracles and Magic Among the Azande, London: Oxford University Press, 1937.

[12] Finley, M. I., The World of Odysseus, New York: Viking Press, 1954.

[13] Firth, R. W., We the Tikopia, Boston: Beacon, 1963.

[14] Frazer, J. G., The Scope of Social Anthropology, London: Macmillan, 1908.

[15] Frazer, J. G., The Golden Bough, New York: Macmillan, 1922.

[16] Gellner, E. A., "Time and Theory in Social Anthropology", Mind, Vol. 67, 1958, pp. 182-202.

[17] Gellner, E. A., "Concepts and Society," Transactions of the 5th World Conference of Sociology, Louvain: International Sociological Association (Naulewaerts), pp. 161-189. [125], pp. 54-104.

[18] Gellner, E. A., Review of Evans-Pritchard, The Position of Women in Primitive Societies and Other Essays, London: Faber & Faber, 1965, in The Oxford Magazine.

[19] Gluckman, M., Politics, Law and Ritual in Tribal Society, Oxford: Basil Blackwell, 1965.

[20] Goody, J. & Watt, I., "The Consequences of Literacy," Comparative Studies in Society and History, Vol. 5, 1962-3, pp. 304-45.

[21] Hempel, C. G. & Oppenheim, P., "The Logic of Explanation" in H. Feigl and M. Brodbeck (eds.) Reading in the Philosophy of Science, New York: Appleton Century Crofts 1953, pp. 319ff.

[22] Jarvie, I. C., The Revolution in Anthropology, London: Routledge & Kegan Paul, 1964.

[23] Leach, E. R., "Concerning Trobriand Clans and the Kinship Category Tabu", Cambridge Papers in Social Anthropology, No. 1, The Developmental Cycle in Domestic Groups, ed. J. Goody, pp. 120-45, Cambridge: Cambridge University Press, 1958.

[24] Leach, E. R., Pul Eliya, New York: Cambridge University Press, 1961.

[25] Leach, E. R., Rethinking Anthropology, New York: Humanities Press, 1962.

[26] Leach, E. R., "The Structural Implications of Matrilateral Cross-Cousin Marriage" in [25], pp. 54-104.

[27] Lienhardt, G., "On the Concept of Objectivity in Social Anthropology" *Journal of The Royal Anthropological Institute,* Vol. 94, 1963, pp. 1-10.

[28] Lienhardt, G., *Social Anthropology,* London: Oxford University Press, 1964.

[29] Malinowski, B., *Argonauts of the Western Pacific,* London: Routledge, 1922.

[30] Malinowski, B., *The Sexual Life of Savages in North-Western Melanesia,* London: Routledge, 1949.

[31] Malinowski, B., *Coral Gardens and their Magic,* London: Allen & Unwin, 1935.

[32] Nadel, S. F., *Foundations of Social Anthropology,* London: Cohen & West, 1951.

[33] Newton, I., *Opticks,* 4th edition of 1730, New York: Dover Books, 1952.

[34] Popper, K. R., *The Poverty of Historicism,* London: Routledge & Kegan Paul, 1957.

[35] Popper, K. R., *The Logic of Scientific Discovery,* New York: Basic Books, 1959.

[36] Radcliffe-Brown, A. R., *Structure and Function in Primitive Society,* London: Cohen & West, 1952.

[37] Radcliffe-Brown, A. R., *A Natural Science of Society,* Glencoe: The Free Press, 1957.

[38] Schapera, I., "Some Comments on the Comparative Method in Social Anthropology", *American Anthropologist,* Vol. 55, pp. 353-61.

[39] Schapera, I., *Government and Politics in Tribal Society,* London: Watts & Co., 1955.

[40] Schapera, I., "The Sin of Cain", *Journal of The Royal Anthropological Institute,* Vol. 85, 1955, pp. 33-43.

[41] Steiner, F., *Taboo,* London: Cohen & West, 1956.

[42] Uberoi, J.P.S., *Politics of the Kula Ring,* Manchester: Manchester University Press, 1962.

[43] Winch, P., "Understanding a Primitive Society", *American Philosophical Quarterly,* Vol. 1, 1964, pp. 307-324.

[44] Worsley, P., "The Kinship System of the Tallensi: A Revaluation", *Journal of The Royal Anthropological Institute,* Vol. 86, 1956, pp. 37-75.

CHAPTER 8

Limits to Functionalism and Alternatives to It in Anthropology

FUNCTIONALISM in anthropology has at least two components. It is, first of all, a theory of how societies *work*. Second, since it conceives of societies working in certain ways, it pre-
scribes a method for their study. As the method stems from the
theory of how they work, one would naturally expect that the two
stand or fall together. This is not the case. On the contrary,
the whole stormy history of functionalism derives much of its tension from attempts to split them apart. Critics have pointed out
that the theory behind functionalism is conservative, restrictive,
or even demonstrably false. Defenders of the faith have again
and again pointed to the splendid and undeniable achievements
of functionalist anthropology. Yet it seems never to have been
seen that the criticisms could be accepted without in any way
damaging the methodology; the separation could be made.

In this paper I begin by discussing the logical and substantial
limits to functionalism, then I enquire into why it was accepted
in the first place, and why it continues to be accepted. Finally,
I consider some of the alternatives and how far they are to be
accepted.

The limits to functionalism are, I shall argue, its lack of explanatory power, its unsatisfactoriness as explanation, and the
constricting effect of its assumptions about the nature and working of social systems. Its merits are mainly heuristic. Alternatives to it should incorporate the heuristic but aim at more realistic assumptions about the social system as well as at genuine

and satisfactory explanations.   After describing functionalism, I
shall proceed to its logical and substantial limits.   These limits
being clearly set out, the question will arise: How did functionalism come to be accepted, and how does it continue to be accepted?
Finally, I shall discuss alternatives to it.

PRELIMINARIES

To start with, what is functionalism?   As a rough first approximation we can say it is a method of explaining social events
and institutions by specifying the *function* they perform.   Such
specifications of function are considered explanatory because of a
cluster of theoretical assumptions about the way societies work.
So much for an abstract formulation; to explain the matter properly some detailed examples are called for.

Most discussions of functionalism—and despite its dominance,
much heart-searching about it does go on—begin, understandably,
with an attempt to survey and sort out the different connotations
of the word "function."   Merton[1] set the trend, and he was followed by Firth,[2] Nadel,[3] Martindale,[4] and others.   As a variant
to this procedure here are four examples of uses of the word in social anthropological statements.   They should sufficiently clarify
the meaning of "function," at least for the purposes of this discussion.

(1) It is one *function*, we could say, of first-fruit ceremonies
which forbid the consumption of new produce before the ceremony, to prevent premature dissipation of food stocks.

(2) It is a *function* of marriage, we could say, to ensure the
legal continuity of a line of descent: marriage is a contract in

[1] R. K. Merton's discussion is to be found in *Social Theory and Social
Structure* (Glencoe, Ill.: Free Press, 1949), pp. 22–24, where he distinguishes
several meanings of the word.

[2] R. Firth's discussion is to be found in his paper, "Functionalism," *The
Yearbook of Anthropology*, 1955 (New York: Wenner-Gren Foundation,
1955), pp. 237–258, esp. 237–240.

[3] S. F. Nadel, *The Foundations of Social Anthropology* (London: Cohen
and West, 1951), has (pp. 368–369) a separation of four distinct meanings
of the word purely within social anthropology.

[4] Don Martindale, *The Nature and Types of Sociological Theory* (London: Routledge and Kegan Paul, 1961), distinguishes (pp. 443–444) four
meanings of "function" which "could be employed for serious sociological
theory construction."

which one family gains rights over a woman's child-bearing capacities and calls her offspring theirs.

(3) It is among the *functions* of incest rules, we could say, to encourage men to seek women outside their group and thus enlarge it by recruitment, and at the same time to prevent internal jealousies over women within the group: men quarreling over the possession of their sisters or their mother.

(4) It is one *function*, we can say, of the leopard-skin chief among the Nuer to settle feuds.

These are examples of what probably would be agreed to be explanations typical of those found in the functionalist literature of anthropology.   My formulations are already loaded in that I write "a function," "one function," and the like, instead of "the function."   When I was an undergraduate we would be set essay topics like: "What is the function of cross-cousin marriage?" Only rarely would we be set: "What is the functional explanation of marriage?"   This might seem to indicate interest in functions rather than explanations.   Anthropologists might reply that in asking for and specifying functions they make no claims to be explanatory.[5]   But it is easy to show that the only reason anthropologists became interested in functions was because they were thought to be enlightening explanations.   The question being asked in this paper is: Are they enlightening explanations or, indeed, explanations at all?   The difficulties that have to be overcome in answering these questions are considerable.   For instance, all the statements above are so obviously *true* that one has to begin by giving assurances all round that in saying that they are not explanations at all one is denying neither their truth nor their importance and interest.   Second, anthropologists have been accustomed for such a long time to regard these functionalist statements as genuine explanations, and they have done so on what seemed like such impeccable and authoritative assurance,[6] that

[5] Cf. E. Gellner, *Words and Things* (London: Gollancz, 1958), where he discusses the various evasion-strategies of language philosophy.   I have heard anthropologists rebut criticism by saying: "I am interested in functions, in how things connect up in society; kindly leave me to get on with my work in peace."

[6] Particularly that of A. R. Radcliffe-Brown and S. F. Nadel, authors with a high degree of methodological sophistication.

these habits of thought tend to prevent them from considering criticisms of functionalism objectively.

The criticisms of functionalism are, I hope, objective. There seem to be insuperable logical and methodological reasons why such statements as are listed above are not explanations. They *are* answers to questions of the form: "What functions has such-and-such?" But the interest of studying such questions turns entirely on the interest and importance of functions. So this latter question cannot be evaded by the most hard-headed defender of functionalism. Insofar as anthropology is functional, to raise the question of the validity of functionalism is implicitly to raise the question of the validity of anthropological theories. And to refuse to discuss the former is to refuse to discuss the latter.

My strategy now will be to outline in the next two sections the logical and substantial criticisms of functionalism.

LOGICAL AND METHODOLOGICAL LIMITS

A deductive explanation is a valid inference with a statement describing the state of affairs to be explained—the *explicandum*—as its conclusion.[7] It is usual to divide the statements which constitute the premises of the inference, and which, so to speak, do the explaining—the *explicans*—into statements of theory and statements of fact—or "initial conditions" in physicists' and methodologists' usage. The presence of statements both of theory and of fact is not logically necessary, of course, since we could equally well put the *explicandum* in as its own premise. The inference then would certainly be valid, because it would have the same statement as premise and conclusion and any statement can always be derived from itself. Such an explanation, let us write it:

explicans	People go to church
explicandum	∴ People go to church

is called "circular" and is obviously not the sort of thing we want. So, clearly, this first purely logical characterization of the nature of explanation is not adequate. It is not enough to demand a deductive explanation; we also ask that the explanation be *satis-*

[7] See K. R. Popper, *The Logic of Scientific Discovery* (New York: Basic Books, 1959), pp. 59 ff.

factory.[8]   Now by satisfactoriness we mean, roughly, the opposite of circular.   A satisfactory explanation is one that says more than a circular explanation, that is, the *explicans* contains statements which go beyond what is to be explained.   We call this the requirement of independence.   The fact that the statements of the *explicans* go beyond those of the *explicandum* means that we can test the truth of the *explicans* independently of the *explicandum*. If we explain "people go to church" by "people believe in God," we know that we can test people's belief in God independently of their church-going.   On top of this, all scientific explanations should, of course, be empirically testable.   It will be my contention that not only does functional explanation not satisfy the demand for satisfactory explanation, it does not even satisfy the demand for logical validity of the derivation.

Let us consider the problem: Why do people go to church? The *explicandum* is the factual statement, "people go to church." This is a very vague, and possibly even false, statement.   But if we decide to explain it, then we take it as true by assumption. We now have a conclusion and we want a valid inference which will entail—or explain—that conclusion.   We find that the simplest such inference is where we write "people go to church" as premise.   The conclusion then certainly follows logically, but we do not feel that this "explanation" has taken us very far.   So we proceed to try to find something better.

Durkheim tells us that going to church is a way of expressing and reinforcing social solidarity.   Now how are we going to make that into a premise in the explanation of "people go to church"? Logically we should write:

(x) People in all societies must express and reinforce their social solidarity;

(y) The only way to do so in this society is by going to church;

and then think to write: therefore:

(c) People go to church.

This may be logically in order, but it is hardly acceptable functionalist anthropology.   The problem lies not in the theory, (x),

[8] See K. R. Popper, "The Aim of Science," *Ratio*, 1, 1958.

contentious though that may be, but in the absurd initial condition (y), which allows "only" one way of expressing social solidarity. Clearly social solidarity can be "expressed" in a number of ways. But unless the word "only" appears in (y) the inference will not be valid. If, for example, we weaken (y) into:

(y') Going to church is one possible way of expressing social solidarity,

then if people do not go to church it does not follow that they are not expressing their social solidarity—since they may be doing it in some of the other "possible" ways. Now it is a defining property of valid inference that if the premises are true the conclusion must be true, and if the conclusion is false at least one of the premises must be false also. But here with (y') we have a case where the following three statements are compatible:

(x)	People in all societies must express and reinforce their social solidarity	TRUE
(y')	Going to church is one possible way of expressing social solidarity	TRUE
(c)	People go to church	FALSE or TRUE

Whether (c) is true or false, it does not clash with (x) and (y'); therefore the derivation is not valid because a counterexample, an inference of the same form with true premises and false conclusion, can be constructed, since (y') covers only some possible cases. Thus if church-going is only one possible way of expressing social solidarity, it does not follow that church-going is explained by the need to express social solidarity. We can only conclude that

(c') In some societies some people may go to church.

At the very most, the expression of social solidarity constitutes one possible explanation of church-going. There may be others. Again, if we weaken (y) into

(y'') all church-going expresses social solidarity

we get no further. From (x) together with (y'') we cannot derive "people go to church"; we can only derive some statement like

(c'') all societies which have church-going members express their social solidarity; those that do not have church-going members may express it in other ways.

Only if the word "only" appears can we make an inference from which we can deduce "people go to church."   Thus to make functionalism a valid explanation, we must strengthen it unacceptably.

Let us look at a more complicated and realistic example:

(x) People in all societies must express and reinforce their social solidarity
(p) All societies have ritual foregatherings
(q) All ritual foregatherings express and reinforce social solidarity
(r) Church-going is a ritual foregathering

It is interesting to note that we cannot deduce from these premises the conclusion:

(c) People go to church

We can only deduce:

(c''') When people go to church they are expressing their social solidarity

But is that an explanation of why people go to church?   It may be an explanation of one of the things they are doing in going to church, but unless it is the *only* thing they are doing when going to church, it may not have pinpointed their *reasons* for going to church.   Their reasons for going to church may have very little to do with what they are doing in going to church.   I shall take up this point later.   But in any case, unless the explanation is made valid, the functionalist theories explain nothing; they have no explanatory power.

So much, then, for validity.   What now about satisfactoriness?   Even given that functional explanations can have their logical gaps rectified, are they satisfactory?   My contention would be that they are not.

Pocock makes this point inadvertently when he remarks with apparent approval that functionalism does not go beyond the known facts in its explanations.[9]   He is thinking of how it avoids

[9] D. F. Pocock, *Social Anthropology* (London: Sheed and Ward, 1961), pp. 60–61.

historical conjectures, of course, but I think we can use this remark as a springboard for criticism.   A theory makes a satisfactory explanation when it is not circular, not *ad hoc*, and is testable independently of the facts it is intended to explain.[10]   But a functional theory does not go beyond the facts it intends to explain; therefore a certain tinge of circularity, or of *ad hoc*-ness, is an inevitable consequence.   To be told that the function of church-going is to express and reinforce social solidarity and that the main test of the desire to express and reinforce social solidarity is church-going is to get into a circle which cannot be broken in favor of a "deeper" explanation.   Circular, or *ad hoc*, or nonindependently testable explanations do not tell us anything new; they are methodologically unsatisfactory.

The logical criticisms I have put forward are, I think, the most important.   Logic being trivial, if its rules are not obeyed, what violates it cannot even be trivially true.

Substantive Limitations

Functionalism is sometimes conceived of as a way of studying societies, a *method;* sometimes as a theory about how societies *work.*   My criticisms in the previous section have been directed at the logical and methodological faults of the functionalist account of how societies work.   I now want to come on to substantial criticisms of this account of how they work, in the course of which we will come to functionalism as a method.   A great many criticisms of a substantial nature have been levelled at the theories of functionalism.   Levy[11] has explored their teleological character, and his account has been elaborated by Merton[12] and Emmet.[13]   Several authors have argued—especially Leach[14] and Gellner[15]—that functionalism, because of its circular reflection

[10] See Popper, "The Aim of Science," *op. cit.*

[11] M. J. Levy, *The Structure of Society* (Princeton, N. J.: Princeton University Press, 1952), pp. 52–55.

[12] Merton, *op. cit.*, Chapter I.

[13] D. Emmet, *Function, Purpose, and Powers* (London: MacMillan, 1957), Chapter III.

[14] E. R. Leach, *Political System of Highland Burma* (Cambridge, Mass.: Harvard University Press, 1954), p. 7.

[15] E. A. Gellner, "Time and Theory in Social Anthropology," *Mind*, Vol. 67 (1958), pp. 182–202, *passim.*   There is a good discussion of functionalism

back on itself, explains only unchanging social systems where the parts happen to link up into a self-explaining system. This criticism has been elaborated into the suggestion that societies are being conceived of as coherent and consistent wholes, "seamless" as Macrae calls them,[16] and that this is unrealistic. Indeed in Malinowski this seamless idea is virtually explicit. And I suppose the criticism could be answered by saying that the assumption is a working assumption for purposes of simplification and no more a disadvantage than was the model of perfect competition in a perfect market in economics.

To this list of criticisms I want to add one more point. This is a mixture of criticism and rescue. I believe that, while these functional theories are not explanations, they are important and interesting. They are important and interesting, I would contend, mainly because they answer the interesting questions: what feedback and side-effects do these various customs and institutions have in their society? What side-effects does marriage have; does going to church have; do first-fruit ceremonies have; do incest rules have; do leopard-skin chiefs have? People get married because they want to; this has certain effects. First-fruit ceremonies implement certain superstitions; they also have certain incidentally beneficial effects.[17] Incest rules, too, are usually bound up with superstition, but they have socially advantageous effects as well. In other words, functionalist theories draw attention to the unintended consequences of actions. But can the side-effects of an event explain that event? The explanation of social actions and institutions is one of the main tasks of social science; accounting for the unintended outcome of actions within the institutional set-up is possibly the other one. If we ask: "What are the nutritional side-effects of first-fruit ceremonies?" the answer will be that they encourage people to eat the last of their old food stocks and thus to conserve their new stocks and make them last longer. Thus people are better fed for longer than they would otherwise be. All this is to draw attention to side-effects or consequences, and it is clear that while these

in Robert Brown, *Explanation in Social Science* (London: Routledge and Kegan Paul, 1963), Chapter IX.

[16] D. G. Macrae, *Ideology and Society* (London: Heinemann, 1961), p. 35.

[17] Nonbeneficial effects, too. First-fruit ceremonies may prevent one from eating *fresh* food, and this could have deleterious effects.

are enlightening, they do not explain the institutions.   They do, of course, contribute to the explanation of how the society as a whole works.

But to return to the substantial objections to functionalism. If the assumptions about the nature and development of societies are dropped, and functionalists turn their theory into a research guide, all such objections—and the logical ones as well—fall away.

At this stage we can split functionalism in two: the theory that every action or institution has a function or functions, and the theory that societies are well integrated, well adjusted, and "seamless."   The first assumption depends upon the second; it is because societies are seamless that all actions and institutions have a function.   The first theory asserts the *existence* of functions: "There exists a function for all events and institutions." The second theory makes a factual assertion about the character of existent societies: "Present societies contain no nonfunctional elements."   The first is useful but unfalsifiable; the second is restrictive and false.

Insofar as functionalism assumes a well integrated, efficiently adjusted, and "seamless" society, it is taking on the character of a metaphysical theory; that is, a theory that cannot be shown to be false.[18]   A theory which clashes with no possible experience. If a theory clashes with no possible experience, it is compatible with all possible experiences and thus has no power to explain any particular statement of experience.   It is also immune to attack.   Functionalism asserts: "There exists a function for every action and institution," and, of course, failure to find such a function does not refute the theory; it only spurs one to further searching.   It is here that metaphysical functionalism becomes a useful heuristic.   For in order to justify this further search, one does not have to prove the truth of "there exists a function for every action and institution."   All one needs do is show that such a search might be fruitful.   It may not turn out to be fruitful, but it is worth a try.

On the other hand, the theory that existing societies are perfect and seamless is falsifiable[19] and, I suppose, in societies under-

[18] I am here adopting a technical philosophical definition of metaphysics as unfalsifiable statements; I intend the word only as a useful label with no derogatory overtones.

[19] Gellner, *op. cit.*, p. 199.

going radical change, manifestly falsified.   How, then, are we to make sense of a theory which can be divided into two parts, the first dependent on the second, the second false, the first unfalsifiable, the second useless, the first to be accepted?   My answer is this.   The search for functions has manifestly been fruitful. Hitherto unnoticed facts and connections in societies, refutations of common sense or previous theories, have been uncovered by those carrying out the functionalist program.   This is fruit enough.   But the false belief in seamless societies must be given up.   We are thus left with the unsupported metaphysical theory that functions exist.   My own preference would be to say: "Some actions and institutions have nonobvious connections with others. Do not forget to look for these."   Thus the metaphysic can be turned into a harmless heuristic, and the false theory of seamlessness can be dropped.

THE APPEAL OF FUNCTIONALISM

The various criticisms of functionalism I have listed were surely not difficult to understand or anticipate.   This then poses two problems: Why was such a flawed theory as functionalism adopted in the first place; and why, now that so much has been written on its defects, does it continue to flourish more or less unaffected?   I think these two problems—why it was accepted and why it continues to be accepted—are separable.   The answer to the first one is different from the answer to the second.   Roughly, the theory was accepted in an inductivist-synchronic revolt against the speculation and diachronic interests of previous anthropology. It is sustained for quite different reasons, the principal among which, I would guess, being its manifest fruitfulness as an heuristic or methodology, and its metaphysical immunity.

Anthropologists were offered a very good reason for taking on functionalism.   Malinowski, its initiator, was extremely hostile toward nineteenth-century anthropology and its technique of explaining present-day primitive societies by means of conjectures about their previous state and what might have happened since then.   He objected to this historical guessing, or reconstruction— that it was speculative, incapable of test, and more likely false than true.   The explanation of social events had to be grounded in something better than this.

He came on functionalism, I believe, during a formative field work experience which caused him to discover that societies can be understood as interconnected and rational systems, not requiring reference to alleged past states of affairs to account for their characteristics and workings.   In other words, I think functionalism's real appeal lay in the fact that it replaced and superseded something else which was thought to be faulty.   Indeed, I have conjectured [20] that functionalism came first, and the criticisms of previous practice followed.

The appeal of functionalism undoubtedly consisted partly in that it prescribed explanations which required only the known and observable facts.   Conjectures and history, both of which went beyond the observable facts, were unnecessary.   All the parts of society could be explained by reference to their relations to the other parts.   What could be more appealing to the empiricist conscience?   Functionalism was a theory of society which demanded only a thorough and firsthand investigation of that society in order to understand it.   No conjecture or imagination was required. Malinowski, in explaining to himself odd aspects of the Trobriand society, found he was explaining one bit in terms of another. Thus he came to the theory that all societies must be such that they can be explained in terms of themselves.   His particular theory relied on postulating basic social needs, but we can ignore that here.   His theory was commonsense and empiricist; it was intimately tied up with a technique, empirical observation, which was gaining a vogue, and it intimated that those who underwent the experience of applying this technique would undergo an enlightenment, similar to that promised by psychoanalysis or the sociology of knowledge; you would be set free from bias and be in contact with the truth.

Malinowski's initial idea was that societies are like macro-organisms having macro-organic biological needs in much the same way that organisms have biological needs.   The function of social institutions was principally to satisfy the macro-biological needs.   Radcliffe-Brown put forward a slightly different idea, based on a mechanical analogy, stressing the "structure" of society in analogy to the mechanical "structure" of the body.

[20] See my *The Revolution in Anthropology* (London: Routledge and Kegan Paul, 1964), pp. 182 ff.

Every part of such a structure, according to Radcliffe-Brown, was interlocked and interconnected, directly or indirectly, with every other bit. To see it as a whole, and exhibit the interlocked working of its various parts, was the job of the anthropologist. Radcliffe-Brown himself used the metaphor of taking a time-slice or cross-section of a society and thus exhibiting its underlying organization and interrelatedness.

In so saying, Radcliffe-Brown was already indicating the attention functionalism was increasingly to pay to the unchanging underlay of society. But in societies where everything, including the underlay, was undergoing change, the explanatory value of such frozen time-slices was bound to be limited. In a Heraclitian social universe, Radcliffe-Brown's appeal to structure was in vain. Also, Radcliffe-Brown was implicitly abandoning the concept of the "needs" of societies and persons as being not explanatory: they amounted to little more than the definition of what conditions were required to be satisfied if the society was to survive at all. The situation is much as if in economics, instead of plotting the price mechanism at work on graphs, we simply took supply and demand figures at one instant and tried to explain the economic system with the help of such models.

But despite the force, and indeed obviousness, of these criticisms, nine years since the death of Radcliffe-Brown there has been little noticeable retreat from functionalism. My explanation of this is that its practitioners could not separate functionalism from the results they had produced with its help. They rightly attributed their success to functionalism and therefore felt it must be the critics who were wrong: anthropologists could not deny or run down their own successes. To this I add an earlier point: that functionalism as fruitful heuristic is based on the metaphysical or unfalsifiable formulation of functionalism—the formulation, that is, which makes it compatible with all possible experience. Indeed most experience can easily be interpreted as giving it support. Recalcitrant experience can always be dismissed as not sufficiently explored or understood. Ability to absorb all experience, irrefutability, is often taken to be a virtue, to indicate truth. This is an error. "Irrefutable" merely means not open to criticism. But still, irrefutable statements can clash with other irrefutable statements, and because neither is criticizable we cannot know whether either or both may be false.   Thus despite the rising tide of antifunctionalist criticism, the citadel holds firm.   The old guard and the new are equally strong in their conviction that they need have no regard for these criticisms.

And indeed it is difficult to deny the brilliance and profundity of the achievements of social anthropology.   To do so would be foolish.   One has to begin, I think, with a reassurance that to attack functionalism as theory is not to undermine it as heuristic or methodology, or to denigrate results obtained by authors who have accepted it as either theory or heuristic.   My guess would be that it was responsible for these results mainly as heuristic, but that the heuristic can be split off quite cleanly from the theory and continue to be accepted.   But even the theory could possibly have been responsible for the results: false theories can sometimes let people achieve correct results.   But this is no argument to show their nonfalsity and that their replacement had better be effected.

So although both the original acceptance and the continued acceptance of functionalism are explicable, the explanation is not sufficient to justify functionalism as a theory.   Instead, it seems to me that the criticisms of functionalism are so serious that it must be renounced as an ideology: it has practical and logical limitations which are most serious.   On the other hand, its heuhistic components—field work and the suggestion that, as societies are ordered systems with, more likely than not, some rationality behind any of their parts, interconnections should be sought —should be retained.   But for some reason or other such a suggestion provokes anthropologists to rage.   They throw around accusations of armchair advice and so on.   My only comment is that substantial and logical criticisms are criticisms wherever they come from, and must either be answered or met.   Their truth and force are quite independent of their source, however hard that may be to stomach.   Defensive tactics based on vague suggestions that critics who have no field experience cannot be taken seriously are obscurantist.   The field is not a form of mystical enlightenment.   If field experience feeds one with arguments which answer the criticisms, let us have them out in the open for discussion.   Otherwise the next move lies with the anthropologists: They have theories which have been challenged.   Either they can answer the challenge, or else they must abandon those theories.

ALTERNATIVES TO FUNCTIONALISM

For a concluding section I want to discuss briefly in the light of the previous analysis some points in connection with the alternatives there are to functionalism. At the beginning of this paper I said functionalism was both a method and a theory of how societies work. As a theory of how societies work, it seems to me superseded: this is far from being the case with it as a method. And I have already argued that even though the rationale of this method stems from the discredited theory of how societies work, it can still be adhered to independently of that theory. First, a method is to be judged by results, not merely by its rationale. Second, a completely different rationale can be given for the success of functionalist method. This completely different rationale, which I would call situational logic, is an extension or generalization of the method of economics to the study of society in general. It is the view that the only known way to explain social life is to envisage the situation as it is faced by the individual, and attempt to reconstruct those factors in that situation, including his own beliefs and proclivities, which led him to act in the way he did. Of course there may be an interesting contrast between the situation as it was and as the actor *thought* it was. But any way, here is a rationale for functionalist method. Try to understand how the society is set up and what happens here if an actor does that there. Thus will the functionalist method bear fruit. So this is one alternative to functionalism. To a considerable extent this method is embodied in what is somewhat portentously called "action theory." And ideal-typical analyses tend to be involved in all this, too.

What I think must be seen is that although functionalism has limits, these are specific, and it should not be rejected wholesale. On the contrary, its important methodological insights should be incorporated into whatever comes to replace it.

In discussing alternatives to it, we must separate two problems: a new theory and a new method. As far as a new theory is concerned, we want one that at least does its methodological job of answering the questions it is supposed to answer. As far as a new method is concerned, first it is not clear that one is required, nor is it clear what it is for.   Functionalism provides us with a method of studying society.   But men do not study things: they study problems.   One extra fault of functionalism is that it tends to concentrate attention on one kind of problem, interrelatedness—not necessarily the most important or most interesting. Second, there is really no single method of studying problems. One must familiarize one's self with the problem, make an attempt at a solution, criticize one's attempts, and so on, of course.   But solutions are acts of creation and sometimes they come and sometimes they do not; there is nothing any method can do for us. Getting theories, or the psychology of knowledge, seems to me to be a topic on which methodology can have nothing much to say. Any method or technique—from staring at collections of facts and trying to induce, to gulping coffee while burning the midnight oil—which suits the individual, is to be endorsed.   And we all know that there is no technique which *always* helps us to solve our problems; otherwise we would not be left with unsolved ones.

The functional method of studying society, then, must apply to some other part of the scientific process.   My suggestion is that it is very helpful in testing solutions to problems, once we have such solutions.   It insists on taking things in their context and not in isolation, and generally emphasizes the difficulty of getting at the truth.   This method is so general and so true that any alternative method should, I think, be rejected.   But, of course, most alternative methods will pretend to be roads to solutions and not to tests, and will be rejected.   We are interested in exploring and testing our theories for falsity; this can be looked at either as the most we can do, or as the very great deal we can do, depending on one's attitude.

Various alternative methods are available.   Action theory and the employment of models and ideal types, are among them. What seems to me more important than animadverting on their relative merits is to point out that greater attention must be given to the formulation of problems in social science.   When a problem has been formulated properly, it should be possible to envisage what kind of solution to it will be required.   "What is the function of marriage?" is not, for example, properly formulated, since the word "function" is so ambiguous and the word "the" is so specific. The problems must be separated: Why do people get married? what side-effects does the institution of marriage have? why do people approve of and sustain the institution of marriage? The effect of these reformulations is always, as in economics, to direct attention: first to why *people* do things, why they think they do things, why they say they do things, and so on; the second, to the nonintended repercussions their actions have through the institutional network. This method has been named situational logic and seeking the unintended consequences of individual actions.[21] As such it incorporates the other alternative methods. It has been criticized mainly because it was thought to exclude things that sociologists want to include, but I have yet to come across an argument which demonstrates this. Mostly, it seems to me, what is thought to be excluded is in fact included, especially laws about societies. For example, the criticism that situational logic is a reductionism and would exclude laws of human society is easy to rebut. Despite occasional loose formulations, situational logic sees institutions as irreducible parts of the situation. And along with institutions must go any known laws governing institutions, and like institutions themselves these laws need not be reducible to laws about individuals, and so they would be autonomously admissable into a situational logic analysis.

In the end, though, the main point about alternatives to functionalism is that they must not succumb to the faults functionalism has been criticized for, namely, validity as explanations, in a logical sense, and they must not utilize theories that are manifestly and demonstrably false, or make belief in metaphysical theories of society mandatory; such theories can always be accepted innocuously as heuristic rules.

[21] For a further discussion of the ramifications of this method, see *The Revolution in Anthropology, op. cit., passim.*

CHAPTER 9

ON THE OBJECTIVITY OF ANTHROPOLOGY

To raise sceptical doubts about the objectivity of the results of anthropology – or any other social science – is enough to tempt many people into offering a defense that is justificationist; which seeks, in other words, to make arguments that show anthropology *is* objective, which *justify* its claims. This strategy is doomed to defeat in the face of a determined sceptical assault. The only strategy which will avoid the trap[1] is one that goes on the offensive, which says "I hold anthropology to be as objective as any other science. If you do not, give me your arguments and I will try to answer them; I will not justify, and, if you agree anthropology is objective and merely want to see how I justify it, I will set aside your questions as idle." This will be my strategy here, and I apologise to those who would like to see a full-blooded justification of the claims of anthropology.

To simplify this immense topic I shall take 'objective' to mean the opposite of 'subjective, personal biased'; I shall take anthropology to mean social anthropology done by means of fieldwork (or its more intimidating name 'participant observation'). There is some connection between objectivity and truth. But it is not clear what it is.

Objectivity has a somewhat broader use than truth. Only statements can be true or false; but discussions, investigations, methods, judgements, people and many other things besides statements, can be classed as objective. That a person, or an investigation, or a trial, has been objective is not a sufficient condition for it to issue in a truth. Moreover, since we can reach the right conclusion by the wrong methods, objectivity is not a necessary condition of truth either. Words which are troublesome like this can be pinned down in various ways: by scrutiny of the myriad ways in which they are used – but this may be unenlightening; by imposing formal definitions of them on discussion – but this cannot but be arbitrary; by seeking to define the essence of their meaning – but this can lead to circularity or arbitrariness; and finally by embedding them in a context which provides rules for their interpretation as well as their use –

R. J. Seeger and R. S. Cohen (eds.), Philosophical Foundations of Science, 317–324. All Rights Reserved
Copyright © 1974 by D. Reidel Publishing Company, Dordrecht-Holland

such a context is known as a theory. The theory I adopt, which is Popper's, sees the aim of scientific investigation as the pursuit of truth,[2] and the interference of bias or personalities as vitiating progress towards that aim. Therefore, objectivity consists in placing checks on bias. No one is perfect, and no one should be uncritically trusted; the checks therefore must be social.[3] What must be institutionalized in the society of investigators is criticism; all work must undergo the ordeal of public criticism. This is an idealized description of the institutions of science.

Had we access to the truth, and were we able to prove that we had it, we might then have a method without bias (objective) and a result without error (truth). Only the tautologies of logic and mathematics can be proved to be true. They are true of all logically and mathematically possible worlds, whatever position we adopt on the relation of those worlds (subjective or objective) to the minds discussing them. The objectivity, or lack of bias or personal involvement, of logic and mathematics is gained precisely because they are vacuous: they say nothing about these worlds, only about their possibilities; they define them and their properties.

As soon as we try to describe, discuss, or explain which of the logically and mathematically possible worlds is realized in fact, then methods of proof and hence objectivity are lost. We preserve our perfect objectivity only by saying nothing.

Attempting to say something non-tautologically true brings out a connection of some sort between objectivity and truth; namely, in our theory that science makes *progress* in its descriptions, discussions, and explanations. As we test, refine, and modify our descriptions, discussions, and explanations we are implicitly maintaining the metaphysical view that there is a direction to the change, that we are improving them by moving towards the truth. What this amounts to is very difficult to specify fully, but Popper has proposed with his theories of depth and verisimilitude a partial explication of it.[4]

According to the theory of objectivity adopted here, the objectivity of the discipline lies not so much in its capturing what the objective truth about things is, but rather in whether it adopts means to foster maximum progress in our descriptions, discussions, and explanations, namely, subjects our ideas to the standard of intersubjective and repeatable testing. The character of antropological fieldwork is such that this standard of intersubjective testability is uniquely difficult to meet. Anthropology is usually an individual enterprise, conducted at considerable expense, in some inaccessible part of the globe, among people with an esoteric language. Only with the greatest difficulty can this research be repeated. Indeed, in the strictest sense, it cannot be repeated at all. Fieldwork takes place at a particular time, and within the unique network of social relationships established by *that* anthropologist, *then*. In such fluid human situations which change over time, and which differ markedly from person to person, no man's network of social relations, point of view and, hence, information can be duplicated. Fieldwork is a very private affair. It thus seems not to meet the demand for public criticisability, and the anthropologist may have to be uncritically trusted.

This argument need not carry us away. After all, in natural science no two scientific tests are truly identical since their numerical distinctness ensures that they take place in different space-time areas and it is only a hypothesis – and a metaphysical and therefore unfalsifiable one at that – that this makes no difference. ('Physics as we know it is indifferent to space-time parameters' is not a falsifiable statement because any counter-example could be interpreted as not belonging to objectively true physics.)

Can or does anthropology operate with a similar hypothesis to the effect that its research is repeatable to all intents and purposes, and that different time and different investigator does not matter? Is it possible to argue that the descriptive material could have been collected by anyone, and so the fieldwork is as near as no matter repeatable? In other words, that the better part of anthropological results are indifferent to time and the observer? This too would be a metaphysical hypothesis. While it may be unfalsifiable metaphysics, I would contend that most anthropologists would declare it false. Anthropological fieldwork does not involve one in the forging of social relationships in the field contingently, and that ideal of social science which feigns indifference to the fact that it is by men as well as about men is absurd.

A little more deserves to be said about this. Some philosophies conceive of the machine as more objective than the man. This looks plausible, but is a mistake. Machines only do what men have built into them: they are no more objective than their builders make them. Some of the biases, preconceptions and interpretations of their makers will be built-in. More important, whatever result they produce then has to be filtered back through the biases, preconceptions and interpretations of their operators. Science is made by man with the aid of machines; not *vice versa*. Because machine operations are mechanical they make less mistakes; but this is only because, recognizing his own mechanical limitations, man has devised in machines ways of correcting himself. A social science like anthropology, however, cannot possibly be mechanized. Cameras and tape recorders can only record what goes on around them, and that something is going on around them to be recorded can only be decided, evoked, or disclosed by a human being. A machine cannot explore a human society because it cannot enter into social relationships like talking. Either by getting the people to talk to him, or by them letting him overhear what they are saying, anthropologists gather data. Recording conversations on film and tape might eliminate some errors of memory, transcription, etc., but those machines might distract from, distort, or even prevent promising social relations which will in the long run be more enlightening.

Further than this, however, all social scientists are studying themselves: man. They are there to give human accounts of human beings. Martian accounts of human beings, arachnid accounts of human beings, mechanical accounts of human beings, may be very interesting and very different, but they are not part of the aim of the social sciences. The metaphysical and interpretative categories in which social science must be written are given: they are those which preserve the human meaning and significance of what we are privileged to be studying.

Human meaning and significance are properties of poetry too, however, which suggests that the social sciences are in danger of becoming private, or at least not objective and progressive.[5] The difference seems to be in that the poet captures moments, preferably unique, while the social scientist captures not moments, which are private and unique, but typical decisions and events for which he reconstructs a rationale. He concerns himself only with those decisions and events he considers to be typical of a great deal of human actions, and his rationale is thus of a general nature. So, while an individual anthropologist's experiences are not repeatable, similar sorts of events are, and attempts can be made to reconstruct their rationale and see if it checks out.

This must lead us to look rather closely at what goes on in the course of field research. What does an anthropologist do in the field that should put him on the road to objective descriptions, discussions, and explanations? To tell the truth, what fieldworkers do is wander around observing, learning the language, getting the feel of the place, chatting with people, interviewing them about their relatives, etc. A short name for this activity is 'gossip'. Anthropological fieldwork consists to a considerable extent in gossip – sometimes even structured or directed gossip.

Do I not, in admitting this, jeopardize my previous argument for the objectivity of anthropology? I don't see it: gossip is one of the principal means we have to find our way around in our own society. In many ways it provides us with information sufficient to cope with the world in which we find ourselves. Gossip is the principal means by which a foreigner like myself finds out things like what is the AAAS and what significance is to be attached to a session such as this. The source of my information is independent of its truth; in seeking the truth I must use whatever means seem appropriate.

The answers I would give then, were someone to impugn the objectivity of anthropological fieldwork because it has a profound personal equation, and is heavily dependent on gossip, are these. Martin has argued, convincingly enough, that fieldwork is neither a necessary nor a sufficient condition for successful anthropology.[6] This does not say that its history and its problems can be understood without reference to fieldwork. So a stronger argument is required and that is this. The personal equation and gossip do no more damage to the objectivity of anthropology than does the coffee or whisky imbided by Nobel Prize winners. All such things are *irrelevant* to the objectivity of anthropology. The objective truth, or lack of it, of anthropological results, the progress or lack of it in anthropological descriptions, discussions, and explanations, cannot be undermined by *ad hominem* arguments. All our procedures together suggest to us that if our results have been subjected to rigorous tests, the best we can devise, then we have done all we can to maximise the verisimilitude of those results. But we in fact do very little to test anthropological descriptions like field reports; that is the whole point – is this a blunder? No, I would say, we no more look over an anthropologist's shoulder than we do over a natural scientist's. Why should we? If he lies or misperceives so what? So he will be found out sooner or later? Not necessarily; the Piltdown forgery, or such incidents as C. P. Snow discusses in *The Affair*, may be the rare cases where the lie is exposed. He will mislead and misdirect a lot of others? Very possibly; but we either can't, or don't approve of, policing the whole world. Trust and independence are the least that are compatible with human dignity, including the dignity of that uniquely human activity scientific investigation. More than this, though, I suggest we neglect the policing of scientists because we know it is unimportant. Where we know incompetence or fakery might do obvious harm we tolerate some discipline, like in medicine or engineering,[7] usually by professionalizing. In anthropology we rely on people doing their best, and we can ask, what else is compatible with their dignity?

So much, then, for argument to the effect that anthropology is as objective as any other science. Some counterattack on those who deny its objectivity might also be in place. The most disastrous consequence of denying its objectivity is not so much that it makes a science of society impossible, but rather that it leads to relativism. The denial of a sience of society – advocated by those action-new-leftists who only allow as legitimate changing society not studying it – leads to absurdities. You can't change what you don't know, you can't know what you can't study, and you certainly can't know whether what you have tried to change is changed if you do not know how it was in the first place.[8] A similar denial for different reasons by the followers of Wittgenstein leads them either into relativism or into the view that a culture can only be understood in its own terms, from within, and so cultures are incommensurable.[9]

The seriousness of relativism is that – unlike denying the possibility of social science which runs in the teeth of the obvious existence and to some degree success of social science – it appears to be a conclusion forced on us by study of the way things are, and thus has a glossy surface of rationality to cover its deep and underlying irrationality. In the name of honest ignorance, and decent respect for other people, anthropologists declare it impossible to evaluate cultures as a whole, the one against the other or them all against some absolute standard. Arguing that all cultures differ profoundly on fundamental questions of value, and that all systems of value are culture-bound, they conclude that there are no standards universally applicable which would resolve these sorts of conflicts. Any adoption of standards by an anthropologist would make him no better than a missionary, who evaluates all cultures and especially their religions by how closely they approximate to the Judeo-Cristian values he is armed with. Such arbitrary and therefore irrational standards of value have allowed men to commit criminal and atrocious acts against those men and cultures found wanting.

My counter to this is that arbitrary evaluation is indeed irrational, but so is drawing the conclusion from the chaos of competing values that all values are equal. This is both against common sense and against good logic, for it is a *non-sequitur*: it does not follow. The excesses of absolutism are no longer, if they ever were, an excuse for shirking the fundamental human task of making up one's mind on moral issues. Elsewhere, I have tried to argue that our duty to try to behave decently towards others is not abrogated when we become anthropological fieldworkers, still less is it our duty to condone conduct in others we in other circumstances would condemn.[10] True, part of our duty is behaving decently by showing respect for others and their differences of opinion with us, not to mention our duty of self-preservation and the caution it entails. But research shows that to a surprising extent given their relativistic utterances anthropologists do behave decently by the standards they have been brought up in and will return to. This is moral common sense, and a blow against it involves the abrogation of all standards.

York University, Toronto

NOTES

[1] See J. O. Wisdom, 'The Sceptic at Bay', *British Journal for the Philosophy of Science* IX (1958) 159–63.

[2] See K. R. Popper, 'The Aim of Science', *Ratio* 1 (1957) 24–35; and *Conjectures and Refutations*, London and New York 1963, Chapter 10.

[3] K. R. Popper, *The Poverty of Historicism*, London 1957, pp. 155–56; *The Open Society and Its Enemies*, London 1962, Vol. II, pp. 216–23.

[4] These are to be found in the references given in note 2.

[5] I take it that much poetry aims to be intensely personal and subjective; that there is no progress in poetry in the sense of one poet's work superseding or replacing that of another. The question of whether this makes poetry more complex than art – which can be interpreted as a process of 'making and matching' – is puzzling. The descriptive and expressive resources of art constantly expand, but this is the only sense in which art progresses. Cf. E. H. Gombrich, *Art and Illusion*, London 1960.

[6] Michael Martin, 'Understanding and Participant Observation in Cultural and Social Anthropology', in *Boston Studies in the Philosophy of Science, Vol. V* (ed. by R. S. Cohen and M. W. Wartofsky), D. Reidel Publ. Co., Dordrecht-Holland, 1969.

[7] See J. Agassi, 'The Confusion between Science and Technology in the Standard Philosophies of Science', *Culture and Technology* VII (1966) 348–66.

[8] This is Popper's argument to show the irrationality of wholesale radicalism, see *The Open Society, op. cit. supra*, Vol. I, pp. 157–68.

[9] See my 'Understanding and Explanation in Sociology and Social Anthropology' in *Explanation in The Behavioural Sciences* (ed. by R. Borger and F. Cioffi), Cambridge 1970.

[10] 'The Problem of Ethical Integrity in Participant Observation', *Current Anthropology*, Vol. 10, 1969.

CHAPTER 10

THE PROBLEM OF ETHICAL INTEGRITY
IN PARTICIPANT OBSERVATION

1. INTRODUCTION

A curious problem arises in connexion with the notion of the participant observer, a problem partly ethical and partly methodological. It seems not to have been clearly seen and stated, although solutions to it exist — in practice, as it were. The problem arises like this. Standard accounts of the method of participant observation require, I would argue, an anthropological observer to be both a stranger and a friend among the people he is studying. Yet one person cannot be a stranger and a friend at the same time: the roles are mutually exclusive. This being so, it is *a fortiori* impossible to play either role in integrity while trying to combine them, with the result that an uneasy compromise is liable to be forged.

The unresolved identity crisis precipitates an integrity crisis, and only by allowing one role to override the other can the two crises be resolved.[1] The anthropologist must choose the role of the stranger, because only that role allows him to act in what he and the society he comes from would consider to be his integrity as a member of that society in general and as a scientist in particular. However, I would go further and press this to the point of arguing that to some extent the success of the method of participant observation *derives from* exploiting the situations created by the role clashes insider/outsider, stranger/friend, pupil/teacher. If I am right, the standard discussions of participant observation need drastic revision.[2]

2. THE IDEAL OF PARTICIPANT OBSERVATION

Modern anthropology is often distinguished from old anthropology by citing the innovation of participant observer fieldwork. As Forge (1967) has written, there is an official story that this was invented in May, 1915 when Bronislaw Malinowski pitched his tent at Omarakana in the Trobriand Islands and set about learning the local language.[3] Both factors — tent and language — were claimed to be vital: a tent down among the native houses so that the observer is physically close to the native life; and learning the language, not using pidgin or interpreters, so that the observer can participate in the life he wishes to observe just as it is lived. The hardships of thus cutting oneself off from one's own tribe and plunging into another tribe have never been concealed. Recently, some autobiographies have appeared which go into some welcome detail about the experience and which reveal interesting problems of identity and integrity hitherto not much discussed (Forge 1967, Malinowski 1967, Powdermaker 1966).[4]

The very notion of "participant observer" needs a lot of unpacking. Junker (1960) sees a spectrum of positions within it: complete participation; the participant doubling as observer; the observer doubling as participant; and the complete observer. He notes that if one begins as a member of the group and then secretly trains as a social scientist the problems of being a traitor may arise; and that if the social scientist seeks to penetrate from outside he may face the problems of a spy. The complete participant must conceal his character as observer/reporter if he does not want drastically to affect the processes he is observing. At the other extreme, the pure observer, seeing but not interacting, is more imaginary than real. Gold (1958) confines the observer-as-participant to the one-visit interview.

This leaves the participant as observer and the problem, as Junker sees it, of striking a balance between being a "good friend" and a "snooping stranger". On the one hand is the aim of participating fully, of identifying entirely with the alien way of life; on the other is the danger of betraying trust. To observe a way of life best, it seems, involves living that way of life. This assumption invites two criticisms, each of which has both a theoretical and a practical aspect. First, is "the inside" a privileged observation point? There is nothing especially privileged about the observations of a parade made by those in it. Spectators may be in a better position, television viewers in a still better one. Which vantage point you choose must surely be a matter of what you want to observe and why. Second, can one join "the inside", or must one have been born there? For some anthropologists, the question is purely practical: they prefer building or buying a local-type hut to living in a tent. Evans-Pritchard (1937:270) tells us the amusing fact that he used the local oracles for regulating his affairs when he was with the Azande. Participation may mean purchasing and looking after cattle if these are the principal means of assessing status in that society. Some anthropologists are alleged to have taken native"wives" — although Forge believes that in general this is not the practice. In short, participation approaches what is deprecatingly or half-jokingly called "going native".

Such a practical attitude may help, but it makes no impact on the theoretical difficulty of becoming an insider. There are limits inherent in the situation. First, an anthropologist is required not to go native altogether, not even as much as the local white beach-comber, since he is an observer.

According to Paul (1953:438), Goldenweiser has endorsed going native, but Radin says nothing is to be gained by it, and Herskovits says it is neither possible nor desirable for an anthropologist. Vidich (1955:357) argues:

If the participant observer seeks genuine experiences, unqualifiedly immersing and committing himself in the group he is studying, it may become impossible for him to objectify his own experiences for research purposes; in committing his loyalties he develops vested interests which will inevitably enter into his observations. Anthropologists who have "gone native" are cases in point; some of them stop publishing entirely.

Miller (1952) presents some examples illustrating this point.

Further, among the duties the fieldworker accepts — whether rightly or wrongly — is the duty to explain to the native population as clearly as possible the reason for his presence among them. Unlike someone who has dissipated his substance and "honestly" (we say) "gone native", the honest anthropologist carefully avoids giving the impression that he is joining his hosts forever; he even makes it clear that "the ethic of science is ill-served by fraudulent methods of study" and argues that if falsehoods would be necessary to fieldwork in a particular place, it would be better to go elsewhere "to avoid compromise of the value that science is a public process, honestly discussed and conducted". (Cf. also Forge's [1967] touching description of how he had to list all the relatives he would never see again in order to find a strong enough argument to justify his departure from the field to return to his own society.) Thus, from the beginning of his study, the fieldworker is torn between pure participant and pure observer roles (e.g., should he or should he not take a local wife?).

Failure to participate to the full, then, is unavoidable; and in any case, there are few cultures in which an outsider can ever completely overcome his role as stranger. Even when he is highly integrated, he may still occupy some such role as "newcomer". Williams [1967:45] ignores this when he writes, "Most societies can find ways of incorporating the anthropologist . . . given an opportunity to search out positions to fit his roles". Sometimes his attempts at integration call forth institutional means of putting him apart (even in the American and Canadian melting-pots we use the markers "first-generation", "second-generation", and "new Canadians"). Paul (1953) argues that at most the anthropologist achieves partial penetration of the society: he comes as a stranger, and always keeps his outsider status. He cites Nadel (1939):

The anthropologist can only be a freak member of the group, not only because of the conspicuous differences in physical characteristics which often exist but also because of inevitable social incompatibilities.

Lohman (1937:893) goes a little deeper:

The history of a relationship between an individual and the people in the community is a record of growth. One does not settle down and commence to traffic in the life of the community. A person is accepted to the extent that he displays like interests and purposes and to the extent that he fits into the economy of the community. He must carve a place for himself. That place not only involves acceptable and traditional practices within the group, but the relationship of the individual with external society is to be defined as essentially the same which members of the community generally hope with reference to the larger social world. The individual's struggle for a livelihood and certain essential satisfactions is to be regarded as the same one which every member of the group has for himself.

Clearly, then however well the anthropologist may be liked and trusted, however long he has been known and been got used to, he is unlikely ever to become an ordinary insider, a full member of the society he studies.

3. ETHICAL CONFLICT IN PARTICIPANT OBSERVATION

Not only is the anthropologist trying to play two roles, participant and stranger, but he is also liable to confront situations in which these roles violently clash. This brings me to my central point. My concern is with neither the theoretical nor the practical difficulties in the path of the participant observer; whether observing inside is better, whether one can be inside — these are discussed elsewhere in the literature (Kluckhohn 1940, Paul 1953, Schwartz and Schwartz 1955, Vidich 1955, Junker 1960, Bruyn 1966, Williams 1967). Here I wish to air my uneasiness about the fieldworker's uneasiness: his struggle to be honest, fair, and truthful. I believe that there is a conflict between his methodological theory and his practice, and that it is a good thing his practice deviates from his theory. The conflict is easily stated: the fieldworker as a scientist is seeking the truth; that very quest involves eliminating prejudice and bias when studying other societies; and that seems to demand relativism. Anthropolotists sometimes call it the principle of cultural relativity and deny that it involves ethical nihilism. Of course in practice it never does since anthropologists, so far from being nihilists, are usually deeply humane and "committed" men. They see cultural relativity — or contextualism — as a counter to prejudice and ethnocentrism.[5] In Piddington's words (1957:601):

The moral behaviour of individuals or groups of human beings must be considered in the light of what they have learned to regard as right or wrong, as forbidden or permissible.

This is very bold. It exculpates juvenile delinquents as well as cannibals and head-hunters. Prejudice against these groups is bad, but so is what Gellner

(1963) has called The Principle of Universal Charity. This principle is as follows: when faced with a practice that is unintelligible (or objectionable), assume that if enough of its context were known it would become intelligible (or innocuous).[6] Yet the whole point of the practices may well lie in their unintelligible (or objectionable) character. The path between the Scylla of unreasonable ethnocentric prejudice and the Charybdis of Universal Charity is very difficult to steer, and the woolly notion of cultural relativity does not map the currents and submerged rocks.

How, then, do anthropologists in practice avoid falling into relativism while sustaining their aim of seeking the truth? Sometimes, the fieldworker, trying to make it clear that he belongs to another society to which he will one day return, will regale the host people with stories and descriptions of life among his own people. Of course, he may simplify his description and make his "tribe" sound similar to theirs. Suppose he strives to be honest? Easier thought than acted: what shall the honest anthropologist say if he is asked how many cattle his lineage has? Shall he interpret it as a question about his wealth and answer it literally? This, in the societies anthropologists specialize in, will probably make him appear an incredibly wealthy man, even if he lives strictly on a professor's salary. Or shall he be more literal and indicate that he has no lineage or cattle? He may then try to explain that cattle do not signify overmuch in his society. The poor fellow more than likely will fail to get this message over, in which case he will paint himself to his hosts as a rather pathetic case. Whichever way he takes the question, his answer will not help him integrate. What if he is asked how many wives his paramount chief has? Shall he try to indicate that all his fellows have only one wife at a time, and so on? Will he be their informant as they are his? Is such a reciprocity possible? Or should he become as ethnocentrically "bad" an anthropologist as they evidently are?

Let us press the decent anthropologist striving to be honest even harder. What sort of attitude should he adopt when faced with unhygienic food preparation, mutilation of children, human sacrifice?[7] Where is his integrity to be found? Anthropologists sometimes mention dysentery as an essential initiation into the profession; and they are only half-joking. They forget the anthropology of half-jokes; let us bring it home to them. What should the fieldworker confronted with dysentery do? He has a supply of drugs, and he guesses that the water supply is polluted. Does his integrity demand that he get dysentery, like the rest of the population? Obviously not. Should he be unlucky enough to get it, must he abjure all but local remedies in order to observe and participate? This principle might put future research at hazard. So let us allow him to avoid dysentery and to take medicine if he gets it. What now of the people he is stranger/friend to? Does his devotion to observing rather than interfering prevent him from handing out drugs, which might preclude observation of local curative rituals, potion-preparing, etc.? Should he refrain from handing out his magic because it will enhance his status and prestige in the society in a way he wishes to avoid? And what of his knowledge of the polluted water? We allow that he does not have to drink it; should he enlighten the natives, or will that too be both an interference and an acquisition of prestige which might jeopardize further observation?

Should, in brief, our honest anthropologist participate to the point where the boundaries of his freedom to comment on what is going on will be set by the primitive society which he is so anxious to join? It is all too easy to imagine probable situations where the honest anthropologist would be failing in his moral duty as our society conceives it if he did not comment or even protest about some practices. Vidich (1955) thinks this keeps the anthropologist socially marginal and that marginality is an advantage.[8] Other anthropologists, like Herskovits (1948), embrace relativism: to participate in a society, to treat it as worthy of living in, one must respect it. If it has values that clash with yours, who are you to judge? Can you claim to know their values are not right for their situation? This moral relativism is being accepted in the name of science; Schwartz and Schwartz (1955:347) have said,

It is essential [to] recognize the importance of participating with the observed on a "simply human" level ... he must share ... sentiments and feelings with the observed on a sympathetic and empathic level. Thus the observer and observed are bound together through sharing the common role of human being. When the observed become convinced that the observer's attitude towards them is one of respect and interest in them as human beings as well as research subjects, they will feel less need for concealing, withholding, or distorting data.

These authors are generalizing from work among mental patients, which perhaps accounts for the stress on countering willful interference with the facts rather than inadvertent interference. What is more serious is that they underplay the role in normal relations between human beings of argument, dispute, criticism, and censure. Part of respect for strange peoples must include not lying to them and not patronizing them. Let us look at what happens in practice.

4. THE IDEAL VERSUS THE PRACTICE

What in fact do fieldworkers do? Powdermaker (1966:188–90) faced the

dilemma when she was working in the southern United States. She ran
into a lynch mob and had a sleepless night wondering what she could do.
In the end she did nothing, made no attempt to seek out the victim and
aid his escape, expressed no strong opinions to those participating and con-
doning. Instead she observed and recorded it all. This story, fortunately,
has a happy ending. Powdermaker breathed a sigh of relief when the man
(who, it transpired, was innocent) got over the state line. But one may argue,
as she does, that in any case she was helpless; if she had gone to the police,
nothing would have been accomplished; if she had made censorious remarks,
her position as a participant observer would have been seriously jeopardized.

Another example is Hunter S. Thompson's sojourn with the Hell's Angels,
the motorcycle thugs of California. While he was witness to far less moral
and legal crime than might have been expected, he nevertheless observed
fights, thefts, assaults, and a semi-public gang-rape. For all his pains in dis-
closing none of this to the police (that would have jeopardized his status,
although he also acted as an intermediary with the police, thus keeping
one foot outside any total identification with the Angels), he was himself
brutally beaten because he did not accede to the demands of some Angels
that he pay them money for the privilege of observing their activities and
later making money writing about them (Thompson 1967:277—78). His
argument was that journalistic observers make a practice of not paying;
their argument was that he was getting something out of hanging around
them, so why shouldn't they get something out of having him hang around?
The problem is a very sticky one.

It is one thing to agonize over a lynch mob, another to conceal crime
for the purposes of science. But where does integrity start? The scientist
is saying that above all he must be true to the search for the unbiased truth.
In the name of this value of his society, he jettisons ancillary values of his
society — or at least he talks as though he thinks he should. Faced with
a clash of values in his own society, he would not hesitate vigorously to
prosecute an argument over the issue. Why does he hesitate to do so as an
anthropologist? The anthropologist, it seems to me, is in danger of forgetting
that as well as being a scientist he is a member of the society he came from
and will return to and should avoid giving a misleading impression to his
hosts either by words or deeds.[9] Truth cuts both ways — he wants not to
alienate them, but do they want him to mislead them? Again, what happens
in practice?

Fieldworkers watching leaves being put on sores, or incantations being
said over tracoma, will often intervene with penicillin. They thus break out
of the "humble participant" role and enter the "powerful-new-medicine"

stranger role (cf. the incident described by Heyerdahl [1963:220–21]). Williams (1967:46) justifies such intervention in the name of truth: "We could have refused to [give] medical assistance. In doing so, we would have cut off a valuable source of . . . data". La Farge (1947) utilized suspicion that he was a shaman to force retraction of a curse he felt would endanger the lives of those who had worked for him. Holmberg (1955) chose straight-forward intervention to see how it would develop. It seems to me that intervention is probably for the best, since it is more honest both to the natives and to the fieldworker himself. The fieldworker usually comes from a rich and powerful society, possessed of much "strong medicine", and has education in a cognitive system that is more powerful than the one he is confronting: it does not serve truth to conceal these facts, however tacitly.

Once again, what happens in practice seems a better guide than the amateurish philosophy of relativism. The fieldworker as a humble supplicant is obviously not often the case. Many people would not tolerate the white stranger snooping around were it not that he belongs, as far as they are concerned, to the powerful white society which they hesitate to brush with. Churlishness and xenophobia may for this reason be curbed and thereby research forwarded. One could argue that this has been the case with research among the Indians on their reservations in North America and among the Bantu and other people in areas of South Africa, and even with Western research in China. Moreover, fragments of evidence exist which suggest that in the field situation conscious use may have to be made of the "stranger" position of the stranger in order to elicit information. Bribery in one disguise or another, and even a certain amount of direct bullying, seem to be not uncommon. Malinowski is very frank about this in his diary, where he describes shouting at his informants, and even punching one in the face; and although in other respects the diary is a salutary work, he fails to say that he was obviously exploiting a position of privilege in being rude. A true participant in the society would hardly get away with that!

It can be plausibly argued, it seems to me, that the observer does himself no harm if he acts in integrity towards *his* society and *its* values as far as possible. There is no reason to think the host people will not respect him more for this than for attempting to curry favour by pretending to go along with things that in truth offend, horrify, or disgust him. Deception and hypocrisy are difficult enough to defend in the name of science; and integrity *as a scientist* cannot be overridden in the name of science. If we think science is served by entering into a full and equal relationship with the subjects of study, then both human and scientific integrity require that we do not artificially exclude from those relationships the tensions and clashes which enrich normal relationships. By and large anthropologists act on this, but they do not give it due credit in their methodological discussions.

NOTES

[1] For the notions of identity crisis and integrity crisis see Erikson (1958:248–57).
[2] For an acute dissection of the ambiguities of participant observation which I have labelled "role-clashes", see Martin (1969). Jarvie (1967) is also relevant. These two papers and the present one, written quite independently, complement each other in interesting ways. Thanks to Michael Martin and Joseph Agassi, both of Boston Univeristy, for helpful comments on earlier versions.
[3] Doubtless the story involves British claim-staking. The claims of Cushing (fieldwork 1906–84), Boas (fieldwork 1883–84), and even Radcliffe-Brown (fieldwork 1906–8) have been pushed aside by the Malinowski public-relations effort.
[4] Paul (1953), who reviews the literature, and Barnes (1963) confine themselves to the problems of privacy, publication, stratification, and relations with the local authorities.
[5] Williams (1967:61) sees it as a practice: "Cultural relativism is an attitude of mind, an awareness of self that can be imparted only to a very limited extent in the classroom, or gained from a text. It must be gained finally in the experiences of living and working for a long period in another culture . . . the attitude . . . is one of being liberated from the parochial truths of one culture . . .". Cf. Jarvie (1967:230–31).
[6] Benedict (1934) and Herskovits (1948) seem to push this far into relativism. The latter is devastated by Bidney (1953). See also Howard (1968).
[7] For maximum frisson I recommend the paper on subincision by Singer and Desole (1967). At one point the authors comment that their film of "this initiation rite . . . has made medical psychoanalysts and analyzed psychiatrists blanch and look away . . .".
[8] He suggests that remaining marginal permits freer social movement, but that, in addition, the socially marginal anthropologist may find his best sources among socially marginal informants.
[9] There are subtleties here. "Truth above all" is a value of the subsociety of science located within the wider society. Because the wider society values science it does not follow that it endorses all the values of its subsocieties. This is a special case of the general problem that every participant observer is not simply "an example of an often quite alien culture system" (Williams 1967:45) but a possibly atypical product of a society that is to him more of an ideal-type than anything else. Cf. Lohman (1937:890).

REFERENCES

Barnes, J. A. 1963. 'Some Ethical Problems of Modern Fieldwork'. *British Journal of Sociology* 14 118–34.
Benedict, Ruth 1934. *Patterns of Culture*. Boston: Houghton Mifflin.
Bidney, David 1953. *Theoretical Anthropology*. New York: Columbia University Press.
Bruyn, S. T. 1966. *The Human Perspective in Sociology: The Methodology of Participant Observation*. Englewood Cliffs: Prentice-Hall.
Erikson, Erik H. 1958. *Young Man Luther*. New York: W. W. Norton.

Evans-Pritchard, E. E. 1937. *Witchcraft, Oracles and Magic among the Azande*. Oxford: Oxford University Press.

Forge, Anthony 1967. 'The Lonely Anthropologist'. *New Society* 10 221–23.

Gellner, E. A. 1963. 'Concepts and Society'. *Proceedings of the 5th World Congress of Sociology, Washington*, pp. 161–89. Louvain: Neualwaerts.

Gold, R. L. 1958. 'Roles in Sociological Field Observation'. *Social Forces* 36 217–23.

Herskovits, M. J. 1948. *Man and his Works*. New York: Alfred A. Knopf.

Heyerdahl, Thor 1963. Penguin edition. *The Kon-Tiki Expedition*. Harmondsworth: Penguin Books.

Holmberg, A. R. 1955. 'Participant Intervention in the Field'. *Human Organization* 14 23–26.

Howard, V. A. 1968. 'Do Anthropologists Become Moral Relativists by Mistake?' *Inquiry* 11 175–89.

Jarvie I. C. 1967. 'On Theories of Fieldwork and the Scientific Character of Social Anthropology. *Philosophy of Science* 24 223–42.

Junker, B. H. 1960. *Fieldwork*. Chicago: University of Chicago Press.

Kluckhon, F. R. 1940. 'The Participant Observer Technique in Small Communities'. *American Journal of Sociology* 46 331–43.

La Farge, O. 1947. *Santa Eulalia: The Religion of a Cuchumatan Indian Town*. Chicago: University of Chicago Press.

Lohman, J. D. 1937. 'The Participant Observer in Community Studies'. *American Sociological Review* 2 890–97.

Malinowski, Bronislaw 1967. *A Diary in the Strict Sense of the Term*. New York: Harcourt, Brace and World.

Martin, Michael 1969. 'Understanding and Participant Observation in Cultural and Social Anthropology'. In *Boston Studies in the Philosophy of Science*, Vol. V. Edited by R. S. Cohen and M. W. Wartofsky. New York: Humanities Press.

Miller, S. M. 1952. 'The Participant Observer and Over-"rapport"'. *American Sociological Review* 17 97–99.

Nadel, S. F. 1939. 'The Interview Technique in Social Anthropology'. In *The Study of Society: Methods and Problems*. Edited by F. Bartlett, M. Ginsberg, E. J. Lindgren, and R. H. Thouless pp. 317–27. London: Routledge and Kegan Paul.

Paul B. D. 1953. 'Interview Techniques and Field Relationships'. In *Anthropology Today*. Prepared under the chairmanship of A. L. Kroeber, pp. 430–51. Chicago: University of Chicago Press.

Piddington, Ralph 1957. *An Introduction to Social Anthropology*. Vol. 2. Edinburgh: Oliver and Boyd.

Powdermaker, Hortense 1966. *Stranger and Friend*. New York: W. W. Norton.

Schwartz, M. S. and C. G. Schwartz 1955. 'Problems in Participant Observation. *American Journal of Sociology* 60 343–53.

Singer, P. and Daniel Desole 1967. 'The Australian Sub-Incision Ceremony Reconsidered: Vaginal Envy or Kangaroo Bifid Penis Envy'. *American Anthropologist* 69 355–58.

Thompson, Hunter S. 1967. *Hell's Angels*. New York: Random House.

Vidich, A. J. 1955. 'Participant Observation and the Collection and Interpretation of Data'. *American Journal of Sociology* 60 354–60.

Williams, T. R. 1967. *Field Methods in the Study of Culture*. New York: Holt, Rinehart and Winston.

CHAPTER 11

ANTHROPOLOGY AS SCIENCE AND THE ANTHROPOLOGY OF SCIENCE AND OF ANTHROPOLOGY

or

Understanding and Explanation in the Social Sciences, Part II[1]

1. INTRODUCTORY

To begin with, an apology for my subtitle, which consciously but unforgivably alludes to Hollywood's current fondness for numbered sequels to successful films. My intention was to signal that this paper, like a film such as *Halloween II*, will make further use of old materials, partly to bring the story up to date, partly to re-work material of proven box-office value, partly to answer those critics who, perhaps, deserve an answer.

Synoptically speaking the paper returns to the issue of whether anthropology aims to understand or to explain. No claim was made in Part I (Jarvie 1970) that the two are mutually exclusive, only that understanding is a vague idea which derives much of its appeal from poor anthropological information about science and its aims.[2] Part I concentrated mainly on criticising Peter Winch's ethnography of science and of Azande witchcraft. For the plot to my sequel I criticise recent work by three distinguished anthropologists – Mary Douglas (1978), Clifford Geertz (1984) and F. Allan Hanson (1985). Each offers a partial ethnography of anthropology, unpacking its assumptions and recommending, explicitly by saying, and implicitly by example, a philosophy of science. In approaching their efforts I shall conform to the standard anthropological injunction to discount what people *say* and attend seriously but critically to what they *do*. Douglas, Geertz and Hanson are a disparate trio, and no doubt disagree among themselves on many matters; but one thing they have in common is that each thinks anthropologists transact in 'understanding'. Their ethnography of anthropology is that we start out from a culture we understand, namely the culture of which we are members, and we endeavour to improve our

PSA 1984, Volume 2,

understanding of other cultures by trying to grasp their self-understanding. The imperative to fieldwork states that we will get that understanding only by means of the intimate contiguity of participant-observation.

By contrast, it is my ethnographic observation that social science in general and anthropology in particular, despite the drift of much talk, sets no particular store by understanding — whatever that may be. Furthermore, and of the greatest importance, and, again, despite what they *say* a good deal of the time, anthropologists do not begin from an understanding of our own culture. My evidence is that our culture is a mystery to us, a mystery on which anthropologists occasionally throw some light precisely by their efforts to explain other societies that are equally mysterious.[3,4] In particular, Douglas, Geertz and Hanson make ethnographic mistakes about our society that stem from their failure to appreciate the centrality of science. Science marks this society of ours and makes if different in many ways from all the other societies there have ever been. Constantly concerned to stress the continuities in the family of mankind, anthropologists of the 'understanding cultures' persuasion uncritically fail accurately to report the ethnography of the societies with science. It is ironic that what they as ethnographers fail to report on adequately — science — is exactly what makes their ethnography endeavours possible.

Although their criticism of views I hold or of me directly has helped me reach the above formulations, most of the arguments were laid down in Part I. Why, then, write a sequel? Because these latest speeches in the continuing dialogue about the ethnography of anthropology have pushed me towards a better and more comprehensive explanation of our disagreement. My Part I explanation was that anthropologists were bad philosophers (induction, 'understanding', relativism) because of bad teaching, and good ethnographers because what they *did* was not conditioned by what they *said*, i.e. the bad philosophy. Their present counter-attacks have caused me to reappraise their ethnography. Where I can check it, namely when it concerns our society in general and the anthropological subculture in particular, I discover glaring mistakes. This has suggested a more initimate relationship between the bad philosophy and the bad ethnography.

Before I go into further detail let me say a little more continuing within the framework of Part I. At issue is the question of whether anthropological inquiry is scientific. In addition to holding that it is, and relatively unproblematically so, I also offer the thesis that understanding is not a major aim of scientific inquiry (at best a mentalistic by-product) and that emphasising it makes accounts of anthropological inquiry incoherent. The biographical reason some persons become social scientists may, it is true, be their desire to understand other people. At the London School of Economics, where I was educated, an effort was made to shunt such persons into the diploma courses in social work. It was felt that their emotional needs and moral interest in the fate ot the less fortunate would find better outlet in such work. The system of gate-keeping at LSE and elsewhere must have been porous because many spiritual social workers managed to slip into the social sciences. One of their earliest shocks at LSE, I recall, was exposure to Durkheim, who offered neither 'understanding' of suicide nor any intense moral concern about it, but rather treated it as a complex of social facts to be explained.

Durkheim was right. In particular he was right about treating social things as facts. Our society is a fact; and the presence in it of science, both as institution and as tradition, is a fact; the pervasive influence of science is a fact; and the consequences of science, including the immense cognitive and predictive advantages it confers on our society are also a fact.[5] Any general comparison of our society, implicit or explicit, with societies lacking science likely distorts things if science is overlooked. The fact of science must figure in many explanations. Within the facts of cognition in our society lies the effort to explain social facts in a manner recognisably scientific. In the body of the paper I shall give some of Gellner's ideas on what is distinctive of science. Here I merely want to note that it includes disinterested investigation of intellectual problems, including the intellectual problems posed by the workings of the societies in the study of which anthropologists have specialised. Any explanation of why we do anthropology that does not take cognisance of that social fact distorts, it seems to me, the intellectual tradition of the subject, as well as that of the culture as a whole.

Now, finally, I can set Part I aside and concentrate of Part II. The rest of the paper is in four sections. First on the ethnography of anthropology as science. Then I look at Mary Douglas on Frazer (1978), arguing that her confusions about him (praising with loud damning) flow from her assumption that our society and its science are transparently unproblematic to the anthropologist. For my part I find the ethnography of our society difficult, not least because it has to include accounts of how brilliant anthropologists who come from its tradition cannot describe it correctly. They do not describe the pervasive manner in which science shapes our society, even though several classical sociologists have begun the work. This is a chronic failure because, ethnographically speaking, science does nor permit relativism; it decrees and enforces the view that there is one physics of nature and only one physics of nature; there is no 'Chinese physics', no 'Azande physics', no 'Jewish physics'. The human race is united by its attempts to contribute to physics, and divided to the extent that any part of it reputiates physics.[6] Following Gellner (1975) and Hanson (1985) I will call this ethnographic feature of science its 'monism', and oppose it to 'pluralism'. Both Geertz (1984), in an attack on what he calls 'anti-relativism', and Hanson, in a critique of my new book (Jarvie 1984), try to articulate and defend what I now call 'pluralism'. I tackle them in my last two sections. Because they take the central problem of anthropology to be understanding, and because they wish to correct the general public's ethnocentric misunderstandings about the societies anthropologists study, their pluralism becomes relativism. Their relativism, however, distorts their ethnography of their own society and prevents them from giving a coherent account of the tradition of science and of that branch of it known as anthropology. These problems show themselves in Douglas's retreat to the ineffables of 'symbolic anthropology', in Geertz's evasive formulations, and in Hanson's inconsistent ones.

Once more, it seems, I will be engaged in challenging the self-understanding of working scientists.[7] No apology is needed since I merely propose to take seriously the maxim mentioned earlier, namely discount what people say and concentrate on what they do. It is not as good a maxim as it at first looks, because it assumes without argument that saying is not a form of doing. Be that as it may, it clearly contains an invitation to the philosopher of science to develop his own interpretation of what anthropologists' are doing and, in the course of that, perhaps, to shift from the descriptive to the normative. Less muddled anthropology, or, at least, less muddled anthropological claims, might result.

In a brilliant summing up of the messages of two philosophers of social science he and I revere, W. W. Bartley III (1984) has written, 'I learnt from Popper that we never know what we are talking about, and I learnt from Hayek that we never know what we are doing'. The gnomic formulation is for effect. When unpacked it is quite straightforward. In Popper's case, since the set of statements that logically follows from the statements we make is infinitely large, and since the logical consequences of statements are so to say 'contained' within them, we can never in principle know everything that is contained in what we have said, hence never know what we are talking about. In Hayek's case, since we can never in principle know all the consequences of our actions, and since the notion of doing something or other can reasonably be taken to embrace all those consequences, we cannot in principle ever know what it is we are doing.

It follows from these general claims that anthropologists are mistaken in thinking they know their own culture and hence what they are doing when trying to expand their knowledge. It further follows that in writing and delivering this paper I too do not know what I am doing. It also follows that in this respect there is no important difference between talking and doing and we do not even know the dividing line between them. Why bother to do anthropology, then; and why bother to correct the anthropology anthropologists do?

Three answers occur to me. First, making mistakes should not discourage us. Second, on-going debate does not *lead to* progress, *it is itself progress*. Third, why be afraid of acting while not knowing what we are doing? Let me expand. First, not knowing what we are talking about and not knowing what we are doing are features of the human predicament. It does not follow that things are hopeless, merely that they are difficult, more difficult than we would like. There are, I hold, specific ways in which anthropologists' talking and doing goes beyond what they think they are talking about and what they think they are doing. If I can bring them to that realisation, even to the realisation that some such state of affairs is possible, some small dialogue may be engaged.

Such on-going dialogue is progressive. The arguments of my trio of anthropologists force the dialogue beyond my Part I because they show that the dichotomy between absolutist and relativist theories of truth is not able to sustain the criticism launched against Frazer, myself and others; and that they refrain from criticising other cultures shows that in their actions they are relativists when facing outwards and absolutists when facing inwards. That is to say, they tolerate in other cultures transgressions much more serious than those they will not tolerate in fellow members of the dialogue. If other members of the culture of science express a whiff of antirelativism it is condemned; aggressive absolutism in other cultures is passed over in silence, or even relativistically endorsed. Therefore my Part I critique of relativism is insufficient and must be reworked to comprehend them as absolutists at home but not abroad.

Theories of truth, whether absolutist or relativist, are matters of philosophy of science, within the scope of which anthropology comes. When anthropology is taken to be the science of all human culture, the culture of western philosophy and philosophy of science comes within its scope. There is, then, an unavoidable interlardedness of anthropology and philosophy. This helps us to make sense of the dialogue between the two fields. Hanson (1985) suggests that I am an anthropologist *manqué* because of my disclination to subject my most fundamental assumptions to the challenge and threat of fieldwork (MSS, p. 9). My countersuggestion is that Douglas, Geertz, Hanson and many other anthropologists are philosophers *manqué*. What sort of philosophers are these philosophers *manqué*? There are in fact only two types. Just as every baby that is born is either a little Tory or a little Whig, so, Gellner has quipped (1984), every philosopher that is born alive is either a little positivist or a little Hegelian. The anthropologist philosopher *manqué* born a positivist has few problems; positivism is an anti-philosophy philosophy because it identifies philosophy with Hegelian mush;[8] so not being a philosopher but rather an anthropologist is already to be living up to one's principles. Oddly enough, the Hegelian anthropologist philosopher *manqué* can also rest easy, comforted by the totalising effect of the principle of internal relations; everything is what it is by virtue of its intrinsic relations to everything else, including philosophy, science and anthropology. So the anthropology with a philosophical slant of Douglas, Geertz and Hanson is not accidentally in dialogue with my philosophy with an anthropological slant.

My last point in response to the question, 'why bother!', was to turn the question back and ask, 'why not bother?' Bartley's apothegm is a powerful expression of Popperian scepticism, of our fumbling efforts to master an uncertain world with unreliable apparatus. Science is the preeminent case of knowledge without foundations. Scepticism is a doctrine of which many are afraid. It knocks away the foundations. Geertz flirts with scepticism when he claims credit on behalf of anthopology for knocking away some of the foundations on which people have erected their ethnocentric world view (see below, p. 174). In its place he offers hermeneutics couched in relativist-idealist form. Here is one attempt to describe his view:[9] "[Geertz] argues for what has come to be called a *hermeneutic* method, wherein one interpretation is piled on top of another, one version of a text (or action treated as text) is compared with another, one set of perceptions is set against another. The medium for these comparisons is the symbolic forms that are readily observable and easily grasped. By starting with sets of clearly given symbols and comparing them with other sets, from whatever source — one's own culture or other known cultures — one can slowly build up an understanding (Dolgin, Kemnitzer and Schneider, p. 480).[10]" This makes him seem not a sceptic who does without foundations but a foundationalist in need of new foundations to build on. These foundations are to be found in symbolic forms; a theme echoed by Douglas and Hanson. The relativist staves off the cognitive and hence social chaos he imagines comes in the train of scepticism by offering the fixity, validity, true-for-them character of each cultural framework.[11] This seems to them more secure than absolutism, with its shaky evolutionist idea that there is unilinear progress, and its absurd consequence that things should be getting more cognitively stable all the time. Popperian scepticism, by contrast, repudiates both poles of the dichotomy absolutist/ relativist and seeks stability as an achievement, temporary and partial, in constant danger of crumbling, always in need of improvement.

2. ANTHROPOLOGY AS SCIENCE

Let me begin with the question of the characterization of science. The traditional way of looking at this question is to sequester the scientific way of doing things and then to try and characterise it. Yet the very act of assuming science can be or is sequestered, is, that is to say, not continuous with other social activities, ensures that this approach is no more than an exercise in ingenuity. Since, as philosophers never tire of saying, everything resembles and also differs from everything else, it is a foregone conclusion that some sort of specific characterisation of sequestered science can be achieved. Hence the entire positivist programme can be reduced by a critic inclined to be cruel to an excercise in what the sociologists call labelling, and we as children used to refer to as name-calling.

Much the same is true of the exercises undertaken by those against science, in the social sciences and the humanities. If one strings together music, art, literature, religion, feeling, warmth and the excercise of understanding (Gellner's Hegelian mush) and points out that cold positivism with its facts, theories and predictions leaves out all those marvellous things, one will have no difficulty in characterising the difference in any number of ways and of showing either the weak conclusion that there is more to understanding the world than science, or the strong conclusion that science does not offer any understanding of the world worth having.

When I referred to the traditional way of looking at the question of characterizing science I had it in mind to suggest that there is a non-traditional way to approach this problem. That non-traditional way might be called the approach from anthropology. Science is, to the ethnographer, a distinctive set of institutions and, if Lord Snow (1959) is to be followed, a distinctive culture. It follows that societies without science may in some specifiable ways be distinct from societies with it. There appear to be societies without it even today; and there are societies that appear to be in the process of getting it. This looks like a marvellous anthropological opportunity, the sort of controlled ethnographic comparison rarely vouchsafed us in the social sciences.

'Does science make any difference, and what is the difference it makes?', may be questions susceptible not only to speculation and argument, but also to empirical investigation. The greatness of Sir James Frazer, it always seemed to me, was that although he never left his own society, he got the most important fact of world ethnography right namely, science makes a difference. Science is not like any other cognitive or social formation, it has a palpable cognitive power of its own, and it cannot but stand high in its own self-regard. This self-regard seems self-serving, but is is unavoidable. Anthropologically speaking the difference science makes is that it makes anthropology possible. It does not take much reading of Herodotus, Caesar, Gibbon or Hume to grasp just how impossible anthropology was when no concept resembling our scientific ideals was present. In particular science problematises the world in a different way from idle curiosity, invidious comparison, chauvinism, or moralising, which are among the reasons earlier writers looked at other societies. Science seeks disinterestedly to explain, and moreover to explain reflexively, that is, to explain how human social life works in a way that includes explanation of the sort of social life we live and in which we conduct such scientific anthropological investigations.

Before pressing this line of reasoning a stage further I must pause to consider a challenge to an earlier part of it. It is logically possible to argue that science is not a distinctive set of institutions and culture. Or, rather, it may be a separate set of institutions and culture now, but at least in its rudimentary forms, it is found in all human society. To adjudicate this counter-claim is not easy. No advocate of science is going to pretend science emerged *ex nihilo*. There have to be precursors. Nevertheless, to say there are precursors is not to deny the possibility of claiming there is a take-off point, a critical mass, or a sea-change in the emergence of science, where it begins to have extensive and ramifying influence on many aspects of the society, including such apparently non-scientific areas as art, religion, myth, social relations, the developmental cycle, kinship, economic organization, etc., etc.

To my mind the best attempt to sketch the ethnography of science has been made by Ernest Gellner. He began by trying to characterise non-scientific thought systems. These were the characteristics he found (1975, pp. 158–67): (a) The use of idiosyncratic norms; (b) Low cognitive division of labour accompanied by the proliferation of roles; (c) Diffuse and pervasive entranched clauses in the cognitive constitution; (d) Cognition has little or no extra-territorial status.

In a later work (1984) Gellner turns to the positive side, what characterises science is: (1) Exclusion of the transcendent, stress on the observable world; (2) Insistence on intelligibility and logical consistency; (3) Insistence on maximum separation of questions, whatever can be separated in thought should be thought about separately; (4) Exclusion of idiosyncratic explanation and again: (5) Though not completely consensual, consensual to an astonishing degree; (6) Inter-cultural in some sense; (7) Cumulative in some sense; (8) Requires arduous and prolonged training in thought-styles in no way continous with those of everyday life; (9) Its continually growing technology is immeasurably superior to and qualitatively distinct from the practical skills of the craftsman.

To Gellner, then, science is a new sort of thing in society and having it makes a difference, among other things a social difference. One way anthropologists had of refusing this sort of view was, as mentioned, to deny that science was a new sort of thing. Hence we have been told many anthropological tales of how tribes order their cropping of the land; how they construct and navigate canoes; how they construct tools or pottery. The implication is that these sorts of doings are continuous with science, only perhaps slightly less developed. A philosopher would criticise this move by suggesting it confuses science as a system of thought, with technology, which is a species of practical action. That gardners have rules of thumb in no way makes their procedures or thought-styles similar to those of science. The sociologist wants to press rather on the huge differences of scale that are being overlooked. The science and technology of modern societies enables transformation of the social and natural environment on a scale that dwarfs the activities to which it is being compared.

Another way anthropologists have of refusing to anthropologise science as making a difference is to accept it and denigrate it at the same time. That is, Gellner-type claims about scientific thought and science-based societies can be accepted and denounced. This we might call the small-is-beautiful argument; the argument that says a little bit of techno-scientific thought and action is a feature of every society, but when it starts to grow out of proportion it wrecks the possibility of living in harmony with nature.

Notwithstanding its fatuity, this position has received some serious consideration, often by anthropologists. Perhaps exasperated by trying to show its fundamental complacency-that is, the irony of its being forwarded only by members of societies anything but small and sweetly in harmony with nature — Gellner has bluntly suggested (1964) that humanity is voting on the issue. Despite ripples and the occasional doubt so strong is the urge of the underdeveloped to join the developed that governments have to promise the transition to bolster their legitimacy.

3. DOUGLAS ON FRAZER

This digression concluded, we can now press on with the implications of the view that science distinguishes some societies from others and is fundamentally involved in the characterisation of our own. Earlier I invoked the name of Frazer, a device for which I have often been chastised (Leach 1966, Jarvie 1966). Just when I thought that debate was settled, and Frazer would be accorded his qualified but rightful place amongst our honorable ancestors, I came across Mary Douglas' 1978 Introduction to a new and brilliant abridgement of *The Golden Bough*. Oddly, since an Introduction might be thought to be intended to entice the reader, Douglas expends most of her space on situating Frazer and the book in his time, and quietly but insistently denigrating it and him. She points out his failure to change his ideas over successive editions. He is described as insufferably arrogant, superficial and a kind of proto-racialist. His problem (the dawn of human thought, possibly, the essence of religion) was not modern. He piled up facts beyond the breaking point. She retails Wittgenstein's, 'What narrowness of spiritual life we find in Frazer'. Frazer's prose is commended for its irony and wit, but when serious is described as portentous, false, unctuous and sniggering. He lived a sheltered life, the bill of indictment continues, oblivious to the cruelties of the world of his time. He had a professorial chair in Liverpool, but preferred to work in Cambridge and did not think it necessary to resign from Liverpool. Apart from the insults of Durkheim (1912), which Douglas does not quote, it is hard offhand to think of a less enticing essay about Frazer. Perhaps Professor Douglas hopes readers will merely glance at the pictures and not get infected by Frazer's ideas.

Is there a central point in Frazer that agitates Douglas? It cannot be his sniggering because both anthropologists and tribesmen do a lot of sniggering between themselves and at each other. What then? Frazer takes it for granted that on the basis of western science rain makers do not make rain. He knocks away their foundations, cognitive as well as social. Here we are reminded again of Durkheim, only this time he was mistaken. He declared that human society could not be based on *error,* i.e. religion. So, he set out to show how religion was not error, *contra* Frazer and others. In place of Frazer's arrogant sniggering Douglas offers: "The modern approach to Frazer's chosen problem is to emphasize the symbolic side of human behaviour, the rites of celebration, without trying too much to distinguish what is symbolic and what is practical, a task that is much more difficult than it appears (p. 14)." Douglas apparently sees no need to explain how a process like emphasizing the symbolic side of human behaviour can do any explanatory work with the problems of anthropology. How the symbolic side will explain anything at all, including the origins of human thought, is not clear.[12] "The anthropologist homes in on the local culture as if it was a complete system with all its explanations contained within itself". Indeed. So societies are self-explanatory? Is that the source of their stability? What, then, one wonders, constitutes the problems of anthropology? Merely teasing out those explanations where they are not manifestly available? But why are local cultures' explanations of themselves to be taken seriously? Aren't anthropologists supposed to treat the testimony of informants (what people say) with the same sort of scepticism that historians adopt towards historical documents? And if that is so, why should 'local cultures' be privileged? Why should their explanaions not be regarded with the same or more scepticism?

After putting Frazer in his place, and after more outline of this modern approach, we come to this: "There is a concentration on tools, on methods, and with it a humility amounting to doubt as to whether we can ever understand another culture. For the moment, the major problem that interested Frazer's contemporaries so passionately is laid aside (p. 14)." The modern approach to Frazer's chosen problem, we are told, is to lay it aside; and, meanwhile, to distract our attention, we are given some prestdigitation about symbolism. And of course there is humility, always humility. The spirit of Uriah Heap is alive and well in anthropology. Amusing though all this is, the issue of the ethnography of anthropological science and its mistreatment of Sir James Frazer is serious business. Douglas ends her piece by offering further humble thoughts about our society and its culture. "Some of us are shocked at Frazer writing that ignorant and dull-witted people tend to magic beliefs. But to balk at that seems to be rather mealy-mouthed for anyone convinced of the invincible superiority of our modern science. Less than a hundred years from now our own attitudes will seem as patronizing as Frazer's. By then we may have met people ignorant of science yet perfectly versed in the meaning of dreams, or able to speak with animals, or able to master their own thoughts and bodies in ways that our science cannot comprehend (p. 15)." As John Wayne said in *The Searchers,* "That'll be the day"; not, I must insist, because Douglas seriously puts forward magical-science fiction possibilities for the future — this I might call her Carlos Castañeda side. Rather because, despite her previous disclaimer, the passage insinuates that she understands not 'another' culture, but her own, scientific culture. Continuing this excerise in showing that she doesn't know what she is talking about, her ethnography of our scientific culture is badly mistaken. Whether or not science is invincibly superior, which I must confess I think it is, is not a question for the ethnographer. What the ethnographer has to note is that in the culture of science the natives take it for granted that science is invincibly superior. It would not have its status without that. Furthermore, within the cultural surround of science right now there are people who are perfectly ignorant of science and who claim to be perfectly versed in the meaning of dreams, able to speak with animals, able to master their own bodies and thoughts. The culture of science deplores their ignorance and treats their claims not as ones that cannot be comprehended, but as ones perfectly easy to explain as the delusions of madmen or the deceptions of charlatans. In the culture of science it is not possible for such claims to be accepted as the result of ways which 'science cannot comprehend'. Science subjects such claims to scrutiny and admits them to the status of genuine events only when it can offer some explanation of them.

For my final comment on Mary Douglas I draw ethnographic attention to the situation of a western child watching television on which the adventures of Superman are to be seen. This seems to me an occasion neither for sniggering at the child, nor for interpreting the watching and reaction behaviour symbolically. Anthropological hackles will rise at this, since they will read it as an insulting and possibly sniggering comparison of primitive peoples with children. Varying the example to calm them is easy. Consider the ethnography of those Catholics who make a pilgrimage to Lourdes to seek a cure for what ails them. Whether or not the anthropologist is a Roman Catholic, and whether or not his Roman Catholicism is symbolic or literal or both, there is no occasion for sniggering at the pilgrims seeking cure and their behaviour is not rendered one iota more explicable by being interpreted symbolically.

4. GEERTZ'S ANTI ANTI-RELATIVISM

If Douglas seeks cognitive and social stability in symbolism, Geertz seeks it in hermeneutic interpretation.

In July of this year (1984) I published a book entitled *Rationality and Relativism* arguing that relativism when fully worked out implies that learning from experience is impossible. The heart of learning from experience, I suggested, was sifting out the false. Relativism, which denies that ideas can be false *tout court* but only false-for-them, is confined to asserting that something is learning-from-experience-for-them but not necessarily learning-from-experience for us. Thus we learn from experience about elementary particles, they learn from experience about their ghoulies and ghosties. Azande physics and Jewish physics.

Although arising in the context of anthropology the point at issue seems to ramify well beyond. Many a teacher of physics or of biology has in fact encountered the same claim and hence the same dilemma. What they are excessively shy about is that science makes univeral claims. The laws of particles rule the world of the Azande as well as the world of the atomic scientists (despite Mary Douglas' forlorn hopes). In opposing relativism I took it that I was working out the consequences of scientific universalism – a view I espouse.

Soon after the contractual copies of my book arrived, so did the June issue of *American Anthropologist,* in which the lead artical, by Clifford Geertz, attacks anti-relativism – a doctrine he partly defines by quoting my own writing and attributes to Spiro, Sperber, Midgely, Gellner. The question that teased me as I read through Geertz was, 'is he or isn't he?' – a relativist, that is ? Like a striptease performed by a transvestite, this question becomes consuming and yet, as we shall see, it it not at all clear that Greetz answers it, or, if he does answer it, what his answer is. Perhaps he swings both ways.

Geertz makes some strong claims for the relativist bent. Relativism lies at the heart of the anthropological heritage (263), "is . . . in some sense implicit in the field as such" (264), which presumably entails that, since Geertz attaches himself to the field, that he is. Each man, he quotes approvingly, calls barbarism whatever is not his own practice, for we have no other criterion of reason than the example and idea of the opinions and customs of the country we live in. Anthropology discourages rushing to judement; the provincialism of most of humanity is worse than relativism. Here I have strengthened his argument. He in fact implies that European provincialism is worse than relativism. He does not explicitly address the problem that most tribes are absolutist and provincial with a vengeance. The relativising anthropologist may be more tolerant than those on behalf of whom he peaches tolerance.

However, Greetz teases us on the main question by complaining that his anthropological challenges to hard rock foundations for cognitive, aesthetic or moral judgements have led to accusations "of disbelieving in the existence of the physical world" (264). I take it that, if one does not like being accused of disbelieving in the physical world then one does, indeed, believe in the physical world, although apparently one's belief is without 'hard rock' foundations. He isn't, then?

Not so fast. Most of the Geertz article is taken up with the question of human nature and the human mind. Geertz says he does not want to place morality beyond culture or knowledge beyond both (276). At this point the stripper is moving the fans so fast that our vision blurs. Apparently the deconstruction of otherness is the price of truth (274). And I commend to cognoscenti the following virtuoso example of arguing by indirection: "There is the same effort to promote a privileged language of "real" explanation . . . ; and the same wild dissensus as to just which language . . . that in fact is. There is the same tendency to see diversity as surface and universality as depth. And there is the same desire to represent one's interpretation not as constructions brought to their objects — societies, culture, lanuage — in an effort, somehow, somewhat to comprehend them, but as quiddities of such objects forced upon our thought (272)." These chastisements of others are well said, but the phrasing is such that no simple series of negations will tell us what Geertz holds. Are our constructions, for example, immune to the quiddities (= essences) of things, or are there no things to have quiddities, or are there things without quiddities, or what? If we bring forward our constructions in an effort to understand is that not to reach for 'real' explanation; are those efforts not even in theory rankable on some scale?

At such a place in the argument resort to the concrete helps. Geertz describes anthropologists as merchants of astonishment, peddlers of the strange; but also as providing counter-examples that aid progress. But if the truth is divisity, pluralism, if it amounts to the Wittgensteinian doctrine that there are many different things going on, and that's that, in what sense is anthropology making progress? The only way to make that claim amount to much is to assert that anthropology is converting more and more people to the profundity that tells them how diverse things are. With this a small problem arises. Is the diversity of things not itself the quiddity that forces itself on anthropological thought? Why is anthropological thought privileged in its constructions? While cognition is without foundations, while constructions are brought, while the world has no quiddity, while reason is just the custom of the country we live in, nevertheless: "We [anthropologists] have been the first to insist on a number of things: that the world does not divide into the pious and the superstitious; that there are sculptures in jungles and paintings in deserts; that political order is possible without centralized power and principled justice without codified rules; that the norms of reason were not fixed in Greece, the evolution of morality not consummated in England. Most important, we were the first to insist that we see the lives of others through lenses of our own grinding and that they look back on ours through

ones of their own. That this has led some to think the sky was falling, solipsism was upon us, and intellect, judgment, even the sheer possibility of communication had all fled is not surprising (275–6)." Do I read too much when
I hear, echoing away in some of these phrases, Geertz still assuming that the
anthropological task is to exorcise the ghost of Frazer, who Douglas accuses
of being so supercilious to savages? And would it be heartless to point out
that when Geertz compares the reaction of 'some' to Chicken Licken, who
thought the sky was falling, he may fairly be accused of sniggering? Douglas
sniggers at Frazer, Geertz at 'some'; the act is not at issue, only the target.
Would it labour the point to say again that by paying attention to what is
done rather than said we find our ethnographers not knowing what they doing,
not knowing what they are talking about?

We come, then, to the anthropology of the anthropological profession.
Geertz includes me in it, which is flattering but incorrect; I am that most
threatening of beings, a participant observer. And, consistent with my own
principles of fieldwork, not liking some of what I see I think it is a moral and
a scientific duty (and Gellner has taught me these are not separate) to say
so.[13] Anthropologists distinguish what people do, from what they say they
do. Anthropologist are people too, and subject to this ethnographic principle.
Some are dewy-eyed humanists and liberals who want to assist the weaker
members of the species. Some aspire to science. That both groups, the one
tending to reject science for morality and understanding, the other over eager
to embrace it, are deeply muddled about science, is a fact one can reach only
by being critical of both what they say and what they do. Geertz's catalogue
of anthropologists' contribution to knowledge lists imaginary enemies of long
ago. It is no longer an accurate anthropology of the peoples anthropologists
study, which can and should include themselves; it is also an inaccurate
anthropology of anthropology.

Anthropologists can coherently argue for tolerance, provided they are
alert to the paradox of tolerance created when the object of tolerance is
intolerant. They cannot be relativists for different reasons. The first is that
the intellectual tradition of science out of which anthropology comes is not
relativist. In so far as it is a scientific tradition it is cumulative, unversalist,
disinterested and progressive. Universality explains, diversity does not; to say
of things that they are diverse is not to explain them; it is the problem, not
the solution. In so far as that tradition is liberal and humane, it does not
excuse illiberality or inhumanity in others that it criticises at home. Geertz
himself is an expect in Muslim societies. To this participant observer one of
the principal questions an anthropologist must answer about some of these

societies is, do they or do they not oppress women? If they do, what is the anthropologist's stance? Does he suspend his own culture's spreading commitment to the emancipation of women and murmur, 'other cultures other mores'? Or does he, after representing the social system as thoroughly and conscientiously as he can, address the question of what hope there is for progressive social change in this matter?

And how about other aspects of anthropological tradition? There is much woolly thought and equivocation in anthropology's intellectual background, and anthropologists give it voice. Again, this participant observer is prepared to discount much of that, cut through the wool and try rationally to reconstruct such core thought as is there. To me, Hanson and Geertz's picture of anthropology as a lot of academics sitting around telling everyone old stories, describing themselves as peddlars of the strange, and being funded to go on doing so is grotesque. The only legitimacy their enterprise can have is as a contribution to knowledge. These merchants of astonishment need themselves to be rudely surprised out of fighting the battles of the nineteenth century and coming to grasp what the procedures and responsibilities of scientists are. These involve eschewing what Gellner acidly refers to as communing with ineffables.

For my final comment on Clifford Geertz I draw ethnographic attention to the extraordinary events surrounding Derek Freeman's book *Margaret Mead and Samoa* (1983). Freeman argues that Margaret Mead got her Samoan ethnography wrong and then he tries to explain how she got it wrong in terms of poor ethnographic technique, the power of controlling assumptions and a certain personal gullibility. His concerns are matters of ethnographic fact about Samoa, about Margaret Mead and about the community of anthropological scholars to which she belonged. An astonishing deluge of polemic has descended on Freeman's head, more of it philosophical-moral than ethnographic. Douglas and Geertz would tempt us to interpret this behaviour of the anthropological community in terms of readily available symbolic forms. This will hardly explain a special section of *American Anthropologist* devoted to attacking Freeman, a special issue of *Canberra Anthropology* containing a mix of papers and his reply. Among the former is Wiener's paper (1983) which argues that since anthropology is about making interpretations one does not and cannot go round refuting it. I pass over in silence those anthropologists who offer a direct challenge on matters of philosophy of science. My own contribution (1983) was to say there remains the problem of the ethnography of Margaret Mead's career as anthropologist and pundit. Since her authority in the latter depended on her status in the former two groups have an interest in defending her. That anthropologists may be more interested in defending their profession than in factual truth is not one iota better explained by a hermeneutic layering of interpretations.

5. HANSON'S REFORMULATION AND DEFENSE OF RELATIVISM

Geertz, we noted, will not come right out and say he is a relativist, he seems to sense its cognitive and social instability. One who openly espoused relativism, has always done so, and who cites Douglas, Geertz, Turner, etc. as his heroes, is F. Allan Hanson (1975, 1981). In a new piece, stimulated by my recent book, he argues that the key to understanding(!) anthropological relativism is the experience of fieldwork. Robert Murphy describes it thus: "Fieldwork is a reflexive affair; the anthropologist transforms raw behavioral data into norm and pattern through the fallible and refractory instrument of the mind, and he or she is in turn transformed by the experience. This sense that the observer and the observed are not independent of each other is at once the source of our uncertainties and the strength of our method, for no other social science seeks to enter so deeply into the lives of its subjects (Murphy 1984)." This immersion in a strange society radically de-ethnocentries the anthropologist, alters his whole outlook on his own society as well as exotic ones. In my book I quoted Descartes (1637) to the effect that foreign travel was mind-broadening provided it was not dragged out too long, in which case there was a danger of becoming a stranger in one's own land. Hanson passes over the quotation as 'vapid', seemingly quite missing its relevance to one of the themes of the book, namely, the de-ethnocentrised anthropologist may have succeeded in losing his bearings in his own culture, particularly as regards the ethnography of science and anthropological endeavour itself.

Hanson defends relativism that is descriptive not prescriptive. While expressing his revulsion at cannibalism per se, he carefully distinguishes two cannibalistic traditions, one as cruel and the other as moral. Like Geertz's examples cited above, this one from Hanson seemed to me rather musty. Are anthropologists still motivated by the travesties of exotic society publicised down to the early years of this century? Is not that a trivial matter to which to devote extensive scholarly resources? Given the complexity and elaboration of the books of Douglas, Geertz and Hanson one might suspect them of overkill if this is their purpose. If they want to correct the simple-minded they should keep their rebuttals short and simple-minded.

Anyway, the upshot of Hanson's pluralism is the argument that we can learn from the peoples who are anthropological subjects just as they can learn from us. Concretely, "From the Hua the West could learn something about the debt that the present owes to the past, how a closer and more trusting relationship between the generations might be established, and perhaps even a more positive attitude towards death — since among the Hua death may have less sudden finality to it than among us because one's *nu* or life principle is constantly in process of transferring to the next generation and contihues in one's descendants (MSS, p. 18)." Notice the similarity to Margaret Mead on the one hand, and Carlos Castañeda on the other. The first embroiled in controversy over whether her fieldwork was incompetant and hence her argument that the West could learn how better to manage adolesence from the Samoans vacated; the second embroiled in controversy over whether the teachings of Don Juan and their travels through space and time (Douglas' future already here) are fiction.

Anthropologists would do well, I conclude, to retreat from the pundit-guru posture, peddling the vast wisdom of those other peoples so much closer to nature than ourselves. There is no progress and little rationality in such endeavours, only the sad and embarassing confrontation with our gullibity, It is a sentimental dream to talk of understanding what (other) people do and think in terms of their own cultural values and categories. For the simple fact is that their cultural values and categories rarely embrace ours (since the tradition of science is still found in only some of the societies of the world), whereas ours do usually embrace theirs. This relationship is asymmetrical, however guilty that may make the anthropologist feel. The guilt is irrational, of course. If social facts are things in the way Durkheim taught, then they can be theorised about, become problematic and be explained without at any point needing to be involved with the local cultural values and categories. Insofar as the asymmetry bothers one, it should be resolved not by pious talk of mutual learning, but by educational talk between scientist and layman.

Forget anthropology for the moment and think of suicide and of cigarette smoking. No doubt the suicide has cultural values and categories. These are of scarcely any interest in the explanation of the problems posed by Durkheim. Yet I think that were there wider social understanding of Durkheim's theory of suicide and social integration, and were that theory true, suicides might fall in numbers. Similarly, cigarette smokers have their cultural values and categories by means of which they make sense of what they do. The psychologist in the withdrawal programmes probably needs to know these. But Durkheim-like questions about rates of smoking, fluctuations in those rates and so on are not to be answered from those values and categories, still less should scientists investigating lung cancer think they have something to learn from the smoker. The relationship is asymmetrical and is to be rectified by making the smoker see the value of the values and categories of the scientist, not vice versa. As to the symbolism of suicide and smoking . . .

Hanson's bold last-ditch attempt to rescue relativism by calling it descriptive, and by suggesting that unless we adopt it we will be horrid to primitive peoples is worthy but, I conjecture, miscalculated. Failure to recognise this leads to errors of logic. Consider the sentence (S): "cognition and morality are contingent upon culturally variable rules and no super-cultural standards exist for the adjudication of those rules (MSS, p. 17)." The sentence (S), is offered by Hanson as a scientific result of doing fieldwork, itself a supercultural discovery about cultures in general, a quiddity imposed on thought by its objects. It has to be a discovery at the supercultural level because, as far as my ethnographic knowledge goes, every native culture, from the Azande to present day United States would deny (S). Yet from (S) Hanson derives the maxim, 'be pluralist'. One must respect the agony of Hanson's position. However absolutist he is in his ethnography of anthropology, however relativist he is in his ethnography of other cultures, he is impaled on the spike of absolutist at home, relativist abroad. This is, truly, relativism (not science) in thought, word and deed.

NOTES

1 Part I would be my paper (Jarvie 1970), revised and expanded as Chapter 2 of (Jarvie 1972).
2 My argument for this is fully set out in (1972).
3 In Popperian circles the tag usually is: natural science explains the known by the unknown; social science explains the unknown by the known.
4 Hanson (1985) claims that 'functionalism is the *bête noir* in everything' (MSS, p. 8) I write. While it is true that my (1964) was critical of functionalist excesses (e.g. ancestor-killing, ahistoricalness), generally speaking I endorsed functionalism as a powerful and revolutionary new tool in anthropology. Hanson's ethnographic information that I am seen as an hostile critic of functionalism is evidence of what I shall maintain below, that no-one is in control of what they say or do. (Connoisseurs should register the way my vocabulary of 'societies' and 'explanations', rather than 'cultures' and 'understanding' indicates that my structural-functionalist training is still intact.)
5 This is argued forcefully in Gellner (1964).
6 Since relativists, who are themselves subject to physics, encourage the thought that 'other *pays* other physics', they cannot escape the charge that their doctrine helps reinforce the divisions of mankind.
7 Philosophers of science often seem overly shy of admitting that their inquiry is normative as well as descriptive. Even while opposing all authority, it is important to

discriminate scientific expertise in the science of nature from scientific expertise in the science of science. These are not necessarily transferable.

It should be said that in his critique of my book Hanson remarks that its most serious shortcoming is that, so far as anthropology is concerned, the book is seriously out of date. 'It was fair enough for Jarvie ... in *The Revolution in Anthropology* of 1964 ... Jarvie's present book does not come to grips with the realities of current anthropology' (MSS, p. 6). Alas, even in 1965 it was not fair enough; Professor Lucy Mair warned readers that I was 'a writer who is not fully aware of the way in which theories have developed since Malinowski's time' (1965 p. 47). What we have here is honest disagreement about the ethnography of anthropology disguised as the suggestion that Jarvie is out of date. To accuse someone of being out of date is to say, you *were* right about us, but we have moved on, try to catch up. Its apologetic character is obvious.

[8] The ingredients for making this mush are spelled out in Gellner (1985), especially in Chapters 1 and 4.

[9] In utilising an abstract of one of his papers, prepared by other hands, I am owning up to the difficulty of summarising this elegant author. To judge by its auspices, the abstract is by sympatheitc hands; judging by its content, it is highly critical. A fascinating minor issue in the ethnography of anthropological publication.

[10] *A propos* of note 9 above, I read the abstract as a perfect recipe for Hegelian mush.

[11] Fear of scepticism, so well expressed by Geertz, cannot be unaffected by the parallel to the self. Many philosophers find the uncertainties of scepticism so intolerable they rather adopt dogmatism or fideism.

[12] I have explained the reasons for this in Jarvie and Agassi 1967 and my (1976). The full original version of the much-discussed paper with Agassi will be published for the first time in 1985 in J. Agassi and I. C. Jarvie (ed.), *Rationality: The Critical View*, The Hague: Nijhoff.

[13] 'In my view, epistemological principles are basically normative or ethical: they are prescriptions for the conduct of cognitive life. The pseudo-psychological, pseudo-logical or pseudo-linguistic forms in which they are often formulated obscure that. They are ... covert pieces of cognitive ethnics. The rest is rhetoric or mystification' (Gellner 1985, p. 34).

REFERENCES

Agassi, J. 1977. *Towards a Rational Philosophical Anthropology*, The Hague: Nijhoff.
Agassi, J. and Jarvie, I. C. (ed.) 1985. *Rationality, The Critical View*, The Hague: Nijhoff.
Bartley III, W. W. 1984: 'Knowledge is a Product Not Fully Known to its Producer'. In *The Road to Serfom after 40 Years*. Edited by Kurt Leube and C. Nishiyama. Munich: Philosophia Verlag.
Descartes, René 1637. *Discourse on Method*. Trs. Haldane and Ross. New York: Dover Bks 1955.
Dolgin, Janet L., Kemnitzer, David S., and Schneider, David M. 1977. *Symbolic Anthropology*. New York: Columbia University Press.
Douglas, Mary 1978. 'Introduction'. In Sir James George Frazer, *The Illustrated Golden Bough*. General Editor Many Douglas. Abridged and Illustrated by Sabine MacCormach, London: Macmillan.

Durkheim, Emile 1912. *The Elementary Forms of the Religious Life*. Trs. J. W. Swain. London 1915: Allen and Unwin.

Freeman, Derek 1983. *Margaret Mead and Samoa*, Cambridge, Mass: Harvard University Press.

Geertz, Clifford 1983. *Local Knowledge*. New York: Basic Books.

Geertz, Clifford 1984. 'Distinguished Lecture: Anti Anti-Relativism'. *American Anthropologist* 86 263–78.

Gellner, Ernest 1964. *Thought and Change*. London: Weidenfeld and Nicholson.

Gellner, Ernest 1975. *Legitimation of Belief*. Cambridge: Cambridge University Press.

Gellner, Ernest 1985. *Relativism and the Social Sciences*. Cambridge: Cambridge University Press.

Hanson, F. Allan 1975. *Meaning in Culture*. London: Routledge and Kegan Paul.

Hanson, F. Allan 1981. 'Anthropology and the Rationality Debate'. (In German) in *Der Wissenschaftler und das Irrationale*. Edited by Hans Peter Duerr. Frankfurt: Vol. I, pp. 245–72.

Hanson, F. Allan 1985. 'Strictures and Ratiocinations: I. C. Jarvie's Philosphy for Anthropology'. *Philosophy of the Social Sciences* 15.

Jarvie, I. C. 1964. *The Revolution in Anthropology*. London: Routledge and Kegan Paul.

Jarvie, I. C. 1966. 'Academic Fashions and Grandfather Killing'. *Current Anthropology* 7, 568–9.

Jarvie, I. C. 1970. 'Understanding and Explanation in Sociology and Social Anthropology'. In *Explanation and the Behavioural Sciences*. Edited by R. Borger and F. Cioffi. Cambridge: Cambridge University Press, pp. 231–48.

Jarvie, I. C. 1972. *Concepts and Society*. London: Routledge and Kegan Paul.

Jarvie, I. C. 1975. 'Epistle to the Anthropologists'. *American Anthropologist* 77 253–66.

Jarvie, I. C. 1976. 'On the Limits of Symbolic Interpretation in Anthropology'. *Current Anthropology* 17 687–701.

Jarvie, I. C. 1983. 'Freeman on Mead'. *Canberra Anthropology* 6 80–5.

Jarvie, I. C. 1984. *Rationality and Relativism: In Search of a Philosophy and History of Anthropology*, London: Routledge and Kegan Paul.

Jarvie, I. C. and Agassi, J. 1967. 'The Problem of the Rationality of Magic'. *British Journal of Sociology* 18 55–74.

Leach, Sir Edward 1966. 'Frazer and Malinowski'. *Encounter* 25 November, 24–36.

Mair, Lucy 1965. *Introduction to Social Anthropology*. Oxford: Oxford University Press.

Murphy, Robert 1984. 'Requiem for the Kayapo'. *New York Times Book Review*, August 12, p. 34.

Snow, C. P. 1959. 'The Two Cultures and The Scientific Revolution'. In *Public Affairs*. London: Macmillan 1971, pp. 14–46.

Wiener, Annette 1983. 'Ethnographic Determinism: Samoa and the Margaret Mead Controversy'. *American Anthropologist* 85 909–19.

CHAPTER 12

Epistle to the Anthropologists[1]

Lack of theoretical progress, among other things, indicates a genuine intellectual crisis in anthropology. Previously, the author advocated a more consciously critical and falsificationist set of methodological rules as a remedy. Fabian has shown that this is not sufficient. He argues that there is an uncritical positivism built-in to anthropology, which leads to ontological, epistemological, and moral error. Metaphysics as well as method needs rectification. The paper urges doing this by rebuilding links to the broad philosophical concerns out of which anthropological theory grew.

THIS PAPER addresses itself to two problems: first, is there a crisis in anthropology; second, if there is, what caused it and what will resolve it. As a springboard for discussion, we look at the allegation of crisis and its diagnosis that has come from anthropologists of a phenomenological or "critical theory" persuasion. While agreeing with them that there is a crisis, the paper attributes it to theoretical stagnation, not to the influence of "positivism." A possible cure for theoretical stagnation is seen in critical reflection on the history of anthropology, and especially in coming to terms with the continuities (or lack of them) between its present concerns and those of the tradition of inquiry to which it belongs.

THE CRISIS

Crises in science are of great interest because they frequently presage an intellectual transformation of some kind (Agassi 1959). They are also treacherous, because some talk of crisis is spurious. There are those who take the view that there is a crisis when people say there is (Jarvie 1972:147-172). I am inclined to use "crisis" in a more objective manner, to refer to an insuperable intellectual difficulty—whether recognized as such or not. To take an example, was there a crisis or a sense of crisis immediately preceding the revolution in social anthropology initiated by Malinowski and Radcliffe-Brown in 1922? I see little evidence of a *sense* of crisis, but plenty that a crisis existed. The crisis was this: the ostensibly competing theories of evolution and diffusion had become so rubbery that they could be reconciled with each other and with all facts. They were better described as metaphysical frameworks or research programs. Neither could specify facts that might refute them and hence would constitute a test, still less a crucial test that would decide between them. Theories which clash neither with other theories nor with the facts are said to have no explanatory power: even though no one denies evolution and diffusion go on, they do not serve to explain any society or social feature. The anthropologist in the field experiences this sharply: according to these theories, what should he look for and record?[2] Almost by accident, both Radcliffe-Brown and Malinowski found themselves plunged into lengthy and intense field experiences. If they were to present "their" people's lives in a coherent and intelligible manner it would virtually be necessary to reinvent anthropology. This they proceeded to do. The result was an immensely powerful new method which treated societies as integrated wholes peopled by recognizably human beings. This transformation and improvement of the practice of anthropology was all to the good; the new pseudo-theoretical dogma was bad. Its

Submitted for publication November 12, 1974
Accepted for publication December 10, 1974

worst effect was that instead of continuing and extending the debate on traditional anthropological problems, the new anthropology dismissed them as misconceived or speculative (Jarvie 1964:7-28, 170-176). Anthropology was claimed to be beginning anew, free from the errors of the past. This absurd radicalism merely succeeded in suppressing the past, not freeing us of it. If we junk the concerns of the past, where do we begin, what can anthropology now be about? This question was rudely shoved aside in the haste to get on with applying the new method. And the method was such a powerful novelty that it has powered the subject ever since. Now, however, that old question "What is anthropology about?" has re-emerged. Therein lie the fifty-year-old seeds of the present crisis. Anthropologists no longer know what their subject is about, they have lost the thread of those long-ago debates (Kuper 1973; Jarvie 1975a).

Outlining as I just have the intellectual origins of the present crisis—as it were its objective component—is to put things backward. Although the elements of this explanation of mine were developed ten years ago (Jarvie 1964), it was only five years ago that I began to see that a new social and psychological crisis in the subject was actually in the making. Fifty years after *The Andaman Islanders* and *Argonauts of the Western Pacific* flopped from the presses, what is the present situation in social anthropology? We have, I would say, all the signs, indeed a veritable syndrome, of intellectual crisis. There is, for example, the pursuit of intellectual fads, such as structuralism—whatever that is. There is reversion to the comfort of long-discredited theories, such as Marvin Harris's espousal of cultural materialism. There is the invocation of such gadgets as computers, linguistics, systems theory, communications theory, and animal ethology as the answers to all problems. Above all, perhaps, there are strenuous calls for radical reform of the subject, politically, ethically, theoretically, and methodologically. Anthropology, we have even been told, may have to be reinvented once more. So much, then, for the general syndrome of disorder.[3] Let us now look a little more closely at some of the things which are pointed to as causing the crisis. My list mixes the serious with the frivolous, but is none the worse for that: crises have their funny side.

First and above all there is the loss of recruits: the growth boom seems to be over in anthropology, student numbers are said to be levelling off or even falling. Even if this were true, the passing of a fashion for anthropology may be salutary.

Second, there is the loss of the great men: no one, it is said, now leads the subject. Malinowski and Radcliffe-Brown are long dead; their most brilliant pupil Evans-Pritchard had ceased to be a creative influence for some years before he joined them. Lévi-Strauss is looked to by some, but he has an off-putting habit of kicking away those who come to pay him homage that prevents effective leadership (Anonymous 1974). Besides, no Anglo-Saxon can seriously contemplate ceding the leadership to a Frenchman.

Third, as a result of the loss of recruits and loss of the great men, there is social disorganization: *anomie*; charisma has been routinized into professorships; segmentary fission and fusion has been bureaucratized into departments; *rites de passages* have been secularized into university degrees; there is loss of the clear sense of what it is to be an anthropologist and hence of the direction to proceed.

Fourth, in addition to social disorganization, there is intellectual disorganization: instead of vigorous theoretical debate there are increasingly specialized and technical quibbles.[4] The reason is clear; expansion and specialization cause people to forget or neglect the broader debates on the basic issues.

Such disorganization leads to the fifth contributory cause to the crisis, and that is intellectual stagnation. There has been little movement, little new theory in anthropology since the fifties.[5] When I was an undergraduate at the London School of Economics in the fifties it was the anthropologists' proud boast that the subject was so dynamic and vigorous no one had the time, inclination, or opportunity to write a textbook. We learned the subject without benefit of textbooks. Nowadays there are many textbooks.[6] For this to be at all possible, the pace of the subject must have slowed down.

The dreary catalog of causes could go on, but I will halt at a sixth, in some ways the most serious, and also the best known. I refer to the loss of subject matter. Untouched simple societies are fewer and fewer, and newly decolonized governments are openly hostile and obstructionist toward anthropologists.

Six gloomy portents of a parlous state of affairs. If we add a seventh, to which I shall come later, namely the sweeping claim that the basic epistemological categories of anthropology are inadequate, it is no wonder some scholars develop an urge to throw it all up and begin again *ab initio*: to reinvent anthropology. It is my opinion that we must resist this urge, not so much because the problems and difficulties are not real, but more because the program of trying to start again from scratch is an impossible one: *ex nihilo nihil fit*. Instead, I suggest that we renew ourselves, refresh ourselves, by reexamining assumptions, by looking again at the history and metaphysics of anthropology, by trying to forge links to the past from which we have cut ourselves off, to recapture the identity of self and re-address ourselves to the central unsolved problems.

PHILOSOPHICAL DIAGNOSES

Two kinds of philosophical difficulties have been advanced as causes of the crisis in anthropology: one, that anthropology participates in the general methodological short-comings of the empirical social sciences; the other an objection to empiricism itself. To begin with, I want briefly to consider the general methodological shortcomings of the social sciences. Methodological shortcomings in the social sciences are frequently alluded to. It was Poincaré who jibed that sociology was the subject with "the greatest number of methods and the least results" (n.d.:19-20). Why are the social sciences preoccupied with their own method? One answer might be that when you have nothing to say, you talk about method. No one would claim there is a shortage of first-order problems in the social sciences; they are awash in problems. War, inflation, poverty, injustice, crime, neurosis, unemployment, racialism, underdevelopment, challenge us still—both socially and intellectually. To talk intelligently about a problem, however, one has to have something to say, a solution or a theory to meet the problem, or a novel criticism of earlier solutions. In contrast to the problems and the methodologies, both of which abound in the social sciences, there are indeed pathetically few fully worked out theories on offer. Classical and neo-classical economics constitutes one such body of theory, a basis for debate at least. Marx, the great critic of classical economics, is also one of the few social scientists to have developed anything resembling a broad and linked theoretical system.[7] By contrast, his critic Max Weber left us only fragmentary insights in the form of a long drawn out critique of Marx. In social anthropology it could be said that the metaphysics of evolutionism, diffusionism, and functionalism were briefly specified as theories able to do explanatory work. They did not however solve any of the above problems. Moreover, all the examples we have given—classical economics, Marx's theory of society, evolutionism, diffusionism, and functionalism—have it in common that in all precise versions they are false,[8] known to be false, and have been known to be false for a long time; in all vague, imprecise, qualified, or otherwise hedged versions, they are irrefutably metaphysical.

Unlike many anthropologists, I regard theoretical breakdown as a fundamentally healthy event. If what we want is intellectual progress, better explanation, then the breakdown of existing theories is a prerequisite: we cannot supersede a theory until we know where it goes wrong. The more orthodox way to look on theoretical breakdown is that we must have used the wrong method, or not been conscientious enough in employing method to have landed up with false theories. The difference here is that I equate the discovery of error with progress; the more orthodox view is that error, mistake, going wrong, is a lurch that needs explanation. One often finds it suggested that there is a correct methodology that is like a path leading from our present state of error or shortcoming or lack, to a future state of possession of the truth or adequacy or wholeness.[9] Alas, to the best of my knowledge no such path exists; or, even if it does, there is no pathfinder to guide us along it. Method is not an algorithm. Method is the general set of rules governing rational or critical debate; it guides us in the appraisal of theories once we have them; it offers us no guidance as to how to get theories when we are without them. This is why theoretical crisis spawns methodological debate: to assess what has happened and its implications, whether a low-level theory, a global theory, or an entire type of theory has been undermined, etc. However critical our debates are, we may still go on making mistakes, or get nowhere at all, and there may be nothing for it but to go on arguing and thinking and hoping that ideas will come.

No doubt all this sounds hard, but life is hard. It is not as hard, however, as many social scientists like to maintain. There is the constantly reiterated complaint that social life is very complex, unpredictable, and afflicted with multiple causes, and that this accounts for whatever theoretical difficulties are current. Yet every methodological remedy proposed in its turn fails. Like cargo cultists, social scientists have yet to learn the basic lesson that spells are an inefficient way to get anything. A related complaint is that social scientists, being human, cannot escape human bias. The implication is that only Martians or perhaps viruses will ever produce a genuine social science, and in the meantime, social scientists should try to empathize the Martian or the viral viewpoint. The well-known answer to this complaint is that it is highly unlikely that the Martian or the virus would even notice man and his social life as a separate category of phenomena demanding a science to themselves; such beings would have no access to what is sometimes called the world of meanings which man inhabits. And this privileged access man has to himself. This grasp every human necessarily has of his social predicament actually simplifies the alleged complexity of social life.

Failure to appreciate this undoubtedly has to do with the tissue of misunderstandings known as scientism. Scientism is the "slavish imitation of the method and language of science" (Hayek 1955:15). Originally exposed and criticized by Hayek in 1942, we nevertheless find it rearing its ugly head in anthropology as recently as Marvin Harris (1968).[10] The irony is that often enough what is so slavishly imitated are methods better known to philosophers than to scientists, e.g., observation, induction, operationalism, experimentalism. Much science obviously (e.g., astronomy, historical geology, and pencil and paper physics) does without experiment. All science is done without induction and operationalism, whatever scientists and philosophers may *say*. It would be doubly ironic if anthropologists of all people did not attend to what scientists do rather than what they say, and hence underestimate the influence of positivism or positivistic *talk* about science. The true methods of science are hard to get at.[11] That may explain why successive methodological revolutions are necessary, as each fails to deliver the goods to the waiting social scientists. Like the cargo cultists they study, anthropologists do not easily lose their credulousness toward mana from heaven.

Theoretical poverty cannot, however, be entirely explained by lack of method or misunderstood method. For such problems have not held back the natural sciences. Another possibility is that what little theoretical progress there is is simply not recognized as such by social scientists. Scientism, positivism, cultural materialism, refuse to recognize progress as such when it occurs unless it conforms to their mistaken ideas of what scientific theories should look like. Thus the sense of crisis brought on by the sense of getting nowhere may be simply a mistake. But I am not inclined to think so, at least as far as anthropology goes. It does seem as though anthropological theory has been stagnant for about twenty years. The question is, why? My answer: because anthropology constantly refuses to debate and acknowledge its philosophical, and especially metaphysical, ingredients. The fundamental philosophical problem of anthropology, as I have argued elsewhere, is how to reconcile man's apparent diversity with his real unity (1964:8n, 1968). This problem is a metaphysical problem, and the theories proposed to solve it give birth to concrete physical, biological, and sociological problems.[12] Scientism, and especially its positivistic variant, constantly tries to cleanse the social sciences of metaphysics, on the mistaken premise that this will make them more like the natural sciences. Yet without this metaphysical problem of the unity of mankind and its surrounding debate there simply would be no anthropology.

So much then for the general malaise of the social sciences and the suggestion that methodological change is what they require. Provided, it seemed to me, we were more critical in a perfectly commonplace and well-understood way, and given a little luck, our theoretical troubles should eventually go away. Or so I once thought. I found myself shaken out of this dogmatic slumber by an anthropologist of phenomenological persuasion—Johannes Fabian—who argued that the critical method was not critical enough (1971), that anthropology contained within its training, its setting of problems, and its scientific and critical outlook, a host of assumptions which were not themselves subject to criticism and yet which could seriously inhibit or distort the anthropologist's work. Starting from some fairly commonplace field problems with the religion he had gone to study, he ended up developing arguments that challenged basic assumptions on which empirical anthropology rests, and seeing in this the source of crisis. Because he captures arguments widely current, and because these arguments are at least an alternative explanation of the crisis, I shall expend some space and effort on them. Even if in the end I bring down a different explanation, Fabian's deserves close and serious discussion.

Fabian set off to study an obscure cult movement in Katanga known as *Jamaa* (meaning "family" in Katanga Swahili). He set off to find it with, he admits in retrospect, no proof that there was such a distinct entity or a specific historical process maintaining its identity through time. He then found no ritual paraphernalia, no insignia, no attire, and no buildings, only weekly meetings, highly localized in organization and content and virtually indistinguishable from other pious meetings in the parish. There were no records and no formal leaders. The founder and prominent members denied founding anything. *Jamaa* was a way of life, not an organization; but not a new way of life, merely a return to the oldest and purest doctrines of the church. So neither ritual nor doctrine was there to be studied.[13] In the end he found that *language*, words, preaching, reading, discussion of *mawazo*—ideas, thoughts—added up to a distinctly marked system of beliefs and norms. Language, then, was the place where *Jamaa* had its reality and showed itself to Fabian. Only through the language could he get at what was going on—there was nothing to see, no hard facts.

Once Fabian had decided to become critical of even the basic categories in terms of which he had been trained to operate, he found parallel arguments had been directed at empiricism by phenomenologists.[14] I liked Fabian's bold strategy. To argue from the empirical field situation straight back to underlying metaphysical assumptions like "hard facts" is what being critical, in the sense I would endorse, pretty well amounts to. But, as I shall try to show, this anthropologist himself allowed his argument to lead him down a dead end, namely, advocacy of a methodological-cum-philosophical revolution in the foundations of anthropology. The revolution would involve: abandoning the subject/object distinction because it is positivistic; most curious attempts to evade what I take to be the inherent ethical ambiguities of the anthropological enterprise; and an epistemology where the so-called social reality and the language in which it is described become entangled in the very process of interaction between the anthropologist and his subject.

My suspicion is that Fabian noticed the phenomenological critique of empiricism, but overlooked the empiricist critique of phenomenology.[15] Thus, denials notwithstanding, I feared his revolutionary doctrine of anthropology as process would aim to become a new regime. It is a fact of comparative sociology or anthropology that all regimes have a tendency to become rigid and uncritical. The only known solution, in politics as in intellectual endeavor, is pluralism, exchange, and debate; in other words not the dictatorship of an all-wise, all-good successor regime.

I was at one with Fabian in looking, as it were, to philosophical reflection upon anthropology as a way out of the crisis. I did not believe, however, that a revolution was required, nor did we agree on which philosophical moves would be the fruitful ones. Before I make our disagreements clearer, let me look more closely at what Fabian has in mind when he attacks the philosophical foundations of anthropology. To begin with, I think he has doubts about ontology. He wants to re-open discussion of the entities which conventionally populate anthropological works—not just cult, doctrine, and ritual, but even such a basic pair of entities as the observer and the observed, the subject and the object.

Fabian's argument is that anthropology should not be divided into an unproblematic part (data gathering) and a problematic part (theorizing). The isolation, observation, and description of the data, the entities, is itself highly problematic, and the anthropologist needs to be very critical. The knowing, data-gathering subject himself enters into a problematic communicative relationship with his objects of study (Fabian 1971:34). Fabian suggests that we reject the subject-object distinction and replace it with the communicative process model of anthropology, in which the anthropologist and his informants jointly construct a *lebenswelt* which itself becomes the object of anthropology. In opposition to what he refers to as positivist methodology—roughly, the idea of a distinction between the observer and the observed—he is seeking to ground the anthropological experience in intersubjectivity, a notion familiar to us from the writings of Schutz (1964) and Berger and Luckmann (1966). He illustrates all this with the Jamaa cult, showing how the units of analysis, the "things" we observe and collect data about, should emerge from this process of intersubjective interaction, and not be imposed upon experience beforehand.

Much of Fabian's argument strikes me as incontestable. There is still a lot of philosophically very naive positivism around in the social sciences, assuming that the objects of experience are "given," are somehow or other "out there in the world." In protesting that we are in the age of post-Kantian epistemology, Fabian is correctly emphasizing Kant's point that the way things "really" are out there is something we cannot ever know for sure; our experience must be in terms of the categories of the understanding (and that this is a product of intersubjectivity—a point Kant would not take). Thus our ontology, or the categories in terms of which we do the anthropology of, say, religious movements ("religion" and "movement" are also categories, of course), will not necessarily be adequate even to the task of capturing the reality of the social organization from which the anthropologist himself comes. Consequently, in striving to come to terms with novel situations and experience, the anthropologist needs to restructure his understanding by means of a cooperative endeavor with the people who are themselves organizing the thought and action which constitutes the structures of society being studied. This is not vague advice, but ties up with the centrality of language in the study of anthropology. Fabian argues that what we might call the social reality itself emerges from the process of interaction between people, a process that takes place within, through, only because of, and is constituted and articulated through, a language of communicative interaction. Hence the anthropologist who comes to a society armed with problems, theories, preconceptions, etc., has to cast all these aside, or perhaps "bracket" them for the time being, and begin by identifying the boundaries of the ongoing interacting linguistic community, and entering it by mastering its means of articulating itself, namely, its language. The social reality of a people is a function of the people and the anthropologist.

This particular examination of the philosophical foundations of anthropology by Fabian challenges current views on the objectivity of the science, indeed its fundamental epistemology. He says, "objectivity lies neither in the logical consistency of a theory, nor in the givenness of the data, but in the foundations of human intersubjectivity" (1971:12). Or again, "objectivity in anthropological investigations is attained by entering a context of communicative interaction through the one medium which represents and constitutes such a context: language" (1971:16). In opposition to the epistemology of what he chooses to call positivism-pragmatism, Fabian writes that his position

> holds that particulars of empirical reality cannot be perceived apart from a totality and that this totality is a genetic process, not just a logical ensemble. It also implies that consciousness of reality is constituted only through real interaction with phenomena and that generalisation is a communicative process, not a solitary abstractive function of a mind imagined to operate outside of space, time, and the context of other minds [p. 25] .... The particulars of observation are not just contingent indications of an underlying necessary reality. They are not seen as 'cases of' but as results of a process in which a totality realises itself [p. 13].

Fabian has certainly indicated ways in which anthropology can be more critical. Yet his stress on language accords very well with what anthropologists in fact do. Malinowski, it bears emphasizing, argued vehemently that the way into a culture was through its language—in order that one could come to see the world as its members do. He knew of the horrendous examples of misunderstanding and damage which had been caused by uncritical imposition of the categories suggested by *our* social life on alien social life, and of the insight to be gained by trying to describe our social life in categories imported from elsewhere. So I see little to dispute here apart perhaps from some minor matters of emphasis and rhetoric.

It is along these sorts of lines that Fabian and other radical anthropologists have tried to explain the crisis in anthropology, and suggest ways of resolving it. My opposition to them is not just based on the specific criticisms of their arguments I shall present below, but on two other grounds. First, I am not convinced that such philosophical criticisms are ever sufficient to account for crisis in empirical science. A crisis is a social phenomenon, and, while conceptual difficulties can give rise to social difficulties (indeed in some ways are social difficulties[16]), we also know that science can often advance despite grave conceptual weaknesses—as witness the forty successful years of functionalist anthropology. The second reason for skepticism about radical philosophical criticism as explanation of the crisis is this: it argues for another attempt to break with the past. That, I contend, is just what is not needed. We need to reclaim the past. It is loss of continuity, losing touch with the tradition of discussion in the subject, especially its central (metaphysical) problems, that has produced the crisis. What anthropology needs is to recapture its aims, to come to terms with itself as an intellectual tradition centering around certain key problems, the successive solutions to which, and the surrounding debate, provide the change and novelty and sense of movement and progress. It is only in relation to its past that a tradition of enquiry can regain a sense of progress. Fabian does not offer this, and hence I make some specific objections to his ideas.

Furthermore, most philosophers of science—who would doubtless be classed as positivist-pragmatists by Fabian—would explicate *objectivity* in terms of *intersubjective testability*; that is, see objectivity as a property of the institutional structuring of the community of thinkers. This concession would not, I fear, be epistemologically radical enough for Fabian. He argues that *reality itself*, not simply the method of study of reality, depends on intersubjectivity.[17] He found it impossible to do justice to, indeed, as it were to find and observe, the Jamaa movement while operating within the standard categories of the anthropology of religion, namely: dogma, organization, rituals, specific beliefs. The Jamaa movement turned out to be unified more by the words and ideas which constituted it (as opposed to being analytical aspects of it).

The immediate and obvious difficulty which Fabian's anthropologist faces is that of communicating with his peers, i.e., other anthropologists. The language of communicative interaction in *this* case is English, and if the anthropologist is to offer to the anthropological public such knowledge of other peoples as he has acquired, he has to do so in such a way that those of us who know no Katanga Swahili, and do not wish to, can grasp what he has learned. He has in other words to *translate* his understanding into *our* language, *our* categories. He has to extend his field of communicative interaction with the Jamaa to include us. If he cannot do this, then he cannot do anthropology. If he does this, his strictures about our present anthropological language and the restrictiveness of its categories or conceptual scheme are disposed of.

The result of the efforts of Fabian's anthropologist may also conform to anthropological practice, since they are unlikely to be in ordinary English and hence will not be bounded by the conceptual limitations of that medium. Anthropological literature is nowadays written in a semi-technical language with a vocabulary drawn from sociology, biology, law, and so on, and from many primitive languages. *Taboo, mana, kula,* and *kwoth*, not to mention Fabian's *mawazo* (ideas, thoughts) are introduced not simply as foreign names, but as foreign *concepts* or categories which the anthropologist will often expend pages if not chapters to explicate. The language of a science, whether of physics or of anthropology, has to draw most of its key categories and concepts from diverse sources, and thus is not subject to the limitations of any one language or reality-production. Fabian has found in the Jamaa movement a case which calls for critical scrutiny of the categories in which the anthropology of religion is done. But I fear this concession also will not be enough to satisfy him.

There are theoretical as well as practical difficulties for Fabian, however: language simply cannot *constitute* or make up the social context, the totality within which particulars come into existence. There is *something* to this; but there is also something very misleading about it. Language, in addition to constituting or shaping the social context (and, doubtless, being shaped by it), is not *entirely* dependent upon it—this is as true of natural language as it is of the language of science. On this relative independence turns the possibility of language being powerful enough to distinguish and discuss real and imaginary alternatives, to question classification and individuation, to pose alternative explanations of why things are as they are. It is true that besides using language to map the social world as we see it, *the social world as we see it may well be influenced by our language-mapping operations.* But the vital capacity of languages for enabling us to discuss whether a map is veridical, to compare alternative and even competing maps of the same world, is what makes social science possible (Jarvie 1972:159-165). If language not only incorporates theories about society, but is itself inextricably entangled with the society it articulates, it is not clear how language can ever be used—either ordinarily or in science—to describe a society, compare it to others, improve upon our knowledge of it, etc. Any propositional knowledge of society becomes impossible. (As a corollary, any propositional knowledge of language itself becomes impossible. Language, we are told, constitutes a social context. I say that it also is a way of discussing and modifying that social context. Moreover, it also becomes a way of discussing and modifying itself—language. We can discuss a language in that language, so that language must in some way transcend or stand aside from itself.)

While the stress on language and on intersubjectivity is fine, the privatization of anthropology, its ultimate inability to issue in a set of explanatory propositions, is disastrous. Anthropology is in grave danger not only of trading in incommunicable mysteries, but also of treating the categories of the actors' languages as somehow sacrosanct, forgetting that the very problems which gave birth to the subject in general and this or that individual field study in particular, are not a product of those indigenous languages and conceptual schemes. Anthropology is, after all, debate about certain problems—such as the rational unity of mankind—and, while these problems are in principle accessible to all languages and cultures, as a fortuitous matter of fact they originated and are mainly pursued in the civilized Western world. We are deceiving ourselves if we ever imagine we can approach the Jamaa without that background. More harshly, the Jamaa cult is of no anthropological interest unless it bears on, connects up with, that background. The entities and categories in terms of which anthropological discussion is conducted may only partially correspond with the way the actors see the world. But *seeing the world the way the actors do is emphatically not the aim of anthropology.* It is at best a *means,* sometimes useful, sometimes not, for furthering the true aim, which is to solve some problems of the tradition of inquiry known as anthropology.

Tradition is what gives continuity to anthropology, what gives the enterprise order and sense. Bold argument, thinking about the problems, pursuit of ever more general theoretical explanations, *that* makes sense. A complete break with the past is a contradiction in terms. Revisionist thinking about the tradition and its problems can, though, go very deep indeed. My colleague J. O. Wisdom has suggested (1972) that there are at least three analytically distinct layers of theory in the tradition, and criticism is deep to the degree it penetrates those layers. There are: empirical theories; the embedded ontology often common to competing empirical theories; and the Weltanschauung or metaphysical systems behind whole clusters of theories. Change of theory is almost routine ("normal"); change of ontology can cause an upheaval; change of metaphysics or Weltanschauung is an earthquake. The current crisis manifests itself in stagnation at the theoretical level. Fabian wants reform at the level of embedded ontology. I suggest that current debate needs to re-connect itself to its metaphysical roots, perhaps to shift back for a while to reconsideration of those seemingly vague and woolly, but actually clear and germane metaphysical issues connected with the rational unity of mankind. Radical change is not on the agenda, I suggest, since the ultimate metaphysical scaffolding for the study of man is unlikely to change, but it needs reconsideration and reinterpretation.

Hence, although I acknowledge crisis, I am not pessimistic and I resist radicalism. In what follows I shall explain why anthropology is healthier than it looks.

CRITICISM NOT REVOLUTION

My first point would be a simple one: radical anthropologists have been critical of anthropology while remaining anthropologists. In a certain sense, this is a vindication of the critical openness of anthropology. Openness is a feature of its social organization, a feature copied from the natural sciences, a feature that is conducive to deeply critical reflection—as deep, that is, as the problem seems to warrant. My second point is that Fabian's experience in the field, that he could not carry out his investigations according to his preconceptions, is absolutely the rule rather than the exception. This is partly why fieldwork is set up as an open-ended activity, the researcher following where his nose for interesting material leads him. My third point would be, then, why does Fabian—not to mention his radical cohorts Diamond, Hymes, Scholte, Wolf, et al. (Hymes 1972)—consider that the crisis demands a fundamental overhaul of anthropology, why do they think anthropology cannot continue as before, steadily changing in response to the growth of knowledge? Because, I suggest, they are overwhelmed by the inconsistency between anthropology's claim to be scientific, and its manifest absence of a body of true doctrine. Here is where we part ways once more, because I view science as a mode of organizing intellectual activity, a social model for openmindedness; they seem to regard it as a stock of true knowledge. Agreed that its aim is true knowledge; that any particular piece of alleged knowledge is not true is not a legitimate general complaint. That science can slide from straightforward empirical criticism right back into scrutiny of its metaphysical, methodological, and categorical underpinnings is what makes it science. So Fabian is exemplifying the method he criticizes.

It would be complacent, I think, to dismiss the possibilities of a phenomenological *putsch* too lightly just because it is unnecessary and because it hasn't happened yet. For one thing, the discipline does perceive itself as in crisis, so people are looking for a release from the tension. For another, the tension is increased by two aspects of present-day anthropology which arouse faculty and student *guilt*. One is that anthropology is about Third World peoples. This in itself provokes guilt, only partly because these peoples were often colonized or enslaved by ancestors of those now studying anthropology. The other is scientism. There is abroad some kind of revulsion from science that is not easily gainsaid. It stems not only out of what might be called the argument from the atom bomb or the argument from the use of technology to manipulate and exploit; but, more generally, because of a visceral feeling that the world of science is a cold, inhuman, mechanical place. Hardly an appropriate mood in which to study the lives of other humans. Phenomenology has the appeal that it overcomes both guilts simultaneously. By seeing anthropology as a process or outcome of *human* interaction between anthropologist and tribesman, it makes the scientist an equal participant with his subjects, and science no longer prevents them from falling into a warm and communicative embrace.

From all this I dissent strongly, although not, I hope, from warmth, humanity, and equality. But I do not see how we can abandon the subject/object distinction, and I think the ethics are inherently ambiguous. Those who think they can be pure are deceiving themselves. On the first of these, the observer/observed distinction, I am a realist. Science argues about the world, a world that was there before there was science, and which will be there after science has gone, hence a world in some if not all respects existing independently of science. There is a world and a science of that world, phenomena and observers of those phenomena, facts independent of theories, knowledge independent of social status, kinship connection, cultural or linguistic membership, political power, or ritual condition. The objects of this world are not arbitrary; they are what has been found problematic and hence what wants explanation. Anthropology is cross-cultural, implicitly where not explicitly, and hence inevitably and correctly uses concepts and categories that are not indigenous but as it were external to the *lebenswelt* of the culture described (Gellner 1973:199). True, the cultural and social process constituted by [subjects plus anthropologist] is not the same as the cultural and social process constituted by the [subjects without the anthropologist]. There is a problem of interference. It does not follow that the anthropologist should make no attempt to subtract his influence and see the society as it was without him.

As for ethical ambiguity, anthropology is a Western science, a product of a specific society and its culture.[18] That culture teaches that there is a vast gulf between cognitive systems which separate the knower from the known and those which do not. Yet one cannot wish the gulf away, and one cannot cross over to the other side and pretend it isn't there. The gulf is a modern version of the irreversibility of gaining the knowledge of good and evil. If one's guilt at this is overwhelming, one had better not pretend to be an anthropologist.

Phenomenology, then, in anthropology as in philosophy, is an anti-science revolt (Agassi 1972). It suggests science presents us with a cold, inhuman, mechanical world and develops a manipulative and exploitative attitude to that world:[19] hence the link-up with the humanistic and socialist objections to science. There is some truth in this. Should therefore science be abandoned? Should we give up the search for cognitively powerful, hopefully true views of the world? Should we substitute "deep subjectivity" for not being judges in our own cause? My answer is no; we cannot give up, and we should not give up (ought implies can). We cannot give up because we must strive continually to come to terms with the world we inhabit, and that is all science is. We should not give up because to try and fail is better than not to try at all. Moral power goes with cognitive power, the ability to make the world a better place develops hand in hand with the power to make it so. This assumes that we can use the analytic if unreal device of standing back from the world, of trying to see it as it is and not how we want it to be. We can do this to our own selves, so why not to other selves? Moreover, a social group is there before an anthropologist visits it, and I see no logical or moral objection to the anthropologist wishing to get an approximate picture of what that social group is like and how it works when he is not there. Of course he can do that only by going there and hence altering the situation, but again, he can make a harmless analytical abstraction.

I dissent, then, from those who wish an end to scientific anthropology, although this may be more on account of my view of what science is than a defense of current practice. One thing is clear enough: anthropology is not currently displaying much vigor or theoretical progress.

Here we are at the heart of the matter as I see it. Evolution, diffusion, function were all pretty *thin*; they were hardly ever theories in any full-blooded sense at all. Anthropology was long powered by fieldwork—a practice, not a theory. Excellent as that practice was, its promoters oversold it with thoroughly bad arguments. Among these were scientistic or positivist arguments that fieldwork would build an empirical science, undermine racial prejudice, and eliminate such Bad Things as speculation about the history of mankind and about the metaphysics of cognition and valuation. These bad arguments were used to transform eager but malleable students from lovers of adventure or of the exotic and bizarre or of the problem of the cognitive and moral unity of mankind into working social anthropologists.[20] Now the bad arguments have come back to haunt and disappoint, for in the end, people do anthropology because they love the exotic and the bizarre, or because they are fascinated by racialism, or because they wish to speculate on the history of mankind and the metaphysics of cognition and valuation. Disappointment awaits those who ever get out from under the fieldwork and the training and realize that the promised land hasn't been sighted, that the science hasn't been built, and that those crude early speculations of the pioneers are still the basic starting point. The crudity and naïveté of anthropological debate on issues such as the unity of mankind, race, social evolution, relativism, and so on, takes the breath away. I recently had occasion to review the so called relativism literature of the immediate post-war period, in which distinguished names like Herskovits, Kluckhohn, and Linton took part, and my philosophical hair stood on end at the dogmatism and confusion. An all-time classic is the pathetic and embarrassing statement on Human Rights of 1947 (*AA* 49:539-543) which couldn't even come up with a clear doctrine that would avoid re-endorsing, say, binding the feet of women in China or internal passports in Russia. So far from years of anthropological research yielding new and deep insights into such questions, the dismaying fact is that earlier debates were of higher quality. Relativism, e.g., is better argued by St. Paul (Romans 14:10-23). The reason is not far to seek. Serious debate of these issues was for long discouraged, but positions on them were built into much anthropological work. Hence they became dogmas that people had forgotten how to defend.

One of the key points is that fieldwork practice was a-historical. So far as fieldwork was concerned, primitive peoples had *no* history, only a present. Even their recollections were part of the present. Curiously, and amusingly, this a-historism was self-referring, and post-revolutionary anthropology tried to pretend that *it* had no past; that the crazy, wild, exciting debates about whether there were men before Adam, whether slaves had souls, whether animals were machines, whether primitives were promiscuous, whether savagery was inherent, and a whole lot of other charged issues, had no connection with the bold new anthropology. Of course they had, as could be seen by examining what the new anthropology put in place of history, namely orally transmitted historical myths about the speculative and racialist darkness in which pre-anthropology was cloaked. This legitimated dismissing history once revolutionary enlightenment was achieved.

It is here that we may hope for a transformation. It is time for anthropologists to do genuine history of anthropology, to cease treating their own predecessors the way they accused those predecessors of treating savages, namely as backward, stupid, etc. (Jarvie 1969), to cease, in other words, transmitting oral myths about anthropological history which smack of the armchair on the veranda, and buckle down to some fieldwork, with its hardships and rewards, in the history of anthropology itself. The problems and debates of our anthropologist ancestors deserve our concern and respect, partly as a matter of right, and partly because we have a lot to learn from them. What anthropology is about cannot be understood without its history, and the more flippantly its history is dismissed as an embarrassment, the poorer self-understanding will be, the more the signs of crisis will grow. Anthropology should perhaps seek resurrection in the anthropology of anthropology.

NOTES

[1] Earlier versions of this paper were read to anthropology seminars at McMaster University (February 28, 1974), at York University (March 8, 1974), and at the State University of New York at Buffalo (March 14, 1974).

[2] Boas's fieldwork was buried in 10,000 pages of unreadable prose, in which there were contradictions, vacillations, and no coherent account of the social organization (White 1966:6-7).

[3] This syndrome is not noted by that specialist in crises of science, Kuhn (1962).

[4] The *American Anthropologist* is occasionally ludicrous in this respect, as one can test by reading aloud a typical contents list (say, for October 1973, 75:1187) to an audience of colleagues in neighboring fields.

[5] Bidney's survey (1953) is now more than twenty years old.

[6] Beattie (1964), Lienhardt (1964), Mair (1965), Harris (1971), Fried (1973), etc.

[7] Which is one reason why sociology takes as much of its subject matter what amounts to commentary on Marx (cf. Jarvie 1972:124).

[8] What is true and what false (the sum is false) in Marx is discussed in Popper (1962, Chs. 18-21). Classical and neo-classical economics consist of models based on theoretical assumptions (perfect knowledge, free entry, infinite divisibility and elasticity of supply and demand) which are *known* to be quite false. The results are then compared to reality and adjustments made to the assumptions to improve the approximation. The falsity of all current anthropological theories is precisely the reason for the sense of crisis.

[9] Popper (1963:3-30) calls this the theory that truth is manifest, there for all those with eyes to see it. On this theory, error equals blindness, distortion. It is falling into error, rather than the achievement of truth that needs explanation. Popper argues that the situation is the other way around.

[10] In his remarkable work, the author of that surrealist fantasy *The Nature of Cultural Things* (1964), comes forth with dogmatic pronouncements on complex philosophical questions such as what truly or genuinely constitutes science and scientific method, and proceeds to berate almost every figure in the long history of anthropology. Under the odd impression that Marx, White, Steward, and himself have found the secret of the universe ("cultural materialism"), he orchestrates the whole history of anthropology up to this climax (climacteric?). That there is a protracted and bitter debate about the nature of science; that the status of the social sciences has several quite odd features; that Hayek has warned about the dangers of aping science in garbled form; all this has apparently escaped Harris's selective reading. Of course it makes for exciting reading. History has a plot and the plot has a climax—the revolutionary take-over by cultural materialism. Unfortunately the plot is a travesty of the real dialogue going on in the history and encourages a cavalier hindsight attitude to the great minds of the past. Another inauthentic debunking and devaluing revolution. Malinowski at least had fieldwork to offer.

[11] May in a certain sense not exist. Popper's classic (1959) is in terms of proposed methodological rules (conventions) for science, not factual generalizations about science.

[12] Such a view of science has been developed by Agassi (1964), Popper (1963:97-119, 184-200), Watkins (1958) and Wisdom (1972).

[13] Cf. my remarks about "study the ritual not the belief" (1964:44).

[14] Lucidly expounded by Cowley (1968).

[15] Especially the four moderate and sympathetic papers by Ryle (1971:167-224).

[16] I have tried to show this in my 1975b.

[17] There is deep error in this formulation. See Popper's (1970:56-57) critique of Mercier.

[18] More precisely, of a sub-society and its sub-culture. This qualification is extremely important.

[19] Interestingly enough, Marx, like Bacon, thought the aim of dominating nature was a Good Thing.

[20] This process is beautifully described in the autobiographical section of Fox (1973:3-40).

REFERENCES CITED

Agassi, J.
    1959 Epistemology as an Aid to Science. British Journal for the Philosophy of Science 10:139-146.
    1964 The Nature of Scientific Problems and their Roots in Metaphysics. *In* The Critical Approach to Science and Philosophy. Mario Bunge, Ed. New York: Free Press.
    1972 Sociologism in Philosophy of Science. Metaphilosophy 3:103-122.
Anonymous
    1974 *Review of* Tristes Tropiques, by C. Lévi-Strauss. *In* Times Literary Supplement, Feb. 22:188.
Beattie, John
    1964 Other Cultures. London: Cohen and West.
Berger, Peter, and Thomas Luckmann
    1966 The Social Construction of Reality. New York: Doubleday.
Bidney, David
    1953 Theoretical Anthropology. New York: Columbia University Press.
Cowley, Fraser
    1968 A Critique of British Empiricism. London: Macmillan.
Fabian, Johannes
    1971 Language, History and Anthropology. Philosophy of the Social Sciences 1:19-47.
Fox, Robin
    1973 Encounter with Anthropology. New York: Harcourt Brace Jovanovich.
Fried, Morton
    1973 Explorations in Anthropology. New York: Thomas Y. Crowell.
Gellner, Ernest
    1973 Cause and Meaning in the Social Sciences. Boston: Routledge and Kegan Paul.
Harris, Marvin
    1964 The Nature of Cultural Things. New York: Random House.
    1968 The Rise of Anthropological Theory. New York: Thomas Y. Crowell.
    1971 Culture, Man, and Nature. New York: Thomas Y. Crowell.
Hayek, F. A.
    1955 The Counterrevolution of Science. Glencoe: The Free Press. (Originally in Economica 1942 9:267-291; 1943 10:34-63; 1944 11:27-39.)
Hymes, Dell
    1972 Reinventing Anthropology. New York: Random House.
Jarvie, I. C.
    1964 The Revolution in Anthropology. New York: Humanities.
    1968 The Emergence of Social Anthropology from Philosophy. Philosophical Forum 1:73-84.
    1969 Evans-Pritchard on the Anthropology of Religion. International Journal of Comparative Sociology 10:286-291.
    1972 Concepts and Society. Boston: Routledge and Kegan Paul.
    1975a *Review of* Anthropologists and Anthropology, by Adam Kuper. Philosophy of the Social Sciences 4:302-305.
    1975b Cultural Relativism Again. Philosophy of the Social Sciences (forthcoming).
Kuhn, Thomas
    1962 The Structure of Scientific Revolutions. Chicago: University of Chicago Press.
Kuper, Adam
    1973 Anthropologists and Anthropology. The British School 1922-1972. London: Allen Lane.
Lienhardt, Godfrey
    1964 Social Anthropology. New York: Oxford University Press.
Mair, Lucy
    1965 An Introduction to Social Anthropology. London: Oxford University Press.
Poincaré, H.
    n.d. Science and Method. New York: Dover.

Popper, Karl R.
    1959   The Logic of Scientific Discovery. New York: Basic Books.
    1962   The Open Society and Its Enemies. London: Routledge and Kegan Paul.
    1963   Conjectures and Refutations. London: Routledge and Kegan Paul.
    1970   Comments. *In* Physics, Logic and History. W. Yourgrau and A. D. Breck, Eds. New York: Plenum.
Ryle, Gilbert
    1971   Collected Papers, Vol. I. London: Hutchinson.
Schutz, Alfred
    1964   Collected Papers, Vols. I and II. The Hague: Martinus Nijhoff.
Watkins, J. W. N.
    1958   Confirmable and Influential Metaphysics. Mind 67:344-365.
White, Leslie A.
    1966   The Social Organisation of Ethnological Theory. Rice University Studies 52:1-66.
Wisdom, J. O.
    1972   Scientific Theory: Empirical Content, Embedded Ontology and Weltanschauung. Philosophy and Phenomenological Research 33:162-177.

CHAPTER 13

ON THE LIMITS OF SYMBOLIC INTERPRETATION IN ANTHROPOLOGY[1]

I

This paper offers some sceptical arguments against "symbolic" interpretations of human action. The general doctrine criticised is nowhere very clearly or explicitly stated; still less is it argued for. Before attempting to formulate it, I give an illustration (Leach 1974:1074):

> An ethnographer observes a man killing a sheep by cutting its throat. A bystander, when asked what is going on, replies: "He is making an offering to the ancestors". What is the logical status of such a statement? What does it "mean" apart from its standing as a description of the sacrificer's actions? How does it come to mean what it means? Does it always mean the same thing? These are issues of great complexity and, for anthropologists anyway, of great importance.

To my mind, the bystander's explanation of what is going on is quite enough.[2] The subsequent questions are frequently leading, in that they rest on assumptions (e.g., who says they "mean" anything, apart from . . .?) — if they did not, they would have no answers; in that any complexity is self-created; and in that they are of no explanatory, i.e., scientific, importance whatsoever. I shall argue that when I describe a man peering down a microscope as "doing research on enzymes", the cognitive status of that statement is no different from that of "He is making an offering to the ancestors". Cognition is univocal, I shall maintain. The approach of looking for symbolic meanings adds unfruitful complication to anthropology, is fundamentally arbitrary, and is morally dubious.

A preliminary attempt to formulate the doctrine to be criticised might be: all human actions have a significance beyond any stated or manifest purpose, namely, they symbolise, stand for, or say something or other.[3] A weaker version would be: human actions "which are not immediately explainable as a rational response to a given situation, or in which the explanations offered do not appear to relate directly to the observable facts" (Leach 1974:1074), symbolise, stand for, or say something or other. The strong thesis would lead one to see symbolism everywhere; the weaker thesis looks for it only when rationality or observation give no immediate explanation.

197

Common to the two is a distinction between practical or instrumental (or rational or observable) purpose and symbolic or communicative purpose. I shall contest this distinction.

Among anthropologists the fashion for trying to "read" the symbolism of myths, religions, taboos, ceremonies, social arrangements, social structures, meals, classification systems, etc., is so widespread that criticising it may seem about as effective as spitting into the wind. Further, to do this with very general arguments risks bypassing the blinkered and decidophobic[4] specialist. It is the values and limits of the whole enterprise of symbolic interpretation that I want to call into question, so transcendental arguments are unavoidable. However, they will be directed, not at an extensive literature survey, but at a single, in some ways representative piece. While constituting an exemplar of the whole symbolic-interpretation approach,[5] and hence a suitable focus for my discussion, its suitability is enhanced because it also has atypical features. The atypicalities stem from its authorship: E. R. Leach is a bold and forceful writer, a thoroughgoing rationalist, an anthropologist willing and able to follow the argument wherever it leads. Unlike that of so many other practitioners of the symbolic-interpretation approach, who trade in hint, allusion, insinuation, nonsequitur, and free association, Leach's work makes argument not just worthwhile, but possible.

II

The Royal Anthropological Institute of Great Britain is an old and prestigious learned society. Among the honours in its gift are several annual public lectures, named in honour of distinguished ancestors.[6] An invitation to deliver one of these is recognition of high status,[7] guarantee of a distinguished audience,[8] and (usually) promise of subsequent publication. In 1966 E. R. Leach[9] delivered the Henry Myers[10] Lecture,[11] which was published are next year in the Institute's *Proceedings*. Entitled "Virgin Birth", the lecture takes up a controversy Leach himself had triggered. Leach (1961) had argued that reports of primitive peoples who did not know the connection between coition and pregnancy were not to be trusted. He suggested that this connection is known in every society and that denials should not be taken at face value. Leach uses the occasion of this lecture to develop in more detail his ideas about how such denials are to be taken, using the Malinowskian device of drawing attention to a similar aspect of our own society — the Christian doctrine of virgin birth — to highlight his points. He also takes the opportunity to argue vigorously the strength of his approach and the weaknesses of those who maintain that belief in virgin birth should be taken at face value.

With characteristic directness, Leach goes to the heart of the matter. Belief in virgin birth is belief in something that cannot be true (Leach 1967:44—45):

> How should we interpret ethnographical statements of palpable untruth? . . . say that it is a species of religious dogma; the truth which it expresses does not relate to the ordinary matter-of-fact world of everyday things but to metaphysics. It is plain . . . that Christians who say that they "believe" in the doctrine of Virgin Birth . . . are not ordinarily arguing from a position of ignorance. . . .Frazer's childish savage should be eliminated from anthropological discussion once and for all; in his place we should put a slightly muddle-headed theologian . . . .

A slightly muddle-headed theologian is he who believes palpable untruths. Clearly not stemming from ignorance, such untruths must be metaphysical. "Metaphysical" is here distinguished from "the ordinary matter-of-fact world of everyday things".[12] In metaphysics, virgin births can be affirmed; in the ordinary matter-of-fact world of everyday things, they cannot. To do so would make the affirmers look childish.

The distinction between the everyday world and metaphysics is familiar enough (at least to a philosopher). In the distant past it was used by positivists to deride metaphysics. Leach uses it to rescue palpable falsehoods from ridicule by calling them metaphysics.[13] In a similar way, after the Second World War, philosophers of religion used the positivist's own distinction to shield religion from positivist attack. Another notable use made of it was in social anthropology, where it became a device to get anthropologists to take religious, magical, paradoxical, and absurd statements seriously (see Agassi and Jarvie 1967, 1973). Broadly speaking, the key idea is to divide beliefs and actions into two kinds: practical, instrumental, and functional ones and meaningful or symbolically expressive ones. Hence, statements about virgin birth, or babies arriving by stork and being found under gooseberry bushes, have to be taken with a grain of metaphysical (or symbolic) salt. Statements about how to wield an adze, sail a canoe, plant a seed, or cast a fishing net are, by contrast, practical, instrumental, and functional: in short: they mean exactly what they say,[14] no more and no less. Why the difference between the instrumental and the symbolic? Clearly, because if we do not make the distinction, cognition becomes univocal, and statements about virgin birth are to be treated exactly as the statements about studying enzymes. By introducing an element of symbolism or expressive meaning, statements that might otherwise have been dismissed as superstition or muddle can once again be taken seriously. If a man tells me I am losing the game because I am

holding the squash racquet incorrectly, I will take what he says at its face
value. If, however, he tells me my game is poor because I haven't found
Christ,[15] likely I will smile condescendingly. Why? Because I don't share the
cultural context needed to unpack all he means by "finding Christ". It could
be that, translated, it means, 'obeying the coach in the name of the Lord".
Once I saw this, I would take his comment seriously, even if I didn't agree
with it.

Presumably this makes clear why Leach entertains symbolic interpretations. It allows things to be taken seriously that in another context might
be dismissed. It explains how intelligent Catholics who know the connection
between intercourse and pregnancy can affirm the Immaculate Conception;
it similarly rescues the Australian Aborigines, not to mention flat-earthers
and fundamentalists. Leach himself instances the saying of Latin grace in
Trinity College Hall (Sir James Frazer's college). Neither superstition nor
devotion can be inferred from this, it is merely a sign that the meal is about
to begin or has just ended — "the actual word content is totally irrelevant"
(p. 41). Similarly, the English marriage ritual tells us about the formal social
relations being established between the parties.

This basic doctrine — that what people say and do has a symbolic dimension — is very widely diffused in the intellectual world, including anthropology. And no wonder; it is very plausible. Observing Leach in the act of
pounding the typewriter keys, we might say he is acting instrumentally —
writing his forthcoming Henry Myers Lecture. Observing him later mounting
the steps to the rostrum with crossed fingers, we might say he is signalling
the importance of the occasion and perhaps his own hope that he will be
well received. This is much kinder than suggesting he is superstitious and
trying to ward off bad fortune. Now consider that subclass of actions we call
speechacts. A ritual performance like delivery of a lecture to the Royal
Anthropological Institute is functional; murmuring grace in Trinity College
Hall is symbolic expression. No doubt the boundaries between functional and
symbolic may shift over time, and no doubt every action is partly symbolic
and partly functional. Nevertheless, the two can be kept analytically distinct,
and different approaches to them by anthropologists are in order. Statements
or ceremonies connected with virgin birth cannot be treated as anthropologically equivalent to the lectures of a social scientist discussing that same
doctrine on a cross-cultural basis. Hence religious actions and utterances,
magical rituals and utterances, and otherwise absurd or unintelligible actions
and utterances cannot just be labelled as such and critically explained; they
must be scrutinised for their symbolic "meaning", how they came to mean

that, and whether they always and everywhere mean the same thing. Doctrines of virgin birth, wherever they are found, should be taken symbolically, not literally. They cannot be taken literally because they are false and well-known throughout the world to be false. It is "impossible on common-sense grounds" (p. 45) that what is well-known to most of mankind should not be known to all.[16] To say that Mariolaters do not know the connection between pregnancy and coition would be to accuse them of childish ignorance or stupidity, and, in anthropology, ignorance is a term of abuse (p. 41). Furthermore, Leach argues, causal or historical explanations of the idea of virgin birth are not acceptable because they are "inaccessible to observation or verification" (p. 43).

Agreeing to label his own position "vulgar positivism", Leach suggests that to those who practice symbolic interpretation "insight comes simply from seeing how the facts fit together" (p. 39), rather as the pieces of a jigsaw puzzle (p. 44) fit together to form a pattern. It is a comparative attempt to examine the variety of forms in which a single ethnographic pattern can manifest itself (p. 44).

In the case of ideas of virgin birth among Aborigines or in Christian doctrine, Leach develops further the idea that they refer not to the everyday world but to metaphysics. That is, they are about the difference between the physical and the metaphysical (p. 46), i.e., the split between the here-and-now and the not here-and-now, between the living and the no longer or not yet living, between men and gods. Virgin birth is a way of saying men and gods can interact (sexually). For Leach and, I suspect, for others of the symbolic-interpretationist persuasion, "there are different kinds of truth" (p. 44).

III

That the assumptions involved in symbolic interpretation should be replete with bad philosophy is one thing; that they contain bad anthropology as well means they shouldn't be let pass. Such patternings as symbolic interpretation discloses have, I submit, neither interest nor point. In his usual disarming way, Leach himself asks, "What is the point of arranging the facts in this way? How do I *know* that such patterns are significant? I don't. I find them interesting" (p. 45). This may be an argument-stopper in certain anthropological circles, but perhaps a philosopher can be forgiven for being a sceptical spoil-sport. Leach has himself suggested that "anthropological theories often tell us more about the anthropologists than about their subject matter" (p. 46). This excellent anthropological principle applies very well to the symbolic-interpretation theory espoused by Leach, even though he is not like those anthropologists of a crypto-religious persuasion, but a self-proclaimed positivist and a rationalist. The anthropology of symbolic interpretation is thus highly interesting.

Leach's central argument is that error = stupidity and abuse. that the contradictory and incoherevnt views of 'good Catholics" are easier to respect than those of earlier anthropologists such as Hartland, McLennan, and Tylor. This incomprehensible preference for the sophistries of theologians over the condescension of his rationalist predecessors makes anthropological but not philosophical sense. We remember that, after grace, the Provost of Kings has to eat with the former, but not with the latter. Leach's predecessors' turning in their graves counts less than the comfort it must bring to so many of his colleagues that positivism presents such a toothless mouth towards religion. Yet I feel there is something cheap in this kind of argument, even though Leach himself uses it against his oppenents (living and dead).[17] If philosophically sophisticated religious men and sociologically sophisticated anthropologists at Cambridge, Oxford, and elsewhere have this symbolic-interpretation approach to religion and magic in common, it is possible to take it two ways. The first is to take the symbolic-interpretation view, like the virgin-birth view, as merely a symbolic expression. That is to say, we should view Henry Myers Lectures and the like as rituals, perhaps as sermons, exhorting us not to condescend. Argument and scholarship are just a kind of conjuror's patter to keep the audience distracted while the social signals are being made. How, though, do we know that the patter is to be read symbolically, not instrumentally? By the same reasoning, obviously, that Leach uses to persuade us to view the virgin birth doctrine symbolically: its author is not a child or an ignoramus, but a slightly muddle-headed theologian.

Now, how do we decide that the dogmas of Mother Church or the Henry Myers Lectures are the work of slightly muddle-headed theologians? The answer again is the same: because the "patter" is palpably false and cannot be taken seriously, i.e., instrumentally. Underlying this point is a point of agreement between Leach and his critics which should be stressed, because Leach plays it down. Even those who indulge in symbolic interpretation do not take everything to have a hidden meaning. Most statements and actions do not; and anyway, we always have to begin by taking the text, whether dogma or lecture, seriously, i.e., at its face value. This is a kind of moral obligation upon those who do not wish to condescend: we must give a text and hence its author the benefit of the doubt. To begin with, even virgin birth and symbolic interpretation beg to be judged true or false. Only when we fail on that assumption to get any sense may we, perhaps, allow ourselves to be condescending, to say "this cannot mean what it says". Hence, to have a "different kind of truth" is a consolation prize for being false, plain and simple. "Different kinds of truth" is symbolic-interpretationist talk for "What status can we possibly confer on palpable falsehoods?" As we have seen, to read even this manoeuvre as a piece of symbolic expression involves the prior move of trying to take it at face value and failing. In the rest of this paper I shall stick to looking at the face value of the symbolic-interpretation view; but in the event that the reader comes to agree with me that it is false, he may then wish as I do to declare the symbolic-interpretation view symbolic, and I shall offer occasional hints as to how this can be carried through.

IV

Against the view that human actions and statements can be explained or understood by means of an interpretation of their hidden symbolism, I would like to begin with a very simple but transcendental argument. This is that there are many different systems of symbolic interpretation on offer. These systems compete with one another. Possibly someone might argue that the competition is a muddle, and in fact they are consistent and could be mapped onto each other in order to form a single coherent system. Good luck to anyone who tries that one. Meanwhile, for purposes of my argument, I assume that the systems of symbolic interpretation of Durkheim, Freud, Jung, Malinowski, Radcliffe-Brown, Lévi-Strauss, Leach, Turner, Douglas, Sperber, et al., are incompatible.

Now, either they all have an equal claim on our attention, in which case their incoherence and inconsistency are bewildering, or one is correct and the others are not (merely symbolic expressions, if you will). In the latter case, which is the correct one? How do we check its correctness? Why is there no agreement on it? There being no answer to any of these questions, one is inclined to conclude that the proliferation of systems of symbolic interpretation is an anarchy brought about by there being no standards in the field. This may be why Leach simply says he can't defend his own system of interpretation, but finds it interesting. Many people find many different things interesting; many people find many different things a bore. I find arbitrary proliferation of symbolic systems (or facts) a bore. Moreover, the science of anthropology not being coincident with Leach's undefended interests, I conclude that the unresolvable conflict between systems of symbolic interpretation possibly signals arbitrariness and hence allows us to declare them either false and uninteresting, false and symbolically revealing, or whatever.

A second, equally simple, and closely related argument explains this possible arbitrariness. To seek the meaning or symbolic interpretation of an utterance or ceremony presupposes that a determinate meaning exists. Supposing it does, how did it get there? When a signaller waves his flags, or a Balinese dancer caresses the air, we know the gestures carry an intentional meaning. The code has a cipher. What reason have we to think that the religious and magical actions of people contain (coded) messages over and above the intentional meaning of the acts and words? Is Leach not here a prisoner of his metaphors? Society is after all neither a language nor a jigsaw puzzle. The symbolic-interpretationist's metaphors, then, are highly misleading. they make him no better than a muddle-headed theologian. Since no account of how any alleged meanings got there is available, we are forced to withdraw the supposition that a determinate meaning does indeed exist. Meanings, patterns, symbols that are determinate are there only when they have been put there. Symbolic-interpretationists sometimes resemble those who scrutinise the works of Shakespeare for the hidden messages from Francis Bacon, Ben Jonson, or Christopher Marlowe (with the difference that such scrutinisers assume that Bacon, Jonson, or Marlowe put the messages there). No one has yet considered the pattern Shakespeare's use of individual letters makes on the printed page and dismissed objections to the pointlessness of it by declaring that he found it interesting.

I am not saying that every social pattern or regularity is (consciously or unconsciously) intended. On the contrary, I follow the tradition from Mandeville and Smith to Hayek and Popper in thinking most of what we call society to be the product of human action, but not of human design. I do no more than invoke a principle of intellectual economy against looking for hidden messages that are not there, and more so against hidden messages that are not quite messages, whose interest cannot be explained, and which appear to explain nothing and proliferate in a confusing way. Against such muddle-headed theology the dogma of virgin birth is a paradigm of clarity.

Are we not to conclude from these first two arguments that nothing is gained by hunting symbolic interpretations of palpable falsehoods? That such interpretations are arbitrary and will proliferate bewilderingly because of the false assumption that a determinate interpretation exists? In fact there is no determinate interpretation; still less is there a canonical one. Or is it perhaps the case that these two transcendental philosophical arguments are hard to grasp? Since I have accused Leach of anthropological and moral, as well as philosophical, error, let me come at the issue again from a different angle, using other arguments.

Let us take some quite uncontested platitudes: One reason people do things (say grace, perform rain dances, give lectures) is habit. Another reason is beliefs they hold which convert easily into imperatives to action (if you don't attend mass regularly, things will go badly for you later; if you don't bring your children up in the faith, how will they be saved? if you neglect the rain dance, you might be responsible for the drought; scholars have a duty to give lectures). I say that all the resultant actions should be explained by the beliefs. Let us put, as it were, this question to Leach. What status does he accord to such beliefs? Some are palpably false, at least one is not; all lead to concrete action in the matter-of-fact, everyday world. Are they metaphysics, symbols? Although he doesn't believe in taking the contents of the words too seriously in every case, Leach clearly wants to separate beliefs that are palpably untrue from all other beliefs a person professes to be holding. How that is to be managed without attending to the contents of the words is unclear; what criterion demarcates word content that can be taken seriously (e.g., Henry Myers Lectures) from word content that is irrelevant (e.g., the wedding ceremony, Latin grace in Trinity College Hall) is nowhere stated. Nor can it be, for, to repeat, Leach must himself operate on the principle that we take a text or an utterance literally and seriously at first and desist from this only when we fail. Fail to do what? Make it come out true, of course. Hidden lemma: utterances and texts which fail to come out true represent a failure on our part to take them sufficiently seriously, i.e., to come up with a symbolic reading, or a notion of different kinds of truth, such that they can be taken seriously, i.e., to be true. This raises at once the intriguing possibility of an argument that would give us a symbolic reading that was false. The doctrine of virgin birth can be read as a way of saying men and gods can interact: the trouble is, they can't (because there are no gods). What does the symbolic-interpretation view tell us to do now?

The issue simply does not begin as Leach naively declares with his question, "How should we interpret ethnographical statements about palpable untruth?" (p. 44). For one thing, it is this very assumption of untruth which is preceded by taking the utterance seriously (i.e., not symbolically). The alternative is a priori to declare it the result of benighted ignorance or stupidity, and this kind of condescension Leach is at pains to rule out. For another thing, the question comes too quickly, while skipping the stages I am insisting on, and as a result they come all too easily: the people we are talking about do not for a minute agree that their beliefs *are* untrue. This fact has been waved aside. Says Leach: "I find it highly improbable on common-sense grounds that genuine 'ignorance' of the basic facts of physiological paternity should anywhere be a cultural fact" (p. 41). Wow![18] And what of the speaker who affirms a gospel he actually does think false, but nevertheless means literally, intending to overrule his own ability to reason and his own judgement because of a decision to accept those of a priest or partyleader? Here we see how Leach's philosophical errors lead to anthropological errors: what he finds highly improbable may be an ethnographic fact.

An altogether more fruitful set of anthropological questions is, By what means are (what look to us like false) beliefs shielded from refutation? How do societies continue to function while their members act on the basis of false beliefs? and, When beliefs change, what brings the change about? Some beliefs — as Gellner (1973) has observed — are shielded by being so vague, ambiguous, absurd, or mysterious that they can hardly be refuted at all; other beliefs, as Evans-Pritchard (1937), has reported, even though refutable, are shielded by multiple ad hoc evasion strategies; others, as Orwell observes, have no power to judge questions of truth or falsity; still others declare such questions illegitimate. Despite this, a society with beliefs completely out of key with the environment doubtless would not survive, so change of and progress in beliefs is a very difficult problem to explain.

Leach's "statements we know to be untrue" (p. 44), then, begs the question of the line between the known truth and the rest — doubtful statements and errors — and this line is the problem, not the solution. The very idea of a boundary between true statements, where word content matters, and untrue statements, where it does not, is a product of the positivist cast of much of Enlightenment, post-Enlightenment, and neo-positivist thought, and hence of much of anthropology. The anthropologically hard thing to grasp seems to be that some people believe not only that two times two equals four, that a canoeist needs a paddle, and that fish can't be caught in trees, but also that the sky is up and the earth down, that Jesus was conceived through the ear, that an infinity of angels can dance on the head of a pin, that Christ bodily ascended into heaven, that transubstantiation occurs during the Eucharist, that the stars govern our destinies, that magic makes the world go round, that a full moon brings out the werewolves, etc. — and, moreover, that some societies and some people believe all of these simultaneously, often enough together with their negations and refutations. Without consideration of their word content, there would be no problem here.

If word content is irrelevant, why do we use the words we do? Why, for example, at grace do we not intone: "Eeny, meeny, miny, min, Let the present meal begin?" Obviously, the answer is because these words are meaningless; not just lacking sense, but lacking religious or traditional legitimation. They could, it is true, perfectly well serve to "say" that the meal is about to begin, but they would not be grace. Conclusion: the content of the words we utter is *far* from being irrelevant. Grace says that God has provided and that we are thankful. *It is totally irrelevant whether those present any longer believe (or even understand)*[19] *what they are saying.* Thanking God happens to be what they are doing when they say grace — regardless of whether He exists. Leach's English bride may indeed be an atheist, be insincere, be getting married in bad faith. Nevertheless, the words of the wedding ceremony are highly relevant to understanding what is going on. It is the content of the words that legitimates the ceremony both to her and to the state. One does not say grace in place of wedding vows, any more than one says "eeny, meeny, miny, mo". In a religious society, major social occasions seek religious sanction; religion may then atrophy, but its form of words can continue as a traditional or legal sanction. Either way, the content of the words counts. Those modern brides and grooms who revise the wording of the ceremony rightly consider the words and vows of very considerable relevance.

Leach looks upon religious utterances such as the wedding ritual as pieces of a jigsaw puzzle "structured in an extremely clear and well defined way" and argues that "not one bride in a thousand has an inkling of the total pattern" (n. 2). This is not only condescending, but unenlightening. The patterns of a person's behaviour do not explain it; the patterns or structures in ritual, doctrine, and myth are neither objectively there nor explanatory. The projected patterns, or the anthropologist's belief that he can discern patterns, are where we begin, not end.

Of course, it is all too easy to explain the bride's acceptance of a wedding ceremony. She may be a believer in the religion to which the ceremony belongs; she may be pleasing her believing or at least traditionalist relatives; or she may believe that following accepted custom is in itself a good — perhaps because she is a disciple of Leach.[20] Or she may believe in magic (Agassi and Jarvie 1967, 1973).

Does it bespeak respect to the bride to admit that she believes in magic, or is it better for this end to deny her her right to believe in magic?

True respect for others, which Leach is so convinced his predecessors Hartland, McLennan, and Frazer and his contemporary Spiro lack, begins by taking others' words seriously — as Spiro suggests anthropologists should, as Leach did to Spiro (in part), as I am doing to Leach. If the ideas expressed by those words seem confused, incoherent, internally inconsistent, manifestly absurd, or empirically false, it does no service to anyone to weasel out by saying these persons must be speaking symbolically. Soon it is necessary to add a buttress and claim that there is a whole hidden area of symbolic speaking and acting of which the actors are totally unaware, or which they always put in inverted commas (Leach 1974). Further to support this view, some anthropologists go so far as to suggest that this symbolising activity is backed by an imaginary process called "symbolic thinking" — which is presumably to be contrasted with ordinary, straightforward, rational thinking. It is a short step from this to a kind of symbolic cognition, or, as Leach calls it, different kinds of truth.

Instead of all this, I suggest the economical principle that we explain the acts and speech-acts of believers in Azande witchcraft, Henry Myers Lecturers, and Christian theologians in exactly the same way: they believe what they are saying and act (including speak) upon their beliefs. Only if we have strong counter-evidence, such as that the bride is an atheist, the college men unbelievers, or the Henry Myers Lecturer not really as attached to Christianity as he sounds, need we offer further explanation of their actions. That further explanation should be not symbolic but sociological. When theologians trade in vagueness, muddle, or sophistry, and when Henry Myers Lecturers find this preferable to Frazer, we need to look into the social functions of the absurd (Gellner 1973). Anthropologists were enlightened when an earlier Leach distinguished what people *do* from the *norm*, and those two from what they *say* they do (Leach 1945). Leach needs to apply his earlier insight to the Christian practices he indulges, namely the significantly named "apologetics": it is odd to find him instead identifying action, norm, and account among muddle-headed theologians in the name of justice to the intellects of primitive people. Religion is a mode of social organization, as well as intellectual organization, and the organizational status quo always has a vested interest in self-preservation: hence the sophistical manipulation of mysteries, different kinds of truth, different levels of meaning, symbolic meaning, etc.

V

It has not been my purpose to deny that people make, take over, use, and manipulate symbols. Ballet, the Morse code, the cross, the swastika, the flag, the authority of uniforms, the magic of pomp and circumstance, etc., are real enough. But these symbol systems, like language itself, are transparent, because they are accessible to their participants and users: they may be intentional, customary, or unconscious; they may even affect us in ways we do not understand. They nevertheless are not in a separate cognitive domain. To assume they are is really to multiply universes of discourse beyond necessity. There is no hidden meaning in belief in virgin birth, astrology, or the order of dishes in a meal. And when the anthropologist meets absurd dissembling about virgin birth, symbolic interpretation, or whatever, he should report it as such and do the sociology of dissembling and the absurd.

I have tried to explain the factual, moral, epistemological, and anthropological mistakes upon which the symbolic-interpretation view rests. Is there in that view a central philosophical error? We get a clue when Leach argues that we cannot infer from a wedding ceremony or the saying of Latin grace that anyone present believes what the words say. This is true enough, but it is poor anthropology to report it as an ethnographic discovery. It is but a particular case of the general sceptical problem that we have no access to other minds. Who knows what people believe? How can anything as elusive as belief explain what they do?[21] The best policy when faced with such a sceptical challenge is to bypass it. Never mind how we know what they believe; concentrate on reconstructing the cognitive claims that could explain their action. The truth of the cognitive claims makes no difference to how well they explain action. The Azande are philosophically interesting because they apparently have a *Weltanschauung* in which a force called witchcraft is diffused through the world, causing action at a distance. This contrasts interestingly with the crazy idea of Michael Faraday that the world is ultimately made of up of fields of force (see Agassi 1972, Berkson 1974). Moreover, the sociology of these two sets of ideas is fascinating. The Azande problem is how the ideas are sustained in the face of the evidence; the Faraday problem is how his ideas were ignored despite his arguments. Metaphysics and their social repercussions are highly problematic and interesting. The metaphysics of transubstantiation are less interesting because they are so vague and poor. They are a kind of degenerating research programme, while the Azande's metaphysics are progressive. Far from rehabilitating the "savage" by comparing him favourably with muddle-headed theologians, I would argue, Leach has denigrated him and conferred underserved status on the muddle-headed in our culture. The alternative view which I have argued here follows Horton (1962, 1964, 1967) and others in comparing Africans with Faraday and characterizing those hunting for symbolism as engaged in desperate attempts to salvage ideas that are erroneous or muddle-headed. We need to be clear about what is mistaken but nevertheless interesting and what is hedged **about and hence** innocuous but nevertheless uninteresting. For myself, I would far prefer to regard "savage" ideas as in the former category than in the latter.

1 My thanks to Joseph Agassi, J. N. Hattiangadi, and J. O. Wisdom for their comments on this paper.

2 It is an entirely satisfactory piece of "situational logic"; see Jarvie (1972: Chap. 1).

3 Symbol: "Something that stands for, represents, or denotes something else (not by exact resemblance, but by vague suggestion, or by some accidental or conventional relation); *esp.* a material object representing or taken to represent something immaterial or abstract, as a being, idea, quality, or condition; a representative or typical figure, sign, or token" (*Oxford English Dictionary*). This admirable definition anticipates a number of my arguments, especially those from vagueness, arbitrariness, and conventionality. See also Gombrich (1972).

4 For the concept of the decidophobe, and his connection with blinkered scholarship, see Kaufman (1973).

5 Perhaps one way to render the approach more coherent would be to interpret it as a metaphysical (because unfalsifiable) research programme, with a fairly solid central idea (something like "deep symbolism or hidden meaning lies beneath most social activities") and variant ways of making it concrete and guiding research (heuristics). This would enable us to deal with both the common features in, and the differences between, hunts for phallic symbolism, power symbolism, structural meaning, archetypes, binary discriminations, ordered classification, and so on. The notion of a metaphysical research programme comes from Popper (1959) and Agassi (1956), some of the terminology from Lakatos (1970).

6 Examples include the Huxley Memorial Lecture, the Frazer Lecture, etc. Medals (the Rivers Memorial Medal, the Patron's Medal, The Wellcome Medal), essay prizes (the Curl Bequest Essay Prize, the Hocart Prize Essay), and, of course, election to Institute office are also honorific.

7 As I understand it, a named lecture, like a named chair, indicates endowment and hence especially high status in the scholarly world (see Freedman 1967).

8 The officers of the Institute make an effort to attend, as does the membership, in expectation of an "occasion".

9 E. R. Leach, a student of Malinowski and Firth, has had a very distinguished academic career, which culminated in his being knighted in 1975.

10 Henry Myers, a Fellow of the Institute, provided a sum of money for a lecture on "the place of religious belief in human development".

11 Previously delivered by scholars such as A. R. Radcliffe-Brown (1945), Sir Raymond Firth (1948), Sir Edward Evans-Pritchard (1954), Claude Lévi-Strauss (1962).

12 A philosopher can only protest that this matter-of-fact everyday world is full of metaphysics; and so is everyone else's, did but they know it.

13 One can bridle at the positivist insult to metaphysics. Most of the really interesting ideas in science and philosophy are metaphysical, and some of them may be true!

14 Some philosophers think there is a deep problem in how we mean what we say.

15 Or Chairman Mao, or the ultimate now.

[16] There seem to be many counter-examples to this principle.
[17] Note the passage on p. 43 where by association Leach charges 19th-century anthropologists with imperialism and sexual fantasies.
[18] Or, if you prefer more detail, see Spiro (1968).
[19] Notoriously, Buddhist monks in places like Hong Kong know no Sanskrit, even though much of what they recite is in that language.
[20] Or she may have no choice: there is no secular marriage in Israel.
[21] This appears to be the reasoning behind Needham (1972).

REFERENCES

Agassi, J. 1956. 'The Function of Interpretation in Physics'. Unpublished Ph.D. thesis, University of London, London, England.

Agassi, J. and Jarvie, I. C. 1967. 'The Problem of the Rationality of Magic'. *British Journal of Sociology* 18 55–74. (Reprinted in *Rationality*. Edited by B. Wilson. Oxford: Oxford University Press, 1970).

Agassi, J. and Jarvie, I. C. 1973. 'Magic and Rationality Again'. *British Journal of Sociology* 24 236–45.

Berkson, William. 1974. *Fields of Force*, London: Routledge and Kegan Paul.

Evans-Pritchard, E. E. 1937. *Witchcraft, Oracles and Magic Among the Azande*. Oxford University Press.

Freedman, Maurice. 1967. *Rites and Duties, or Chinese Marriage*. London: Bell.

Gellner, E. A. 1973. *Cause and Meaning in the Social Sciences*. London: Routledge and Kegan Paul.

Gombrich, E. H. 1972. *Symbolic Images*. London: Phaidon.

Horton, W. R. G. 1962. 'The Kalabari World-View: An Outline and Interpretation. *Africa* 32 197–220.

Horton, W. R. G. 1964. 'Ritual man in Africa, *Africa* 34 85–104.

Horton, W. R. G. 1967. 'African Traditional Thought and Western Science'. *Africa* 37 50–71, 155–87.

Kaufman, Walter 1973. *Beyond Guilt and Justice*. New York: McKay.

Lakatos, I. 1970. 'Criticism and the Methodology of Scientific Research Programmes'. In *Criticism and the Growth of Knowledge*. Edited by I. Lakatos and A. Musgrave. Cambridge: University Press.

Leach, E. R. 1945. 'Jinghpaw Kinship Terminology'. *Journal of the Royal Anthropological Institute* 75 59–72.

Leach, E. R. 1961. 'Golden Bough or Gilded Twig'. *Daedalus*, Spring, pp. 355–78.

Leach, E. R. 1967. 'Virgin Birth'. *Proceedings of the Royal Anthropological Institute*, pp. 39–49.

Leach, E. R. 1974. 'Acting in Inverted Commas'. *Times Literary Supplement*, October 4, no. 3787, pp. 1074–75.

Needham, R. 1972. *Belief, Language, and Experience*. Chicago: University of Chicago Press.

Popper, K. R. 1959. Postscript: After 20 years. MS.

Spiro, Melford E. 1968. 'Virgin Birth, Parthenogenesis, and Physiological Paternity: An Essay in Cultural Interpretation', *Man*, n.s., 3 242–61.

CHAPTER 14

THE PROBLEM OF THE ETHNOGRAPHIC REAL[1]

Stated simply, the problem of the ethnographic real is, what exactly is it that the ethnographer sets out to record and study? It is a serious problem not because ethnographers do not know what reality is, but because they constantly invoke it as a standard (Heider 1976: 79); this renders vicious the otherwise possibly innocuous and unavoidable fact that the activities of perceiving, recording and thinking are fraught with distortion. It is an interesting problem because the aims of ethnography are vague, and the philosophical assumptions behind those aims poorly understood. By looking at this problem from the angle subtended by ethnographic film, rather than that of clasic one-man field work, it may be possible to illuminate philosophical issues in the basis of anthropology as well as of film.

I

The most popular philosophy of science is inductivism, which alleges that science begins with the gathering of data. When social scientists were unself-consciously inductivist, they could and did argue that ethnography was the data-gathering base of their science (Jarvie 1964, 1967). Out there in the world were societies and cultures about which anthropologists wished to collect the facts. From the data-bank accumulated by their collection efforts anthropologists would be able to make generalisations, at first locally, then covering cultural areas, and finally comprehending mankind as a whole.[2] This antiquated methodology, which I have seen seriously put forward as recently as 1979 in the inaugural lecture of the current Professor of Social Anthropology at Oxford (Needham 1979), is only good when naive. And as such it has great and obvious appeal to naive documentary film makers. Thinking perhaps in the tradition of those uncritically inductivist social scientists Sidney and Beatrice Webb,[3] John Grierson defined documentary film as an excercise in the creative treatment of actuality (Grierson 1946: 78–82). The actuality he had in mind was the ordinary lives of ordinary working folk: the lives of the rich, comfortable or intellectual being thought of as artificial and unreal and thus in some way as unappealing as those of the creatures of fiction film. More to the point, Grierson combined a

212

romantic temperament with the approach of a preacher, hence he was able to draw in both earnest young men and government support. It was the romantic in him that allowed an alliance to be forged with the explorer Flaherty. To the true romantic, however sentimental, even the working classes seem to live somewhat artificial lives; the only truly unspoiled and hence real people are those out of touch with civilisation, but in touch with nature: primitive people. While romanticism is part of the impetus behind anthropology, one must be clear how superficial and naive romanticism + preaching would seem to such as Boas, Kroeber, Malinowski and Radcliffe-Brown.[4] Their concern was the building of a science. On this base an axis was possible because inductivism was a shared philosophy of film makers and anthropologists (Jarvie 1964, 1967).

Romanticism, then, made the anthropologist's bailiwick of Aran, Hudson Bay, or the Kalahari desert attractive to film makers. We must be careful, however, not to confuse this coincidence of interest in places and people with comparable aims and results. Flaherty is more appropriately studied with Cooper/Schoedsack, Grierson with Riefenstahl, than either with Chagnon/ Asch, Gardner, MacDougal, Marshall, or Smith. Unfortunately, film makers were a little behind anthropologists in the development of their sensibility. Even if their initial impulse was a sentimentalised attraction to the noble savage, anthropologists spent a good deal of the first third of this century freeing themselves from some of the grossest of those assumptions. Romanticism and its associated ethnocentrism were eschewed. On the contrary, the 'savage' (the need for scare quotes indicative of self-consciousness and uncertainty) came to be portayed as tough-mindedly interested in wealth, power and manipulation. Anthropologists taught themselves to be sceptical not only of their own preconceptions, but also of first impressions, and the accounts offered of their behaviour by the objects of study (Leach 1945:59, Brown and Barnett 1942:31–2). Rather, anthropologists increasingly brought to their ethnographic field work intellectual problems and categorial difficulties 'imported' as it were from their training. The clash between this and inductivism created a sense of crisis in the foundations that has inspired a range of works (Nadel 1951, Bidney 1953, Steward 1955, Harris 1968).

Film makers acknowledging the element of creativity in the presentation of reality were philosophically more sophisticated than, say, Margaret Mead who, in the late nineteen fifties, could be heard at the Royal Anthropological Institute extolling the virues of the camera and the tape recorder as boons to the anthropologist (Mead 1963, 1973). At last the technology was available definitively to record what went on in another society. Just set up the equipment and get out of the way and countless hours of priceless and informative data would be yours. On hearing this I was dismayed: not so much because of the naive inductivism of Mead's implicit philosophy of science, as because she seemed not to be aware that even Grierson was unable to leave out the word 'creative' from the use of the tape recorder and camera to capture reality. Inductivism is more defensible than the view that the natural attitude of film technology is inductivist. More on this later.

Some film makers and anthropologists long ago had arguments to make it clear that what they were seeking to record in film and in ethnography was not unproblematically 'there' waiting to be recorded. Anthropologists were looking for things, constructing things, interpreting things that they observed utilising selection and relevance rules that were set not by the peoples they were studying but by the academic discipline within which they were operating. Film makers knew full well that they were engaged in a creative endeavour in which their pre-production, shooting and post-production procedures might all interact, that the controlling factor of that interaction was their own imaginative vision, not some given reality which so to say obtruded its way into the film (Mead and Bateson 1977).

To make sense of this is really not very hard. The fault lies less in what anthropologists and film makers do, and more in what they say they do — perhaps in what they say only in their more unguarded moments. Anthropologists take it as a commonplace that there are worlds of difference between what people do, and what they say they do; and also between what they try to do and what they say ought to do. Even literate people, not to mention preliterate people, manage to behave pretty clearly and consistently despite their muddled views and demands upon themselves. The same, reflexively, is true of anthropologists and film makers. In particular, both anthropology and film making seem to be activities in a fairly healthy state, despite the muddles uttered by their practitioners. Both the observer and the observed then, at times do the right things while giving as explanations for their actions poor reasons. The wrong reasons have their price: the rigidity of the society in question, whether observer or observed. Overcoming the rigidities of observed societies is beyond my present concern. To overcome the rigidity of the society of the observers I propose to eliminate the muddle in the philosophy of science and so offer right reasons as explanation for doing the right things.

Inductivist philosophy of science has been used to legitimate scientific activity at least since Newton. Interestingly enough, it leads to incoherent accounts of cases of scientific endeavour, including Newton's own. There are

many reasons for this incoherence, but the most striking as far as our purposes go is that the theory which leads to the making of such accounts is
plainly and obviously false: there is no pure and securely grounded data-
base upon which the generalisations of science can be erected. Every statement of fact, every observation-report already embodies a selection procedure, point of view, theoretical assumptions and so cannot serve as a
logically prior base. Theory-ladenness is easily shown by the fact that the
command 'Observe!', evokes only the response, 'Observe what?', and that
the explanation, 'The facts,' evokes only the further response, 'Which facts?';
whereas, if we say, 'Observe and record the facts of kinship in this society!,'
assumptions pour out into the open in both the command and the response.
Kinship is assumed to be a category, some things are in it and other things are
not (and this boundary is presumed relatively unproblematic); it is assumed
to be observable and recordable; it is assumed to be significantly different
from one society to the next (otherwise why record it?); and so on. Once this
much is clear, we realise we have donned categorial spectacles manufactured
by the theoretical system in which kinship is significant and through which
we must now observe. What we observe can then hardly provide secure
grounds for theories, since it is already theory laden (Popper 1959:59 and
chapter V). The indiscriminate collection of data thus comes to seem wasteful,
but not useless, for, buried in the mass, there may be nuggets that in some way
challenge or contradict the implicit or explicit ideas of their collector. When
this contradiction is noticed we have an intellectual problem, and the discovery
of such a problem constitutes intellectual progress. What once we thought we
knew or even took for granted, we now know we do not or cannot.

An argument like this shifts the legitimation of the recording function of
field work away from a mythical base of pure fact from which science can
be synthesised. This is not to deny all value to data-gathering. Rather, its
value is not to serve as a basis for future induction. Data-gathering, thus, is
no longer indiscriminate and wasteful but becomes a search for some definite
material, e.g., for anomalies, exceptions and, if the philosophy of Sir Karl
Popper is correct, best of all, a search for counter-examples to current
theories.

As to film making. It is no more an objective or mechanical recording of
what is there than is painting. Already Popper's follower Gombrich has
plausibly argued in *Art and Illusion* that the history of representative
painting can be reconstructed in terms of a process he calls 'making and
matching' (Gombrich 1962). That is to say, a painter wishing to capture some
aspect of the visual world seeks, tests and improves devices to represent

it in paint on two-dimensional canvas. Gombrich reproduces the wonderful *New Yorker* cartoon of the drawing class in Ancient Egypt all holding their pencils at eye level to take the measure of a model who happens to be an angular two-dimensional woman! The same point could be made about film by drawing a film studio in which there are actors and actresses whose bodies are flat, or who are cut off in mid-chest, or who have voices but no body. In other words, like Gombrich's painter, film makers too have striven long and hard to make and match: to portray emotions, the logic of dramatic action, parallel action, inner thoughts, deception, and also, most subtly, a point of view that is neither of the characters, nor of the audience, but akin to the voice of the narrator in prose: namely the point of view of the film maker himself. So successful have they been in this that, far from being inductivist, the majority of film makers practical and academic alike, hold that film is irremediably subjective. There is a failure of logic here: subjectivism is the despairing redoubt of the disappointed inductivist, but it is an error to imagine that induction is identical with the method of science. Induction is *a* theory of science. Among alternatives, Popper and Gombrich offer us a philosophy of science which even allows us to speak of the effort 'to show that the undeniable subjectivity of vision does not preclude objective standards of representational accuracy' (Gombrich 1962:xi).

The upshot of this section, then, is that neither anthropologists nor film makers see their task as definable in terms of recording given and unproblematic facts. Each has a different aim, anthropologists to advance the problems their subject treats; film makers creatively to express their vision. Hence it is not surprising that the anthropologist rarely makes a film satisfactory to the film maker, the film maker rarely makes a film satisfactory to the anthropologist. The continuing controversy in Great Britain over such television documentary series as 'The Disappearing World' echoes in its concerns the controversies between film makers and historians over the series 'The Great War' and 'The World at War' (P. Smith 1976). What is at issue is not the inclusion or exclusion of phenomena themselves, but the argument that the so-called phenomena are constituted by the activities of the anthropologist or the film maker. What an anthropologist sees in New Guinea, and therefore wants to record and reflect upon may be invisible and inaudible to a film maker without the intellectual concerns and categories of the anthropologist (Heider 1976: 10–11). What the film maker wishes to do when let loose in New Guinea may strike the anthropologist as not much more than a rather sentimentally presented set of pretty pictures. At best, the pictures may be unsparing yet enervating (*Dead Birds*). Think of *The Ax Fight* (1975) and of *Nanook of the North* (1922), the one a re-working of some intricate footage of a fight that broke out in a Yanomamo village that the anthropologists were lucky enough to capture on film, the other a laboriously re-staged and faked but gorgeously photographed reconstruction of the struggle to survive in the frozen north (Jarvie 1978a). A recent example of the *Nanook* style is Hilary Harris' elegant travelogue masquerading as ethnography, *The Nuer* (1970), justly criticised by anthropologists (e.g., Heider 1976), yet appreciated by no less than Evans-Pritchard (Evans-Pritchard 1972).[5] So much confusion. The trite though of course possible solution that has been advocated is, let anthropologists become film makers and film makers become anthropologists (Loizos 1977). Though this could work and certainly would be good for enrollments at film schools and diploma courses in anthropology, the solution misses the point; it attemps to overcome the dissatisfaction rather than explain it. Perhaps the aims of film makers and anthropologists are at variance, if so, we may explain their mutual dissatisfaction even if we do not come across a solution.

How much at variance? Well, film makers cannot assume a captive audience; they must keep their audience entertained; their primary responsibility is to their imaginative vision: there lies the source of their integrity. Film makers employ their skill in the service of that vision. Anthropologists by contrast are academics and scholars and, while they may by pedagogically flexible, their values will be those of science: caution, responsibility, accuracy, a critical attitude, and scrupulous attention to the demarcation between what is agreed and what is controversial. Above all, to be sententious, their responsibility is to truth. Film makers' audiences are a frame of reference; anthropologists share with their audience partnership and criticism and a transcending frame of reference: the traditions and goals of their discipline, So, if we find the concept of truth hard to handle (Wiener 1978) we can get by relating their responsibility to the tradition and activities of the intellectual discipline and the peer group.[6] Anthropologists portray a tribe not because of its aesthetic appeal (although they need not ignore that); not because they have an imaginative vision (although they may); but because that tribe or that aspect of culture/society they are showing is of anthropological significance. This means it is a contribution to research or teaching or both. What is of significance is a function of the traditions and activities that make up anthropology. Anyone trained in both film making and anthropology, then, might indeed be notable for being able to do both, but not necessarily for being able to combine these disparate aims in one creation.

II

So far, so simple. Now things get less simple. The account I have given thus far of anthropologists and film makers avoids a more basic challenge to their joint enterprise. This challenge is to the model of ethnographers or film makers as detached observers, isolated from rather than interacting with their subjects. This is sometimes expressed by saying the model positivistically assumes there is a real world available for recording and study independent of the observer. Another way it can be put is to say that we cannot penetrate appearance and touch reality: an anthropologist doing ethnography is entering into social relationships with the persons he is recording/studying and so what he is aware of is essentially appearances and even of a specific kind, namely the reactions his presence generates, his own social interactions. Another anthropologist, then, with different interests or a different personality, at another time, might provoke or generate different interactions and hence record and study the ap-pearance of a different process (Fabian 1971).

The trouble with this challenge, indeed the trouble with taking the problem of appearance and reality too seriously, is that it becomes a *reductio ad absurdum* on itself. Starting from the idea of anthropologists as interacting, it ends up not allowing them anything to interact with. If the product of ethnography is a record of interaction it is all-too-easy to say this breaks down the distinction between observer and observed and this easily collapses into ethnographic solipsism: all ethnography is no more than a report on the eth-nographer (Jarvie 1971, 1975). There is nevertheless something to the idea, the issue is to prevent it running amuck. The commonsense model of an an-thropologist (subject) non-interactingly observing (an object) is naive; it is the same as the model of perception as some sort of 'within' (the mind? the inside of the skull?) peering out of 'windows' (the cortex? the eyes?) at the 'external world' (things? other people?); nevertheless, in order that some sort of learning take place there must be a two-place relationship if we are to talk of *someone* learning *something*.

At this point I shift gears briefly, to deal with the issue of appearance and reality in a general manner. It will perhaps be remembered that Bishop George Berkeley used the duality of appearance and reality to show that a radical empiricism demanded the permanent vigilance of an all-seeing God. From the contradictions in sense experience such as seeing a straight twig in water as bent, and feeling the same vessel of water to be hot to one hand and cold to the other after the hands had been plunged one into hot and one into cold water, he argued for not altogether trusting the unaided sense as guides to what is there, for not admitting apperances as a guide to reality. Clearly at times we perceive things that are not there. From the further point that people (and things) did not disappear when we turned our backs on them, or at least the people said they did not, and gardens appeared to go on growing when nobody was there, and adding to this his radical empiricist principle, *esse is percipi*, Berkeley concluded that in order for it to be true that things were there when no one was perceiving them there had to be as it were a Supreme Perceiver always around to ensure that the permanent possibilities of perception awaited us (Berkeley 1910).

Berkeley was one of the ablest arguers in philosophy, and his position, which is logically the same as a highly respectable doctrine called phenomenalism (Wisdom 1953: 1—94), espoused by, among others, the non-bishops John Stuart Mill and Bertrand Russell, was not easy to rebut. The place to start, perhaps, is the argument from illusion. What follows from the universally admitted fact of perceptual illusions? Most obviously, to repeat, the general unreliability of perception as a guide to what there is, of appearance as a guide to reality. Is this, however, cause for despair? Does it follow from the fact that a person makes a mistake that therefore everything they do or say should be put under suspicion as unreliable? Only, I suspect, if one has in mind some paragon of reliability, some error-free algorithm. If a calculator tells you 2 + 2 = 5, then you would do well not to trust it to multiply 2345 by 67. The reason is because its operations are mechanical, and if they have gone wrong in one simple place they may be and probably are wrong in others, because of the interlinking of the mechanisms.[7] But if one morning a bank clerk mis-adds a page of figures it is doubtful if that bank will then recalculate everything that person ever did.

So: sense illusions provide one with a reminder to keep a watching brief on the evidence of the senses, but they do not undermine them completely. One might formulate the correct conclusion as follows: rely on the senses by all means, but where good reason is offered for not trusting them, be careful. Thus, don't trust the desert because of mirage; orient yourself in fog by different means than on clear days; compensate when reaching under water or using the driving mirror. Thus one can hold on to the project of a science like anthropology utilising the evidence of the senses in studying part of what can be called the external world, even while being cautious about identifying any part of it as the real world. The real world is not the external world, the real world is not the perceived world. The real world is not the world as it seems from any particular privileged vantage point. The decision as to what the real world is, as to what objects populate it, is a judgement, a judgement in which perceptual evidence plays a part, not the sole part since a great deal of other kinds of evidence plays parts in it such as logic, mathematics, the body of theories we hold, and common sense. It is a little misleading to say that the real world is a construct; rather our picture of the real world is a product of, or an attribution made in, a judgement. To say we construct the real world leans towards idealism, for we also construct dreams, illusion, fantasies, myths and fictions. Rather should we say this: we designate as real those entities, states and processes that in our judgement best explain the evidence of our sense and which best suit and cohere with the demands of our theories. Thus we decide what the real shape of a coin is by deciding it is the one that explains best the many different-shaped perceptions it can give, fits our theories of optics and metallurgy, our geometry and our knowledge of minting. The advantage of this view is its minimum concession to idealism, namely, the notion that knowledge is the outcome of an interaction between the observer and the observed, the knower and the known, the mind and the world, yet its retention of a stable, mind-independent knowledge of things in the real world the objects and processes of which are nevertheless subject to reconsideration.

Unresisting to puns, I cannot help but now ask, what is the real world to the reel world? The answer flows I think fairly naturally: it is advisable to trust film even less than to trust the evidence of the senses. Film is not the evidence of the senses, it is the highly processed evidence of other people's judgement put into sense-representation. It cannot, therefore, come even remotely close to the status of data. Already an anthropologist's informants' reports are advisedly treated critically: how much more critical is one justified in being towards selected film of informants, which has therefore about as much standing as *hearsay*?[8] Film can not normally be primary evidence, not even in the way that field work yields primary evidence, or in the way for an historian documents do (Jarvie 1978b). To be a little more encouraging, film can be treated as a primary course, but only if its use is hedged about with severe restrictions. Basically, it must be possible to situate the piece of film in the context of some other, unproblematically primary, materials thus lending it the credence usually accorded to primary materials (never total). For example, a film shot by a field worker who can describe exactly the time, place, and circumstances of its making, allay fears about the intrusion effect of the machinery, report that nothing is missed because of limited angle of view, necessity of changing film, quality of sound recording, and so on. So much information of this kind is required, however, that for anthropological purposes one is inclined to suspect the film will be no more than an illustration to the written field report and usually redundant. If the field worker can verbally and in writing give such situating assurances, he lets us know we can use the film at the same time that he is reducing it to the level of an item in his notebook. Apart from such things as the visual appearances of things, people and ceremonies, it is difficult to know what film would add to such an entry. But take such an abstract item as a conversation (between two objects, or subject and object) and it is at once obvious that one hundred words in a notebook could summarise, make sense of, and contain anthropological insights based on that conversation in a manner that film or tape could present only clumsily and at full length. Film, that is to say, is not good at intellectual gisting.

To give a parallel example from history: of what value is a piece of film showing Winston Churchill speaking with F.D.R. at one of their wartime rendezvous? To begin with, the war, their position as leaders, and the significance of their different meetings, all have to be established by primary documentary means. Even then, to be of historical value the film must be authenticated (by literary means); we need assurance that these are the real people, not impersonators. Suppose we 'overhear' them talking. We need to know much that the film cannot supply: whether this was staged, or was a bit of genuine eavesdropping that they later approved for release. We also must, as historians, connect whatever information we take from this film with all the other information we have: for example, just because they smile and seem amiable would not be a reason for concluding that F.D.R.'s well-documented suspicion of Churchill as an old imperialist warrior can be discounted. In summary, film can be used as primary evidence only when other primary evidence permits. Film then is the opposite of optical illusions. They, I have argued, do not in any way yield the conclusion that all perception is to be mistrusted because of occasional illusion; yet because film is at one or more removes from perception, it is to be mistrusted as a matter of course. Perception is usually to be trusted though at times rejected; films are usually to be mistrusted though at times accepted. Film is, as historians say, 'a tainted source'. Indeed, I will go so far as to suggest that fiction film may be less tainted than factual film.

III

In looking at the problem of appearance and reality we have so far used examples from the physical world of objects, not from the social world of processes, structures, classes and institutions. It is widely believed that these social entities are in some serious way less substantial than physical objects and that hence the study of them is harder to ground, harder to carry out, and that therefore it is permissible and even recommended that they be done creatively and frankly subjectively. This is not a view I share. My thesis to the contrary would be that human beings, so far from inhibiting self-study with their unpredictability or what not, positively cooperate with and facilitate social studies; that it is easier, not harder, to study people than things. Studying human beings is in certain decisive and noticeable ways easier than studying the natural world. The behaviour of people in society is anything but the random and unpredictable chaos of the motion of gas molecules; it is as orderly as and in some ways more predictable than the behaviour of all but closed and very simple physical systems (Popper 1957:§27, 1972:Chapter 6). How can this be so? The answer is that men simultaneously are part of society, constitute it and conceptualise about it. This latter is the most important. Men's society-making activity is primarily conceptual: they order and organize their actions depending on how they think things are (Jarvie 1972). Thus a strategically placed informant is of the greatest value in anthropology because he or she is, as it were, the horse's mouth. The informant may not operate with anthropologists' concepts, but anthropologists bring their own concepts into relation with the informant's concepts and end up giving an account of the society or culture that is congruent with the informant's conceptions. More than one informant is needed for purposes of comparison, checking and access to areas of the society that are closed to outsiders.

Now this really simplifies matters. Beetles and rolling stones do not cooperate with the naturalists and physicists studying them in offering their conceptualisation of the situation as a starting point to be checked, supplemented, corrected and used. We have to guess and test, guess and test, endlessly. Some systems, admittedly, may be less volatile than human systems, but only in some respects and a certain degree; others, like the weather, volcanoes, explosions in laboratories, all attest to the unpredictable volatility of physical nature too. Motiveless crimes, riots, fecklessness and unreliability testify similarly about human nature. But in proper social settings the opposite holds: most of the time, the bus drivers arrive at their garages at shift time just about as reliably as the diesel fuel in buses' cylinders explodes to order. Indeed, we have a higher expectation of our understanding of the human storm than the stormy weather: we still allow freak storms and so on to pass without explanation, yet we strive to offer rational accounts of motiveless crimes (Lejeune 1977; Posner 1979), riots and fecklessness. We employ what philosophers of social science call the rationality principle and press it through to an extraordinary degree. The rationality principle is where we commence our attempts to understand human beings by attributing to them rationality, that is, behaviour directed towards an intelligible aim by feasible means. Where our initial effort fails, the principle urges us to try again: to alter our model of the situation, the actor's model of the situation, his appreciation of the means and his putative aims. Only if all our efforts fail do we consider action unintelligible. Whether the ascribed aims and appreciation of means are themselves allowable as rational demands an appraisal of the wider context in which the actor operates. This almost empty but regulative principle that people act appropriately to their situations renders the cloudy open systems of human interaction into almost a clock-like predictable closed system (Popper 1967; Jarvie 1972: Ch. 1).[9]

On a philosophical level, then, the contrast between appearance and reality is somewhat less of a problem with social objects than with physical objects. To a considerable extent, society is what society seems to be to its own actors, for they will act on the basis of how it seems, and so the consequences of their acts, namely the configuration of the society at the next time-slice we take, will be a product, will have been formed, by how it seemed. This is why anthropologists are strongly interested in tuning in on how the actors see things: as a first approximation to figuring out how they are, i.e., what construction of them best explains the empirical evidence given current theories.

This formulation of the status of the ethnographic real avoids the two extreme positions of emics (accept their categories) and etics (impose our categories). Whereas Marvin Harris dismisses the emic position (Harris 1968: 568–604), and Peter Winch dismisses the etic position (Winch 1964), I allow neither dismissal. Anthropology is the record of discussion of the discovery of emic inadequacies and hence the development of etics. This brings us to the trickiest and hardest point to explain: simply characterising intellectual work in the subject of anthropology in this manner puts the ethnographic film in even graver difficulties than the foregoing arguments suggested. Before coming to that, just to emphasise once again the point made, anthropologists trade in conceptualisations of societies: their informants' and their own. Film is not especially adept at recording or explaining such conceptualisations, still less their dispute. Film concretises things, responds to the skill of acting and presentation and carries with it dangerous overtones of its own authenticity. It has a tendency to present appearance as though it were reality so far as the physical world goes, and undoubtedly skews the bias towards members' accounts[10] when representing the social world. This interferes with the process that anthropologists are engaged in, which might be summed up as attempting to mediate between different members' accounts by arriving at an account of their own that incorporates and explains all those members' accounts. This is a dialectical or discursive process, and the greatest cognitive weakness of film is its clumsiness in presenting material discursively (Jarvie 1978b).

Earlier, I drew a contrast between the society of the observers and the society of the observed, and showed how the society of the observers differs radically for the anthropologist and the film maker. I placed less stress on the contrast of a society of science versus a society of art, than I did on the society of co-workers under the regulative ideas of truth, community and tradition, as opposed to the society of imaginers and their audience. Scientists are part of their own audience in a manner that creators cannot be. Let me now flesh out this sketch of what a scientific discipline like anthropology is. Intellectual disciplines can be (and are I think best) characterised as chains of argument or debate around certain sets of problems (Popper 1959; Hattiangadi 1978–79) that are fought over by various schools of thought (Agassi 1975), who advance and defend explanatory theories intended to solve these problems. As in the adversarial trial process, evidence is marshalled, witnesses are called, speeches are made on each side. The scientist himself moves easily and naturally between being an advocate and being a member of the jury, which in a way he is, because science is a self-governing activity and the verdict is pronounced by the jury of this peers. However, both verdict and sentence are always subject to review, as the problems on trial proliferate along with the solutions offered to them. This picture of the nature of science is very different from the inductivist picture with which we began. Science no longer appears out of a neutral data-base that can be gathered by the neutral observer, as objective and detached as the camera and tape recorder are alleged to be.[11] Science is a process of on-going debate in which evidence is marshalled for partisan purposes and yet the marshalling is subject to certain rules regarding its public and repeatable character and its empirical or observable nature and its conformities to the laws of logic such that interim assessments of the states of our knowledge are possible. Knowledge is simply the best surviving theories. Where no theory is clearly the best by any of the established criteria, or where the criteria are uncertain or under challenge, candour demands that we present whatever competing alternatives there are. One may conceive of filming a textbook, it is unclear how one films endless scholarly debate. How rarely film as opposed to slides is used in the hard sciences deserves noticing, and then as a visual aid to lectures, not as part and parcel of research.

To my mind this poses a grave challenge to claims about the value of film in ethnographic endeavour: even to employ a piece of film as speech in the debate requires that its viewers are reassured by its being situated and its public and repeatable character being attested. Film as it were embodies in itself a vision of the ethnographic real, when anthropology, the very exercise it is intended to feed, is engaged in attempting to judge how to describe what the ethnographic real is. For in my view the ethnographic real is not a given, a piece of some unproblematic external world, subject only to some minor troubles to do with disentangling appearance and reality. Rather is the ethnographic real a misleading label for what statisticians call the best case hypothesis; by this they mean the curve which best fits the data, by this I mean the theory that best solves the problem. The inductivist thinks he studies, observes, classifies and generalises about something he thinks of as real world objects out there. I, on the contrary, prefer to think that reality as it presents itself to us comes in the form of problems, conundrums, practical tasks, aims to be pursued. The real then is whatever entities our best-tested theories need to assume in order to do their work: neither stones nor social institutions have a god-given permanence independent of the vagaries of human enquiry.

IV

I have now switched over from critical and sceptical arguments towards some articulation of a positive point of view of my own; a point of view, about both the doing of ethnography, and the value of film in ethnography. Beyond ethnography there lies anthropology in general, and the value of film in that. Were I to sum up my negative views I might say that film is at best a supplementary recording device, a useful illustrating medium, a visual aid in teaching, a poor expository and argumentative device, and in general, in view of its expense, complication, and discursive poverty, very much a mixed blessing.

Let me begin the project of expressing more positive views by means of an analogy, that of the map. A naive inductivist view of maps is that they simply represent what is there. Yet it is obvious that there can be an infinite set of maps of any one piece of earth, ocean or sky. Even after deciding on projection and on scale, there remain all the many things that go on that can be put on a map: isotherms, isobars, isoclines, isogeotherms, population density, elevation, geological character, rainfall, means of communication and transportation, crust thickness, extent of ice-age coverage, and so on. To a non-inductivist geographer there is no such simple real as a piece of land, sea or sky with these and those characteristics waiting to be mapped. There are problems and tasks which direct one's attention to certain sorts of sense that can be imposed on a landscape and then transcribed in many varying ways to maps.

In other places (Jarvie 1972:159–65) I have compared the task of the social scientist to the map maker, stressing the additional difficulty that the social scientist is poised uneasily between the entities or categories employed and hence operated by the actors he is studying, and the entities and categories he brings to his task from his disciplinary training. The social scientist, I have argued, maps not only the society he fancies he is interacting with, but also the mental maps of their own society carried around by the actors (Jarvie 1972:159–72).

To this argument it is sometimes objected that either the actors' maps are enough or else that the actors' map are redundant and should be ignored. My rebuttal consists in saying that the outcome of action is a functional relationship between the way things seem to the actor and the way in some sense they actually are. The social scientist uses his informants' view of the way things seem as his first clue to the way they are. If an actor acts on the basis of a mistaken supposition about the way things are, the outcome will clearly be a product of his action plus its impact on the situation as it is. If a lone rider believes he is being pursued by a murderous gang and as a result rides his horse to death and perishes himself soon thereafter, his death cannot be explained if we ignore his mistaken belief. Similarly, in accounting for the death of James Dean his view of the situation as embodied in his reported last words is highly germane: Don't worry, he sees us. He'll stop'. On a more complicated level I have argued that in a certain way the question of whether there is a system of social class in any sense can be short-circuited when we know that, whether there is or there isn't, a great many people believe that there is and, in acting accordingly, thereby generate phenomena that constitute a class system of sorts. In a beautiful argument in the 'Arrest' section of *The Gulag Archipelago*, Solzhenitsyn stresses the degree to which the entire system of oppression which he is describing derives its effectiveness from a certain voluntary surrender of legitimacy to it by countless of its victims (Solzhenitsyn 1974:3–23). The actors constitute and sustain the social system.

What role can we see for film in all this? For one thing: a lot of talking heads. Society and culture are to a considerable extent invisible and inaudible, but they can be described in *talk* (MacDougal's and Smith's work illustrate this). Interaction and transaction are the primary modes by which an ethnographer does his work. To an ethnographer busy interacting and transacting a camera might simply be a rather inconveniently large and obtrusive pencil.

Moreover, few are the subjects of anthropological inquiry nowadays who do not know what a camera is, and hence are very much 'on' when it begins to roll, in a way they are not with an ethnographer who takes discreet notes or even stores it all up in his mind, for diary-writing in the evening.

Apart, then, from the value of seeing, and the accidental recording of something valuable, i.e., uninterpreted material at the time of shooting, I am sceptical of the value of film as a vehicle for scientific anthroplogy. To wind up my argument I want to consider some apparent counter-examples: one a case of a film in which a casual remark to the camera can be thought to typify an aspect of the culture in a much smoother way than it could in print; a second case of film makers stumbling on valuable material and learning from the attempt to understand it (the event itself so bewildering that note-taking might have been too slow); and finally an attempt to be discursive, even didactic, in film, an effort documentary-political rather than ethnographic, but one also widely respected and hence useful for my purpose. If these counter-examples go though the film can accomplish more than I have so far allowed.

Case one: a casual remark vividly illustrates a point. In the *Viracocha* film of the Bolivian Series of the Amercian Unversity Field Staff's "Faces of Change" film series, a radical set of attempts to see just how much can be accomplished with the medium of film, there is an already notorious episode where a mestizo landlord is speaking to the camera about his Aymara peasants and there suddenly appears a subtitle to the effect that he is lying. Since the man is no near the beginning of the film its makers may have thought they had to correct what they thought was misformation as it was given. But if the information was so misleading, why not edit it out? Answer: it may typify mestizo attitudes to Aymaras so it has some ethnographic validity. Clearly, unless there is further evidence we will assume this landlord acts towards his peasants in conformity with the picture of them he is describing. To describe a point of view, even a prejudiced one as a lie, however, is to intrude a naive view of the difference between appearance and reality, and of the nature of social and cultural processes. All evidence is equal to the ethnographer, even socially sanctioned lies, prejudices, and confusion.[12]

Case two: luck and anthropological expertise produce something unique. Napoleon Chagnon and Timothy Asch's *The Ax Fight* (1975) is held up as an exemplary piece of ethnographic film making because the fight they photographed just began happening when they were otherwise occupied, but they were fortunately able to turn their cameras on it, and utilise the footage three times. They illustrated some important social and cultural facts as they were displayed in the fight itself, and showed the anthropologist at work learning about what he has observed. Without detracting at all from their feat and its ingenuity, what is all the fuss about: is there anything in the film that Chagnon and his pencil would not have caught? Maybe so. Just possibly events moved so fast that only capturing them on film in order to go over them at leisure made all the difference. Here then we have a slim argument for the value of film in the ethnographic enterprise that allows it to contribute to academic study. Whether the benefits would justify the expense of including filming budgets in all field trips is doubtful, especially as one might argue the whole thing was a fluke, unlikely to be repeated in hundreds of field trips to societies less volatile.[13]

Most ethnographic films are the merest fragments of putative contributions to ethnography: Hilary Harris's beautiful-to-look-at film *The Nuer* lasts 75 minutes and contains only a tiny fraction of the information covered in Evans-Pritchard's book of the same name. For the parochial undergraduates of North America just the chance to see *National Geographic*-style pictures of how others live is perhaps salutary. Be that as it may, where are the filmed attempts to address the major questions that agitate anthropologists intellectually: where the discussions of structure and sentiment, where the films about etics versus emics, where films about Australian kinship, about Choctaw terminology, about the structure of unilineal descent groups, primitive knowledge of the connection between coition and pregnancy? Nowhere to be found I afraid, and any student unfamiliar with these matters has not been seriously trained. So for my third case, which I do grant more to than others, I take a documentary of the utmost seriousness and even pretention: *The Sorrow and the Pity*, the film Alvie Singer (in *Annie Hall*) sees time and time again. This film wants to be taken seriously as a study of collaboration under German occupation in Clermont-Ferrand. To this end, Germans, Frenchmen (collaborators and resisters), and outside statesmen are all given time on screen to explain their point of view. The film is very long, as perhaps befits the gravity of its subject, and skillfully made. And yet . . . how different is it from what is laughingly known as trial by television? How aware are those who talk of the image they cut on screen? How honest was the director in letting them talk and then editing so that they condemn themselves out of their own mouths? How close is the film to propaganda and how far is it from history? I raise these questions because I believe the film does not conform to the methods of social science and history and therefore itself is a tract rather than a primary document. One wishes there were sequences where those coming off worst could be viewing it on the Movieola and have the chance to comment and gloss what they said and what the film maker is saying, rather in the way The Rolling Stones do in *Gimme Shelter*.

These three cases witness the role I have already assigned to ethnographic film, and the final case goes to my point that anthropology (or history or socology) cannot be done on film. The medium itself is unsuitable, even though film makers try valiantly to be reflexive and deposit their 36,000 feet of film in the Smithsonian (H. Smith 1976:24).

V

In an eariler aside I said that feature films might be a richer source for ethnographers than consciously ethnographic or anthropological film. This is because the value of a primary source has great deal to do with it not being used for the purpose it was intended. We do not take Shakespeare's histories as guides to the interpretation of the events they pretend to depict. We are suspicious of all memoirs as likely to be self-serving. Historians hunt for documents that throw light where they do not intend; similarly, social scientists seek clues to social processes that people scarely notice, still less are contriving to confect. But this raises a serious question about the value of film versus the value of discursive language. It is a fact that history is largely a matter of documents and talk, and society is largely a matter of institutions, actions and talk. Film is integrally involved in neither. Briefly in the thirties and forties film was utilised for political purposes, but now that function has passed to television. Film is outside the major processes we call history and society. Zapruder's footage of Kennedy's assassination is valuable because Zapruder captured what he did with a minimum of contrivance. Fiction film is valuable too because in hosts of ways of which it is not aware it depicts people, mores and landscapes of its time. It is fragmentary and tantalising, but nevertheless available to the acute observer.[14] The socially conscious film, however, is far less useful to the scholar, except in so far as the film is typical or generic.

Where do we arrive at finally? The real is created, not given. The artificial is part of the real world: the standing street set in the Burbank studio is a real-world physical object. Film makers are traders in appearances and illusion, whether they are Busby Berkeley and his impossible effects; Flaherty and "The March of time" faking it; or Emile de Antonio editorialising to a captive audience. The possibilities of ethnographic film seem very limted, because film cannot suspend belief: What appears is real, while in science the whole debate is about what to call real given the conflict of evidence before us.

NOTES

[1] Read to the Society for Cinema Studies Annual Conference, San Francisco State University, 24.3.79. Thanks to Joseph Agassi, J. N. Hattiangadi, Sari Thomas and Annette Wiener for critical comments.

[2] A classical statement of this line is Isaac Schapera's *Government and Politic in Tribal Society* (Schapera: 1956). Leach traces the ancestry of the idea to Radcliffe-Brown (Leach 1951: 53).

[3] The Webbs argued that you only had to reveal the facts to make the necessity of reform apparent (Webb and Webb 1932: Chapter XII).

[4] Although it should not be denied that 'scientific' anthropology became pretty preachy too, and still is.

[5] My own preference among Harris' work is his early film *Highway* (1958).

[6] In her complex and sensitive examination of several films about the Trobriands (Weiner 1978) Professor Wiener finds the epistemologies of direct realism, perspectival realism and idealism at work in the practice of different film makers. Although disclaiming any preference among these, the paper ends with a call to address the film as construction rather than as truth. I take issue with this because I offer what I consider to be a philosophy superior to all three, although closest to direct realism. The regulative idea of truth, and the philosophy of empiricism as the main route to it, strike me as ethical as well as epistemological components of the scientific quest (cf. Gellner 1976).

[7] This lovely idea is probably the only lovely thing about a neglected RKO Radio film of 1951 entitled *Double Dynamite*, starring Jane Russell, Franck Sinatra and Groucho Marx.

[8] The standing of hearsay in law is interesting: 'Hear-say is good evidence to prove, who is my grandfather, when he married, what children he had, etc., of which it is not reasonable to presume that I have better evidence', Gilbert's *Law of Evidence*, 1762, quoted in the OED.

[9] In this paper, Popper shows concisely how Freud is a sort of archrationalist who even makes neuroses and psychoses, hitherto uncontroversial paradigms of irrationality, rational, i.e., actions appropriate to the situation as the actor sees it.

[10] The jargon is Harold Garfinkel's (Garfinkel 1967).

[11] (Mead (1963). Photographs 'provide an impersonal check record against which field observations can be placed', (p. 175), moreover, such impersonal photography should take place before the hypotheses are formulated 'for, once the hypothesis was formulated, the anthropologist might become too selective in what he photographed' (p. 172).

[12] The film maker in question is not convinced of this, and he does not describe and defend the incident mentioned (H. Smith 1976).

[13] Of what value can such film be? 'To be unused and unknown has long been the fate of all too many ethnographic films stored in the vaults of museums or the garages of anthropologists' families' (de Brigand 1975: 17). Compare this to the following: White's account of how Boas' field work was buried in 10,000 pages of unreadable prose (White 1966: 6–7).

[14] 'It is usual to define ethnographic film as film that reveals cultural patterning. From this definition it follows that all films are ethnographic . . . ' (de Brigand: 13). The play here is on 'reveals'. Film may reveal cultural patterning intentionally by showing, which is O.K.; or inadvertently by being what it is, which is perhaps best.

REFERENCES

Agassi, Joseph. 1975. *Science in Flux*. Dordrecht and Boston: Reidel.

Berkeley, George. 1910. *A New Theory of Vision and Other Writings*. A. D. Lindsay (ed.), London: Dent.

Bidney, David. 1953. *Theoretical Anthropology*. New York: Columbia University Press.

Brown, G. Gordon and Barnett, James H. 1942. 'Social Organisation and Social Structure'. *American Anthropologist* 44 30–36.

de Brigand, Emilie. 1975. 'The History of Ethnographic Film'. In *Principles of Visual Anthropology*. Paul Hockings (ed.), pp. 13–43. The Hague: Mouton.

Evans-Pritchard, E. E. 1972. 'Review of the Nuer'. *American Anthropologist* 74 1028.

Fabian, Johannes. 1971. 'Language, History and Anthropology'. *Philosophy of the Social Sciences* 1 19–47.

Garfinkel, Harold. 1967. *Studies in Ethnomethodology*. Englewood Cliffs: Prentice Hall.

Gellner, Ernest. 1976. 'An Ethic of Cognition'. In *Essays in Memory of Imre Lakatos*. R. S. Cohen, P. K. Feyerabend and M. W. Wartofsky, (eds.), pp. 161–77. Dordrecht and Boston: Reidel.

Gombrich, E. H. 1962. *Art and Illusion*. Second ed. London: Phaidon.

Grierson, John. 1946. *Grierson on Documentary*. Forsyth Hardy (ed.), London: Collins.

Harris, Marvin. 1968. *The Rise of Anthropological Theory*. New York: Crowell.

Hattiangadi, J. N. 1978–79. 'The Structure of Problems, Parts I and II'. *Philosophy of the Social Sciences* 8: 345–365 and 9 49–76.

Heider, Karl G. 1976. *Ethnographic Film*. Austin: University of Texas Press.

Jarvie, I. C. 1964. *The Revolution in Anthropology*. New York: Humanities.

Jarvie, I. C. 1967. 'On the Theory of Fieldwork and the Scientific Character of Social Anthropology'. *Philosophy of Science* 34: 223–242.

Jarvie, I. C. 1971. 'Reply to Fabian'. *Current Anthropology* 12 231–232.

Jarvie, I. C. 1972. *Concepts and Society*. London: Routledge.

Jarvie, I. C. 1975. 'Epistle to the Anthropologists'. *American Anthropologist* 77, 253–266.

Jarvie, I. C. 1978a. 'Review of Nanook of the North'. *American Anthropologist* 80 196–197.

Jarvie, I. C. 1978b. 'Seeing Through Movies.' *Philosophy of the Social Sciences* 8 374–397.

Leach, E. R. 1945. 'Jinghpaw Kinship Terminology'. *Journal of the Royal Anthropological Institute* 75 59–72.

Leach, E. R. 1951. 'The Structural Implications of Matrilateral Cross-Cousin Marriage'. *Journal of the Royal Anthropological Institute* 81 23–55.

Lejeune, Robert. 1977. 'The management of Mugging'. *Urban Life* 6 123–148.

Loizos, Peter. 1977. 'Review of Ethnographic Film'. *American Anthropologist* 79 758–759.

Mead, Margaret. 1963. 'Anthropology and the Camera'. In *Encyclopedia of Photography*. Willard D. Morgan (ed.), Vol. 1, pp. 166–184. New York: Greystone Press.

Mead, Margaret. 1973. 'The Art and Technology of Fieldwork'. In *A Handbook of Method in Cultural Anthropology*. Raoul Naroll and Ronald Cohen (eds.), pp. 246–265. New York: Columbia University Press.

Mead, Margaret and Gregory Bateson. 1977. 'For Gods Sake Margaret'. *Coevolution* (Summer).

Nadel, S. F. 1951. *The Foundations of Social Anthropology*. London: Cohen and West.

Needham, Rodney. 1979. *Essential Perplexities*. Oxford: OUP.

Popper, K. R. 1957. *The Poverty of Historicism*. London: Routledge.

Popper, K. R. 1959. *The Logic of Scientific Discovery*. London: Hutchinson.

Popper, K. R. 1967. 'La Rationalité et le Statut du Principe de Rationalité'. In *Les Fondaments Philosophiques des Systèmes Economiques*. Emil M. Claassen (ed.), pp. 142–150. Paris: Payot.

Popper, K. R. 1972. *Objective Knowledge*. Oxford: OUP.

Posner, Judith. 1979. 'Reply to Lejeune'. *Urban Life*. Forthcoming.

Schapera, Isaac. 1956. *Government and Politics in Tribal Society*. London: Watts.

Smith, Hubert. 1976. *A Filmmaker's Journal*. AUFS Fieldstaff Reports, West Coast South America Series. Vol. XXIII, No. 2.

Smith, Paul (ed.). 1976. *The Historian and the Film*. Cambridge: CUP.

Solzhenitsyn, Alexander. 1974. *The Gulag Archipelago: An Experiment in Literary Investigation I–II*. New York: Harper and Row.

Steward, Julian. 1955. *Theory of Culture Change*. Urbana: University of Illinois Press.

Webb, Sidney and Beatrice. 1932. *Methods of Social Study*. Cambridge: CUP.

White, Leslie A. 1966. 'The Social Organisation of Ethnological Theory'. *Rice University Studies* 52 1–66.

Wiener, Annette B. 1978. 'Epistemology and Ethnographic Reality: A Trobriand Island Case Study'. *American Anthropologist* 80 752–757.

Winch, Peter. 1964. 'Understanding a Primitive Society'. *American Philosophical Quarterly* 1 307–324.

Wisdom, J. O. 1953. *The Unconscious Origin of Berkeley's Philosophy*. London: Hogarth.

CHAPTER 15

ANTHROPOLOGISTS AND THE IRRATIONAL

Sir Raymond Firth, most distinguished living representative of the great tradition of British social anthropology, once wrote, 'Science and magic ordinarily represent to two poles of reason and unreason, but it is not easy to draw a rigid line between the rational and the irrational spheres of human activity'.[1] Anthropologists have not always found the drawing of this line to be as difficult as Firth makes it out to be. Sir James Frazer, for one, had no doubts that bloodthirsty savages dancing about in the skins of their enemies were irrational, whilst scholars writing about these matters in their studies in Cambridge were rational. To anthropologists, the irrational has meant the dark forces: magic, superstition, witchcraft, voodoo, and the like. Since anthropologists adopted participant-observation they can reasonably claim to have greater intimacy with such matters than anyone except the initiates themselves.

Intimacy with the irrational has had its effects. The armchair anthropologists of the nineteenth century, and most of the fieldworkers of the twentieth century, through about 1950, were scientific, rational and detached in their outlook. Hence they regarded the irrational as something in need of explanation. Without for a moment believing that the subjects of anthropological investigation were enslaved by the dark forces, as travellers tales and priests had tended to suggest, they nevertheless acknowledged that other than rational ideas played a quite considerable role in the social organisation of many of the peoples they studied. But so too did many ideas that any European social scientist could identify with, such as technology, wealth, power, legality, sexuality, and so on. If, then, these societies had ideas and institutions that were quite intelligible in their structuring and operation to the European mind, how could they co-exist with ideas about the dark forces and together constitute a coherent and integrated society? Why would not societies wracked by accusations and counter-accusations of sorcery and witchcraft not pull themselves apart, rather as in the cases of the Witchfinder General in England or Salem in Massachusetts?[2]

The attempt to explain interest in the dark forces looked, to some observers, like an attempt to explain them away. Anthropologists have always vacillated between curiosity about others and a guilty admiration. This sets them up for the reaction of relativism. Maybe anthropologists should not be explaining the dark forces but learning about them in order to comprehend their power in the society studied and in our own society. An anthropologist has only to pick up a tabloid newspaper and turn to the astrological section, or to notice the myriad religious and quasi-religious cults that flourish in his own society, to come rapidly to the conclusion that there are more things in heaven and earth than are dreamed of in scientific philosophy, and that perhaps a more humble attitude is appropriate. Thus whereas once the legends were about which anthropologist slept with his or her subjects, now the additional question arises as to whether the anthropologist was initiated into the tribe, embraced their religious ideas, or keeps a juju in his office.

Perhaps a third way can be charted. Is it not possible to explain the things people do without setting out to explain them away; is it not possible to allow that people may believe different things without concluding that all beliefs on offer are equally valuable; is it not possible to examine the dichotomy between the irrational and the rational upon with both reactions draw and to break it down? Perhaps rationality lies not in beliefs, but in the manner in which beliefs are held. Perhaps rationality is a matter of attitude. The anthropologist can escape patronising the poor superstitious savages, escape patronising his own culture as naive and ethnocentric, and instead attempt to secure for his subject an attitude that is both tolerant and yet rational, open to the ideas of others yet not uncritical of them; infused with human sympathy yet not irresponsible.

My plan will be to explore the first two reactions to the irrational in order to expose their weaknesses and deficiencies, and to conlude by building an approach that supersedes them, partly by defusing the issue itself. Perhaps we can cease to be prisoners of the asumption that there is an irrational, some dark forces, to which we must react. All that there is is the flux of experience, bewildering and incoherent as it presents itself to us, and there is our yearning to give it order and thus to be able to enjoy it, to no longer be afraid of and threatened by it.

This account is general, because it is clear enough that anthropological subjects, mired in the dark forces as they are supposed to be, display the same kind of fascination and repulsion towards western man and his works, as the anthropologist displays towards witchcraft, voodoo, etc. etc. And the anthropologist capitulating to the native world in the style of Castaneda[3] is a form of crisis or breakdown of imposed order that is similar to frenzied reactions on the other side, such as the cargo cult.

Long ago, in a study of anthropology refracted through the experience of the cargo cult, I tried to suggest that anthropology was an academic cargo cult. I should also have added that there were elements of cultural cargo cult too. Anthropology was the cutting edge of scientific man's self-confidence. They would go to the remotest societies and show that they made perfect sense on quite humdrum principles. Their members would be seen to be organising their lives around power, wealth and beliefs; engaged in the struggle for survival; obeying law, pursuing their livelihood, contracting marriages, and so on. This needed saying and became a sort of crisis-point in western self-regard because they were a living alternative to the barve new world of progress, industry and science. The cultural loss of self-confidence that this induced was slow, perhaps because it was easy to reject their consiness with the heart of darkness. But anthropology was a reflexive cargo cult, it insidiously undermined the self-regard of the cultures doing it, bringing home the elements of caprice, arbitrariness, and even darkness to be found even among ourselves.

1. REPULSION

Repulsion from the dark forces can be seen in reactions that range from 'ye Beastly Devices of Ye Heathen,' through to moderate old Evans-Pritchard's view that, neat though the Azande system of witchcraft, oracles and sorcery might be, unfortunately, chaps, witches simply don't exist. In the case of the cargo cults, the strongest repulsion was expressed by the colonial official-cum-anthropologist F. E. Williams, who chronicled the cult called the Vailala Madness.[4] This was a prototypical cargo cult among people living on the Vailala River in Papua. The belief became widespread that the ancestors were going to return, bringing with them vast quantities of cargo, that is, material goods, that belonged to the people, but had been misappropriated by the white colonists. Great excitement surrounded the beliefs. The traditional religion and its implements were rejected, new organisations, such as dummy police and dummy civil service were set up, and preparations went ahead to receive and store the coming cargo. Particularly notable to the observing Europeans was the affliction of mass hysteria in which large numbers of people became giddy and staggered around, sometimes pouring out utterances in what appeared to be glossolalia.

Williams reaction to this cult was that it was muddle-headed nonsense. Somehow, the natives had to be brought to realise that cargo goods were worked for, earned, manufactured, and that they did not rightfully belong to anyone but their manufacturers and purchasers. They also had to be calmed down, got back to productive work and perhaps educated into an outlook less fantastic and occult.

At about the same time Peter Lawrence and I published studies in which we in effect rehabilitated Williams' view.[5] Our contention (developed entirely independently) was that cargo cults were attempts to impose meaningful order on the flux of experience, especially the experience of western colonialism as it had impacted on these dwellers of the western Pacific. Fusing the received stock of ideas of their traditional thought systems with the events surrounding the arrival of white men led, by no very great leap of thought, to doctrines we call cargo cults, where traditional magico-religious means were applied to current colonial situation problems, especially that of relative deprivation. My reasoning was from a philosophically sympathetic cognitive reading of the cargo cults ideas, Lawrence was able to show how in the historical succession of cults in one area there was manifestly some improved grasp of what was actually going on in the culture contact situation. Although Lawrence was far from the point Peter Worsley reached, when he suggested the cults were the beginning of a political or class consciousness of the exploited.[6]

Looking back, I see now a grave weakness in my reasoning, at least; the account was too specific. Here apparently are cults that grow out of culture clash; but, were there not millennial or end-of-the-world cults in our own society, also expecting such things as reversal of the social or economic order, and how could these be related to anything like culture clash? I have in mind the sort of cult studied by Festinger in *When Prophecy Fails*, which concentrated on the problem of what happens to cults that predict a millennium that then fails on the given date to arrive.[7] I also think of the True Light Church of Christ in North Carolina that believed Jesus' Second Coming was due in 1970, who had quit their jobs in anticipation of being the only 'elect' who would be saved.[8]

These cults in the heartland of the United States could hardly be laid to culture clash. But they could be looked at as stemming from the desire to give order and meaning to diverse elements of experience. They grow up among people who have taken the Christian scriptures very seriously, including lots of dark sayings, numerological and cabbalistic passages, references to what seem like real events, and so on, and some attempt has been made to decipher these hidden messages from God and to act accordingly. The difference between these cultists and the anthropologist is easy to discern: while the anthropologist believes in gods, he probably doesn't believe in God, he doesn't take the holy scriptures awfully seriously, and he finds order in his life by trying to fathom the order other people make of their lives. But by what argument does he elevate his own seeking for order over that of his subjects?

By the argument of the priority of science. Can this argument by sustained? Not, I believe, in its progressivist or positivist forms. Science does not have a priority that is god-given. Science has a priority only in the sense that it is an attempt at a more comprehensive ordering of experience, that in its turn makes ordered sense of our earlier attempts at ordering. But it does not and need not exempt itself, or earlier versions of itself. Science can be treated as merely one more religion among others, but it can also be treated as a meta-religion that makes sense of other first-order religions and is itself open to being made sense of in its turn. It teaches curiosity and scepticism towards objects of repulsion (and attraction). The dark forces may be the ancestor of enlightenment.

In the history of the encounter with cargo cults, then, we can see a development. Bewilderment and disgust is the initial reaction: the Papuans are acting childishly, or like the stupid savages they are. This is followed by two related and rather high-falutin, explanations, similar in that they do not find it tolerable to treat what the savages are doing without either attraction or repulsion. I am alluding to structural-functional and to symbolist explanations. Structural-functional explanations are those that relate the workings of social institutions to the basic functional ordering necessary for social life to go on at all. Most subtly worked out in Evans-Pritchard on Nuer Kinship and Azande religion, it was most pithily formulated for the dark forces by Max Gluckman in his classic radio talks published as *Custom and Conflict in Africa*.[9] After chapters with such titles as 'The Peace in the Feud', 'The Frailty in Authority', he set out to demonstrate 'The Logic in Witchcraft'. By 'logic' I think he meant 'reason', and what he tries to do is show the sociological reasonableness of witchcraft accusations. They systematically follow, he says, lines of tension and dispute in social institutions; they provide a means of concretising the bad feelings that grow up among those living in proximity, rivalry, subordination, kinship and so on. And though they may appear to be deeply divisive of themselves, perhaps what they do is externalise and canalise bad feeling. Furthermore, many societies have means of counter-acting witchcraft, or deciding whether an accusation is true, and employing customary means to diffuse it. Among the Azande the witch does not neces-sarily know that he or she is hexing his or her victim, and so the accused too has an interest in deciding and discharging the accusation.

This picture is very neat and impressive except that it relies on a homeo-static model of society that offers no account of the transition from, or the decay of, useful social institutions like witchcraft. Cargo cults are, for the purposes of this argument, even more acute. Manifestly they are in Melanesia phenomena of culture clash and social change, and hence only partly amenable to structural explanation. They are in no way part of a homeostatic system, if anything they are disruptive interruptions of social change. As for cults in the American heartland, one might look at them with less than glassy-eyed trust, as structural phenomena, certainly, but not central or homeostatic. They might be looked at rather as marginal patterns of bonding between individuals and families who feel socially isolated and threatened. Their ready acceptance of themselves as an elect who must keep together and act on instructions shields them from the realisation that perhaps their way of life and beliefs play no functional role in the present social set-up.

As a consequence of these weaknesses, symbolist explanations came to the fore. Fascination and repulsion were fused, then mixed perhaps with a little patronage. Could it be that cargo cults are not discourse at the literal level at all, but rather at the symbolic level, whatever that is? Here there is a difficulty, because some anthropologists are Freudians, others are Roman Catholics, still others Lévi-Straussians and so on, and each author hunts for different sets of symbols at work in religious ideas. At an obvious level, of course cargo cults are symbolic. To believe in the return of the ancestors bearing great wealth, thus inverting the present social relations of colonialism and dependence between natives and the powers that be, might almost be described as wish-fulfilment. Much more sophisticated vocabularies can be introduced and much more cryptic symbolic purposes can be entertained, as when Mary Douglas reduces notions of purity and danger, of the ordering of meals, of the abominations of Leviticus to the social need to classify, to order, to impose sense upon inchoate and threatening nature.[10] So cargo cults too would be amenable to such reasoning. The people on the Vailala River perhaps re-ordering their world in line with the orderings they see Europeans manipulating in the hope that they too will be able to manipulate successfully.

Both structural-functionalists and symbolists rely heavily on the ideas of Durkheim and Mauss; on confronting the dark forces and noting how marvellously they integrate the society. Structures and symbols can be interpreted as struts and buttresses that hold the working society together. But cargo cults are resistant to these sorts of interpretation, because they usually stand at a juncture where standing, ordering and integrating structures are being eroded, challenged, undermined by the cult, where symbolic pictures of the world are being added to, changed, overthrown. Hence at the very best cargo cults can be seen as though they were presaging future integration of society, at some time when the present turbulence is passed.

Integrationist theories have difficulty in accounting for situations of change or flux, when lack of integration is precisely what is happening. Feuds and witchcraft accusations are stabilising and integrating factors by comparison. There is a repetitive, patterned and cyclical character to them, making them integral parts of the social fabric. Cargo cults are bizarre, infrequent, individuated, and sometimes highly disruptive of all forms of normal social life. Cultists may destroy their wealth or property, cut themselves off from their neighbours, withdraw their wage labour, engage in collective building and ritual activities that set them apart from those not involved, and so on. Of course, in the long run some case can be made that they are integrative. But then everything is integrative. That such disruptions are responses to plights goes without saying, and that these reponses are forms of coping and hence over-coming is clear also.

2. ATTRACTION

Attraction and repulsion are of course opposites that often contain the other. Thus it might seem that one reason archrationalistic anthropologists made a study of 'primitive peoples' was because of a hidden attraction to the irrational. Thus Frazer seems positiviely to wallow in ever more bizarre and sanguinary customs. Impeccably atheistic anthroplogists meticulously document the detail of ceremonial and belief among their subject peoples, a courtesy they would be unlikely to extend to the practices and ideas of their co-cultural cohorts. But in others the attraction was nearer the surface, especially in those of High Church or Roman Catholic learnings. There we see the fascination with the things divine, the tendency to take religion at face value, the desire, in the case of Evans-Pritchard, to write for the Nuer the sort of account of their religion they themselves would have written had they theologians to hand. The resultant book, *Nuer Religion,* alarmingly assimilates the Nuer to a conception of religion and belief that is unmistakably ethnocentric and sent, I remember, a frisson through the anthropologists at the LSE when it was published.[11]

Rightly so, for what Evans-Pritchard had done was to confront the irrational, the dark forces and to try to defuse them by bringing them into coherent comparison with things thought to be more familiar or accessible, western theological concepts. This makes the book a sad sequel to his masterpiece, *The Nuer,* and to his *tour de force, Witchcraft Oracles and Magic Amongst the Azande.* Absorbing and ramified as is Evans-Pritchard's account of Zande beliefs, the reader is given a coherent system of ideas that are then dismissed our of hand as ideas. There are no witches. This robust attitude is no longer present in

Nuer Religion. We long for and do not get the assertion; of course, there is no *kwoth.*

Beginning perhaps with Peter Winch's astonishing 1964 attack on the Azande book[12] we have gradually seen anthropologists looking for arguments to get out of those necessary sceptical denials. Instead we have western scientists off in the wilds arguing away to themselves that maybe there is some-things credible in mumbo jumbo. Winch argued that Evans-Pritchard's asser-tion that there are, after all, no witches, was impermissable. In an argument so tortuous none of his critics has been able to reproduce it to his satisfaction, Winch reasoned that the witch system of the Azande constituted a complete universe of discourse, and there was no meta-universe of discourse in which the adequacy, accuracy or truth of that universe of discourse could be appraised. His motive was clearly infatuation. He wanted to be able to find an argument that would prevent the assertions 'God doesn't exist'. or, 'religious beliefs such and so are mistaken' being legitimate. Not being legitimate, they could hardly be a condition of social science.

Widely discussed by philosophers down to this day, I suspect that the implicit (and denied) relativism of Winch's account was what percolated through to a whole new set of anthropologists who were off to their own confrontations with the dark forces of religion in the Far East, and Africa. From being a curiosity, the savage had moved towards being a repository of wisdom, living in harmony with nature and perhaps in communion with forces and things not vouchsafed to jaded and science-satiated westerners. Leaving aside the pragmatic paradox of the assertion of this idea by westerners, we can look instead at its more extreme forms in phenomenological anthropology.

Here the attack goes right down to the basic premiss that there is a sustain-able distinction between the subject and the object of anthropological inquiry. We shall set aside the obvious objection that if there is not such a distinction then it is unclear who is studying whom, why and why bother? Fabian has suggested a milder version of this: that what anthropologists study or, perhaps more accurately, what anthropologists constitute, is an interactive process between the participant observer and his subjects in which a social reality is constituted and it is this the anthropologist so to speak writes up.[13] Fabian, who studied the Jamaa, seems to have retained his detachment from life in the congo, but another student of the area, Jules-Rosette went so far as to herself become a believer in the religion she was studying.[14]

Jules-Rosette I shall come back to in my final section. Fabian's argument I have discussed independently.[15] What I want to do here is diagnose. Fabian's own encounter with a diffuse movement like Jamaa, and the encounters of like-minded colleagues,[16] seems to flow from attraction and sympathy with his anthropological subjects. While it may be understandable that I criticise being repelled or ambivalent towards the irrational dark forces, I can imagine puzzlement that I should frown on attraction and sympathy. The reason is because there is a confusion over what anthropology is about. It is about intellectual problems involved in explaining the unintended consequences of human action.[17] That the subjects of study are humans with many irrational attitudes is part of the problem, not a solution. It is irrelevant and confusing to allow either attraction and repulsion to influence one's work. More appropriate is to be detached and sceptical. Neither the rational nor the irrational is its own explanation.

Cargo cults have produced their western adherents too, Edward Rice in his forceful and impassioned *John Frum He Come* gives an account of life on Tanna and of the cult of John Frum that is so sympathetic the author more or less declares that he accepts that John Frum is a reality for the Tannese, and hence is a reality.[18] This reality may be denied the colonialists, but he, Rice was made privy to it. Preposterous as these conversions may seem, and as destructive as they undoubtedly are of any anthropological perspective, I propose to treat them as important indicators. The error behind them seems to have to do with observationalism. If you conceptualise anthropology as a field, with subjects and topics that have to be observed and recorded, then you must concede that sympathy and the insider's viewpoint is to be acknowledged. But then your are a perfect patsy for the Winchian pitch that only believers can discuss the nature of the reality of God.

3. NEITHER REPULSION NOR ATTRACTION

My discussion of the third view will turn around two concepts. One is *encounter* between the self and others (anthropology), and between the self and former self (anthropologists). The other is *commitment*, whether to anthropology as a humane enterprise, to one's self, or to the people studied. Encounter, it seems is always a threat to commitment: it is not easy to maintain one's commitments in alien surroundings; the ways of alien people have a way challenging the assumptions one may not even have noticed one was committed to. Encounter with the dark forces can be so harrowing that the the anthropologist may be repulsed; or may convert; or may come to look at anthropology as itself a form of social and cultural adaptation to a changing world, a form of cult or magic itself; that the anthropologist is like the prophets and magicians he studies, using the dreams, fears and desires of the culture in the presentation of their message.[19]

Though encounter has this effect on commitment we still seek it: this might seem ordinary enough: encounter is a part of our experience, and we all hope to learn from experience. Yet two things are worth nothing here as rather extra-ordinary. One is that commitments are often taken to be just those things on which we predicate our learning; not at all the sorts of things it is possible for us to chop and change in the course of learning and under the impact of new experiences. Commitments are usually thought to lie behind a protective belt of epistemological and psychological devices that prevent experience inflicting any damage on them.[20] Yet George Orwell noted (*Clergyman's Daughter*) that commitments come and go and cannot be kept; that their changes are somehow linked with experience, with encounter. The other point is that among the commitments being challenged here are not just first order but also the metacommitments — commitments, that is, to this or that tradition of enquiry.

One might not normally expect that experience would penetrate the protective belt and affect both commitments and metacommitments. For if and when it does so, it invalidates commitments as the (unquestioned) *grounds* of enquiry, and for logical reasons. That is to say, even if facts can threaten commitment, this suffices to deprive it of its ascribed foundational status. So: either the protective belt does its job unfailingly; or, other grounds for inquiry must be sought. A third conclusion is possible: enquiry needs no grounds; presuppositions are always only for the sake of argument and can at will become themselves subject to further argument. Such a third alternative is one that I have explored for many years, trying to draw the consequences it appears to have for anthropological enquiry.

The clash between encounter and deep commitment or metacommitment is one that I can hardly but welcome. In my first book I tried to show how cargo cults, or rather, the attempts of anthropologists to grapple with cargo cults, could tell us something about anthropology itself.[21] There seemed to me to be deeply buried philosophical commitments in anthropology that cargo cults could show up to be the prejudices that they were: inductivism, sensationalism, and essentialism were among those I picked out. It was and is my view that there are no commitments so deep as to be unreachable. Everything is negotiable with experience, including the notions of experience and of the objects of experience. In a way, precisely such negotiation is what (western) philosophy is.[22] So, it is not unexpected that anthropologists prepared to follow the argument wherever it leads, might detect a clash between their field experience and the endeavour which brought them to the field in the first place — attraction or repulsion.

The question I want now to pose is whether they should take the further step of concluding that it is not commitments that yield to experience, but the principle of commitment itself, the idea that commitment is the foundation of all experience. The step, that is, of arguing that once one's commitments have been shaken, one can no longer settle as comfortably into new commitments as before. For once shaken, commitments no longer have that feeling of being entrenched clauses, out of reach, lived by rather than intellectualized.[23] The commitment to a way of doing anthropology leads to discoveries that shake the commitment to anthropology itself, and that in turn shakes confidence in commitment itself. Or does it?

My hesitation stems from a remark of Bernadetta Jules-Rosette, which I say frankly, quite took me aback. The diviner John Marinke asks her: 'Are you skeptical of African science?' *And she shakes her head.* This is in the course of an absorbing and sensitive paper that repudiates romanticism, and strives (wo)manfully to regain the enterprise of science. She has it that in the end, whatever understanding the anthropologist has gained must be translated back into the language of social science.

Why am I taken aback? Because I take the oxymoron 'committed science' to be in fact a contradiction in terms.[24] It would seem to me incumbent upon anyone purporting to be a social scientist to answer the question with a nod of the head. (Perhaps adding a disclaimer like, 'And also of many other things'.)[25] And here I find it terribly hard to disentangle my own personal scepticism from the sceptical attitude I feel to be a deep part of science, especially science that has been engaged in self-reflection.[26] If I was studying the arcana of nuclear physics or medicine and was asked whether I was sceptical of western science, I am afraid I should nod my head as vigorously as I would were I asked the same question about Uri Geller. John Marinke is not Uri Geller and Bernadetta Jules-Rosette is not ICJ.

Scepticism, I would hazard, is a mandatory part of the scientific attitude, because only scepticism allows one to be ruthlessly critical not only of the ideas of others, but, more especially, of one's own pet ideas. The very thought of being unsceptical towards African science gives me vertigo. Scientists — anthropologists included — are, or should be, *professional* sceptics. They are reporters, commentators, on the human condition; a condition in which they participate, of course. But they are not reporting on those aspects of it in which they participate with all men, they are reporting on those aspects of it which seem different, alien, exotic, inexplicable, irrational. They are professionally marginal men. It is often remarked that the sorts of people who become sociologists and anthropologists are people marginal to their society: outsiders, immigrants, members of minorities, etc., and that the social sciences as it were rationalise their situation. Perhaps so. Social science might also be seen as the struggle to become marginal; the effort to differentiate oneself from the rest of mankind; to free oneself from the assumptions and preconceptions other men take for granted, live by; the attempt to transcend one's society in order the more clearly to see it and oneself. Social understanding does not mean one ceases to be a social being: that is impossible. Similarly, self-understanding does not imply that one ceases to be a self. What one endeavours to do is to achieve distance from one's society, to achieve distance from one's fellow man, ultimately, to achieve distance from oneself. This distancing, which we already experience unreflectively in what we call self-consciousness, and which ethnomethodologists achieve by 'throwing'[27] is very hard to achieve, and even harder to maintain. There are those who question its value or its legitimacy. My argument would be that there is no going back now: it is rather like being naive or unselfconscious; once one lost those pristine states, they are gone forever. Social naiveté and unself-consciousness went out long before the Greeks. Men have been able to view themselves and their social arrangements with detachment at least since then. Given that there is no going back, no lost community of self, society and fellowship that we can regain, the most rational policy is to try to do the job well.

Part of the problem here has to do with commitment. If we could get rid of commitment, that is, if we could get rid of the commitment to commitment, the anthropology of religious experience might be more progressive, we might learn from encounter more than we now do. Far too many anthropologists take religion suspiciously seriously. When I say 'suspiciously,' what I am suspicious of is that they may themselves be believers, or former believers, who remain committed to the view that religion is an authentic experience to which the anthropologists must do justice, pay due respect, etc, and take this pretext to be commitment to scientific anthropology. Thus, in a classic case, Evans-Pritchard is scathing about Durkheim's views on religion, when one suspects this is because Durkheim is not committed to religion, is neither attracted nor repelled. Perhaps this is a problem that will never be solved, for it arises in philosophy as well as anthropology: the problem, namely, of whether or not one should allow oneself to be committed to religion. Not to this or that specific religion, but to religion as such or in general. Committed to religion or to the religion of anti-religion, anthropologists undergo an encounter which makes them change or modify self and commitment, including commitment to self. Were they from the start more professionally or methodologically sceptical — of themselves, of science, of anthropology, certainly of religion, of all human activity — cognitive as well as behavioural — perhaps their unease would be lessened. But their aim to preserve commitment effects their habit or methodology. This is as it should be, of course, for recommendations about methods turn on views of aims. I therefore think we need to discuss the aim of anthropology. A standard view is that anthropology aims to describe. This aim can be criticised as inadequate since it does not specify what is to be described, and because an argument can be made that everything can be described in infinitely many different ways. Another view is that anthropology aims to explain why people do things. This seems to be a misunderstanding. Freud may tell us why we do things, but subjects like anthropology, sociology and economics concentrate instead on the consquences of the fact that we simply do do things.[28] My present view is that the social sciences aim to explain what might be called the unintended consequences of people's action,[29] and I follow Popper in holding that anthropology is best regarded as the general, cross-cultural form of sociology.[30] Take automobile accidents. The social scientist's aim is not to explain automobile accidents, unless they are true accidents, when we seek those unintended aspects of the physical and human situation that brought them about (bad weather, poor signs, distractions, etc.); otherwise, the reasons road-signing is poor, or the reasons the driver is distracted or drunk, what one might call the causes of the accident, are the purview of applied rather than theoretical social science. Rather, theorists concern themselves with things like markets, kinship systems, land tenure, political arrangements, religious ceremonies, and the like. Malinowski on the *kula*, Mauss on the potlatch, Durkheim on the elementary forms, Evans-Pritchard on the Nuer lineage and feud, Radcliffe-Brown on Australian marriage rules, Fortes on Tallensi kinship, etc., all these great anthropologists were exploring the unintended consequences, the systemic outcome, of the actions of actors. In the immortal phrase of Adam Ferguson, the result of human action, but not the execution of any human design. Because no human design is involved, such results, outcomes, systems, are problematic, require explanation. Or, to be more precise, many will be taken for granted, even unnoticed. It is when some theory goes wrong, when human design is thwarted, that we notice the gap in our understanding of our own social system. An anthropologist merely magnifies this. He finds almost the entire system he is endeavouring to enter problematic, the more so as his efforts to enter it are thwarted. From this encounter, anthropology stems; this encounter is the individual microcosm of the global and persistent phenomenon of culture contact and culture clash, which may be the engine of all intellectual and cultural progress.

Problemstellung, which can by no means be taken for granted, can be seen as contrasted with, even opposed to, a different aim, one so diffuse it is hard to formulate, but one might caricature and call it 'acting out one's love for mankind,' and hence stressing empathy, *engagement*, understanding, mutual interaction, shared reality production, and the like. All this is very moral and very earnest. One might ask what it is all for? What problems is it supposed to solve? The problem perhaps of human misunderstanding, or lack of communication? If this, then I would argue it is both misconceived and naive. No class of mediators is needed to cope with the problem of communication. Nations and societies can communicate through their diplomats, their interpreters, travellers, etc. There is no point in financing people to go on expensive expeditions to the ends of the earth to gratify a yearning for empathy with their fellowman, or to chisel away at problems of human communication. The naiveté is to think of the problem of communication as a specifiable and hence solvable problem like the problem of whether to grant diplomatic immunity. Communication problems, even within the same culture, the same family, are a part of the human condition with which we all continually struggle, but which can hardly legitimate a specific academic endeavour like anthropology.

My view is, I acknowledge, an intellectualist view. And I note how few allies I have in anthropology. The ordeal-by-fieldwork has been replaced by fieldwork-as-personal-odyssey-and-self-discovery. So I find myself in the awkward position of speaking for the older anthropological tradition, which concerns not the doer but the deeds. Following that tradition I ask, 'What problems have we solved, with what theories, to which tests have they been put, and to which further ones should they be put?

One might compare the situation, as Jules-Rosette does, to the learning of a language. One reason to learn the language of a faraway place might be that one wants to go and live there. This is rather an odd aim if one has never been there; but never mind. Another reason might be that one wants to learn the language in order to be able to translate from that language back into one's own, to tell people things. This is a public purpose, to which the methods of total immersion, empathy, etc., may be appropriate, as may many other methods, including course-work and private study. In the first case the end is private. If you don't wish to bring them to us (or us to them, as medical missionary, e.g.) then the purpose is private and of no legitimate intellectual or academic concern. Empathy may be all right as a moral or methodological stance, but it is not itself sufficient.

Jules-Rosette says that unless this translation back is accomplished then why call the result of one's endeavours science? This is too weak. What needs to be said is that science has presuppositions — among them a basic realism. Realism has notoriously many philosophical difficulties, as has a realistic empiricism. Bishop Berkeley thought that that showed one had to retreat into idealistic phenomenalism.[31] This is a mistake. Phenomenalism and idealism have even more notorious difficulties. That the basis of science is realistic, more so in the social sciences, seems to me blindingly obvious. We do not allow the problem of other minds to drive us into solipsism; no more should we allow arguments from the social construction of reality to drive us away from realism.[32] For all the difficulties of realism, it still has obvious and very powerful arguments in its favour, including those from evolution.

Having come so far, and having focussed the issue in philosophical terms, I now turn to a brief autobiographical offering.

By profession, I am a philosopher of science. I teach in a philosophy department and am without formal standing among social scientists.[33] My B.Sc. Econ. was in social anthropology, but my Ph.D., also within the Faculty of Economics, is in Scientific Method. This, I suppose, makes me an officially certified methodologist. Anyway, whatever I am, or take myself to be, I seem to be a stranger or outsider to anthropologists.[34] Especially when their concern is reflections on their field experience, and their estimate of the impact is has had upon themselves and their ideas. However, I have long been struggling with my own fieldwork and conversion experience. The experience in question was with a secular cult known as British social anthropology.[35] Unlike some anthropologists, my struggle was to *avoid* conversion, to refuse assent to the community, to stay marginal, to insist on accepting only what I chose. To avoid attraction and repulsion. It was in this posture that I commenced my research into cargo cults twenty three years ago. My desire to do a philosophical-cum-methodological Ph.D. thesis in the library, rather than an anthropological-fieldwork one, was an expression of my resistance to conversion to anthropology, whose high priests at that time considered fieldwork mandatory.[36] I had no desire whatever to do fieldwork, even in a remote part of Britain as was then fashionable, as I imagined it to be a form brainwashing, an irrational condition.

It was a blow to me when my mentor, the late lamented Maurice Freedman, told me that my philosophical/methodological research proposal was unacceptable to the anthropologists even though he had kindly passed it on to the philosophers. They, it turned out, were very willing to help me develop my ideas, and so I became a student of philosophy quite despite myself. This crisis of indentity has never been resolved, and I have learned to exploit the status of a marginal man: to play philosopher to anthropologists, anthropologist to philosophers; to exploit an intellectual niche, whether it be called interdisciplinary studies, philosophy of the social sciences, or methodology.

In the course of developing my critique of social anthropology, under the auspices of philosophy, a critique which could fairly be described as my apologia for not converting, I decided that cargo cults, being weird but fascinating, might give me a clue as to why conversion was not for me. Unexpectedly, the harvest was very great. These cults taught me to de-ethnocentrize myself (so far from being weird and bizarre, they approximate closely to the religious norm of much of the world over much of recorded time), and to see the institutionalized religion of my native British as the exception not the norm. They also taught me that the anthropology of anthropology, indeed the anthropology of the intellectual world, was a rich seam which could be mined for many years to come.

Religion, I confess, always had been rather distasteful to me. Virtually my only background was the diffused Protestantism of secular British culture (school hymns and prayers, public ceremonies, etc.). From early adolescence I had decided the arguments for agnosticism, at the very least, were overwhelming.[37] Later on, however, my resistance to conversion became stronger, perhaps because of my tussle with social anthropology, and I concluded that the utter absurdity of religious beliefs and practises forced me to be atheistic.[38]

Omitted from these autobiographical comments so far is my encounter with the system of ideas to which I do attach myself, a unique system of ideas that does not demand, indeed discourages, conversion; does not articulate and defend particular beliefs, but encourages a certain policy towards all beliefs. This is the philosophy of Karl Popper. As indicated, I had already developed something of a sceptical temperament where it came to attachment to systems of ideas. In my first year at the London School of Economics, I took logic and scientific method under Popper. After that, I thought no more about him for a while, until I began to miss the critical stimulation of his lectures. This was during my second year. So, as a substitute (he gave no second- or third-year lectures in those days), I decided to read *The Open Society and Its Enemies* — the only book of his then available in English. This must have been in the Spring of 1957. Here suddenly was a coherent articulation of my scepticism; here was a critical philosophy which explained to me why I resisted intellectual conversion experiences, whether studying economics or social anthropology. Soon after, I decided to take my honours degree in anthropology, and requested permission, as a senior undergraduate, to sit in on Popper's graduate seminar. This was granted. That seminar, which I attended regularly for the next four-and one-half years, gave me completely new aspirations in the world of ideas. It was an institution in which diverse people came together to reason about all sorts of topics. Research students and visting academics from diverse fields came and aired their latest ideas for critical scrutiny. In practise, Popper's philosophy consisted of no more than the endeavour to carry these explorations forward with the utmost vigour and rigour. Some people could not stand this; their open-mindedness and critical attitude had limits. Religion, I soon realised, was often at the root of the trouble, since it meant taking some ideas for granted, rendering some immune from scrutiny. Limits of open-mindedness seemed intellectually indefensible, yet I began to detect something like them at work in social anthropology. Social anthropology was not just a field or a method, it seemed like a system of methodological and substantial ideas which the student was expected to swallow. This indeed, is how Polanyi and Kuhn have since described science.[39]

Hence, when I was passed on to the philosophers as a research student, I was able almost immediately to settle down to my main problem: disentangling the open- and closed-minded aspects of anthropology. I took as my case study, disentangling the open- and closed-minded aspects of Melanesian thinking as embodied in their cargo cults, and of anthropologists as embodied in their thinking about cargo cults.

Where did all this leave me? Rather distant from the anthropological commitment. A sceptic and a marginal man who very much wanted to remain one, and did not secretly admire or yearn for the security of a lost faith or lost community. Someone not prepared to be more charitable to the religious ideas and systems of native peoples than he was to the religious ideas and system of his own people. Hence, when Jules-Rosette is asked whether she believes in African science, she replies yes; and proceeds to be initiated. I had in effect been asked whether I believed in social anthropology and had replied 'no'; so my initiation was strictly circumscribed. That was fine by me. If someone asks me whether I believe in western science, Chinese science, or African science, my answer is 'no.' As E.M. Forster said, 'I don't believe in belief'.[40] Belief takes away from me a distance, a scepticism, a reservation, which I want always to have, and which I think is essential to intellectual intergrity.[41]

Coming, then, to the literature on cargo cults, was a bit like coming to any ancient or remote text. All sorts of error and nonsense would likely be buried there, but this was not my main concern. Starting from a sceptical point of view, I did not feel that it was false or nonsensical ideas that need explanation; it seemed to me that all ideas were in need of explanation. Perhaps we have made a little progress in the small realm of scientific ideas, however, that was a debatable matter, and the debate itself highlighted the precarious-ness and need of explanation of even such minimal claims. Rather, the problem seemed to me to be to employ imagination and insight in a manner that would make sense of the cargo cults whilst preserving the apparent falseness, even absurdity, of some of their ideas. Neither attraction nor repulsion. Surrounded in my own society by committed people, I felt only the greatest respect for the sceptical over-turning of religious theories of the world that cargo cultists seemed to go in for.

As I struggled to understand cargo cults, and anthropologists' understanding of cargo cults I seemed to see a pattern at work. In remote Melanesia, the eruption of culture contact created an intellectual problem: what is going on? Cargo cult doctrines, garbled, confused and syncretic as they were, made sense as conjectures intended to explain what was going on, and rectify what was perceived as a worsening or intolerable state of affairs.[42] That their ideas were tied to specific expectations at specific times had the disadvantage that the cult might collapse,[43] and the advantage that error would be exposed. (Note how rationalist or intellectualist I was being.)[44] Such an idea had escaped most anthropologists, who had instead displayed their bafflemant by the bewildering array of putative explanations of the cults they offered: stupidity, psychological derangement, irrationality, lack of contact with reality, nativism, oppression, class struggle and so on.[45] Yet I could see pretty clearly that much more research was need.

Soon after my book appeared, Peter Lawrence's masterpiece *Road Belong Cargo* (1964) came to hand, carrying out a programme very close to what I had thought necessary. Little remained for me to do but hail it, analyse it, and note that even in their character as cults, cargo cults were part of a traditional Melanesian mode of response.[46]

But anthropologists were not prepared to come out and debate the issues. Instead, in classic religious or dogmatic school fashion, they closed ranks, made surreptitious changes and modifications, watered down their ideas, and chased hares and fads (structuralism, network theory).[47] Anthropology is like a craft guild, insisting on its master-apprentice initiation through field-work, but trading in uncommunicable mysteries, *Personal Knowledge*, as Polanyi called it.[48] This I felt to be explicable only by taking quite literally the idea that they were a tribe held together by a cult, an ancestral-cum-cargo cult. The religion was the tribe. Festinger predicted that disappointed cultists retreat in on themselves and present a brave face to the world.[49] They then attempt to reduce dissonance by further proselytizing. This certainly seems to have happened in anthropology. Sceptics and wreckers shoved aside, and the subject tramps on, going nowhere , whistling noisily to keep its spirits up.

When I say this, I speak of anthropology conceived of as an attempt to understand and hence come to terms with the human condition.[50] On these matters the subject is not progressing satisfactorily. Exploring cults is also self-exploration; understanding cults can increase self-undersatanding. They can, indeed, increase our understanding of the academic role itself.

4. LESSONS

My argument so far has been that my encounter with cargo cult religion led to sociological discoveries; to spotting parallels between the study of an ostensibly 'academic' subject like anthropology, and millenarian religion. This involves not taking academic subjects altogether seriously at *their* face value either.[51] The parallel has its limitations, no doubt, but it also has hidden strengths. For example, I found that when bringing my thinking up to date in a more recent paper, it felt a bit like writing an epistle.[52] What I had not seen, although it now seems clear enough, was that the parallel can be generalised. I was brought to see this not by reading social scientists, but by reading a novel, one which I propose now to describe and discuss.

Alison Lurie has written a series of novels about academic and intellectual life, among the most brilliant of which is *Imaginary Friends*.[53] This is relevant here simply because it is about the study of a small millenarian cult in upstate New York. The protagonists, besides the cultists themselves, are two university professors; one very young and in his first job, the other middle-aged and securely established as the author of a sociological classic, since which he has not published much. Upstate New York is not far from Cornell, where Ms Lurie teaches, and has for long been an area of intense fringe religious activity. Otherwise, much of the general scheme of the cult has obviously come from reading Festinger's *When Prophecy Fails*.

What the novel does that I had not seen and which illuminates the theme of this volume is simple enough. She shows how the presuppositions of a sociological enterprise like this doom it from the start: the sociologist would dearly love to be invisible, but cannot hope to be; the sociologist wishes to be immune and aloof, selfcontained and untouched, but he cannot be; the sociologist is either attracted or repelled, and both lead to disaster. The study of the cult affects the cult and, more significantly, affects those who study it. McMann the older professor, ends up straddling the border between madness and sanity. The hubris of trying to be god and man at the same time, student and creator, human and super-human , sane and mad, attracted and repelled becomes manifest in McMann. Zimmern, the younger investigator, only just manages to cope and somehow salvage his career. Yet he is unable to understand what has happened; not what went wrong, but was is wrong. Ms Lurie's novel challenges the very enterprise of studying people in society.

Roger Zimmern, an untenured young professor, stands in awe of Thomas McMann, author of the sociological classic, *We and They: Role Conflict in River City*. However, a bond grows between them, and McMann proposes they engage in a joint study of a small cult in the nearby town of Sophis. It transpires that a small group there called the Truth Seekers, meets in the home of middle-aged Mrs. Elsie Novar, where resides also a nineteen-year-old medium called Verena Roberts. Verena has received messages ostensibly from a distant planet, Varna, and its leader, Ro.

The group is quite small, eight or ten people, and both small town and kin. Commuting from the university, Roger and Tom pretend to be intinerant businessmen, although this pretense is later exposed and dropped. Soon after their joining, the group becomes more intense, and a date is set for the arrival of the space men. Rituals are enacted, including dietary and clothing prohibitions. When the prophecy fails to be fulfilled Verena concludes that Ro *has* arrived and entered all of them, and that now life can return to normal. Elsie, however, struggling to interpret the 'message,' concludes that Ro has entered Professor Tom McMann who now is Ro of Varna.

At this point, Verena's boy friend tries to take Verena away, and is himself driven away by Tom, who accuses him of being in league with jealous academic colleagues out to sabotage his study. Ken returns with the police, and McMann resists. In the final scene, Roger visits McMann in the asylum, where the latter maintains that he is playing at being mad in order to do another sociological project. Moreover, he continues, when he gets out, he intends to lead the group forward into a mass movement. Roger's doubts enrage McMann and he chases him away.

So much for summary. Among the fascinating aspects of the novel are how, for example, the two academic strangers give additional weight to the group, the more so after it is discovered that they are among the despised professoriate. It illustrates the virtual impossibility of sticking to non-directive reponses to everything. Roger is very conscientious about this, and as a result becomes the kind of group idiot. McMann, bluff and confident, constantly sails close to the wind, justifying himself in relation to The Study. Allegory, too, is used. The group is called the Truth Seekers, and they meet near a small college town. Explicit parallels are drawn with the University:

The Seekers didn't seem any less crazy, but now everyone else, especially my students, was starting to resemble them. Essentially, they were all converts to the same religion, or victims of the same illusion: they believed in education, in science, in the voice of authority p. 60).

As the time of The Coming approaches:

The Seekers had lectures, they had readings in approved texts, they had assignments (twenty minutes of meditation on set topics before breakfast every day, short essays on matters of special interest). They were expected to take notes at meetings, and copy out the messages received. Between times, they had to study the 'lessons' and memorize the prayers, lists, and definitions dictated by Ro and his friends, preparing themselves to be questioned on them at any time: in effect, called on to recite in class. . . . The whole thing got to be like a relentless parody of higher education. There was the same intense seriousness about a body of the accumulating data which was, to say the least, unverifiable; the same assumption that here was a small group of enlightened. thinking persons who understood the universe correctly. As for the messages from Varna, aren't articles in most professional journals a form of automatic writing? It is another self who speaks there, solemn and oracular, in a cryptic jargon the real man would never use (p. 110).

Just before The Coming, talking over the plan with McMann:

I saw something else too: a connection between McMann's hypothesis about the Truth Seekers and his position in the Department, even in the world. Opposition would never shake his own convictions, so he wanted and expected the Seekers to hold to theirs (p. 184)

Earlier on, when Roger expresses concern about Verena not eating:

"Listen Verena may took pathetic to you," he said in his seminar manner, bluff but highly educated. "But she can take care of herself. You've got to remember, That girl has already changed a number of people's lives rather profoundly. Elsie, Milly, Rufus, the whole lot of them. Don't let her fool you . . . " There were two more lives Verena had changed, I thought, that McMann had overlooked: his and mine (p. 115).

My reasons for bringing up this novel, rather than say some field encounter, should now be fairly obvious. It is true the fieldwork experience has a deep effect on those in it, emotionally, morally and cognitively. It is also true that the endeavours of cultists have great similarities to doing sociology. Moreover it seems that education itself, perhaps especially autonomous higher education, is similar too. This seems to show that there is something universal in the experience of encounter: encounter with new people, new groups, and also encounter with new ideas, dark forces. Since, except for the solitary scholar, most encounters of this kind take place in a social context, where new people, new groups and new ideas are all encountered together, it should cease to surprise us that the encounter with the religious cults of remote peoples has had such an effect on anthropologists and anthropology. Religious experience is after all that place in most societies where individual, group and cognitive encounter are found most frequently and most intensely. In everyday work people are frequently scattered and busy. But at the times of ceremony, rites, religious meetings, etc., they engage with each other and with ideas in their most general form and are attracted or repelled.

Nevertheless, to generalise further, I continue to be impressed by the everyday character of the struggle to be curious and sceptical, not attracted or repelled. Entering a new town, a new university, every term a new classroom, always seems to me to involve these elements, and hence always, to a degree, to affect one cognitively as well as emotionally. MS Lurie may intend her allegory as a criticism of social science. I do not take it as such. I take it that all human encounter is self-making, and human encounter with the ideas and attitudes of others can be self-transcending. But this is an arduous and precarious endeavour that can leave us disillusioned or mad, as easily as enlightened and renewed.

NOTES

[1] Raymond Firth, *Human Types*, Revised Edition, London 1956, p. 155.

[2] Keith Thomas, *Religion and the Decline of Magic*, London 1971; Brian Easlea, *Witch-Hunting, Magic and The New Philosophy*, Brighton 1980; Alan McFarlane, *Witchcraft in Tudor and Stuart England*, London 1970.

[3] Carlos Castaneda, *The Teachings of Don Juan*, Berkeley 1968; *Journey to Ixtlan*, New York 1972.

[4] F. E. Williams, *Papua: Anthropology Reports No. 4, The Vailala Madness, Etc.*, Port Moresby 1923.

[5] Peter Lawrence, *Road Belong Cargo*, Manchester 1964; I. C. Jarvie, *The Revolution in Anthropology*, London 1964.

[6] Peter Worsley, *The Trumpet Shall Sound*, London 1957, Enlarged Edition, New York 1968.

[7] Leon Festinger, Henry W. Riecken and Stanley Schachter, *When Prophecy Fails*, New York 1956.

[8] *New York Times*, January 3, 1971.

[9] Max Gluckman, *Custom and Conflict in Africa*, Oxford 1955.

[10] Mary Douglas, *Purity and Danger*, London 1966.

[11] E. E. Evans-Pritchard, *Nuer Religion*, Oxford 1956.

[12] Peter Winch, 'Understanding a Primitive Society,' *American Philosophical Quarterly*, Vol. 1, 1964, pp. 307–24.

[13] Johannes Fabian, 'Language, History and Anthropology', *Philosophy of the Social Science*, Vol. 1, 1971, pp. 19–47.

[14] Bernadetta Jules-Rosette, 'The Veil of Objectivity: Prophecy, Divination and Social Inquiry,' *American Anthropologist*, Vol. 80, 1978, 549–70.

[15] I. C. Jarvie, 'Epistle to the Anthropologists', *American Anthropologist*, Vol. 77, 1975, 253–66.

[16] See his special issue of *Social Research*, Vol. 46, No. 1, 1979.

[17] I. C. Jarvie, *Concepts and Society*, London 1972.

[18] Edward Rice, *John Frum He Come*, New York 1974.

[19] Mercene Marcoux, in an unpublished paper.

[20] R. G. Collingwood held this view in a most interesting form, see *Essay on Metaphysics*, Oxford 1940, chapter V; *An Autobiography*, Oxford 1939, ch. VII.

[21] *The Revolution in Anthropology*, London 1964; see also 'On Theories of Fieldwork and the Scientific Character of Social Anthropology', *Philosophy of Science*, Vol. 34, 1967, 223–42; 'The Problem of Ethical Integrity in Participant Observation', *Current Anthropology*, Vol. 10, 1969, 505–8; 'On the Objectivity of Anthropology', in R. J. Seeger and R. S. Cohen (eds.), *Philosophical Foundations of Science*, Boston Studies in the Philosophy of Science, Vol. XI, Dordecht 1974, pp. 317–24; 'Cultural Relativism Again', *Philosophy of the Social Sciences*, Vol. 5, 1975, pp. 342–53.

[22] Here I follow Ernest Gellner's intriguing idea that the centrality of epistemology in western philosophy is explainable. See his *Legitimation of Belief*, London 1975.

[23] Cp. Gellner's remarks on Husserl in 'Ethnomethodology: the Rechantment Industry, or the Californian Way of Subjectivity', *Philosophy of the Social Sciences*, Vol. 5, 1975, 446–7.

[24] She does not, and her explicit allegiance to the brilliant but irrationalist Micheal Polanyi, confirms this point. Cf. note 39 and 40 below.

[25] She does not justify her answer by saying information would otherwise be withheld. Whether *deception* is justified as a means of getting anthropological information is an issue I avoid here.

[26] The word 'attitude' should not be taken to mean that science depends upon psychological variables. 'Attitude' can be cashed out as, 'dispositions to act in certain ways', miniature individual versions of the formal laws, rules, and procedures of the institutions of science. These institutions – schools, departments laboratories, universities, libraries, journals, seminars, conferences, colloquia, books – indeed the invisible college itself, institutionalise scepticism.

[27] I borrow the term from Gellner, *op. cit.*, note 23, above, p. 437.

[28] See F. A. Hayek, *The Counter-Revolution of Science*, Glencoe 1953, p. 39.

[29] See my *Concepts and Society*, *op. cit.*, note 17 above.

[30] K. R. Popper, 'The Logic of the Social Sciences', in T. W. Adorno *et al.*, *The Positivist Dispute in German Sociology*, London 1976, pp. 87–104, especially the Eighth Thesis, pp. 91*ff.* (The original of this important paper appeared in German in *Kölner Zeitschrift für Soziologie und Sozialpsychologie*, Vol. 14, 1962, 233–43).

[31] See J. O. Wisdom, *The Unconscious Origin of Berkeley's Philosophy*, London, 1963, pp. 1–80.

[32] See J. O. Wisdom, 'The Phenomenological Approach to the Sociology of Knowledge', *Philosophy of the Social Sciences*, Vol. 3, 1973, 257–66.

[33] I have never, for example, been invited to joint the Association of Social Anthropologists of the British Commonwealth, presumably because their basic qualification is an academic teaching post in social anthropology.

[34] In 'The Problem of Ethical Integrity . . . ' *op. cit.*, note 21 above, I suggested that doing anthropology essentially involves exploiting the ambiguities of the stranger-friend role.

[35] The sociology of religous movements seems to me to incorporate the sociology of intellectual endeavour as its secularised version. Popper has a fascinating distinction between religious or dogmatic schools and critical schools of thought in *Conjectures and Refutations*, London 1963, Chapter 5, especially pp. 149–50.

[36] Gellner refers ironically to the theories of cognition by trauma and knowledge by total immersion in *Cause and Meaning in the Social Sciences* London 1973, p. 126.

[37] I recall the deep impression made on me by Fred Hoyle's *The Nature of the Universe*, Oxford 1950, and by the radio debates between Bertrand Russell and Father Copleston, and A. J. Ayer and Father Copleston. Such was the calibre of the education one used to get from that magnificent institution known as the BBC Third Programme.

[38] I suppose my views are closest to Richard Robinson's *An Atheist's Values*, Oxford 1964.

[39] Michael Polanyi, *Personal Knowledge*, London 1958; Thomas Kuhn, *The Structure of Scientific Revolutions*, Chicago 1962.

[40] See E. M. Forster, in *I Believe*, London 1940, pp. 42–50.

[41] More Puzzling is the social marginality such intellectual distancing induces or reinforces. One can read it two ways: either reflection induces and entails marginality, or, reflection is an effort to overcome marginality and achieve re-integration. The latter I find unconvincing. The open-minded society, the reflective, critical society is one in which the bonds of unreflective community cannot exist. See Walter Kaufmann, *Without Guilt and Justice*, New York 1973.

[42] K. O. L. Burridge in *Mambu*, London 1960, and *New Heaven, New Earth*, Oxford 1969, and Glynn Cochrane, *Big Men and Cargo Cults*, Oxford 1970, are very good on this; but then so is Peter Worsley, *The Trumpet Shall Sound*, London 1957.

[43] Although Leon Festinger in *When Prophecy Fails* suggested another scenario. See note 7, above.

[44] This was quite deliberate, and led me to a fierce defense of Tylor and Frazer and the subsequent controversy. See Robin Horton, 'Neo-Tylorianism Sound Sense or Sinister Prejudice', *Man* Vol. 3, 1968 pp. 625–34.

[45] For details see my 'Theories of Cargo Cults: A Critical Analysis', *Oceania*, Vol. 34, 1964, 1–31, 108–36.

[46] See my 'On the Explanation of Cargo Cults', *European Journal of Sociology*, Vol. 7, 1966, 292–312.

[47] For more details see 'Epistle to the Anthropologists', *American Anthropologist, op. cit.*, note 15, above.

[48] Hence the appositeness of Jules-Rosette's reference to Polanyi, whose philosophy of science strikes me as dogmatic and irrational.

[49] Leon Festinger, *op. cit.*, note 7, above.

[50] A sketch for a reading of the history of anthropology in these terms is my *The Story of Social Anthropology*, New York 1972.

[51] For further discussion of this problem of how seriously to take religious and anthropological doctrines, see my 'On the Limits of Symbolic Interpretation in Anthropology', *Current Anthropology*, Vol. 17, 1976, pp. 687–91 and 700–1.

[52] 'Epistle to the Anthropologists', note 15, above.

[53] Her novels in sequence are: *The Nowhere City*, New York 1965; *Imaginary Friends*, New York 1967, *Real People*, New York 1969; *Love and Friendship*, New York 1972; and *The War Between the Tates*, New York 1975; *Only Children*, New York 1979. Page numbers refer to the Avon paperback edition.

CHAPTER 16

FREEMAN ON MEAD

Malinowski, legend has it, discouraged visits by other anthropologists to 'his' Trobriand Islands — even if their purpose was to look into matters that he had not. He argued that since pre-literate societies were disappearing there was greater urgency in 'doing' hitherto unknown societies than there was in 'redoing' those already recorded. The reasonableness of this argument depends upon the theory of science implicit in it. A theory stressing that science sets high store by description and cataloguing would yield an imperative about the urgency of recording societies in danger of 'disappearing'. Implicit also is a metaphysic that presupposes 'societies' are the sorts of things that can 'disappear'.

Even such a (inductivist) theory of science would authorize some checking up by one anthropologist on another, thus enjoining not only visits to cover previously neglected peoples but revisits to societies already 'done'. Such revisits could provide a kind of spot check, or quality control, on anthropological fieldwork practice. It was perhaps apprehension about quality control, rather than response to urgent imperatives, that lay behind Malinowski's discouraging such revisits. Like any good Baconian, Malinowski rested his hopes for a science of society on method: learn the language, engage in direct (participant) observation, eschew informants if at all possible and, above all, before entering the field prepare the mind by rinsing it of preconceptions and readying it to be the uncontaminated container of experience.

Chemists know, however, that the cleanness of a washed container is a relative matter depending on what is considered a contaminant. If organic residue is the problem, then chemical residue may be overlooked; the expectation of removing all traces not only of organic residue but also of chemical residue may well be one that is impossible to meet. At all events, the containers have to be washed and then tests have to be run on them. Their cleanness is a function of the standard we set.

Cleansing minds of prejudice and preconception is no less fraught with practical difficulties and problems of standards than cleansing laboratory containers. There are no guarantees for science and the best we can usually manage is to spot check our efforts. To a considerable extent those efforts are a creature of our current theories. Our theories of the levels of organic or chemical presence that can cause pollution of the contents of the container have changed in many ways in the last two hundred years. Hence our standards have changed. The same is true of our ideas of the contaminants of the mind. Just as what in the 1920s might have been thought to be a spotlessly uncontaminated laboratory container would be unacceptable now, what in the 1920s would have been regarded as an unprejudiced mind would not be so now.

Since Malinowski died, his field area has been revisited and some of the things he recorded have been challenged, if not corrected. The same goes for the work of other twentieth-century founding fathers, including Radcliffe-Brown on the Australian Aborigines, Firth on the Tikopia, Fortes on the Tallensi, Leach on the Sinhalese, and so on. Anthropologists are not perfect, and the questions they ask, as well as the standards they apply, change over time. Hence, revisits and the correction of previous findings, while too expensive and time-consuming yet to be standard procedure, are hardly subjects of scandal and concern.

Derek Freeman's new Book, *Margaret Mead and Samoa*, subtitled the *making and unmaking of an anthropological myth*, has nevertheless caused rather more ripples than might have been expected. Its thesis is very simple: Margaret Mead's best-selling classic *Coming of age in Samoa* presented a picture of Samoa as a kind of tropical paradise, where, in particular, adolescence and the discovery of sex were managed without any of the stresses and strains so troublesome in our society; this picture of Samoa is factually false. That a major anthropological figure of the twentieth century produced an inaccurate record of a society which she had visited would have seemed a topic appropriate for the scholarly journals. Why has it been written up at book length (and rather repetitively) and published as a trade book? The answer that Freeman gives is that Margaret Mead's book was a very important brick in the building of an anthropological edifice, namely the theory that nurture, not nature, is largely responsible for the forms and ills of our society. The book enabled us to see this for ourselves by simply looking to the South Seas, where there is better social management of universal human biological problems. We could, learn from Samoa — if not to imitate them, then at least that some alternative to our condition is possible. So, nurture, not nature, must be dominant.

Freeman believes that this long-accepted conclusion, in whose terms the biological component in human social life was minimized, is one that has had its day. At the time it arose, its principal advocate, Franz Boas, was fighting against the reverse tendency, namely the pseudo-biology of racialism, which explained everything from Christianity to industrial success by the superior biological endowment of certain lighter-skinned peoples. Freeman's book, then, has an interesting essay in it on the history of anthropology in America as it turned over the question of how causally important were biological and social factors in the formation of social institutions. Although a social anthropologist by training, Freeman has long been an advocate of the view that the study of biology should be re-introduced into anthropology and anthropologists should not shy away from it merely because of its past association with racialism.

But again, despite the *succès de scandale* of sociobiology, this material would seem more in place in the scholarly trade press. To explain his book's impact one has to look not at Freeman's text but at his target. He situates his target, Margaret Mead, within the kinship system of American anthropology. A student of the nurturists Boas and Benedict, Mead's Samoan work practically provided the coping stone for the Boasian intellectual edifice, and was also a best seller. The anthropology of this best seller, and the anthropology of Margaret Mead's subsequent career and position in American society, is something Freeman does not, unfortunately, delve into. *Coming of age in Samoa* clearly presented a message that some in America very much wanted to hear — myth or not. It is part of a large literature of self-reflection on American society produced in the twentieth century, suggesting that in the search for 'a more perfect union' Americans could look to other societies and other standards for models. The book was shorter and better written than Malinowski's *Sexual life of savages*, or the works of Havelock Ellis and Freud, but nevertheless it stands on a shelf with those as part of a whole body of thinking about how to reshape social customs and practices. The book was more popular in America than abroad, which may or may not have something to do with the enormous importance placed in the United States on adolescence and its conflicts.

In criticizing, however scientific in spirit, one of the heroines of the movement for more enlightened views on sexual education and social custom, Freeman is taking on a target not unlike Dr Spock. Just as there are now generations of adults who were raised on and who consult Dr Spock, there are generations of adults whose parents read and who now themselves read *Coming of age in Samoa*. And what Freeman puts in its place is a rather depressing message. Not only did Margaret Mead get Samoan custom wrong, but, over a broad range of social behaviour, Samoan society is not noticeably less tense, conflict-ridden, or productive of unhappiness than is our own. Thus Samoa is not the model for an experimental society like the United States to seek out; rather, it is just another exotic society a long way away, of great technical interest to anthropologists but of only vicarious interest to the layman.

That some of the reviews written in the United States have been defensive not only of nurture, or culture, theory, but also of Margaret Mead's status, is hard to understand. Despite the hope that America might learn to manage adolescence better than it had before the *Coming of age in Samoa*, there is little evidence that it has succeeded in this. America has not noticeably moved its treatment of adolescence towards that pictured in *Coming of age in Samoa*. This quite aside from the question of whether the picture presented in *Coming of age in Samoa* is imaginary.

Perhaps what Mead stood for — nurture — has taken deep root in American social optimism. After all, myths have their functions. You cannot build a new nation along Enlightenment lines if the flaws of the old nations are inheritable. The myth of the potential equality of all men is something that holds America together. Its promise is that despite inequalities and social tensions the society is open to the possibility of individuals and groups improving their position.

So, a book that Freeman threw into the arena of the professional debate over sociobiology has cuased ripples for rather different reasons, related to the sociology of myth. Following from this, my first criticism is that Freeman needed to enlighten us a lot more on the anthropology of anthropologists. Anthropologists have contributed quite a few intellectual best sellers to the culture of this century, have in different countries become pundits, and have thrown their weight behind different sorts of social change. Hence, disputes among anthropologists have a significance that ramifies far beyond the narrow concerns of the profession. Questions of power and of vested interests are involved, and anthropologists could cast a great deal of light on these. Freeman does mention that he confronted Margaret Mead with some of his findings (pp. xvi, 326) but is unclear as to whether she conceded in private that she had made mistakes. His decision to continue the research and finally publish it seems to have been partly brought about by her failure to publish any retractions whether in the scholarly press or in later editions of her work. On the contrary, she seems to have drawn the absurd conclusion that where her evidence was at variance with everything else that was available, some special set of conditions must have existed at the time she was in Samoa. Freeman has little difficulty in disposing of this way out.

How does Mead come out of the discussion? Mainly as a very bad field worker: she had an inadequate grasp of the language, she stayed in the field only a relatively short time, she lived not among the people she was studying but with agents of the government — who were of her culture — and she relied largely on questioning informants, rather than observing things for herself. When, in the 1950s, I was taught social anthropology at the London School of Economics just this short list of sins was something we were constantly reminded about, and the work of Margaret Mead was pointed to, even then, as an example of how superficial and implausible a monograph would be if these sins were committed. Freeman, however, goes even further, and suggests that Margaret Mead was a dupe. Questioning adolescent girls about their social and sexual life, a delicate and embarrassing subject, Mead set herself up to receive reports on the fantasies rather than the real life of these girls. She talked to rather a lot of the girls in quite a short period of time, and there is little possibility that she knew any of them in the sort of depth and detail necessary to keep a check on their reliability. It is because of the possibility of this kind of duping, even when no mischief by the informants is involved, that scepticism is nowadays built into the distinction, drawn by all anthropologists, between what people do, what they say they do, and what they think they ought to do. We learn from the mistakes of our predecessors.

How does anthropology come out of Freeman's book? He dedicates the book to Sir Karl Popper, the great exponent of the idea that the hallmark of science is that it produces testable statements. Mead's statements about Samoa are certainly testable. Freeman has tried to test many of them against pre-existing literature and against his own and others' field observations, and he has found them wanting. It does not follow that either Margaret Mead or the anthropological practice which she embodied is culpable. On the contrary, Sir Karl Popper points out that when new scientific ideas arrive upon the scene it is sometimes the case that no one can see how they can possibly be tested. Devising a means of testing them is often a considerable achievement, but we can only be sure of this achievement when it has been completed. Hence, ironically, the least controversial candidate statements for scientific status are those that are actually refuted. So it was to Mead's and anthropology's credit to have produced testable statements; it is to Freeman's credit to have devised ways to do the testing. And now their scientific status is secure, since they have been shown to be false. This is the way that science progresses.

We have greatly advanced our understanding of a number of problems. We have refuted the idea that biology is unimportant in such phases as maturation and adolescence. We have come to recognize that the stresses of this period in our society are not untypical of human experience elsewhere.

We have perhaps modified our somewhat Utopian expectations of how greatly our society could be imporved. We have deepended our knowledge of Samoan society by challenging Margaret Mead's authority; subsequent work has found much of what she said to be inaccurate, but has used that as a stimulus to find out what the truth is, hence also how it was possible for her to get it wrong, learning thus more about Samoa and more about how to do anthropology well. We have also opened up a new problem, and that is how to take account of such events as the spread of popularized anthropology into the society as a causal contributor to social change. Some of the great men of our discipline, from Frazer to Lévi-Strauss, are themselves part of the anthropology of the society to which they belong.

If Margaret Mead made mistakes, they were mistakes from which science learned, so her place in the growth of knowledge is secure. If she was a myth-maker, and since myths are not refutable, there is much more to be said. Why was the society receptive to her myth? What other myths preexisted here? What is the depth of the social commitment to nurture, to the malleability of man and hence the social need for myths that reinforce it? When a myth derives not from anthropomorphic stories but from putative science, the process of its building and the possibility of its being dismantled are sociological matters on which I wish Freeman had speculated.

PART II

APPLICATIONS AND IMPLICATIONS

CHAPTER 17

THE OBJECTIVITY OF CRITICISM OF THE ARTS

THIS paper is an attack on the widely held view that judgments on works of art are irremediably subjective. Subjectivism, as it will be called, has its attractive and its less attractive sides. It is simple; it plausibly explains why there is so much disagreement in criticism of the arts; and, while arguments for and against it can be deployed, none of the arguments against is conclusive. This latter quality may be thought by some to be unattractive, and even a reason for rejecting subjectivism.[1] Another unattractive feature of the subjective view is that it entails relativism, since from

All judgments are subjective

together with (presumably[2]), the trivial minor premiss

All subjectivities are equal

it follows that

All judgments are equal.

Thus, according to subjectivism, any judgment made by any person at any stage of his life is equal to any other judgment. Naive over-estimations of current fads, the untrained comments of children, the considered views of experts, all are equal. There can be no such thing as progress in our ability to make better judgments as we grow older and learn more, or as works and periods come into perspective. The possibility is destroyed of our saying one work is better than another in some sense other than that 'I' prefer it, and thus the possibility or rational argument about judgments disappears. Of course, if all past, present and future subjects agree that Bach is the greatest of composers, we have an absolute judgment of sorts. But a dissenter may appear, and it is hardly satisfactory merely to outvote him.

My strategy in this paper is to begin by showing how the retreat to

---

[1] Impregnability against rational argument, a common feature shared by scepticism, idealism, irrationalism, and so on, is often admired. But it is important to distinguish intact positions which as far as is known have not succumbed to criticism—this is what we want of our own positions—from positions which one *knows in advance* are *immune* to criticism. Since all immune positions are intact positions, it is easy to confuse them, but to want the latter is unexceptionable, while to want the former is to want certainty even at the price of irrationality. See W. W. Bartley III, 'Rationality *versus* the Theory of Rationality', in M. Bunge (ed.), *The Critical Approach to Science and Philosophy*, Glencoe, 1964.

[2] The denials of this premiss, 'It is not the case that all subjectivities are equal', or 'Some subjectivities are better' or 'more true' or 'more objective than others', all express a judgment on judgments. Such a metajudgment is presumably also subjective, for if it is not we have an objective way to discriminate between competing subjective judgments (according to who made them) and thus they are no longer 'merely' subjective, and the first premiss is denied.

subjectivism can take a rational form: when it is forced on one by the breakdown of rational argument (section 1). Then I shall elaborate the subjectivist solution to the problem created by the breakdown, isolate its two most powerful supporting arguments and show how it merges two things which might better be distinguished: response and evaluation (sections 2 and 3). In criticism of subjectivism I shall then challenge the idea that the two supporting arguments do the job the subjectivist wants them to do; separate out the response and evaluation; and explain diversity and disagreement differently, showing that *agreement* does exist to some extent in art criticism, and that it poses problems for the subjectivist (sections 4 and 5). Finally will come my own solution to the problem of the objectivity of criticism of the arts, locating it principally in the *tradition* of arguing rationally about art, the *institutions* which carry this tradition, and not in the judgments which have emerged from this tradition (sections 6 and 7).

1. *The failure of rational argument*

Consider two people who have just shared an aesthetic experience: they are coming out of a theatre, or a gallery or a concert-hall having just been exposed to a work of art. They begin to discuss it. X says it was a bad play, Y insists that it was first-rate. Where to go from here? X attacks some part of it, say the sententious writing in the first act; Y praises another part, say the construction of the third and final act. Y may deny X's criticism of the writing, or sweep it aside as true but insignificant when set against the virtues of the play. X has the same two choices with respect to Y's praise: to reject it or to accept it as true but unimportant. Both would have some difficulty in accepting the other's point and simultaneously maintaining that the play was bad or first-rate, as the case may be. However X does have the edge, since a bad play may have a good third act, but a first-rate play should not have sententious writing in the first act. If X and Y totally reject each other's points they reach an *impasse*. If they accept them as true but unimportant they again reach an *impasse*. In one case they disagree about what is good and what is bad; in the other case they disagree about what kinds of badness and goodness are important. This looks like a basic difference of taste; and *that* is subjective.

Compare this unsatisfactory situation with that which seems to prevail in science. If two scientists are arguing about whether Newton's mechanics is true or not we feel little doubt that they can make progress. Newton's theory relates to certain facts and has certain consequences. An inconsistency within it, or between it and statements of past or future facts renders it false. A rational argument arriving at a conclusion is in principle possible. Disagreements in science are not matters of personal subjective taste.

There seems to be a clear-cut difference between science, where statements are true or false, and quarrels can be settled, and which therefore is objective; and criticism of the arts, where statements have the appearance of being true or false, and thus objectively decidable, but which in fact reduces to matters of taste. We seem to be misled by our language into thinking there is an epistemological symmetry between the statements 'The heliocentric hypothesis is true' and 'The statement "this play is first-rate," is true' simply because they both predicate the property 'truth' of certain statements. However, since there is no way of testing the second statement we should *not* allow its grammatical similarity to mislead us into thinking there is an epistemological similarity: that there is anything like 'knowledge' of what is artistically first-rate. In art we are merely swapping opinions; in science we are talking about something with an objective correlative. It is a fact that critics give different appraisals of the same works of art. Disputes arise between those holding different views, but these disputes do not get resolved; they end up, as they started, in straight clashes of opinion. From this lack of unanimity, and from the uselessness of argument in trying to settle the differences, it can be concluded that there are no known means of saying whether critics' statements are true or false; no known and accepted standards in criticism of the arts; and thus no objectivity in such criticism.

Implicitly or explicitly this situation is contrasted with that (mistakenly) thought to be the case in science, where there seems to be a certain unanimity, and where those disputes which arise appear to end with one side or the other being proved right. In science there are standards and thus there is objectivity.

Subjectivism can seem, then, to be forced upon one by the critical *impasse*. Attempts to escape from subjectivism nearly always try to locate objectivity in the attitudes and behaviour of individual critics; these have failed. 'Balance', 'fair-mindedness', 'lack of bias': all such definitions fail. This is because they ignore two fundamental arguments against the possibility of individual objectivity. These arguments can be accepted, confuted or evaded. My choice is to accept them as true and as a consequence shift the emphasis away from the individual. By separating the idea of objective criticism from that of individual detachment I believe we can break out of the *impasse* the discussion of objectivity almost always generates. The problem of objectivity can in fact be easily solved, provided only that we locate the desired objectivity in the institutions of criticism, and the critical tradition, and not think of it as a property belonging to the individual critic or his attitudes. Now this shifting of the problem involves the risk that what we end up with may not correspond with some people's ideas of what objectivity really is. This is inevitable, since to some extent the paper criticizes the intuitive notion that objectivity is personal lack of bias. The problem, can however, be formulated without mentioning objectivity: is there the possibility of rational argument about the arts, or is subjectivism forced upon us?

At this point I need briefly to digress in order to make it clear that my notion of objectivity is taken from Popper's critical philosophy of science. In brief I hold that mistaken views on the objectivity of *science* are held; then these views are applied to criticism of the *arts*, which is found wanting. But since these views on science are mistaken, science is wanting in this way too. But if we improve our views on the objectivity of science, criticism of the arts will not seem *so* different.

To return to the two arguments in the subjectivists' armoury. They cannot be ignored; to me, at least, they seem true. It is the conclusions the subjectivists draw from them that are questionable.

First, there is the argument that all human beings, indeed all animals, are inescapably biased. Second, is a supplementary argument that anyone convinced of his own lack of bias is likely to be the most biased of all.

These arguments, if true, destroy the theory that locates objectivity in the attitudes of individuals. Let us look at the two arguments in a little more detail.

Francis Bacon asserted over and over again that our beliefs distort our thinking.[3] He reasoned that even observation of the facts can be affected by our bias. He claimed that we see what we want to see; that if we in any way anticipate what we shall see, we shall see it heavily coloured. Bacon, of course, believed that if the mind was purged of anticipation the problem of bias would no longer arise. In other words, he believed that the solution lay in reforming individual attitudes; the difficulties lay in achieving this pure unbiased state. But his argument needs strengthening only a little to show that these difficulties are insuperable. This strengthening could consist in showing: (*a*) that anticipations or expectations or biases precede observations in the order of time; (*b*) that they also do so in the order of logic; and (*c*) that to imagine one is free of biases is itself a serious second-order bias blinding one to first-order biases.

Much psychological evidence can be adduced in support of (*a*). It can be shown that new-born children and animals have anticipations; it can also be shown that an observer who does not know what he is

---

[3] *Novum Organum* Book 1, Aph. xlix, 1, liv, lviii, lxvii–ix.

looking for does not find it. Philosophers of science have also spent much time on (*b*), and some have argued that statements of observation are riddled with anticipations, or interpretations, or biases.[4] This being a paper on aesthetics I want merely to take all this as results. Again, (*c*), in the light of (*a*) and (*b*), is a pretty well inescapable conclusion; if anticipation or bias is both logically and chronologically prior to observation, then he who believes he has eliminated all bias from his observations is deluding himself.

Accepting, then, the correctness and force of these two arguments, what conclusions are we to draw from them?

One conclusion, the subjectivists', is that these arguments provide a warrant for subjectivism. Since we are all biased, and irremediably so, the best we can hope for is an honest reaction to a work of art; we should expose our biases to public gaze, not conceal them and pretend to objectivity. While I agree that bias is better exposed, and I hope to explain (in section 3) how it can be, I do not think these two arguments force us to accept subjectivism.

An alternative conclusion—the one I shall draw—is that the demand for individual objectivity is excessive. The arguments showing the universality and inescapability of bias apply equally to scientists as to critics of the arts. Yet science is the objective discipline *par excellence*. Now any criterion of objectivity which rules out science is clearly making excessive demands. The criterion of lack of individual bias is thus excessive.

2. *The subjectivist explanation*

Let us now move from the two basic arguments to examine in a little more detail the subjectivist case to see if it is internally consistent and coherent. Only with a fuller understanding of what subjectivists are getting at is it possible to straighten out the confusions and analyse the excessive demands with which they buttress their position. As an example of the arch-subjectivist position we can take the emotive theory of aesthetic statements: the view that evaluative statements about art are to be interpreted as no more than expressions of emotional attitudes;[5] or attempts to engender similar attitudes in others; or both. When we say that Bach is a great composer, all we are saying, on this view, is that we have a strong emotional liking for his compositions, and all the arguments we marshall to back our assertion are no more than rationalizations. All emotions being equal,

[4] In Chapter 1 of his *Conjectures and Refutations* K. R. Popper discusses some of these questions.

[5] Any statement may of course express emotion, and possibly all do. The point is whether that is *all* they do.

my assertion that Bach is great is to be given no greater weight than Lucky Jim's reference to 'filthy Mozart'. What, after all, is more subjective than emotion? And, since different people have different emotions, and there are no criteria for saying whose are the better emotions, all emotions are equal and so all evaluative statements are equal. A complete relativism results: judgments are true or false only relative to particular individuals. The only false judgments are those where the individual is unaware of, or lying about, his *true* emotional response. (Here may be the source of much of the stress on critical sincerity.)

The subjectivist position can be seen to involve two assumptions which together are destructive of any countervailing view. The first assumption merges responses to and evaluations of works of art. In saying that 'work *x* of Bach is great music' is equivalent to 'I like work *x* of Bach very much' one's likings (responses) are being equated with one's judgments (evaluations). Unless response and evaluation are identified in this way the admitted subjectivity of *response* need not carry over into the evaluation or judgment. The second assumption is that different people have different responses and, hence, since they are the same thing, different evaluations.

It deserves to be noticed, I think, that these two subjectivist assumptions converge and reinforce each other. Were critical evaluations objective, it seems to be assumed, there would be agreement and concurrence. Were there concurrence evaluation could not be dismissed as a matter of personal, idiosyncratic response. But since it *is* no more than personal, idiosyncratic response there cannot be agreement and therefore it cannot be objective. But is it correct to identify response with evaluation? And is it the case that people's evaluations differ as much as their responses? To both questions I shall reply in the negative.

3. *Response* versus *evaluation*

To begin with I shall sharply separate response and evaluation. Take as an example Robert Bresson's film of Bernanos's novel *Le Journal d'un Curé de Campagne*. The great majority of critical opinion views this film as an austere masterpiece. One national critic in Britain, however, deplored it as tedious Roman Catholic masochism. Here we can split off evaluation from response. The dissenting critic responded negatively and *also* gave a low evaluation. He was, I think, unique in that. Several of the critics who consider the film to be very great are violently anti-Catholic. One could say that they responded badly to the film. They felt repelled by its religion; but that did not shake their high evaluation. There is nothing remarkable in this. One may be repelled by Creon's respect for the law at all costs without losing one's respect for *Antigone*, or changing one's view that it is among the greatest of tragedies. Or, to return to films again, the number of critics who refuse to acknowledge that *Triumph des Willens* and *Olympische Spiele* are virtually unsurpassed triumphs of documentary film-making on the grounds that they boost a repellent cause is very small.

If we identify evaluation and response, and say that statements like 'I think it is good' or 'I think it is great' say the same as 'I like it', then they should be derivable from statements like 'I like it'. But they are not. From 'I think it is great' you cannot infer 'I like it' and from 'I like it' you cannot infer 'I think it is great'. This is simply because there is no contradiction in saying 'I like it but it is rubbish' or in saying 'It is great but I can't stand it'.

I challenge, then, the over-simplified indentification of evaluation and response. I contend that the two can be, and are in practice, separated. I further contend that there is less disagreement over evaluation than there is over response. If this is true then it will go some way (I do not want to go all the way) to meet the criticisms of those who feel that some agreement in criticism must be achieved if it is to be considered objective. My view is that statements describing response can be (psychologically) true or false. Art criticism is not (or ought not to be) about responses, but about evaluations. Moreover, my belief that there are rational discussions about art which are not reducible to psychological investigations about the effect of art on art critics (responses) presupposes this view.

Given, then, that there is a difference between a response: 'I like Bach's Goldberg variations'; and an evaluation: 'Bach's Goldberg variations are great music'—on the grounds that we can affirm or deny either or both without contradicting ourselves—I shall now argue as follows: first (section 4), that from diversity of evaluation, and failure to settle disputes, it is invalid to infer the subjectivity of criticism of the arts; second (section 5), that the diversities of individual response are far greater than the diversities of evaluation; third (section 6), that within the present institutional set-up it *is* possible to argue rationally about evaluations and that this is shown by the fact that it happens. Sometimes an individual yields, at other times he holds out, but loses the battle for which judgment is to get incorporated into the tradition. So objectivity may be attained, but not necessarily agreement.[6]

[6] I am about to argue (§ 4) that we cannot infer validly from critical diversity to lack of critical objectivity. It may therefore seem odd that I juxtapose critical consensus and critical objectivity. Clearly, though, if I deny that diversity implies lack of objectivity I also must deny that objectivity implies agreement.

4. Diversity and disagreement

First, then, what is to be inferred from the fact that critical opinion is diverse, and the further fact that critics often fail to resolve disputes arising out of these differences of opinion? What is often inferred is that clearly these critcal opinions are merely subjective responses; why else should they be so different; why else should their differences be irresolvable? This inference, in one or other of its various forms, lies behind much subjectivism and relativism in ethics as well as aesthetics.

Why should diversity of judgment be explained by subjectivity? Juries differ among themselves, judges differ, and we don't lightly call them not objective. Scientists differ, even mathematicians differ, and we certainly don't call *them* not objective. Only in popular and rather ignorant mythology about science and mathematics does one find monolithic agreement between all parties.

I would contend that in the matter of agreement: (*A*) science is not as rosy as it is being painted; and (*B*) criticism of the arts is not as black as *it* is being painted.

(*A*) We are asked to believe that in science and mathematics there are not too many disputes and that all those there are can in principle be settled. Yet is that really the case?

Once posed, I do not see how this question can but be answered in the negative. Certainly this rosy picture little resembles actual situations in the history of science, although it does approximate to the pictures certain historians try to paint of the the 'smooth development'[7] of science. In truth the history of science is one long series of disputes, sometimes polite, more often violent and bitter. True enough, most of these quarrels eventually stopped. But they were rarely resolved during the lifetimes of the protagonists. Frequently they were resolved only by death and the acceptance of one side into the mainstream of science thus ending the dispute for the time being.[8]

What about present-day scientific disputes? The idea that science is not wracked by apparently implacable disagreements is an illusion. What 'steady progress' there is usually turns out to be either technological, that is, within a given theoretical framework, or to consist in the mapping-in of areas within the broad outlines of accepted theories.[9] What other progress there is tends to be far from steady or smooth.

[7] See J. Agassi, 'Towards an Historiography of Science', *History & Theory*, Beiheft 2, 1963, § 'The Continuity Theory'.
[8] Becoming part of the mainstream may merely muffle, not prevent, further criticism. Berkeley's attacks on the calculus and 'occult' entities and Einstein's on Newtonian mechanics are examples of attacks on mainstream orthodoxies. And of course once a topic has been opened up again other connected ones are likely to be taken up too.
[9] Since drafting this I have come across a similar view in T. S. Kuhn's *The Structure of*

But surely, the subjectivist can say, scientists are in *broad* agreement, especially about the facts; art critics aren't even that. This *may* be true; but I suggest that art critics *are* in broad agreement too, especially about the facts. Presumably the subjectivist imagines that scientific disputes are resolved by a meter reading. Apart from the fact that there are various ways to interpret meter readings, science is not quite like that. The easily settled scientific disputes resemble disputes about whether this painting is oblong or that colour patch red: these, too, can be settled by simple inspection. *Interpreting* the meter reading is rather like trying to decide whether El Greco did or did not paint this newly discovered picture. Disagreement in art criticism, as in science, is about theories or interpretations. We all see the sun rise and set: how are we to interpret this event? We can all see the framed oblong with the different coloured patches on it: what does it all add up to, do we like it, and is it good? It seems as though neither scientific theories, nor individual critical judgments, can be objective. It makes no more sense, I contend, to say Newton's cosmology is objective (especially as it is false) than it does to say the prevailing valuation of Shakespeare is objective. Objectivity lies elsewhere, it is not a property of *statements*.

To this it could be replied that while it is permissible for individual to differ, if we believe that something like truth exists, then *in principle* all disputes and differences in science should be resolvable.[10] Thus even if there were no monolithic agreement at any particular place or any particular time, one must be able to envisage the possibility; and certainly over specific issues in science some agreement is reached,[11] for a time, at least. But in criticism of the arts there hardly exists anything like truth, and therefore even in principle it seems there is no hope of perfect agreement.

(*B*) Little time need be spent on showing in which respect criticism of the arts is less black than the subjectivist supposes. Suffice it to say that the history of art criticism seems no more wracked with

[10] 'In principle' because belief in truth can be distinguished from belief that it can be known by man or belief that if known to man he will know that he knows it. The separation of these issues is already clear in Xenophanes.

[11] This has been affirmed by Hesse (discussing Harré), 'we are quite sure that we have shown that there *are* bacteria . . .', *Brit. J. Philos. Sci.*, 13, 1962, p. 236, and Alexander, '. . . scientific laws at a comparatively simple level are usually not regarded as worth further testing. The hypothesis that the melting point of gold is 1063° C., the hypothesis that the tides on any one coast recur at constant intervals, the hypothesis that ice floats on water: all these and countless others are so well confirmed that scientists no longer go on to testing them . . .', *Aristotelian Society, Supplementary Volume*, 34, 1960, p. 136. Other frequently cited examples are the disputes over the heliocentric hypothesis and over phlogiston.

Scientific Revolution (Chicago, 1962) where puzzles involved in articulating the paradigm are seen as a normal task of scientists (see Chapter IV).

disputes than that of science. I would willingly grant that disputes in art criticism seem to go on for longer. The great clash between romanticism and classicism, for example, seems to be revived with every generation, neither victory nor reconciliation seems possible.

So while conceding that scientific disputes appear in principle easier to resolve than those in criticism of the arts, I would deny that this makes all that much of a difference. Science is not as perfect as it seems; art criticism not so hopeless as it seems. I see no reason why we should not allow that there are objective values in art which our *evaluative statements* try to capture, and in so far they have something very like truth-values. That scientific disputes are resolvable in principle matters little if they tend not to be resolved in the here and now. That disputes in criticism of the arts are not in practice easily resolved matters little if the regulative idea of values remains something to strive towards. In neither case is objectivity revealed by monolithic agreement or by decisive and rapid resolution of disputes. Moreover, if we upend the whole discussion and discuss not the regulative idea of truth, but that of falsity, there seems to be still less difference between the two. The history of science tends to be a history of the overthrow of one idea after another, *not* of the establishment of a body of ideas as true. Criticism of the arts does both. First, premature reputations and evaluations get overthrown (as with C. P. E. Bach) and then a tradition of evaluations gets firmly established (Bach, Mozart, Shakespeare, Goethe, etc.).

5. *Degrees of diversity*

This brings us to the second of the three points listed at the end of section 3. While critics differ widely in their responses to works, they differ less in evaluations. Many critics agree that *Le Journal d'un Curé de Campagne* is a remarkable, even great film. Yet their *responses* run from hatred, through indifference, to devotion. One could multiply examples. There is, it seems, far less disagreement about evaluations that have gained the status of being part of the tradition than there is between individual critics on individuals or individual works. The tradition seems to get established over a long time on a foundation of protracted disputes. Of course, once it is established, it provides a standing challenge to the bold critic who wants to mount an assault on some part of it. But then this is exactly paralleled by the situation in science where a bold thinker may try to undermine the whole of established theory.

The problem of agreement of *tastes* (responses) is not important— tastes differ, *evaluations* tend to agree more. *This* can't be explained on the subjectivist identification of evaluation and response. Let us turn the problem around and ask: how is it that there is any agreement or co-ordination between the subjective tastes (responses) of independent psyches? A first possible reply might follow these lines. Partial or random agreement between tastes is not a problem requiring explanation. After all, people are not perfectly similar, not entirely dissimilar. Thus, if there was perfect agreement between their tastes we would have a problem; if there was perfect disagreement we would have a problem too. But in fact there is some agreement and some disagreement scattered more or less randomly around, and this we do not have to explain. After all, in physics perfect order is a very rare and problematic state, and so is perfect disorder; but a random hodge-podge is, so to speak, the expected norm and therefore not problematic.

This is a plausible reply. Perhaps I could begin to criticize it by asserting that the evaluations people make are not perfectly randomly distributed, but rather cluster around certain centres. There are, let us say, n serious composers. It is neither the case that only one of these is liked, nor is it the case that all of them are equally liked. The situation is that a few dozen are revered, and a hundred or two are performed, and the rest are consigned to oblivion. This situation does require explanation. Why, for example, do so many people like Bach, Mozart and Beethoven so very much more than any of their rivals? How do so many subjective reactions come to settle down on the same artists? Why is there not a random distribution? The subjectivist, if he considers this problem at all, will have to provide us with some additional theory to show why subjective tastes cluster.

Presumably the subjectivist would assert that our overlapping tastes are a product of our education and upbringing, that in effect we are conditioned to direct our tastes in one direction rather than another. Now certainly it is difficult to deny that we are all conditioned. But the subjectivists' answer does not go far enough since our problem was not, 'how do we come to like what we like?', but, 'how come we like alike? In other words, 'how is it that the conditioning is directed to getting us to like alike?' Let us put this schematically:

(a) We like alike
(b) We like what we are conditioned to like

Now we cannot derive (a) from (b), although it may be that we like alike because we like what we are conditioned to like. But we can derive (a) from (b) together with:

(c) We are conditioned alike

While for the purposes of the argument most of us might accept (a) and (b), provided 'conditioning' was not interpreted too strictly as a sort of brainwashing, we can see at once that (c) is problematic. All sorts of objections can be raised against it. Can myriads of human experience be said to be alike? If it is alike who or what made it alike and how? But we need not enter into the rights and wrongs of this second premiss (c), it is enough that we show that the at first sight simple and straightforward position of the subjectivist falls back on such dubious defences when faced with the problem of explaining co-ordination.

6. *Locating objectivity*

If, however, every judgment can be overthrown and new diversities and disputes thrown up, where can we locate the objectivity, if any, of our judgments? To begin the attack on this problem I want to analyse the whole apparatus referred to so far simply as 'criticism of the arts'. This is partly in order to try to locate more exactly the area of dispute, and partly in order to reinforce the suggestion that even by the citerion of agreement science is closer to criticism of the arts than it at first appears to be.

Criticism begins with the individual critic, armed with his knowledge, tastes and preferences—all, we might think, irremediably subjective. Next there are the institutions connected with criticism: previews, advance copies, reviews in the press and on the air, lectures, conferences, journals, cocktail parties, and so on. These are the mechanisms which facilitate criticism and its dissemination. It is through these that the critic works. Lastly there emerges out of the employment by these individual critics of these institutions a critical tradition (although to some extent the tradition shapes and influences the running of the institutions and so is in that sense prior). By a critical tradition I do not mean minor traditions such as that critics always try to inflate themselves at the expense of what they are criticizing, or that eccentricities of manner and dress are to be cultivated. Rather I mean that from the discussions between the many individuals manning the critical institutions there emerges a set of judgments, and arguments to back these judgments, on which there is broad agreement, and that this constitutes a tradition. Examples I have in mind are the judgments made about certain writers or artists. In the critical tradition of English literature Shakespeare is regarded as a great (seventeenth-century) poet, and Sir Francis Hubert is regarded as a minor (seventeenth-century) poet, and there exist arguments to back these judgments. One could give similar examples in painting and in music. The relative positions accorded J. S. and C. P. E. Bach, for example, completely upsetting the places assigned them by their contemporaries, is well established and easy to back up.

The two examples I have given are well established: but traditions do not necessarily take long to establish. Moreover, they can be overthrown. Yeats, Eliot, Joyce, Lawrence, Woolf are widely regarded as the principal English writers of the first half of the twentieth century. None of us knows whether that will be their position in the critical tradition of the twenty-first century. We believe that our present valuation of J. S. Bach is correct and that C. P. E. Bach was simply overrated by his contemporaries. I do not think that we can allow our judgments are merely a matter of taste for the simple reason that if we did we should have no grounds for believing J. S. is the *greater* of the two. On the *absolute* rights or wrongs of our judgments I do not think we can pronounce; but in their superiority over previous judgments I think we have to believe, otherwise the replacement of C. P. E. by J. S. would be inexplicable, except as whim and the equation of greatness with subjective taste.

My point, then, consists of saying that criticism of the arts is something which embraces three things: individuals, institutions, and traditions. The latter partly emerge from, and partly influence, the individuals and institutions. So, when we say that criticism of the arts is not objective, do we mean that the individual critic is not objective, or that particular judgments of his are not objective, or both; or do we mean that the institutions are not objective; or that the traditions are not objective; or do we mean that some combination of all four is not objective?

Our approach to the problem from the point of view of the breakdown of rational argument made it look as though we meant that the individual's judgments were not objective because he had no rules by which to judge the work of art. To this it might be said that in the same way a jury has no rules against which to judge guilt, although they do so. But now we see that this problem of individual lack of objectivity is only one part of the problem of the objectivity of the complex apparatus which is criticism of the arts. Since objectivity involves lack of bias and individuals cannot escape bias I conclude that all attempts to locate the objectivity of criticism of the arts in individuals are doomed to failure. I do not think a solution lies in trying to lay down rules about the arts that the critic can simply apply. Apart from the horrid mechanical idea of criticism this accepts, I know of no such rules which actually work. Indeed, as I shall later mention, my impression is that widely accepted rules stand more as a challenge, something to be broken with impunity, than a *formula* for making art. To say we do not *want* rules about good or bad art, guilt or innocence, is not to say we have no *standards*, that we accept relativism. On the contrary, standards are of the utmost importance, but these are of critical argument, logic and honesty, not formulae that are once and for all decided. Our standards must be of this general character or else we would leave no room for innovation or overthrow of previous evaluations. In view of all this we should perhaps locate the objectivity of criticism of the arts in the institutions and the traditions of criticism of the arts. Here we can discuss and plan for lack of bias by institutional reform.

Of course, none of this absolves the critic from *personally* trying to be fair and, for example, giving a reasoned defence of his views. But as long as the institutions through which, and traditions within which he works are not too biased, his own failure completely to eliminate bias will not be a disaster. In seeking objectivity what we should seek is institutions that are minimally biased and which have built-in self-criticism and which thus compensate for the bias of the individual critics who man them. From the workings of these institutions emerge traditions of judgment which can also be criticized and in the development of which it may be possible to discern progress. Not only is individual objectivity an unattainable ideal, it is also unnecessary, provided the institutions have been properly designed and there is a strong flourishing critical tradition.

There is a lot of difficulty in saying a piece of criticism is objective; just as there is the same difficulty in saying so and so's scientific results are objective. Yet the body of science, its tradition, and the the body of criticism of the arts, *its* tradition, is or can be objective. That objectivity resides not in the individuals, or the statements, but in the institutional set-up. A magazine may be biased, but the different biases of different magazines may cancel out. Some critics may be blind to the worth of some artists, but the editorial standards of journals will see that not only they are heard. Conference delegates may be party-liners, but they will not be the only delegates, or if they are this will not be the only conference. In, it seems to me, the free and critical discussion within institutions devoted to promoting that free discussion, and not favouring any bias, we have the heart of objectivity. Here too resides any possibility of rationality; for these disputes, debates, arguments, whatever their content, presuppose the worth of disputing critical evaluations.

7. *The objectivity of institutions*

Objectivity, I have maintained, should not be predicated of individuals or their attitudes. Rather is it something to be found in institutions and their associated traditions. It seems to matter no more that an individual critic undervalues an artist or a movement than it does that Priestley died believing in phlogistonism. What is important is that no individual critic gets control of all the institutions and suppresses countervailing views, or that the tradition gets implacably set in an attitude of intolerance towards an artist or a school. *Then* is objectivity really in danger, and subjectivism is a strong incentive. Since subjectivism allows that there is nothing for art critics to be *wrong* about, why not an art dictatorship? It is salutary that our institutions for criticism of the arts are relatively free and competitive and that our tradition of evaluation, however intolerant (of romanticism, for example), also embodies the metatradition of being critical of the tradition.

Objectivity, then, is not to be pictured as the possession of truth by a person, but as a sort of democracy of opinion and criticism, within which the truth may be pursued. Institutions can be more impartial than individuals provided the tradition which governs them is a critical one. Within that tradition we strive to criticize and eliminate bias, but those of us—authors and editors—who are convinced they are without bias are likely to be the most deep-rootedly biased (because it is unconscious). It is absurd even to think of an individual's *response* to art being unbiased. We want objective *evaluations*. But how is this to be achieved? The situation is very complicated. An evaluation can be conclusively shown to be false (e.g. if it is self-contradictory); but it cannot be conclusively established as true, any more than can a scientific theory. Arguments can be deployed, but within limits: the regulative idea of truth is perhaps harder to catch and to know it has been caught than in science. Each work of art, in a way, creates its own standards—and these standards are embodied in the critical tradition. But traditions can also be criticized and reformed, and this might seem to remove any basis and thus to fall back into relativism.

The relativism charge can be rebutted with the following argument. To say all standards are open to criticism is not to say there are no standards. Moreover it is also not to say that all standards can be challenged simultaneously. Provided we proceed piecemeal we can always retain something even if we retain nothing permanently. Let me sum up all this. We can say that an individual evaluation is open to criticism, traditional evaluations are also open to criticism, and the institutions of art criticism are themsleves open to criticism of their objectivity. The standards (traditions) emerge from the process of criticism of the arts and yet they remain criticizable—not established beyond dispute.

F

As for the question of what counts as criticism, that can be left for another paper, but certainly almost anything does; the problem is rather what kinds of criticism are logically strong and interesting. These questions, how much can criticism achieve and what is the point of it, are acute for the subjectivist.

8. *Conclusion*

Why should we bother to read or, indeed, to write subjective criticism? Perhaps it is written to record for posterity how we felt at the time. But why read it? Why should we be interested in other people's views? Apart from sheer human interest, one reason we are interested is, I hazard, a rather commonplace one: simply that we look to critics for guidance in picking our way among the plethora of works available in all the arts. This especially in the matter of new works by new and unknown artists. But since what we read, according to the subjectivists, is mere expression of other people's subjective opinion, how does it help? I don't know what the subjectivist would say, but I do know that the reader, looking for guidance among the overwhelming mass of new art, has to adopt the method of familiarizing himself with the preferences and prejudices of the critics so that he can know how far to trust them. He has to know that in the eyes of Mr. Apple composer Baker can do no wrong and that therefore Apple's recommendations on new works of Baker must be treated with some circumspection. He has to know that Miss Cake feels ill at the thought of violence and that therefore her blanket condemnation of any film which contains violence is not necessarily going to be commensurate with his own opinion. In that critics are honest and allow us to find out their shortcomings, we should to a considerable extent be able to overcome the disadvantages attendant on their subjectivity. This applies to institutions too. We soon get to know when a journal or a society plugs a line, and thus we learn to treat its pronouncements on certain topics with some circumspection. It doesn't really matter that the *Daily Mirror* is Labour and the *Daily Sketch* is Conservative. It doesn't matter that the Royal Academy is 'against' modern art or that some galleries forget that there are painters antedating Picasso. Similarly it is neither to be expected nor desired that critics have no blind spots or soft spots.

Our ultimate aim then, is not a sort of supercomputer (man or institution) which churns out final judgments on works of art. We are thankfully, nowhere remotely near a stage in criticism of the arts where we can take our pencils and cry 'come, let us calculate' and hope to produce some cut-and-dried answer about a work of art.

This is certainly not *my* ideal of objectivism criticism, and in criticizing subjectivism I do not want it to be thought that is what I am hoping to put in its place. Criticism is a human and fallible activity, requiring sensitivity and judgment of an order which soulless machines do not possess. But unless we oppose subjectivism there are *no* standards in the arts, and criticism is worthless.

To be a subjectivist and write criticism seems inconsistent. What would be the point of swapping opinions; and moreover opinions which are couched in language that suggests that they are more than opinions and nearer truths? Possible answers are that the critic, thinking very highly of himself, believes his subjective opinions are worth more than those of others. But that is only his subjective opinion and unless he rates it higher than that he wouldn't act on it. Alternatively, since opinions are so diverse he may consider the more there are to choose from the better for the public. Again he may not regard *all* criticism as subjective; or he may be a complete cynic and do criticism merely as a job which he's grateful to have. None of these is very satisfactory.

In familiarizing ourselves with the prejudices of critics we demonstrate the falsity of subjectivism because we find we go on agreeing with a particular critic. Of course this could be explained by saying that our personalities are stable and that this is the source of our stable tastes. But this merges evaluation and response, and we've been over that. The acquired taste seems to me to reinforce their separation: one may learn to respond to something simply because of a critic's forcefully argued evaluation.

Criticism is pointless unless it has some objectivity, unless there are arguments which count, and unless we can gain from it something like an increase of knowledge (or appreciation, or insight).

CHAPTER 18

THE RATIONALITY OF CREATIVITY

My title links two abstract nouns that are usually set over against each other, seen as contrasting, if not in opposition. The view that informs this paper is that what can usefully be said about creativity is very little, and rather trite; and that it is co-extensive with the rational element in creativity. There may or may not be other than rational elements in creativity; confronted with them, my inclination would be for the first time to invoke Wittgenstein: "whereof one cannot speak, thereof one should be silent." The little I think can be said about the rationality of creativity will be confined to section five. The preceding sections will offer a general critique of the literature, bringing out its poverty and also its irrationality.

Much of the growing literature on creativity,[1] it seems to me, bypasses several quite decisive arguments. Properly understood, these arguments vitiate much of the debate in that literature. These arguments are the following: the problem to be solved by studying creativity is not clearly specified; creativity is treated as a psychological rather than a logical issue; that to explain creativity is to explain it away; and, when we create an explanation that explains creativity, it also, paradoxically, must explain itself. To each of these arguments I shall devote a section.

I. What is the Problem?

What problem is it intended that theories of creativity solve? This, to be sure, is a question rather than an argument. But the absence of a satisfactory answer to the question can be turned into an argument against the enterprise. Einstein remarked in several places that formulating the problem clearly constitutes the better part of the solution. Of course, different writers work on different problems. Were I to *set* problems concerning creativity

D. Dutton and M. Krausz, eds., The Concept of Creativity in Science and Art, pp. 109-128.

for others to work on, I might instance the paradox that the originality of an original idea only becomes "visible" against the background of an intellectual tradition, and those in an intellectual tradition can become trapped in it and blind to new ideas. I might ask whether ideas accumulate, or are reached in one jump. My self-imposed task is not, however, to set problems in this way; it is to express dissatisfaction with a body of literature.

J.P. Guilford,[2] in a paper often cited as initiating the modern literature on creativity, posed two questions for further research. (1) How can we discover creative promise in our children and youth? (2) How can we promote the development of creative personalities? Guilford was, at the time, President of the American Psychological Association, and his setting up of the problems for future research deserves close scrutiny. (1) tells us some children may be creatively promising. (2) implies that there are "creative personalities" (= creatively promising people?), whose development can be promoted. Creativity, then, is envisaged by Guilford as some sort of dependent variable, and the idea is to spot it and get to work on those factors which affect it, in order to foster it.

But what is creativity that we should be interested in discovering it and promoting it? Presumably, it is something like the ability to produce new and original ideas, creations, inventions, and the like. But why should we want to discover thinkers, artists, and inventors, and promote their development? Is it because we want to increase the output of papers, works of art, and patents? Academics, art critics, and patent offices already complain loudly that they can scarcely keep up with the flood. And perhaps much of the flood are ideas, works of art, and inventions that are neither new, nor original, but merely dross. Output alone, then, I take it, cannot be the object of promoting creativity. Obviously, it is output of quality that is to be promoted.

This aim is a rather complex one. Should there be an increase in the output of quality; or that plus a decrease in the output of trash; or merely a decrease in the output of trash? If the second or third, then an overall drop in output as such seems likely; if the first, I would suggest it is impossible — you get more quality only by getting more, and that includes more trash. At the moment, the rate of trash production seems to vary directly with the rate of production. Inverting the relationship might be very desirable. Its

accomplishment strikes me as very unlikely, as I shall argue
below, because part of the price of maximizing output is a great
deal of waste.

Another possible answer to why we want to spot creativity is
not because we want to increase it in general, but because we want
urgently to foster it in particular cases. Think-tanks, brainstorm
sessions, game theory, war games, contingency planning, futurology
and economic model-builders all yearn to be creative in this sense;
so do cancer researchers, unified field theorists, and governments
faced with inflation. All these groups act as though a general
theory of creativity might help them to achieve solutions to their
problems, and might also help to achieve them sooner. These aims
are at once absurdly over-ambitious and perfectly straightforward.
It is absurd to imagine us ever being able to solve such pressing
problems in a relatively straightforward or mechanical way. Our
world does not seem to be made like that. If we routinize a type
of problem, as we have in mathematics with tables, logarithms
and calculators, that only transfers our ambition from what is
now "routine calculation," to deeper and harder problems. The
common sense side of the ambition to crack the pressing problems
of humanity is heuristics and rules of thumb; general advice for
analyzing problems, thinking about them, and so on. These have
been forthcoming since intellectual endeavor began. An increase
in them looks unlikely, on the face of it, to help with urgent
problems.

So far, I have given two answers to the question of why we
should want to discover and promote creativity. One is to increase
quality output, the other is to facilitate the solution to urgent
problems. Both answers are rather pragmatic; to do with practical
social gains. Perhaps this is because we have implicitly equated
creativity with cognition and technology, rather than with art.
We rarely hear cries for an increase in the bulk quantity of art
(even of quality art), unless it be from artists; artistic output is
rarely acknowledged to be socially urgent (although a case can be
made). But for miracle drugs, new sources of energy, even Pola-
roid movies, there is social urgency. As regards artistic creativity,
then, neither output nor urgency constitutes a good reason for
investigation. We need a third answer to the question "why
research into creativity at all," an answer that is not pragmatic,

and that takes account of works of art as well as cognition and technology. My suggestion would be: the simple desire to explain the creative achievement, to understand it better, to get at the truth about it. At the moment, creativity is in the *virtus dormativa* phase: "creativity" is a property ascribed to certain artistic and intellectual achievements by certain creators who are said to possess the capacity to "create," as evidenced by the creativity of their work.

This is a parlous state of affairs indeed − provided only that an explanation of creativity is possible (my scepticism on this score will emerge presently). What, exactly, is in need of explanation; what is the problem? What fact or facts clash with what beliefs, theories, or expectations in the matter of creativity? I confess to not being sure. The obvious explanation of such uncertainty is that different writers have different problems, as we have already noted. There is, however, the possibility that the problems are connected, and hence can be set out in an orderly way. My suggestion for the status of most fundamental problem of all, from which the others branch off, is this. Creative achievements are unique events; explanatory progress is made only with repeatable events. Hence there is something inexplicable about creativity. Or, rather, to all new, interesting, novel, ingenious, pleasing, inventive, gifted: and other cognitive, technological: and artistic acts there is attributed a common property, something they all exemplify, something that can thus be studied and explained: this is called "creativity." Thus the inaccessible uniqueness of creation is made to yield to the belief that nothing is mysterious, remote, inexplicable.

This fundamental problem is, I believe, absorbed during our elementary education. We are taught that artistic, cognitive, and technical achievements are unique events, miracles, strokes of luck (or genius) which we should mainly be concerned to welcome and study.[3] This fundamental epistemological pessimism seems to foreclose the problem: creativity just is an inexplicable "gift." Our rationality is signalled to the extent that we accept and make the best of this situation. That same education, however, also indicates an epistemological optimism: the achievements of science and technology suggest that all problems will sooner or later yield to human thought. We seem to have truth and beauty in such abundance, it is inconceivable that we cannot reach the truth about beauty, originality, etc. Although I claim this problem of inexplicable uniqueness to be the fundamental one behind the creativity literature, I do not claim it is soluble. I suspect that many who contribute to the literature mistakenly believe that because they have found a problem, or what looks like one, it must be soluble. Its insolubility, and indeed ultimate incoherence, in my view vitiates the entire literature.

Given, though, for the moment, that this is a soluble problem, let us continue discussing the attempt to explain creativity. Perhaps if we could explain creativity, specify the laws it obeys and the initial conditions productive of it, then the aims of increased output and/or urgent solutions would be facilitated. The problems of output and urgency would then clearly be subordinate to the problem of inexplicable uniqueness. Were that so, might it not have been better organization on my part to begin with explanation as an aim, and then to move on to increased output and urgent solutions as subordinate or by-product aims? The reason I did not proceed in this way is because of the possibility that an explanation of creativity would not solve the practical problems of output and urgency. Our understanding of earthquakes, continental drift, ice ages, red giants and black holes may make us feel better, emotionally and intellectually, but they do not give us any power over the processes in question. Is it not entirely possible that the concatenation of elements required for creativity obey laws such that human intervention is not possible? Maybe creativity is an outcome of trial and error, and obeys only the laws of chance. We can explain the roulette wheel without being about to gamble on it successfully.

For example, one strand in the literature, which undoubtedly can be traced back to Freud, is the idea that creativity is a manifestation of psychological disorder.[4] The most extreme recent case is Storr's argument that Einstein's genius was a by-product of a psychological condition, namely schizophrenia (could the schizophrenia not be a by-product of his genius?). Confirmations of the neuroses of creative people abound: from Berkeley's concern with the bowels to Einstein's eccentricities of dress and manner; from Bobby Fischer's tantrums to the unbelievable squalor of Francis Bacon's studio. But what of counter-examples? What of

Mozart, Rembrandt, Hume? What of the argument that even if all creators have neuroses, not all neurotics are creative, and hence the creative value of what someone does cannot be fully understood in terms of their psychology? What makes the difference between Einstein's psychopathology and that of the schizophrenic who believes he is a piece of soap? The answer has to focus on the content of their ideas, and thus has to have reference to something like the objective existence of intellectual problems and traditions, and the further fact that Einstein's psychopathology resulted in his contributing to those rather than to the private world of insane fantasy. We cannot, as it were, direct neuroses into science and art rather than intellectual rubbish. This argument goes to undermine the idea that an explanation of creativity, even if found, will lead to practical knowledge of how to foster creativity. We might get further with folk tales and rules of thumb.

So much then for doubts about the utility of solving the basic problem of inexplicable uniqueness. Let me now argue that no such explanations of creativity are there to be found. The case I choose is the movies; not just because they are a speciality of mine, but also because their creative processes are less privatized than those of the traditional arts and sciences (I suppose it is a bit analogous to studying research teams rather than individual scientists). Producers of movies, obviously, have sought for many years to understand what makes a movie a success. Success is an aspect of creativity that cannot be gainsaid simply because popularity is one of its desiderata. In the classical arts, the crucial desideratum of success (so seldom mentioned) was to please the patron, the dedicatee, or God, as well as the artist himself.[5] One might say that in movies, to be a creative success is to make something both interesting *and* popular. By this standard, the most creative periods in Hollywood were between 1914 and 1926, and, again, from the mid-thirties to the mid-forties. The first period marks the maturity and development of the silent movie, the second, maturity and development in the sound movie. What can explain such periods of creative success? Certainly no psychological theory of creativity will do, for this would be to reduce a creative era or a creative place to a fortuitous concatenation of individuals. To give so much to fortune seems excessive.

Two factors are widely bruited:[6] experiment and encouragement. While there may be exceptions, these factors do seem crucial, whether we think of Ingmar Bergman, the French New Wave, or the vintage periods of Hollywood. Freedom to (and security despite) experiment and continuing encouragement are entirely characteristic of Hollywood in the two periods mentioned, less as a policy than as an unintended consequence of institutional arrangements. By 1914, silent movies were twenty years old, technically accomplished, highly successful with the public, and hence not trammelled with rules, regulations, and restrictions. No one really knew for sure and in advance what would click at the box office and be something to be proud of as well. Hence many filmmakers were given their heads as soon as they had a success. This was institutional rather than attitudinal. Doubtless many movie moguls were crass and vulgar and concerned solely with catering to public taste. But they had to work through and with men who had a professional and creative pride; who were not and would not think of themselves as hacks. In some cases their self-estimation may have been excessive, but that is not important. What matters is that men of the caliber of D.W. Griffith, Eric von Stroheim, C.B. DeMille, King Vidor, John Ford, Buster Keaton, and other slapstick comedians were challenged and stimulated by a new medium to an unprecedented degree. At first, they simply enjoyed themselves immensely. Early Hollywood seems to have been a place where any crazy idea could get a hearing, and creators worked at a frantic pace.[7] What sorted out the sheep from the goats was the popular touch, whether in a player or a director. Unawareness may have been something of a blessing, for with public acclaim came self-consciousness and, ultimately, pretension. Griffith and Stroheim are examples, as is Orson Welles in the forties. The most spectacular case, however, is Charlie Chaplin. This London street urchin, who became a brilliant vaudeville comedian of the English music hall, went to Los Angeles to try himself in films in 1913. He worked steadily and quickly until 1916. In that year he was negotiating a new contract with a different company, and this necessitated a trip to New York. He cabled his brother which train he was on, and settled down for the five-day journey. Remarking that in those days he was unrecognized when out of make-up and costume, he recalls being in the middle of shaving when the train was swamped with people in Amarillo, Texas.

They were looking for him! Telegraph operators had spread the word that he was coming, and cities laid on formal welcoming ceremonies.[8] Chaplin himself does not say this, but I detect the beginnings of self-consciousness and decline in his movies from that experience, although there are occasional reversions to form. By 1918, Chaplin persuaded D.W. Griffth, Mary Pickford and Douglas Fairbanks to join him in creating their own film company under the title United Artists. Grandeur indeed.

After the introduction of sound, movies were in effect a new medium. Technical teething troubles over, they conquered the depression business slump and entered another golden age artistically and economically. It sounds incredible, but Los Angeles in the thirties seems to have been a cultural El Dorado. Gathered there were Hugh Walpole, Aldous Huxley, Christopher Isherwood, Thomas Mann, Bertolt Brecht, Thornton Wilder, Scott Fitzgerald, William Faulkner, Raymond Chandler, Nathanael West, Ben Hecht, Igor Stravinsky, Sir C. Aubrey Smith, Sir Cedric Hardwicke, Leslie Howard, Laurence Olivier, Orson Welles, John Houseman, and Vivien Leigh — to name only a few whose fame owed nothing to the movies. The combination of the attractions of California living with the intense creativity and excitement of Hollywood almost produced a cultural center to rival New York. In this atmosphere the individuals sometimes flourished and sometimes suffered, but the movies only flourished.[9]

We can see then that there is some pattern to periods of great creativity. We cannot reproduce them at will. The fundamental strength of public demand for movies cannot be recovered, especially since the arrival of television. Hence, there have been long periods in which filmmakers have been offered anything but encouragement and certainly nothing like freedom. Recently a new phenomenon has appeared: desperate experimentation in the face of bankruptcy. Several of the major American movie companies have gone from success to collapse in the last six or seven years. For a time, there were unrivalled opportunities for innovation and experiment. But that has passed, and a pervading sense of insecurity co-exists with the most profitable year since 1946.[10]

In this section I have argued that the first weakness in studies of creativity is poorly articulated aims. When the aims are articu-

lated it seldom looks as though any of them could sustain the
kinds of explorations of creativity that have been undertaken —
practical or theoretical.

II. A Logical or a Psychological Issue?

Philosophers commonly distinguish between what they call the
logic and the psychology of knowledge; between, that is, the
rational reconstruction of the propositions and inferences which
constitute knowledge, and the subjective mental processes that
go on in those producing it. The aim of making the distinction
is to free epistemology from psychology, to deny that knowledge
has anything to do with belief. In a similar manner, I should like
to distinguish between creativity as an objective matter, a property,
so to speak, of created works; and creativity as a property of
persons or their minds. Much of the research into creativity is in
the latter category and, though I am sceptical of it for reasons
already and yet to be stated, I do not want to discuss it directly.
What I want to stress is the distinction and the consequences of
its neglect. Unless there is an objective logic of creativity, a psychology of creativity can be of no interest. The psychology of
scientists is interesting mainly because they are doing science,
and science means something like exploring the way the world
is. Presumably, creativity is interesting because there is something
going on in creative people that results in objective results: creations.
What are the objective achievements? Here the whole subject
seems to become anecdotal: sayings and stories about the great
geniuses are trundled out. Two things strike one: first, the *virtus
dormativa* effect; second, that the achievements called creative
can be characterized without the concept of creativity and without remainder. Originality, novelty, synthesis, insight, and so on
suffice. The status of creativity as a property in its own right is
highly questionable.

This is the main reason I have postponed saying anything direct
about creativity until the end. So far, we have asked the simple
question, what are the aims of studying creativity? This was an
obvious question with which to begin a discussion of rationality
and creativity, since a rational action is necessarily (though not

sufficiently) a goal-directed action. But this question is also a second-order question: it is about the study of creativity, not about creativity. Here we begin to capture in a preliminary way some elements of what this paper is advocating. I believe that the rationality of creativity has to do not so much with the (psychological) creative process, as with the rationality of the creator towards his own creative process. In other words, rationality is to be located in the actions the creator takes, before, and especially after, any "act of creation" occurs.

For various obvious reasons which I do not here want to go into,[11] Popperians often say that rational belief is only a special case of rational action; they subordinate or even absorb the act of belief or creation into action. Hence those who look on creativity psychologically, as bisociation, or psychoneurosis, and so on, as though there was a ghost in the machine, a Magic Moment when the Muse Speaks, a flash of blinding light, an urge to cry Eureka, are bypassed. Action before and action after eventually squeeze out what is in between.

Rational action is goal-directed action, where the tools are critically-held theories. Rational thought is action directed to the goal of solving intellectual or artistic problems. The rationality of rational action shows itself in critical open-mindedness, trial and error. The rationality of rational thought consists of trial and error, which is a form of action. It is not the problem being tackled that is rational; no more is it the solution being offered that is rational; but the method of trying out the thought, inspiration, idea, against the problem, against other solutions and, in some interesting cases, against the facts, that is rational. This is the case whether the problem be called cognitive or artistic.[12]

One hears the response that this is all very well, but that the theory of creativity comes to explain the new thought, the very thing that is put on trial. This presupposes the mind, soul, ghost in the machine, that receives or creates the new thought, the inspiration, does the bisociation, or whatnot. My counter-suggestion would be that my account allows us to dispense with the mind reified in this sense, and hence creativity hypostatized in this sense, for the mind becomes the product rather than the producer of rational organization, of goal-directed, trial-and-error action. Einstein said: "my pencil is more intelligent than I."[13]

This view also proposes a rather different approach to the practical questions of increasing output, solving particular urgent problems. It suggests no recipe, but general social conditions of encouragement and freedom. Bisociation and the like are mental acts which — whether or not they lie at the root of creativity — is somehow irrelevant since there is no way to foster or induce them. Whereas an institutional setup that fosters freedom and encouragement — while not easy to construct — has been constructed from time to time, sometimes inadvertently. The other consequence of my view is that fostering creativity may turn out to be a less attractive prospect than it sounds. What I have in mind is this. Neither a favorable social setup nor an array of rules of thumb, are a recipe for creative achievement. So much expenditure may be undertaken without promise or even hope of results. Indeed, even if success is achieved, they predict that its cost will be a huge amount of what will later be designated waste: that is to say, we know beforehand that much of our expenditure will be afterwards declared waste, yet we cannot specify in advance what will be waste, and hence we cannot eliminate it. Thus we are denied the comfort of even thinking we can eliminate waste. (Although in my view we can dispense with the moral overtones on waste by declaring waste part of the costs of production.) If we divert the entire budget of the U.S. Pentagon into research into the causes of cancer, say, we can no more guarantee success (however that is defined) than we can assure the gambler that his number will come up (it will, but he could be dead before it does). No doubt, in time, scientific research on this scale would yield the bureaucracy, jobs, and contracting industry that the military budget does: and there are unattractive as well as attractive aspects to there being so many men and women in white coats. It is unlikely such expenditure and such waste would ever be agreed to because, while the military has a task at which it is very rarely tested, cancer research is tested every time a patient dies.

So much, then, for the question of what problems are being tackled in the literature on creativity. Not only are these problems not often formulated, formulating them inclines one to the conclusion that they cannot be solved: not simply because they are difficult or intractable but, much more seriously, because they reveal muddles that may vitiate the enterprise. Creativity may not give rise to clear problems because on no known theory is it presupposed as a definite property of the physical world or the world of mind. To avoid concluding it is chimerical we shall have to seek it elsewhere.

III. Creativity a World 3 Event

The groundwork for the second main argument, about to be developed, has been extensively laid down in the discussion so far. Creativity, like knowledge or discovery, can be seen to have a logical as well as a psychological aspect. A solution to a problem can be judged creative; so can the mind which produced that solution. However, a solution that was in fact creative can fail to be recognized as such at the time, and its creator can similarly be thought not creative. The problems we are talking about can be cognitive or artistic. J.S. Bach is my favorite example: a composer virtually dismissed in his own time as a competent but rather pedestrian fellow, far outshone by his brilliant sons C.P.E. and J.C.[14] While those sons are by no means forgotten, they can hardly now be mentioned in the same breath as their father, who has serious claim to being one of the (if not the) greatest composers who ever lived.

With cognition the question becomes more involved. For one thing, there is a popular prejudice in favor of positive science being called creative at the expense of negative science. Positive and negative are connected with the simpleminded distinction between, say, a theory (positive) and its criticism (negative). Sometimes, lord help us, a distinction is made between negative and constructive criticism. Hence, Copernicus is creative for inventing heliocentrism, but the many critics of Ptolemy are not even well-known. Along these lines one might as well say Plato was creative and Aristotle was not: but this shows up the absurdity. Aristotle created beautiful arguments against Plato which were enormous creative achievements in themselves. Newton was a creative genius, but so too was Berkeley, who picked holes in Newton's mathematics and metaphysics.

All this discussion is in the logical realm. Solving a problem is creative; devising a criticism of a theory is creative. Creativeness cannot be unpacked in any precise way, and indeed I have hinted

earlier that it may be a dispensable term. What I want to emphasize here is the different point that whether or not an idea or a
criticism is a creative one has nothing to do with psychology, with
whether an act of creation, inspiration, or bisociation has occurred.
Indeed, the extensive discussion of humor by both Koestler and
Freud demonstrates this. So far as this paper is concerned, there
is nothing creative about jokes. I find the expressions, "what a
creative joke," or, "he's a really creative comedian," very odd.
Odder, is the attention given to humor by those interested in
creativity.

If there is rationality in creativity it is of course going to be
located in the public, objective, logical realm, and not in the
psychological one. Hence the importance of this distinction and
the fact that it plays haywire with the literature on creativity.
On this view, "creativity" is a cognate of "simple," "powerful,"
"unifying," "exciting," "trail-blazing," and other sorts of adjec-
tives that might be attached to new theories, new criticisms,
or new works of art. The rationality of creativity then consists of
it being successful action directed at solving an artistic or cognitive
problem. Calling something "a creative failure," might simply
indicate ingenuity. Degrees of creativity are also sometimes
alluded to, but I see no way of explicating these in any discussible
manner.

Perhaps the notion of creativity, then, is that of a socially
defined event in the world of ideas or art, what Popper has called
the world of objective mind, or mind objectified, the third world
or world 3.[15] This rather than a "property of the mind." A new
theory or work of art undoubtedly has its physical or world 1
aspects — marks on paper or daubs on canvas. It also undoubtedly
in some sense had its origins in certain mental acts of its creator,
in world 2. But neither of these is of much importance or interest.
What makes it a theory, a new theory, a work of art, an original
work of art, is the objective relationships it bears as a world 3
object to other world 3 objects, other theories and works of art.[16]
These in turn have gained their significance because of the bearing
they have on those especially important world 3 entities known as
problems, that is to say, former theories, or means of portraying
the world in art that have now become inconsistent or otherwise
unsatisfactory. The standards of what is new or what is a creative

addition to art are similarly a judgment within world 3, constantly subject to world 3 debate. Art and cognition are the mind striving to achieve objective existence in the external world 3, transcending space and time, and they achieve that when something is created (a theory, a solution, a new problem, a new argument, a "match," a discovery, etc.). Put it like this: to seek in the physical world a recipe for, or an explanation of, what physical conditions bring about Einstein's pencil marks is no more absurd than asking us what kinds of mind or mental process brings about Einstein's great thoughts. Just as Einstein's pencil marks have no meaning unless their significance in the third world is understood, so his thoughts have no interest unless there is a third world significance. This is precisely my objection to Storr's view of Einstein as a psychopath. What possible explanatory value does this hold? What counts is not psychopathy, but the world of objective ideas. This is the logical aspect of creation and cognition; creativity in a certain sense only exists as a vector in world 3.

IV. To Explain Away

The third decisive argument undermining the entire enterprise of studying creativity in the manner it is currently studied has been most eloquently expressed by Einstein in his beautiful essay on Newton.[17] Conceding that reason is weak when measured against its never-ending task, Einstein hails Newton as the first to succeed in explaining a wide range of phenomena mathematically, logically, quantitatively, and in harmony with experience. How, he asks, "did this miracle come to birth in his brain?" Then he apologizes for the "illogical" question, "for if by reason we could deal with the problem of 'how,' then there would be no question of a miracle in the proper sense of the word" (p. 220).

In other words, what Einstein is saying is that creativity is interesting precisely because and to the extent that it is uniquely mysterious. Were it not such, it would not be creativity. We can show this by imagining what the reaction would be were we to pinpoint the creative element in many cases of creation. I contend that what would happen then is that we would set out to isolate other, alternative special features of creativity as "the miracle."

The problem here is that this argument shows that creativity is such that were it to be explained it would be explained away. Usually an explanation of something does not explain it away. When it does, something is wrong.

V. Self-Reference

The fourth decisive argument is this. Suppose we had an explanation of creativity. *A fortiori,* that would be an explanation of new explanations. *A fortiori,* it would be an explanation of that new explanation itself that we have just devised (namely of creativity).

Were we to say, (T) "All creation is a product of neurosis," we should also have to say that (T) itself, being a creation, was a product of neurosis — regardless of who first uttered it. But how are we to know that this neurotic manifestation is to be taken seriously, whereas the belief that someone is a piece of soap is not?

VI. Trial and Error

Having, then, looked at four arguments which seem to me not only not met but quite impossible to meet, the grounds for my scepticism towards the literature on creativity have been exposed. Towards the beginning of the paper I said that what could be said about creativity was rather trite and rather scanty. At the risk of now being both trite and scanty, I present a few remarks on the matter additional to what has emerged in the foregoing discussion. Bertrand Russell, W.A. Mozart, and moviemaking are my examples of creativity; Russell in the cognitive area, Mozart in the area of individual artistic creation, movies in the area of collective artistic creation; Russell and Mozart fluent and individual geniuses, movies made by committees.[18]

In his essay, "How I Write,"[19] Russell reports that, when bothered by a problem, he tried the method of writing and rewriting, but he invariably found the first version to be the best. This was a discovery about himself (his mind, but, more importantly, its world 3 achievements). Eventually, he adopted the following method. After concentrating reflection on the problem at hand, possibly writing nothing, he had planted it in his subconsciousness and would turn to other things. At some point the solution would re-emerge into his consciousness, and it only remained for him to write it out. This is a very striking passage in Russell. It gives concrete and helpful hints ("Turn to other things for a while"). It explains the sense of inspiration or revelation (as the rush created by the surfacing of subconscious mental work). It is also followed by a careful disclaimer. Russell points out that not everything he produced in this manner was creative or valuable or true. He says merely that this was his conscious method of working, which he had discovered by trial and error. After the fact he decided whether what he had written was publishable. Even after he had published he might later decide that some of the things he had said were false. He emphasized, however, that his aim was simply to try to do the best he could at the time. The Russell Archives at McMaster University are filled with early drafts of books and articles that never saw the light of day. Hence we see at work in Russell a conscious process of trial and error, a totally rational approach to creativity as ultimately a world 3 matter.[20]

Similar in some ways is the fluency reported of Mozart, whose subconscious seems to have been working on music the whole time. Hence, he could compose in his head, play from memory, and write down the piece later; compose while playing billiards; even compose a prelude while copying down the already thought-out fugue.[21] He left very few notebooks or sketches, and yet is known to have corrected and improved works a great deal, often turning aside to easier, lighter commissions while struggling hard with problems in more intense works.

I have picked on examples like Russell and Mozart because on the surface they look so fluent and "inspired," the opposite of the hesitant, diffident, groping, trial-and-error creator I have in mind. In close-up, however, this impression disappears. Russell and Mozart have to be rational about their own creativity too. Russell reports a harrowing exception to his own method of work when he was writing *Principia Mathematica*. He tried consciously to work hard and creatively. The strain of working on the abstract and difficult problems of that book from 1902–1910 was so severe that "my intellect never quite recovered . . . I have been ever since definitely less capable of dealing with difficult abstractions than I was before."[22]

Artists and intellectuals work as they can, as they find they have been most successful (in the world 3, not public opinion, sense) and exercise much of their critical faculties on the question of what is good enough to release. Painters throw away canvasses, or store them away incomplete, perhaps to be finished one day, perhaps not; writers submit themselves to editors (who may be themselves, their wives, as well as others), the most startling case of which came to light recently with the publication of Ezra Pound's editing of T.S. Eliot's poem "The Waste Land." Some people went so far as to wonder whether publication didn't detract from Eliot's stature as a creative innovator.[23] The short answer to that, I suppose, is that Eliot could have restored any cuts Pound made had it been his judgment that they did not serve to solve the poetic problem with which he was grappling. Furthermore, many artists and intellectuals show their work to friends, wives, children, professional peers, editors, publishers and the like long before it sees the light of day. Academe has a tradition of acknowledging such help. Because that tradition is not general does not at all imply the practice is not.

It is not hard, then, to see the process of trial and error not only at work, but consciously employed, in cognition and the individual arts. A fortiori it is not going to be difficult to detect it in collective arts, whether architecture or the cinema. Film-making not only employs trial and error, but, to the extent possible, institutionalizes – even bureaucratizes – it. This is not necessarily all to the good, as, obviously, excessive trial is a form of caution. Once Russell knew that earlier works he had written contained mistakes, or did not sell, he might have been justified in publishing nothing. Capable of error and yet wanting to avoid it, the cautious policy is to do nothing.[24] Capable of failure, yet desperately trying to avoid it, cautious movie producers compromise – that is to say, they interpret trial results too soon and too harshly. This permeates the creative process in movies, which is an institutionalized clash between art and commerce, each side with its own problems, its own integrity, its own series of trials and errors to be avoided. Money being the necessary, but by no means sufficient, condition of there ever being any films made at all, commerce holds a powerful position. The subtlety is not that the bureaucratic organization is split between commercial people and creative people, but that commerce and creation coexist in most film people. Hence, a script may be written and rewritten until it has shape and coherence; it then may be rewritten some more to improve its commercial possibilities. The same will apply to casting, to decisions on sets, costumes and locations, to editing the picture, to the manner in which it is publicized. The writer, the director, the actor, the cameraman, the set designer, and the editor are all simultaneously in search of a solution to their creative problems which is also commercially viable. Some trials are creative (does that scene cut well?), some commercial (does the preview audience like it?), many are a mixture of both. For sure, the box office is neither physical nor psychological; I suggest that the creative side similarly is a sort of objective matter.

In film, as in the other arts, but less so in philosophy and still less so in science, there is a tedious avant-garde with a romantic view of creativity as mainly consisting in not interrupting while the Muse speaks through the favored individual. Life is easier that way. Being rational and self-critical is very hard and sometimes impossible. It is nevertheless the key to anything deserving the label creativity.

Notes

1. See J.P. Guilford, "Creativity," *American Psychologist* 5 (1950): 444–54; Arthur Koestler, *The Act of Creation* (London: Hutchinson, 1964); P.E. Vernon, *Creativity* (Harmondsworth: Penguin, 1970); J.W. Getzels and P.W. Jackson, *Creativity and Intelligence* (New York: Wiley, 1962); Anthony Storr, *The Dynamics of Creation* (New York: Atheneum, 1972); and the *Journal of Creative Behaviour,* 1967.
2. J.P. Guilford, op. cit.
3. In the same way that chess masters record and study the grand masters and their great games. No one seems to be trying to find out what makes a great game great and thus deprive it of its mystique. Cf. section 3, below.

4. Storr, op. cit., pp. 61ff. Jean Cocteau somewhere compares being creative to being pregnant. Salvador Dali expresses similar ideas in *The Secret Life of Salvador Dali* (New York: Dial Press, 1961), as does the brilliant and tormented British painter Francis Bacon. See David Sylvester, *Interviews With Francis Bacon* (London: Thames and Hudson, 1975).

5. When I was first introduced to Rembrandt's painting known as "The Night Watch," it was remarked that its bold, active, almost chiaroscuro style had shocked those who commissioned it, and Rembrandt's intransigent artistic temperament on this point contributed to his financial downfall. The idea was that crass patrons always failed to understand geniuses, who had to be tough to maintain their integrity. Later, I noticed this story was declared a legend by contemporary historians, who claim that the picture was always hung, that Rembrandt's commissions did not dry up, and who attribute his downfall to expensive living (especially the house). The theory that all creative artists are misunderstood by hoi polloi is a widespread and pernicious one, since it can be used to rebut all criticism, and even self-criticism and doubt.

6. See J. Agassi, "The Function of Intellectual Rubbish," *Research in the Sociology of Knowledge, Science and Art* 2 (1979): 209–27.

7. Charles Chaplin, *My Autobiography* (London: The Bodley Head, 1964; Penguin edition, 1966), p. 154. Chaplin was amazed when Mack Sennett said to him, "We have no scenario. We get an idea, then follow the natural sequence of events." So different from what he describes as the "rigid, non-deviating routine" of the theatre.

8. Chaplin, op. cit., pp. 175–79.

9. The most evocative account of Hollywood in the thirties and forties is by Charles Higham and Joel Greenberg, *Hollywood in the Forties* (London: A. Zwemmer, 1968). The only book I know which attempts seriously to discuss the creative process in movies without reference to individual genius, but rather to collective endeavor, is Lawrence Alloway, *Violent America: The Movies 1946–1964* (New York: Museum of Modern Art, distributed by the New York Graphic Society, Greenwich, Conn., 1971).

10. See Pauline Kael, "On the Future of the Movies," *New Yorker*, August 5, 1974, pp. 43–59.

11. See J. Agassi, "The Role of Corroboration in Popper's Methodology," *Australasian Journal of Philosophy* 39 (1961): 82–91, and J. Agassi and I.C. Jarvie, "The Problem of the Rationality of Magic," *British Journal of Sociology* 18 (1967): 55–74.

12. What I have in mind is Gombrich's notion of art as "making and matching." See E.H. Gombrich, *Art and Illusion* (London: Phaidon Press, 1960).

13. Einstein is quoted to this effect in K.R. Popper, *Objective Knowledge* (Oxford: The Clarendon Press, 1972), p. 225 (note).

14. I.C. Jarvie, "The Objectivity of Criticism of the Arts," *Ratio* 9 (1967): 67–83. Tovey comments that Bach's art was neglected "as old-fashioned and crabbed" by his younger contemporaries. We owe his rediscovery to Mendelssohn and Schumann. (See "Bach, J.S." in *Encyclopedia Britannica*, 11th edition.)

15. K.R. Popper, *Objective Knowledge*, chaps. 3 and 4.
16. This may explain my total opposition (not to modern art but) to modernism in art, the philosophy that traditions must be broken with. How someone trained as, or pretending to be, an artist can even think of this is something of a mystery; it is a bit like an English speaker deciding to utter only gibberish.
17. Albert Einstein, "Isaac Newton," in his *Out of My Later Years* (New York: Philosophical Library, 1950), pp. 219–23.
18. See I.C. Jarvie, *Towards a Sociology of the Cinema* (London: Routledge and Kegan Paul, 1970), chaps. 1, 2, and 3.
19. In Bertrand Russell, *Portraits from Memory* (London: George Allen and Unwin, 1956), pp. 194–97. Storr, op. cit., pp. 42–43 attributes a similar idea to Graham Wallas.
20. To show that Russell's cool detachment has nothing to do with his endeavors being logical and cognitive, one could cite the superb American painter Edward Hopper, who not only creates by "painting, scraping off, and repainting," but also is dominated by the objective logic of creation: "I find, in working, always the distracting intrusion of elements not part of my most interested vision, and the inevitable obliteration and replacement of this vision by the work itself as it proceeds. The struggle to prevent this decay is, I think, the common lot of all painters to whom the invention of arbitrary forms has lesser interest. I believe that the great painters, with their intellect as master have attempted to force this unwitting medium of paint and canvas into a record of their emotions. I find any digression from this large aim leads me to boredom." (Quoted in Lloyd Goodrich, *Edward Hoppper* [New York: H.N. Abrams, 1971], p. 161.)
21. See the account in Erich Hertzmann, "Mozart's Creative Process," in Paul Henry Lang, ed., *The Creative World of Mozart* (New York: W.W. Norton, 1963), pp. 17–30.
22. Bertrand Russell, *The Autobiography of Bertrand Russell, 1872–1914* (London: George Allen and Unwin, 1967), pp. 152–53.
23. T.S. Eliot, *The Waste Land*, a facsimile and transcript of the original drafts including the annotations of Ezra Pound, ed. Valerie Eliot (New York: Harcourt, Brace, Jovanovich, 1971).
24. In the movies this becomes interesting in the political dimension. From time to time Russia and China made it so difficult to avoid ideological error (because of unpredictable shifts in the party line) that filmmaking shrank almost to zero.

CHAPTER 19

TECHNOLOGY AND THE STRUCTURE OF KNOWLEDGE

The problem with which I want to engage your attention this evening requires a little more specification than is given in my title. It would seem obvious enough that technology is a species of knowledge. Our so called 'age of technology' seems to have more of this commodity we can call 'technological knowledge' than any previous age or society. You would expect, then, that technology as a species of knowledge would be highly revered, widely studied, and generally well understood in our society. You would think, in fact, that a talk with my title would be no more required than one on 'science and the structure of knowledge'. This happens not to be so. Technology is *not* generally revered, especially by intellectuals, *not* well understood and studied, and even has its claims to be a species of knowledge disputed. I take it as my task to try to dispel such views. What I shall suggest in the course of what follows is that from one angle technology is only a part of the logical structure of our knowledge; and that from another angle the whole of our knowledge can be regarded as a substructure, as included under technology. Viewed logically, technology is a substructure of knowledge; it is knowledge of what physicists call the 'initial conditions'. Viewed anthropologically, knowledge is part of man's multiform attempts to adapt to his environment which we call his technology. Resistance to recognition of these facts is fed, I shall suggest, partly by ancient snobbery and partly by sheer mistaken identification of technology with machine-technology.

Some philosophers — and it is not a new thing to find philosophers in the role of villains of the piece — fail to classify technology as knowledge at all. Before taking issue with them, and perhaps explaining their attitude, some review of their arguments may be called for. Professor Gilbert Ryle of Oxford University has drawn a very well-known distinction between two senses of the word 'know'; namely, knowing *how* to do something, and knowing *that* something is the case.[1] We know *that* we live on an ovoid planet so many miles from the sun, with certain rotation periods, along with so many other planets, etc., etc. We may know *how* to tie a reef knot, swim the breast stroke, or drive a motor car without in any way being able to articulate this knowledge, or to explain what it is *that* we know when we know *how* to do these things. Moreover, although tieing knots and swimming are learned, we

302

can forget them or forget that we know them. Not having ridden a bicycle for many years we might be inclined to say: 'I can't do it' or 'I've completely forgotten how to'. Yet, when placed in the saddle we are off without any trouble at all. What Ryle is saying is that there is a kind of knowing, namely the mastery of a technique, which is very definitely not knowledge in the traditional sense of the word. One can even be unconscious of having it. Politics is a particularly vivid case of this: political acumen, skill, and good sense is widely regarded as a talent or instinct which it is impossible to analyze into a series of statements saying *that* such and such is the case.

This knowing *how* to do things is called in America, 'know-how'. It is highly regarded and prized here. In England, where I come from, and Europe generally, this 'know-how' is spoken of rather slightingly as 'mere know-how'; the implication being that the really important thing is knowing *that* such-and such, from which the know-how will follow, if one can be bothered to sully one's hands with such prosaic matters. (Unfortunately, there is no such short locution as 'know-that', such that one could say 'he has the know-that' in parallel to 'he has the know-how'. When we say 'do you know that', 'know' is a verb and 'that' a preposition and they do not combine to become a noun like 'know-how'. So I shall have to persist with the clumsy expression 'knowing that'.)

I shall argue that know-how certainly isn't enough by itself, although it is not to be despised either. It seems to me that know-how is more intellectual than it is being made out to be by Ryle; but that essentially either knowing that without know-how or know-how without knowing that is seriously deficient. Both know-how and knowing that are indispensible parts of human knowledge.

The problem, then, is whether technology or know-how is knowledge, and if it is, what kind of knowledge it is, what its place is in the structure of knowledge. Personally I dislike mystery stories and I always read the endings of tense novels first. So you will not be surprised if I proceed to outline my answer to the problem at once, and then proceed to elaborate on it for the rest of my allocated time.

My answer, then, is as follows. Technology does have somewhat different aims than science, it aims to be effective rather than true — and it can be the one without the other. Yet technology is knowledge of sorts; such know-how as we have tells us about what works in this world. Its position in the structure of knowledge is thus peculiar, because, what happens to be effective in our part of the world may be a purely contingent matter and will also depend on what degree of effectiveness we happen to demand of technology. It may be enough for us to say of this drug that it cures this illness 90% of the time. We may then feel that we know *that* drug x cures illness y. But we do not. We know *that* drug x has a 90% effectiveness in curing illness y. We also know *that* it has a failure rate of 10% with illness y. The causes of illness y and the reasons drug x cures it may be completely unknown. Some of our drug technology, then, is based on the contingent fact that drug x sometimes cures illness y. Now in much of our medical technology we regard 90% effectiveness as very good; if we raise our demand — as we tend to do, human beings never being satisfied — we also make more urgent the question of cause and cure in its pure form. For except in the few cases where we stumble across an 100% effective cure by accident, the obvious way to effect an 100% cure is to find out the cause of the disease and devise a true cure that deals with that cause in a well-understood and controllable way.

This argument aims to show the sharp differences created by making the aim of an activity effectiveness rather than truth. What is effective may be true, or it may be false — Newtonian celestial mechanics is a very effective navigating tool but has been superseded in science by Einstein's relativistic mechanics — or it may be unknown, as in the case of drug x. Now, because we also value truth, attempts will be made to find out why drug x works as it does, but meanwhile it will go on being good technology, effective 90% of the time.

So truth is not the same as effectiveness. And when we talk of knowledge we usually mean knowledge of truth. What I shall suggest is that knowledge of effectiveness is knowledge of truth too, even if it is on a different logical level. It is, so to speak, true knowledge of *what* is effective. It is not true knowledge of *why* it is effective; it does not *explain* anything. But it is part and parcel of the whole truth, nevertheless.

The ancients left us with an idea of knowledge as proved truths. Contemporary philosophy has smashed this idea to smithereens and decreed that only the tautologies of logic and mathematics can be proved, but tautologies like 'all tables are tables' can hardly be knowledge, since they don't tell us anything. So a new conception of knowledge has arisen which discards proved truth and places the following mental reservation before all scientific assertions: 'this is a hypothesis, the best we can suggest at the moment. It will be revised as soon as we have reason to doubt it'. Nowadays, then, knowledge with a capital 'K' is generally taken to be putatively true statements; that is, statements tentatively advanced in the belief that they might be true and should be tested. Scientific knowledge is generally taken to be putatively true statements about the *structure of the world*. That water boils at 100 °C is not a truth about the structure of the world, but a contingent fact about our local environment. Technology, it seems to me, is closer to knowing a lot of things whose *logical* status is like that of water boiling at 100 °C, rather than like Newton's laws or Einstein's mass-energy equations. That there is a difference of level between these will be clear. It is perhaps not so easy to specify. Put briefly in a way that should become clearer later on, I would say that science aims at true laws which cover the entire physical world and explain the facts of the case about it. Know-how is knowing what works, how to do things in a small part of that world, with a precision as high as is demanded.

In expanding on all I have said so far about the problem of the place of technology in the structure of knowledge I want first of all to draw some distinctions which are often overlooked. The first is to note that technology is a portmanteau-word which includes under itself applied science, invention, implementation of applied science and invention, and the maintenance of the existing apparatus — these last two being something like planning and engineering.[2] For the present I do not want to talk about engineering and maintenance, since they seem such purely practical matters that their status as knowledge doesn't arise. But invention and applied science do seem worth separate treatment.

First of all, invention. Invention can be as important in pure science as much as in other fields. Invention is discovering a way of doing something we already know to be possible. Persistence of vision makes the motion picture possible; but a great deal of inventiveness was required in order to make this possibility an actuality. Einstein's mass-energy equation and Rutherford's demonstration that the atom could be split made it clear that the atomic bomb was possible — although it was not clear to everyone at the time. Physicists were hotly divided about whether ways could ever be invented of sustaining a chainreaction long enough to release a significant amoung of energy. Now how does invention come into pure science? Mainly in the devising of experiments with which to test theories. Certain physical theories entail that light has pressure; some attempts have been made in the last few years to invent machines that will detect this pressure; and so far all these attempts have failed. But this leads me to a qualification about invention of experiments. The attempt is to invent an apparatus to do a job which will be possible if the scientific theory under consideration is true. However, should that theory be false, the experiment will not work. Michelson and Morley's apparatus should have detected the ether wind. That it did not was not a reflection on the experiment they invented, but on the ether theory.

What is the character of the inventor's knowledge, then? It seems to me that the knowledge generated by an inventor is not on a fundamental level in the sense that pure science is. What it is, is a sort of ingenuity in bringing together separate pieces of mechanical and other information and applying them to a particular problem. The information is sometimes quite prosaic facts about our locality of the universe. The inventor shows us how, when these are put in a certain combination, they do a certain job. A special kind of ingenuity and mechanical intuition seems to be the property of the inventor, a talent seemingly very different from what makes the pure scientist.

Now once something has been invented, it still has to be implemented. Very often mechanical drawings do not specify all details and materials, not to mention dimensions, etc. The building of the prototype and then subsequent modification, all this is technology too. Just as the word of the builder in carrying out the architect's blueprints is technology. But again, this I leave aside as purely practical.

Applied science, I am going to suggest to you, is far more like pure science than it is like invention. For what really is applied science? It is the applying of abstract theories to the world. 'Applying' here means deducing from scientific theories, with the help of some statements of fact, consequences that can be tested and applied. Now this kind of deductive exercise is abstract and theoretical and is performed by pure scientists all the time. Why do I assert this: precisely because it is the aim of pure science to explain certain given facts. When a pure scientist is possessed of a theory in order to show that it explains the facts he is working on he has to do the deductions. It would have been no good Kepler proclaiming all planets move in ellipses if he had not had the ability to deduce from this that at certain times the configuration of stars would appear thus, then later thus, later again thus, and so on. These predictions followed from his theory. They were tested against the superb observations of Tycho de Brahe. Had Kepler not attempted the deduction but simply put forward his theory, science might have been held up for a long while until the observations could be shown to be deducible from the theory.

When I say scientific theories are abstract and fundamental, I mean it literally. Concepts like space, mass, force, coordinate system, quantum jump, and so on are abstractions in the highest sense. They are suggestions as to what constitutes the basic structure of the world. Applied science is the attempt to show just how they can do this by actually deducing those descriptions of the phenomena that they do explain.

Now where does technology come into all this? Technology is our tools, invented by the inventor, shown to be possible by the pure scientist, and actually explained by the deductions and calculations of the applied scientist.

Technology, *qua* know-how, *qua* tools, however, cannot be knowledge. A tool is not knowledge. A chisel is not knowledge, nor is a lathe: they are things. Knowing *that* real chisels exist, knowing *how* a chisel can be used, knowing *how* to construct a chisel, *these* may be knowledge, but the chisel itself cannot be so considered. So perhaps those philosophers who have suggested that technology was a 'knowing how' rather than a 'knowing that' were right after all.

To sum up so far: if technology is tools, or what the inventor invents, or what applied scientists do to show how a theory explains, then it has no place in the structure of knowledge. Such a view may sound odd, but it has often been entertained by philosophers. Some have gone so far as to identify all of science with technology; to say that science itself is no more than a tool or an instrument for predicting and controlling nature. It follows from their view that this tool can make no claims to be knowledge.

One of the most famous occasions when this argument was used was during the Inquisition's hearings on the Galileo case. Galileo was claiming that Copernicus was quite right: the earth *did* move around the sun and not *vice versa*, and he had many sophisticated arguments to back up his case. This was contrary to Biblical teaching and therefore placed Galileo in some jeopardy. Cardinal Bellarmino proposed a rather ingenious solution to the impasse. Bellarmino urged Galileo to concede that what he meant was that the assumption that the earth moved greatly simplified astronomical calculations and should therefore be adopted by all practical astronomers. Bellarmino proposed, if you like, that the heliocentric hypothesis be considered a piece of know-how for making stellar calculations. Bellarmino suggested Galileo should not bring down the wrath of the Inquisition on his head by going further and claiming this useful piece of know-how was also *true*. Like a chisel, it was neither true nor false but useful.

Bishop George Berkeley, whose name is enshrined in that center of anti-establishment protest, the University of California at Berkeley (although I don't know how his name came to get mispronounced), revived Bellarmino's argument in the eighteenth century when he was confronted with a serious problem, again with religious roots. A devout Bishop of the Church of England, he saw what he thought was a wave of religious disbelief sweeping the land, basing its claims on science and especially Newtonian science. This was the entire truth about the world, it was proclaimed; religious teaching was ignored. Many are those clergy who have been outraged at this use of science as a weapon with which to beat religion. Berkeley was cleverer than most, however, and some of the arguments he devised to prick Newton's bubble were strong. But most important, his overall position was that Newton's theories were a very useful and powerful predictive tool: but they were no more than that. To claim that man was discovering in science true knowledge was blasphemy and *hubris*. Mathematical tricks or knacks such as the equations of Newton should not, he argued, be accorded the status of truths, any more than should a chisel be awarded such status. Truth was the business of religion and religious teaching. Thus did the establishment Bishop legitimize his role.

One awkward consequence of identifying science and technology, as Bellarmino (and Berkeley) did, is that technology is a tool and thus seems not to make knowledge claims. Two solutions to this are available. Bishop Berkeley simply denied that science-technology was knowledge in any sense. It was to be found elsewhere. The other move is that of pragmatism: knowledge simply means: what works. Knowledge here is completely identified with know-how. And knowing *that* is simply dismissed as a philosophical smoke-screen. The only way you *can* know that you know *that* something is by trying it out, by making it work. So what counts is what works, know-how.

The view that technology = science = not making knowledge-claims, strikes me as both dangerous and as having some truth in it. The view is dangerous because of the stress in technology on effectiveness. And as we have already seen, effectiveness is by no means coincident with truth. But when we compare the celestial mechanics of Newton and Einstein, the results differ so minutely in so few cases, and the equations of relativity are so much more involved, one wonders whether or not if they were judged by their effectiveness Newton would not still be accepted uncritically. Here lies the danger of pragmatism, that we can go on with a theory because it works, making adjustments here and there and blinding ourselves to the possibility that it is just false and needs to be replaced by a theory in better accord with the facts. Merging technology and science, I would suggest to you, could actually inhibit scientific progress since it would allow only doubts about effectiveness but not doubts about the overall truth of the theory. The grain of truth which I said could be found in the identification of science with technology I will come to at the end. For the moment I think we can separate sceince from technology by saying the following: the laws of science lay out the boundaries of what is possible, but within these boundaries there are many contingent variations closely connected with technology. What technology does is to explore and explain the fine detail of the facts of our world. This is to take technology as embracing applied science, invention, engineering, and so on.

When I say that science lays down the boundaries of what is possible, I mean what is physically possible. But what, you may wonder, is physical possibility? Let me illustrate what I mean. We might usefully imagine a set of four concentric circles, each of which represents a greater area of possibility. The outside circle we can call the circle of logic which bounds the area of what is logically possible; that is, what can be said without violating the law of contradiction. This is the area of maximum possibility. Within the circle of logic is the circle of what is mathematically possible. Bertrand Russell's theory that these first two circles coincided turned out to be a mistake.[3] Within the circle of what is mathematically possible (e.g. n-dimensional space) is the circle of what is physically possible, and here we find the fundamental laws of science. The first two circles circumscribe all logically and mathematically possible worlds; the circle of science circumscribes the actual physical world. Inside these three circles is the narrowest circle, the boundaries of what we can imagine as possible, what we can visualize with our mind's eye. You might be surprised at my suggestion that what we can imagine is smaller than what is, especially as our notions of what is, our scientific theories, are products of our imaginations. All I want to say is that what any one of us can imagine hardly encompasses all the marvels of nature there actually are: truth *is*, I would say, stranger than fiction. But since science is a product of our imagination, and since sometimes we imagine impossible states of affairs we had better make these last two circles overlap, rather than encapsulate one in the other.

Now while science sets the laws of the physical world, these are quite general laws. Technology, however, is quite specific. Even on the surface of the earth what is good technology in one place is not in another. Technology is what we might call 'environment-specific'. The technology of house-building in Greenland, Tokyo and Arizona is quite different because of the different environments. If you consider some of the basic problems technology constantly grapples with, such as food, shelter and transportation, you will see how the demands that are made on technology and the kinds of solutions it suggests are environment-specific. What is suitable food in Greenland may go bad in hours in Arizona; what transports man efficiently over Greenland snow, may get him nowhere in Arizona. What will shelter a man in Arizona will not shelter him in a jet airplane, or on the moon. What technology knows is, within the general laws of nature, how to solve these problems of feeding, housing and sheltering in different parts of the universe. Physics places no barrier to spacetravel: but our technology is only slowly getting to a point where it can solve all the environment-specific problems of the space environment. Our know-how is only slowly beginning to catch up to this task.

So when I say that technology fills in the fine detail within the framework set by the laws of nature I mean it this way. Technological knowledge is knowledge within the boundary of the circle I have described which coincides with the laws of science. What technology handles within that boundary are the practical problems set it by the society.[4] Whereas science in a way puts the question to nature; technology puts the question both to society and to nature. When a physicist seeks the relationship between mass and energy he does not ask society what it wants the outcome to be. But in technology it is not as simple as that. Ask a traffic engineer to solve the problem of traffic congestion in a city and he will counter-question: 'how far are you prepared to go, how much can you spend?' The asker may be a politician who needs votes and who says, 'don't ask me to ban cars and don't ask me to raise taxes more than a percent or two'. Within that limit the engineer goes to work. We all know traffic is eased if you ban cars. Few of us knew that one-way street systems, banning turns, sychronising chains of stop lights, isolating pedestrains, building flyovers and bypasses could do this until the traffic engineers taught us it was so. They have increased our knowledge, but it is not knowledge of the deepest, in the metaphysical sense of deep, kind. Let me add that this 'metaphysical' sense of 'deep', carries as far as I am concerned no snobbish overtones. It is not necessarily more difficult, or more worthwhile knowledge: it is simply not knowledge about the structure of the world.

Much of what counts as a problem in technology will depend on the society. The technology of clean air, auto-safety, eliminating poverty and avoiding depressions in the economy and the individual were not problems which actively engaged our society 100 years ago. Now the society has decided they are problems and must be tackled. In this development it seems that science must lead the way and suggest what is possible. To a primitive with a magical attitude to custom and taboo, to a social philosopher who sees society as an organism we dare not tamper with, social technology hardly arises. They have to change their metaphysics first. But even with a metaphysics that allows that we can intervenc in our environment, specific theories of how the environment works may block progress. To a laissez-faire economist the idea that depressions could be controlled was unknown: he believed in the self-righting tendency of the economy, given time. Keynes' work was galvanized because the Great Depression, far from righting itself, went on worsening; eventually he was able to explain this by means of a new theory about the structure and working of the economy, and to show how to apply that knowledge to the practical situation. However, even if the environment is not considered sacred, intervention can have undesirable consequences. The slaughter of the Buffalo affected the Red Indians in terrible and unintended ways; some of the consequences of the widespread use of insecticides and detergents are coming to light. These pose new technological tasks, requiring further intervention with further undesirable consequences. Our tendency to raise our standards, to demand better and better performance of our technology, includes the demand to minimize undesirable side-effects. The facts that pretty well all tampering with the environment will have these undesirable effects, and that only further tempering will alleviate them, ensure that technological problems must grow at an ever increasing rate.

Society sets the limits on the kinds of solutions that can be seriously entertained, and closely scrutinizes those that are tried. There seems to be an inescapably social element in technology. Science only sets the outer limits to the problems that can be tackled in that, e.g. it tells us that no good will be served by the society asking the technologist to make a perpetual motion machine.

Before I come to my final point, I would like to expatiate briefly on the fact that technology is not widely studied and admired by intellectuals. This is I think because of the identification of science with technology and the identification of technology with grubbing around in the workshop. There is a snobbery about the workshop which is at least as old as the Ancient Greeks, and which can be found earlier and even more nakedly expressed in China. One can perhaps understand the desire not to dirty those long tapering hands, and it is easy nowadays to confuse an experimental laboratory with a workshop, since in many ways it is one. What is confused is the identification of technology with dirty hands. Every emperor of China who made reforms or legislation was a technologist; Plato's *Republic* was a technological thought-experiment; the groves of academe themselves are a product of a medieval experiment in self-help education.

That this obvious point has not been taken for granted is perhaps explained by the superficial identification of technology with machines. In turn this may perhaps be explained by the impact on man of push-pull physics and its embodiment in the Industrial Revolution, or the Age of Machinery. This was an historical break-point, making such extraordinary wealth possible that man's life was to be transformed. However, it also blinded everyone to the continuity of this development with other kinds of attempts to change the environment. It is especially important to gain this perspective now because the age of machines is rapidly drawing to a close. Marshall McLuhan's semi-serious ideas at least point this out clearly and excitingly: the electronic age has begun.[5] I would add that the bio-chemical ages, not to mention the thermophysical ages, are near at hand. Our technological breakthroughs now get consolidated and implemented at an accelerating rate, and our curricula will find it hard to keep up as long as they are machine-oriented.

And this brings me to a point I left aside previously. You remember that I said the identification of science with technology had a grain of truth in it? That is what I now want to explain. To begin with I must take you back to the argument that a tool, like a chisel, cannot be knowledge. Is this really true? I would suggest that we may be being mislead by a word. Certainly a tool like a chisel is not, in addition to being a thing, a piece of knowledge. What about a piece of knowledge, though, isn't it a thing, and can't it also be a tool? '$E = mc^2$' is a piece of knowledge, a theory or an equation, if you like. Is it not also a tool? Did we not use this piece of knowledge to plan and build and calculate the effect of the atomic bomb? Isn't a tool simply something man uses to increase his power over the environment? Isn't in this sense the whole of scientific and even intellectual endeavor an outgrowth of our attempts to cope with our environment by learning about it?[6] My own teacher Sir Karl Popper, in a beautiful lecture, has suggested this view. Placing us firmly in the struggle for survival in a hostile environment, he sees language and the quest for understanding as superb adapting mechanisms, no longer blind and chance-like like mutations, but controlled and intelligent.[7]

Technology for me, then, is coterminus with our attempts to come to terms with our world; that is, our culture and our society; and as such it contains within it both pure tools and all knowledge.

NOTES

[1] See G. Ryle, Chapter 1 of *The Concept of Mind*, London 1949.
[2] For this point see Joseph Agassi, 'The Confusion Between Science and Technology in the Standard Philosophies of Science', *Technology and Culture*, Vol. 7, 1966, pp. 348ff.
[3] Russell's theory led him to write *Principia Mathematica*, but it later transpired that not all of mathemarics could be so derived.
[4] For a brief discussion of this see my 'The Social Character of Technological Problems', *Technology and Culture*, Vol. 7, 1966, pp. 384–390.

[5] Marshall McLuhan, *Understanding Media*, New York 1964.
[6] See my 'Is Technology Unnatural'? *The Listener*, March 9th, 1967, Vol. lxxvii, pp. 322–3 and 333.
[7] K. R. Popper, *Of Clouds and Clocks*, St. Louis (Washington U.) 1966.

CHAPTER 20

The Social Character of
Technological Problems

There is a great deal in Professor Skolimowski's very interesting paper
with which I fully agree, especially, perhaps, his thesis that technology
is not to be identified with science and that it has a different philosophy
and methodology. If there is a single problem that is central to Skolimowski's paper it is perhaps his statement that science has a single aim,
the pursuit of knowledge or truth; can a similar, simple aim be ascribed
to technology? Skolimowski's answer is "yes" and that that aim is efficiency, the construction of ever more efficient solutions to technological
problems. So while scientific progress is toward truth, technological
progress is an increase in efficiency.

In the last half of his paper Skolimowski pursues the question of in
what exactly efficiency consists. His view, roughly, is that it is different
in different branches of technology. Different patterns of thinking lead
to efficiency in different technological subjects. These differences of
patterns of thinking he outlines with respect to surveying, civil engineering, and mechanical engineering. Efficiency in surveying consists
largely in the pursuit of accuracy; in civil engineering it consists in
durability; in mechanical engineering it consists in "efficiency" in the
technical sense of the word. Skolimowski expresses the hope that from
these beginnings patterns can be discerned for technology as a whole,
and indeed that this might even lead to "a new methodology of science."

Technology seems to have been treated like Cinderella by philosophers of science. It has always been put in the second-best place, mentioned almost as an afterthought. This is perhaps understandable, since
the received notion of the role of technology is that it is the province of
engineers and other such non-gentlemen, and its philosophy thus is

314

not a matter of great concern to the philosophical purist. This attitude of the philosophers is especially baffling to the present-day public who expect the philosophy of science to discuss such achievements as the atom bomb, space rockets, supersonic airplanes, television, and so on. Whenever one of these examples is introduced in a discussion philosophers of science are tempted to say: "But that is *technology*, of no *scientific* importance at all."

The philosophers of science have so far disdained technology despite the fact that we are living in an age of technology and not an age of science. Whereas ancient Greece and the seventeenth and eighteenth centuries were the eras of science, with discussion and progress going on apace, today we have had, for example, an impasse in quantum physics for a generation. Technology, on the other hand, grows and progresses all around us. Little new *science* is involved in a manned landing on the moon, but a great deal of new technology is. In setting 1970 as a target date for the accomplishment of this feat, NASA's technologists boldly proclaim that they expect to be able to make enough technological progress before then—to iron out the wrinkles, as they say —to carry the program through. Can one imagine someone setting a target date for the completion of a project that involved a unified field theory? How then to approach this neglected subject of a philosophy of technology?

Skolimowski very correctly began with an extensive review of what technology is or, rather, what it is not. He then passed to two problems: first, that of distinguishing technology from science (he did this with reference to the idea of progress in both); second, that of isolating the characteristics of specifically technological thinking.

I would like to break the philosophy of technology into three main philosophical problems: (1) In what ways does technological knowledge grow and progress? (2) What is the epistemological status of technological statements? (3) How are technological statements to be demarcated from scientific statements? These problems overlap, of course, and perhaps are not of equal importance, but they seem to me to pretty well cover the main initial questions any philosophy of technology must answer.

1. To begin with, then, how does technology progress? My own field of competence is social anthropology, and hence I shall refer to primitive societies in dealing this problem.[1] It is, I hope, obvious enough

[1] Although in anthropology I am *against* functionalism (the doctrine that things ought to be explained solely in terms of their social function) and instrumentalism (the doctrine that scientific theories make no claim to truth, only to being useful instruments), in the philosophy of technology, following Skolimowski, I am *for* both.

that all societies have to cope with technological problems. Their ability to solve them obviously will be a function of the clarity with which they are posed, the resources and experience available, and, as Agassi has very rightly emphasized,[2] luck and ingenuity.

Societies do not face the same set of technological problems of course; African tribes are not faced with the problems involved in going to the moon or with the problem of coping with excessive traffic in cities. These are cases where highly developed technology has created, so to speak, its own further technological problems. Yet all societies face the common problems of food, shelter, and transport, to take only three examples. Skolimowski touched on shelter when he discussed house-building and on transport when he discussed bridge-building. He did not touch on food. One might think that before the era of canned and frozen foods, food was not a technological problem. But of course domestic animals like cows, pigs, and hens—and especially battery hens and crops like high-yield wheat and seedless oranges—are as much technological achievements as Metrecal. In the field of transport the carefully bred horse is as much an invention as the motorcar or the airplane; in the matter of shelter, the mud hut is a forerunner of the skyscraper. I find quite unintelligible the idea that technology means only machines, especially in an age when the dividing line between animate and inanimate matter is increasingly hard to draw.

So in a sense all societies have technology of sorts, and the problem of progress involves comparing them with each other in as unprejudiced a manner as possible. Not all primitive technology has been superseded. There are parts of this great country where only a horse can take one—the horse, as has been said of the bicycle, has reached its own plateau of evolution; there are times and places where a shack or even an igloo is as effective a shelter as a modern house; and of course we have by no means progressed beyond the food inventions of earlier generations.

Not all technological progress is replacement and abandonment of previous means. New means used to solve old problems, old means used to solve new problems, and new means used to solve new problems are all easy to illustrate. The old problem of flying was solved with the new means of the airplane; the new problem of high-speed calculation was solved with the old means of the circuit, the switch, and binary numbers, that is, the latest computers (although perhaps the combination was new, but certainly the new problem of going to the moon is being tackled with the old, old means of the rocket); and finally the new

[2] See Agassi, "The Confusion between Science and Technology in the Standard Philosophies of Science," this issue, pp. 348–66.

problem of traffic congestion was solved by the new means of freeways. Technology seems to me to progress in all these ways.

But is this a specific enough treatment of how technology progresses? Can we say no more than that progress is a function of the clarity, resources, and ingenuity that can be brought to bear on a technological problem? Is there no heuristic special to technology? Skolimowski seems to be moving in this direction when he posits that the general aim of efficiency and the means of achieving it in different branches of technology is to give emphasis to particular qualities, like accuracy, or durability, or "efficiency" in its technical sense.

Some arguments occur to me which indicate that efficiency is by no means the aim always underlying technological progress. Take Skolimowski's suggestion that efficiency in civil engineering primarily consists in thinking in terms of *durability*. Is durability necessarily an aim of building? Does it not depend on what the building is for? Blockhouses of World War II were very highly durable, and as a result they still scar parts of the European landscape—because of the expense of removing them. Americans *could* build fireproof, floodproof, typhoonproof, and earthquake-proof houses, but they are discouraged by the expense. They are also discouraged by the fact that they cannot make them progress proof. They cannot, that is, build houses that will not be out of date sooner or later—and these days it is sooner rather than later. Built-in obsolescence is as important a consideration in houses as in motorcars. Similarly, I think one could argue that in surveying, *accuracy* is only a relative aim, relative, that is, to the problem the surveyor and his cartographer are set. Terrain maps may ignore land use, road maps and tenancy plans may ignore terrain, maps of the London and New York subways ignore all but the most general features of what they are depicting.

What these criticisms move toward is something like this: it is the problem that is posed to the technologist which determines the character of the thinking required or, as I would prefer to say, the overriding aim that is to govern the solution. The engineers who devised the Bailey Bridge and the pontoon bridge were given civil engineering problems in which *speed of construction* was far more important than *durability*. A map-maker may be far more concerned with a clear general outline than with particular details. The designers of American cars certainly are not much concerned with the efficiency of their product so much as the appearance, the smoothness of ride, etc. American cars could be much more durable and much more efficient (in terms of cost per mile) were manufacturers prepared to raise the unit cost. But the unit cost must always be considered alongside the problems of worker or consumer satisfaction, aesthetic attraction, and social cost. Whether the overriding concern is with accuracy, durability, "efficiency," or what, is always dictated by the socially set problem and not the technological field. Here, then, I take issue with Skolimowski when he says there are patterns of thinking in technology specific to the branch and independent of the sociological background.

The very fact that we live in an age of great technological progress in itself suggests we are not in dire need of a heuristic gift from philosophers, always provided that we can give some explanation of this technological success, an explanation to the effect that a heuristic is already in use or one is not needed. My own suggestion is that the success is explained by the increasing clarity with which technological problems are posed, by our improved ability to think ahead. Less and less are inventions made and then found uses for; more and more are they sought when there is a demand or a potential demand. The element of inventiveness is still very great, but all that can be done in the way of a heuristic has been done. This tremendous concentration on single problems tends to accelerate progress, since not only solutions but multiple solutions may be found, and then *these* may turn out to have other applications.

2. I come next to the problem of the epistemological status of technological statements. I am puzzled as to why Skolimowski contrasts science as the exploration of the real, with technology as the creation of the artificial. It seems to me that the contrast is less between the artificial and the real as between the artificial and the natural. Science and technology are both concerned with a world that is equally real, but the latter is concerned to interfere with it. Science, of course, aims to investigate the whole universe and to describe the most general laws it obeys. Technology is quite different; it works within what these laws allow, concentrating on what is possible in narrow localities of the universe and definitely not everywhere. For example, much of our technology must be changed when we enter weightless or low-gravity environments, just as big Tokyo buildings are different from big New York buildings on account of earthquakes. In terms of the logical analysis of the statements of science, then, technological statements are part of the factual description of conditions in a circumscribed locality of the universe, what are called the "initial conditions."[3]

[3] In the model of scientific explanation proposed by Karl Popper in 1934 (see his *Logik der Forschung* [Vienna, 1934], translated as *The Logic of Scientific Discovery* [New York, 1959], pp. 59–60) a statement is explained if it can be validly deduced from premises containing one or more universal laws (UC), together with one or more particular statements of fact—the initial conditions (IC). An example

And, of course, very often we can discover initial conditions, such as the fact that a certain drug cures a certain illness, without having any explanatory theory of why they are so, just as fish swim without hydrodynamics and primitives grow crops with no scientific theory of how this occurs. Here we seem to have some explanation of why there are societies that have technology but nothing we would recognize as science; we hardly find the reverse situation (since there are no societies without technology). This leads me to dissent from Skolimowski's view that technology is not concerned with the pursuit of truth, although I would concede that successful technology sometimes can be in conflict with accepted science. For example, ships and space ships navigate with tables based on Newtonian celestial mechanics, which is part of Newton's physics—and Newton's physics is superseded. Thus truth cannot be the principal aim of technology. However, technological information is not unrelated to truth. The fact that the stresses to which the fuselage structures of high-speed aircraft are subject result in a phenomenon called "metal fatigue" was an important discovery about the world, and our airplane technology had to take it into account. Like gravity it is a very localized phenomenon. A scientific explanation of the fact of metal fatigue was not a necessary prerequisite of a technological solution to it.

3. This brings me to the last of the three problems mentioned above, namely, the demarcation between scientific statements and technological statements. Agassi has discussed this, and Skolimowski's views are not particularly dissimilar. We all agree that the aims and methods of technology are different from those of science and that truth is not the overriding aim of technology. Wherein, then, lies the core of the differences? The answer is, I am sure, that there is no absolute demarcation: it is very much a matter of context, and particularly of problem context. Scientific statements are posed to solve scientific problems; technological statements allow that certain devices are not impossible.

When a problem is or is not scientific can hardly be formally characterized, but in a general way science must involve questions about the nature of the world. Which problems are in fact studied seems to depend upon the scientific tradition and also upon the empirical character of the theories from which the problem arose.

Similarly, no formal criterion of technological problems can be ex-

---

of this would be: (UL) All men die when their heads are cut off. (IC_1) King Charles I of England was a man. (IC_2) King Charles I of England had his head cut off. Therefore, King Charles I of England died. For extensive discussion see C. G. Hempel, *Aspects of Scientific Explanation* (Glencoe, Ill., 1965), *passim;* and W. W. Bartley III, "Achilles, the Tortoise and Explanations in Science and History," *British Journal for the Philosophy of Science,* XIII (1962), 15–33.

pected. It is again a question of the aim. If the aim is to manage to accomplish something practical which science allows as not impossible, rather than to discover some universal truth, then technology is what we call it. Both science and technology are, as Skolimowski pointed out, goal-directed and thus amenable to praxiological analysis. The question remains whether our agreement that the structure of technology is complex and its methods diverse can be maintained in the face of our disagreement over whether there are specific ways of thinking peculiar to branches of technology independent of a social and traditional context.

CHAPTER 21

IS TECHNOLOGY UNNATURAL?

A year ago Mr Tom Wolfe, that careful documenter of our *mores*, published a magazine article which told the story of Carol Doda. Miss Doda is the girl who pioneered topless dancing in San Francisco cabaret. Reflecting on the way Miss Doda's natural endowments had been enhanced by false eyelashes and polyethylene injections, Wolfe labelled her 'the perfect put-together girl'. He speculated that sooner or later we might find ourselves confronted with people who are almost totally put-together. Consider what is already technologically possible, reading down, so to speak: dyed hair, lightened skin, coloured contact lenses, remoulded features, lifted face and neck, inflated bosoms, stretched spines, transplanted organs, artificial limbs, and so on. Wolfe welcomes Carol Doda as a portent of something most of us find faintly sinister — the intrusion of technology into even the most intimate areas of our experience, including relations with the opposite sex.

Carol Doda then brings to the surface a widespread attitude to technology: not just that it is getting more and more powerful, but that it is getting out of control. It may bring about the time when we cannot distinguish between the natural and the artificial, between a woman and a robot. Fierce expression of this antipathy to technology is given in Peter Simple's *Daily Telegraph* satire column. In particular Simple portrays with loathing one Dr Heinz Kiosk, an ogre in the guise of a devotee of social engineering, who campaigns against everything old-fashioned and inefficient.

Coexisting, if somewhat uneasily, with this suspicious attitude to technology is the totally different attitude that regards technology as the wonder of the modern age. We live, we are told, in an age of technology. We can hurtle round the world at ever increasing speeds or plug our sensorium into media that change the entire mode of our experience. Everything, from the food we eat to the shelter we live in, is a product of the age of technology. Our lives are unimaginably richer and more comfortable because of it.

Our society, then, displays two strongly contrasted attitudes to technology. On the one hand, an uncritical adulation; and, on the other, suspicion, mistrust, and even fear. Out of the tension between the attitudes of adulation and suspicion, a number of problems arise: for example, the familiar reaction of fear that the machines are taking over is brought on by the complacency of those who adulate technology. The dangers of technology would appear much less if everyone was aware of them and trying to do something about them.

I shall not be discussing these sorts of fears and dangers here. The problem I shall discuss is more obviously philosophical, and concerns the ancient distinction between man's handiwork and that of mother nature. It could be formulated like this: is the distinction between the natural and the artificial more confusing than useful in an age of technology? All distinctions and classifications are, I believe, manmade; they usually embody theories, and in criticizing any distinction I shall be indicating that the underlying theory is untenable too. It may turn out that the underlying theory has been jettisoned long ago, although the distinction still remains to cloud our language and our thinking. Moreover, I think that here is a much more interesting source of unease regarding technology — namely, that it is making an assault on some of our basic categories.

These two problems which Carol Doda evokes, what attitude to adopt towards technology, and where to draw the line between nature and artifice, are part of a growing discussion of the philosophical problems raised by technology. Philosophers of science, who might have been expected to be interested in technology, have, in fact, largely ignored it. To be frank, I hope there will never exist an academic subject called 'the philosophy of technology', with the paraphenalia of professorships, library subdivisions, examinations, and, worst of all, text-books. Such developments stifle the excitement of new ideas and problems, and swamp everyone under a flood of publications the vested interests feel obliged to produce. This sad fate has already befallen the philosophy of science. But given that growing out of technology there are genuine problems which need discussing, it was encouraging that a year ago in San Francisco there was held a first symposium on the topic, and last December saw another one in Washington.

A COMING PHILOSOPHY

The philosophy of technology, then, is a coming thing. The specific question within it that I am concerning myself with here is: what remains of the distinction between the natural and the artificial when we are confronted with modern technology? This distinction is of interest mainly, I suppose, because it has been the habit of previous ages to overestimate the range of what is God-given and natural in their theories of the world. I do not mean 'natural' in the sense of what we are used to, but in the sense of what could not be otherwise. An extreme case of this view was suggested by André Gide in *Corydon*; he argued that everything which exists — and specifically homosexuality — was natural. Notice how the word 'natural' takes on more and more meanings. Gide is mistaken if he thinks that just because something exists it is also normal, what we are used to, or could not be otherwise. Gide's extreme of making the natural coterminous with what exists is quite rare. The other extreme is to make a hard-and-fast distinction between the natural and the artificial, and this is very common.

Usually when the natural is contrasted with the artificial the word 'natural' is intended to connote the world as we human beings came upon it — its ecology, flora and fauna, succession of day and night, cycle of seasons, and so on. These might be regarded as the stable factors in man's environment: while he was technologically poorly developed man had reason for believing these factors to be fixed and unalterable. The most striking version of this belief was the theory that society itself was a part of the fixed environment and had something like divine sanction behind it. The theory of the Divine Right of Kings, the Puritan theory that wealth and position were marks of God's favour, the semi-religious attitude adopted towards the Confucian theory of society in Imperial China, are all examples of the belief that social arrangements were part of nature. Not only did these theories reduce society to nature, and what exists to what is right, they also implied both that nature could not be altered and that if in our *hubris* we tried to alter it, dreadful things would happen. Two positions are being maintained here: that present social arrangements are good; and that they could not successfully be otherwise. But if they are unalterable they do not need the sanction of God; and if they are good there is the implication that they could be otherwise. Eventually a different philosophy was invented.

THE NOBLE SAVAGE?

Perhaps because the handiwork of the Author of Nature must by definition be good, there arose the doctrine that original man, nature boy, the noble savage, was pristine pure, uncorrupted by technology or the artifices of human society. Rousseau used this view to turn the tables on those who regarded society as natural; he said that so far from being natural, human society was a monstrous perversion which enslaved man and corrupted his nature. Hobbes's view that nature was violent and cruel and society a necessary means of protecting ourselves against it was here being stood on its head.

Lately our ideas of man's origins have changed in ways that bear interestingly on this issue. It appears that men could not be Robinson Crusoes, but are naturally social animals: we came down from the trees bringing society with us. Although we are part of nature's creation, the environment we inhabit is sufficiently hostile for us to be forced to organize against it on account of our long periods of gestation and rearing. So in a sense it could not be otherwise than that man should strive to tame his environment: partly by modifying it, partly by interposing devices between it and him, devices like social institutions and various forms of machine. These devices are his technology.

As the tool-making animal, man was perhaps from the start going to be chafing at what, it seemed, could not be otherwise. It is curious that it was already after man was on the road of progress, gradually mastering his world, that the conservative philosophies of the rightness of what exists arose. In practice, what Plato called just, and the sort of society which truly conformed with Divine Right, was the *status quo ante*. It is a testimony to the power of these ideas that sometimes they did succeed in stopping the clock, if not in putting it back. Perhaps because a more powerful rival philosophy developed which was not hostile to technology, namely Greek and Renaissance science, progress was not halted for ever. As a result of that progress we have now reached a stage where we can remake the landscape, the flora and the fauna, very much as we wish; we cannot control day and night or the seasons, but we can for many purposes disregard them. From the first stone axe to the latest atomic power station there has been only one process at work: control of the environment in the interests of man's comfort and wealth. That is all technology is.

ADJUSTING TO ENVIRONMENT

If that is all it is, how do we explain the unease about it? Man is and always has been a technological animal. Moreover, he is well adapted to his environment: he adapted to the seasons when they were the biggest factor in his life; he has adapted himself to cities now that they are becoming the biggest factor in his life. Of course this adaptation is not by mutation, but by constantly adjusting the environment, by interfering with it and adding to it. And why should this unease come now? A large number of technological ideas are beyond the grasp of many of us. Technology is thus mysterious: yet its rate of progress, and the impact of that progress is everywhere manifest. It is characteristic of human beings to react badly to changes of environment: they at first feel disorientated, even bewildered. We have to live nowadays in an environment in constant, unpredictable, and sometimes radical processes of change. Yet we can understand neither exactly what is happening nor why it is happening. Striving to adjust to something which gives us no respite or peace, we ask: what will happen next, where is it all going, when will it end?

They strike me as questions to which straightforward but comfortless answers can easily be given. We do not know what will happen text, we don't know where it is all going, we think it will not end. Here is perhaps another source of anxiety; we profess ignorance and thus evoke the fear of the unknown. This hankering after a stable environment with expectations not being constantly disappointed, and some sort of an end in sight, seems to be very deep-rooted. For example, I am inclined to think the special atmosphere of war-time Britain is explained by it: everyone knew what the aim was and in general they knew what was expected of them, and so they gave of themselves.

This digression aside, it seems important to say that technological progress itself has no specific overall goal and assigns us no specific roles in what is to come. In this respect it is like science, which is also a blind trial-and-error search for truth. Technology is undertaken with the vague aims of making us richer, more comfortable, and better informed. Technologists tackle the jobs man gives them. In other words, society guides technology. Yet we feel that technology feeds back on society and somehow begins guiding it: and we are right. But technology is not a monster with aims of its own — the feedback is controllable too. If it is to be controlled, though, we must make choices and decisions — and here comes another disturbing aspect of technology: it forces on us lots of decisions that were formerly taken by our environment; our power to manipulate the environment compels us to choose exactly what we want manipulated and how. Once upon a time weather and time of day dictated what we could and could not do. Now, given only a proviso on cost, we can decide independently of these factors. Our increasing awareness of how little there is that could not be otherwise forces us to decide which parts of what could be otherwise shall be otherwise. Again, it is a commonplace that people do not like taking decisions, still less having more thrust upon them that they never asked for.

So far, then, where has the argument brought us? If there is nothing unnatural or artificial about ploughing fields and hunting game, then there is nothing unnatural or artificial about propelling ourselves around the world to the music of sonic booms; or indeed about Carol Doda herself.

It is no more natural for man to be a slave to the seasons, I suggest, than it is artificial for him to be a slave to the time-clock. Each is merely a phase in the development of man's relationship with his environment. Man's nature, if such an entity exists, is to be curious about his environment and to try either to adjust to it or to adjust it to him. Technology is part of us, and this forces us to re-examine the old distinction between the works of nature and the works of man. Scrutinizing such a well-entrenched distinction in itself makes us uneasy. But the unease has other roots in the restlessness and instability of the environment created by technology, the fear of the unknown that technology is leading us into, and dislike of the decisions it is forcing us to take.

Underneath all this, however, we must seek the deeply embedded theory which sustains the distinction between the natural and the artificial. My guess is that what is involved is a self-image – perhaps it should not be dignified with the name of a theory at all. Man has a self-image of being something special in creation. Man is the one animal with any significant power over nature: he feels he can bend it to his will. He therefore feels he is above nature, or at least at its centre. This self-image is misleading and has to be replaced with something at once more modest and more challenging. Man cannot alter nature in the sense of what could not be otherwise. That is a tautology. The laws of nature and of logic place absolute limits on man's activities. Man's special place in nature consists in his greater degree of ability to tinker with the contingent features of his environment. The framework, the laws of nature and of logic, cannot in any sense be tinkered with or manipulated. Man's previous mistake was to confuse contingent features with invariant laws. Here lies the biggest factor which separates man from his fellow creatures: his ability to grasp those laws and thus trim his endeavours. His ability to learn from experience is highly developed and this gives him an enormous edge over all other living things.

Technology then, I contend, is the most natural thing in the world, in the sense that given man's questing nature and instinct to survive he could hardly do otherwise. Peter Simple's Dr Heinz Kiosk and his band of twisted social engineers on the rampage is no more than a talented satirist's nightmare. Yet, of course, as we expand our ability to control our environment obviously our decisions will affect more and more people. The decision to take a rock and make it into a stone axe affected almost no one else. The decision to drive an eight-lane highway from London to Edinburgh will affect millions both adversely and to their advantage. And this, clearly, is a political problem created by technology. The solution to it, equally clearly, is to make the decisions as broad-based as possible, so that those affected are involved in the decisions. Here again it is technology forcing us to decide. If we choose Dr Kiosk, or choose him by default, that is our responsbility, not his.

The case of Carol Doda, then, the perfect put-together girl, reminds us that man is a physico-chemical machine that has a talent for making, and an mclination to make, other machines that help him adjust to his environment. The only limits to this activity, which we call technology, are set by the laws of nature and the laws of logic. As the misestimates of the past are corrected, we constantly adjust our ideas of what latitude these laws allow. No longer do we regard them as imprisoning. Inside this framework of what is physically and logically possible there is more than enough room for freedom of choice. If we do build robot women, perhaps there will be a public demand for them to be clearly marked. They are, after all, not the real thing. How long such an invidious new caste system could last is anybody's guess. Far more sensible to jettison the false philosophy on which it is based.

CHAPTER 22

Utopian Thinking and the Architect*

I

The problem I want to discuss might be put, first of all, like this: How can architects and planners build for the future when they happen to be imprisoned — for lack of what H. G. Wells would call a "time machine" — in the present? The future is open; we do not know what it will bring. Yet, "planners have to imagine the future as a matter of routine. Whether you are building a motorway, a chemical works or a school, you are making a forecast of the continuing need for such a thing over its economic life."[1]

What planners and builders do now will frame the future. How *can* they plan and build rationally and responsibly in the face of a total ignorance about what is to come? The answer I shall try to develop is that we can explore the future in our creative imaginations and subject our ideas to severe criticism and evaluation. Pentagon officials call it "contingency planning." They try to conceive of every possible situation that could arise and plan what they would do. The plans are not really there to be acted upon but constitute a library of ideas some of which may be useful. Also it is felt that we can better face situations that we have, in part, anticipated and thought through or, at least, trained ourselves to think about.

---

* Professor Jarvie's lecture was preceded by a showing of H. G. Wells's movie *Things to Come* (1966 was the centenary of Wells's birth and the thirtieth anniversary of this film).

[1] Nigel Calder, "Wells and the Future," *New Statesman*, Vol. 72, No. 1854, p. 427.

It follows from my thesis that it would be both irrational and irresponsible for planners and architects to avoid such critical dreaming about the future and its possibilities.

It is a corollary of my thesis that such speculative thinking should be as bold and extreme as possible, that tentativity in this part of the endeavor will defeat its object. Similarly, timidity in criticism will render it useless.

My strategy in arguing these points will be first to consider the question of ignorance, mistakes, and responsibilities and then to tackle some possible objections to the program of critical speculation. This will bring me to Wells's film, from which I shall try to draw some material to illustrate the argument.

II

When a philosopher of science finds himself invited to give the opening address at a conference organized by planners and architects, it is not unreasonable for him to suspect that what is expected of him is a sermon. Philosophy is often conceived of by nonphilosophers (not to mention some philosophers) as a rather vague and general subject, and philosophers consequently are thought to be good at giving vague and rather general advice. If you are a philosopher of science, the only difference is that the sermon is supposed to be about methodology. It doesn't take a philosophical training to know that it is best to get sermons over first. Since I see sermonizing as what sociologists call my "ascribed role," and since I have decided to play the role to the full, I need two things. The first is a text; the second, a salutary example.

For my example I shall take H. G. Wells's ideas as realized in William Cameron Menzies' film *Things to Come*, 1936. This is perhaps especially appropriate in the year of Wells's centenary, Wells being an author who constantly tried to get us to take the problem of the future seriously. As my text I shall take — not something biblical, although perhaps almost as well-worn — a corny joke:

Question: What is the difference between a doctor and an architect?
Answer: The doctor can bury his mistakes, but the architect has to live with his.

The first thing to do with a text is to analyze it; analysis will ruin any joke, but that hardly matters if the joke wasn't much good to start with.[2] However, the joke may be instructive. What interpretations can be put on a joke that says doctors can bury their mistakes but architects cannot?

It is undoubtedly a cynical joke, whichever way you look at it. One implication is clear: we all make mistakes — doctors, architects, everybody; the problem is that of getting away with them. There is also a hint that these mistakes will be painful or damaging. They may cause us embarrassment. The doctor can try to forget — "out of sight, out of mind"; the architect is not allowed to forget, and he must suffer.

The joke could be read as congratulating the doctors, who, because they can hide their mistakes, need not worry about them. Those responsible can forget, for the public has no means of discovering who is responsible. If the public did know, of course, they would hold doctors responsible, just as doctors hold themselves responsible. Why else, after all, do they try to forget, to bury, to repress unpleasant thoughts?

But does not the joke conceal an even more cynical message: that you need not take responsibility for your mistakes if you can conceal your connection with them and the damage they do? Does not the joke hint that architects must be especially circumspect merely because their responsibility is clear for all to see? And is not this view cynical? Responsibility for damage is being equated with identifiable responsibility.

Even the meagerest text can bear a great amount of interpretation, some of it not altogether consistent. There is one other idea concealed in the use in my text of the word "mistake" which I would like to analyze, and this is that we are in some sense responsible for our mistakes. Yet at the same time the joke says we all, doctors and architects, do make mistakes. This strikes me as very peculiar. One would agree that we can have the responsibility

---

[2] For examples of corny jokes and of good jokes ruined by analysis see Sigmund Freud, *The Psychopathology of Everyday Life*, Standard Edition of the Complete Works (London: Hogarth Press, 1960), Vol. 6, pp. 77 ff., and *Jokes and Their Relation to the Unconscious*, Standard Edition, Vol. 8, pp. 16 ff.; see also A. Koestler, *The Act of Creation* (London and New York: Macmillan, 1964), especially pp. 32 ff.

not to make mistakes, but to say we shall inevitably make them *and* that we should feel responsible for them is harsh doctrine, indeed. In going wrong we show our imperfections, our inability to meet our ideals; and even before we say anything or have any ideals, we are tainted by this proneness to be mistaken. The view is a variant, perhaps, of the doctrine of original sin.[3]

Leaving the joke aside, can we make sense of the problem of mistakes and responsibility? It is true that we are fallible creatures and shall make mistakes. Perhaps even more discouraging, Xenophanes was probably right when he said that even if we were in possession of the truth, there is no reason to believe we should be aware of it.[4] Consequently, we might expect all our endeavors, including our attempts to look into the future, to go awry. But if whatever we do will turn out to be mistaken, where does our responsibility lie? It can't lie in the responsibility not to be mistaken. Sir Karl Popper, in *The Open Society and Its Enemies* and elsewhere, has suggested that our responsibility is to minimize our mistakes by being severely critical of our ideas.[5] That is our responsibility. It is this suggestion of Popper's that I wish to ponder and develop in the rest of this essay.

I shall proceed by examining four critical arguments which are directed against utopian thinking in general and which I can also use to expand on what I mean by critical utopianism. These criticisms are, first, that the future is unknown, so thinking about it is futile; second, that utopias are remote possibilities, and we might do better to concentrate on the available data and the trends they reveal; third, that utopias will trap us, morally and

[3] Cf. Ernest Gellner, "On Being Wrong," *The Rationalist Annual* (London, 1957).

[4] The fragment is translated in G. S. Kirk and J. E. Raven, *The Presocratic Philosophers* (Cambridge, England: Cambridge University Press, 1957), Fragment 189 at p. 179. Compare the translations of the same fragment by J. Burnet, *Early Greek Philosophy*, 4th ed. (London: A. & C. Black, 1930), Fragment 34 at p. 121, and W. C. Guthrie, *A History of Greek Philosophy*, Vol. 1 (Cambridge, England: Cambridge University Press, 1962), Fragment 34 at p. 395.

[5] See K. R. Popper, *The Open Society and Its Enemies*, 4th ed. (London: Routledge & Kegan Paul, 1962), *passim*, and *Conjectures and Refutations* (London: Routledge & Kegan Paul, 1963), especially the introductory chapter and Chapter 1.

imaginatively, so they are to be avoided; and fourth, that utopias are produced by a selective and dogmatic imagination, and one could as easily show them to be antiutopian hells.

III

There can be no doubt that the future is open. Popper again has constructed a decisive argument to show that since what happens next is dependent on our future state of knowledge, and since our future state of knowledge is, in principle, unpredictable,[6] the future is, in principle, unpredictable.[7] Does it follow from this argument that all utopian thinking is useless and futile? This depends, I think, very much on the aim of the utopian thinking. If the aim of the utopian is to know the future, then I think Popper's argument is a knockdown winner. He constructed it to attack doctrines of historical inevitability which claimed to predict the future. But what if the aim of writing about or designing utopia is to tax our imaginations to their limit in order to maximize the choices available to planners, increase our creative freedom, anticipate, however imperfectly, some of our coming problems? Then I think Popper's argument is salutary but not destructive.

Take as an example Plato's *Republic*. There is some doubt about his aim in writing it. It may[8] or may not[9] have described a state of affairs Plato wanted to see actualized. Whatever his intentions, however, he threw into focus some very interesting

[6] Perhaps it is worth making a distinction here. Of course, there is a sense in which we can say that when a successful soft landing on the moon is achieved, we shall know what the composition of its surface is. We can predict that we shall then know a certain fact. We cannot know the content of this prediction; we can only guess. If we could predict what theory will come to replace relativity in due course, we should not need to wait for due course but could move on to it now.

[7] K. R. Popper, *The Poverty of Historicism* (Boston: Beacon, 1957), pp. ix-xi.

[8] For the view that *The Republic* is a utopia see Vol. 1 of Popper, *The Open Society, op. cit.*

[9] Northrop Frye argues that *The Republic* "is not a dream to be realized in practice; it is an informing power of the mind." See his "Varieties of Literary Utopias" in F. E. Manuel, ed., *Utopias and Utopian Thought* (Boston: Houghton Mifflin, 1966), p. 34.

sociopolitical problems: for example, that the main problem of a stratified society is strictly to control mobility, or otherwise its structure will be undermined; or that the main problem of politics is "who rules the rulers?" These by-products of Plato's dream of a utopia have been of the greatest value to all later discussions. One of the disappointing aspects of the H. G. Wells film on utopia, which I shall come to presently, is that he raises almost no problems with which the future will have to grapple. There is very little by-product from his exercise. This is a general fault of uncritical utopianism, although the film is not entirely uncritical.

Northrop Frye[10] has drawn attention to a passage in which the utopian John MacNie[11] in 1883 foresaw not only that travel would be by horseless carriage but also that traffic problems would arise, and he suggested in 1883 that these be resolved by drawing a white line down the center of the road and making it a rule that traffic stays on the left except when overtaking. That sort of thinking-through as a by-product of utopianism is very impressive. It takes relatively little imagination to see that the problems of sprawling urban areas or of population increase could become quite serious in the near future. It takes only a little more imagination to pursue some possible solutions and find out the sort of further problems which will be generated. Indeed, it would seem to be the duty of any planner or reformer to do this and to try to think out all the consequences of any change. Unless we try to do this, it seems to me that we are acting irresponsibly in seriously proposing that such solutions be adopted.

A solution to the size problems of urban sprawl might be rapid transit. I hear that at M.I.T. they have gone so far in such studies that in some systems passengers would have to be anesthetized. Another solution might be higher and higher buildings, allowing existing urban areas to be frozen at their present size, thus halting the sprawl. But this again would depend on improving and expanding transit systems and on people finding high-rise living congenial. Much thinking along these lines has contemplated community centers among the high-rise buildings to take pres-

10 Frye, *op. cit.*, pp. 30–31.
11 John MacNie, *The Diothas* (London, 1883).

sure off the transportation system. But, of course, the magic of London and New York and Paris is the amenities of their centers, which disappear with decentralization. These amenities are economical only because of the massive support they suck into the city, and they are supported massively only because they are so conveniently close to each other — many choices are available in a small area. As education advances, more and more people want to be near these amenities, and the cost of expanding them increases. So community centers are no solution, and at this point I break down, because I don't see any solution to this particular problem.

Now, to come directly to architecture. When British planners are given, as they just have been, the prospect of creating three new towns for perhaps a million people each, they cannot really be allowed to get away with such slogans as trying to merge "the visual delights of the village with the economic and social benefits of largeness."[12]

The same author goes on to say, in self-contradiction, "it is impossible to build a city without a clear view of the society that will live in it." A community of farmers will center on a market, whereas seamen will live where ships can dock. According to this same writer, two main suggestions to be taken into account in building such a future community have been put forward. One suggestion is that you start with transport and work outward in the planning; the other is that you start with buildings and a balance of concrete and green. Are these really premises from which to build "cities for the next millennium"? Consider the following questions: Who can predict that the separation of work and home will go on into the next millennium? Who can say whether permanently located cities will continue to be the only way to house large numbers of people? Are planners really planning for choice, or do they intend simply to offer people much the same in these new towns as they have already — with a few improvements in the way of essentials of life? I am making a very general point: not simply that portable or disposable buildings ought to be considered, but that the planner is being forced to

12 Terence Bendixson, "Cities for the Next Millennium," *The Spectator*, Vol. 217, No. 7201 (July 1, 1966), p. 15.

arrogate to himself the role of creative — or uncreative — anthropologist.

The plans of the planners will mold the lives of men. Towns and buildings are, above all, places where people live and have their being. A new city will both positively and negatively constrain the lives of its citizens, just as unplanned New York and London force large numbers of their work force to commute. If a planner does not think about the limitations he is placing on the choices open to the future society that his plans will create, then he is not doing his job in a critical manner. He is becoming that most dreadful of things, a utopian planner remaking the world to his blueprint; he is not building cities fit to live in, but challenging people to be fit to live in his cities.

Yet of a creative anthropologist we should demand at least, it seems to me, a profound understanding of his own society, as well as a respect for it and its members and their way of life. Then he will not tamper with it lightly and certainly not undemocratically. Simultaneously, I plead for architects and planners to be bolder and freer in thinking through their ideas yet more constrained in carrying them out — for them not to be allowed to influence our lives by fiat, without letting us have any say in the decision. Planners' plans are, it seems to me, far too conservative — from Nikita Khrushchev's drab dream of Russia in 1980 to the rather dreary so-called "new towns" scattered around the British Isles. This is a reason why we should not allow any more of them to be imposed upon us, for they reduce our choice and are in that way a form of dictatorship. Certainly, then, thinking about utopia is not futile.

IV

This brings me to the second criticism of utopianism that might be put forward: namely, that it is far too fanciful, too up-in-the-air. Neither the feasibility nor the likelihood of the plans is known. But one thing surely *is* known: utopia will cost a lot, take a long time, and cause much social upheaval. The only rational course for those burdened with the responsibility for planning is to focus on present trends and tendencies, collect data, and from them estimate the probabilities of this or that happening (on computers perhaps), and plan accordingly.

In fact, once we have isolated the data and sorted out the trends, the environment will, so to speak, design itself — rationalization and cost analysis will point to a definite solution.

It is not possible to challenge the contentions that utopias are fanciful, possibly not feasible, possibly expensive, time-consuming, and disturbing. It does not follow from this that hardheaded data collection or trend projection is the only rational course of action. It is neither rational in and of itself, nor is it in any way realistic. Indeed, it is another form of speculation.

Take the *non sequitur* first. However fanciful and incredible utopian thinking has been, later generations have laughed at ideas they find prosaic. Many, many things that are part and parcel of our daily lives now — like electricity, jet travel, and, of course, moon travel — were once incredibly fanciful speculations, thought to be impossibly expensive, disruptive, and not very likely. Thus what we now regard as fanciful may tomorrow be ordinary, and therefore fancifulness is no criticism of thinking about the future.

Moreover, the hardheaded approach contrives to substitute something equally fanciful: namely, the hypothesis that things will go as they now seem likely to go. The *hubris*, not to say the historicism, of this assumption is considerable. Are we now such gods that we can tell which of the many possibilities in our society will be the ones that are going to grow stronger? No, but don't data and computers surely help us? This reply is nothing but mystification with science. Data must be selected and collected and computers programmed to produce the results wanted. The whole exercise is only an elaborate way of dressing up what you already believe. There isn't a trend or tendency that can't be reversed, and there is no reason whatever for believing it won't be. There is no way of estimating probabilities in this matter.[13]

As to the environment doing anything even remotely like "designing itself," I find it difficult to settle on an argument to contest

[13] This is a "controversial" issue, of course, but I think the arguments are decisive. See K. R. Popper, *The Logic of Scientific Discovery* (London: Hutchinson, 1959), and the various discussions of probability therein.

it. It is not necessary to argue that there is an enormous area of choice in architecture and planning at any stage — that decisions will never make themselves. If efficiency is proposed as a guide in making a choice, it would not be hard to show that efficiency itself is a very problematic idea and that even such a highly sophisticated treatment as *The Statistics of Extremes*, by Emil J. Gumbel, shows clearly that although you can make certain efficient decisions with the help of statistics, there is still a very large and quite unavoidable area of free choice. This crushes the idea that the environment can plan itself, even in terms of efficiency. Anyway, planning is not really about efficiency or solely about efficiency; it is about freedom, and it is about flexibility and the maximization of both. There are no "data," no clear-cut choices. There are people who have different ways of life. There are the decisions they are prepared to make.

If the hardheaded critic is merely saying that we should beware of fanciful solutions to our problems and proceed piecemeal in our actual building rather than our thinking, then, of course, he has a point. But since the future is unknown, each step is taken at hazard, and its consequences and ramifications are unforeseeable. Given a plan, we should proceed piecemeal because the possibility exists that the ramifications of any particular part of the plan could obstruct or prevent the rest of it from being realized. In war the good strategist phases his plan to allow time to modify and develop the plan as he goes along. Let me give some examples of how aims and plans can interfere with themselves: To expand universities may defeat the object of expanding the universities by undermining standards and thus turning them into nonuniversities. Simply to slam freeways through a city may destroy the city and turn it into something else. We can, however, dream or think wholesale rather than piecemeal in order to anticipate and think through.

I have already said that trying to impose a blueprint on society is authoritarian. The question is whether some problems are not so large that they must be attacked all at once. Thus a great problem facing American planners is the trend of migration toward California and the possibility of a continuous urban sprawl stretching from Sausalito to San Diego. The question everyone

thinks of is less whether or not this is desirable than how to ameliorate its horrors. Such planning for urban renewal and building
of superhighways is highly necessary and desirable. Why should
we think or dream or plan on a wholesale basis, considering the
urgency of such problems? One argument I shall marshal is that
trends are reversible and that there should be contingency planning in such a case; and this planning must be large-scale. The
trend to California, of course, could be reversed.

Another argument might be that advances like the total separation of motor traffic in town centers — such as Coventry —
seem to have taken their cue from wholesale dream cities like the
Wells-Korda-Moholy-Nagy vision in *Things to Come*. Only the
over-all vision allows one to see whether, for example, present
patterns of dispersing homes so that people must cluster for work
and entertainment are sustainable if cities are developed in different ways. There is no reason, then, why piecemeal planning
should not follow on and benefit from utopian dreaming.

V

This brings me to the third of the arguments directed against
utopianism in general, and one that actually contradicts directly
the previous sentence: namely, the view that we become en-
thralled by and enamored of our utopian dreams — constructed
so often in accordance with what we conceive as the highest principles. Not to desire this utopia is like not desiring the Good Life.
Utopianists are thus tempted to impose their dreams upon their
fellow creatures, even if the latter are reluctant. Sooner or later
their fellows will come around to recognizing the Good Life for
what it is; and in the meantime, for their sake, a little persuasion
may be justified.

Even dreaming is dangerous, then, because it produces authoritarianism. This argument draws attention to a very serious danger
in utopian speculation. Our awareness that this danger exists and
our actual experience of the bureaucratic tyrant who would love
to make society "well ordered" and "well run" must put us on
guard. However, it seems to me that architecture and planning
are here being connected with a very general political concern:

"Beware of blueprints of society." To the planner this should be translated to read: "We want to dream of utopias in which men could better live the lives they now lead and even broaden their range of choices of life styles. We do not want you to tell man how he should live.Your dreams are for us to choose from and learn from, not for us to live up to." What we obviously cannot do, of course, is censor people's thinking. There is nothing we can do to stop dreaming. It may, therefore, be as well to encourage it in a critical spirit.

From the point of view of the planner, another reason that utopias trap us is that they involve our imaginations. This argument cannot easily be bypassed. What it says is not so much that we fall in love with our utopias as that we are so involved in them and their concepts that we cannot be critical of the concepts, categories, and terms in which they are set. For example, in our present way of life, home and play are frequently separated spatially and are put in different categories. A dreamer might conceive of a city in which this separation is calculated, built-in, and beautifully organized. But if you suggest that not thinking beyond these categories is a rather conservative approach, he might recoil, uncomprehending — what kind of life would it be without them? They are fundamental. Well, of course, the answer is simply that it is not even bold to imagine a life without the separation of work, home, and play. Such living already goes on around us: namely, by anyone who loves his work and does it at home. Most academics will probably, like me, be in this category. Most of my research and writing work is done in my home, and I go to the university only because it is a matter of convenience; the teaching and libraries are centrally organized at the moment. I can well imagine this changing, and indeed there are signs that it is already doing so. Why not imagine a city in which certain housing units for teachers included a large room in which students could foregather? Why not? Because the transport problems, administrative problems, and library problems created would be insufferable. But in the age of conference television telephones and such things, do administrators need to be housed together? Librarians already are thinking beyond readers having to go to libraries. Could we not imagine dialing a number for the catalogue, turning a knob till we found the entry, dialing another number, and having a microfilm of the book appear on our screens, or even having a Xerox copy of its pages made?

So far are we from a utopian university of this kind being worked out in detail and explored that we hardly conceive of it — as shown by the deplorable conservatism of the new British universities, none of which has, as far as I know, a single innovation of this kind.

Yet this dream is, in fact, rather prosaic. Most of the technology required has already been invented.[14] By contemplating problems it might create, it certainly opens up multiple choices to us.

In advocating utopianism I am going much further, however, since we should try to dream critically of situations which are yet beyond the technologically possible. If we are uncritical of dreams, then such dreams become a rather aimless kind of science fiction; but if we are critical and proceed only with particular problems and discipline ourselves, then it could be, I think, very fruitful; and the more disciplined by criticism, the more fruitful.

To reinforce my case — perhaps some of you are impressed by our new universities — I shall refer to two British planners' works: Gordon Cullen's *Townscape*[15] and G. A. Jellicoe's *Motopia*.[16]

Cullen's book is one that I found almost as depressing as some of the townscapes he praises. It is a book in which design and function are somehow being pushed so that one can imagine life going on much as before in the suburbs, with a little tidying up. One gets a picture of endless vistas of suburbia, slightly prettified, but not requiring any major changes. This will be his ideal townscape. Not only does he ignore the aesthetic core of much that he discusses, but he doesn't go behind the buildings to the way of life that is being produced by them and discuss whether it is in any way satisfactory.

---

14 That it is not so startling is perhaps evidenced by the appearance of these ideas in "2000," a series of articles in the British popular magazine *Woman's Mirror*, October 1966.

15 G. Cullen, *Townscape* (New York: Reinhold, 1961).

16 G. A. Jellicoe, *Motopia* (New York: Praeger, 1961). Motopia is only the latest neologism in a long chain. Besides "utopia" itself, which is a synthesis of "outopia" and "eutopia," we have had "antiutopia," "dystopia," "kakotopia," and even "pornotopia."

The same is true, to a less extent though, of the more critical look at the future possibilities to be found in *Motopia*. Jellicoe's explicit premise is that the motorcar will be with us for the foreseeable future. We have, therefore, to design dwellings working outward from the motorcar. Jellicoe takes the simple ideas of rooftop roads and buildings in grids and produces an efficient way of fitting the motorcar and its owner into the suburban landscape. But Jellicoe is too critical in many ways, or uncritical of his criticism. For example, he rules out putting roads underground because of cost. If anything changes over time, it is relative cost. That is obvious. Then, after seeing his monotonous apartments my first thought was, "Why aren't they underground, too?" Because, after all, at least Wells went that far in the film we have seen. And again, Jellicoe's plans are bedeviled by his uncritical attitude toward the way of life in motopia. All he does, in fact, is assume that life patterns will be exactly like today's in suburbia, and his aim is to organize the town a little more efficiently around them. He assumes, for example, that regular shopping will continue to be a part of life and that every block will have to have a certain amount of shop space.

In Hong Kong, where I have been living for almost five years, and which is generally regarded as rather old-fashioned, much shopping is done by telephone and order book because delivery is cheap. Again, it is a question of the relative cost. It is not hard to imagine the relative cost of delivery coming down perhaps because of some mechanical means, and this kind of regular avenue of shops for household goods would then be quite out of date. In a decade or two it would already be wasted space. This is not even considered in the course of the argument. He could have considered the possibility of such patterns of shopping more or less being abolished — at least regular shopping, as opposed to specialized shopping, for which we might continue to go a long distance.

Jellicoe might reply that shopping is not just an economic necessity, that it has a certain social function in a community, especially for unoccupied married women. The answer to this, after one thinks it through, would be: (1) to find ways to occupy the women and (2) to dream up alternative social activities for those still unoccupied. Shopping is only a substitute. These women want to socialize together, but why do they *have* to do it through shopping?

Apart from Jellicoe, the problem is that while architects have no business moralizing about our present ways — none of us have — they should also avoid being too conservative in accepting patterns that exist now as though they were essential to our way of life. When they do this, they limit our choices. Some of our present social institutions are already very abstract and could become much more so — like the university I have envisaged. Others, like the family, are not, and the architect could offer to make them still less abstract by, for example, constructing a city in which separations within families are minimized. We have a regular separation now. The worker or provider goes away from the home, comes back, and so on. Maybe he doesn't want to stay at home. That is another social problem which one has to consider, but why not give him the choice? We can dream of a community in which the organization is different and see what the consequences are.

The architect, then, has scope for being a social force. He can point out possibilities. The London County Council planners were presented with the problem of transferring the Bethnal Green community to Roehampton. The main specification they were given was that Bethnal Green as a community was to be preserved as much as possible. They did not interpret this as meaning that the working-class terrace houses should be reproduced in the countryside. They tried instead to create an environment which would not kill any valuable aspects of the community as it was but which might create opportunities for the community to develop and change if it so wished. The unfortunate part about this was that the community wasn't really brought in on the planning; it was done by government fiat.

In suggesting the architect is a "creative anthropologist," I mean that his buildings are frameworks around man's activities, and the activities that men want should be the basic decree for the planner, for the architect; it is a mistake to take our present life patterns as fixed and unchanging. An argument to underline this last point is that technological progress is accelerating and there are consequent changes in the patterns of our activities; the frameworks are going to have to accommodate stranger and stranger social patterns. What thinking critically about the future can do for us is partially to ameliorate that strangeness or to prepare us for it and thus to help us adapt to it, to think in terms of it more quickly and effectively than otherwise.

So much, then, for the first three criticisms of utopianism. I seem to have refuted them all, at least to my own satisfaction, but not without conceding and learning a great deal. My position at this point can be summed up by saying that our proneness to error, the openness of the future, the blindness of present trends, our self-set moral and imaginative traps — all of these should make us hypercritical of any utopian exercise; but we blind ourselves if we give up altogether.

VI

From the very first dream of utopia it has been distrusted and disliked. There has been a flourishing tradition of antiutopias beginning with the horror stories of Jonathan Swift and proceeding through Butler's *Erewhon* to the gloom of Orwell, Huxley, and Michael Young. The criticism which these authors direct again and again at utopianism is that it is naïve and optimistic, and this is also my fourth criticism. These authors adopt the reverse stance — pessimism. Then selected tendencies in the present are extrapolated, and the result is a monstrosity. This technique yields a very powerful argument against those who simply extrapolate from the so-called "hard data" of the present situation. We can see that the selection is everything, and whether the result will be hell or paradise depends on whether the governing vision is optimistic or pessimistic.

Between these two poles of optimism and pessimism there has hitherto been virtually no middle ground. To present this schematically, the future could be confronted or thought about in three ways:

1. Things will go on as they have — with a few small changes. This is a rather conservative prediction about the future.

2. Certain present tendencies will become dominant. This is inductive prediction.

3. Wild speculation about the future; or we have no idea, but maybe such and such will happen.

My contention about these three possibilities is that they are all on the same level of likelihood. There is absolutely no way of telling whether we are in for a period of quiescence (1), whether certain present trends will grow stronger and become dominant (2), or whether drastic wholesale change will occur without warning (3). The advocates of 1 and 2 are simply conservative and inductive in their refusal to face this fact, that we really don't know.[17] However, those who approach wild speculation and prophecy in a critical way might at least learn something unexpected and conceivably useful.

This plea for a critical utopianism can, of course, be easily argued with hindsight. One can make a case for saying that the planners of the Los Angeles freeways did not make it clear that their ideas might create a noncity like nothing else known previously. I don't say this in any moralizing spirit. Some people, and I would number myself among them, appreciate very much the special way of life possible in Los Angeles. But I also say that the flood of criticism of Los Angeles suggests that it was not created with foresight.

Any action we take, like building freeways, will have countless social and other repercussions, many of which we cannot foresee.[18] Some, however, might have been foreseen. Since city planning goes back to the Greeks, does it not shame us when we contemplate the hideous suburban sprawl which surrounds our major cities? Not only is it horrible to look at, but it stultifies and limits whole ways of life. Apart from making people commute and imprisoning housewives in home and garden, it has also ruined the cities socially. Increasingly, only the very rich and the very poor live in the cities themselves — the poor because they can't afford to get out, the rich because they can purchase the en-

[17] See K. R. Popper, "Probability Magic, or Knowledge Out of Ignorance," *Dialectica*, Vol. 11 (1957), pp. 354–374.

[18] See my *Revolution in Anthropology* (London: Routledge & Kegan Paul, 1964), pp. 216 ff.

vironment they want there. It is difficult to know if this is inevitable — whether, for example, if we tried to diversify the cities, having houses at all prices available, the natural forces of the city environment wouldn't drive house prices up or "slum" them all down. But certainly the sprawl seems to me a product of diffidence by authorities and planners. What happened could have been foreseen and fought against. Why it wasn't or, if it was, why resistance failed, I don't know.

The only way to avoid such things in the future is to put before the public, through the elected government, or whatever, in the boldest possible terms all the choices and all the consequences we can see at this time. As we implement whatever choice is made, we must then constantly reappraise the whole set of choices we adopted at the beginning. Perhaps in order to dramatize matters we should resort more seriously to the world of science fiction. This brings me to the film *Things to Come*, because all science fiction writers from Jules Verne and H. G. Wells through to Isaac Asimov have from time to time looked at social design and other problems in the futures they envisage. Asimov conceives of the entire "rise and fall of civilization" in one of his works.[19] In the movie we can see all the elements of looking into the future that I have discussed and some others. We have there utopia, anti-utopia, prophecy, shrewd projections of trends of 1936, wild miscalculations, and other conservative miscalculations; and we also have critical utopianism.

We have in addition, and I had better get this out of the way now, a rather bad film. As Alistair Cooke remarked, "It is just a fancy dress ball, here and now, at the R.I.B.A."[20] A critic in *Era* said that it was "based on what is possibly . . . the worst scenario that has ever been written."[21] The tale it tells after the portentous caption "Whither Mankind?" is of how the world plunges in 1940 into a war that devastates Europe. But somehow, somewhere,[22]

[19] See Isaac Asimov, *Foundation* (New York: Gnome Press, 1951); *Foundation and Empire* (New York: Gnome Press, 1952); and *Second Foundation* (New York: Gnome Press, 1953).

[20] Alistair Cooke in a review of the film in *The Listener*, March 18, 1936, p. 545.

[21] G. A. Atkinson in *Era*, February 26, 1936.

[22] *The Times* film critic commented that the world will be saved by

civilization is rebuilt by the scientists and engineers. They proceed to subdue the war lords and deal firmly with reactionaries before shooting off two of their *Herrenvolk* on a journey to the moon. Will mankind, Wells asks, listen to the reactionaries or to the forces of science, reason, and light?

Let me isolate from this film some of the different strands as they relate to the critical exploration of the future. First, there are the conservative elements: In the film there is something irresistibly of the thirties and Wellsian about the furniture on the one hand and the personal relationships in the film on the other. A writer in the journal *Design for Today* commented in 1936 that "The glass couch is somehow reminiscent of Burlington House."[23] And several writers have noted the pseudo-Grecian garb adopted especially by the female characters. But, above all, the posturing, speechifying, and the self-righteousness of the scientists make one feel very uncomfortable if this is the world of the future.

Second, there are projections of current tendencies: Here we note the prediction that the airplane is becoming an important weapon and will fight the next war. The tendency to high-rise apartments and to artificially controlled lighting and air-circulation systems is also carried through. The increased use of glass and plastic was also what looked like a reasonable guess. So much for projections.

Third, there are elements of prophecy: The amazing one, of course, was the prediction of the war in 1940. Nobody knows how Wells came on that idea. The other was the journey to the moon. We are apt to be impressed by these superb guesses. But they were only that and cannot be systematically repeated by even, I think, a critical utopianism.

What about the strictly utopian aspects of the film? Utopia is the paradise on earth, simultaneously here and nowhere. For Wells it comes after the holocaust. Antiutopia in the conscious sense is portrayed in the scenes of war, destruction, disease, and

---

mechanics, research students, and airmen. The latter emerge from the war ruins they made, mysteriously endowed with wisdom, detachment, and nobility. What happened to make them like this is a moot point — a mystic communion with machinery, perhaps?

[23] A. Vesselo, "Design for Tomorrow," *Design for Today*, April 1936.

dictatorship. This is when the antiscientific forces get the upper hand, when men try to run their affairs in the same old muddling way. They almost succeed in destroying civilization on earth.

Wells is an optimist, however, and so we get a fourth element of utopia: the scientific civilization of pure air and light, the benign reign of the scientist-airman. Wells is so optimistic that he fails to realize that his picture of the airman's civilization is in many ways repugnant. The all-knowingness of the new leaders, their self-righteousness, and the artificiality of their perfect environment are very depressing. He seems to take it for granted that people would be happy to be dressed and housed more or less homogeneously.[24] It didn't occur to him that our present diversity is not solely the result of our society having grown up piecemeal but also something we have chosen.

As Colin Welch wrote apropos of Wells in general, and it applies beautifully to Wells's caricature of the reactionaries in the film, "The idea that people should be taught to think; the idea that, thus taught, they might reach conclusions different from each others', even from his own: these were . . . repugnant to him [Wells]."[25] This is where Wells's utopianism is uncritical and, I think, authoritarian.

Finally we come to his critical utopianism. Despite his naïve optimism and trust in science, scientists, and engineers, Wells put into the mouth of the reactionary sculptor some critical remarks about his monstrously dehumanized vision; there is the suggestion

[24] "I would say to *our designers*: 'For God's Sake let yourselves go'. . . . Being inventive and original is not being extravagant and silly." Wells said this in a memorandum to everyone concerned with designing *Things to Come*; reprinted in *Two Film Stories* (London, 1940), p. 16. How, then, did the following come to be Alistair Cooke's judgment? "It must be heartbreaking for Mr. Wells to be told that the costumes he predicted they'd be wearing in 2030 are to be the very thing in beach-wear this summer. But there is a category of less inevitable error: the aeroplanes drone away from exhaust trouble. The chairs are any modern chair done in glass: they have glass elevators but, the point is — they still have elevators. . . . "Things to Come" shares with most Utopias the primary error of making today the premise, of pretending that new civilizations do not differ in kind but only in degree of decoration, luxury, leisure, and so on." Cooke, *op. cit.*

[25] Colin Welch, "Father of Little Superman," *Daily Telegraph*, September 21, 1966.

that a society with a surfeit of comfort, leisure, and beauty might suffer serious and disruptive tensions. The fundamental objection is that the whole civilization has lost the human scale, and the scrambling after progress has become completely pointless and cannibalistic, feeding on itself. Now, certainly this is a serious architectural and planning problem, the human scale; interestingly enough, Jellicoe in his *Motopia* harped quite a bit on the necessity of considering it.

These are some of the ideas of the future to be found in the film. But where, for instance, do we place the speech in which the airman tells the war lord his way of life will not be permitted to go on? Is that utopian or antiutopian? What, too, of Wells's theme that the reactionaries would be the artists?[26] Is that a prophecy that the present two cultures of the sciences and the humanities will be increasingly separated? I confess ignorance.

VII

What are the implications of my argument for architects and planners? Most of them were spelled out as I went along. The main one is that looking into the future is almost impossible, and our only hope is to pool our ideas and criticisms. None of us, by magical prophecy or cryptomagical induction from data, can know what is to come. But if we explore critically and creatively, we may be able to do a better job than the urban sprawl which spoliates our countryside, the dull grid patterns of Manhattan and motopia, or the hygienic inhuman and synthetic world of *Things to Come*.

If the problem of expense is raised, then I am tempted to answer with the following cheap argument: If we can afford to fill the archives of the Pentagon with libraries of so-called "contingency plans" for wars that may never take place, why can't we afford to do the same for civilian life in peacetime?

---

[26] "Mr. Wells as applied scientist probably gave a lot of help with the detail of the sets. But Mr. Wells as sociologist should surely have called in Mr. Lewis Mumford, who would have told him, what Korda's settings visibly demonstrate, that the artist as beauty specialist will be a vulgar survival." Cooke, *op. cit.*

One of the main problems is to see that the attack — that is, the criticism of the utopian — reaches even the most deeply entrenched categories and institutions to see if they are essential. I have touched on the idea that the termination of the rigid work-play separation is not very utopian. Wells imagined an environment controlled so that night and day and the seasons were eliminated. Further lines of thought are that the tables might be turned on my opening joke and that buildings might become much less monuments of indestructibility and immobility. The town-country dichotomy might disappear. The whole idea of separate buildings might give way to continuous ones. And on the moon we may get the situation where the outside appearance of buildings is of little concern and all the emphasis is on the interiors.

Concerning architectural education, I have only one suggestion as to how we can teach students to be less imprisoned by their received categories and concepts — and that is to teach them comparative sociology and anthropology. This follows directly on my suggestion that in an important way an architect or planner is a creative anthropologist. This would require, for me, that when he is planning a scheme, he should do what is called "field work." That is, he should live as a participant observer in the firm or institution he is going to build for, get to know its way of life, its aspirations, and so on, while he starts designing. But at each stage he should try to expose his ideas to criticism by those who may have to or may choose to live in what he is designing. All this will be anathema to those imprisoned by the romantic idea of art as self-expression; I can't help that.[27]

Acquaintance with different ways of life through the study of comparative social institutions has of itself a liberating effect. But some deeper study of sociology would also be of value. The nature and persistence of social institutions are very peculiar, and their intractability has to be studied. In some ways an institution is like a rule of the road, which is more effective in getting drivers to drive on one side than is a physical thing like a big sign saying

[27] I have tried to criticize the idea in my article "The Objectivity of Criticism of the Arts," *Ratio*, Vol. 9 (1967), pp. 67–83; see also E. H. Gombrich, *Art and Illusion* (London and New York: Phaidon, 1966), *passim*.

"drive on the right." This applies to planning and architecture. For example, it is not good enough to clear the slums and build nice new buildings if the society which produces slums will turn the new buildings into slums — this is what has happened in England again and again. It seems to me that the planners are trying to treat this problem purely architecturally. The old houses are ugly, so they build beautiful new houses, and they become slums.

Finally, consider critical utopianism itself. Utopia is the perfect place, the perfectly good place. Utopian thinking is probably most fruitful if it narrows its focus and takes only one aspect of this perfect life at a time. In methodology we stress the importance of concentrating on a single problem and its ramifications; otherwise, it can't really be followed through. I have mentioned contingency planning; Herman Kahn, who has explored the methodology of war games, contingency planning, and scenarios very extensively, also has come to exactly the same conclusion: that the main technique is to decide what problems you are talking about and then to break them down into as many manageable subproblems as you possibly can. In this way, you find that a large number of them have obvious solutions and that others are very difficult; but you have at least narrowed the points of concentration. This seems to me one of the easiest ways to break down existing categories and preconceptions.

I end with some direct ways in which I think the utopian dream can be strongly criticized without being put into practice. The first is to follow the ramifications as far as you can and to find out whether the utopia is self-defeating. This is like looking for internal consistency in the dream. A second check or criticism would be to see whether the dream would be destructive of certain things you value, whether there is some conflict with other things you consider important. The third and very important mode of criticism would be to see whether the utopia actually solves whatever problem you began with. Let's say it is suburban sprawl. You may find that the solution does other things but doesn't solve the exact problem. The fourth and final kind of criticism you could make is to ask whether the utopia accords with present facts.

When I began, I said that I would play my ascribed role to the full. So, as promised, I have preached a sermon in which I have reasoned my way to vague and rather general conclusions. Not *so* vague and *so* general, I hope, that they are without consequences which you find of interest.

CHAPTER 23

Nationalism and the Social Sciences*

The new 'clerks' declare that they do not know what is meant by justice, truth, and other 'metaphysical fogs', that for them the true is determined by the useful, the just by circumstances. All these things were taught by Callicles, but with this difference; he revolted all the important thinkers of his time.
—Julian Benda, 1928

Introduction

The task I will take up in this essay is that of explaining how nationalism can be an issue in the social sciences. My explanation is that, while both the social sciences and nationalism are outgrowths of the Enlightenment, they are not wholly consistent with one another, and the issue is how to square them. As long as nationalism was to be an instrument of liberation; and as long as one of the aims of liberation was to set reason free to seek the truth; and as long as one of the aims of the social sciences was the attempt to bring reason to bear on human affairs, to understand rationally the rational animal; the two had to be consistent. But, as they developed, they diverged. The later development of each was to be inconsistent with its earlier form, and, hence, inconsistent with the earlier form of the other. Nationalism in political practice turned loose the forces, not so much of sweet reason, but of fanaticism and domination. The social sciences, in their turn, came to endorse an argument (or pseudo-argument) which was to become the foundation of a new sub-discipline in sociology, called "the sociology of knowledge." This argument seemed to show that the rational animal could never be liberated from his chains, his reason was limited; in particular, that rational argument was no more than propaganda of one sort or another (with some exceptions that render the argument inconsistent, hence, pseudo).

Those of us who still trace our intellectual descent through the tradition of the Enlightenment have come to be properly sceptical of the unreason thus displayed by both nationalism and the social sciences. When the two conflict, as when nationalists denounce the pseudo-objectivity of the social sciences and social scientists repudiate the demand that they submit to causes of state, we can observe the double-bind situation and help retrace the argument and the history to the point where, we suppose, they went wrong.

* My thanks to Professor Joseph Agassi for discussion of my ideas for this essay and for critical comments on an early draft.

Nationalism, science, and social science

On the face of it, there is something like a natural antipathy between nationalism and science in general. Nationalism is particular, science is universal; nationalism has an emotional ring, science is the exemplar of reason.[1] Hence, the rational universality of science should be in basic conflict with the emotional particularities of the diverse manifestations of nationalism. So it would seem; and, it cannot be denied, there has been a tradition of thought which has affirmed this conflict. Science, that is, reason, has been viewed as a liberating force. Science was taken to be the embodiment of the rational unity of mankind, transcending all natural and conventional barriers between men, especially wealth, class, station, and nation. Its prophet, Sir Francis Bacon, explicitly held up science as the great equalizer: all men are equal when they put the question to nature. His was the egalitarianism of research teams. Subsequently, many scientists, in practice, have been radicals and visionaries, socialists, internationalists, and Marxists.[2] This has led to suspicion of them, that they might put science— higher good as they see it—above the interests of the nation in which they work. Scientists of various stripes have suffered on account of this presumption. Yet, their inspiration was traditional and benign: a devotion to reason and knowledge as great liberating and equalizing forces. Reason is where the rational animal recognizes his unity, his community, and it epitomizes itself in science; emotion is what creates particularity and division, hence nationalism and war.[3] So the visionary, religious, or political attachments of scientists were stridently defended as reasonable rather than emotional and the more strongly held for all that.[4]

So, we see how a chain of reasoning results in scientists, so far from being paragons of enlightenment, being flawed in all the usual ways, including naïveté, self-righteousness, and, ironically, nationalism. Believing so fervently in the rationality of science, and their own rationality as practitioners of it, can easily lead to loyalty to other scientists on the team and in the community and so to the nation. English smugness about Newton's physics vanquishing Descartes's enrages some Frenchmen, as the claim is implicitly made that dissent is *unreasonable*. The French physicist and historian Pierre Duhem goes so far as to try to characterize the French mind and the English mind as they express themselves in science. He expresses a clear preference for the former, which he sees as logical and imaginative; the latter is empirical and plodding.[5] Such nationalist pseudo-argument is an embarrassment to those who must teach this brilliant philosophy of science.

However that may be, present-day natural scientists vacillate between professions of internationalism in theory and hard-headed pragmatic nationalism in practice. Foreign work is not treated lightly merely because it is foreign. When funds are sought, however, great play is made with the argument that The Country must maintain its (competitive) position. If it does not, woe and lack of material benefits will result. In practice, at least, science cannot readily claim to be the antithesis of nationalism. Both have their origins in the radicalism of the Enlightenment, and both share the deep element of unreason that is in all radicalism. That element is totalism: the idea that if there is something wrong, the only rational thing to do is sweep it all away and start again. In so far as it is totalistic, science is irrational; in so far as nationalism seeks freedom from foreign domination, it is rational.[6]

So much for nationalism and science in general. What of nationalism and the social sciences in particular? Are they similarly at odds? Can they turn the tables on each other's claims to rationality? A great many social scientists seem to take the whole issue of nationalism very seriously. This, in itself, differentiates them from natural scientists, who certainly do not take current nationalist controversies seriously at all. National boundaries are relevant to money but not to knowledge. Social scientists are not so clear-headed.

Readers of this *Journal* have as background knowledge a debate of some years' standing concerning nationalism and the social sciences. Not so long ago, people were noting with alarm that American academics were flooding into Canada. To the argument, "so what?" (of which I have always been a passionate exponent), a distinction was drawn between "hard" subjects like mathematics and physics and "soft" subjects like history and the social sciences. It was argued that hard subjects were immune to national boundaries; soft subjects were "sensitive." (Other subjects, like English, or my own, philosophy, did not generate much heat. Thus are one's fond illusions shattered.) It was said to be as if Americans had taken over Canadian newspapers and filled them with American items and an American slant. Draconian measures (e.g., citizenship quotas) were bruited, as the issue fused traditional Canadian and leftist anti-Americanism, fear of external domination, and the disgruntlement of the unsuccessful into an articulate pressure group. To the extent that the issue was a political one, the pressure group was defeated. A cooler approach prevailed.

In the course of the debate, however, one argument was taken seriously by those who should have known better, namely: the social sciences are "soft", that is, not cut-and-dried, that is, not factual, demonstrated, proved, unbiased, and so on. So, while American mathematicians are no matter, American sociologists are. The argument is bogus, yet most social scientists were helpless in face of it; some even embraced it. This was because of the argument from the sociology of knowledge: a whole slew of work in the social sciences has been predicated on taking this argument seriously, and the argument from "soft" social science is but an instance of it. Hence, when it was turned against its inventors, and joined to the bullying tactic of invoking the success of the natural sciences, no answer was available to social scientists.

The natural sciences did seem to be successful, and rightly so. They had "hard" results which transcended national, social, and racial barriers. Not only did the social sciences not have these results, but they were soft and vulnerable because of the sociology of knowledge argument, because they could not break free of the total ideology of the society they came from.

A series of arguments to the same point
Faced with this quandary, social scientists could be expected to attempt a counterattack. If it could be shown that the natural sciences were not at all empirical, demonstrated, proved, unbiased, or whatever, then social scientists need not feel one down. All so-called sciences could be brought (down) to more or less the same level. This would sit well with the fashionable view that the natural sciences were conjectural, imaginative, personal, etc. And, while the philosophers Popper and Polanyi had each painted such a picture of science, social scientists did not take to their (very different) sociologising of science[7] because each still held up natural science as something special and gave compelling reasons. The godsend for the social sciences was Thomas Kuhn, who, despite protestations that he revered science and the patronizing remarks he made about the social sciences, actually had no good arguments in his system for doing so. His theory of paradigms, normal science, and puzzle-solving totally undermined the authority and prestige of the natural sciences vis-a-vis the social sciences.[8] The latter now knew the (sociological) secret of success and, hence, had hope of achieving it. Under Kuhn's view of science, nationalism can come back in. The illusion of "hardness" and value-neutrality is dispelled, and we should be as concerned about American mathematicians and physicists as we are about American sociologists. Such a Kuhnian counterattack produces a shift of ground, namely the admission that the "hard"/"soft" distinction is irrelevant, if not bogus, or at least a mere matter of degree. Even this slight modification, namely the admission that even natural science is not absolutely hard—as sociologists of science must admit anyhow—will suffice to turn the tables, as it will show that the real issue is a consequence of the involvement of the social sciences with their subject matter, of the fact that they are men studying men, which is that people in such a position cannot be trusted.

For the nub of this argument about (political) "sensitivity" to which the social sciences have played host sounds as if it defends them, whereas, in the logic of it, it obviously exposes them. And though I too wish to expose them, I will not use this argument. The particular application of the argument to the "sensitivity" of the social sciences to national boundaries says that the reason the social sciences are "sensitive" is that they are the work of men, and men are products of their society, and, hence, their social sciences are a product of their society. So, if the nation or social class to which they belong suffers from false consciousness, the social science they produce will suffer similarly. The consciousness an American has of Canada almost inescapably has to be false. False consciousness is undesirable; hence, American social scientists are undesirable in Canada.

Is the logic of this argument valid? One tests validity by substitution, by a parallel argument. We get, here, physics is produced by men, and men are a product of their society; hence, their physics is a product of their society. So, the false consciousness of Americans will make American physicists likewise undesirable in Canada. But wait. Can there be a mistake in the substitution? Can we say all the original premises are true but not all the substitute ones? Clearly, one premise can be questioned after the substitution. We can say, though Canadian and American social scientists differ so radically as to make migration harmful, Canadian and American physicists are almost identical.

This argument sounds very plausible. Again, it is a valid argument, but, while it seems to restore the sham argument, it exposes its sham. We need only ask why are Canadian physicists so similar to American physicists whereas Canadian social scientists differ so from their American colleagues? Are the Canadian physicists better than the Canadian social scientists in this respect or worse?

This is a matter of opinion. Lenin denounced all non-materialist physicists as bourgeois. He would have denounced Canadian physicists as lackeys of the American ones.[9] Others may say physical reality hardly differs in Canada and the U.S.A., whereas social realities differ greatly, and all bias, inadequacy, values, presuppositions, etc., of a given society go into the society's social scientist and make him, of necessity, different than his peer in another country. This argument is peddled by Gouldner in his *For Sociology*.[10] Criticising Becker's utterly modest and reasonable *The Outsiders*, Gouldner suggests Becker's liberalism is that of an establishment; that all establishments have reasons to lie; and that liberalism just like any other ideology is a cloak for the lies of an establishment. At pages 5 and 6 there is a subtle change from the conditional mode (establishments *can* lie) to the assertoric ("The sociologist also lies because . . ."). The flaw which shows through the grammatical shift is that liberalism (i.e., rationality plus tolerance) is a delicate plant. It has produced our society and much of the world's real intellectual achievement. When it gets established here and there, its partisans do indeed sometimes protect it by means that belie its whole philosophy. So, liberalism must be self-critical. If it is not, it is not liberalism. Gouldner, however, cannot bring himself to affirm the liberalism to which he owes his intellect and his career.[11] Desperately worried about how to be a sociologist and a whole man, or, perhaps, a whole-man sociologist, he ends up concluding that lying propaganda is all pervasive. Nor is Gouldner a voice in the wilderness: he is influential[12] and representative of the uses to which the argument from the sociology of knowledge is put. It is a mere accident that nationalism is not his particular cause. What happens is that social scientists declare their knowledge parochial[13] and then, in the name of parochialism, demand closed boundaries. But, is it not better, if that is the situation, to demand that the social scientists never stay home?[14]

Whether it is a tape-worm or a tumour, this argument needs to be expelled. To begin with, the argument is intellectually dishonest: either those who make it have to exempt themselves from its findings or else they contradict themselves. After all, if every doctrine is a function of its total ideology, then the doctrine that every doctrine is a function of its total ideology must itself be a function of its total ideology.[15] So, the sociology of knowledge dismisses itself as easily as it dismisses bourgeois ideas. To make an exception of freely poised intelligentsia is inconsistent and self-serving and, hence, intellectually dishonest. Nevertheless, within sociology itself, it has long been the practice to take this very damaging argument seriously— and even to give courses that centre around it—under the title "the sociology of knowledge."

Sociology, then, has come to a pretty pass. Inspired by the hope of progress and enlightenment, it suffered disappointment when neither came to pass. So, an attempt is made to get sociology and sociologists harnessed directly to working for progress and enlightenment, that is, to political action. But this immediately produces an intolerable conflict: what is O.K. in one place ("one party democracy", military dictatorship) is not in another (liberal democracy). So reason and enlightenment offer no clear guide, sociology offers no clear guide, to action. Why not? Because knowledge is a social product and suffers from the defects of the society producing it. In other words, there is no general social knowledge; no general sociology; no science of society—only a sociology embodying the ills of its society which it is unable, thus, to remedy. There can be limited, partial, and particular knowledge but nothing very general, certainly not universal.[16] The generality and universality of science are not dispensable features. A particular statement just cannot explain satisfactorily another particular statement.[17] So, sociology has issued in an argument that defeats the idea of a science of society and leaves it vulnerable to political attacks and interference. Sociologists have thrown away their own chances of making a stand. That their enemies have not yet rushed in and laid waste must be because they haven't noticed the breach in the defences, or they do not care, or they suspect a trap. But, there is no trap: it is the social scientists who are trapped. Hence, too, they cannot avoid being humiliated by the example of the natural sciences. Those disciplines do not harbour an argument which undermines the enterprise itself: although the argument holds there; natural scientists find it a challenge, not a barricade. Or, if they do, it is a well-guarded secret like the irrationality of the square root of two.[18]

The argument from the sociology of knowledge is only the most obvious and self-wounding of a number of arguments which indicate sociologists suffer from low self-esteem. Their taking seriously the nationalist challenge, their ambivalence about politics (eagerness to preach, yet resistance to any interference), and their wild inconsistencies are clues.[19] All the arguments are variations of one kind or another on the one and only sociology of knowledge argument.

Let me itemize them one by one. *Item:* There is the widely diffused view that sociology issues in no product: no general facts, theories, or testable explanations that can be pointed to as clear and unassailable achievements. Physicists have their atom-smashing machines, their equations; doctors have their cures, their heart-lung machines. What have sociologists to offer? Only projections of their false consciousness. As I have indicated, an unauthorised reading of Kuhn can be used to relieve anxiety on this point; with the consequence that, in debunking natural science, the whole Enlightenment ideal of the rational pursuit of knowledge is destroyed.

Item: Such putative product as sociologists may offer is said to have political colouration, hidden values, extra-scientific overtones of one kind and another.

This is because of the sociology of knowledge.

Item: Which is further reinforced by a most curious argument, one which concerns the connection between theory and practice. Theory divorced from practice is held in some suspicion; for practice, especially work, is not just *an* activity, it is men's self-making activity. Hence, the sociologists' detachment from practice means that they cannot connect up with reality and that they cannot make themselves into anything. Furthermore, since sociologists' work is a form (their form) of practice—although they convince themselves that it is not—they are unwittingly making themselves and so are involved in self-deception and false consciousness.

Alas, this argument, too, falls back into the sociology of knowledge, the hapless declasse intellectuals unable to manage theory or practice.

Item: From anthropology comes another curious argument, based on a strange requirement. This requirement is to the effect that social scientists should serve the interests of those they study; that they should endeavour to help and assist those they study; that they should orient to the natives' concerns rather than their own. Assume it to be a reasonable demand. Assume, further, that anthropologists serve best their object of study if they share their beliefs. It follows, then, that they should accept the natives' view of their world, rather than try to see things in the categories of science.[20] Again, the trouble is rooted in the fact that the sociology of knowledge has made the anthropologist excessively self-conscious about, and deprecatory of, the whole enterprise. Why should an anthropologist serve the people he observes? How does that serve science? Why should he serve them by, for example, believing in their limited medicine? Only if one denies the universality of science, including social science, and adopts a relativistic attitude to what is studied does it make sense. Such a relativism is a consequence of the sociology of knowledge.

The sociology of relativism
This whole series of arguments (and others) feeds on and into a relativism which can take both general and specific forms. Specific areas of thought,

belief, knowledge, and so on, can be declared "incommensurable"—that is, non-comparable—yet sound within bounds (e.g., western medicine is only good for modern western man). This can also be generalised, so that nothing that is done or said in one society can be evaluated against standards in any other society; and there is nothing outside of that society except other societies. One can go still further and say, in any tolerant society, that nothing one individual does can be evaluated other than against that individual's own standards. This latter view amounts to little short of a social philosophy known as nihilism;[21] the former is collectivism, which is nihilistic in the international sphere. Hence, all these relativistic doctrines, far from being half as neutral as they are meant to be, are very specific and very destructive.

One could, of course, take these arguments apart one by one, showing their inconsistencies and other weaknesses. But that has been done elsewhere.[22] My purpose in assembling them here is to point to a common feature, which might be called their self-defeating character, their function as reinforcers of low self-esteem, their spoliation of the nest. If such arguments were taken to be unassailable and serious, one would expect the discipline to wind itself up, declare bankruptcy. It would be intellectually honest of its practitioners to become politicians, street sweepers, plumbers, taxi-drivers, and the like—or perhaps intellectuals of another kind.[23] Yet, they do not. So—either they equivocate and dissemble or they do not take the arguments altogether seriously: in which case honesty demands that they should say so and give their reasons. Perhaps delinquency in this regard explains the low self-esteem. Other factors are important too. Clerks in general have seen their social value and status decline. Generalists and humanists have felt the pinch more than others.[24] Sociologists and anthropologists may have hoped to become scientific and so join the few specialist and valued clerks. Their attempts failed. So, either soldier on; or slip helplessly back into generalism; or become social activists, planners, social engineers, propagandists, and the like.

So much, then, for the argument from the sociology of knowledge and its variants. It is this argument which allowed social scientists to discuss the issue of American social scientists coming to Canada, and it was the absence of this argument that allowed natural scientists to laugh the issue off. (Which is not to say, of course, that there are not perfectly good reasons for restricting the influx of American academics. But, these arguments would be part of the general arguments for restricting immigration.) Whatever the background to this argument, it is, to my mind, a highly dangerous and destructive one. It tries to fuse science and ideology, facts and values, knowledge and belief, truth and opinion, argument and propaganda. These parallel pairs are variations of a crucial distinction between trying to get at the way the world is and trying to persuade people to believe something. A scientist, I take it, wishes to understand the general features of the world; it is none of his business to convince people, to make them believe things. Argument is the dialectical process (in Socrates's, not Hegel's sense) of attempting to understand the world; propaganda is the attempt to make friends and influence people to see the world in a certain way. Argument makes itself subservient to the world and to reason's attempts to capture it; propaganda is subservient to those manipulating it and trying to manipulate others. Argument trades on truth and falsity; propaganda trades on persuasion and lies. Near argument lies the heart of intellectual values and responsibilities; near propaganda is the heart of intellectual dishonesty and irresponsibility.

Science aims to explain *nature*. The social sciences are perhaps special among the sciences because they concentrate on that part of nature (mankind) which has invented *convention*. The question is always, in the social sciences, how can you have a natural science of convention? Nature and convention are (by convention, of course) opposites. The question is the harder, the more we stress the polarity, nature: convention. Crucially, the issue turns over the idea that the objects and laws of nature are a "given", there before science or scientists, autonomous; whereas conventions, while perhaps predating any particular scientist, do not predate or antedate man. Hence, there is something limited, partial, artificial, invented, uncertain, uncontrolled, unknown about social things and any laws they may obey.

Some things about men, luckily, are natural (including their having some conventions): bi-pedallism, sexual reproduction, group living, kinship—even power, wealth, belief. What of nations? Are nations a natural or a conventional condition of man? The Greeks, naturally, were divided on the issue. In the chequered history of western Europe, it was natural that conventionalism prevailed. There were, before the Middle Ages, no European nations to speak of; indeed, the conventional history of Europe from then till now is the history of nations forming from non-natural groupings. As they formed, they divided mankind, and as they did so, they offended the preferences of Enlightenment thinkers concerned with the rational unity of mankind. Then came Hegelian nationalism, which, with relativism, denied the thesis of the unity of mankind. Marxists denied that the units were nations: they are classes. There can be unity of the classes, but the reunion of mankind comes only with the end of class divisions.

Now, suppose a social scientist accepts relativism. How is he to discuss the questions, are human groupings natural? Which grouping is the natural one whose prejudices the social scientist cannot avoid?

The American and Canadian social scientists look alike, not only to the Marxist who denounces both as in the wrong class (bourgeois), but also to the third world (western), even to Continental Europeans (North American). In other words, accepting the parochial argument of the sociologist of knowledge, which is my parish? Should, perhaps, Canadian social scientists stay each in his Province? City? Borough? House?

Which divisions get organized has to do with the desire for propaganda. It is a fact that French-speaking Canadians can and do argue in a vein similar to those Ontario social scientists who fear Americans. In short, · nationalistic theorizing goes with nationalistic propaganda, and propaganda requires the public's ear!

Enlightenment today

The traditional ideals of the Enlightenment were affected by two crucial events, the American and French Revolutions. The one was encouraging; the other, though in part inspiring, was also deeply discouraging. It was so deeply discouraging, indeed, that there seems to have been a loss of faith in reason and enlightenment themselves, a disullusion that paved the way for romanticism and its reactionary variant. The American Revolution of 1776 was an entirely encouraging event. It encouraged enlightened men to think that the old constricting social order which divided men from one another could be overthrown and a rational system put in its place. Tyranny could be overthrown; self-govenment and freedom instituted. Thirteen years later, the other attempt was made to do it—in France in 1789. Whereas the American Revolution could be seen as a victory for and a vindication of the ideas of the Enlightenment, 1789 came to be seen as a defeat for freedom, reason, and humanity. Enlightened men who had overthrown an autocracy nevertheless became worse in some ways: their terrorism, fanaticism, and killing for virtue was quite unmatched by the *ancien régime*. They then undertook a general war against the European powers and created, for a while, a vast Empire. So, the hope of the Enlightenment—the triumph of reason and universality, ended up creating new and better excuses for violence. Moreover, a further irony, both the American and French Revolutions (and the Russian, for that matter) spawned a nationalism resembling nothing so much as a secular religion and, hence, a totally self-righteous imperialism.

The nineteenth century saw a further fusion of the ideas of nationalism and liberation. Strangely, the Romantics who were inspired by the French Revolution stressed its (alleged) nationalist colours no less than its inspiration to freedom. The re-unification of Germany and Italy and the urge to break up the Ottoman and Austro-Hungarian empires were sprung on Romantic soil and were predicated on the view that nations (or, as we should say, cultures) were natural entities, with their own inalienable rights (to be united, free of foreign domination, etc.). If nations were mere conventions, then of course the Ottoman and Austro-Hungarian empires were as legitimate as any of the most monolithic nation-states.

In the wake of the Empire and the Napoleanic wars, a new philosophy was thus forged, and one which made history. Nationalism and liberation went together; however, nationalism and imperialism and, hence, oppression also went together. How was it that one Romantic vision and practice of nationalism could be both a dark force and a liberal force? The logic, if there is a logic here, seems to be something like this. In a situation of oppression, a nationalistic doctrine legitimates rebellion: whether against princes or emperors. However, legitimating creeds are easier to defend and propagandize if they are declared the natural state of things, from which they have been perverted and to which they should be restored. And since liberation is manifestly a good thing, the triumph of nationalism is a good thing, and all deeds done in its name are good things, even natural things; this, then, by the force of propaganda, the inertia of rhetoric, could make anything associated with nations a good thing—including imperialism, jingoism, enforcement of belief, and, the crowning glory, relativism as a generalised ends-justifying-the-means doctrine. If the nation embodies a virtue (any virtue, whether reason and light, or socialism in one country, or any other), then it may employ whatever means seem necessary to defend and propagate itself.[25]

Nationalism flourishes. The third world revolves around it. Emerging nations seem to regard recognition of their nation status as an essential component of their manhood, as natural. Liberation movements assume it as a premise. A country like Canada is always rediscovering it, as lately and as this new *Journal* attests. What then? Natural or conventional? A superb answer has been given by Gellner: conventional, of course, but with quasi-natural components.[26] In a tribal society, a man's identity is his location within a structure. In a de-tribalized society, the only thing which can give man an identity is his culture. His culture is encapsulated in his language and his educational system: every man is a clerk, that is, must be literate; literacy demands education, and education requires a national apparatus, a social and material technology, and these both foster and permit a minimum level of education, knowledge, and ideas shared by (almost) all.[27] Hence, nations are the logical outcome of the changes taking place in the underdeveloped emerging nations, as well as in non-emerging ones such as Canada, Scotland, etc. One cannot dismiss these nationalisms as figments of the imagination, as dispensable social conventions. If ultimately conventional, they are very far from being optional or dispensable.

Gellner's argument is sociological. So, the enlightened reason of the social sciences finds a new explanation of that other Enlightenment idea: nationalism. Science has its modern origins in that period known as the Age of Reason (Bacon, Harvey, Descartes, Boyle, Newton, and the rest), the social sciences and nationalism in the Enlightenment of the eighteenth century. Science was a revolution against the traditional knowledge of the past: unsystematic, folksy, superstitious, ineffectual; the Enlightenment attacked many of the values, including the attitude to politics and the state, of the past. Loyalty to a nation, a culture, rather than a given structure of authority, indeed the measuring of a system of sovereignty against aims and values independent of that authority, hence conventionalising and de-legitimizing authority, was part of that attack.

While the identification of science with the rational enterprise has continued until very recently; nineteenth century liberal, rational socialists and internationalists took nationalism to be a phase, be it a stage, or an aberration, a piece of developing consciousness or of false consciousness. Nationalism has been both praised as liberating from village superstitions and dismissed as a product of the Dark Forces, the Aryan mystique, the pull of blood and soil. While this is historically understandable, I think we must learn from Gellner's *Thought and Change* to make better sense of its function in the modern world.

In this essay, while accepting Gellner's account, I persist in the view that nationalism is a dark force in the limited sense that it is inimical to science and cannot be reconciled with science. Canadians may have certain characteristics, a national style, preoccupations, and the like. This may have much sociological influence on the shape of scientific organization. But when a Canadian does science, whether physics, economics, or anthropology, his work, I contend, can in no scientifically or epistemologically relevant sense be Canadian: it is only Canadian, if at all, in its being limited and not scientific enough!

It is important that my position not be misunderstood. Sociologically, I think nationalism is understandable, a fairly rational and understandable response to certain situations, and, thus, neither wicked nor destructive. Epistemologically, it is a limitation and, when celebrated, nothing short of a disaster. The sociology of knowledge thus leads from nationalistic relativism to the very denial of science.

Perhaps, here, a word is necessary to put my thesis in perspective. Just as I do not condemn nationalism out of hand, I do not hold up science as it is practiced now as the epitome of rationality in all respects. Sociologically and psychologically speaking, even epistemologically speaking, science is a mess. Scientists, so far from being paragons of enlightenment, are often flawed in all the usual human ways, including passionate nationalism. Irrational, dogmatic, emotionally overwrought or detached, intellectually unadventurous, the scientific community is much like any other, as Polanyi and Kuhn have made depressingly clear. When Paul Feyerabend points out (in *Against Method*) that science has become a political pressure group like any other in the U.S.A., evading scrutiny while scurrying after funds; when Polanyi paints a picture of master-apprentice mystique; when Polanyi and Kuhn portray scientific change in terms of authoritatively and forcefully imposed authorized text books and (educated) public opinion; I would not presume to correct them. However, what they say is at best epistemologically irrelevant and, as they describe it, epistemologically pernicious. Epistemological rationality as we know it is epitomised in the institutions of science or even in the merest aspirations behind these institutions.

While I hold that learned societies, conferences, journals, seminars, universities, textbooks, and the like embody the rationality of science—such as it is—it should be stressed that the institutions are no more perfect than the individuals. It is the proliferation and the pluralism of institutionalised science that prevents dogmatism, ideology, and propaganda from completely usurping debate. In a similar way, it is the multiplicity of organizations and institutions in a democracy that resist the totalitarian tendencies of some individuals and institutions. In neither case is success easy, still less is it certain. Constant vigilance, struggle, and criticism is required. Any attempt to break down the distinction between argument and propaganda, reason and emotion, engenders a possibly fatal complacency.

These misunderstandings out of the way, I want now to explain clearly just why nationalism and the sociology of knowledge are mistaken in the scientific enterprise. The central argument upon which I draw is deceptively simple and well-known. It is that nothing follows about the truth of an utterance from who or what utters it. To assert otherwise is to commit the classical fallacy of *argumentum ad hominem*. Let me take myself as an example, since I am taking a stand in this essay. Even if all Popperians are notorious defenders of the *status quo*, it does not follow that, because I am a Popperian, what I say can be dismissed as no more than a defence of the *status quo*. If Hayek says that socialism and planning are the road to serfdom, it is no argument to dismiss what he is saying because he is a "reactionary." One is entirely entitled to take no notice of what he says, not to think about it, perhaps not to teach it, and so on; but one is not at liberty to delude oneself into thinking that in being labelled reactionary his point has been rebutted.[28] That this fallacy is disregarded by so many contemporary social scientists can be explained only if they do not know it or if they do not appreciate its force. I suspect the latter but need not press the point.

When it is claimed that the social sciences are value-free or objective, the following is, I think, all that is meant.[29] The social sciences *aim* to issue in statements (of problems, theories, critical arguments); statements can be true or false, relevant or irrelevant, interesting or uninteresting, progressive or reactionary, moral or immoral, Canadian or American. But, the first pair is different in kind from all the others, in that it does not vary with the others. Reactionaries, nationalists, foreigners, revolutionaries have been a fertile source of true, interesting, thought-provoking statements about societies. The value-neutrality of social studies rests on the possibility that the issues can be debated, that statements put forth by national and foreigner alike should be carefully examined. Hence, calling a statement foreign is in no way a method of handling it or the issue it pertains to. The issues being the intellectual problems under discussion and the statements advanced to solve them. Cynics can dismiss what appear to be debates as charades, cloaking the settling of issues by force. Others may conclude that if values impregnate *everything* rational debate is an illusion; but rational debate is not an illusion, therefore, values do not permeate everything.

Concluding observations

The dismaying thing about attempts to evade the force of the *ad hominem* argument in the social sciences is the sketchy, non-argumentative, excessively casual treatment of it. Logical arguments have the appearance of simplicity, even triviality; it is precisely for that reason that they are the deepest, most powerful, and deserving of serious consideration. Yet, they do not get it. One can search in vain through Gouldner, for example, for such a serious treatment. Some social scientists seem to think that Kuhn has provided it (Kuhn does not think so). And, so on. Issues constantly get confused. The epistemology/sociology distinction is, after all, clear enough. If there is an answer to the *ad hominem* argument, it needs to be very carefully stated.

Instead, a kind of anti-science state of mind seems to be the spring of thought. Sidney and Beatrice Webb thought that it was enough to study society to become a radical. Others think it is enough to know an American is teaching political science or sociology to Canadians to know there is a problem. There may or may not be a problem, this I do not deny. But, I am sure it has nothing to do with the origins or the views of the teacher. A good test of this would be that it could not be solved by substituting one of a different nationality. There is no inference from what a man is to what he says. This is *ad hominem.*

So far in this essay, I have tried to exemplify rather than preach. I have reasoned about reason; I have eschewed emotion or invective; I have argued rather than propagandized. This is because I consider the work of human reason to be the work of human liberation, salvation, self-transcendence, call it what you will. Understanding this world gives man dignity, self-respect, and, possibly, freedom.

It is man's work; it is what makes him. Hence, to smudge reason, to confuse it with propaganda, to invent pseudo-arguments against argument, pseudo-arguments which attempt to show that the distinction between argument and propaganda, reason and unreason, cannot be made, is the worst kind of *trahison des clercs,* comparable to the relativism and nihilism attendant on blurring the distinction between facts and values. Shame is it then to report that some sociologists have been in the vanguard of this intellectual treason, have even bamboozled themselves into seeing it as more progressive and enlightened to be so.

Footnotes

1. Contentious suppressed premise: emotion and reason are mutually exclusive.
2. For example, in our own age, Einstein, Oppenheimer, Fermi, Bernal, Haldane, Blackett, etc. This point is emphasized in C.P. Snow's *The Two Cultures and the Scientific Revolution* (London 1959), as well as his novels *The Masters* (London 1951), *The New Men* (London 1954), and *The Affair* (London 1960). See also, Fred Hoyle's influential science fiction, *The Black Cloud* (London 1957) and *October 1st is Too Late* (London 1966). Consider also the impact of the famous *Science at the Crossroads* volume, edited by N. Bukharin in 1931 and reprinted in 1971.
3. See J. Agassi, "Unity and Diversity in Science" in his *Science in Flux* (Dordrecht 1975).

4. "My philosophy is the philosophy of Marx and Engels, of Lenin and Stalin. It is a living philosophy all right. Millions of men and women live for it and, when the need arises, die for it" [no irony intended]. J.B.S. Haldane in *I Believe*, ed. Clifton Fadiman (New York 1939): 371-374.

5. Pierre Duhem, *The Aim and Structure of Physical Theory* (Princeton 1954 [1914]): especially pp. 55 ff.

6. The irrationality of totalism consists in this: rational action is goal-directed. To achieve a goal by sweeping away whatever exists, both gives us no assurance that things will be better and strong assurance that, even if they are not, we shall not know it, as our standards will have gone with the totality. See Popper on "canvas cleaning" in *The Open Society and Its Enemies* (London 1962).

7. Popper sociologises science in *The Logic of Scientific Discovery* (London 1959), section 8; *The Open Society*, op. cit., chapter 23; and *Conjectures and Refutations* (London 1963), chapter 5. Polanyi sociologises science in *Personal Knowledge* (London 1958), and "The Stability of Beliefs" *British Journal for the Philosophy of Science*, volume 3 (1952): 217-237. See also, J. Agassi, "Sociologism and Philosophy of Science" *Metaphilosophy*, volume 3 (1972): 103-122.

8. Kuhn sociologises science in "The Function of Dogma in Scientific Research." *Scientific Change*, ed. A.C. Crombie (Oxford 1963): 347-369 and 386-395; and in *The Structure of Scientific Revolutions*, second edition (Chicago 1970).

9. Yet Pascal warned us: "Truth on one side of the Pyrennees; error on the other" (*Pensées*, III, 1670). Marxists mistakenly think History is not another name for the Pyrennees.

10. London 1973.

11. At latest report, he has wandered off into some Never-Never Land of subjective objectivity and relative truth. The document in question, his editorial in *Theory and Society*, volume 1, number 1 (1973), virtually constitutes a *reductio* argument against what it advocates.

12. Vide the exaggerated attention given to his forlornly apocalyptic *The Coming Crisis in Western Sociology*—another candidate for that series of books entitled *Whatever Became of . . .?*

13. See my "Cultural Relativism Again." *Philosophy of the Social Sciences*, volume 5 (1975): 343-353.

14. Bertrand Russell remarks in various places that history books should be written by foreigners. Cf. *Sceptical Essays* (London 1935): 114-115; and *Education and the Social Order* (London 1932): 140-141.

15. See chapter 5 of my *Concepts and Society* (London 1972); my review of I.L. Horowitz, *Philosophy, Science, and the Sociology of Knowledge* in *British Journal for the Philosophy of Science*, volume 15 (1964): 266-268; and chapter 23 of Popper, *The Open Society*, op. cit.

16. Just this reasoning has led Peter Winch (*The Idea of a Social Science*, London 1958) and A.R. Louch (*Explanation and Human Action*, Oxford 1966) to doubt the very idea of a social science. Cf. Ernest Gellner, "A Wittgensteinian Philosophy of (or Against) the Social Sciences." *Philosophy of the Social Sciences*, volume 5 (1975): 173-199.

17. For example, the particular fact that the moon shines cannot be explained by saying it is made of green cheese. Unless, that is, one also asserts that this green cheese shines, which is *ad hoc*, or that all green cheese shines. See W.W. Bartley III, "Achilles, the Tortoise, and Explanations in Science and in History." *British Journal for the Philosophy of Science*, volume 15 (1962): 15-33; and my "Toulmin and the Rationality of Science." *Essays in Memory of Imre Lakatos* ed., R.S. Cohen, M.W. Wartofsky, and P.K. Feyerabend (Dordrecht 1976).

18. Alleged to have been discovered by the Pythagorean sect and kept a dark decret. Hippasus is said to have been killed for giving it away. Such things occur in the natural sciences until today; but they are untypical, and natural scientists tend to deny their very existence.

19. Project Camelot is a case in point. Gouldner could as easily argue that those sociologists and anthropologists who worked for the State Department and the CIA are the most honest

and scientific, because they live out subjective objectivity and relative truth. They implement to the full what others resist, the inescapable fact that sociologists are products of their nation, class, or whatever, and, hence, cannot but (and therefore should) serve its interests. Objections are just a product of the false consciousness of the déclassé (yet really bourgeois) intellectuals.

20. For more on this see my "Epistle to the Anthropologists." *American Anthropologist,* volume 77 (1975): 253-266.

21. Literature is surprisingly short on nihilism. For example, A.J. Ayer's nice little piece ("Philosophy at Absolute Zero." *Encounter,* volume 5, October 1955: 24-33) doesn't discuss the question of relativism at all.

22. See my op. cit. note 13 above, and "The Problem of Ethical Integrity in Participant Observation." *Current Anthropology,* volume 10 (1969): 505-508.

23. Could this possibly be why so many sociologists wander off into history, philosophy, politics, and so on, all the while insisting that they are really doing sociology?

24. See Gellner, "The Crisis in the Humanities and the Mainstream of Philosophy." In his *The Devil in Modern Philosophy* (London 1974). Benda is harsher. He says that now that clerks are reduced to the level of ordinary citizens they cannot be detached. The bourgeoisie to which they now belong hates democracy, liberation, and tolerance. It is not surprising, then, that they cook up arguments in literature and the social sciences that serve such snobberies, whether T.S. Eliot's *Culture,* or Karl Manneheim's "freely poised intelligentsia."

25. One might argue that the ambivalent moral character of nationalism is a special case of the ambivalent character of all total ideologies. If the ideology identifies and incorporates virtue, totalism provides a license for any crime—it is, after all, done in the name of virtue.

26. In *Thought and Change* (London 1964), Chapter 7.

27. See also Chapter 11 in Gellner's *Contemporary Thought and Politics* (London 1974).

28. I have in mind particularly the work of Herman Finer, *The Road to Reaction* (Boston 1945).

29. See Kurt Klappholz, "Value Judgments in Economics." *British Journal for the Philosophy of Science,* volume 15 (1964): 97-114.

CHAPTER 24

EXPLORATIONS IN THE SOCIAL CAREER OF MOVIES:
BUSINESS AND RELIGION

> The motion picture commenced as a novel and pleasing type of entertainment, but it has evolved into an important social and cultural force. In some senses it provides a common denominator to the feelings and aspirations of an entire people. Its importance must then be measured in terms other than the conventional one of dollars and cents.
>
> Bertrand 1941, p. 56

> Industry is carried on for the sake of business, and not conversely; and the progress and activity of industry are conditioned by the outlook of the market, which means the presumptive chance of business profits.
>
> Veblen 1904, pp. 26–7.

American society has experienced the movies as a widely sold good/service and as a secularised religion; modes that overlap. Religion is a (big)business; business preaches the religion of success; movies sell both business and religion as forms of success. Hollywood dramatises salvation-through-success as much offscreen as on. Salvation in this Hollywood religion has five overlapping forms: power, wealth, status, sex and immortality (PWSSI).[1] Movie people in general and movie stars in particular are seen to be rewarded with power, wealth and status, as signalled by their expensive presentation of self (clothes, hair, teeth, plastic surgery), large and luxurious homes (subject of guided tours and guide books) and their mobile and extravagant lifestyle. Many of them, even the apparently unpromising, are seen to be endowed with a highly desirable and marketable characteristic: sex-appeal, an asset that can be displayed both onscreen and off. And finally their being 'somebody' means not only that attention is paid to them but, also, they are deathlessly preserved on film, videotape and newsprint forever. PWSSI cannot be distributed equally in society, for such an arrangement would be unstable. Indeed one might say that a society can be characterised partly by how PWSSI *are* distributed and partly by how it thinks PWSSI *ought* to be distributed: its practice and its religious myth. American society is democratic not aristocratic in its religious myth, but there is a strong tendency for aristocracy to re-emerge in its practice. Hollywood movies present stories about the PWSSI rewards going to those talented/determined/lucky enough, and also stories that teach such success to be illusory, unsatisfying (Thomas 1977). The religious myth of the movie business itself is that anyone can be discovered, 'break in'; the practice is that Hollywood is a tightly closed and impenetrable establishment. So both Hollywood itself and the movie stories it makes present object lessons to America. It renders America coherent and hence cohesive: it reconciles in its practices and in its myths the conflict between myth and practice.

To understand this business-cum-religion of movies we shall draw on De Tocqueville (1835/40), Durkheim (1912) and Veblen (1904). Veblen distinguished between industry in the narrow sense, aiming to make a livelihood by manufacturing goods, and business, manipulating industry to make profit. The movie business embodies the religious myth of business, not of industry. Movies were an industry until 1908, when the Patents Trust was started; thereafter more money and creative entrepreneurial effort went into organizing, acquiring and merging business than went into the product, movies.[2] Movies are anyway a somewhat atypical economic good; they are semi-manufactured, semi-hand crafted, not mass-produced; they are not sold but leased (to an intermediary, the distributor, who in turn leases them to an exhibitor, who in turn leases *seats*) like a service; they are physically durable yet perishable, as I explain below; retailing branches of the industry reach out into almost all populated areas; yet the backbone of sales and profitability is in a few large urban areas and, indeed, in a few theatres in those areas.[3] Unlike a typical economic good such as dishwashers or a typical service such as haircutting, movies are an abstraction, the celluloid in cans is marketable because it 'contains' cognitive, symbolic and affective material with rich cultural significance. The dishwasher has the manifest function of being a labour-saving device, plus the latent functions of status and display. Haircutting, similarly, given our social rules about appearance, has manifest functions, but mainly it has the status connected with having someone else do what you could functionally have a family member do, or even, at a pinch, do yourself, as well as a communicative and bonding function deriving from it being an occasion for gossip.[4]

Manifestly, movies function to entertain and to pass leisure time; their status varies with the place they are showing and the price; latently they function to foregather an audience which subsequently constitutes a quasi-group whose members are bonded to each other by the cognitive, symbolic and affective content of what they have experienced.

So much for overview. Even though their social career has not yet lasted one hundred years, the movie business and its products have undergone changes in social position that can be analysed into phases. We must beware, however, of *period magic*: that is, the belief that social phenomena will map neatly onto our usual system of time-measurement, based as it is on the periodic motions of the earth in relation to the sun. Social processes are continuous over historical time and seamless through social space, so our attempts to abstract and systematize them into phases must not be taken too literally.

I shall suggest that movies are now in the fourth phase of their social career. Phase one was a time of small-scale industry, experienced as undifferentiated product with homogeneous content and of peripheral social significance. Phase two saw that industry become a big business, differentiate the product, making possible discrimination of content; it also saw movies become a central cultural phenomenon in America, articulating in their practice and its myth their own practice and myth and the conflict between them. By containing the conflict movies and the movie business latently function to palliate this conflict in society at large and hence to make society more coherent and cohesive. In this second phase their centrality is evidenced by the extraordinary amount of attention paid to them by the paying public, politicans, judges, the press, government agencies, religious organizations, community and veterans organizations, teachers and researchers. Phase three was the second half of the phase of movies as big business, when stability and pursuit of profitability led to restandardization of product and re-homogenizing of content. Towards the end of this phase the industry began a permanent decline and was pushed away from the centre towards the periphery of society. The present phase is residual, one of an as yet unfinished transition brought about by the shrinkage of the business both in absolute terms and as a percentage of the leisure economy, its being superseded at the cultural centre by television and a new situation in which more differentiation and more homogenization of product and hence more individualizing and also more formulaizing of content is taking place.

Phase One: Small Business, Undifferentiated Product, Homogeneous Content (1895–1916): From the Beginning to the End of The Motion Picture patents Company Trust

> With a fuller development of the modern
> close-knit and comprehensive industrial
> system, the point of chief attention for
> the business man has shifted from the
> old-fashioned surveillance and regulation
> of a given industrial process, with which
> his livelihood was once bound up, to an
> alert redistribution of investments from
> less to more gainful ventures, and to a
> strategic control of the conjunctures of
> business through shrewd investments and
> coalitions with other business men.
>
> Veblen 1904, pp. 24–5

The movie industry grew very rapidly (see tables). Movies were made possible by the precision mechanical and chemical technology developed in the second half of the nineteenth century. Beginning as a peep-show, they quickly also became a novelty act in vaudeville, then an exhibition at a permanent place of business, eventually in purpose-built premises. At first films were manufactured before there was anywhere to show them, or any middlemen to wholesale and market them. But once all three functions were in place the industry could in this phase be freely entered in any of its three divisions (production = manufacturing; distribution = wholesaling; exhibition = retailing) for relatively little outlay.

How is it that there was economic and social 'space' for this industry? That is, whence came the factors of production — land, labour and capital — and what were the competitive substitutes from which people might divert time and money? Did movies serve social functions previously given to other institutions and products (such as religion, folklore and broadsheets); or did they serve functions required by the new social forms of evolving capitalist America; or perhaps both?

Land and labour were not problematic. Whether located in Rochester (New Jersey), or Manhattan, there seems to have been no economic barrier to building, extending or adapting premises. The Biograph company located in a New York City brownstone; early companies in Hollywood used barns and livery stables. Unskilled labour was plentiful at a time of massive immigration. Little skilled labour was required, and most of that could be recruited from the theatre, where people were in constant need of steady employment. Proto-cinemas like storefront nickelodeons were usually run by their owners or lessors.[5]

Capital is another matter. Even Edison and Eastman, fortunes made or in the making, were at first frugal about expenditure. In production, distribution and exhibition capital was not to be obtained from the money market or the banks. Movie operations were too risky and fluctuating: apparently healthy cash-flow at the box-office could evaporate if the fad passed. Moguls' biographies regularly report them soliciting funds and loans from relatives and friends. Capital came from private sources until massive amounts were required for studio building, theatre acquisition, and sound installation.

As to the consumer's personal economy of time and money. The organization of life under industrialization and wage labour involves specialization of function. Spaces are divided into work space, home space, play space, common space, sleeping space and so on. Time is divided into work time, rest time, meal time, sleep time, leisure time, etc. Money is allocated to necessities and discretionaries. Specialization increases efficiency and the production of wealth. Hence 'spare' space, time and money appeared. The social bonds required for industrial organization cut across and so to a certain extent de-legitimated traditional community and family bonds. Under this regime the sense of individuality emerged and controlled the disposition of 'spare' space, time, and money; space, time and money that was appropriated neither by traditional social forms nor by industrial organization. Some of the 'spare' was money, and any disposition of that took place inside, not outside, the economy. A competition was set up between traditional forms (e.g. family and religion) and industrial forms for expenditure of the leisure dollar, space and time. The work day and the work week were strictly divided off from 'free' time; space was sold, in the form of larger housing, gardens, and places of public use; means of spending the leisure dollar were devised. Minstrels, strolling players, early theatre, and so on, were not organized like this. They might have religious roots, or rich patrons, or in effect beg after their performances. Industrialization reorganized the economic basis of all the so-called arts, not least the performing arts.

Moreover, precisely because the bonds of industrial society cut across old social bonds and devalue them, precisely because industrial organization in its original form places a high premium on strict organization and predictability, it fosters institutions that will inculcate those values in every way: not just in the content of coherent and clearly shaped stories, but also in the very organization of leisure itself. The myths of kinship, religion, folkore, region and gossip are not structured or economical in their use of space and time, or their depiction of exemplary behaviour for industrial society. Yet efficient industrial workers need reinforcement and shared experience to bond them. Industrialization requires individualism (the worker selling his labour, the putative entrepreneur setting out on his own to exploit his opportunity), social harmony (predictability of behaviour and hence profit) and of course literacy and numeracy. The amber in which all these can be embedded is some form of collective experience, something shared, reinforcing and particular to the group concerned. The need for coherence and bonding is greatest when the society is new, in the process of formation, scattered over vastly separate and diverse regions and accepting immigrants speaking a babel of tongues, as in America at the time movies appeared.

TABLE I
U.S. domestic feature production

Year	Production	Year	Production
1927	668	1955	254
1928	627	1956	272
1929	705	1957	300
1930	514	1958	241
1931	505	1959	187
1932	489	1960	154
1933	507	1961	131
1934	480	1962	147
1935	520+	1963	121
1936	517+	1964	153
1937	535+	1965	153
1938	450+	1966	156
1939	526+	1967	178
1940	673	1968	180
1941	598	1969	232
1942	533	1970	186
1943	427	1971	233
1944	442	1972	229
1945	377	1973	295
1946	467	1974	280
1947	486	1975	362
1948	366	1976	353
1949	356	1977	311
1950	383	1978	217
1951	391	1979	221
1952	324		
1953	344		
1954	253		

Source: 1927–68 *Historical Statistics of the United States*, except for: + Bertrand (1941), and 1969–1979 *Reel Facts*, by Cobbett Steinberg, New York: Vintage, 1982.

TABLE II
Admission to Theatres
$millions

	All Theatres	
1909	167	
1914	191	
1919	336	
	Motion Picture Theatres	Legitimate Theatres
1921	301	81
1931	719	78
1941	809	79
1951	1310	186
1961	921	398
1970	2749	735

Source: *Historical Statistics of the United States and Statistical Abstract of the United States 1984*

TABLE III
Motion picture projectionists

1900	?
1910	4,000
1920	10,000
1930	20,000
1940	24,000
1950	27,000
1960	18,000
1970	16,000

To serve the function of providing collective experience under industrialization we find emerging the popular press, popular fiction, popular songs, melodrama and vaudeville — all language-specific. It was at a high point of immigration to, of the urbanization and melting-pot processes in, America that a method was invented for the mass dissemination of pantomine drama, i.e. movies — significantly a non-language-specific medium. Pictures and (piano) music, culturally rooted yet accessible to outsiders, were able to be mechanically reproduced and hence rapidly distributed to large numbers of consumers. Unlike the electric bulb and the telephone, movies were not a flexible technology able to be used as a substitute for others (viz., candles, letters). Rather were they a flimsy and crude supplement to the many existing dramatic arts and visual novelties. Although it is said they killed vaudeville, one might be sceptical of that. Legitimate theatre, live music, the saloon and later rivals like radio and television, co-exist and compete.

Up to the founding of the Motion Picture Patents Company in 1908 (Cassady 1959) the movies were experienced as a characteristic small business. Entry required little outlay of land, labour or capital, and there were good opportunities to make money. Many tried their hand, some succeeded, more failed. Having about the same social status as circus side-shows, the movies attracted budding entrepreneurs from other serivce and consumer-good industries (Jesse Lasky from Vaudeville entrepreneurship,[6] Adolph Zukor from furs,[7] Samuel Goldwyn from gloves,[8] Louis B. Mayer from scrap,[9] Marcus Leow from furs,[10] Carl Laemmle from men's clothing,[11] William Fox from cloth processing,[12] etc.). Entering the industry to make money, they did not necessarily expect it would last. That realization dawned slowly. At first they traded in undifferentiated product − they rented out seats to view movies, ran the same movies till they were worn out, or later, changed movies that were much of a muchness anyway.

Repeat custom obviously depended on novelty. Movies are curiously perishable. Old movies are a minority taste, re-usable movies a rarity. Whatever the sensation is that movies provide the customer (and we argue this issue still), it is non-repeatable: mostly people do not want to see the same movie twice (buffs and specialists forget this). Continuation of the business would turn on supplying new movies at frequent intervals, sufficiently different to renew the sense of gratification. Further differentiation of product, such as between new and interesting movies and new and uninteresting ones was yet to come.

For many years not only was the product undifferentiated (and sold by the linear foot), but the content was homogeneous. Nickelodeons showed short movies that consisted of a chaotic and bewildering array of actualities, fictions, newreels, faked newsreels, cautionary tales, pantomine versions of well-known books and plays, etc. The settling down of movies to longer dramatic forms, utilizing recognizable performers, and coherently identified and promoted as such, evolved gradually.[13] To those who argue that the public made the differentiation, chose the stars, one could argue that differentiation of product was a business necessity and that those who resisted it were forced out of business.[14] In the dialectic between supply and demand it is foolish to try to identify one or the other as the prior cause.

In all discussion of mass media the term 'the public' is anyway ambiguous. There is, clearly, the public that proffers its nickel to the exhibitor and provides the foundation for the economic pyramid of the movie industry.

There are also, however, leaders of public opinion, such as elected officials, policemen, licensing bodies, teachers, journalists, religious spokesmen and demagogues who, in the name of public opinion, inveighed against this burgeoning new form of popular entertainment.[15] The threat they perceived is not imaginary, although whether that threat is to the public welfare or perhaps to the welfare of those 'spokesmen' themselves, is moot.

Phase Two: Growth, Differentiation of Product, Discriminable Content (1917–1927): From the Formation of the First National Circuit to the Founding of RKO

Various items, of very diverse character, are to be included under the head of "good-will"; but the items included have this much in common that they are "immaterial wealth", "intangible assets"; which, it may parenthetically be remarked, signifies among other things that these assets are not serviceable to the community, but only to their owners.

Veblen 1904, p. 70

Democracy encourages a taste for physical gratification; this taste, if it becomes excessive, soon disposes men to believe that all is matter only; and materialism, in its turn, hurries them on with mad impatience to these same delights; such is the fatal circle within which democratic nations are driven round ... Despotism may govern without faith, but liberty cannot. Religion is much more necessary in the republic which they set forth in glowing colors than in the monarchy ...; it is more needed in democratic republics than in any others. How is it possible that society should escape destruction if the moral tie is not strengthened in proportion as the political tie is relaxed? And what can be done with people who are their own masters if they are not submissive to the Deity?

De Tocqueville, 1835/40, Vol. II, p. 154, vol. I, p. 318

Most of us prefer an orderly and easy life and business men are no exception. The early movie market was promising but chaotic and uncertain. Hence the basic situational problem for its entrepreneurs was (and remains) how to reduce risk: how to make the business orderly, steadily profitable and growing. The supplier no more wants to be at the mercy of the vagaries of the market than does the consumer. The rational entrepreneur always pursues the strategy of trying to get some control of the market: partly by supplying product he thinks the public will demand in preference to that of his competitors; partly by trying directly to squeeze out his competitors, by buying theatres, rationalizing wholesaling and moving into production; i.e. by horizontal and vertical intergration. The aims: to make entry difficult, to reduce the numbers already in; to be able to earn monopoly profit.

Legend has it that Edison was so unaware of the financial potential of the movies that he refused to spend $150 to get foreign patents. By 1908, when the Edison Company led in the formation of the Motion Picture Patents Company, he must have been clearer about the money to be made. But, because his monopoly was of projectors, cameras and film, but not of distribution or exhibition, there was a structural tension between the monopolists and their customers, the distributors and exhibitors, because the latter were not offered the incentive of a share of the monopoly profit to induce cooperation with the monopolists. William Fox and Carl Laemmle, in particular, saw no advantage in cooperating with the Patents Company.

One of the means they found to compete with the Company was product differentiation: to offer films they thought the public would find more attractive. No sooner had the Motion Picture Patents Company been declared a trust in restraint of trade (1915, affirmed 1916) than First National Theater Circuit was formed (1917), forcing Zukor, two years later, to begin theater acquisition on a scale that impelled him to approach a major lending institution, namely Leob, Rhodes and Co. No sooner was one kind of monopoly outlawed (patents), than a different kind was initiated (theatres). Is the risk in this business excessive, or is the climate of business such that once a certain size is reached the product becomes subordinate to the potential profit? Is perhaps this tendency meliorated a little by the character of the early entrepreneurs who loved show business, and were the gloves finally off when Hollywood companies were swallowed by conglomerate corporations who appoint officers solely concerned with balance sheets?[16]

In the struggle to control the market, worsting the competition is part of the battle. As firms grow, they begin to differentiate product, and heterogenize content. A simultaneous struggle is going on to expand the size of the market. The shiftless urban mass is hard to cater to: they have little surplus of time or money; an element of caprice in their choices, lack of steady habits; and uncertain lines of communication to them making them difficult to reach and manipulate. Higher up the class scale there is more time and money, for sure, more regularity and predictability; and much clearer lines of communication.

One begins to discern, in this phase, product differentiation and content difference developing strongly. Films ceased to be sold outright by the linear foot and instead were hired, first by the foot, then by the reel, and finally much more logically, by the title. It is in this period too that we see the perfection and extension of narrative cinema, from very brief movies to multi-reeled ones, the heavy promotions of films as such and by company names, and of course the emergence of stars, both on-screen and off.[17] In the course of the years such directors as D. W. Griffith (1874–1948), John 'Jack' Ford (1895–1973), Cecil B. DeMille (1881–1959), producers such as Samuel Goldwyn (1882–1974), David O. Selznick (1902–1965), Darryl F. Zanuck (1902–1979), producer-directors such as Alfred Hitchcock (1899–1980) and Orson Welles (1915–1985) all endeavoured to have their names associated with their films in titles and advertisements. But of course those on-screen were the most successful at such self-promotion. A film starring Pickford or Chaplin would be sold at what the market would bear, and eventually that market would be broken down into first, second and later runs, each getting the film a little later and less fresh, each charging lower admission, each catering to different sectors of the population. A film starring no-one would have quite uncertain market potential.

Why are stars so important? Unlike the theme or the plot, the on-screen star is concrete, not abstract; unlike the producer, director or writer, however famous, the star is visible; but, especially, the star 'belongs to' or graces, another abstract entity, the company. To the audience the star functions as a representation of the individualist fantasy of a self that is its own free creation. A traditional society with fixed roles and statuses, ascribed not achieved, allows little leeway for the notion that the individual person can be something else and hence someone else than he or she is. Indeed, identity and ascription are fused. Industrial society, with its stress on ranges of achieved roles and statuses, demands that the individual have a notion of self-identity detachable from tradition, family and ascription. The actor or actress moving smoothly from role to role in movies, from humble origin to stellar status in 'real life' (an ironic way of having to refer to off-screen Hollywood), epitomises this tendency to be or to be able to be a self who is also and constantly someone else.

Content differences in movies began to reflect the aspiring or real bourgeois character of their makers, as well as the large section of the movie audience that is proletarian, poor or very young. At it were, an official morality pervaded the films that was chivalrous, Victorian and bourgeois, with prurient interest catered to in moral melodrama (wickedness can be shown but then must be condemned). Risqué subjects such as white slavery, illegitimacy, concubinage, and various crimes were treated in the stories. Despite this content, their atmosphere was suffused with respectability. Their appeal, one would suspect, lay mainly to those aspiring to or having, respectability, the skilled workers, the petty bourgeoisie and the bourgeoisie. But there were also films of action, both dramatic and comic, which operated on a much more visceral level, often defiant of respectability: the bandit at the end of *The Great Train Robbery* exultantly fires his gun at the camera; Roscoe Arbuckle and Charles Chaplin in their early films are contemptuous of authority and respectability. Perhaps the rude and anarchic energy of action westerns and slapstick comedy were the fare for the wage-labourer and for children. Without carefully coded content analysis correlated with box-office returns it is chancy to interpret. Notoriously, what survives is only a percentage of what was made.

It is in this phase of their development that the movies began to take on some of the characteristics of a religion. DeTocqueville in the motto argues the necessity of religion in democracies, and misses only the point that there are non-Christian cults in America, including the cult of the nation itself. My analysis in this paper suggests that the movies became the second great secular cult after the American patriotic religion. It is complementary to the religion of the nation in that it offers fulfilment to the individual directly, rather than through subordination to the social whole, and it makes concrete some of the promise of the American Dream, the more perfect union where the more perfect and the more fulfilled human being will dwell. Both in its devotional texts (the movies themselves) and in the lives of the priests, scribes and acolytes who tend the texts in Los Angeles, it reiterates these hopes. A quality as ordinary as sex-appeal becomes a route to fame, which becomes a new kind of route to immortality. The movies' shift in social space from the periphery of society to its centre (Shils 1975, Jarvie 1982), where they integrate with the sources of power and of value in the society, is facilitated by their quasi-religious function.

The boundary of this Phase was the foundation, by the Rockefeller/RCA/

G.E. interests, of the RKO Radio company. This was the last of the five major vertically integrated companies to get in place, and it crystallised the shape of the American motion picture industry until the nineteen fifties. Only then, under consent decrees entered into with the Justice Department to settle the anti-trust suit, did the integrated companies break themselves up. Part of the fall-out from those changes was the displacement of the movies away from the centre of society and back towards its periphery.

Phase Three: Big Business, Block Booking and Homogenizing of content (1928–1956): The Apogee and Decline of the Majors

> Business enterprise ... conduces mildly to the maintencance of archaic ideals and philistine affectations, and inculcates the crasser forms of patriotic, sportsmanlike, and spendthrift aspirations. ... The literary output issued under the surveillance of the advertising office is excellent in workmanship and deficient in intelligence and substantial originality. What is encouraged and cultivated is adriotness of style and a piquant presentation of commonplaces. Harmlessness, not to say pointlessness, and an edifying, gossipy optimism are the substantial characteristics, which persist through all ephemeral mutations of style, manner, and subject-matter.
>
> Veblen 1905, p. 185

As I stressed at the beginning, the phases are not necessarily distinct in time or space; they interpenetrate one another. In search of market control companies merged and radical vertical integration was entered into, with producing/distributing merged companies setting out to acquire chains of theatres. Adolph Zukor, William Fox, Marcus Leow, Louis B. Mayer, and the Warner Brothers pressed this policy. The large, vertically integrated companies became known as the big five (MGM, Paramount, Twentieth Century Fox, RKO and Warner Brothers), those with fewer theatres or none were the little three, Columbia, Universal and United Artists. This was the pattern until the movie business was overtaken by television in the fifties and its structure was broken up by a successful government anti-trust suit (decided in 1947 and upheld by the Supreme Court in 1948).[18]

Once locked into theatre chains these companies were forced to keep up a certain level of output if they were to provide weekly changes of programme for their theaters. As the double-bill made its appearance, for the demands of weekly programming they needed a minimum of fifty-two 'A' features, 52 'B' features, and an unspecified number of short subjects, every year. No studio ever managed such an output. There was always room for some independent production, for re-issues, and for the big picture that ran for more than a week. The optimum size of studio output seems to have been something more like forty to sixty per annum with the latter figure very hard to sustain.[19]

Despite their assault on the market, the development of oligopoly, and the relative lack of competition, the movie industry did have a business cycle, which has been said to be every seven or ten years.[20] The important thing is that this cycle was not directly correlated to the general business cycle: for example, it was possible for movie attendance to be quite steady or even go up at times of economic distress (e.g. 1929—32), similarly for attendance to slip in good times (1947—8). In the prosperous consumer society of the twenties, movies did well at first, poorly later. The phrase 'the affluent society' was coined for the fifties, yet the movies went into a severe downward spiral in 1956. So much for the vaunted inelasticity of demand.

All this made the movie business a worrisome, but rewarding enterprise, and it is no wonder that lending institutions, banks and even the stock exchange were eventually to participate in its financing.[21] Ownership of theatres, with their large cash-flow and real-estate, was good security for loans needed to finance 40—60 productions a year.

All was not roses. In 1933 four of the majors (RKO, Paramount, Universal, Fox) were in bankruptcy and reorganization, and RKO never fully recovered.[22] But that the depression should eventually deepen enough to hit the rather inelastic movie demand, especially with the debt from the conversion to sound scarcely amortized, is hardly a surprise. Upon recovery (well ahead of national recovery) the industry went into its most prosperous period (1940—46).

As a middle-sized industry it gained disproportionate amounts of publicity. Louis B. Mayer was for several years the highest paid corporate executive in the United States, and it was widely bruited abroad that the movies were America's fourth largest industry — an absurd claim by any measure.[23] Still, the glamour and visibility of Hollywood, and the controversial content were meant to draw attention. However, they also drew the attention of the Temporary National Economic Committee of the NRA, which set out to study industries with a view to developing codes of conduct to aid recovery.

What was disclosed was a woeful pattern of oligopolistic practice and hence profit.[24]

The government concentrated on two features of the industry, the vertical integration, and block booking. The latter was simply the practice of selling a studio's output in blocks: you took all of the movies in the block or you got none of them. This was a way of ensuring all the product was unloaded, it in effect ensured the cross-collateralizing of movies was carried through and, like vertical integration, it undoubtedly made life hard for those trying to enter the industry.

The demands of market control and predictability also ensured that studios needed ways to homogenize product. Unless they did, there was just no possibility of being able to manufacture enough product to fill the theatres. (The same is true of television today: the 'series' is a marvellous invention for quasi-mass production.) So the feature was balanced by the second feature or 'B'. Features themselves were broken down into vehicles (a Gable, an Astaire-Rogers), to formulas (boy meets girl, boy loves girl, boy loses girl, boy gets girl), and to genres: western, slapstick, weepie, romance, musical, war, gangster, horror, science fiction, Biblical spectacle, sophisticated or screwball comedy, private eye, and so on. These forms were I think the product of economic necessity: they broke down the problem of the production schedule into smaller and more manageable parts, and they ensured that writers, directors, producers did not start from *tabula rasa* forty to sixty times a year. An unintended consequence of this routinization and bureaucratization of what the naive see as a creative artistic process (auteur theory) was the discipline and challenge it presented to film workers. Working and re-working familiar ground was a way of developing tremendous craftsmanship, density of texture, turning limitations to advantage by seeing how far they can be stretched, and therein lies the richness of American commercial movies.

The picture I am painting is fairly complex: business encourages homogenization, yet homogenization turns out to be the spur rather than the gag of creativity. Very sophisticated conventions and dramatic forms are developed that nevertheless can be marketed and advertised because they are familiar.

If we think of content, then we have to relate it to these genres, vehicles and stars, the opposite of the romantic individualized conception of creativity. These works are the products of committees, and committees sometimes have identity and style, but not always. Furthermore, each company was structured somewhat differently, so that the committees making movies within each studio would differ significantly: Fox and Warner musicals were not at all like those of MGM. The sorts of units producing socially conscious films and gangster films at Warners did not exist at RKO. For a period, Irving Thalberg was the uncredited chairman of all committees at MGM and he gave their product its final shape, etc., etc.

There is one thing about a committee: it is more of a slice of society than is any one individual. Hence in the working of committees one might see an explanation of possible ways that social and cultural preoccupations and mind-sets can get on to the screen, but I am sure this cannot be done at the level of individual films. Indeed, I am sure that content analysis of the individual film in the literary-critical style is a methodological mistake at this and any earlier period (it makes more sense in the next phase). Films are never attributable to one person but to a committee, the committee is always a creature of the social and economic system of the film business, the committee is always assembled in a curious West Coast outpost of civilization, a company town cut off from the rest of the world: Los Angeles. A film such as *Casablanca* is, as a result, utterly transparent. None of the persons who produced, none of the cast who performed, it, saw it as other than a routine chore.[25] Its Academy Awards and financial success were an unintended consequence of the sheer professional skills, the purposeful sleepwalking the studio system was able to produce. To treat it as a unique work amenable to analysis of its significance is a mistake. Its later popularity is so amenable.

It is at this point that we can gain a general view of the movies as religion, as they developed in parallel to movies as a business. The movies were a religion of salvation, both in the sermons they preached onscreen and in the models of life that were demonstrated off-screen. In a competitive and theoretically egalitarian society there is great uncertainty. What is in store for a person is not determined by their family, what their parents did, what ethnic group they come from, what relgion they belong to. It seems as though the possession of talent or of luck, or of a combination of them is what will be the determinants. But if what you are born into no longer determines what you will become then, in addition to the uncertainty, there is also the solitude: the individual is on his own. In such a society to be unknown, to be nobody, to be unnoticed and unmemorable is perhaps to be obliterated and powerless.

American movies are, from the first, remarkable in that their stories are not always about the wealthy and the literate, but also about the poor, the ordinary, working people, criminals. All the great silent comics, Chaplin, Turpin, Keaton, Arbuckle, Lloyd, Laurel and Hardly embody this. They play, naturally, the upper class part in the occasional film. But they equally or more often play the ordinary and even the downtrodden. And despite luck and talent, the stories will also tell of how individualism and determination help them realize goals they have set for themselves.

In eerie parallel there is the rise of the movie stars themselves; some are richly talented, some unpromising, some merely lucky. All however are admitted to the Los Angeles Valhalla where the only value that counts is success in the business, and continuing success at that.

One needs to bear this in mind to understand why what might seem penumbral matters such as fan magazines, gossip collumns, fan clubs, autographed photographs, product endorsements, star interviews, promotional tours and the very desire to become a movie star itself were and are so important. They are not penumbral but integral to a grasp of the position of the movies as secular religion. Movies themselves offer fantasy versions of fulfilment, while becoming a movie star offers concrete fulfilment. No wonder that so many intellectuals, baffled by these two seemingly disjoint sides of movies, have written novels in which their characters step out of life and into the movies. This is ingenious but incorrect. When Judy Garland sings 'Dear Mr. Gable' in *Broadway Melody of 1938* she sings not to the character in a film but to the 'Mr. Gable' who is a movie star.

As we shall see, in the next phase, the movie industry went into an absolute decline, and also into a relative decline in social importance. It was replaced as the central mass medium of America by television, and its star-system was much reduced. Yet the star system itself showed enough resilience to overcome this blow. Television production was relocated from New York to Hollywood and so television stars cropped up amongst and in the haunts of movie stars. And then, such is the public appetite, there was incorporation into a unified star system of other celebrities from show business (Las Vegas) and popular music. There was a vicarious element here, but I continue to stress that salvation is the main focus of interest.

Phase Four: Tansition (1956 to date) From Major Mass Medium to Minor One: Medium Size Business Semi-Monopoly, Product Differentiation (+ Formulae)

> The work of the greater modern business men . . . is . . . strategic. The dispositions which they make are business transactions, 'deals,' as they are called in the business jargon borrowed from gaming slang. These do not always involve

> coercion of the opposing interests . . .
> It may often be that the several parties
> whose business interests touch one
> another will each see his interest in
> reaching an amicable and speedy arrange-
> ment; but the interval that elapses
> between the time when a given 'deal'
> is seen to be advantageous to one of the
> parties concerned and the time when the
> terms are finally arranged is commonly
> occupied with business manoeuvres . . .
> intended to 'bring the other to terms' . . .
> Veblen 1904, pp. 32–3

After television, the consent decrees and the wrecking of Hollywood morale by HUAC, the experience of movies in American society began to change. Some perspective becomes possible on them as they shrink and change economically and culturally. Hollywood comes to seem rather a wretched and bewildered social institution, not at all good in a crisis. The challenge of television was fled from, mutual betrayal surrounded HUAC, and the sordid oligopolistic practices were exposed for the world to see in the anti-trust suits. Later, as domestic tranquility and the old puritan values were dismantled by the large and articulate new class of student-intellectuals, created by university expansion and war resistance, movies changed too.

RKO was sold off. All other companies consented to sell their theatres, so such familiar logos as lion, mountain, shield and searchlights now only designated production-distribution organizations. Many theatres across the land, especially in small towns and run-down districts, closed. The senior generation of movie businessmen died or retired or were forced out of what were by this time public companies capable of being raided and taken over. Without theatres and with a shrinking market, output fell sharply. All B production and most short production stopped. Studios shrank from 40, to one dozen, output from 4–600, to around 150–200 movies per year for theatrical release. Before the obvious but slow-to-come invention of movies for television, and the shift of television production from New York to Hollywood to take advantage of available factors of production, the big companies shrank. They sold off assets: first their backlog of old movies in their archives and libraries; then their excess real-estate, large amounts of land formerly kept for location work; then they began to rent their sound stages to independent production companies, and finally to television production companies; MGM quit distribution.

Fundamental changes took place in the market. Instead of demand seeming insatiable and predictable any more, it became more capricious and harder to predict than it was when movies were a novelty. Waterman says a stochastic relation to factors of production now prevails.[26] Without block booking and producer-ownership to theatre circuits each movie has to be marketed on its merits. This means that the apparent greater freedom of independence, no mass-production and personal control, is off-set by greater caution in launching unusual projects. Production costs rose, not just because of inflation but also because there was no cross-collateralization within a studio, no invisible overhead, and especially because each movie had to be carefully and possibly heavily advertised on its own, especially on the extremely expensive medium of television.

As the movie business shrank it receded from the centre of American popular culture to the periphery (Shils), serving less to make coherent and hence cohesive the whole culture, more to serve the needs of sub-cultures within the general culture (Gans). Yet in their content movies could now draw on and enrich a stock of myths and formulae in the popular culture forged by previous movies. So the possibly divisive effect of sub-cultural specialization was meliorated. Although in numerical and pecuniary terms movies are secondary to television and popular music, they are still a rich seam of myths, formulas and meaning. Television mines movies for ideas to use in series spin-offs far more than movies do the same to television. The movies during this period, then, become a smaller if still noisy business, a mixture at the levels of product and content of the remarkable (Robert Altman and Woody Allen) and the dreary sameness (the endless sequels to successful movies, the blockbuster, the latest version of the formula + follow-up). The genres, vehicles and formulas still dominate, but the harsh studio discipline is lacking and hence there is much economic and creative sloppiness and self-indulgence. Were one to try to sum up the movies as they are now as a social experience one could say they are a massive cult among young people, ranging from college buffs to drive-in yahoos, and an occasional outing for the rest of the population. They range from the safe and rather old-fashioned values of many outdoors and Disney films, to those that press the cutting edge of language, theme and attitude to the limits of current social tolerance. In this they are quite unlike television. In religious terms, movies are now the Greater or Higher Tradition, Television the lesser of Lower Tradition when it comes to articulating what post-affluent America is and thinks it should be. Television is family-centred at a time when the nuclear family has been exposed to unprecedented challenge from anomic individualism. Movies are the Higher Religion of PWSSI: television is parasitic on movies this way, in the same way that the television industry is parasitic in Hollywood, and television stars copy and aspire to the classic movie star style. Yet as an industry the movies are no longer a largish business geared to produce enough to dominate the culture, they dominate by other means and have become instead a moderate size business dealing in specialty products for subcultures of the popular culture.

Sub-cultures (Gans) are abstract, not concrete. There are no films for *real* sub-cultures, such as South Boston Irish; what there are are films that weld a number of such concrete sub-cultural groups into the audience for a film, such as the audience for Clint Eastwood or Charles Bronson or CB/Truckers/Good ol'Boy vehicles. We can then speak of these audiences as the sub-culture *evoked by* the film. A primary latent function of movies now is to evoke these subcultures and their sentiments. Audiences participate in movies more than they have since they were a novelty. Hit films such as *Rocky, Jaws, Exorcist, Star Wars, E.T., Raiders of the Lost Ark* constitute a solidifying collective experience for all those many who saw them. But equally, to be a fan of Clint Eastwood or to stay away from movies altogether because the violence or language give offence, is to set oneself over against some of one's fellow-citizens in interesting ways. My analysis will stop here because I believe that the present phase will not focus itself until it is over. Like history, content analysis should be a retrospective activity, and right now the movies, like American society generally, are in some sort of transition, the outcome of which is unknown.

NOTES

[1] Sociologists conventionally focus on power, wealth and belief as central to their concerns. Clearly my five overlap somewhat, e.g. sex can be a function of power or wealth or status, just as status can be a function of power or wealth. Immortality (viz. 'fame'), like its sub-class, belief, is an under-rated urge.

[2] Very few of the many executives in the movie industry are 'gatekeepers', i.e. concerned with decisions about which movies to make.

[3] See Bertrand 1941, pp. 11–13. Toronto, for example, presently accounts for 45% of Canadian receipts, and only 10% of the Canadian population.

[4] Max Gluckman, 'Gossip and Scandal' (1963) explains the group-creation and boundary-marking function of gossip in small groups and expresses a certain hesitancy about its function when about public figures and film stars.

[5] For example, Jack Warner sang, his sister played piano, his brother Sam ran the projector and Albert sold tickets at their first theatre according to his charming *My First Hundred years in Hollywood*, New York, Random House, 1964. On the other

side of the globe much the same was true of the brothers Shaw, *now* moguls in Hong Kong who model themselves and their logo on the Warners, and who were *then* owners of a Shanghai theatre which they operated themselves. See my *Window on Hong Kong: A Sociological Study of the Hong Kong Film Industry and Its Audience*, Hong Kong: Centre of Asian Studies, University of Hong Kong, 1977, Chapter 1.

[6] Jesse Lasky, *I Blow My Own Horn*, New York: Doubleday, 1957.

[7] Will Irwin, *The House that Shadows Built*, New York; Doubleday, 1928; Adolph Zukor, *The Public is Never Wrong*, New York: Putnam, 1953.

[8] Carol Easton, *The Search for Sam Goldwyn,* New York: Morrow, 1975.

[9] Bosley Crowther, *Hollywood Rajah*, New York: Holt, Rinehart, Winston, 1960; Samuel Marx, *Mayer and Thalberg: The Make-Believe Saints*, New York: Random House, 1975.

[10] Robert Sobel, *The Entrepreneurs: Explorations Within the American Business Tradition*, New York: Weybright and Talley, 1974, Chapter VII.

[11] John Drinkwater, *The Life and Adventures of Carl Laemmle*, New York: Putnam 1931.

[12] Upton Sinclair, *Upton Sinclair Presents William Fox*, Los Angeles: The Author, 1933; Glendon Allvine, *The Greatest Fox of Them all*, New York: Lyle Stuart, 1969.

[13] Discussions of *Life of An American Fireman* by Charles Musser and André Gaudreault in *Cinema Journal*, Vol. XIX, 1979, No. 1; John Fell, 'Motive, Mischief and Melnodrama: The State of Film narrative in 1907', *Film Quarterly*, Vol. 33, 1980, pp. 30–7.

[14] Zukor vigorously prosecutes the theory that the public chooses the stars (*op. cit.* note 7 above); but in the forties and fifties the studios did manufacture stars.

[15] See Robert Sklar, *Movie-Made America*, New York: Random House, 1975, Chapter 8; Garth Jowett, *Film: The Democratic Art*, Boston: Little, Brown and Co., 1976, Chapters IV, VI, IX; I. C. Jarvie, *Movies as Social Criticism*, Metuchen (N.J.): Scarecrow 1978, Chapter I.

[16] This is the thesis of Pauline Kael, 'Why are Movies so Bad? or, The Numbers', *New Yorker*, June 23, 1980, pp. 82–93.

[17] There has been little scholarly reconstruction, as yet, of the manner in which the star system was fed and promoted by the rise of fan magazines, clubs, etc.

[18] Michael Conant, *Antitrust in the Motion Picture Industry*, Berkeley and Los Angeles: University of California Press, 1960.

[19] So hard to sustain that they resorted to selling unmade and even undreamt-of films, partly to raise expectations and money, partly to galvanize themselves. See Lasky, *op. cit.*, note 6, above.

[20] Anthony Dawson, 'Patterns of Production and Employment in Hollywood', *Hollywood Quarterly*, Vol. 4, 1950, pp. 338–53.

[21] Seen by many as a sinister development, e.g. F. D. Klingender and S. Legg, *The Money Behind the Screen*, London: 1937; and their faithful disciple Henri Mercillion, *Cinéma et Monopoles*, Paris: Armand Colin, 1952. Dramatization of the fantasy, with a happy ending, is carried through in the movie *Stand In* (1937).

[22] Exhaustively documented in Richard Jewell, 'A History of RKO Radio Pictures Inc., 1928–1942', unpublished Ph.D. thesis, University of Southern California, 1978.

[23] Exploded by Mae Huettig, *Economic Control in the Motion Picture Industry*, Philadelphia: University of Pennsylvania Press, 1944.

[24] See Bertrand 1941.

[25] Howard Koch, *Casablanca: Script and Legend,* Woodstock, N.Y., Overlook Press, 1973, and *As Time Goes By,* New York: Harcourt, Brace, Jovanovich, 1979.
[26] David Waterman, 'Economic Essays on the Theatrical Motion Picture Industry', Palo Alto: Department of Economics, Stanford University, Studies in Industry Economics, No. 101, December 1978.

BIBLIOGRAPHY

Bertrand, Daniel. 1941. *The Motion Picture Industry – A Pattern of of Control.* Investigation of Concentration of Economic Power, Temporary National Economic Committee, Monograph No. 43, Washington, D.C.: U.S.G.P.O.
Cassady, Jr., Ralph. 1959. 'Monopoly in Motion Picture Production and Distribution: 1908–1915'. *Southern California Law Review* **32** 325–90.
De Tocqueville, Alexis. 1935/40. *Democracy in America.* Various editions.
Durkheim, Emile 1912. *Elementary Forms of the Religious Life.* Trs. J. W. Swain. London 1915: Allen and Unwin.
Gans, Herbert J. 1974. *Popular Culture and High Culture.* New York: Basic Books.
Gluckman, Max. 1963. 'Gossip and Scandal', *Current Anthropology* **4** 307–16.
Jarvie, I. C. 1982. 'The Social Experience of Movies', in S. Thomas (ed.), *Film/Culture.* Metuchen, N. J.: Scarecrow, pp. 247–68.
Shils, Edward. 1975. *Center and Periphery.* Chicago: University of Chicago Press.
Thomas, Sari. 1977. *'The Relationship Between Daytime Serials and their Viewers'.* Ph.D. dissertation, University of Pennsylvania, unpublished.
Veblen, Thorstein. 1904. *The Theory of Business Enterprise.* New York: Scribner's.

CHAPTER 25

METHODOLOGICAL AND CONCEPTUAL PROBLEMS IN THE STUDY OF PORNOGRAPHY AND VIOLENCE [1]

1. PREFACE

This paper has grown out of a long-standing interest in motion pictures and their social effects (Jarvie 1970, 1977, 1978). The controversy over them which began in the early years of this century continues to this day. A literature survey carried out for my (1970) made it apparent that few of the controverters based their assertions on research, and that much of the research was methodologically flawed, hence unable to support any conclusions. Some of the research was disinterested; some clearly sought evidence to justify alarm. By and large this latter research never remotely approached its aim, which was to dent the arguments for there being no prior restraints on free speech. The current state of play will emerge in this paper.

In the early nineteen seventies a remarkable new element entered the situation. Hard core pornographic films, formerly an illicit and black market item, began to be publicly shown and sold in many parts of the United States (and later in France, Japan, etc.). The path had been blazed in Scandiavia in the nineteen sixties, but the American change was on a different scale: massive investment was soon made in theatres, distribution networks and the production values of the films themselves. Full-length pornographic feature films in colour were screened in regular theatres. Within a very short time such films were widely reviewed and discussed, and an entire specialized press grew up alongside them. My own attitude was to welcome and take advantage of this alleviation of part of the condition of sexual repression. Rather naïvely I predicted that it would only be a matter of time before my home country of Canada would follow suit, and then possibly other European countries. How mistaken I was.

Far from being generally hailed as a victory for freedom of speech and of choice, this newly available good quality pornography faced a swelling chorus singing the song of social degeneracy and, specifically, suggesting pornography was part of a male plot to dominate and exploit women. Canada thus remains in this as in other ways sexually repressed. My decision to write on the subject was made when Canada's National Film Board (NFB) released their contribution to the debate, a documentary film entitled *Not a Love*

Story – A Film About Pornography. A stir was caused when it was not passed for public showing by Ontario's Board of Censors. So a Canadian film singing a song of woe about pornography was itself found pornographic and not permitted normal commercial showing in Canada's most populous Province. The Board did allow it to be shown in special educational contexts. In the United States *Not a Love Story* was shown commercially and became the most profitable film the NFB ever produced. This was a nice irony: absence of prior restraint in the United States permitted both pornography and a film attacking pornography to be freely accessible, while the most populous Province in the country where the film was made, consistent with its policy of prior restraint, severely restricted its showing because it showed too much pornography of a kind not legally available in Canada. There is something absurd in all censorship, and especially when it is so strict that it does not permit a film that in effect endorses it.[2]

What could a methodologist offer to the debates over this whole issue? Perhaps two things: one, help in sorting out which points at issue were subject to decision by research; second a review of that research to seek out its strengths and weaknesses and hence, where relevant, its reliability. My procedure was as follows. I began with *Not a Love Story*, viewing it closely, studying a transcription, collecting articles about it, and discovering who the various experts in it were, and reading their writings. Many belong to a group in the feminist movement who have organised campaigns against pornography, and so I have subjected their arguments, philosophical as well as empirical, to close scrutiny. On field trips to the United States (1972, 1975, 1979–1984) I visited theatres showing X films and took careful notes on their contents, the make-up and behaviour of the audience. Finally, I discovered a great deal of secondary literature, in the press, in the learned journals of social and sexual studies, and in the specialised fan press that has grown up around pornographic films and videos. While the research was underway the focus of the industry shifted from public showing of pornography in theatres to making those films available on video-casette for home viewing. Even this development is not permitted in Canada.

2. *THE FILM* NOT A LOVE STORY – A FILM ABOUT PORNOGRAPHY (*NALS*)

This documentary film adopts the personal approach. Its director, Bonnie Sherr Klein, is the narrator. She is, she tells us, the mother of a school age daughter who was surrounded at the candy store by pornography; what did the little girl make of it? Klein also suggests, over shots of a woman doing bumps and grinds, that this woman "could be me". The form of the film is a quest into the underworld, the dark side of life, behind the closed doors, in search of understanding. Klein encounters an outspoken striptease artiste, Linda Lee Tracy, who concludes her act with the cry, "God bless the working woman". They team up for the rest of the film, discussing their reactions with each other. Proceeding by way of the wide-eyed interview, they take us to peep-show arcades, coin-in-the-slot and other live shows, demonstration marches against pornogrpahy by women's groups, to meet actors and actresses in pornography, a magazine publisher, a woman photographer in her studio, miscellaneous feminists, all of who give us their interpretation of pornography, a male consciousness raising group and all of this intercut with brief glimpses of pornographic material, moving and still.

Much, if not all of the material which is excerpted or talked about in the film is material not legally available in Canada. Hence Klein's decision to explore into it in the United States remains puzzling, as is her failure to alert the feminist spokeswomen to this fact about Canada. There is a complex logic here, which it took me some time to disentangle. A clue came during the late summer and autumn of 1984 when several Canadian policeman were killed in the line of duty, at least one by a young man modelling himself on a deranged veteran in a violent film starring Sylvester Stallone. The grieving police chiefs took the occasion to denounce violent films and TV programmes which they saw as causes of the deaths of their officers. That Canada has much more stringent censorship of sexual and violent material than the U.S.A. deterred them not at all. If stringent censorship does not stop the rot, the logic seemed to be, the solution is to make it more stringent still. The interest of the police in such matters is clearly less than disinterested. Law enforcement is a dangerous and time-consuming job, involving much that is repulsive and much that is frustrating (Ericson 1982). Hence laws against sin, where action is easy to take, there is no danger, and no failure, are very attractive to the police because they give them the feeling they are really getting something accomplished and they give the public the feeling that the police are fighting the forces of sin, which are the forces that produce crime.

Some Canadian vice is home grown, for example, prostitution and homosexuality. Most pornography, however, originates in the United States. It is a constant source of self-congratulation for Canadian mayors and police chiefs that they preside over cities with a fraction of the crime rates of comparably-sized American cities. With its vigorous criminal underworld and general business rapacity, America is taken to be engaged in ceaseless attempts to extend its activities to Canada. America is both a moral and social object lesson; and a threat. Hence Canadians can, as Ms. Klein does, justify examining closely the seedier sides of America whilst reassuring themselves that their interest is uplifting, not prurient. Much of the imagery of the film plays on the light/dark, dirty/clean polarities. The feminist spokes-women are for the most part scrubbed-looking, and sometimes backlit by sunshine. The pornographic participants and dealers are seen in dimly-lit night scenes, or under red lights and behind closed doors. The final scene of Linda finds her on a beach in a white bathing suit writing poetry, chastened, cleansed, even redeemed by her journey through sleaze.

The presentation of men and women is similarly polarised. The men are often worried or guilty-looking, sometimes overtly wimpish by con-trast to the articulate and animated women. And one absence is impossible to overlook. Klein's daughter presumably has a father, but Klein never ventures the possibility that sexuality in general and pornography in par-ticular might be contextualised for her with the cooperation of the male parent.

Many commentators took it that the film was an attack on pornography as degradation of women and possible incitement to violence towards them and so was advocating censorship. Ms. Klein vehemently denied in inter-views that the film was suggesting censorship, saying rather that it presented material for people to make up their own minds. Clearly the Ontario Board of Censors thought it gave people rather too much opportunity to make up their own minds to permit its commercial showing. Despite the negative context in which the film presented pornography, these censors suspected that Ontario's starving pornography audience would go to the film for the wrong reasons. While I am quite unsure what the wrong reasons are, and still less clear what the right reasons would be, or what would make either set of reasons 'wrong' or 'right', my research at this point turned away from the film and towards its content. The film aroused much controversy, being hailed by feminist journalists in the mass media, and attacked by feminist writers for the small magazines. The leading Canadian social scientist in the field, Thelma McCormack, is thanked in the credits, was consulted, but seeks to disassociate herself from its attitudes:

in the finished film, there was no intelligent discussion of [social theories of pornog-raphy] at all. They simply used shock for shock value ... I find that using American content distances the whole problem for Canadians, and turns the production into voyeurism (Kruk 1982).

These words were not, however, my inspiration, for my own research had already begun. We shall return to McCormack's ideas in Section 17.

Like the film's makers, Canadians who wish legally to see hardcore pornographic films and shows must cross the border. Indeed, most of NALS was shot in New York, which is extreme even by American standards. My own research was not done in New York but in Los Angeles and Miami. Although NALS has on-screen interviews with performers and purveyors of pornography it has none with consumers — unless one counts the confession group of males excoriating themselves. This is a serious methodological defect both in the film and in most of the scholarly literature. Almost no-one is prepared to acknowledge that they can enjoy pornography; they seek instead to speculate about what makes for the demand.

One word above all sums up the feeling of NALS: pornography is *frightening*. Several times in the film disturbing images are lingered on: a woman disappearing into a meat grinder; a child in a pornographic film; a woman bound and apparently being hurt. Sometimes the soundtrack carries a heartbeat, one of the surest ways to create panic in a film audience. Given that the images frighten some women it is natural that in speculating about who consumes this material monsters are conjured up: men who attack, rape, mutilate, possibly even murder women. Evidence is to hand: some social scientists have long claimed that there is a connection between crime and pornoraphy, a connection disclosed in the numbers of criminals convicted of attacking women who possessed large quantities of pornography.

We shall be disentangling the threads of all this somewhat later, but it is only honest to declare my hand now. The first is that NALS blurs the distinction between sexuality and violence: all the images that are frightening or disturbing are violent, or hint at coercion (the child). If the subject is pornography — 'A Film about Pornography' was the subtitle of NALS — then the question is why concentrate on violent images; why not also show some non-violent but graphic depictions of sex? As we shall see the film here takes over a blurring that its feminist mentors make. Secondly, speculating about what this pornography is for is no substitute for finding out. Thirdly, there are many people who possess a great deal of pornography and evince a great deal of interest in it who have no connection to criminal attacks on women at all (e.g., some social scientists; some censors; some policemen). Clearly, then, pornography is not a sufficient explanation of violent attitudes to women, and the attempt so to link it is a classical case of the fallacy of affirming the consequent.

3. SOME GENERAL CAVEATS

Invalid argument helps nobody's case. Not all pornography is the same – this is as true of pornography as it is of books, films or people. Hence some sort of controlled statistical sampling is a minimum requirement if generalisations or interpretations are to be taken seriously. Similarly there is the danger of *parti pris*: if some feminists are against pornography and declare its very presence offends them those of us sympathetic to the feminist cause may want to give their views credence. We must guard against *parti pris*.

And then there is the problem of textual interpretation: hermeneutics. All too often the social effects of the mass media are approached in the following fashion. Since they involve narratives in a recognisably human world, the social critic reduces them to a plot summary, adduces from that summary certain themes and then argues that people who watch the mass media copy what they see and directly absorb the messages or themes. So if *Birth of a Nation* portrays mulattoes as treacherous, negroes as childish, and the Ku Klux Klan as heroes its viewers are thought likely to imitate the anti-mulatto, anti-negro and pro-KKK behaviour by imitation or modelling; to soak up the attitudes directly.

There is a particular proneness to foist this kind of interretation on the mass media, even or especially by literary intellectuals who would never dream of reasoning so crudely about literature. Why should the one text be treated as complex and subtle in its meanings and effects and the other obvious? A text in question would be NALS itself, anti-pornography, yet seen as dangerously pornographic by Ontario's censors. It evades the question of censorship yet is widely taken as a plea for (more) censorship. Ostensibly a documentary film with serious informative intent, it operates as a narrative: a descent into the underworld by the director madonna-figure to redeem the stripper-whore. It informs us by titillating us. Some of these double messages arise because of poor translation of intentions into execution; but some are simply due to a film being a complex text, as texts go; difficult to interpret and not having a coherent conception of its intended audience.

Sex itself is a notoriously tricky subject on which to write. Most of us would like to appear expert and confident. It is fanciful to imagine that we are. Our very desire to appear knowledgeable and confident about sex compensates for the fact that usually we are neither. Taking the plunge into discussion of pornography, which is a subfield of sex, would be easier if the fancy of knowledge and confidence was warranted. Far from it. The subject of sex is a deep and murky ocean in which the ships of many people's knowledge and confidence have sunk. The latest vessels to flounder were launched under the flag of the women's liberation movement. They look at first knowledgeable and confident sailors, but they navigate with the help of anger, passion and indignation. Unfortunately, these powerful sentiments seem to have swept overboard careful writing, logical argument and respect for common sense. To navigate without them is impossible, to stay afloat is difficult.

Such expertise as I have is in argument; on sex I make no claim to knowledge and certainly not to confidence. Purely by scrutiny of argument I think it can be shown that pornography is poorly misunderstood by NALS and by the American feminist writers on which it bases itself. Although I shall offer tentative fragments of a defence of pornography, this merely shows my hand, it does not of itself serve as rebuttal. Scrutiny of arguments will, I hope, make it clear that, if pornography is to be criticised, neither the grounds chosen nor the argumentative level achieved will do. These ships are on the rocks.

A final caveat: the relations of pornography, feminism and gender are not simple. Males and females have declared all four possible combinations (Table I). Hence to support feminism it is not necessary to oppose pornography.

TABLE I

		FEMINISM	
		For	Against
PORNOGRAPHY	For	Gloria Leonard[3] Molly Haskell[5]	Linda Lovelace (*Inside*)[4]
		A. Sarris H. Hefner	Al Goldstein[6] M. de Sade
	Against	Gloria Steinem L. Lovelace (*Ordeal*)[4]	Phyllis Schlaffly Anita Bryant
		R. Gwyn J. S. Mill	J. Falwell R. Reagan

4. NALS AND THE AMERICAN SCENE

With the single exception of Margaret Attwood, a Canadian writer, all the experts interviewed in NALS are American: Susan Griffin, Kate Millett,

Robin Morgan, Kathleen Barry, and Ed Donnerstein. Attwood's token appearance simply has her read in a flat monotone, a very poor "poem". All the intellectual content of the film comes from the Americans. Fair enough, at least they have in their country direct experience of what they are talking about and so opportunity for analysis. However, in the film they offer to instruct us, rather than engage in argument. Hence I turned to their writings, beginning with the anthology *Take Back the Night* (Lederer 1980) and following through on the cross references in that to Barry (1979), Carter (1978), Dworkin (1981), Griffin (1981) and Faust (1981). To begin with, what was the setting in America?

For the last decade the anti-pornography sections of America's blue laws have been weakened, Canada's have not. A principal manifestation of this has been the proliferation in major U.S. cities of cinemas showing only hard-core pornographic films and of Canadians crossing the border to see them. And in the last half dozen years hundreds of these films and earlier 'loops' have become available on video-cassette which have to be smuggled into Canada. Indeed, pornography makes up more than one half of the prerecorded video-cassette market in the U.S. Concomitantly, a subindustry of fan magazines has proliferated (*Cinema X, Velvet, Adam Film World, Starlet, Porn Stars, Studflix, Video X*) to promote pornographic films and tapes. Doctored versions of these magazines are on sale in Canada. A star system has emerged, featuring some very good looking men and woman.[8]

Predictably, there are groups in the society who oppose these developments, along with all other manifestations of the so-called 'sexual revolution'. Surprisingly, some of it comes from the otherwise radical women's liberation movement. There is now a substantial body of feminist writing about pornography, most, but not all, of it against. All too little of this writing deals with films and video cassettes, all too much with picture magazines and prose. Andrea Dworkin, for example, describes in some detail (PMPW) a handful of picture spreads and fiction to support an analysis of some 224 pages that scarcely mentions movies. The many contributors to *Take Back the Night* (TBTN) cite few examples at all, and almost no movies, although quite a few of their Women Against Violence in Pornography and the Media street demos have focused on movies.

Arguing from anecdotage or from unspecified pornography in general rather than carefully selected and representative examples implies that all pornography is the same. Needless to say, this is as untrue of pornographic films as it is of almost any human endeavour. Pornographic films differ in content (e.g. hetero-and homosexual), in mode (e.g. sex loops versus feature films), in popularity (viz, box office returns and cassette sales) and in quality. And, like sexual behaviour in general, what is depicted ranges from normal, though deviant, to grotesque and psychopathic. No surprises so far, I imagine. But what would we make of someone who argued that because some human behaviour was grotesque and psychopathic, it followed that all human behaviour, being human, was to be condemned? We would see the fallacy: human behaviour covers a range; there is no reason to condemn the range in order to condemn the extremes. Pornography is only the latest victim. Popular entertainment has often been the victim of the hidden premiss that it is undifferentiated. Time was when intellectuals used to think all westerns or musicals were the same, even that all Hollywood movies were the same. One occasionally still hears this said about television.[9] Now it is the turn of pornography to be rescued from such unthinking general dismissal. The genre ranges widely along many parameters, including sexual practices and film making skills.

Thus, if there is on the pornography market some deviant material that some find atrocious it does not follow, though it may be true, that the genre is identical with that material and hence that the genre is atrocious. Time and again however, this pattern of argument is found in the feminist writing under discussion: the author describes some violent or sadistic pornography, offers interpretation of it, then slides imperceptibly towards indictment of the entire genre. Indeed pornography comes to be *identified* with violent pornography:

pornography is in itself a sadistic act . . . the pornographer is not sane (PAS, pp. 111, 125).

Such a slide only makes sense if it is assumed that pornography is destabilising material whose consumers, like drug addicts, slip in deeper all the time. Hence I shall call this The Slippery Slope Argument, the idea that from *Playboy* to rape and murder there is a continuous downward path.

5. THE CONTENT OF PORNOGRAPHY

Like Justice Potter Stewart (cited in TBTN, p. 40) most of us allow as how we know pornography when we see it. If we permit this ostension to be grafted onto The Argument from the Slippery Slope a powerful rhetorical weapon is created. It permits pressure groups to label as 'soft porn' illustrations in elementary school readers that show boys and girls in tight trousers or shorts or riding on 'phallic bicycle seats' (*Los Angeles Times*, Aug. 4, 1982, Part I, p. 27). Are the feminists under discussion more scrupulous?

Susan Brownmiller: Pornography is the undiluted essence of antifemale propaganda (TBTN, p. 32).

Helen Longino: verbal or pictorial explicit representations of sexual behavior that . . . have as a distinguishing characteristic the degrading and demeaning portrayal of the role and status of the human female . . . as a mere sexual object to be exploited and manipulated sexually (TBTN, p. 42, see also Ann Jones at p. 183, and Diana E. H. Russell at p. 218).

Charlotte Burch: symbolic violence against women . . . part of an international slave traffic in women that operates as a multinational corporation (TBTN, p. 93).

Judith Bat-Ada: pornography is a hate campaign (TBTN, p. 132).

Ann Jones: pornography is a genre depicting the physical exploitation, humiliation, wounding and skilling of women (TBTN, p. 179).

Robin Yeamans: any use of the media which equates sex and violence (TBTN, p. 248).

Andrea Dworkin: pornography means the graphic depiction of women as vile whores (PMPW, p. 200).

Kathleen Barry: pornography is a practice of cultural sadism as well as a means of diffusing it (FSS, p. 206).

Consider these definitions in light of the film that is the emblematic beginning of the present phase of controversy over hard-core pornography: *Deep Throat*. Is there any violence in the film? Not that I can discover. Is the film anti-female propaganda? It all depends upon the way you look at it. A natural construal is that it is about female liberation. The heroine and her friend are sexually active unmarried women and 'Linda' is looking for not just causal pleasure but true bliss. The conceit of the film is that the secret of the bliss for her is an anatomical quirk (infra). This premiss is absurd, of course, but then the film *is* a comedy. An obvious reading of the film is that women can get and want as much pleasure from the physical act of sex as men, and that most people, men and women, have assorted sexual quirks and hang-ups.

An objection could be that Linda's quirk is not just any old comedy premiss, but one which pleases men and which humiliates women, hence is part of sexist male fantasy (PAS, p. 61, fn.). How then are we to interpret the Dagwood syndrome of comedy in which men are humiliated by women and come back for more? The objector may protest that this is irrelevant since the Dagwood structure does not mirror sexist power relations whereas Linda's quirk does. If we stick consistently to this line of defence, then we must conclude that the trouble with pornography is sexist society and its sexism, not pornography, whatever that is. How sexist is Linda's saga?

This question is not incidental. *Deep Throat* is a central case in discussions of pornography. That a film of this overt content was the single biggest box office winner in the short history of the pornographic film [10] might be thought to tell us something of the genre, of the audience, of its gratifications and of evolving attitudes towards sex. It appeared in 1972 and was a major event in the campaign to bring sexual issues out of the closet and propagate the idea that sex is not shameful, not sinful, not for marrieds only, not for men to take and women to give, not something to be frightened of, but rather a source of mutual pleasure to willing participants. Sad to report, then, that none of the material under discussion offers alternative feminist readings of *Deep Throat* to reveal its sexism that I could report and discuss (save for that mentioned in note 58 below).

Instead, the feminist writers under discussion here take as their standard example the Marquis de Sade.[11] I have yet to meet anyone who enjoyed, or even managed to read right through, still less 'got off on' or recommended de Sade — as pornography or anything else. In the circles that I travel he is taken to belong to a certain genre of philosophy of life, degrees away from, but all of a piece with, such mortifiers of the flesh as St. Paul, St. Augustine, Luther, Kierkegaard, Nietzsche, even Sartre; to be studied, if at all, only to extract the bizarre nihilism and destructiveness of his ideas. In these circles Sade is not the archetypal pornographic author, his fictions are not sexually stimulating. Why do the feminist writers under discussion bother with him, then? Perhaps because he too is a writer and so is an antiseptic way for those trained in literary study to write about pornography. Without The Slippery Slope Argument his works are no guide to the population of pornography. More characteristic samples are feature films and video-cassettes and it is the general shape and position of that industry and its audience that will teach us most about pornography. Some of the feminists have challenging ideas of which X-rated films are a more severe test than is Sade.

6. THE BOOKS BEHIND NALS

Although a closely connected (and cross-referenced) body of literature, each of the six books takes a different tack. The earliest published was Angela Carter's *The Sadeian Woman and The Ideology of Pornography* (SWIP) (Described by Andrea Dworkin as 'pseudo-feminist' (PMPW, 84): in every movement there are none so pure as the purest of the pure).

Carter's volume is a monograph, a continuous piece of writing on a single topic: de Sade. After a polemical introduction that shows she is unafraid of rude words, each chapter summarises and interprets a major work: *Justine, Juliette* and *Philosophy in the Boudoir*. The purpose seems to be to show that de Sade was ahead of his time in acknowledging female sexuality and connecting sexual revolution to social revolution; ahead, but not far enough ahead. Great play is made with his evasion of the issue of taking pleasure in pain: Eugénie's atrocious rape of her mother in *Philosophy in the Boudoir* is about to bring her mother to climax when she faints:

Were Madame de Mistval to have come, then all the dykes would be breached at once and chaos and universal night instantly descend: pleasure would have asserted itself triumphantly over pain and the necessity for the existence of repression as a sexual stimulant would have ceased to exist. There would arise the possibility of a world in which the concept of taboo is meaningless and pornography itself would cease to exist. Sade, the prisoner who created freedom in the model of his prison, would have put himself out of business; he is as much afraid of freedom as the next man. So he makes her faint . . .

He makes her faint because he can only conceive of freedom as existing in opposition, freedom as defined by tyranny . . .

The Sadeian woman, then, subverts only her own socially conditioned role in the world of god, the king, and the law. She does not subvert her society, except incidentally, as a storm trooper of the individual consciousness. She remains in the area of privilege created by her class, just as Sade remains in the philosophic framework of his time (TSW, pp. 131–3).

Compared to the American feminists under discussion Carter, who is a British novelist, writes with lucidity and control. She performs a valuable service in summarising the tedious, repetitious and repellant works of de Sade thus freeing us from the necessity. Like much production of the literati, however, it is hard to say just what problem is posed, just what thesis maintained.

The thesis of Barry's book (FSS) is that women were not born free and yet it is a scandal that they are everywhere in chains. From white slave traffic in the Near East, to mistrust of Patricia's Hearst's account of her enslavement by the men of the SLA, the phenomenon is pervasive. Although a world-wide conspiracy of men is hinted at, and male notions of intimacy are attacked, Barry makes a plea only for emancipation: for the freedom to choose without coercion. It is not difficult to imagine her more 'Marxist' sisters generalising the dilemma and arguing that, since the social system is inherently coercive it is hardly likely that it will forego oppressing any of its classes, hence it has to be overthrown.

Believing the experience of pornography to be different from the experience of art, Barry stresses the social isolation of the consumer of pornography,
hence the free play of fantasy and reality, thereby 'reducing the need for'
sex partners 'to relate to each other' (p. 213). Although 'usually men do not
leave pornographic stores or theatres to act out what they have just seen'
(p. 211), if they let their fantasies enter their interactions then 'taken to its
fullest form it becomes the literal acting out of private fantasy on to another
through force' (p. 214), i.e., cultural sadism. The film *Swept Away* set off
a trend for men and women to enjoy SM. It was made by a woman and
displeases many feminists.

Take Back the Night (TBTN) is an anthology of pieces by feminists of
diverse views, anchored around writings produced under the auspices of
Women Against Violence in pornography and Media. Like any work by many
hands this anthology is hard to summarise. There is a strong network of
inernal cross-reference, but also serious disagreements and contradictions
between authors. Take only the issue of censorship. the editor, Laura Lederer,
writes:

We want to see banned all pornography which portrays rape, torture, murder, and
bondage for erotic stimulus and pleasure. (TBTN, p. 29).

Robin Yeamans is narrower, wanting suppressed

any use of the media which equates sex and violence. This . . . would not cover material
which is simply degrading to women. (TBTN, p. 248)

Wendy Kaminer, a lawyer, by contrast, insists:

Feminists need not and should not advocate censorship. (TBTN, p. 241).

What to make of the editing? By some standards it is atrocious. The
pieces vary widely in quality of thought and writing, they contradict one
another and repeat the same points time and again. In an afterword, however,
Adrienne Rich declares the book to be a 'microcosm of the American feminist
movement as it standards at the beginning of the 1980s' (TBTN, p. 313).
To accomplish this was no mean fact of editing and what blame there is
shifts from the editor to the movement itself.

Both Andrea Dworkin and Susan Griffin appear in TBTN, and they
have also written interpretative monographs about the cultural meaning of
pornography. Dworkin's *Pornography Men Possessing Women* (PNMPW)
sees pornography as a manifestation of the male desire to subjugate women.

Griffin's *Pornography and Silence* (PAS) sees it rather as a projected denial of the very existence of any tender and thus vulnerable aspect to masculinity.

Dworkin's writing is strident and also freely indulges coarse language, and a less than constrained anger against all men, as witness her conclusion:

We will know that we are free when the pornography no longer exists. As long as it does exist, we must understand that we are the women in it: used by the same power, subject to the same valuation, as the vile whores who beg for more.

The boys are betting on our compliance, our ignorance, our fear. We have always refused to face it. The boys are betting that we cannot face the horror of their sexual system and survive. The boys are betting that their depictions of us as whores will beat us down and stop our hearts. The boys are betting that their penises and fists and knives and fucks and rapes will turn us into what they say we are — the compliant women of sex, the voracious cunts of pornography, the masochistic sluts who resist because they really want more. The boys are betting. The boys are wrong. (PMPW, p. 224).

Griffin also gets excited, but the tone is different:

And thus the pornographic hero rejects himself. He excludes from his conscious idea of himself that part of his soul which pornography calls 'feminine'. But this is precisely what society in reality does. Culture excludes women. Yet if culture has successfully rejected the feminine, then, we must ask, why must pornography continue to humiliate and punish the feminine? Why is such a prodigious effort, such a massive amount of paper and print and celluloid, dedicated to this task, when the feminine has already been made silent?

Because . . . this self cannot die. (PAS, p. 66).

Faust's book is a contrast to the others. Although published at about the same time, it is a critique, by an Australian feminist, of the sentiments that were rising within the movement and which were to culminate in the other books. Faust asserts that both women's and men's sexuality varies along a range from, as it were, tough to tender. In this she is consonant with Griffin. She admits her own attitudes were towards the male end of the female scale. Because of this, and if it is true that Australian men are more unabashedly male chauvinist than their brothers elsewhere in the world, she has a basis for the excellent grasp of the problem she displays. She castigates here sisters:

Feminists in both the radical and the reformist wings of the movement accept the blanket statement: 'Porn is not about sex, it is about male power over women.' By adopting such a lazy and shallow approach, feminists lose a crucial insight on female sexuality and sexual politics (WSP, p. 10).

The alternative is to use pornography and its differing effects on men and women as an entry point to trying to understand what separates the sexes and what brings them together. This is done with sensitivity and verve and a thorough review of the research literature. Unlike Dworkin, who attacks Kinsey, Faust argues he had wise things to say we still have not learned. Her final chapter sets out reasons why there will always be tension in the relations between men and women.

Let us come back to *Not a Love Story* . . . it is a documentary about pornography and the porn industry, and a feminist critique of both. The film, like the feminists it draws upon, blurs any boundary between cheesecake, *Hustler*, soft and hard core and also overlooks the national boundary between Canada and New York's Forty Second St. This generous sweep makes sense only if we introduce The Slippery Slope and reason that such soft porn as Canada has is as alarming as what is traded on Forty Second Street. But if we do not grant use of The Slippery Slope what relevance has the American material to Canada? A gesture of solidarity with the suffering American sisters? A hint that there but for the grace of God go we?[12] Either would suffice, but Dworkin's words above suggest a third line of thought is at work: the existence of pornography anywhere hurts and humiliates *all* women. Gloria Steinem argues like this:

> our bodies have too often been the objects of pornography and the women-hating, violent practice that it preaches. Consider also our spirits that break a little each time we see ourselves in chains or full labial display for the conquering male viewer. (TBTN, p. 39).[13]

Although she writes 'our' we are to understand she is talking about someone else; to the best of my knowledge there are no such pictures of Gloria Steinem. Why do photographs of others break her spirit? Perhaps because she is a woman and empathises with womankind? How valid is this reasoning? Apply it to men. A man contemplates pictures of men erect and exposed or chained and degraded (by women or other men), does it break his spirit a little, make him feel 'conquered' by the viewer? Not so far as I can introspect. In addition to the fact that pornographic photographs are usually done for money and may to a hard-working prostitute look like easy money at that,[14] Steinem fails to empathise with the exhibitionist streak in some of her sisters and brothers. Striking evidence of this is the number of Polaroids published in soft-core and 'swingers' magazines at the ladies' and gentlemen's own behest.[15] Steinem's prose specialises in this kind of argumentative slide, a form of the pathetic fallacy, namely, if I share some characteristics with you, then what is done to you is done to me:

Our bodies had borne the health burden of endless births and poor abortions. (TBTN, p. 39)

Since men also share many characteristics with women it could with equal plausibility be argued that their bodies had suffered from endless births and poor abortions. This logical point makes us uneasy; after all, births can happen to women but not to men.[16] So whether or not 'endless births and poor abortions' haven't happened to Steinem, they *could* have; they could not have happened to man. It all looks so simple, yet it works as an argument only if the institution of the *couvade* is ignored. Does the argument go through in other cases? Does membership in a group privilege one in relation to the suffering of that group, or is such a claim groupisme?

Better to appreciate the unsoundness of Steinem's argument, onsider the example of dwarfs. Who empathises better with the suffering of dwarfs, other dwarfs or other sufferers and potential sufferers? Introduce gender into the equation: who empathises with the poor abortion of a female dwarf, another woman of normal height such as Gloria Steinem, or a male dwarf? Clearly, the specific answer is a function of context: no general answer is possible. When the context is consideration of the status of women, on the face of it it is another woman who empathises best; when the context is the problems of being dwarfs, on the face of it other dwarfs empathise best.[16] Steinem's argument is sound, then, only when and because the context is sexism and not pornography.

7. EROTIC/PORNOGRAPHIC

As their definitions indicate, the feminist authors discussed here differ about the boundaries, the character and the social meaning of pornography. Laura Lederer and her WAVPM followers call pornographic *Playboy, Vogue* advertisements and certain record album covers. As Humpty Dumpty made clear to Alice, we are all free to use words as we see fit.[17] For certain purposes *Playboy* and *Deep Throat* may be in the same category —images of women objected to by some women and men. But on the matter at issue, pornography, the two are on different sides of the hard-core fence. The difference may be a matter of degree that becomes a difference of kind. Without denying borderline cases and problems of specification, this fence still is an important one to keep in mind. A particular reason here is that this fence coincides with the border fence between Canada and the USA: hard-core is banned on one side, legally available on the other. In general terms the fence is easy to point to: hard core is pictorial matter which shows males fully erect, and/or persons in sexual contact with others, male or female. Soft core, the rest, is thus a residual category.

All the works under discussion make a distinction between the erotic and the pornographic, which they equate with the difference, roughly, between the light and the dark. Yet in TBTN only three contributors try to define the erotic. Gloria Steinem: the erotic is 'mutually pleasurable, sexual expression between people who have enough power to be there by positive choice' (TBTN, p. 37). Helen Longino emphasises 'mutual respect' (TBTN, p. 42). Interestingly, both these definitions would seem to exclude from the category of the erotic all pornography except a few Polaroids and home movies notarished as to the qualities desired. Diana E. H. Russell: '*Erotica* differs from pornography *by virtue of its not degrading or demeaning women, men, or children*. Like pornography, erotica is often intended to turn people on sexually. And like pornography, erotica may also be sexually explicit — though it tends to be more subtle and/or artistic' (TBTN, pp. 218–9). Reviewing NALS B. Ruby Rich (1982) comments: 'Fixing the dividing line is rather like redlining a neighborhood: the "Bad" neighborhood is always the place where someone *else* lives. Porn is the same. If I like it, it's erotic; if you like it, it's pornographic.' (I have heard Julia Lesage make the same point).

Neither pornography nor erotica, then, is a sub-class of the other: there is non-pornographic erotica, and non-erotic pornography. But there is also an intersection which is where the issue must be joined. Steinem wants mutual pleasure and equal power, Russell wants no degradation. Most male homosexual pornography fails to degrade (or show) women and children, though some does degrade men. Anyway, to satisfy Steinem's requirements, would we have to decide whether mutual pleasure and equal power were displayed in films or pictures? How?

Consider the tussle between Clarence Darrow and William Jennings Bryan in *Inherit the Wind*. The balance of power and/or mutual respect between them is not a function of the individuals Spencer Tracy and Frederic March; nor does it lie in the acting ability and performances of these two star actors; nor in their comparative status in the star system; nor in the direction they receive. It lies solely in the total conception of the drama. The artistic conception of some pornography is to humiliate women, definitely not to show balance of power and/or mutual respect. Some of this is even made by women, as we have seen (n. 15). William Jennings Bryan and his fundamentalist followers are humiliated in the movie; whether the fundamentalist viewer is humiliated or not through empathy depends on the position of fundamentalism in society's pecking order. No child is humiliated when Oliver is humiliated in *Oliver Twist*; no black is degraded when the hero of *Black Like Me* is degraded; no Jew or Presbyterian is humiliated when seeing *Chariots of Fire*. If women are always humiliated when the pornographic scenario calls for their sisters to be humiliated, then the issue is once more of the social context: it is sexism which makes her condemn pornography.

A different thought on equal power and consent might be that players in pornographic films not only act, they actually have sex. This violates the assumptions of their acting in much the same way as if an actress were actually to give birth for a scene, or an actor was actually to die in a death scene. We would be intruding on and appropriating for purposes of viewing private, intimate and important human events. The initial plausibility of such thinking cannot survive two counter arguments. (1) Exposure of their sexuality is continuous with all the other exposures actors accept. Birth and death are hard to arrange (although the reality of their own dying was used in their last films by such as Edward G. Robinson (*Soylent Green*), John Wayne (*The Shootist*), Henry Fonda (*On Golden Pond*) and Ingrid Bergman (*Golda*). Where each actor sets the limits of emotional and physical exposure has to do with their approach. (2) We know that much of the sex seen on the screen is constituted by the editor, not enacted by the players. It would take too much space to do a detailed analysis, but it is clear that shot and reverse shot, master shot and close shot, all require actors, sets, lights and cameras to be repositioned and adjusted even though, when cut together, the resulting celluloid appears to depict a continuous encounter. On-screen sex is not as real as it seems but largely an artifact of filmcraft. We shall advert to the problem of the reality of on-screen sex acts again below in section 14. So whether and in what sense the actors "have sex" is moot.

It is also said that pornography 'objectifies' women while erotica does not. Full discussion of this distinction is better postponed until we discuss the *functions* of pornography in section 12.

8. EXAMPLES OF PORNOGRAPHIC FILMS

Meanwhile, how far have we come in our quest for content? Not far. Having argued that pornographic feature films are of central importance let me remedy their neglect by the feminist authors under discussion by sketching in some of them. Had I space, I would like to exhibit the complete works of the directors Gerard Damiano,[18] Chuck Vincent [19] and Anthony Spinelli [20]

A. K. A. Armand Weston. But not to weary the reader let me concentrate on two well-known classics of the genre, *Deep Throat* (1972) and *Behind the Green Door* (1972), and a more recent pair that were big hits, *Talk Dirty to Me* (1980) and *Roommates* (1981).

My examination of these examples will confirm the reader's suspicion that I implicitly defend pornography. A legitimate question is, how far does this defence go? The answer is, at least as far as liberal tolerance, and anything further is not required for the argument of this paper. The question of how far liberal tolerance should go is hotly debated, but not here, since, for the sake of the following argument, I will concede that humiliating or degrading any member of the audience is beyond what liberal tolerance permits.

Let the sensitive reader be warned: I now summarise hard core pornographic material and skipping straight to section 9 is an option I recommend to those not inured to it.

Deep Throat is an odyssey, a woman's quest for sexual fulfilment, a picaresque tale. The heroine Linda (Linda Lovelace), with the help of her sexually aggressive roommate Helen, searches for sexual fulfilment: not just recreational or pleasurable sensations but bells ringing and rockets bursting. Helen stages a party whose several males give Linda a chance to explore straight, anal and oral sex. She enjoys it but says it is not truly satisfying. So Helen suggests a sex therapist, Dr. Young (Harry Reems), who when Linda confesses that of all sexual activity 'giving head' pleases her best, makes the startling discovery that her clitoris is in her throat; this being so, the path to fulfilment involves her mastering 'deep throat'. This she does so successfully that Dr. Young makes her one of his therapists and sends her out to service those in need of sexual stimulus. We also learn that the doctor is sexually involved with his nurse and that the combined demands of the two women make him ill. Linda's success with a man who drinks Coca Cola from a glass dildo in her vagina (to the music 'Love is Strange') and with a geriatric case lead to her assignment to a client who must play out a burglar-rape scenario. She falls in love with him because of his charm and his enormous member. Dr. Young promises to cut it down to perfect size.

Shot hastily and crudely on a shoestring budget at Miami locations, the plot of the film is at times barely coherent; but its sex scenes are always very graphic.[21] In her self-denunciatory book *Ordeal*, Linda Lovelace tells how making the film was a relief from the pressures of her battering husband. Her smiles into the camera may not connote enjoyment but they probably do connote pride in a job well done.

Behind the Green Door, originally just *The Green Door*, is an abduction fantasy framed within the reminiscing of two truckers in a diner. A young girl sits alone at an outdoor cafe, then is abducted as she walks home.[22] The trucker and his pal enter an exclusive club where members wear evening dress and masks. The girl is brought in the back door and told by a woman that she will not be harmed, that undreamt of pleasure is going to be hers, that she has only to relax and open herself to the experience. She massages her. On stage a mime acts out putting on faces like putting on clothes. The woman is led blindfold into a spotlight where six other women in black robes remove her white robe and begin to caress all parts of her body with hands and mouths. Almost swooning with pleasure the girl is carried to a raised platform in the center of the room where more intense caresses and cunnilingus are applied. Through the green door comes a black man dressed only in white tights with a hole cut for his genitals. He takes over the cunnilingus and, eventually, enters the woman. A long, and growingly intense copulation takes place, the latter part of which is synchronised to rhythmic music. From time to time we cut away to the audience, who become excited at the events they witness and, as they continue, start groping and undressing each other as a prelude to their own sexual activities. When the woman reaches a prolonged (and very real-looking) orgasm the scene shifts as some trapezes are lowered and she is offered a means of handling four men, one she fellates, one she sits on and two she masturbates. Unlike the first part, this is clumsily shot, so that what is happening is not always clear. When the men ejaculate there is a slow-motion color-reversal sequence of her facing penis after penis as they shoot out semen. These shots are repeated, reversed, shown in negative and rotated to a *musique concrète* sound track. Suddenly one of the audience dashes onto the stage, picks up the girl wrapped in a sheet and exits with her. Back at the diner the truck driver slyly indicates no one knows what became of her, but then we see him heading home in his truck knowing that the woman is waiting for him and we see in his mind he anticipates their sexual coupling.

Again the shoe string budget, again the sexual odyssey: the lonely or depressed girl needs help to open herself to sexual pleasure, in this case by an abduction in which she is not harmed. Indeed, once the woman explains to her what will happen the girl yields to it, albeit a little hesitantly, a little frightened. After a seven year hiatus Marilyn Chambers returned to pornography in *Insatiable* which was less an odyssey and more a pursuit of the rainbow, since its heroine's pleasure in sex is simultaneously a torture because she can never get enough. This cribbing from Sartre's *Huis Clos* is also used in *The Devil in Miss Jones*.

Talk Dirty to Me (1981) and *Roommates* (1982) are considerably more skilled pieces of movie-making than the early seventies classics. *Talk Dirty* posits two young men, Jack, sexually successful (John Leslie), Lennie inept and timid (Richard Pacheco). They are poor, so when one has an accident the other seduces the (Lady) doctor (Chris Cassidy) to avoid paying the bill. The film is true to its title, since the characters are always talking about what they are going to do before, and then what they are doing during, the sex. Jack vows to have the beautiful Marlene (Jessie St. James) in 3 days. They move in next door and spy on her and work on her garden. Jack seduces the real estate agent (Juliet Anderson) and two nymphs who come over to visit, then he finally conquers Marlene while his friend loses his virginity downstairs.

This escalation of the porno film from showing it to talking about it was pioneered by Gerard Damiano in *The Devil in Miss Jones* and *Portrait* but carried further in *Talk Dirty* and *Outlaw Ladies* where the makers trade on the well-known erotic value of talk in connection with sex. *Talk Dirty* centres on male rather than female characters, and, while humiliating the virginal Lenny, also keeps its distance from the impossibly confident Jack. The film was so popular that a sequel was put out continuing the basic polarity between the rake and the believer in love, and the latter scenes are much the most erotic (*Nothing to Hide*). (A rival sequel, *Talk Dirty to Me Part II* was less effective.)

I have selected *Roommates* because it also has been very popular at the box office and has gained favourable comment in the press. It is the story of three women sharing an apartment in New York. Billie is a production assistant on commercials (Samantha Fox), Sherry a model (Kelly Nichols), Joan an aspiring actress (Veronica Hart). The aspiring actress believes her professor loves her but whenever they make love he allows himself to climax quickly and leaves her unsatisfied. By the end she gets wise to his selfishness and falls for a gay actor friend. The model lives in the fast lane, is gang-raped, and gets involved with a seedy pill pusher (Jamie Gillis) who severely beats her up. The production coordinator, after confessing to her roommates that she was once a hooker, finds herself ensnared by former contacts who blackmail her into continuing to practice that profession. At a stag party one night one of the guests turns out to be the producer she was falling for. After this depressing experience of men the menage breaks up and the former hooker is seeking roommates again.

As with the first two films, this one is women-centred. It is harder to classify. All the women experience bad sex and bad treatment from men.

Fellatio, a favourite porn film commodity, is shown as humiliating in one case and unenjoyable to the inexperienced. Writer-director Chuck Vincent clearly is offering a fresh departure with this film, one in which sex can be seen as an illusion for women when they let themselves believe in men. Although all the principals are porn veterans, they manage to acquit themselves quite well as thespians. The film has rough spots, especially in speaking and editing rhythms, but its success and its unusual theme raise the question of whether the pornographic genre is really such a creative strait-jacket as is sometimes made out.

These examples, it could be objected, load my argument just as much as do the persuasive definitions of section 5. This is fair; the examples are crucial. The ones chosen are very well-known and widely distributed, took in considerable sums of money at the box-office and are fairly typical of the more than 200 pornographic feature films I have examined over 5 years; NALS ignores their existence. They put some speed bumps on the Slippery Slope. The examples do not dispose of the claim that there is a "rising tide" of pornography, but they do challenge any assertion that its content is 'getting worse'. Rape scenes, child molestation scenes, torture scenes and killing scenes are said to be on the increase. One has to wonder whether this impression comes from taking 42nd St. in the mid-nineteen seventies as typical of what was to come in the United States as a whole. Beverly LaBelle says the 'turning point' for many women came with the film *Snuff* (TBTN, p. 274). This exploitation film was released in the wake of New York police claims that there were in circulation South American films in which a woman was actually killed on the screen — so called "Snuff films".

Since the *Snuff* episode was a turning point we should look into it. When the film opened in New York feminist groups picketed outside the theatre and demanded that it be banned. The *New York Times* sent two reporters to see it, and both reported that while the idea sickened them, the film's killings were transparently fake and that current Hollywood offerings were more convincing.[23] Police and feminists seem to have been victims of a shrewd publicity campaign for a trashy film. Only feminists who wanted to believe the film was real could have been fooled. John Leonard mentions that *none of the women protesting had seen the film*. It was the idea they were protesting. Once the District Attorney had made sure the film was a hoax[24] one might have expected the protests to fade away. But no, a leaflet LaBelle quotes (TBTN, p. 276), says real or simulated is not the issue. Laura Lederer, the editor of TBTN, adds a footnote to LaBelle's article precisely on the point, what was to be done when the hoax was exposed: 'feminists quickly moved to state that the murder of one woman was only the first of many concerns we had about "snuff" films' (TBTN, p. 276n). What then is the issue? The removal of a film of which a pressure group dissapproves. Why do they disapprove of it? Because it incites crime, namely murder and torture of women. On the principle of not showing any film that incites crime it shows merely by its being shown censors would be given wide power. The issue here is not pornography, not sexism, not the law, but only, as Humpty Dumpty said, who's in charge, that's all.

The New York police seem to have been quiet after the hoax was exposed but a strange Hollywood film maker, Paul Schrader,[25] incorporated the idea, as though he believed it, in *Hardcore*. In that film, widower George C. Scott's daughter disappears during a church outing to Los Angeles. With the help of a private detective and a girl who works in a sex arcade he discovers his daughter has been recruited to the pornography industry. The man she is involved with makes 'snuff' films and he must rescue her before she is the next victim. Thesis: sin is a slippery slope: if your daughter wanders off from a church trip to Los Angeles next thing you know you"ll see her doing multiples on pornographic loops, and being lined up for a snuff film. The Slippery Slope Argument is not the exclusive property of feminist attacks on pornography.

The legend of snuff, like the legend that the Nazis flooded Poland with pornography,[26] seems to be central to a mythology that permeates the feminist writing on pornography that stands behind NALS. Other myths broadcast are: that the pornography industry is bigger than the film and rock music industries combined;[27] that there is a hidden agenda in pornography which aims to break down sexual taboos and thus keep women in their place (Bat-Ada, TBTN, p. 121); that there is a connection between viewing/producing pornography and crimes against women;[28] and so on.

9. THE FUNCTION OF MYTHS IN DISCUSSIONS OF PORNOGRAPHY

It would take excessive space to track down and expose each myth, so I will subject only one to the test of common sense. On p. 103 of her book Andrea Dworkin writes: "feminists calculate that in the United States one woman is raped every three minutes, one wife battered every eighteen seconds. There are currently an estimated twenty-eight million battered wives in the United States." So far as one can tell from the text, these statements are meant literally and their bonafides are on 'FBI statistics'. (Incidentally, for Robin Morgan, the rape rate is probably an underestimate since she holds that all sex under any kind of pressure is rape (see below) — which means there are lots of rapes of men by women too.) Consider literally and in good faith those twenty-eight million battered wives. Published in 1981, the present tense in Dworkin's prose presumably refers to 1980. But let us use only general knowledge. The population of the United States is 225 million. Slightly more than half of these are female, let us say 113 million. Again, roughly one-third of these are juveniles and so are neither wives nor batterees. There are then 76 million women in the marriage age band. Twenty-eight million is 36% of 76 million. So feminist calculations tell us that more than one out of three marriageable women is battered. Such a statistic makes a feminist rightly horrified at our society; such a statistic makes me question the statistician.

The concoction, circulation and desire to believe myths is a social phe-nomenon subject to sociological explanation, not necessarily feminist in character. A group that believes it is persecuted but knows it is disorganised may seek to re-order experience in a manner that validates and enhances its sense of persecution, sharply marks its views off from those of the surround-ing, persecuting society, and hence promotes solidarity. Since the women's movement is largely one of intellectuals, many of its myths are couched in intellectual terms, using statistics, other social scientific impedimenta, psychoanalytic interpretation, literary-critical 'reading' of texts. All offer the same functional message: look at it this way and it will order (or reorder) your experience, explain to you what is *really* going on and thus pull you into our group. Indeed, the myth is summed up boldly: 'pornography is the ideology of a culture which promotes and condones rape, woman-battering and other crimes of violence against women' (Lederer, TBTN, pp. 19–20). The rising tide of pornography and the debased content of pornography is to be explained as a strenuous effort by patriarchical males to keep women in their place. Pornography makes propaganda for attacks on women, people do what propaganda tells them to do, hence ever more women are attacked and frightened into keeping their place. In other words, the increase in pornography in general and violent pornography in particular is a response to the women's liberation movement.

Leaving aside the question of rising tides as an appropriate metaphor for social change, let us look further at the role of myth. The function of myths is to organise and explain experience in ways tht make it seem subject to human will (projected). Myth-making and myth-sustaining is probably essential for group creation, and for maintaining solidarity and continuity. But, it should be noted, in enshrining and endorsing myths, a group pays a price. There will be those to whom the myths are unacceptable, either because they conflict with other myths or with facts, or because in some way they blacken a cause to which those others are devoted. In general, in so far as the writers and the movie under discussion propagate myths hostile to men, they alienate the male half of the population. Myths such as that male sexuality is in some inherent way violent, and that males like or tolerate pornography because it is all of a piece with that sexuality, are offensive to men: most males are going to disassociate themselves from what is being said, from the group that says it and that is sustained by it.

Furthermore, a question of policy towards myths is in question. Groups can be aware of their myths but not take them seriously (this is a feature of much progressive religion). Groups can, alternatively, take seriously and hold fast to belief in their myths. But there is a third, and more weird, policy, found especially in certain religions such as Catholicism and Communism, where the myths are known to be false yet belief in them is explicitly demanded. It is here that perhaps the feminist writers under discussion are unclear. All kinds of what ifs, thought experiments, metaphors and myths are innocuous in the course of making a point. They are innocuous because once the point is made we are free to deny the literal truth of the myths utilized. It is quite interesting to conceptualise the oppression of women in terms of myths like that of the patriarchal society, of a male hegemony, or of a male conspiracy. The policy question is, is subscription to such myths a mandatory condition for obtaining a membership card in the cause of women's liberation?

We may find it hard to empathise with this practice even when it happens in full view, but then we are naive: it happens quite frequently. The most flagrant example in the literature under discussion is the thesis that pornography *is* violence against women, *is* sadism against women, *is* the ideology of male dominance. Its authors, one can be sure, know perfectly well that there is a flourishing all-male pornography industry for homosexuals.[29] In most of these films no women appear; therefore these films are decisive counter-examples to such claims. What is the reaction? Retraction? Certainly not! Qualifiers? No. (Inserting the word 'most', or, being supercautious, 'much' before 'pornography' would suffice to block the counter-example). Then what? A sophisticated rebuttal is Dworkin's attempt to interpret male homosexual pornography as consisting of one of the men taking a female role and then suffering violence, degradation, etc. (PMPW, pp. 42–3). She hardly notices that this renders symbolic the thesis that pornography *is* violence against women, etc., and raises the new question of why oppose symbolic violence? Not because it fosters real violence. Our literature and art could hardly exist without symbolic violence and to accuse it of causing what it represents is to perpetuate muddle. But all this is academic: Dworkin's move is clearly an ad hoc manoeuvre in the face of awkward facts. Much male homosexual behaviour has nothing to do with male-female role-playing. Allowing all cases where there is dominance-submission to be freely interpreted as symbolising oppression of women is partisan. Moreover, it endorses the excessively sexist myth which deems a dominant woman the male of the family.[30] Similarly, it stereotypes male homosexuals into masculine and feminine roles, which is sexist/homophobic. Definitions of pornography as violence towards women etc. fly in the face of obvious counter-examples, yet authors quote each other reaffirming them — presumably to give them currency. This is obviously membership-card behaviour.

10. RESEARCH DESIGN AND FINDINGS

The feminists interviewed in NALS and writing in the books cited are aghast not just at the rising tide of pornography, but also at what — they assert — is its increasingly violent content. They attribute this to male desire to batter women into their place. The evidence offered is rather sketchy: visits to Manhattan porno strips for a three-month period and anecdotes. No run down of companies and their catalogues is undertaken, no comparative statistics on what kind of material sells best (*Deep Throat* is still the box-office champion), no controlled investigation of any kind. Lists of unpleasant scenes and rough and ready counts of their frequency (TBTN, p. 15, 17) are, of course, of little use and less reliable than the more elaborate but equally questionable jeremiads of Gerbner about television violence.[31]

   With these cavils in mind I counterpose at this point some observations of my own. A mind trained in philosophy and film study may get a different impression than a mind trained in feminism. I draw on the work of Jim Holliday, the leading writer of consumer's guide material about pornography, on scant reading of the trade press, on many hours of dutiful viewing at the VCR and in Pussycat theatres and on a review of the academic literature (Section 17). My opening observation is that there is a parallel between the evolution of the history of film in general and of the pornographic genre in particular. Ontogeny recapitulates phylogeny. The principal overt content of feature film pornography is the promotion of films with attractive and versatile actors and actresses. Very early silent films, like clandestine porn loops, used mostly anonymous players. In the new situation the customer for pornography is encouraged to know his or her stars and to attend films, buy tapes, picture books and loops in which they feature. Fan magazines have grown too. Very much secondary as a selling point is plot; sometimes the trailers do not even indicate what the plot is, concentrating instead on the stars and the "hot" action scenes. Two characteristics, however, stand out when plots are considered; these are the satire, and the journey into a person's fantasy world (usually a woman's, but not always). In such fantasy a paradigm taken from mainstream movies can equally often be *Rebecca* as *Deep Throat* — the latter set a tone since it was both a lighthearted-comedy that never took sex too seriously as well as a woman's fantasy (albeit male-pleasing rather than female-pleasing). *Behind the Green Door* is the other archetype, since it also is an exploratory journey through inner space. Subsequent fantasy premisses in films have concentrated on reminiscence: hookers reminiscing, housewives reminiscing, men reminiscing and, a reflexive variant, porn stars reminiscing.[32] That the characters on screen are so often dreaming, day-dreaming, and reminiscing is a fact not without significance. It tells the audience that we are inside someone's head: this is fantasy. As for comedy, just as early Hollywood mined every conceivable source for stories, stealing from standard works and even from other films, so in pornography; and just as satires of current films was a speciality of movie comedy from the earliest days, viz., recently *Airplane, Young Doctors in Love*, so in pornography there is a steady supply of satires on current movies and television programmes: *Naughty Network, Sex Boat, Take-Off, Gums, Debby Does Dallas, Genital Hospital, Urban Cowgirls, San Fernando Valley Girls*, and so on.

So much for the evolution of the genre — unintended, no conspiracy, entirely explicable by the aim of pleasing the audience. As to content, contrary to the allegations quoted above, little perversion, little violence, almost no gore. The bulk of feature films and tapes are straightforwardly hetero-sexual and relatively unadventurous. Anal sex, for example, is not at all frequent,[33] and 'fisting' or 'water sports,' are often cut.[34] Such deviations are more commonly shown in all-male homosexual pornography, a fact which may indicate — perhaps — that they are everyday in the sexual world of male homosexuals. Violence and sadomasochism are infrequent[35] and when found, as in *Taxi Girls, The Private Afternoons of Pamela Mann, The Story of Joanne* or *Roommates*, there is a deliberate lack of conviction about them, a sense of playacting. Contrary to what might be expected, the kind of violence towards women which the film and books under discussion here object to not is to be found in pornography but in mainstream Hollywood movies. The gang rape scene at the beginning of *Death Wish*, the rape scene in *Clockwork Orange*, the homosexual rapes depicted in *Deliverance* and in *Spetters* (none an X-rated film, incidentally), the murders in *Dressed to Kill* and *Body Double* are a quantum leap ahead of pornographic films in emotionally gruelling the audience while insistently forcing them to suspend their disbelief.[36] The equivalent scenes in pornography seem insistently rather to force disbelief: this is mere fantasy, they insist.

To assert all this is not to deny that the scenes in question may be distasteful, even offensive — in both Hollywood and pornographic movies. *Behind the Green Door*, a classic of the pornographic film genre, is reported by some men and women to be, and by others not to be, a sexual turn-on. It represents itself as possibly dream, possibly real, the fulfilment of a female fantasy of female total surrender. At all points the film makes clear that the heroine suffers no hurt or harm. Supposing it is a fantasy of both men and women,[37] the question arises as to whether it is a 'healthy' one, should one have this fantasy and from that presumably flows an answer to the question, should a film of this fantasy be permitted on (a) the public and (b) the home screen? Without deciding the question of 'healthiness', as a practical matter question (b) can be disregarded. Pornographic video-cassettes by the million are in circulation in the United States, as is duplication equipment. Any attempt to clean up home screens would merely drive up the price. But even if suppression is impractical in this case (*Toronto Star*, 14–11–81), the desirability or otherwise of this material being available remains for discussion; that discussion is taken up in section 15, below.

To sum up: the bulk of commercially available movie pornography is thoroughly safe and bourgeois in that it portrays a limited number of familiar variations on sexual intercourse, exhibiting mutual pleasure of both male and female, regularly portrays people as getting pleasure in exciting the other and by taking them to climax before following suit. There is a specialist fringe of what 'Jehovanists' (Davis 1983) call perverse or degenerate pornography but no evidence is presented to suggest that the bulk of ordinary porn viewing males seek it out or enjoy it. (For further discussion see section 12, below.)

11. WHO PRODUCES PORNOGRAPHY?

The modern era differs sharply from earlier eras, and films differ from books, paintings and other media. As long as pornography was clandestine it was difficult to know who produced it. The Kinsey Library, and the researches of the authors of *Dirty Movies*, have sometimes been unable to identify even the country of origin.[38] My own best guess would be that it was at first a cottage industry with output from professional photographers, organised crime, and amateurs, drawing female models from the ranks of prostitutes and good time girls, aspiring models and actresses who had already dabbled in grey areas. Male recruiting was more haphazard and it is said that these actors were rarely paid; ability to perform and visible assets being less pretested than among females. No regularised distribution or exhibition channels existed; reels passed from hand to hand.

The gradual increase in the distribution and exhibition of soft core pornography films in the late fifties and sixties brought other kinds of capital into the production of this material. The break-through was *Deep Throat* which, Damiano has clearly indicated, was backed by somewhat unsavoury people,[39] yet was shown in regular cinemas hastily cobbled together into adult film circuits in any jurisdiction that seemed promising and where legal harassment might be defeated. Once the profitability of the form established itself there was a gradual increase in the level of investment in pornographic features,[40] with the establishment of regular circuits, distributors and producers, the latter now organised into the Adult Film Association. Pornographic film making presently resembles the fringe operations of classic-period Hollywood, those concentrated in Poverty Row and Gower Gulch.

The corporate entities involved in the industry have shaken down to a handful, as have directors and producers (parallel to classical Hollywood again). The performers seem more transient. Linda Lovelace says she has drifted into normal life; Tina Russell became anorexic and died.[41] Harry Reems was harassed by legal authorities[42] but surfaced again with a new film, *Society Affairs*, (1982). After starring in three films in 1973, Marilyn Chambers drifted into other things, but in 1980 released a new hit, *Insatiable*, and others have subsequently appeared. The screen already has its lady veterans: Georgina Spelvin, Carol Connors, Gloria Leonard, Annette Haven, Jessie St. James, Seka, Vanessa Del Rio and others have been a decade in the life. Among the men veterans, John Holmes, Jamie Gillis, Eric Edwards and John Leslie seem like permanent fixtures. There is too a phalanx of actors and actresses of the second rank who have shown considerable staying power. Fringe activity though it be, this shows the Hollywoodisation or embourgeoisement of the pornographic movie industry has proceeded far enough for its denizens not to appreciate the advice and sympathy of Laura Lederer, Gloria Steinem and their colleagues.

It remains necessary to situate the pornography industry in the social context of American society. Thesis: pornography is a specialised branch of prostitution and the classical sociological treatment of prostitution by

Kingsley Davis (1937) applies — with some modification (see also Benjamin and Ellis).

when coitus is practised for money its social function is indeterminate, secondary and extrinisic. . . . Where the family is strong, there tends to be a well-defined system of prostitution and the social regime is one of status. . . . But where the familial controls are weak, the system of prostitution tends to be poorly defined. (Davis 1937)

Davis interprets the function of prostitution to be that of protecting the family. What is the family threatened by? Lack of controls on sex. All human societies encourage or at least permit sexual relations of certain sorts, and discourage or even forbid sexual relations of other sorts. Where there is a strong emphasis on the family and on the legitimacy of offspring, there is usually a sharp line between respectable women and prostitutes. The money paid to the latter can be interpreted as compensation for loss of status. It was predicted that if the family weakened as an institution then the line between the respectable woman and the prostitute would blur. This is, I believe, the case, as witness the proliferation of prostitution under different names: hostess, escort, masseur, good-time girl, actress.

Another aspect of Davis' analysis, however, has not been born out. He suggested that a climate of greater sexual permissiveness would reduce the incidence of prostitution: 'free intercourse for pleasure and friendship . . . is the greatest enemy of prostitution' (p. 754). If anything, the reverse might seem to be the case, especially as many of the actresses at the beginning of the pornography boom in the nineteen sixties would be better described as promiscuous free spirits than as prostitutes.

Interviews with the actresses reveal a good many of them were call-girls. The sexually liberated amateur of sixties legend (and loops) has disappeared.[43] But Marilyn Chambers says she was recruited directly from photographic modelling,[44] Georgina Spelvin from the production crew.[45] Males drift in from the fringes of the acting/modelling worlds largely, it would seem, through contacts.[46] Initially their pay was low, but those whose endowments and performance were appreciated eventually made modest incomes (Brady and Montesano, 1982).

The changed sexual climate has enormously enlarged the demand for one service of the prostitute often described in stories of the sentimental education: education. Prostitutes provided not only sexual services and pleasures: they traditionally provided education or, if you like, initiation. If, however, the structure of sexual expectations has altered then the former system will not do, for two clear reasons: if really large numbers of males want this education there simply are not enough prostitutes around. The other reason connects with deeper changes: what once would be called 'respectable' women want equal access to sexual choice and hence to knowledge. It is no longer acceptable that the knowledge should be transmitted to them at the pleasure of males. Thus the proliferation of forms of prostitution is explicable as means to cope with the size and diversity of the new demand for education as well as pleasure, and the particular growth of pornography as well as its content can be explained by changes in the structures of control of sex. What is perhaps surprising is that in content the pornography tends to be highly orthodox and mainstream, failing in this to acknowledge what we might call the polymorphously perverse possibilities and practices of the population. Pornography thus succeeds in being part of rather than undermining the system of social controls on sexual life. Let me elaborate.

The classical prostitute was a (perhaps the) sexual specialist in society; the classical brothel, a 'house of pleasure'. Sexual relations in other settings had to do with duty and procreation, less with pleasure or art. Our society has, consequent on industrialization, rejected both these premisses; parallel to the demand for universal literacy is the demand for universal mastery of the sexual arts. The prostitute no longer monopolises expertise; every person wants to be sexually expert. As a corollary of this, it is understood that sexual relations wherever they are undertaken should never be matters of duty, still less unpleasant duty, but always freely undertaken and pleasurable. These are fine ideals, but they are difficult to realise in a world in which sexual ignorance and superstition is widespread, in which powerful groups resist the implied secularisation of the sexual act, in which powerful forces isolate and condemn certain forms of sexual practice, and in which there are many sexually willing people whose situation makes it virtually impossible for them to find fulfilment.

The continuation of prostitution in our permissive climate is explained by these factors. However, as we know, very few jurisdictions in Canada or the United States have ever come to terms with prostitution as serving those social functions which would be implied in its regularisation. It has been regularised from time to time in French Canada, the Yukon, New Orleans, on the Barbary Coast, in the vicinity of military bases, and in Nevada, but neither its legal base, nor a proper understanding of its social roots, has ever been deeply enough established to ensure that there would not be moves by pressure groups to eliminate prostitution.

Like alcohol, attempts to eliminate prostitution merely make it more difficult, possibly impossible, to control. Hence both street and organised crime step into the vacuum and disease, exploitation, robbery and the ensnaring of children are associated with prostitution. In the city in which I recently did some research, neighbourhood groups were pressing the police to 'clean up' the prostitutes from Hollywood. Since being a prostitute is no crime, and acts of prostitution are rarely in evidence, the police were pushed to the borders of legality, using forms of entrapment, indiscriminate round ups, and stop and search tactics. In all the discussion what surprises the sociologist is the failure of any functional understanding. If neighbourhoods dislike prostitution because of solicitation and associated crime, and if they want an uncorrupted police, one would have thought the obvious conclusion would be that means of solicitation are needed that will not cause offense, means of conducting prostitution business are needed that will minimise the opportunities for crime.

Of course the reformers and cleaners-up are utopians, that is, people for whom prostitution, if not all sex, is sin, and a world without sin is just around the corner.

What has all this to do with pornography? It should be obvious. I interpret pornography as a branch of prostitution, one serving overlapping social functions. It is intriguing how so much of America has come to terms with controlled permitting of pornography, but not with prostitution in general. More strongly, it has not come to terms with use of the media for prostitution.

Now to explicate the assertion that pornography is a branch of prostitution. In the classical brothel, pornographic pictures, songs and performances were often part of the facilities. What are now called live shows were supplemented by such devices as one-way mirrors and peepholes (cf. Cleland). Brothels also catered to fantasy. In Genet's 'The Balcony', which takes place entirely in a brothel, the characters act out the parts they would like to play in life, from dominance to abject submission. Pornographic films are only an outgrowth of this aspect of the brothel trade. Without any doubt the very first women to act in sexually explicit films were prostitutes.[47] This continues to be true today, although semantic dissembling is widespread and hence needs to be deciphered. Linda Lovelace's third autobiography confesses candidly that she worked as a prostitute, with her husband as pimp.[48] Interviews with other actresses identify them as call-girls, escort service, showgirls, go-go dancers, good time girls, gold diggers.

Perhaps the major revelation of the last ten years of pornographic films has been this: prostitution, both amateur and professional, is a flourishing trade in the United States, despite its blue laws, and despite the sexual revolution, and there is a sufficient well of talent that film makers have been able to find very good looking people witting to perform in their films. Depressed looking girls with pimply bottoms performing in poorly lit home movies are one thing, raving and healthy-looking beauties are another. After all, if you are putting your sexual assets on the market and what you have is rather good quality, is it surprising that film work appeals, since its working conditions and the amount of wear and tear it entails can hardly be worse than real world prostitution?

But here one needs to note the element of advertising and the element of exhibitionism. Increasingly, magazines indicate that porn actresses do live shows and, one need not be born yesterday to suspect, other side lines too. Exhibitionism is another matter. To lose self-consciousness, to be able to act convincingly, to relax and enjoy being in front of the camera, are qualities everyone in film work needs. That there should be flagrant exhibitionists among prostitutes and among the men recruited to serve them, need be no surprise.

If anything, performing in films has to be a form of moving up-market for prostitutes since it gives them high wages for relatively few sexual acts, with very few partners. After all, the top of the prostitution profession is the woman kept sufficiently well that she need sleep with no-one but her benefactor unless she chooses. The degradation of having to say yes to a customer because you want the money, the dangers of physical abuse and of disease are greatly minimised by working in films. The more successful actresses undoubtedly make enough from films alone to live on. Those eager interviewers who ask them repeatedly how they feel concerning certain sexual practices undertaken on screen may seem naive. Do they not have any idea of what a free-ranging prostitute may as a matter of course engage in in the interest of pleasing her clients? Further to ask them whether they enjoy this or that act, or where they draw the line merely compounds the folly. Everyone draws the line somewhere, in life and in job. But a professional may undertake with equanimity something they are used to, without at all relishing it. But of course such 'interviews' are contrived to serve the legend. One of the persistent legends of our society is the prostitute with a heart of gold, who loves her work and her clients. This seems to be a relic from the time when sexual expertise and sexual pleasure were connected with outlaw sex and not with that within the family. After all, we all want the professionals who care for us, especially those engaged in skin trades — nurses, doctors, dentists, masseurs, hairdressers — to really care about us (O'Neill 1972). In pornography this shows in the eager articles and interviews maintaining that the performers not only relish what they do, but genuinely experience something as they do it. A characteristic feature of the trailers in pornographic theatres is what Nichols calls the mode of direct address.[49] That is, the female star of the up-coming film, directly addressing the audience, will sing the praises of her film in terms of gross sexual excitement. She will, for example, maintain that she had great pleasure making it, that her male stars were carefully chosen for their looks and sexiness, that even remembering it and telling us about it makes here sexually excited. Noticeably, these come-on ads are never voiced by the male stars, although the pornographic cinema has a more permanent stable of males than it has of females.

Many writers of our time have thought of sex as a subversive force. If it is, then prostitution tames it. And that is how pornography functions too. There is an irony here, because the anti-pornography crusaders have always agreed with the radicals that sex is a dangerous and destructive force that, if not tightly controlled and canalised, would do everything from destroy the family to bring down the Roman Empire!

Ten years after *Deep Throat* brought pornography out from the darkness of smokers to the glare of trial and publicity we see nothing of the sort happening. Pornography is now well-established as a solid market with steady growth in video-cassettes. In his *Movie-Made America* of 1976 Robert Sklar could reprint a whole page of a newspaper advertising pornographic theatres in Los Angeles. Nowadays there are only a handful operating in the whole South Coast basin, although those remaining seem to have a steady and established business. Bookstores and peep shows have also settled down to a few, mostly in areas already sleazy for other reasons and hence subject to minimum attention from authorities and neighbourhood groups. The biggest growth area for the business has been in one where those who continue their opposition to the free circulation of pornography have a lot of trouble making any inroads: video-cassettes.

Many record and electronic stores have opened branches with small circulating libraries of video-cassettes in both the VHS and Beta formats. Examining the extent of the shelving quickly reveals that adult cassettes take up about 1/3 the space of the legitimate cassettes. Sales of these cassettes are however said to account for more than half of the sales. Since these are just boxed tapes, rented only to people with credit cards and ID, involving no advertising or materials that can possibly offend, they obviously can be little cause for complaint. That they are a steady and flourishing business means that pornography has finally found a means of circulation about which its opponents can do very little.[50]

12. WHAT DOES PORNOGRAPHY PORTRAY?

The first thing to note is that these films show sexual relations strictly in the era of contraception. Although the naive might take the visible ejaculations to be birth control by coitus interruptus, the truth is that no-one in these films acts as though pregnancy is a real threat. Hence contraceptive preparations are never shown; but then no-one, in these films, ever gets pregnant. Sex thus is detached from one of its major traditional responsibilities: procreation.

Sex also, in these films, is detached from marriage. In many of the films those engaged in sexual encounters are not and have no intention of being married. It would not be correct, however, to assume that sex is desacralized in these films. Some of the sex is, but frequently the ideal of sex held up is sacralized: that is, sex is a sort of holy ritual that transports its celebrators into an ecstatic state and creates between them a special and possibly permanent bond. Lovers who find this find what they are seeking, married people without it set out on the quest, often returning to the partner to cement it into the marriage. We might say sex has become a secularised yet sacred ritual.

By and large sex is also shown as easy to obtain, and easy to enjoy. We never see in these films anything like mutual uneasiness between the partners, hesitation, missed cues, delight in drawing out the situation, difficulty in mutual accommodation. It is quite amazing how infrequently either frigidity or impotence is ever touched on. *Deep Throat*, as cognoscenti of primitive forms of the art will recall, was about the Search for True Orgasm.

The sacred form of the Simultaneous Climax has not been a prominent feature. Indeed, the most frequent pattern taken by a straightforward sexual encounter in these films is as follows. The partners engage in mutual foreplay, whereupon the man sets about bringing the woman to climax. Following this, she urges him to come to climax too, which he does. Most acts of sex, then, end with the male climax. Virtually no acts of sex end with the partners eschewing climax. (Now here I am of course talking of events in the dramatic plane of the film, I am not talking of the parallel or different transactions that may take place between the actors on the set.)

These films never deal seriously with fumbling or with ignorance. For example, it surprises me that one of the classic erotic tales, Colette's *Le Blé en Herbe*, in which the older but still desirable woman initiates the young boy into sex, is scarcely ever used. It is as though film makers fear that if they expend the time required for such material the film will not be able to contain the mandatory eight or so acts of sex, and the customers will complain. My own judgement would be that, as the professor said about the student, they don't complain if they're satisfied. Only one or two films have given careful treatment to the theme of two inexperienced lovers discovering sex for themselves. Such material is erotically very potent and would seem a natural.

As to compatibility. When people are lovers one of the things they have to negotiate is their actual sexual practice: its frequency, location, time, and form. One of the oddities of current pornographic materials is how it completely blinks away these questions. It is as though if both are willing, anything goes. This may be the reader's experience, and the film makers experience, but it is certainly not mine, or those I have interviewed informally. Most people have ranked preferences, all the way down to what they will not do for anyone. In the latter category, there are certain kinds of exhibitionistic display at which most people baulk. Also there is a wide range of personal preference when it comes to position, orality, anality, S and M, urolagnia, scopophilia, scatology, and the use of aids, devices, tapes, and the presence of other persons. All of these magically disappear in these films and when the partners get down to something a little out of the ordinary, they do it like well-trained animals in circuses. Scarcely so much as a 'will you' or 'can I?' is ever exchanged.

What to make of all this content? Above all it makes sex unproblematic, unmysterious, impersonal and safe. The defenders of the American way of life under democracy and god have nothing to fear, sex is being marketed as a consumer commodity, mass produced and hence somewhat homogenised, the extremes and rough edges of craftsmanship rubbed off, the exquisite personal taste of the individual chef merely simulated. For a rental price of $2.50 the American adult can buy themselves TV-dinner-style sex. Increasingly the bodies involved look as plastic perfect as those in *Playboy*, the pleasures to be obtained guaranteed like the US Recommended Daily Minimum Vitamins and Iron on your breakfast cereal, and the practices engaged in eagerly and easily carried out by the partners, whatever their age or state of health. Personal hygeine is never treated and so one has to assume everyone in these films has taken care of it. The disease and disorder which is a part of the reality of most people's bodies is banished.

How does this variant of prostitution function to protect the family? Answer: it suggests that in a democratic society good sex is democratically available to everyone, that it is only a question of education, and that equality of opportunity will lead to equality of achievement: that not only can and will everyone enjoy a healthy sex life, but that all will find it fulfilling. All anxiety-creating topics are eschewed: there is little interracial sex; little use of drugs; and male homosexuality is totally absent. If homosexual tendencies and practices are as widespread as Kinsey found, this avoidance reveals considerable latent anxiety. This is further revealed in the proclivity for scenes in which more than one man is present and a certain comradeship is displayed, as well as in the loving treatment the camera so often gives male bodies. It seems OK for these film to portray women as bisexual, but never to portray men as such, even when they service women together in the same scene. Why is the bisexuality of women unthreatening, even erotic? This asymmetry must connect to an asymmetry in our society that is not easy to understand. Obviously there is strong denial of any bisexual element in the male make-up, but that is no explanation. Why this denial? Psychology will not help here because it is universal and there is no reason to think that this asymmetrical denial is present in all societies, e.g., there is every reason to think it was not present in ancient Greece. The common male homosexual activities of fellation and pedication are shown on the screen, but the first only by women on men, the second only men on women. These weaknesses indicate that although pornography should function to educate both sexes its makers are both consciously and unconsciously prisoners of the homophobic male viewpoint.

The threat of sex, sex as an explosive force that will cause people to behave in rule-violating ways is studiously underplayed in these films. The bonded couple is the vessel for good sex, and both the stud and the easy girl are portrayed as searching for The Real Thing. But if unadulterated and uninterrupted sexual excitement is The Real Thing, what then? While not myself convinced that sex is such a subversive force, still less that it is a hydraulic quantity whose pressure has to find a release, I would not dismiss these ideas out of hand. These films support rather than undermine the family, emphasise pair bonding even if they ignore the two usual responsibilities that go with it: children and concern for the other. These films allow concern for the other to be exhausted by sexual concern, as though the sum total of human relations between the sexes was sexual, as though sex was the most important component in relations between the sexes.

Once upon a time I thought the proliferation of pornography was a healthy thing that might help loosen up America's puritan heritage. It has done that but only at the cost of reinforcing other forms of insularity and complacency that may now loom larger. The kind of pornography that is needed now is not willing gals and guys romping around as though the whole thing was utterly straightforward. What seems to be needed is films that deliver on their promise rather than create dissatisfaction — which is what I believe many films now do. What is missing is pornography that intimates something of the genuine power of sex in people's lives (which has only some connection with getting it on), and also more realistic expectations regarding its complex forms of expression; and, of course, what is needed in Canada is any pornography at all.

13. WHO CONSUMES PORNOGRAPHY?

There is no statistical breakdown of the population frequenting pornographic movie houses or purchasing pornographic video cassettes. They are primarily males, according to the film and books under discussion. This surmise I would accept, provided it is stressed both that no small number of these males are homosexual and that the population of females who attend pornography, though small, is not negligible. Once again, when the trade was largely clandestine the question of who were its consumers was not rewarding. It was hard to get hold of without money or contacts. Frats and men's clubs often found the police were their best source. Since pornography surfaced in the United States and even for a while became chic, the audience has grown and diversified. It is available in the United States to anyone near a cinema showing X films or with access to video tape equipment. There are regions of the United States where these are still not easy requirements to fulfill, but United Parcel Service end-runs Post Office regulations for the enterprising. Alas, Canada is still Prohibitionist.

Notwithstanding the inflated feminist claims, pornography has grown only to a modest-sized industry.[51] It dominates the sale of pre-recorded video-cassettes, monopolises a handful of theatres in almost every big Amerian city, supplies a section of the magazine racks at larger news-stands, and fills arrays of specialist bookstores and arcades.

The double bill of *Deep Throat* and *The Devil in Miss Jones* ran for nine years at the Pussycat Theater on Hollywood Boulevard. In major American cities regular movie theatres show hard-core films, and repertory theatres mount programmes of 'porno-chic'. The observable audience is too large to be entirely made up of raincoated centre-city transients. In suburban shopping centres there are large numbers of women present at X theatres. Surprising numbers of couples go too. Who are these customers? To repeat, data is scarce; but a commonsense distinction between curiosity-seekers, one-time tourists and 'the regulars' is obvious. The transients may be opaque to analysis prior to a proper field study. But here our concern is with the regulars, those whom the film and books under discussion utterly fail to observe or analyse adequately.

Who are these regulars? Clearly they are different from the tourist. The books under discussion although not the film incline to the view that the customers are male rapists, actual or potential:[52] Robin Morgan is credited (TBTN, p. 134) with the ringing slogan 'Pornography and Rape: Theory and Practice'. But the basis of her claim is neither empirical nor porno-related. It rests on her other claim that all sexual relations not initiated by the female spontaneously are rape.[53] Hence, the point that audiences may use these movies as a mild sexual fantasy can justly be turned into an accusation of harbouring the desire to rape; after all, the fantasy is unrelated to sex with a 'woman out of her own genuine affection and desire'.

An aspect of the discussion here deserves notice. The argument has now slid down a different slippery slope; the slippery slope we noted before was from innocuous to vicious pornography; the one we have here is different: from talk about pornography to instruction on proper attitudes to, and conduct in, actual sexual relations. Let us not slide from one to the other; but we may nevertheless make a proper transition. Presumably there is one connection or another between what happens on the screen and in real life. One may be against things on the first, then, because one is against them in the second. What this transition amounts to may be salutory; one may benefit, however, from noticing what it is. The study of life and art and their interaction in the manner pursued by the authors under discussion here is the study of the possibility of interaction and interchange of (sex) taboos in real life and (censorship) taboos in art. But are not these feminist authors against taboos altogether? It seems not: they seem to be saying that taboos are OK; that the thing is to have the right ones. Susan Brownmiller's contribution to TBTN is boldly entitled 'Let's Put Pornography Back in the Closet'. Judith Bat-Ada condemns pornography for showing anal sex. Why? Because viewers may pressure 'wives and lovers into having anal sex'. And what is wrong with having anal sex? It is 'generally uncomfortable at best and dangerous at worst' (TBTN, p. 129).[54] Anal sex is often derided in the books under discussion. Robin Morgan cites it, along with fisting and kinky sex, as an example of the Bad Things pornography is so-to-say 'selling' to its audience. In addition to their Jehovanist distaste for certain specific variations of sexual intercourse, the feminist writers under discussion want to proscribe another more abstract cross-over phenomenon from pornography to life: 'objectification' in human relations. What this amounts to will be discussed later (Section 14(6)). At the moment I want only to highlight how assent to the argument demands assent not only about certain features of pornography, but also assent to certain premisses about proper sexual conduct.[55]

This, then, is the analysis which the feminist literature under discussion offers — by sliding rather than walking into it, but never mind that — of the regular pornographic viewers: they are there to consume propaganda for sexual misconduct. Who then are the consumers of such propaganda? That is, who needs to be told about the joys of sexual variation? Who, in our society, reaches adulthood without knowing about them already? Given that these topics are widely discussed in books about sex, in magazines, advice columns, school courses, and so on, not to mention the scuttlebutt that all juveniles and adolescents are exposed to, only those of limited and narrow upbringing could continue to be ignorant. (There are a great many people in that category.) A well established principle of modern secular attitudes to sex is: if you both feel like it and no harm is done to anyone, then it is your own business. No doubt this does not solve all problems. Harm may be hard to define; quite ordinary missionary sex helps spread vaginitis, trichomoniasis, herpes, and more serious venereal infections; such dangers affect individual choices. Some may find flirting with possible danger (e.g. in using drugs) feeds their excitement; certainly the "danger" of limerance plays that role in the intense causal encounter. For all that, it seems ill-advised for anyone, including feminists, to dogmatise; to say, as some do, that this or that kind of sexual activity is in itself a Good Thing or a Bad Thing.

May we now draw the modest conclusion that those who consume this pornography in some sense want or even need it? That it offers them, or tells them, something they don't know? Whence were their needs fulfilled in past times? By underground circulation of pornography. In brothels. By visits to other countries. By day-dreaming. Sometimes not at all. Some of what comes out of our psychic wells is unspeakable, some not so bad. Is the horror at the content a refusal to face it? Is the attempt to suppress a denial?

14. WHY PORNOGRAPHY IS CONSUMED

On this most vexed of questions maximum confusion reigns. The film and some of the authors under discussion believe pornography is part of the symbolic affirmation and reassertion of male hegemony, of propaganda against women, perhaps on the rise as a vicious reaction to the women's movement. The last argument seems rather far-fetched and can be disposed of right away. For, do viewers of pornography know much about that movement? So much as to fear it and enjoy a back-lash in the form of pornography? The women's movement does indeed get media attention and publishes its own mass products, such as *Ms* and the paperbacks under discussion. But as it failed to get the ERA passed, why would the conspiracy of men be so worried about it that they would foster tacit symbolic propaganda against it? Anti-feminists — of both sexes — are quite able and willing to use overt propaganda and do not seem to be subtle enough for tacit propaganda. This however is not to deny — not in itself — that pornography is the assertion of male supremacy. Is it? Will a pornographic movie asserting female supremacy light a red light in the minds of Laura Lederer, Bonnie Sherr Klein and her colleagues? The answer is hard to discern. Mutuality is given as desirable yet, as we have seen, is hard to display. Suppose that problem is overcome. Logically, all objections should thereby fade away, even the label should be changed from pornography to erotica. My hesitation about expecting this to be the reaction goes back to Steinem's remark about labia and the conquering male viewer. It is true that men violate women with their gaze in a way that women do not symmetrically violate men. This may have biological roots (visual stimuli) but there is also a social dimension too — in most cultures women's bodies usually belong to some men (father, brother, mother's brother, husband) in ways that men's bodies rarely do (except perhaps, in slavery). The connection of this with the fact that the work women can do includes bearing children is obvious. Also obvious here is that the problem with mutualist pornography will, once more, be sexism not pornography.

There is very little else in the film and books under discussion that could be described as answers to why is pornography consumed. One paper in TBTN is devoted to it. The author is Phyllis Chesler and I will number the points I think she makes. Pornography functions for men at a symbolic level where it enables them to: (1) deny loss of prowess; (2) learn to await sexual rewards; (3) assuage the bitterness of being deprived of sex; (4) ward off thoughts of intimacy and incest with their mothers; (5) deny inadequacy; (6) contain their violence towards other men by projecting it onto women (TBTN, p. 156–7).

Chesler employs her own framework which will remain unchallenged as stated above. Also, her argumentation reveals two hidden premises which pertain to factual matters and are palpably false. This should suffice to undermine her detail. The first hidden premiss is that there is no pornography for women; the second is that there is no pornography for homosexual men. Both premisses are hidden because to state them, when they are so obviously false, would evoke self-ridicule. All her interpretations of pornography have to have qualifying phrases like, 'some pornography can be read as', 'pornography intended for males means' added. These innocuous qualifiers have an enervating effect. Consider a parallel case. The force of the following two assertions is quite different: 'feminist indignation is (always) just penis-envy writ large', and, 'it is (sometimes) possible to interpret feminist indignation as penis envy writ large'. One need not be a feminist to want vigorously to contest the first assertion; as to the second, everyone who wants to can safely waive it away with a 'so what?'. The only way to attach any force to Chessler's presentation is to have no discrimination between the two kinds of statement.

A quite different source from either the women's movement or psychoanalysis might be sought to explain the 'flood' of pornography and why it is consumed. Since World War II America has been engaged in a general process of dismantling its own puritanism. The society that once wouldn't wear the bikini because it exposed the navel, or which cut British films because they showed too much cleavage, has loosened, through a series of court and legislative actions, its controls on dress, language, the printed word, contraception, abortion and pictorial pornography. That sexual mores have also liberalised over this time may be evidenced by statistics on premarital chastity, rate of spread of venereal disease, and out-of-wedlock births. Not all these developments are pluses. This process in turn has to do with changes in American society summed up as urbanisation, affluence, immigration, secularisation and cosmopolitanisation. The coincidental or connected development at the same time of a new phase of the movement for women's liberation should not tempt us to confuse that with the sexual revolution. Just as, in Table 1 above, we saw how attitudes for and against pornography cut across attitudes for and against feminism, a similar table could be devised showing how attitudes for and against the sexual revolution cut across attitudes for and against women's liberation. Greater freedom of sexual thought and action can be turned to male advantage just as was sexual repression. Some feminist thinkers toy with the idea that women had a more secure and possibly powerful position before the sexual revolution. These changes affect the way the political liberalism and the actual social illiberalism of America evolves.

Can all *this* be seen as part of a male conspiracy? That would be difficult since some feminists approve of some of it. Moreover, who is the pornography for? If men are in control, their propaganda should be directed at brainwashing their slaves, making them happy and cooperative, not sullenly docile. But, notoriously, women do not like a great deal of pornography. Perhaps through it men vent their fury on women. This too is unwise — only a docile population is manageable. By the logic of management women should be fed material that will keep them quiet. Judging by the anger, if there is a male conspiracy it has been bungled. Let us try to get away from male conspiracy explanations.

One of the reasons that so little is written about pornographic films and tapes is that the writing reveals at least as much about the writer as about the material. If it is true that most women are not sexually intrigued by the average piece of pornography we may think they can write about it with ease since they reveal very little about themselves. Yet if my previous discussion has shown anything, it is that NALS and the feminist writings have within them some very strange ideas and, in the vehemence, a good deal of anxiety about pornography. But these women have had the courage to expose themselves in this way so it behooves a critic of theirs to plunge into the question of functions despite the anxiety such self-revealing discussion may entail.

To begin with I want to recall an earlier point: pornography is diverse. Along its spectrum are widely different materials which might very well serve widely different purposes. In particular, we may remember a general point of psychopathology, relating to pornography as it relates to other material: any material, psychopathic or not, functions differently for the psychopath than for the relatively normal person. We may take the case of John Hinckley Jr., well known because he attempted to assassinate President Reagan. His reaction to the Hollywood film *Taxi Driver* was bizarre enough to set him aside from the bulk of moviegoers for whom that film functioned as an enthralling experience. But Hinckley's fixation on the actress Jody Foster, who played the role of the child prostitute Easy/Iris in the film, and his inability to distinguish between her and her screen role, is not something to be anticipated and prevented; film makers, film censors and anyone else in the film industry are not obliged to take account of it. What is these people's civic responsibility? As a rough criterion I propose the following: movies are a medium of entertainment which people enjoy partly because there is an illusion of something happening although they are always aware that none of it is real. Those who cannot separate the screen from real life are special and peculiar cases whose unpredictable delusions the film industry does not have to consider.

Going on from there: (pornographic) films portray a variety of (sexual) situations that people enjoy partly because they know it is only a film. What is the nature of this enjoyment and in what way does it connect to off-screen life? Feminist writing concentrates on the social question of the effects of (pornographic) movies on the rate of crime and mistreatment of females. What of the individual? The feminist books are largely silent; the exceptions are Phyllis Chesler and Susan Griffin (PAS) who offer elaborate psychoanalytic interpretations of the connection of pornography to the mother, to hatred of the body, to denial of feeling and of attraction to death. This sounds bad, but since it is mild by comparison with psychoanalytic readings of such simple processes as normal middle-class growing up, it is not really an indictment of anything, nor even a characterization of anything beyond psychoanalysis proper. It thus calls for no comment.

That there should be so little in either the film NALS or the books mentioned about the process and meaning of consumption of pornography doubtless relates to both the absence of research and its intrinsic difficulty. Here I will expatiate on only one sort of difficulty: the pornography we are discussing is visual: films and magazines. There is no general understanding of the manner in which we consume either. Arguments that leap from representations on the page or the screen over to life, which suggest a direct causal connection, are moving far beyond any established results. Someone once put the claim to me thus. Suppose in a film we see a woman standing in the kitchen stirring soup. Nothing more than a plot point. Suppose however that almost invariably when we see women in films they are literally or figuratively in the kitchen stirring soup. Are we not then free to interpret these films as telling us that this is the 'natural' place of women? Do not then movies help to reproduce and perpetuate the system that puts women into that 'place'?

If we accept this argument, then the interpretation of pornographic films does not come out showing that the natural place of women is in the kitchen stirring soup. Rather do they show women as sexually active rather than passive, seeking relationships rather than sheer pleasure; or seeking forms of pleasure that will break the chains of their inhibition. Whatever one may think of such messages, they hardly perpetuate but are highly subversive of the current repressive attitude to sexuality, especially in certain regions of the United States and in Canada. Similarly, one could shift the attention from soup stirring to clothes and bodies. Is the woman in the kitchen dressed in an apron and standing in a slouch, etc. From the pornographic films we learn that women are usually young, have healthy bodies with often some excess body-fat, and wear under their street clothes highly provocative lingerie. Is this their natural 'place', or is this the constant representation of an ideal, an aspiration?

There are two methodological weaknesses in all such interpretations: the illusion of counting; and the phenomenology of discount. Notoriously, the meaning of an action seen can be quite different to the participants from what it seems to be to the viewer. Even stirring soup is deceptive. To a film critic counting kitchen+soup scenes each such scene is the same. To a moviegoer watching the narrative one such scene may be an incidental detail, another may be a crucial plotting point to do with poisoning, a third may be a woman taking her turn in the kitchen, a fourth may be a desolate scene of a lonely person preparing food for herself, a fifth may be a moving scene of a missionary preparing food for starving children, etc., etc. The presumption of counting is that there is a common denominator of signification in all these scenes, namely: woman+kitchen+soup+stirring = natural place. But the equation presumes too much.

The phenomenology of discount is similar. Countless numbers of people have been watching movies for generations and have been exposed to men and women of great beauty and talent. This has not destroyed the capacity of those with less beauty or talent to cope with life; if anything, the reverse. How so? We do not know. But we can certainly infer that a discount mechanism must be in place that enables the moviegoer to be aware of the disjunction between the movie world and the world he or she inhabits, so the difference is marked not missed. Hence expectations within movies are not uncritically transferred into expectations in real life. There may be some transfer, but it is not easy to know what it is, its extent, or the extent of its individual variation.

With these caveats in mind, let us turn our attention back to the pornography under discussion and try to supply some of the things that need to be said about it that were conspicuous by their absence from *Not a Love Story*. Commonsense suggests a number of functions pornography can serve for the individual.[56]

(1) *Information*. Films, books and so on can give us information, misinformation, they can guide us, mislead us, and so on. That is why they have long been used for instructional purposes and for propaganda purposes. A great deal of theoretical debate surrounds their achievement, however. There are those who treat the film or book as a stimulus and the human being as a response and the relationship between them as one-to-one. But, rather as it was once discovered that hypnotic subjects will not obey any and all instructions, so was it discovered in mass media research that the stimulus could *boomerang* and produced the opposite response to the one desired. Propaganda against prejudice, for example, could be reinterpreted to reinforce the prejudice. Thus even the claim that there was a statistical

relationship between the stimulus and the human response seemed too strong, since a boomerang effect would produce a negative result. We have seen this problem already in the Ontario Censors' decision to restrict showing of *Not a Love Story*. Although clearly a propagandist documentary against pornography the censors feared that users of pornography could integrate it into their needs. The Canadian feminist author Margaret Attwood's novel *Bodily Harm* has been criticised for the same reason. A further complication comes from depth psychology, which seeks out hidden messages operating on the audience's unconscious. And a final wrinkle is added by the Marxist tradition which noses out the implicit ideology of the status quo reproduced in the work and hence produced in the society.

Since the issue is vexed let us begin at the level of instructional films: To grasp this function all one has to do is try to empathise with the sexually ignorant — imaginatively to understand the sexual ignorance typically found in our society — and hardly anything else. One added premiss required is that it is easier to enjoy sex if ignorance is removed. This added premiss, however, is hardly ever objected to, least of all by enlightened feminists such as are under discussion. From pornographic films male viewers can gain information about the detail of female anatomy, its variety, how best it can be approached. Exactly the same is true for female viewers. Not only is it unquestionable that techniques of love-making can be learned, especially that extensive foreplay can be a pleasurable extension of and improvement to sex; not only is it generally agreed that it is one thing to read or be told, and quite another thing to watch foreplay with both partners enthusiastically enjoying it; the point is particularly pertinent for all those who are so sensitive to the sufferings of sisters taken for granted by their male chauvinistic mates: what better can they do for the suffering of wives in bed but to teach men to be gentle (and perhaps vice versa)! This sort of obvious, commonsense, even pedestrian, point seems to be forgotten all too often — perhaps revealing woeful ignorance both of how ignorant on matters sexual many people still are, as well as of how harmful this fact is, and how supportive of sexism.

TBTN offers a counter-argument to education/information, namely, propaganda for misconduct: (male) lovers returning from pornographic viewing to demand at home what they have seen on the screen (pp. 224–8). This delicate issue must be faced, despite the general caveats entered above. One function of film in general — especially films of social commentary (on the very rich; on the very poor; etc.) has always been anticipatory socialization, that is, teaching the ways of segments of the social world to the still alien viewer. It is much more than idle curiosity. Not just socially mobile adults but also children, for a conspicuous example, can learn about adult behaviour from watching other adults, from instruction and from movies. And what they learned may be salutary or objectionable. No-one wants them to learn the objectionable. It goes without saying that some of the activities pornography shows may be unfamiliar to the viewer who thus learns from them — something salutary or objectionable. Should their learning be curbed even if they are children no longer? The feminists under discussion are adamant: any force or pressure, they protest, is wrong. Agreed. But what about instruction about force and pressure? And what about gentle (pornographic) attempts at persuasion, at try-it-you-might-like-it? Robin Morgan would have to declare this rape. She seems to leave out of her view of sexual connection a crucial kind of sexual pleasure, namely the pleasure of giving pleasure to the other. Men may learn from pornography some things that excite women: if this makes men better lovers and thus gentler to women (in matters sexual) will the feminists under discussion object? The reverse argument, no doubt, should be made also: women may learn from pornography, mediated through male viewers, how to be better lovers. Since being better lovers means behaving as an equal to, rather than imposing one's way on, one's sexual partner, the feminists under discussion who endorse mutuality must be in favour of being better lovers. This is supported by all the anti-pornography arguments rehearsed in this study; hence, these anti-pornographic remarks are in error by their own premisses.

They do suggest two moderate defensive points: pornography may not be the best source of information. This should be conceded at once. It is not an argument for withdrawing this source, however. The second point is that at best what pornography may be a source for is better sexual technique. Is sexuality to be equated with technique? Again, an immediate concession. Sexual relations are part of human relations and the best quality of human relations are not reducible to matters of technique. This again is not an argument for withdrawing any source of information on technique.

The matter, to repeat, is simply commonsense and concedes much of the complaint of the authors under discussion. The discussion has been general, it only become truly delicate when we descend to specifics. The range of sexual practices lovers may enjoy be very large — far larger than some of the feminists under discussion allow. Let us return to the example which may be objectionable a priori: Judith Bat-Ada thinks anal intercourse is such. This is indeed a delicate case, because it obviously may be true, a priori, that anal sex is never enjoyable to women. But is it in fact so? Her willingness to make the claim a priori, with only a nod at empirical evidence, is evidence about

Bat-Ada rather than about sex.[57] In particular about her willingness to dogmatise about controversial subjects.[58] Can one counter her dogmatising by the simple declaration that some women disagree with her? After all, plenty of women and homosexual men affirm that anal intercourse is a pleasurable erotic activity, inherently neither dangerous nor uncomfortable, to be indulged in only voluntarily. The last goes without saying, but I do not want to confront Bat-Ada with empirical testimony. She may want to deny it, and I defend her right to do so. My question was about attempts at persuasion. Will she refuse to leave room for persuasion? Both boys and girls may need persuasion to try any sex practice the first time. If the idea comes from a pornographic film is that any worse than if it comes from spontaneous urge? If suggestion is allowed, however, will a suggestion be wrong if compliance with it is attempted only once? And even if the compliance is different, does that alone render it rape?

(2) *Masturbation*. Solitary sex is a practice that has come out of the closet during the sexual revolution; formerly declared by teachers and priests to be a sinful perversion and by doctors and Boy Scout Manuals to cause all manner of harm from pimples to madness, it is now taken for granted both that it is an integral part of most people's sex lives, whether alone or together, and that it is quite innocuous. Pornography often has protracted and detailed scenes of masturbation. So far from it being negatively sanctioned, it is now acknowledged that a person may enjoy the sight of another masturbating.[59] What goes on screen also goes off. Pornography offers material to play and the mind over while masturbating, not solely in the theatre, but also in memory later. Home-viewable video-cassettes are here preferable to the large screen, as they make the conjunction of viewing and masturbating easier.

Of course, some people need no props to masturbation, others may find the stimulus of their actual sex-lives sufficient. But we may need our powers of empathy just here: it should be remembered that numbers of elderly people, handicapped and the imperfectly formed may have no other replenishable reservoir of masturbation material. One could go further and say the same for pubescents, but this touches on the taboo around children and sex. I will come back to this in Section 14.

(3) *Arousal*. The most obvious function of pornography is to get people sexually excited. Some would suggest that sex life enhanced by pornography is inadequate. But this comment only sounds as if it were a dismissal of the usefulness of pornography, when, logically, it lends it support. It is true that sex-life is often inadequate that, quite generally, inadequacy and the need for help are one; that, particularly in the matter at hand, staleness, difficulty

of arousal, lack of stimulus, invite such help as can perhaps be gained from viewing pornography. Here again the video-cassette market is a great break-through, making stimulus available where and when it is called for. Fairly reliable information has it that in those gay clubs where sexual activity is permitted, the showing of pornographic cassettes is a standard feature of local entertainment and that some viewers are passive watchers, others engage in active sex simultaneously with viewing. If this is true, if in the already highly erotically charged atmosphere of all-male gay clubs pornography is invited as extra stimulus, then we may conclude that even when sex stimulation is quite adequate, enhancement may be wanted and welcome. It is clear that no liberal writer can consistently object to this.[60]

(4) *Celebration and play*. Pornographic theatres and their trade goods are temples to celebrate and play with sex.[61] They celebrate pan and eros, they specialise in depicting sexual activity in all its intricacy, and vigour – be it performed in joy or in joylessness. Our society singularly lacks ceremonies around this basic human fact, something that many other civilizations enact to diverse degrees of intensity and in diverse manners. Eros is not reproduc-tion or marriage or mutually respecting tenderness, although all those should have their own ceremonies too. Eros is in itself the enjoyable carnality of sex, something it can be a pleasure to be reminded of, to face without shame, to accept in all its diversity. At the same time as being a powerful and real force, it is also something we can defuse fear of by playing with it, by not always taking it too seriously, even profaning it (McCormack 1980, p. 58). It is intriguing how many of the pornographic films are in fact comedies, where sexual quirks can be laughed at as they are enjoyed. No doubt the hostility to pornographic comedy which some authors exhibit is silly in the same way as is the hostility which other authors exhibit towards the violence in Disney cartoons. It is neither the sex nor the violence but the exuberant joy which is stressed by the artist and is overlooked by the critic. Of course the critic may have ample room for complaint about poor artistry-both in pornography and cartoon – but artistic merit or its absence is not the topic of either the feminist anti-pornography or my critique.

(5) *Anxiety*. All the functions so far and the final one I discuss next, fantasy, can be connected to the need to reduce anxiety concerning sexual matters. Anxiety has such sources as ignorance, what Mary Hartman called "performances problems', a sense of sin, deficiencies in one's relations to the target sex, inexperience, fear, of being unattractive or inadequate, or disgust. Men and women in pornographic films do all sorts of gross and carnal things while apparently thoroughly enjoying themselves. This is doubtless

acting, since film making is in reality a tiresome business; it is clear, then, that the acting comes to convey a message.

Why is it, though, that most pornography is male-oriented in this respect, that most pornography does not attend to female sexual anxieties? A simple answer would be that females do not have any anxieties on this count; but commonsense dismisses that answer. If, as Beatrice Faust claims (WSAP, passim), the sexuality of men and women is different, it would follow that both their anxieties and the means of allaying them may be different. It is even possible that pornography serves to increase female sexual anxiety. NALS articulates the view of those feminist writers who say that they do not want to be measured by the fashion models, *Playboy* nudes, and sexual athletics that saturate the imagery available to men. Real people, they say, do not look that good or perform that smoothly; they even object to the portrayal of real people as if they were ideal — on the ground that such a portrayal is painful: it makes people feel less than their perfect portraits and so at fault. This is a good point. If one accepts Faust's further argument that men are more geared to visual stimuli than women, one might conclude that *Playboy*-style idealization makes it hard for women to live up to men's image of them. Faust however thinks that the high level of men's visual orientation is biologically given and so not something that can be 'cured',[62] just as women's greater sensitivity to tenderness and touch is biologically given. Indeed she argues that this asymmetry in male/female sexuality creates permanent sexual anxiety in both sexes. This raises a simple question: what artifact serves female biological peculiarity the way pornography serves male biological peculiarity? Presumably the answer is any enhancement or depiction of female tactilism.

If the truth be told, according to Faust, women do have their functional equivalent to pornography: soap opera, women's magazine fiction, gothic and Harlequin-type romances (she should have mentioned *Cosmopolitian*). In these stories women's peculiar anxieties are allayed by the heroine's finding happiness with a man who is strong and appealing, but also tender, attentive and secure. But this kind of artifact — art geared specifically for women — is notoriously sexist and anti-feminist. The feminists in NALS are interested in differences that are political not biological: oppression of women. Are there kinds of sexual anxiety which come from very deep differences between men and women perhaps even purely biological differences that cannot but be relevant to their sexuality? Perhaps. Not only child bearing is given to women only. Women are fertile for only a short band of their lives; men can be fertile from puberty to death. Women can have at most a small number of children; man can father very large numbers. Women's level of sexual interest has a different rhythm from men's — affected as it is by monthly cycles, by childbearing, by menopause and their attendant anxieties. Admittedly there are traces of these variations in men, but they are muted. Nor is that all. A man must have erection and orgasm to reproduce, a women needs neither. If it is permitted to add to this list of biological differences the different responses to visual stimuli that make men able to respond to a far broader range of women than do women to men, then it almost looks as though men are built to roam sexually, women built to seek longevity and security. If this is so, nature goofed as far as those are concerned who identify equality with sameness. If nature goofed we may have an explanation of the importance of *fantasy*. If feminism is egalitarian in the face of such a broad and anxiety-generating natural difference, then feminism wants to combat nature. If so, then it can use all the services of fantasy it can get, not least of which should be openly feminist pornography, aimed at allaying female anxiety in present day society. Faust seems to want this.

(6) *Fantasy*. Fantasy may be the most glaring ommission from the feminist literature on pornography on which *Not a Love Story* draws. It is mentioned from time to time, but never seriously discussed. From a film maker like Bonnie Sherr Klein this has to seem especially odd, since films deal in fantasy. Fantasy overlaps masturbation and arousal but deserves separate treatment because of its broader significance. Fantasy is our way of reconstructing the world as we might like it to be, or as we might like that part of it to be which we can visit. Faust reports that, asked to construct their sexual utopia, men will usually include an element of sexual free-for-all, women often will not (pp. 84–5). Women, she reports, tend rather to fantasise about a man always and renewably strong, sexy, passionate and loyal.

This explains much about pornographic films: they often present fantasy situations that men enjoy but women do not. The pornographer who could manage to combine fantasy pleasing to both sexes seems set to be the money-maker of all time.

This view of pornography as sexual fantasy is too simple. Graphic sex (for males) may not sit well with tactile eroticism (for females); especially as the element of voyeurism enters. Slade (1975) makes the point that explicit sex on the screen ousts all other material and becomes the only reality. He discusses how distracting would have been pornographic illustra- tion of Bibi Andersson's speech in *Persona* where she describes a high erotic encounter on the beach. One could think of other examples: suppose, in the scene that made *Shampoo* famous, after Julie Christie announces that what she would really like to do is fellate Warren Beatty, suppose we had then seen rather than had suggested her doing this? I argue it would have brought the whole narrative to a halt, the only reality would be that one had seen two famous film stars actually doing it. To a degree this is already true of nudity on screen, as a magazine like *Celebrity Skin* attests. Actors and actresses are always asked what it was like to face or to do nude scenes, just as once they were asked about kissing scenes, and titillating legends circulate about whether they got carried away and really "did it" while filming. This legend has surrounded *Boxcar Bertha, Don't Look Now, The Postman Always Rings Twice* and *Bad Timing* in recent years; the ability to see what isn't there and to forget the conditions under which films are made suggests a lot of wishfulfilment at work. But it is not only that — it has to do with gut reaction. Violence, too, fills the screen, and audiences may see more of it than is explicit on screen, especially when they strongly sympathise with the hero — regardless of whether he is donor or recipient. Hence, looking at nudity, and more so, at sex scenes, is sometimes quite visceral in itself. Which brings us to voyeurism.[63] One of the very few things I agree with Stanley Cavell about is the voyeuristic side of the pleasures of the cinema. Both he and I have said all movie watching is voyeurism (my 1970, his 1971). It would seem to follow from this that pornography is the ultimate use of the medium, since the voyeur's quest is always to look upon sex itself. Filmed pornography is as old as film, yet it hardly seems like the culmination of the medium. The subsection of the film industry that produces pornography has become a profitable and stable part, but not a dominant one. Other genres — science fiction, adventure, mystery, romance, comedy and so on — continue to flourish. Why? Is the movie not a voyeuristic pleasure after all, or is watching sex not voyeuristic? Neither. What the availability of pornography enables one to think is that possibly the voyeur's curiosity is about anything hidden or tabooed; but that once disclosed it moves into perspective.

I do not know if women are as avid voyeurs as men. I do know it is hard to fathom why on-screen sex stops the narrative. Why does it stop movies more than does violence or heights? Partly because the sexual action is real, unlike everything else in the film. Other real things, such as the killing of real animals on screen, or the use of actual surgical footage or horrifying newsreels (think of Bergman's use of the footage of the burning Buddhist monk in *Persona*) certainly for this viewer have the capacity to bring the narrative to a full halt. If it is true that hardcore scenes halt the narrative then they will never be successfully integrated into mainstream Hollywood films. Pornography will be a genre that cannot be blended into others. A pornographic film with a horror plot will be a pornographic film first; a pornographic film with a gangster plot, etc. Slade may have been refuted by Oshima's *In the Realm of The Senses* and Riploh's *Taxi Zum Klo*.

These responses to killings or newsreels are personal and may be merely to do with my being uninured. Even now it is hard for me to empathise with the uninured audience's reactions to their first sight of explicit sex (as at college screenings of NALS). Maybe I do not want to be inured to animal killing or concentration camp footage. This could be turned into an argument supporting the position of the feminists under discussion: they do not want us to get inured to sex. Pornography inures, therefore pornography is bad. This is what Dworkin dismisses as the liberal argument that pornography hurts us all. Being not a liberal but a paternalist who knows best what is good for us she will have none of it.

So we seem here to have some sort of breakdown of the fantasy: pornography is fantasy yet it trades in unambiguous footage of people actually engaging in sex, a reality that can be contained only within its own genre. Perhaps a reminder of an earlier point will help clarify matters. To say pornography shows real sexual acts is slightly to misstate the case. What filmed pornography does is to edit together selected fragments of photographed sexual activity in order to give the impression of a continuous sexual encounter. Different angles on the same encounter may have been shot on different days, sound and music may be added later, inserted or clinical close-ups may use "doubles". None of these elements would satisfy fantasy; it is only the pseudo-event created by putting together the elements that creates a surface over which our fantasy can play.

What is fantasy? How essential is it? Not being any kind of expert on such matters, I will confine myself to observations. Sex, like a number of other subjects, is one on which we may imagine, because we participate in it, that we are all experts. This is self-deception. We have minds and bodies and so cannot avoid possessing some knowledge about them, but we are not experts on them — we are no psychologists or physiologists for that reason. Moreover, since it has been claimed that culture preserves bizarre and repressive ideas about sex, the likelihood is that our sex-related folk knowledge and introspection are highly misleading.

In trying to understand the appeal and value of filmed pornography I want only to think through two other points. One is the centrality of fantasy in many people's sex lives, the other is this vexed question of whether pornography objectifies women.

Fantasy plays many roles in people's sexuality. Some people act out their fantasies — even with equipment, costumes and the like. Others think it out or talk it out. Some fantasy people keep to themselves and hide even from their intimates: one might suspect this is common where a predominantly heterosexual person has occasional homosexual fantasies. Other people find it particularly intimate and also exciting to have their partner disclose fantasies. This says enough to reveal the subject as highly personal and highly variable and in so far as sexual relations also involve the pleasuring of each other seems to argue against any attempt to lay down a party line on what is and is not truly erotic.

There is a grain of truth in the constant accusation that pornography objectifies women; Slade (1975) counters this by noting that it equally objectifies men — if not more so. Surprisingly, although the concept is one central to their thinking, there is little discussion of this claim in the film and books under discussion. The very word 'objectification' belongs to philosophy — it clearly derives from the phenomenological-cum-marxist tradition. As a professor of philosophy I should be able to explicate the concept yet in truth I have never been able quite to get the hang of it. It is closely connected with the viewing of another person as being there primarily in order to serve one's own ends. To a degree, most social relationships in modern society involve objectification, the treating of others as anonymous ciphers, such as check-out clerks at supermarkets. (Sociologists call it 'impersonalism'). This indeed is the source of some philosophers' rejection of the modern world. There is substance to their rejection, as is shown by the very presence of strict rules of comportment and polite distance towards people one 'objectifies', designed to ensure no mistreatment. Yet this does not bespeak rejection: both clerk and customer accept the reduction of their personhood to temporary and well-delineated objectified roles as the price of social lubrication. Here we may also take a clue from the argument of Steinem and others that the labial exposure of a woman exposes and humiliates all women:

as her likeness shines out from the public sidewalk, she has become all women: any woman walking by this image may feel the urge to turn her head away in shame. For this picture of the body of one woman has become a metaphor, in its anonymity (and in the general anonymity that belongs to women), for all women's bodies. Each sale of a pornographic image is a sadistic act which accomplishes the humiliation of all women (Griffin, PAS, p. 112).

First I think a point should be repeated and conceded: similar displays by men would not necessarily shame men. Presumably the argument would go that men are the dominant class so displays of their genitalia are displays of their power. Women are the subordinate class and whatever sexual power they may have is vacated by its promiscuous display in public places. Whether feminists like it or not, this point seems to me central to the anthropology of sexism: women's bodies, along with their dowries, have traditionally been articles of trade. Their bodies were valued for childbearing first, capacity to work second, and sex very much a third and sometimes insignificant factor.[64] But increasingly in modern society sexual favours have over-taken the capacity to bear children and to work as a woman's bargaining chip. Hence those who give out their bodily favours either for straight cash or for free are a threat to the exchange value of the female body, as traditionalist defenders of the traditional norms of society know only too well. By parallel argument, I suppose, liberated women are threatened too because they feel others' promiscuity devalues their assets. They wish for an egalitarian market in which to seek an erotic partnership based on mutual esteem. Women who sell sex, trade it, give it away, allow themselves to be filmed doing it, women who in any manner play traditional man-pleasing roles, are obviously a serious threat to the exchange values established in this egalitarian market. The little power that women have depends on scarcity and repression, to end those *before* equality is achieved make all women worse off. In a sociological study of such groups as Citizens for Decent Literature and Morality in Media, Inc., Zurcher and Kirkpatrick (1976, passim) interpret them as groups engaged in defence of their threatened status by reaffirming allegedly 'basic' social values. Sadly, despite their declarations to the contrary, not only are the feminists under discussion making common cause with such groups seeking to reverse change, their actions are subject to *exactly* the same sociological explanation.

That the desire for women's liberation produces ambivalent anxiety about status-loss goes some way to explain the stridency. The anger may be a deeper matter, due to disappointment. Dworkin (TBTN, pp. 148–54) was clearly deeply upset to find, when she joined the left in the sixties, that the men were sexist and enjoyed pornography. Might one infer that here anger at the sexism diffused over to the pornography which she took to be an integral part of the outlook of the sexist males?

Secondly, being human, and so, in a metaphysical way, all parts one of another, all human encounters must range along a scale from objectification to particularity: men and women only recognise each other as such because of strong resemblances between the sexes and because of the archetypal image they have of the two opposite sexes. To be blunt, when interacting with the opposite sex one is always simultaneously and dialectically interacting with the unique and with the typical, one makes love to this specific person, and also to one's own self, thereby making one's partner an object: man or woman, as the case may be.

Thirdly, the process is reciprocal. We objectify ourselves: in sex talk it is not uncommon for us to refer to ourselves impersonally or even in the third person. The increasing invasion of such talk in pornographic films heightens their erotic intensity. Again I stress that this process is true of men as well as of women. Indeed I would go so far as to say that intimacy with the unique other is to some extent a turn-on precisely because that unique other is one's embodiment of one's own archetype of the opposite sex, and thus also one's channel to communion with the powerful universal force of sexual energy; once that energy begins to flow one is an object to one's own self as well as to others.

Fantasy, then, is part of objectification. In fantasy we conjure with possibilities without the intrusion of responsibility and consideration: if men concentrate on women's appearance that stems from their visual sensitivity; if women concentrate on men's personality that stems from their sensitivity. In real life, responsibility and consideration induce men to overcome their vulnerability to the visual; but women also compromise by taking their appearance seriously. Compromise is a strain, as are all prolonged human relations. That each should seek an outlet, dream about and become excited over imaginary scenarios in which responsibility and cosideration can be disregarded, seems harmless enough.

We can now assess the core of Gloria Steinem's objection and find her condemnation grossly misplaced. She says erotica yes; pornography, no. Why? Because pornography objectifies and thus degrades. At times objectification degrades, we have seen: when proper rules of distance and delineation are not observed. Otherwise not. The source of objectification is fantasy. To the extent that erotica is the better fantasy, it objectifies more, not less. Indeed, in its very elusive and allusive nature, erotica is devastated by the sex-object's capacity to cook, wash dishes and change diapers. By its very stark realism, by its very crudeness, pornography can take place in the kitchen, in the office between (male) employer and (female) employee.[65] What is more sexist? A fantasy sex-object who does not wash dishes, or one who does? Gloria Steinem is confused about this and so views *Playboy* — the paradigm of non-pornographic erotica — as pornography proper. There is reason in that: she attacks the enemy and the enemy is not at all sex, erotic or pornographic, but sexism. She sees sexism in pornography and confuses the two, but the enemy remains sexism – and perhaps her confusion, but not pornography.

15. PORNOGRAPHY IN ITS SOCIAL CONTEXT

The major political problem regarding pornography is that of censorship. The political framework for discussing censorship is liberalism. Liberalism is notoriously problematic. How liberal should a liberal political system be? Fortunately for the present discussion, the weakest, simplest, and most straightforward liberal philosophy – eighteenth century liberalism – will do here. How liberal are and how liberal should be the feminists who examine pornography for its illiberal sexism? The answer is given in the best paper in TBTN, Wendy Kaminer's quoted above (section 6).

Eighteenth century liberalism would approve of such developments as liberalised divorce laws, as sex education, as popularly available means of contraception, as tolerance of sexual deviation; to this I should add the separation of sex from both marriage and love (viz. 'trial marriage' and 'recreational sex') as part of a process of reducing sexual repression. Like any social change, this one disturbs and distresses some people, it thus meets reasonable resistance which may point to side-effects that are both real and distressing. The argument 'the freedom you demand offends me in and of itself, hence should not be granted in order to spare my feelings' is often used by resistors but is an unreasonable argument. This argument, together with, 'freedom does not include the freedom to tell lies' constitute the acid tests of classical liberalism. Everybody is deeply offended by something or other (even if we can confine ourselves to things not involving harm to others, although those offended can rhetorically claim they are being 'harmed' by being offended) and so such an argument from the giving of offense would cut a wide swathe; and criteria of truth and lies can be made broad also. If one's liberalism falters in the face of either distress or the accusation of lies then one may as well concede entirely and accept a degree of repression that mirrors the strengths of the forces presently desiring repression as they are deployed in society. Accusations of dishonesty against some of the feminists whose works were under discussion have not been absent from this paper but liberals need not press them. Why they wrote and who wants to read them will be taken up in the next, and penultimate section.

Freedom to read, write, publish, depict, caricature, ridicule, distort, hurt, satirise, offend, and, yes, to lie, seem to me all of a piece. Once one follows an affirmation of freedom with a 'yes, but . . . ' then the unpacking of the 'but' can lead anywhere. This is not to say that freedom equals utter freedom. Utter freedom nowhere exists and never has. Only a utopianist expects it to. Issues of social policy are practical matters. The society in which we live and witness the growth of both pornography and anti-pornography has its own limits on freedom: the question always is, should these be tightened or relaxed? Whereas once American social illiberalism put fairly high on the scale of repression all sorts of religious, political and especially sexual thought, American official political liberalism has gradually became a world leader in freedom in these very matters while the rest of the world (U.S.S.R., China, India, Saudi Arabia, Iran, Eire, Greece) adopt severe measures of suppression and persecution.

The anti-pornographic material under discussion is, then, ideological. Let us examine the ideology. It takes over from Marx the idea that society is divided into two classes, one of which owns/exploits/mistreats the other. The name of the exploiting class is 'men', of the exploited class 'women'. There is a split over the Leninist view that a revolutionary change is brought about by polarising the two classes, and its gradualist complement that change is achieved slowly by reform and persuasion. Those feminists exercised by pornography argue that it is made by men for the consumption of men and so graphically depicts the manner in which women are exploited for the pleasure of men. Of course, if men are the source of the suffering of women and if men are unredeemable then it follows that women must seek out other women for equality and fulfilment. Such polarisation is assisted by the Jehovanist (Davis 1983) view so widespread in our culture that sex is harmful. Men's enjoyment of pornography can thus be used to make them feel guilty and to make women feel indignant and threatened. Thus we see why an item relatively low on the social agenda has been successfully pushed almost to the top. The issue is the relative social and political positions of men and women all of which can be focused in depictions of their carnal connection. So those feminists who are heterosexual, liberal and gradualist still rightly feel the need to address the pornography issue. Their liberalism makes any censorship or thought control repugnant. Yet some of them reach such a conclusion. How? It is not yes-buttery; it is rather an attempt to argue that freedom should be curtailed in order to foster certain highly beneficial social aims that, it is hoped, when they are achieved, will yield a much better society (non-sexist) and also one in which the lost freedom to enjoy pornography will not be missed by anyone anyway. This argument may be overlooked, perhaps, by some who have no interest in pornography. But if they have interest in liberty, they should respond, and even sharply so. For it is a classical fact that revolutionaries ready to control, suppress and kill for virtue have always used this very argument. Whether one chooses to believe it has to do with one's gullibility, not with attitudes to pornography. The liberalizing record of repressive regimes is not encouraging, and their ability to self-correct, that is, to admit that their projected future state is not now going to come about and hence previous stolen freedoms should be restored, is not tested, since a thousand and one ad hoc excuses for failure can be found, some demanding further curtailment of freedom. (On the internal feminist politics of pornography see Rubin and *Signs*.)

What about the offense pornography causes? A fundamental conceptual confusion is to merge obscenity and pornography. Separating the two is at least as important as separating pornography and erotica. Pornography, we have seen, is best identified by practical test: pictures of erect penises and actual sexual contact. This gets a film an X rating in the U.S.A. and prevents it being shown in Ontario. Obscenity is the label for material of any kind that is grossly offensive. It may have been an unintended consequence of the US Supreme Court's Miller criterion judging obscenity by community standards that juries have been found that are not offended by *Deep Throat*.

Obscenity is a far wider category than pornography: some obscenity is certainly not pornography and, it seems, some pornography is not obscene (Williams, 1979). My suspicion is that the most grossly offensive material nowadays is that which shows explicit violence or vicious prejudice, not sex. Hence, a San Francisco showing of *Birth of a Nation* was recently cancelled after protests;[66] pornography continued unimpeded. One of the most obscene moments I have ever experienced was when, in the course of the teleplay *QB VII*, authentic footage of the Nazi medical 'experiments' on children was shown. Close shots of pathetic children whose suffering was real was cheapened by inclusion in a third rate television programme. Obscenity (offensiveness) here is strictly a matter of context. Filmic records of terrible events are viewable in other circumstances without offense.

In my suggestion that hard-core pornography be defined as graphic depiction of sexual acts there is implicit acknowledgement of the etymology of the word, "writing about whores". We now extend its sense to writing or depicting sex. In addition to being much narrower than obscenity, pornography so defined is also less context-dependent. It makes sense to have a community standard with regard to obscenity, I would argue; it does not make sense to have a community standard with regard to pornography. It also makes sense for some communities to declare that they find pornography obscene.

The trouble with the concepts of obscenity and pornography, then, is that some people find obscene all pornography, indeed the very idea of sex itself. The main contributors to the feminist film and books under discussion come close to this. In order to be able to agree with them one needs to delineate a context, however broad. In what kind of a context can we place the problem of social desirability so as to facilitate rational discussion?

One possible context would be the background of a sexually repressive and inhibited society such as the United States was until the sexual revolution began. By any indicator — pre-marital chastity, number of sex partners, frequency of sex, degree of diffused sexual knowledge, variety of sexual practices, the double standard — the base-line America started from was puritanical. Although journalists exaggerate the degree to which the whole population has changed its habits,[67] there has been deep erosion of this base and changes in all the indicators. Then came a backlash (for example the Moral Majority) not, I think related to any excesses, but explicable by the same underying processes that fostered the sexual revolution itself. The fundamental qualitative changes that have taken place in American society in the last fifty years stem from its earlier structural change from a rural to an urban society. Urbanisation was followed by secularisation against which backlashes have been sporadic (Reform, Prohibition, Revivalism) and, later, general affluence. The social controls of religion and repression weaken because they no longer provide a set of sanctions and rewards that integrates smoothly into the industrialized city. They stress community and conformity, but industrial capitalism rewards individualism and opportunism. Conducting sexual relations according to competitive individualism rather than communalism leads naturally to the sexual revolution as we know it. Sex becomes first of all a field of privacy, a personal property not be interfered with. Then, within that property space, its pleasures are highly individualised: do what pleases you as long as it does not hurt others. These same social changes and this resurgent individualism are what the backlash resists, trying to reimpose community standards and control. Once sex as such has been declassified as sin the process is not reversible; but the extent to which its further classification as a pleasant recreation is reversible is still hotly contested. One expression of this is the fact that heterosexual sex clubs are subject to more police harassment than homosexual ones. Perhaps because the threat to the major market is too close.

Another possible context might be that of erotic stimulus itself. Whether or not pornography is available, its origins lie in the capacity of images and sounds to trigger and to arouse sexual desire. Taking all cultures, straight/gay, west/east, developed/third world, it would be hard to deny that the images that arouse, foster or sustain sexual desire cover a very broad range. Some of them are very graphic, some are fantastic, some involve scenarios with no overt sexual component (these were deemed by Freudians as fetishisms even when they were quite conventional). Such images are employed in various ways: to re-charge flagging desire, as a trigger, as an aid to masturbation. This varied context is important because it is not gender-asymmetrical: people of both genders have fantasy sexual images even if their specific content is different.

Two objections could be raised here, one that private fantasy is altered when it enters commerce, the other that some people's fantasies may offend or frighten other people. Both are good points. It is doubtful that fantasy is ever private: whether the images employed are socially learned or archetypal imprints, they have received patterns. But then realisation and sale still may both debase and cheapen them. Of course, a priori they may also sharpen and heighten them. And if the fantasies are offensive or frightening to some people or other, their free circulation amplifies the offense and fear.

The film and books discussed here clearly are offended by some of the fantasies to be found not only in pornography but in all the imaging of women in ads, magazines, pin-ups, fashion, etc. They express great fear of the eroticisation of children (e.g. Brooke Shields in *Pretty Baby* and her jeans ads) not to mention child pornography. They attack the glazed, sensual look of fashion models. They object to the portrayal of women in pornography as either sexually voracious or as apparently reluctant but really 'she wants it, they all do' (Dworkin, PMPW, *passim*). They object to the suggestion that restraining and beating women may be forgiven and even enjoyed. Above all they are excercised by exhibitions of women enjoying rape or forced sex (*Drama Review* 1981). This, they rightly complain, has little to do with real life rape (but it may cause it; see section 17).

Some questions are in order: (1) are these objections symmetrical, that is, if we look for men in the same positions do we find them? The point is that if we do, this may be an argument that there is nothing sexist about these images. (2) Have any of these images to do with real-life enactments? Diana F. H. Russell, (TBTN, pp. 224–8), is deeply shocked that after seeing pornography men suggested that they would like to try something they saw on the screen. It is not clear in what context and how these responses were gathered, but it is at least also shocking that in this day and age the men whose responses were gathered have to learn about sex variants at the cinema (hence section 14(1) above). The issue of forced sex is real in many contexts;

it is a red herring in the context of the pornography debate. One may object to this: one may claim that everything connects with everything else to make up the one world view. We can characterize the world view which embraces the current pornography and permissiveness as a centuries old, patriarchal conspiracy to oppress women. Now everything does indeed connect with everything else in one way or another. Yet real life is a subtle matter in which not only does everything not connect up with everything else, but also much of the connection there is is not known and much of it is not understood. In order to know and to understand we need to study. And in order to study we need problems in context. Consider one who objects to bringing to the surface erotic feelings about children because this is a perversion that if not so rehearsed will go away. Is this correct? Or will the repression cause harm? One may object for even more exotic reasons, such as the general claim that 'men are sexually attracted to children' (Florence Rush, TBTN, p. 72) and expressions of this attraction should not be allowed. This is an insult to the truth and to the male members of our species. Does the author have the right to testify about his feelings towards children or must he admit the truth of Ms. Rush' claim that (unknowingly, perhaps) he is a pedophile? If the claim is denied will that reveal male chauvinism? Since he is not allowed a proper defence may he not resort to a counter-attack? Freud may be a dirty word with some feminists, but would they dispute his sense of the pervasiveness and power of sex, among males and females, children and adults? Here we see the importance of frameworks for rational discussion. Suppose one is Freudian and asserts that everyone is attracted physically to everyone else, males, females, children' adults, then that renders Rush's dictum 'men are sexually attracted to chidlren' merely a corollary and non-sexually specific: another corollary would be 'women are sexually attracted to children'. To make it the indictment of men it is clearly intended to be one has to postulate a vast difference between the sexes. But what psychological theory offers such a framework?

Is our taboo on facing up to the erotic content of our relations to children a social failing? [68] Children onlooking adult sexual activity and even playfully participating is tolerated in more 'natural' cultures than our own. We rigidly keep the dirty secrets of sex away from our intensely and rightly curious children. This may be a reason why as children we are forced to imagine the details of the important secrets that are hidden from us and these perhaps spurious images become life-long erotic triggers. [70] Rush's empathy with children would be vindicated were she to recommend greater laxity regarding children and sex after having been shown that repressive taboos are harmful.

This does not close all issues. For, if there is one prohibition that we must uphold, it is the prohibition on rape. What is the status of rape? It is not a common theme in the bulk of pornographic feature films, although it is a favourite topic in Hollywood movies. One pornographic classic is devoted to it, *Behind the Green Door*. In that film, to recall, there is a non-naturalistic rape, a fantasy of rape. Its fantasy character is carefully preserved by allowing no hint of harm or violence and constant reassurance to the character and the audience that none is to come. Is this explicit sex plus fantasy rape better or worse than those Hollywood rapes with explicit violence and fantasy sex? In some ways the atmosphere of the pornographic film is far healthier and less threatening. What the film does is to fantasise about overcoming inhibition and repression, *not* about the acceptance of rape. No-one is misled into thinking this is how they can or will be overcome, but the message they take from the film is the rewards of pleasure that await the overcoming of inhibition and repression.

Behind the Green Door does not preach that rape is OK or that women will resist but really want it, although with minor mental gymnastics it could be read that way. A far stronger example of that message, however, would be Lina Wertmuller's *Swept Away*, where the arrogant rich-bitch heroine is forced into sexual submission and finds it fulfilling and conducive to true love.[71]

The question is can any action in relation to pornography reduce rape? Leaving aside total suppression, what content changes in pornographic movies would best serve the end of reducing rape? To use categories mentioned above, we can ask which combination of the many possible is conducive to the reduction of rape. For example, if deleting sadomasochistic scenes from pornography were shown empirically to reduce rape we might, after a consideration of other costs, agree that they should be deleted. This would be very difficult to establish because there are quite a number of categories and hence combinations of pornographic and sadomasochistic material. There is hard and soft core, male homosexual, male heterosexual, fantasy and realistic, erotic and pornographic. Perhaps a reason the feminist writers under discussion place a blanket condemnation on pornography in all categories is precisely because these categories make the issue too complex for empirical resolution. If what happens on the screen is a general threat to any section of the population then to protect women from degradation, violence and rape the blanket should be cast over a wider field than pornography, and we cannot even assume pornography to be its centre or weightiest part. Many Hollywood and European mainstream movies exploit scenes and situations in which women and violence are blended and the audience worked up. These too would be targets for deletion. This project now begins to escalate out of control and we see, once more, that the issue is sexism not pornography, and, as it escalates, that the little qualification written above, 'after a consideration of other costs', begins to loom.

So we can see there is no solution in the direction of deletion and this without invoking thresholds of offense, tolerance and the obscene. Thus I would not propose deletion of the offending scenes from *QB VII*: not only because offense is not a reason to criminalise an action, but because the problem lies elsewhere.

16. WHO MAKES/CONSUMES ANTI-PORNOGRAPHIC MATERIAL?

The short answer is well-educated, bi-coastal women in academic or journalistic jobs. Highly educated, highly literate, high achieving members of the professional middle class. Women who, if they have not already made it in traditional employment, are using the feminist movement itself as a way of making it. By their own account of the sexism of our society they must have overcome many impediments in their rise to prominence. That there are barriers to anyone's advancement, that the barriers inflict pain, are serious problems for our society. All members of the society have a vested interest in the relief of such social problems. It is odd, then, that we have found a tone of mistrust and even hatred towards men in these writings and this film.[72] This tone is politically unwise and creates a pragmatic self-contradiction. By making all men the enemy, this tone at least halves the potential political base of the movement for women's civil rights, more than halves it if we remember the female 'collaborators' with the chauvinists. It contradicts Gloria Steinem's demand for 'mutually pleasurable sexual expression between people who have . . . choice'. Hatred of, one is tempted to say objectification of men into, 'the male' can hardly be a component of sexual relations centred around mutual regard, tenderness and equality.

So the problem now becomes, why do these high-powered feminists we are discussing write in this way, what is the potential audience? To answer this we have to diagnose self-destructiveness and self-contradiction as phenomena of the sociology of movements in general. We have touched on the latter when we discussed membership card behaviour in Section 9 above. What can we make of that behaviour when it is combined with deliberate alienation of those who have an interest in the cause, even a sexual interest? A few ideas. One is that those who discover social problems take a proprietory interest in them, hence by some convoluted logic or other, women's liberation becomes a women's problem. Generalized, this means poverty is the poor's problem, racialism the discriminated's, neurosis the neurotic's. Why futilely try to possess problems and exclude others? Because then you create a secure inner world of ideas and doctrines which can be imposed as an entry price and to which you can refer as a source of answers to life's problems. Hence the phenomenon of what might be called the professional feminist. In writing this I must stress how these feminist manoeuvres are by no means unusual, so much so that Walter Kaufmann was able to list adherence to a movement as a fundamental form of decidophobia, where by decidophobia he meant refusal of autonomy.[73] Autonomy is thinking for oneself, advocating women's civil rights but not subscribing to self-destructive or self-contradictory demands simply to preserve a rhetorical solidarity with 'sisters'. Sexism not pornography is the problem but the problem of sexism does not belong either to women or to feminists.

Decidophobes may be one group that makes/consumes anti-pornography — and here again the film *Not a Love Story* makes common cause with its natural enemies the Moral Majority, et. al. The latter too are decidophobes; they too shy away from autonomy by banding together into groups tied together by logically incoherent doctrine and practice; they too fear autonomy and the autonomous and expend much energy in opposing it and them. Billy Graham, it should not be forgotten, in getting decisions for Christ, doesn't tell you which sect to join, only urges you to give up your directionless autonomy and join something. Some feminist anti-pornographers are stricter: only their faction of their group is the right group, but if you are a male you cannot join. One further parallel with the Moral Majority enemy is striking, and no doubt will be strenuously denied: titillation. The oldest device for allowing hypocrites to toy with that of which they disapprove is condemnation (See 1974, p. 156). Under this rubric one has a dispensation to gaze upon and think about the forbidden; to react and observe other reactions; to probe like a tongue at a cavity. Feminist writers under discussion mention their extensive files of material, their frequent visits to movies, arcades and stores, the plaintive tales of shop owners that distributors force them to accept the horrible stuff.[74] Has radicalism such a short memory? Have we to remember the imputations of prurience against Havelock-Ellis, Krafft-Ebing, Freud, Stekel, Reich, Kinsey, the counter-charge that the critics dwell on the condemnation to enjoy the titillation? How long ago did we learn to be deeply suspicious of those who most heatedly condemn homosexuality, legalized alcohol, etc? And what else can we make of an agitated anti-pornographic film and writings that generate so much heat and so little light? (See Rich 1982.)

As we look at this anti-pornographic crusade a certain complementarity begins to show itself. Economists polarise goods into those that are substitutes for one another and those that are complementary. Sugar and honey are substitutes, left and right shoes are complements. Most goods are partly one, partly the other. Substitutability affects elasticity of demand, namely how readily people respond to changes in price. It they buy the same quantity whether the price rises or falls then demand is inelastic, if demand varies inversely with price, it is elastic. Clearly, goods which are substitutes can have high elasticity, because price rises for one good can lead to substitution of the other. Goods that are complementary are a different case. A rise in the price of left shoes or of cups can bring about either no change, if demand is inelastic, or, drastic change, if it is. The demand for pornography was, I conjecture, inelastic in the past. Those who consumed it when it was illegal had to have it and were prepared to pay; all other sales were a matter of opportunity. When pornography became relatively freely available in the America of the 1970s there was a surge in demand as the price fell, but this then levelled off. Scandinavian experience was similar. It would seem that anti-pornography is like our example of right and left shoes; it is an economic complement of pornography. As pornography grew so anti-pornography grew (See 1974, p. xi). This confutes those who thought that pornography's appeal was its being forbidden: it is no longer forbidden in much of the United States and it continues to have appeal. Hence taking away anti-pornography will not eliminate pornography, but will eliminating pornography also eliminate anti-pornography? One possibility is that rather it will escalate: if violent pornography is banned, then sexist pornography may be next, then all other hardcore, then *Playboy* and so on. Think of the Canadian situation. In Sections 1 and 2 I referred to the oddity of NALS in the Canadian experience. There is a vigorous anti-pornography movement in Canada, and now NALS shows us there is a feminist faction in it too. *Yet Canada has no legal pornography*. It has erotica, and pin-ups and soft-core but legally none of the real thing. *Deep Throat* opened to Toronto's Yonge Street for a few hours in the early seventies and was hastily closed down. Students attempting for a lark to screen *Deep Throat* on campus found plainclothes Mounties with walkie-talkies prowling around. Bonnie Klein and her film crew had to go to New York to film the pornography industry and to sample its product for their movie.

What sense can we make of an anti-pornography crusade in Canada with no legal pornography to crusade against and when only 12% of the population think it a serious problem (*Toronto Star*, 24.11.84)? That the well-springs of anti-pornography are not pornography but must be something else. One could be uncharitable and suggest sexual repression and hence fear as a source. But then again one can be charitable and say that in the works under discussion the source is sexism not pornography. Pornography is simply a focus for feminists to coalesce around and I have tried to argue that it is a bad choice. Where there is no pornography, as in Canada, the possibility of an alliance between the feminist forces of repression and other more traditional forms of repression is one we must confront.

17. SOCIAL SCIENCE AND THE STUDY OF PORNOGRAPHY

Speculation about and research into the possible effects of the mass media is as old as those media themselves. To take movies as an example, there is active discussion by an experimental psychologist in 1916 (Munsterberg) and historians have chronicled vigourous debates (Jowett 1976; Sklar 1976; May 1980). A great deal of empirical research has been commissioned over the years by both private and public bodies. The Payne Fund series eventually resulted in 12 volumes on 'Motion Pictures and Youth' in the years 1933–1937. During and after the second world war there was much government sponsored research into the effect of propaganda films on civilian populations, and the effectiveness of film for mass military education (Hovland, Lumsdaine and Sheffield). There have been several Presidential Commissions in the United States which have commissioned massive technical studies; there has been a Royal Commission in Great Britain; and both a Provincial and a Federal Inquiry in Canada.

Luckily for these bewildered by the sheer bulk and diversity of the literature there is also the institution of the literature review, which lists, summarises and discusses the research and findings. The Payne Fund studies had a separate summary volume. At the end of the war Joseph Klapper undertook a general survey of the whole field of the effects of mass communications, which eventually became his (1960). The Public Inquiries usually include such reviews, as do private ones (Pornography 1972; Eysenck and Nias 1978). Hence a vast body of research, some of it coming to pessimistic conclusions, some to no conclusions at all, exists, but no-one would ever guess this from *Not a Love Story* or the writings of those interviewed.

My own modest contributions were a *bibliographie raisonnée* in my (1970) and a brief chapter in my (1978). It might be interesting to bring this up to date from a Canadian perspective and to comment on the feminist literature from the same point of view. Two colleagues of mine, Thelma McCormack and James Check have made intervention into the debate. McCormack (1978) makes the excellent move of treating the results of research as a social fact in its own right. She notes that research into violence finds the effects serious while research into pornography finds the effects innocuous. She asks the awkward question, who is doing the research, on what sorts of subjects? In both cases the overwhelming answer is: males. If our perceptions of and responses to inequality in life or in art are structured by our own positions in the social structure, as these are modified by our reference group identification, then it is possible that much of the effects research is seriously flawed.

Check's work is perhaps the male feminist's attempt to do properly what the feminists have flubbed: namely to confirm feminist views about pornography, rape, etc. 'The present findings constitute the first demonstration in a nonlaboratory setting not vulnerable to criticisms in terms of laboratory artificiality and "demand characteristics" of relatively long-term antisocial effects of movies that fuse sexuality and violence' (Malamuth and Check 1981, p. 443). Three years later this first demonstration has become a minor industry: 'Recent research has suggested that exposure to sexual violence in pornography can have antisocial effects, such as (a) increased acceptance of rape myths and increased acceptance of violence against women (Check and Malamuth, 1982; Malamuth and Check, 1981a, 1981b), (b) increased laboratory aggression against a female confederate (Donnerstein, 1980; Donnerstein and Berkowitz, 1981), and (c) decreased future perceptions of rape victims' suffering (Malamuth and Check, 1980a; Malamuth, Haber and Feshbach, 1980)' (Check and Malamuth 1984, p. 15).

Bernard Berelson once summed up the effects of mass communication research thus: 'Some kinds of *communication* on some kinds of issues, brought to the attention of some kinds of *people* under some kinds of *conditions*, have some kinds of *effects*' (Berelson 1948). Check and colleagues have 'demonstrated' that male researchers can alter their reference group and hence produce data that 'confirm' or are 'supportive' of theories that suit certain kinds of feminist argumentation. It is interesting to have this move actually carried out, even though the logical situation is such that we know a priori that it could: confirmation of almost any hypothesis can be found to any desired degree. This is one of the reasons philosophers of science argue that only attempts to refute hypotheses, attempts that fail, add any kind of evidential weight. Furthermore, there is much dispute as to how that weight can be interpreted.

McCormack and Check are recognisable as social scientists. Is any of the feminist work so recognisable? During the course of this paper we have touched upon a number of places where the feminists under discussion raise issues within the social sciences. First, the problems: the most general problem of social science they deal with is, 'what is the relation, if any, between what happens on the screen and what happens in life?' The most specific form in which they discuss it is, 'is there a causal effect on behaviour from viewing violence, degradation or humiliation on the screen?' Another problem that organises much of the discussion is, 'are there social, psychological, biological differences between the sexes?'

On methodology they are guided by three general considerations concerning *bias, behaviourism* and *reductionism*. Research conducted by males is suspected of male-*bias*. *Behaviourism*, the doctrine, 'don't study the mind study the behaviour', underlies many of the attempts to show cause and effect at work on the screen affecting life. *Reductionism* is found in two forms: the insistence that sexism can be reduced to a cultural problem and biological factors discounted, and the argument that a social phenomenon, pornography, can be subjected to a kind of collective psycho-analysis.

The relation between off-screen and on-screen is said to be direct and hence to vary in its desirability with the desirability of what is depicted. Findings to the contrary by the President's Commission on Obscenity and Pornography are questioned by Professor Irene Diamond of Purdue with arguments no stronger than that some of the data can be interpreted differently and

a better case can be made for a model hypothesizing a relationship between pornography and the repression of women . . . the evidence supports this proposition. Other data worthy of more careful examination . . . include reports from some cities that tracts with large numbers of pornographic outlets tend to have disproportionately high rape rates, reports from police officers that rapists are often found with pornographic materials in their possession, as well as reports that wife-batterers are often devotees of pornographic literature (TBTN, pp. 200–201).

To subject this to the scrutiny serious thought deserves would be cruel.

Pauline Bart, by contrast, in surveying experimental and social psychological research into pornography prefaces her paper thus:

It is difficult to demonstrate the real-world effect of pornography (or even that of violence in pornography) through research because we do not know the relationship among any of the following: what people believe and what they tell researchers they believe; what kinds of things they think they will do and what they *actually* will do and under what circumstances they will do it . . . and material that is not pornographic in one context may be in another. (TBTN, pp. 204–5).

After such an opener we know we are in for a treat, and, sure enough we are presented with a highly useful summary of the findings of other social scientists and then some properly tentative and open-minded conclusions. Effects on women not enough studied, catharsis model inadequate, imitation model inadequate, science not value-free, most research done by males before violence pervaded pornography, not to assume men and women have the same interests, pornography is not in the interests of women. The slight tone of querulousness that creeps in is redundant; otherwise this paper, and Wendy Kaminer's masterly setting out of the legal situation are the cream of the TBTN crop and excel by any current standard.

Dr. Diana E. H. Russell, who teaches at Mills College, looks into what the 'New' research on pornography says. 'New' here is code for post-Presidential-Commission-on-Obscenity-and-Pornography-Report-research-conducted-by-women-or-non-sexist-men. 'New' may even be code for 'which we find more congenial'. Russell declares herself in favour of pornographic erotica provided it shows respect, affection, tenderness and caring as going along with sex, thus being educative. Regrettably she then turns to a bogus (pornographic) 'research' photo magazine on rape, probably dating from the time 'redeeming social significance' was a popular defence of pornography, runs through the contents, and comments: 'Do we really need research to tell us that such material reinforces or even fosters dangerous myths about rape?' (TBTN, p. 221). She then detours through feminist books, including her own, as though they were authorities who had established that all men are sexually coercive to some degree at some point in their lives, hence many men have a propensity to rape. She finds confirming evidence in an article by Malamuth, Haber and Feshbach. She then turns to the issue of learning from pornography. She asked women whether they had ever had upsetting sexual suggestions from their partners traceable to something seen in pornographic movies. Ten percent of the female population of San Francisco apparently had. She admits that she cannot conclude that pornography is causing this behaviour but thinks she can conclude that it '*does* have some effect' (TBTN, p. 228). A more cautious conclusion would be that her subjects *say* it does – and refer back to Bart's warning. Not denying that some women have masochistic and/or rape fantasies, Dr. Russell wonders whether the propensity of men to rape means that these are bound to be misunderstood. Eysenck and Nias thinks they can create a rapist in the lab. by behaviour therapy so Russell comes down in favour of limited censorship.

Russell's article is rich in its selectiveness, its wanderings and its mixing of research with recommendation. Bart's warnings, which are basic doctrine in sociology and anthropology, need to be printed in bold red block capitals where the research concerns sex: on few subjects are respondents less likely to be reliable in their answers, reports, etc. The usual problems of unreliability are compounded by the intense interaction in sexual matters between people's reports and their hopes, wishes, fantasies. All sex research is gravely suspect. Asking people what they do, or their feelings about what they do must be treated with the greatest caution; observing them is notoriously full of pitfalls, as readers, say, of Szasz on Masters and Johnson, will know. As we find time and again, we learn about the researcher, her predispositions, obsessions, taboos and foregone conclusions in all this more than we learn about sex. There may be ways out of this maze, but if so, I for one do not know them.

Griffin is no more a social scientist than her mentor Hannah Arendt was. She psycho-analyses our culture and men in general to show that the image of femaleness women try to conform to is the pornographic image of denial, emptiness, silence. She also maintains that the Nazi scenarios of anti-semitism and the holocaust exactly parallel pornography (of the degrading kind). She doesn't quite say we have the one because we have the other but I think she believes it, since the apocryphal story of the Nazis flooding Poland with pornography is once more rehearsed. 'In the ideology of pornography' the Poles 'had to recognize the same hatred and abandonment of the self. Men or women immersed in the pornographic ideology would more easily surrender themselves to authority' (PAS, p. 194). Those diabolically clever Nazis, knowing all that.

Literate and sensitive, preposterous and hyperbolic ('the pornographic mind is identical both in form and in ultimate content to the Nazi mind', p. 194), the main thing to note is its reductionism. Culture is the product of 'minds', pornography issues from the 'pornographic mind', and so on. This reductionism leads to ghastly errors like psychologising and hence misunderstanding the Nazis, whose causes and crimes are simply not susceptible to such explanations as, 'images must accelerate in their violence until they become actual events, events with devastate countless human lives' (PAS, p. 158). Argument will be to no avail in light of her endorsing this:

There is no such thing as objective, value-free science. An era's science is part of its politics, economics and sociology: it is generated by them and in turn helps generate them. In short, science is not fact: it is culture (PAS, p. 96).

Such a doctrine was highly congenial to, and endorsed by, the Nazis.

Dworkin's contribution to social science is strictly confined to her bibliography. In praising it, McCormack (1980b) is a trifle too charitable, since it overlooks her own work, also such as Henson, Laws, Mayer, Mishan, Slade, Williams, Zurcher and Kirkpatrick, etc., which I have included in mine.

Perhaps the most fundamental of all methodological problems that needs to be addressed to the studies of pornography and violence is, indeed, rarely so addressed. This is, what is the purpose of these studies of pornography and violence? The answer we have given already is that it is to test the hypothesis that pornography and violence have a social effect; and also to test the further hypothesis that this social effect is, generally speaking, undesirable. But the question then arises, suppose we were to find that there was some effect and that it was undesirable, then what? Clearly, again, the answer is that such results would lead to the conclusion that the social group through the organs of the State apparatus, should take steps to control, and possibly even prevent, the circulation of pornographic or violent material.

There is, however, a classic objection to this course of action that holds whether or not some effect is found. This objection is that any such attempt to employ the apparatus of the organs of the State against any form of speech is more dangerous than could be any demonstrated effect. Let us suppose there is a demonstrated effect. The production of pornographic and violent material takes place in a free market. That is to say, it is a sporadic reaction to anticipated demand. Thus, if there is a great demand for it, it will be produced. If the demand lessens it will not be produced and other kinds of material, possibly less pornographic and less violent, or possibly pornographic and violent in different ways, will be produced. At all events, the social group has quite a close control over the matter through the market mechanism.

The organs of the State apparatus are a different matter. These are set up by laws and the administrative consequences of laws, which include regulations and the appointemnt of people to jobs. However finely laws, administrative arrangements, and creation of jobs are tuned to the situation at the time, once they are in place, they have a vested interest in continuing to be in place, and not in responding to changes. Although the coalition of interests that was articulated in order to pass the laws and take the other actions may have dissolved, there will be other coalitions both in the legislative process and in employment who now have an interest in things continuing. And the articulation of a new consensus in order to overthrow the law and dismantle the apparatus is much more difficult to achieve than the original initiative.

Furthermore, laws, administrative arrangements, and people in jobs, are all very human. Laws are simply written phrases given a special status. When a law against pornography and violence is passed, pornography and violence have to be defined, and the law has to explain why they are to be forbidden. So, for example, one of the classic definitions of obscenity, that it tends to deprave and corrupt, is simultaneously the reason why it is to be suppressed, namely because the society apparently does not wish its members to be depraved and corrupted. Nowadays the overtones of these words 'deprave' and 'corrupt' are almost exclusively sexual. It does not take too much histroical imagination, however, to recall a time when the depravity and corruption referred to might have nothing to do with sex but much more to do with religion, for example the depravity and corruption of one's soul thought by Protestants to be attendant on Papistry. Thus a law that said that written or pictorial materials that tended to deprave or corrupt should be prevented from circulating, could in a different context be used to suppress works advocating Roman Catholicism.

Again, however, the inertia of the system is such that even if flagrantly prejudicial steps of this kind are taken by the administrative apparatus and the people employed to run it, it is by no means a foregone conclusion that a coalition will articulate itself ready to change the law.

Law already makes certain acts crimes. One ludicrous aspect of this, is that things that regularly take place in the bedrooms of people, are crimes in certain jurisdictions, crimes that are usually simply never detected and the law never enforced. Consider the situation with representations of pornography and violence. Where the acts depicted are of a criminal character, the law as it exists already contains the power to prosecute those engaged in them, or abetting them on the grounds either that they are committing a criminal offense or that they are inciting its committal by their presentations. This, for example, completely takes care of the so-called child pornography and 'snuff' movies. Why would anyone want more police powers than those already given?

And so we come back to the original point. The research is, in a certain sense, beside the point because the research itself cannot make the bridge from showing an effect to telling us what to do about it. And the arguments about what we should do about it turn on quite different matters than the alleged effects of the original offense, but rather on our social scientific knowledge that censorship and its instruments always have unintended effects that are far worse than whatever it was set up to 'protect' us against (see note 2 and the text thereto).

18. CONCLUSION

Andrea Dworkin: 'we will know that we are free when the pornography no longer exists' (PMPW, p. 224), suggesting the non-sexist society of the future will lack pornography. We do not know the shape future society will take, especially if a radical social change such as the elimination of sexism occurs. Mishan offers a possible view: a Pornographic Society 'in which all existing restraints have vanished . . . there are no legal checks . . . Facilities for autoerotism . . . participating in any activity . . . Provided actors, audience and participants are willing, provided there is a market for the 'product', no objection is entertained' (p. 24). Without any argument, Mishan thinks this state of affairs would be grounds for alarm and something should be done to 'stem the tide' (that metaphor again). Women's liberationists and neo-conservatives converge on an irrational fear of a society in which no more fuss is made about sex than food.

Meanwhile, the strategy of attacking pornography strikes me as counter-productive for the movement against sexism. It divides the women's movement against itself, if divides the women's movement from those of its male supporters unconvinced that sexism and pornography are intrinsically connected, it makes common cause with groups opposed to the main planks of women's liberation. It plays fast and loose with social science. The issue is sexism, not pornography. A wiser strategy might be to concentrate on the struggle for a non-sexist society and let pornography find whatever place it will. That analysis of *Not a Love Story* and the thinkers it draws on has led us to this conclusion may be its best defence.

NOTES

[1] Sections of this paper were read at the Culture and Communication Conference, Philadelphia, March 26, 1983; to the Department of Sociology and Anthropology faculty/graduate seminar, University of Guelph, February 1st 1984; and to the International Communications Association Meetings, San Francisco, May 26, 1984, Honolulu May 26, 1985. My thanks to all who contributed comments on those occasions. A draft was widely circulated and I want to thank everyone who sent me criticisms. Whether they agreed or disagreed with me, I learnt from them all: Joseph Agassi, Judith Buber Agassi, Brian Baigrie, W. W. Bartley III, Allan Casebier, Murray S. Davis, Fred Eidlin, Michael Gilbert, Ruth Gilbert, Ron Gottesman, Karen Gottlieb, Leo Groarke, Florence Jacobowitz, Suzanne Jarvie, Stephen Kresge, Paul Levinson, Thelma McCormack, Iris Mor, Peter Morgan, Jay Newman, P. H. Nowell-Smith, Linda Ozin, Judith Posner, Brian Sanders, Robert Stoller, John P. Sullivan, Alex Szatmari, Sari Thomas.

2 As a result, Toronto cinemas have been unable to show very important movies such as *W. R.: Mysteries of the Organism* (Dusan Makavejev 1971), *In the Realm of the Senses* (Nagisa Oshima 1976) and *Taxi Zum Klo* (Frank Riploh 1981). Each autumn as the Toronto Film Festival rolls around, there is a cliff-hanger about which internationally acclaimed films the censors will disallow. In 1984, to facilitate discussion, a Festival of Banned Films was staged, complete with scholarly discussion. Predictably, four films the organizers wanted to include were disallowed.

3 Gloria Leonard is the publisher of the skin magazine *High Society*, and has directed and starred in several pornographic films.

4 Linda Lovelace is the stage name of the star of *Deep Throat*. She has published two (even three) autobiographies. Her first (*Inside Linda Lovelace*) talls how she loves sex and making pornographic movies. Her second (*Ordeal*) tells how she married a battering husband who forced her into prostitution and pornography, which she hated. Gloria Steinem (1980) believes *Ordeal*. I prefer the legal view that a witness confessing to lying throws *all* his testimony into question.

5 Molly Haskell, a feminist film critic (see her 1974) and her husband Andrew Sarris, who writes for the *Village Voice*, were among the jurors at the Sixth Annual Erotic Film Awards organised by the Adult Film Association of America. See *Los Angeles Times* July 10, 1982.

6 Al Goldstein is the founder and editor of the sex tabloid *Screw*.

7 Richard Gwyn is a columnist for the *Toronto Star*.

8 Two women, Linda Lovelace and Marilyn Chambers, were the first stars in big-screen pornography. The latter is still a star in 1984. The following women have also had long careers: Georgina Spelvin, Gloria Leonard, Carol Connors, Annette Haven and Jesie St. James. Aside from those who admit in interviews that they were hookers, several of the others were mannequins or dancers. Despite Slade's claim (1975, p. 132) that the men are interchangeable, a stable of male stars also has shown staying power. Lovelace's co-star in *Deep Throat*, Harry Reems returned to the screen in 1982. John Holmes' career was brought up short only by his imprisonment on burglary and contempt charges unrelated to pornography. After agreeing to testify to a Grand Jury he was released and soon re-appeared in Marilyn Chambers 1983 film *Up 'n Coming* (*Santa Monica Evening Outlook*, 23/11/82). Jamie Gillis, Eric Edwards, Paul Thomas, R. Bolla, Bobby Astyr and John Leslie all have distinct on-screen styles that have lasted them through the decade. To be emphasized are the escalating good looks of both sexes. To speak only of women, and of course subjectively, I would describe Marilyn Chambers. Annette Haven, Beth Anna, Veronica Hart and Loni Sanders as raving beauties. Although less visible, there is also a flourishing star system in the male homosexual pornographic film industry and one or two actors cross over from one system to the other. All my remarks above concerning stars of 'heterosexual' pornography apply mutatis mutandis to the homosexual sub-genre. Quotation marks just placed around 'heterosexual' will be explained when the narcissistic factor in sex is raised in Section 14, and note 63, below.

9 An example would be the following comments by the late Walter Kaufmann, professor of philosophy at Princeton University:

the opposite of creative use of leisure time: collapsing in front of a television set watching – or not even watching – whatever fare is offered.

This is the ultimate in uncreative passivity. The viewer is offered merely predigested pap, in a predetermined sequence, at a speed – or rather lack of speed – beyond his poor control, and his autonomy is reduced to switching channels (1973, p. 155).

10 *Variety*, which originally listed it on its box office tables, has quietly dropped it from its list of all time box office winners (May 12, 1982). Farley and Knoedelseder, two investigative reporters for the *Los Angeles Times*, confirm that it earned at least $30m and may have made as much as $100m. The initial investment was $22,000. Their explanation of how the film was distributed explains why exact figures are impossible to obtain. See their fascinating 1982a, b, c.

11 Carter's entire book, a chapter of PMPW, a section of FSS, numerous references in PAS are devoted to 'the divine Marquis'. Awkwardly for feminist solidarity both Simone de Beauvoir (1955) and Susan Sontag (1967) have found good things to say for him.

12 See Richard Gwyn, *Toronto Star*, 10.12.81. My interpretation of the film is that despite its makers' anti-censorship comments (off-screen), the film itself provides a set of arguments that can and will be used to shore up the repressive but eroded Canadian system of Provincial censorship. Canada now has a Constitution that guarantees freedom of speech. It remains to be seen whether the language can be used to loosen the censors' grip and substitute a purely advisory rating system as in the UK and USA.

13 See the parallel passage in PAS, top of p. 112.

14 This point is made by Patrick Lucas in NALS and by 'Jane Jones', TBTN, p. 63.

15 Clearly a response to this is possible: no-one denies many women in this culture accept their male-imposed role. Hence women in the pornography trade are highly suspect, possibly 'collaborators' (TBTN, p. 133) with 'sexual fascism' (TBTN, p. 127ff). Gloria Leonard, the publisher of *High Society*, Marilyn Chambers, who is the publisher of *Club*, and the film directors Carol Connors, Jennifer Welles, Svetlana, Gail Palmer and Annie Sprinkle are not to be dismissed so lightly. These are women doing well out of pandering to male fantasy. For that they deserve feminist kudos. That they may, as they so often assert, thoroughly enjoy what they are doing, can be treated with circumspection: since their avocation is to tell men what they want to hear, the pleas may be discountable. It is a regular feature of all fan magazine interviews that the actors and actresses heartily endorse what they are doing. But, then, what else would they tell the customers? It is not customary for prostitutes, for example, to tell their customers that they loathe 'the life'.

16 'On the face of it' because were this reasoning generally true, normal-sized, non-neurotic psychiatrists would be unable to treat anyone different from themselves.

17 'A woman who has *Playboy* in the house is like a Jew who has *Mein Kampf* on the table' Steinem quoted in TBTN, p. 122). At the very least both woman and Jew may have the items in the house on the principle of 'know your enemy'.

18 Gerard Damiano not being a household name, even amongst film scholars, a word is in order. A former hairdresser, he began by making loops (q.v.) and rose to prominence under the pseudonym Gerry Gerard as the director of *Deep Throat* 1972. Since then he has maintained a fairly steady output including: *The Devil in Miss Jones* (1973); *Memories Within Miss Aggie* (1973); *Portrait* (1974); *The Story of Joanne* (1975); *Joint Venture* (1978); *Waterpower* (1978); *All About Gloria Leonard* (1978); *Odyssey* (1979); *People* (1979); *Skinflicks* (1979); *Fantasy* (1979); *For Richer for Poorer* (1980); *The Satisfiers of Alpha Blue* (1981); *Beyond Your Wildest Dreams* (1982); *Consenting Adults*

(1982); *Never So Deep* (1982); *Whose Fantasy is it, Anyway?* (1983); *Throat – 12 Years After* (1984); Damiano has to be pornography's first *auteur*. Recurring themes in his work are bizarre sexual scenarios, careful cutting to music, erotic talk between his characters, plundering literature or other films for plots, and a curious tendency for his camera to wander into sex scenes already in progress and then, having shown us enough, to slide out again, sometimes before the usually mandatory 'come' shots. As the director of the most financially successful of all pornographic films he also pioneered the technique of building an impression of continuous sex scenes by cutting together close and long lens shots from 'impossible' viewpoints, as well as preserving good rapport between his players by filming with several simultaneous cameras. He is now often referred to as a veteran, and certainly has to look to his laurels with the likes of Henry Paris, Radley Metzger, Anthony Spinelli and Chuck Vincent on the scene.

19 Vincent's principal movies include: *Bon Appetit* (1980); *Fascination* (1981); *Games Women Play* (1981); *Roommates* (1982).

20 Spinnelli's principal hard-core movies include: *Seduction of Lynn Carter* (1979); *Take Off* (1978); *Easy* (1979); *Sex World* (1979); *Hot Line* (1980); *Talk Dirty to Me* (1980); *Vista Valley PTA* (1980); *High School Memories* (1981); *Skin on Skin* (1981); *Between The Sheets* (1982); *Nothing to Hide* (1982); *The Dancers* (1982).

21 There are accounts of the making of the film by the leading actress (Lovelace 1973, pp. 73–91, 1980, pp. 105–40), leading actor (Reems 1976, pp. 75–87), director (Damiano in Smith 1973) and others (Turan and Zito, p. 157–65).

22 I can find nothing in the film to warrant Griffin's assertion that the girl is virgin (PAS, p. 21).

23 *New York Times*, 27.2.76, p. 21; 7.3.76 by Richard Eder, Part 2, pp. 13, 24.

24 *New York Times*, 10.3.76, p. 41: 'Morgenthau Finds Film Disembowelling Was Indeed a Hoax'.

25 Schrader scripted the menacing *Taxi Driver* and wrote and directed *Blue Collar, American Gigolo, Cat People.*

26 This myth is copied (TBTN, p. 202) from Pamela Hansford Johnson's *On Inquity* (London 1967), p. 18 where no source whatsoever is given. Robin Morgan repeats it in NALS, Griffin in PAS, p. 194.

27 No source is given for this factoid (PAS, p. 249, PMPW, p. 10, 201 and NALS).

28 Heavily indebted to the writings of one Dr. Court of Flinders University in Australia. These are scrupulously dissected and found wanting in the Williams Report (1979) pp. 69–86.

29 A documentary on the evolution of male homosexual hard core movies, with some interesting early footage and a nice light touch is *Erotikus.*

30 This is no minor point. The feminist literature under discussion is weak in the technical anthropology of the position and power of women in societies around the world. One wonders, in particular, what they make of cases where women do assume male roles – as in ghost marriage or female kingship. One interpretation of these is that power distribution over male roles is incidental to the fact that they are filled by members of the male sex. Doubtless social anthropology could be dismissed as male-biased science, but if the formulation is this: 'studies of the effects of pornography, like other social science studies, so often confirm the presuppositions of the researcher. And so-called "raw data" can be cooked to different tastes' (Ann Jones, TBTN, p. 180) then all the pretensions to research of TBTN are swept away too.

[31] Gerbner's studies of television violence – 'cultural indicators' and 'cultivation analysis' and listed and severely criticised by Paul Hirsch 1980–81.

[32] Viz. *Inside Marilyn Chambers, Inside Jennifer Welles, Inside Desiree Cousteau, Inside Seka, Deep Inside Annie Sprinkle, All About Gloria Leonard, Serena.*

[33] Slade (1980) reports it as the 'leading deviation' (p. 129).

[34] For example, Holliday notes that the original *Candy Stripers* had a fisting scene that was cut (1980, p. 26); so had *Satisfiers of Alpha Blue*, which is nowhere to be seen in the film as exhibited. Also in the latter film and in *Deep Inside Annie Sprinkle*, that eponymous actress performed her specialty only to have it left on the cutting room floor 'for legal reasons'.

[35] Slade reports that violence and rape were rare, turning off most customers, and came bottom of a survey of audience preferences (1980, p. 129).

[36] In a letter defending TBTN against Carolyn See's adverse review (1980) in the *New York Times Book Review*, Elizabeth Dworan instances not pornography but *Dressed to Kill, When a Stranger Calls, Halloween, He Knows You're Alone, Friday the 13th*, and *Silent Scream*, all Hollywood movies (NYTBR, Jan. 25, 1981, p. 29).

[37] In *Inside Marilyn Chambers* the star of *Behind the Green Door* avers that it was a fantasy of hers.

[38] See Knight 1967, and Di Lauro and Roblin 1976.

[39] See Damiano interview in Smith 1973. Financial backing of the film has now been fully documented by Farley and Knoedelseder 1982a, b, c.

[40] A 1982 production, *Nothing to Hide*, cost $400,000. *Los Angles Times* 31.7.82.

[41] See her memorial article Jackson 1982.

[42] The extraordinary legal tactic was tried of Federal prosecution for conspiracy to engage in interstate traffic of obscene materials. See U.S. v Peraino CR 75–91 (W. D. Tenn. May 6, 1976) in Mayer 1977. Reems was acquitted on a technicality and not re-charged.

[43] See Slade 1975, Russell 1973.

[44] On Chambers see her autobiography 1975.

[45] Spelvin interview in Smith 1973.

[46] See Stevens 1975, Reems 1976, and James 1982.

[47] As is clear from the growing literature on the history of the genre.

[48] Linda Lovelace, *Ordeal*, New York.

[49] Bill Nichols, *Ideology and Image*, Bloomington 1981.

[50] Even rental or sale, provided it is for personal use, can obviously be covered by the individual's right to view in private what he or she sees fit. Where the vice squads still have some leeway is in interstate shipment of the cassettes and laws against sending obscene material through the mail. The latter is circumvented by the private parcel companies; the former would require the kind of surveillance that it not warranted by the importance of the trade. Hence it is relatively easy and inexpensive to buy on either coast materials made on the other coast. Unlike drug deals, the massive raids on tape warehouses made in Los Angeles two years ago did not drive up the price of cassettes.

[51] The claim that it is bigger than the motion picture and record industries combined (PMPW, p. 10 and 201 PAS, p. 249) reminds one of the times movies were claimed to be the thrid larges industry in the US (Huettig 1944, pp. 55). Such figures as are quoted usually come from the police, a source with an interest in inflating them.

52 If only men can rape, then this is trivially true, since all and only men are potential rapists.

53 She italicises the phrase 'the pressure is there' (TBTN, p. 136). If pressure, even gently persuasive pressure, is what makes for rape, then much sex does indeed become rape and women regularly rape men, on this stipulation. One wonders if the pressure of logic applied by the author of the present paper makes him by Morgan's lights a rapist of his reader.

54 Bat-Ada's pronouncements come in the course of a discussion of how breaking down taboos creates a situation advantagesous to the male hegemony. Violence, anal sex and child sex are her examples of taboo-breaking. Other taboos, cannibalism, miscegenation, sex-dirt and bisexuality are mostly avoided in mainstream pornographic features films. For this reason I regard them as muffling the subversive power of sex, and basically presenting a very middle of the road view of sexuality.

55 Of the major variations in sexual intercourse, the remaining ones are treated differently. Masturbation and cunnillingus are sacarely mentioned. I come to the former in Section 14. Fellatio, by contrast, is mentioned with distaste by several of the feminist writers under discussion, who also aver that they are not alone in their opinions. Ignoring the most obvious point (Gans 1973) that fellation is the easiest sexual act to film and that the customer may think ejaculation shows the sex act is not faked (but see my remarks at the end of Section 7), Russell quotes Eysenck and Nias:

Even when they do not overtly depict scenes of violence and degradation of women at the hands of man ... the tone is consistently anti-feminist [sic – a Freudian slip] with women only serving to act as sexual slaves to men, being made use of and ultimately being deprived of their right to a sexual climax – in the majority of such films, the portrayal ends with the men spraying their semen over the faces and breasts of the women (TBTN, p. 220).

Note the confusion between feminine and feminist, between pleasure and rights, between a woman having a climax and men having a climax, and between what happens on the screen and what happens in life. The sex acts on screen are largely constructed in the editing room (Section 7).

A more moderate feminist, Beatrice Faust, gives a more commonsense analysis:

Since ejaculating into blank space is not much fun, ejaculating over a person who responds with enjoyment sustains a lighthearted mood as well as a degree of realism. This occurs in both homosexual and heterosexual pornography, so that ejaculating cannot be interpreted as an expression of contempt for women only. Logically, if sex is natural and wholesome and semen is as healthy as sweat, there is no reason to interpret ejaculation as a hostile gesture. Healthy semen is not like feces, which may smell offensive, dirty the sheets, and carry germs. Some women and men enjoy the silky feel of fresh semen, some enjoy the smell and some find it excites the imagination (WSP) here.

56 In addition to commonsense I also draw on Faust (WSP) here.

57 She mentions 'the homosexual men who are in hospitals receiving treatment for acute or chronic problems related to anal intercourse' (TBTN, p. 129). This is anecdotage and does not display any facts or figures. Most such cases derive from the use of foreign objects or the fist.

58 For example, Offit 1981 takes a very different attitude. Compare Susan Griffin who

declares 'the entire humor of *Deep Throat* hinges on the observation that many women do not even take sexual pleasure in fellatio' (PAS, p. 61 fn). Whose 'observation' is that? As mentioned in Section 8, above, the heroine of the film declares that 'giving head' is her favourite sexual act. And what does 'many women do not even take sexual pleasure in' imply? Is women's sexual pleasure a context-free category? A solitary activity? Or does their pleasure, like all our pleasure, have an ingredient of pleasure that comes from pleasing the other? What else is mutuality? These may be analytically distinct but are they distinguishable at the level of affect or that of behaviour?

59 I notice a contradiction here between the definitions of the erotic in Section 7 as 'mutually pleasurable, sexual expression' and masturbation. Images of a person masturbating are a zero case of something being erotic (for some are erotic to some) without involving anyone else. Come to think of it, the same goes for cheesecake and beefcake, the most potent examples of which often project the idea that the subject is having erotic/pornographic *thought*.

60 Which may explain why so many of the feminist writers under discussion contemptuously dismiss the liberal view (PMPW, p. 10; TBTN index refs).

61 Other temples in this sense are gay steam baths, brothels (indistinguishable from temples in some ancient cultures), swingers clubs. How impoverished and sleazy is this list. But then what is being worshipped and profaned at the same time is a religious/romantic view of sex, with the bed or other site of sex as the domestic altar. As Thelma McCormack (1980) points out, people are always going to want to profane the sacred. These complements can hardly exist one without the other. See my comments on the complementarity of pornography and anti-pornography in Section 16.

62 As opposed to Dworkin quoting Pankhurst, 'Men have a simple remedy for this state of things. They can alter their way of life' (PMPW, p. 10).

63 Further to my remarks on stars in note 8 above. The narcissism and ambivalence in sex means that viewer identification with and projection onto the stars is complex. Its phenomenology does not fully unravel for me, but it seems clear that heterosexual and homosexual elements are there simultaneously. Since most of the movies are in the third person — that is, we viewers gaze at both the women and the men — all the sex acts permit us to project ourselves into both the donor and receiver positions. Thus one can read the loving attention these films devote to male members and secretions as allowing the male viewer to experience virility, but one must also realise that one is being placed in the position of recipient too.

64 Any attempt to dismiss this as male-biased anthropology will not go through. Anthropologists have defended women against the charge that in marriage they are bought and sold. See the extensive technical literature on bride-price.

65 But see the reversal in *All About Gloria Leonard* where she is the predatory boss.

66 *Los Angeles Times*, 13.6.80.

67 See Gay Talese, *Thy Neighbour's Wife*, New York 1980.

68 This taboo is so strong that when, in the nineteen thirties, Graham Greene suggested that Shirley Temple's appeal included an element of the coquettish he and his magazine were successfully sued for libel. Not so remarkable? Yes, but forty years later, when his film criticism was collected for a book, his piece on Shirley Temple still could not be printed. See Greene 1972, p. 2.

69 E.g., photographs in C. Lévi-Strauss' *Tristes Tropiques*, Paris 1955.

70 I acknowledge this thought and much impact on the paper elsewhere to a long conversation with Stephen Kresge.

[71] Highly recommended is Joan Mellen's (1980) amusing attempt to show that Wertmuller is 'the most profound of feminists' because of her Marxism. Freed from the class necessity to be selfish, Mellen argues, the heroine of *Swept Away* responds with excess, portraying 'the byways of a personal liberation that are accessible to men as well as women were they not to turn their backs on the suffering of their time' (Mellen, p. 105). The vulgar Marxism of Wertmuller (the upper classes are selfish), combined with the vulgar Marxism of Mellen (the selfishness is psychological and voluntaristic and by turning to face suffering we can end the 'strain' and experience 'relief') is a good example of how to make black (a sexist film) into white (a non-sexist film).

[72] This is not my imagination. A man, John Weightman (1982), and a woman, Carolyn See (1980), both detected it in their reviews. In a letter to the NYTBR the editor of TBTN, Lederer, distinguishes anger from hate and says her contributors have the first but not the second. She also says the anger is justifiable. One can only conclude from this either: (a) she has not read some of the material in her own book, which would be a charitable explanation of the atrocious editing; or (b) she doesn't know hate when she sees it. Readers of this paper have only to glance back at some of the quotations.

[73] Kaufmann 1973. Other forms of decidophobia are: adherence to a school of thought, religion, Manicheism, and moral rationalism. All are found in the writers under discussion. Such determined refusal of autonomy is in need of explanation.

[74] TBTN, p. 126n. Feminists were told this by a small bookstore owner. They apparently never heard of the possibility that interviewees will tell the interviewer what they think she wants to hear.

[75] A mysterious 13th volume, *Boys, Movies and City Streets* by Paul G. Cressey and Fredrick M. Thrasher is listed as part of the series but appears never to have been published. Inquiries to Macmillian publishers and the hiers of Cressey and Thrasher have turned up no trace of a MSS. It is thus surprising to find my own mistaken listing of it in my 1970) turning up in Brody (1977) and Eysenck and Nias (1978).

BIBLIOGRAPHY

Brief annotations are added to some of the more fugitive items.

Barber, D. F. 1972. *Pornography and Society*. London: Skilton.

Beauvoir, Simone de. 1955. *Faut-il Brûle de Sade?*. Paris: Gallimard.

Benjamin, Harry and Ellis, Albert. 1954. 'An Objective Examination of Prostitution', *International Journal of Sexology* V. 8 100–3.

Berelson, Bernard. 1948. 'Communications and Public Opinion', in W. Schramm (ed.), *Mass Communications*. Urbana, Ill.: University of Illinois Press.

Berger, Arthur Asa (ed.), 1980. *Film in Society*. New Brunswick: Transaction.

Bettelheim, Bruno. 1976. 'Reflections, Surviving'. *New Yorker*. Vol. 52, Aug. 2, pp. 31–52. On concentration camp survival, *Seven Beauties*. rape.

Brady, Jared and Montesano, Louis. 1982. 'Blow Away!?!'. *High Society*. Vol. 6, No. 10, March, pp. 24–7. Background article on the arrest of pornographic star John Holmes, detailing his career and life style.

Brody, Stephen. 1977. *Screen Violence and Film Censorship — A Review of Research*. Home Office Research Study No. 40 London: HMSO.

Cavell, Stanley. 1971. *The World Viewed*. New York: Viking.

Chambers, Marilyn. 1975. *Marilyn Chambers: My Story*. New York: Warner Bks.

Champlin, Charles. 1982. 'Porn: Not a Pretty Picture'. *Los Angeles Times*. 3.9.82, Part VI, pp. 1, 5. Review of NALS.

Check, James V. P. and Neil M. Malamuth. 1984. 'Can there be Positive Effects of Participation in Pornography Experiments?'. *The Journal of Sex Research* **20** 14–31.

Check, James V. P. and Neil M. Malamuth, Submitted. 'Pornography and Sexual Aggression: A Social Learning Theory Analysis'.

Check, James V. P. and Neil M. Malamuth, In press, 'An Empirical Assessment of Some Feminist Hypotheses About Rape', in P. Caplan, C. Larson, and L. Cammaert (eds.), *Sex Roles II: Feminist Psychology in Transition*, Montreal: Eden Press Women's Publications.

Cleland, John. 1974. *Memoirs of a Woman of Pleasure*. London.

Connor, Colette. 1982. 'Porno Stud Profile, John Leslie'. *Porn Stars*. Vol. 3, No. 6, Nov/Dec, pp. 48–52, 80–2.

Davis, Kingsley. 1937. 'The Sociology of Prostitution'. *American Sociological Review* **2** 744–55.

Davis, Murray S. 1983. *Smut*. Erotic Reality/Obscene Ideology, University of Chicago Press.

Dean, Malcolm. 1981. *Censored: Only in Canada*. Toronto: Virgo.

Di Lauro, Al and Roblin, Gerald. 1976. *Dirty Movies*. New York: Chelsea House.

Donnerstein, Edward. 1980. 'Aggressive Erotica and Violence Against Women'. *Journal of Personality and Social Psychology* **39** 269–77.

Donnerstein, Edward and Berkowitz, Leonard. 1981. 'Victim Reactions in Aggressive Erotic Films as a Factor in Violence Against Women'. *Journal of Personality and Social Psychology* **41** 710–24.

Drakeford, John W. and Hamm, Jack. 1973. *Pornography: The Sexual Mirage*. New York: Nelson.

Drama Review. 1981. special issue on 'Sex and Performance'. Vol. 25.

Ericson, Richard V. 1982. *Reproducing Order: A Study of Police Patrol Work*. Toronto: University of Toronto Press.

Evening Outlook. Santa Monica, 8.7.82. 'Porn Star Convicted on 1980 Charge'. p. A6.

Eysenck, H. J. and Nias, D. K. 1978. *Sex, Violence and The Media*. New York: Harper Colophon.

Farley, Ellen and Knoedelseder Jr., William. 1982*a*. 'Family Business: Episode One, The Pornbrokers'. *Los Angeles Times*. 13.6.82. Calendar Section, pp. 3–13.

Farley, Ellen and Knoedelseder Jr., William. 1982*b*. 'Family Business: Episode Two, The Hollywood Years'. *Los Angeles Times*. Calendar Section, 20.6.82, pp. 3–9.

Farley, Ellen and Knoedelseder Jr., William. 1982*c*. 'Episode 3: The Fall'. *Los Angeles Times*. 27.6.82, Calendar Section, pp. 3–8.

Farley, Ellen and Knoedelseder Jr., William. 1982*d*. 'The Real Texas Chain Saw Massacre'. *Los Angeles Times*. 5.9.82, Calendar Section, pp. 1, 3–7.

Farley, Ellen and Knoedelseder Jr., William. 1982*e*. 'A Tangled Web Clogs "Chain Saw"'. *Los Angeles Times*. 12.9.92, Calendar Section, pp. 3–5.

Feinberg, Joel. 1980. 'The Idea of the Obscene'. Lindley Lecture, University of Kansas.

Foddy, William H. 1981. 'Obscenity Reactions: Toward a Symbolic Interactionist Perspective'. *Journal for the Theory of Social Behaviour*. Vol. 11, No. 2, July, pp. 125–46.

Freely, Grace. 1980. 'Men of X'. *Playgirl*. Vol. VIII, No. 2, July, pp. 44–9, 112–5. On male stars Gillis, Leslie, Morris, Holmes, Thomas, Jeremy, Morrison. Includes Interivew with Morrison and Morris.

Gans, Herbert. 1973. 'Deep Throat: The Pornographic Film Goes Public'. *Social Policy*. Vol. 4, No. 1, July–Aug., pp. 119–21.

Gordon, George N. 1980. *Erotic Communications, Studies in Sex, Sin and Censorship*. New York: Hastings Hourse.

Grant, Lee. 1979. 'Red-Carpet Treatment for "Girls"'. *Los Angeles Times*. 7.11.79, Part IV, p. 22. Reports Gala premiere of *The Ecstasy Girls* at Pussycat Theatre in Hollywood.

Grant, Lee. 1980. 'Awards Given for Best Erotic Films'. *Los Angeles Times*. 12.7.80.

Grant, Lee. 1982. 'Weston: X Still Marks His Spot'. *Los Angeles Times*. 31.7.82, Part V, pp. 1, 6. About Sam Weston, aka Anthony Spinelli, Armand Weston, a director of the Hollywood film *One Potato, Two Potato* in 1964, now as established director of pornography (see note 20 to text): 'the image of sleazy people, creeps and backalley types is not accurate'.

Greene, Graham. 1972. *The Pleasure Dome*. London, Secker.

Gwyn, Richard. 1982. 'Film on Pornography an Agonized Cry for Censorship'. *Toronto Star*. 10.12.81, p. A10.

Hart Veronica. 1981. Interview. *Video X*. July, Vol. 2, No. 5, pp. 50–1.

Haskell, Molly. 1974. *From Reverence to Rape*. New York: Holt, Rinehart and Winston.

Haven, Annette. 1982. Interview. *Adult Video Plus*. Vol. 1, No. 1, pp. 3–4.

Henson, Donald E. and Rubin, H. B. 1971. 'Voluntary Control of Eroticism'. *Journal of Applied Behavior Analyis* 4 37–44.

Henson, Donald E., Henson, Claudia, and Williams, Jessie R. 1977. 'Temperature Change of the Labia Minora as an Objective Measure of Female Eroticism'. *Journal of Behavior Therapy and Experimental Psychology* 8 401–410.

Henson, Donald E. 1978. 'A Comparison of Two Objective Measures of Sexual Arousal of Women'. *Behavior Research and Therapy* 16 143–51.

Henson, Donald E., and Henson, Claudia. 1978. 'Consistency of the Labial Temperature Change Measure of Human Female Eroticism'. *Behavior Research and Therapy* 16 125–9.

Henson, Donald E., and Henson, Claudia. 1979. 'Analysis of the Consistency of Objective Measures of Sexual Arousal in Women'. *Journal of Applied Behavior Analysis* 12 701–11.

High, R. W., Rubin, H. B., and Henson, Donald. 1979. 'Color as a Variable in Making an Erotic Film More Arousing'. *Archives of Sexual Behavior* 8 263–7.

Hoffman, Jan. 1982. 'The Bride Wore Clothes'. *Village Voice*. Dec. 30- Jan 5, pp. 11, 23. On the marriage of porn star Marc Stevens (cf. NALS).

Holliday, Jim. 1980. *How to Build Your X-Rated Film Library*. Beverly Hills: Skull Mountain.

Holliday, Jim. 1982. *The Top 100 X-Rated Films of All Time*. Hollywood: WWV Inc.

Holliday, Jim. 1982. Review of *Deep Inside Annie Sprinkle*, in *Adult Video Plus*. Vol. 1, No. 1, p. 8.

Hovland, C. J., Lumsdaine, A. A., and Sheffield, F. D. 1949. *Experiments on Mass Communication*. Princeton University Press.

Huettig, Mae D. 1944. *Economic Control of the Motion Picture Industry*. Philadelphia: University of Pennsylvania Press.

Hughes, Douglas (ed.). 1970. *Perspectives on Pornography*. New York: St. Martin's.

Jackson, Norman. 1982. 'Farewell to Tina Russell, First Lady of Porn'. *Starlet*, Vol. 3, No. 1, J/F, pp. 75–9.

Jaehne, Karen. 1983. 'Confessions of a Feminist Porn Programmer'. *Film Quarterly* XXXVII, Fall. 9–16.

James, Kevin. 1982. 'Stuntcock, Interview'. *Velvet*. Vol. 5, No. 10, June, pp. 56–9, 70, 76. Got into the business because Mike Ranger lived next door.

Jarvie, I. C. 1970. *Towards a Sociology of the Cinema*. London: Routledge and Kegan Paul.

Jarvie, I. C. 1977. *Window on Hong Kong*: A Sociological Study of the Hong Kong Film Industry and its Audience, Hong Kong: Centre of Asian Studies, University of Hong Kong.

Jarvie, I. C. 1978. *Movies as Social Criticism*, Metuchen, N. J.: Scarecrow Press.

Jarvie, I. C. and Agassi, J. 1967. 'The Problem of the Rationality of Magic'. *British Journal of Sociology* 18 55–74.

Johnson, Pamela Hansford. 1967. *On Iniquity*. London: Secker and Warburg.

Jowett, Garth. 1976. *Film: The Democratic Art*. Boston: Altantic Little Brown.

Kaufmann, Walter. 1973. *Without Guilt and Justice*. New York: McKay.

Klapper, Joseph. 1960. *The Effects of Mass Communication*. Glencoe, Ill.: The Free Press.

Knight, Arthur. 1967. 'The Stag Films'. *Playboy*. Vol. 14, November, pp. 154ff.

Kruk, Laurie. 1982. 'McCormack Displeased with Pornography Film'. *Excalibur*. April 8.

Lane, Penney. 1982. 'Censorship: Canada'. *Porn Stars*. March/April, Vol. 3, No. 2, pp. 76, 69.

Laws, D. R. and Pawlowski, A. V.. 1973. 'A Multi-Purpose Biofeedback Device for Penile Plethysmography'. *Journal of Behavior Therapy and Experimental Psychiatry* 4 339–41.

Lederer, Laura. 1981. Letter to the *New York Times Book Review*. January 25, p. 29.

Lesage, Julia. 1981. 'Women and Pornography'. *Jump Cut*. No. 26, pp. 46–7, 60.

Los Angeles Times. 13.6.80. ' "Birth of a Nation" Dies After Attack'. by Philip Heyer, Part I, pp. 3, 17. Three days after left-wingers vandalized Richelieu Cinema in SF film was withdrawn.

Los Angeles Times. 25.8.81. 'X Rated Movies Less Violent Study Shows'.

Los Angeles Times. 4.8.82. 'Text Review's Significance Shows in Revisions'. Part I, pp. 3, 26–7.

Los Angeles Times. 26.6.82. 'Porno Film Star Holmes Acquitted in Four Canyon Murders'. Part II, pp. 1, 8.

Los Angeles Times. 10.7.82. 'Spices of Life at the Erotic Film Awards'. Part V, pp. 1, 5.

Lovelace, Linda. 1973. *Inside Linda Lovelace*, Los Angeles: Pinnacle.

Lovelace, Linda. 1974. *The Intimate Diary of Linda Lovelace*. Los Angeles: Pinnacle.

Lovelace, Linda. 1980. *Ordeal* (with Mike McGrady). New York: Citadel.

Malamuth, Neil M. and Check, James V. 1980a. Penile Tumesence and Perceptual Responses to Rape as a Function of Victims Perceived Reaction'. *Journal of Applied Social Psychology* 10 528–47.

Malamuth, Neil M. and Check, James V. 1980b 'Sexual Arousal to Rape and Consenting Depictions: The Importance of Woman's Arousal'. *Journal of Abnormal Psychology* 89 763–66.

Malamuth, Neil M. and Check, James V. 1981a 'The Effects of Mass Media Exposure to Acceptance of Violence Against Women. A Field Experiment'. *Journal of Research in Personality* 15 436–46.

Malamuth, Neil M. and Check, James V. 1981b. 'The Effects of Exposure to Aggressive Pornography: Rape Proclivity, Sexual Arousal and Beliefs in Rape Myths'. 89th Annual Meeting, American Psychological Association, Los Angeles.

Malamuth, Neil M. and Check, James V. 1982. 'Factors Related to Aggression Against Women'. Annual Meeting, Canadian Psychological Association, Montreal.

Malamuth, Neil M., Haber, S., and Feshbach, S. 1980. 'Testing Hypotheses Regarding Rape: Exposure to Sexual Violence, Sexual Differences, and the "Normality" of Rapists'. *Journal of Research in Personality* 14 121–37.

McCormack, Thelma. 1978. 'Machismo in Media Research'. *Social Problems* 25 544–55.
McCormack, Thelma. 1980*a*. 'Feminism, Censorship, and Sadomasochistic Pornography'. *Studies in Communication* 1 37–61.
McCormack, Thelma. 1980*b*, Review of PMPW and PAS. *Fireweed*. Issue 11, 97–9.
McCormack, Thelma. 1982. 'McCormack Displeased with Pornography Film'. *Excalibur*. 8.4.82. Interview about NALS.
MacDonald, Scott. 1983. Confessions of a Feminist Porn Watcher'. *Film Quarterly* **XXXVI**, Spring, 10–17.
Marchetti, Gale. 1982. 'Readings on Women and Pornography, An Annotated Bibliography'. *Jump Cut*. No. 26, pp. 56–60.
May, Lary. 1980. *Screening Out the Past*. New York: Oxford.
Mayer, M. F. 1977. 'New Approach to Obscenity: The Conspiracy Doctrine'. *St. Louis University Law Journal* 21 366–73.
Mellen, Joan. 1980. 'On Lina Wertmuller'. in Berger 1980, pp. 99–108.
Mishan, E. J. 1972. 'Making the World Safe for Pornography'. *Encounter*. Vol. XXXVIII, No. 3, March, pp. 9–30.
Munsterberg, Hugo. 1916. *The Photoplay: A Psychological Study*. New York: D. Appleton and Co.
New York Times. 27.2.76. 'Commentary: Cretin's Delight on Film'. by John Leonard, p. 21. Report on a visit to *Snuff* with liberal guinea pigs who it turned out, were protesting a film they had not seen.
New York Times. 7.3.76. 'Snuff is Pure Poison', by Richard Eder, Part 2, pp. 13, 24. Repeats Leonard's points.
New York Times. 10.3.76. 'Morgenthau Finds Film Disembowelling Was Indeed a Hoax'. p. 41. Manhattan District Attorney Robert M. Morgenthau confirms NYT story of special effects, actress in final scene alive and well and interviewed by police. Original was Argentine film *Slaughter*, with added scenes.
New York Times. 7.3.82. 'Feminist Group Pickets Meeting on "Adult" Films'. p. 22.
New York University Review of Law and Social Change. 1978–9. Colloquium, Violent Pornography: Degradation of Women versus Right of Free Speech, special issue, Vol. 8, No. 2.
Newsweek. 1973. 'The "Throat" Case'. January 15, p. 30.
Offit, Avodah K. 1981. *Night Thoughts, Reflections of a Sex Therapist*. New York: Congdan and Lettes.
O'Neill, John. 1972. *Sociology as a Skin Trade*. London.
Peckham, Morse, 1969. *Art and Pornography, An Experiment in Explanation*. New York: Basic.
Petty, Rhonda Jo. 1982. Interview. *High Society*. April, Vol. 6, No. 11, pp. 18–23, 88. At p. 23 she indicates she was a good-time girl but 'I never thought of myself as a prostitute'.
Pornography. The Longford Report. 1972, London: Coronet Books.
Reems, Harry. 1976. *Here Comes Harry Reems*, Los Angeles: Pinnacle.
Rich, B. Ruby. 1982. 'Anti-Porn: Soft Issue, Hard World'. *Village Voice*. 20.7.82, pp. 16–18, 30. Highly critical review of NALS.
Rist, Ray C. (ed.). 1975. *The Pornography Controversy*, Changing Moral Standards in American Life, New Brunswick: Transaction Bks.
Rollin, Roger B. 1982. 'Triple X: Erotic Movies and their Audiences; *Journal of Popular Film and Television* 10 2–21.

Rubin, Gayle. 1984. 'Thinking Sex: Notes for a Radical Theory of the Politics of Sexuality'. in Carole S. Vance (ed.). *Pleasure and Danger: Exploring Female Sexuality*, London: Routledge.
Rubin, H. B. and Henson, Donald E. 1975. 'Voluntary Enhancement of Penile Erection'. *Bulletin of the Psychonomic Society* 6 158–60.
Rubin, H. B., Richard, E., and High, R. W. 1979. 'The Relationship Between Men's Endogenous Levels of Testosterone and their Penile Responses to Erotic Stimuli'. *Behaviour Research and Therapy* 17 305–12.
Russell, Tina. 1973. *Porno Star*. Houston: Lancer. See Jackson 1982.
See, Carolyn. 1974. *Blue Money*. New York: McKay.
See, Carolyn. 1980. 'Angry Women and Brutal Men'. *New York Times Book Review*. 28.12.80, pp. 4, 14, 15. Review of TBTN and WSP.
Signs. 1984. Special issues on 'The Feminist Sexuality Debates'. Vol. 10, Fall.
Slade, Joseph P. 1975. 'Pornographic Theatres off Times Square'. in Rist (ed.), pp. 119–39.
Slade, Joseph P. 1977. 'The Porn Market and Porn Formulas: The Feature Films of the Seventies'. *Journal of Popular Film*. Vol. VI, No. 2, pp. 168–86.
Slade, Joseph P. 1980. 'Recent Trends in Porn Films'. in Berger (ed.). 1980, pp. 121–35.
Smith, Richard. 1973. *Getting Into Deep Throat*. Chicago: Playboy Press.
Smith, Kent. 1982. 'Director of the Year: Anthony Spinelli'. *Adam Film World Annual Guide to X rated Movies and Video*. Vol. 1, No. 4, May, pp. 30–4.
Sontag, Susan. 1967. 'The Pornographic Imagination', in her *Styles of Radical Will*. New York: Delta, pp. 36–73.
Steinem, Gloria, 1980. 'Linda Lovelace's "Ordeal"'. *Ms*. May, pp. 72–6.
Stevens, Marc. 1975. *Ten and One Half!*. New York: Zebra.
Symons, Julian. 1976. 'New York's Hard Corps'. *Times Literary Supplement*. April 9, No. 3865, p. 428.
Time. 1973. 'Wonder Woman'. January 15, p. 34.
Toronto Star. 15.5.82. 'Curb, Dont Extend Censorship'. editorial.
Toronto Star. 14.11.81. 'Police Find Hands Tied Fighting Boom in "Video Porn"'. p. A1, A6.
Toronto Star. 19.11.81. 'Pornogate Tickles Their Fancy in Quebec'. p. A11.
Turan, Kenneth and Zito, Stephen F. 1974. *Sinema: American Pornographic Films and the People Who Make Them*. New York: Praeger.
Variety. 1982. 'All-Time Rental Champs (of US-Canadian Market). 12.5.82. pp. 59ff.
Varney, Ginger, 1982. 'Pornography Vs. the Feminist Religion'. *Los Angeles Weekly*. Sept. 3–9, pp. 16, 21. Review of NALS.
Video X. 1981. 'Video's Virginal Vixen'. Vol. 2, No. 5, July, pp. 37–41. Excellent on-the-set pictures of a porn shoot centred around an actress of legal age who looks like a Lolita.
Weightman, John. 1982. 'The Abominable He'. *Times Literary Supplement*, Jan 1st, No. 4109, pp. 5–6. Review of PAS and PMPW.
Williams, Bernard. 1979. *Report of the Committee on Obscenity and Film Censorship*. London: HMSO.
Zurcher, Jr., Louis A. and Kirkpatrick, R. George. 1976. *Citizens for Decency, Antipornography Crusades as Status Defence*. Austin: U. of Texas Press.

SOURCES

I am grateful to the editors and publishers who have given permission for the reprint of the papers in this volume. The original places of publication are as follows:

Chapter One in H. K. Betz (ed.), *Recent Approaches to the Social Sciences*, University of Calgary Press, 1979, pp. 76–88; Chapter Two, *Journal for the Theory of Social Behaviour*, Volume 11, Number 3, October 1981, pp. 223–240; Chapter Three in R. S. Cohen and M. W. Wartofsky (eds.), *'Epistemology, Methodology, and the Social Sciences*, Dordrecht: Reidel, 1983, pp. 107–21; Chapter Four, *British Journal of Sociology*, Volume 34, Number 1, March 1983, pp. 44–60; Chapter Five in Paul Levinson (ed.), *In Pursuit of Truth*, Atlantic Highlands, N. J.: Humanities Press, 1982, pp. 83–107; Chapter Six, *The Philosophical Forum*, Fall 1968, pp. 73–84; Chapter Seven, *Philosophy of Science*, Volume 34, September 1967, pp. 223–242; Chapter Eight, *Annals of the American Academy of Political and Social Science*, Monograph 5, Functionalism in the Social Sciences (ed.), D. Martindale, Philadelphia, February 1965, pp. 18–34; Chapter Nine in R. J. Seeger and R. S. Cohen (eds.), *Philosophical Foundations of Science, Boston Studies in the Philosophy of Science*, Volume XI, Dordrecht: Reidel 1974, pp. 317–24; Chapter Ten, *Current Anthropology*, Volume 10, Number 5, December 1969, pp. 505–8; Chapter Eleven, P. D. Asquith and P. Kitcher (eds.), *PSA 1984*, Volume 2, East Lansing, MI: Philosophy of Science Association, 1985, pp. 000–000; Chapter Twelve, *American Anthropologist*, Volume 77, Number 2, June 1975, pp. 253–66; Chapter Thirteen, *Current Anthropology*, Volume 17, Number 4, December 1976, pp. 687–91; Chapter Fourteen, *Current Anthropology*, Volume 24, Number 2, June 1983, pp. 313–25; Chapter Fifteen (in German) in Hans Peter Duerr (ed.), *Der Wissenschaftler und das Irrationale*, Volume 1, Frankfurt: Syndikat 1981, pp. 213–44; Chapter Sixteen, *Canberra Anthropology*, Volume 6, Number 1, 1983, pp. 80–85; Chapter Seventeen, *Ratio*, Volume 9, June 1967, pp. 67–83; Chapter Eighteen in Denis Dutton and Michael Krausz (eds.), *The Concept of Creativity in Science and Art*, The Hague: Martinus Nijhoff 1981, pp. 109–28; Chapter Nineteen was the banquet lecture to the annual conference of educators in technology, delivered at, and printed by, the Division of Industrial Engineering and Technology, State University College, Oswego, NY, 1967; Chapter Twenty, *Technology and Culture*, Volume 7, July 1966, pp. 384–90; Chapter Twenty-One, *The Listener*, Volume 77, March 9, 1967, pp. 322–23 and 333; Chapter Twenty-Two in Stanford Anderson (ed.), *Planning for Diversity and Choice*, Cambridge: MIT Press, 1968, pp. 8–31; Chapter Twenty-Three, *Canadian Journal of Sociology*, Volume 1, Number 4, 1976, pp. 515–28; Chapters Twenty-Four and Twenty-Five not previously published.

LIST OF PUBLICATIONS

1958a   'Pictorial Erotica: An Analysis', *Clare Market Review*, Michaelmas 1958/Lent 1959, Vol. LIV, pp. 19–22.

1958b   'In Memoriam Wittgensteinii', (review of N. Malcolm, *Wittgenstein, A Memoir*), *Clare Market Review*, Michaelmas 1958/Lent 1959, Vol. LIV, pp. 42–3.

1959   'Notes on the Films of Ingmar Bergman', *Film Journal* (Melbourne), No. 14, November, pp. 9–17. (See 1961d and 1963d).

1960a   'One Man, One Vote', *Crossbow*, New Year, pp. 34–8 and 49. Reprinted in Vol. 55, *Clare Market Review*, Spring, pp. 14–19.

1960b   'Ginsberg and Ethics', *Enquiry* (Nottingham), Vol. 2, June, pp. 19–27.

1960c   'Professor Passmore on the Objectivity of History', *Philosophy*, Vol. 35, October, pp. 355–6.

1960d   'Preface to Film Criticism', *Film*, No. 25, Sept.–Oct., pp. 13–14.

1960e   'Beat, Square and Cool', *Film*, No. 25, Sept.–Oct., pp. 15–17.

1961a   'Sociology and the Film Critics', *Film Journal*, No. 17, April, pp. 101–2.

1961b   'An Old Problem Still Unresolved' (review of A. Munn, *Free Will and Determinism*), *New Scientist*, Vol. 10, May, pp. 269–70.

1961c   Towards as Objective Film Criticism', *Film Quarterly*, Vol. 14, Spring, pp. 19–23.

1961d   'Notas Sobre los Films de Ingmar Bergman', *Film Ideal* (Madrid), No. 68, Spring, pp. 18–25 (Spanish translation of 1959).

1961e   'Love Death and Destruction: Antonioni and L'Avventura', *Motion* (London), Summer, pp. 7–10.

1961f   'Nadel on the Aims and Methods of Social Anthropology', *British Journal for the Philosophy of Science*, Vol. 12, No. 1, May, pp. 1–24.

1961g   Review of Peter Winch, *The Idea of a Social Science*, in *British Journal for the Philosophy of Science*, Vol. 12, No. 1 May, pp. 73–77.

1961h   Review of Quentin Gibson, *The Logic of Social Enquiry*, in *British Journal for the Philosophy of Science*, Vol. 12, No. 1, May, pp. 77–79.

1961i   'Hysteria and Authoritarianism in the Films of Robert Aldrich', *Film Culture*, No. 22–23, Summer, pp. 95–111.

1961j   'Comeback', *Film*, No. 28, March–April, p. 18.

1961k   'Short Rant', *Film*, No. 29, Summer, p. 9.

1961l   'Fanny', *Film*, No. 30, Winter, p. 15.

1963a   Review of D. F. Pocock, *Social Anthropology*, in *British Journal for the Philosophy of Science*, Vol. 13, No. 4, February, pp. 327–29.

1963b   'Production in Hong Kong', *Film Journal*, No. 21, April, p. 112.

1963c   'Theories of Cargo Cults: A Critical Analysis, Parts I and II', *Oceania*, Vol. 34, September, December, pp. 1–31 and 108–36.

1963d   'Recent Films of Ingmar Bergman', *Film Journal*, No. 22, October, pp. 14–18.

1964a   'Hong Kong Notes', *Sight and Sound*, Vol. 33, Winter, p. 32.

1964*b*   'The Celluloid Revolution', *The Bulletin* (Sydney), February, pp. 41–2.

1964*c*   'Key Problems of Sociological Theory', (Review of John Rex, *Key Problems of Sociological Theory*), in *British Journal for the Philosophy of Science*, Vol. 14, No. 4, February, pp. 352–55.

1964*d*   *The Revolution in Anthropology*, London: Routledge; New York: Humanities. Reprinted in 1967; paperback Henry Regnery, Chicago 1969, pp. xxii + 256.

1964*e*   'Second Hong Kong Dialogue', *Crossbow*, Vol. 7, April, pp. 47–50.

1964*f*   'Explanation in Social Science' (article-review of Robert Brown, *Explanation in Social Science*), in *British Journal for the Philosophy of Science*, Vol. 15, No. 1, May, pp. 62–72.

1964*g*   'Face and Facade in Hong Kong', *New Society*, Vol. 3, No. 91 June, pp. 13–15.

1964*h*   Review of Helmut Schoek and J. Wiggins, eds., *Scientism and the Study of Man*, and *Relativism and Values*, in *British Journal for the Philosophy of Science*, Vol. 15, No. 2, August, pp. 151–8.

1964*i*   Review of J. Passmore, *Philosophical Argument*, in *British Journal for the Philosophy of Science*, Vol. 15, No. 3, November, pp. 264–66.

1964*j*   Review of I. L. Horowitz, *Philosophy, Science and the Sociology of Knowledge*, in *British Journal for the Philosophy of Science*, Vol. 15, No. 3, November, pp. 266–68. (see 1965*c*).

1964*k*   'Hurray for Cinema', *Film*, No. 41, pp. 16–17, 19, 20, 25, 27, 28, 29.

1965*a*   'Limits to Functionalism and Alternatives to it in Anthropology', *Annals of the American Academy of Political and Social Science*, Monograph 5, *Functionalism in the Social Sciences*, ed., D. Martindale, Philadelphia, February, pp. 17–34. Reprinted in R. O. Masters and D. Kaplan (eds.), *Theory in Anthropology: A Source Book*, Chicago: Aldine, 1968, pp. 196–203.

1965*b*   'Far East: Backing the Americans', *Crossbow*, April–June, pp. 37–8.

1965*c*   'Reply to Professor Horowitz', *British Journal for the Philosophy of Science*, Vol. 16, No. 3, November, pp. 241–2.

1965*d*   'In Praise of Romantic Comedy', *Film*, No. 42, pp. 39–41.

1966*a*   'The Language of the Screen' (Review of R. Schickel, *The Movies*) in *The Bulletin*, March.

1966*b*   'Academic Fashions and Grandfather-killing: In Defense of Frazer', *Encounter*, Vol. 26, April, pp. 53–55. Reprinted in *Current Anthropology*, Vol. 7, December 1966, pp. 568–9.

1966*c*   'The Social Character of Technological Problems', *Technology and Culture*, Vol. 7, July, pp. 384–90; reprinted in Carl Mitcham and Robert Mackey (eds.), *Philosophy and Technology*, New York: Free Press, 1972, pp. 50–53; also in F. Rapp, ed., *Contributions to a Philosophy of Technology: Studies in the Syructure of Thinking in the Technological Sciences* (Theory and Decision Library 5), Dordrecht: D. Reidel, 1974, pp. 86–92.

1966*d*   'On the Explanation of Cargo Cults', *Archives Européennes de Sociologie*, Vol. 7, No. 2, pp. 299–312.

1966*e*   'Onibaba', *Film*, No. 47, Winter, pp. 22–3.

1967*a*   'Is Technology Unnatural?', *The Listener*, Vol. 77, March 9th, pp. 322–23 and 333.

1967*b*   (with Joseph Agassi) 'The Problem of the Rationality of Magic', *British Journal of Sociology*, Vol. 18, March, pp. 55–74; reprinted in B. Wilson (ed.), *Rationality*, Oxford: Basil Blackwell 1970, pp. 172–193, (See 1978*d*.)

1967c   Review of W. Goldschmidt, *Comparative Functionalism: An Essay in Anthro-pological Theory*, in *Man* (N.S.), Vol. 2, March, p. 139.

1967d   *The Revolution in Anthropology*, reprinted with a new appendix, London: Routledge; New York: Humanities.

1967e   'The Objectivity of Criticism of the Arts', *Ratio* (English), Vol. 9, June, pp. 67–83.

1967f   'Die Objektivitat der Kunst Kritik', *Ratio* (German), Vol. 9, June, pp. 63–78 (German translation of 1967e).

1967g   'Technology and the Structure of Knowledge', the banquet lecture to the annual conference of educators in technology, delivered at, and printed by, the Division of Industrial Engineering and Technology, State University College, Oswego, New York. Reprinted in Carl Mitcham and Robert Mackey, *Philosophy and Technology*, New York: Free Press, 1972, pp. 54–61.

1967h   'On the Theory of Fieldwork and the Scientific Character of Social Anthro-pology', *Philosophy of Science*, Vol. 34, September, pp. 223–242.

1967i   Review of R. Rudner, *Philosophy of Social Science*, in *American Anthropologist*, Vol. 69, December, pp. 782–3.

1968a   'Utopian Thinking and the Architect' in Stanford Anderson (ed.), *Planning for Diversity and Choice*, Cambridge: MIT Press, pp. 8–31, discussion pp. 31–41.

1968b   'The Emergence of Social Anthropology from Philosophy', (article-review of J. Burrow, *Evolution and Society*), *The Philosophical Forum*, Fall, pp. 73–84.

1969a   (with Joseph Agassi) 'A Study in Westernization', in 1969c, pp. 129–163.

1969b   'A Postscript on Riots and the Future of Hong Kong', in 1969c, pp. 361–69.

1969c   *Hong Kong: A Society in Transition*, edited with an Introduction, London: Routledge; New York: Praeger. Pp. xxix + 378.

1969d   Review of C. W. Churchman, *The Systems Approach in Science*, Vol. 163, March 21st, p. 1315.

1969e   'Media and Manners', *Film Quarterly*, Vol. 22, Spring, pp. 11–17.

1969f   'On the Relevance of the Philosophy of the Social Sciences', (Review symposium on M. Brodbeck, *Readings in the Philosophy of the Social Sciences*, with Percy Cohen and Alasdair MacIntyre), *British Journal of Sociology*, Vol. 20, June, pp. 220–3.

1969g   'The Problem of Ethical Integrity in Participant Observation', *Current Anthro-pology*, Vol. 10, No. 5, December 1969, pp. 505–8 (See 1971c, 1973b, 1982b.)

1969h   'Evans-Pritchard on the Anthropology of Religion', *International Journal of Comparative Sociology*, Vol. X, Nos. 3–4, pp. 286–91.

1969i   Review of Bertrand Russell, *Autobiography 1914–1944, Clare Market Review*, Vol. 65, Nos. 1 and 2, pp. 30–33.

1969j   'Film and the Communication of Values', *Archives Européennes de Sociologie*, Vol. X. No. 2, pp. 205–19; reprinted as an appendix to 1970c and f.

1969-   (ed.), 'Myths and Mass Media', papers by Jarvie (1969j), Thelma McCormack,
1970a   Michael Burrage, A. J. Brobeck, Eliska Freiova, Paul Filmer, Judith Agassi, Roger Pincott, over two issue of *European Journal of Sociology* (*Archives Européennes de Sociologie*), Vols. X–XI, Nos. 2 and 1.

1970b   'Cargo Cults', in *Man, Myth and Magic* (part-Encyclopedia), British Publishing Corporation, London, No. 15, pp. 409–12.

1970c   *Towards a Sociology of the Cinema*, London: Routledge and Kegan Paul. Pp. xix + 394. (See 1970f, 1974f, 1974h, 1977f.)

1970*d* 'On Explaining Cargo Cults' and 'The Problem of the Rationality of Magic' (with J. Agassi), in Bryan Wilson (ed.), *Key Concepts in the Social Sciences: Rationality*, Oxford: Basil Blackwell, pp. 50–61 and 172–93. (Reprint of part of chapter 4 of 1964*d* and of all of 1967*b*).

1970*e* 'Understanding the Explanation in Sociology and Social Anthropology', and 'Reply', (to Peter Winch) in Robert Borger and Frank Cioffi (eds.), *Explanation in the Behavioural Sciences*, Cambridge, Cambridge University Press, pp. 231–45 and 260–9. Reprinted in Fred R. Dallmayr and Thomas A. McCarthy (eds.), *Understanding and Social Inquiry*, Notre Dame: University of Notre Dame Press, 1977, pp. 189–206. (See 1978*c*.)

1970*f* *Movies and Society*, New York: Basic Books. Pp. xix + 394. (American edition of 1970*c*).

1971*a* (with J. Agassi and T. Settle) 'The Grounds of Reason', *Philosophy*, Vol. XLVI, January, pp. 43–50.

1971*b* Review of Richard Hughes, *Hong Kong – Borrowed Place, Borrowed Time*, in *Journal of Asian and African Studies*, Vol. VI, No. 1, January, pp. 56–7.

1971*c* 'Reply to Fabian', *Current Anthropology*, Vol. 12, No. 2, April, pp. 231–2.

1971*d* 'McLuhan, System-Study, and Technological Determinism', *Philosophy of the Social Sciences*, Vol. 1, No. 3, September, pp. 245–51.

1972*a* *The Story of Social Anthropology*, New York: McGraw-Hill, pp. xii + 131.

1972*b* *Concepts and Society*, London: Routledge and Kegan Paul, pp. xxi + 214. (See 1974*e*.)

1972*c* Review of W. G. Runciman, *Sociology in Its Place*, in *Philosophy of the Social Sciences*, Vol. 2, No. 3, September, pp. 271–4.

1972*d* 'The Social Character of Technological Problems' and 'Technology and the Structure of Knowledge' in Carl Mitcham and Robert Mackey (eds.), *Philosophy and Technology*, Readings in the Philosophical Problems of Technology, New York: Free Press, pp. 50–61. (Reprint of 1966*c* and 1967*g*).

1972*e* 'Cargo Cults' in *Encyclopedia of Papua and New Guinea*, Melbourne University Press, Vol. I, pp. 133–7.

1973*a* *Functionalism*, Minneapolis: Burgess. Pp. 39.

1973*b* 'More on Positivism and Professional Ethics – Reply', *Current Anthropology*, Vol. 14, No. 3, June, pp. 321–2.

1973*c* 'America's Sociological Movies', *Arts in Society*, Vol. 10, No. 2, Summer-Fall, pp. 171–80.

1973*d* Review of S. Andreski, *Social Sciences as Sorcery*, in *British Journal for the Philosophy of Science*, Vol. 24, No. 2, June, pp. 193–9.

1973*e* Review of K. Hopkins (ed.), *Hong Kong: The Industrial Colony*, in *Sociology*, Vol. 7, No. 2, May, pp. 300–2.

1973*f* (with J. Agassi), Preface to and editing of, *Cause and Meaning in the Social Sciences* by E. Gellner, London and Boston: Routledge. Pp. xi + 228.

1973*g* Review of R. Nisbet (ed.), *Social Change*, in *Social Science Quarterly*, Vol. 54 No. 3, December, pp. 669.

1973*h* (with J. Agassi) 'Magic and Rationality Again', *British Journal of Sociology*, Vol. 24, No. 2, June, pp. 236–45.

1973*i* 'American Movies About Marriage', *Journal of Popular Film*, Vol. 2, Summer, pp. 278–299.

1973*j*   'Comment on Blok', *Human Organization*, Vol. 32, No. 1, pp. 95–107.

1974*a*   (with J. Agassi), Preface to and editing of, *Contemporary Thought and Politics*
          by E. Gellner, London and Boston: Routledge. Pp. xi + 207.

1974*b*   'Foreword' to P. M. Yap, *Comparative Psychiatry*, a theoretical framework.
          Toronto: University of Toronto Press, pp. xiii–xv.

1974*c*   (with T. Settle and J. Agassi), 'Towards a Theory of Openness to Criticism',
          Philosophy of the Social Sciences, Vol. 4, No. 1, March, pp. 83–90.

1974*d*   'On the Objectivity of Anthropology', in R. J. Seeger and R. S. Cohen (eds.),
          *Philosophical Foundations of Science, Boston Studies in the Philosophy of
          Science*, Vol. XI), Dordrecht: D. Reidel, pp. 317–24.

1974*e*   *Die Logik der Gesellschaft*, München: Paul List Verlag. Pp. 314. (German
          translation by Wilhelm Höck of 1972*b*).

1974*f*   *Film und Gesellschaft*, Stuttgart: Ferdinand Enke Verlag. Pp. xv + 362. (German
          translation by Modeste zur Nedden Pferdekamp of 1970*c*).

1974*g*   Review of W. W. Bartley III, *Wittgenstein*, in *British Journal for the Philosophy
          of Science*, Vol. 25, No. 2, June, pp. 195–8.

1974*h*   (with J. Agassi), preface to and editing of *The Devil in Modern Philosophy* by
          E. Gellner, London and Boston: Routledge. Pp. x + 262.

1974*i*   Review of Adam Kuper, *Anthropologists and Anthropology*, in *Philosophy of
          the Social Sciences*, Vol. 4, Nos. 2–3, June–September, pp. 302–5.

1974*j*   'Recent Books on Chinese Films' (Review of Jay Leyda, *Dianying*, Alex Ben
          Block, *The Legend of Bruce Lee*, Wolfram Eberhard, *The Chinese Silver Screen*),
          in *Journal of Popular Film*, Vol. 3, No. 4, Fall, pp. 351–55.

1974*k*   *Sociologia del Cine* (Spanish translation of 1970*c* by Joaquin Fernandez),
          Madrid: Ediciones Guadarrama. Pp. 351.

1975*a*   Review of S. Toulmin, *Human Understanding*, Vol. I, in *Philosophy of the
          Social Sciences*, Vol. 5, No. 1, March, pp. 91–4.

1975*b*   Review of Frank Cunningham, *Objectivity in Social Science*, in *Contemporary
          Sociology*, Vol. 4, No. 2, March, pp. 97–8.

1975*c*   Review of Andrew Tudor, *Image and Influence*, Studies in the Sociology of
          Film, in *Time Higher Education Supplement*, April 11, No. 182, p. 21.

1975*d*   'Epistle to the Anthropologists', *American Anthropologist*, Vol. 77, No. 2, June,
          253–66. (see 1976*c*).

1975*e*   Review of F. Henriques, *Miscegenation*, in *West Indies Chronicle*, Vol. 90, No.
          1527, May/June, pp. 63–5.

1975*f*   Review of Verina Glaessner, *Kung Fu. Cinema of Vengeance* and Linda Lee,
          Bruce Lee: The Man Only I Knew, in *Journal of Popular Film*, Vol. 4, No. 3,
          pp. 270–1.

1975*g*   'Cultural Relativism Again', *Philosophy of the Social Sciences*, Vol. 5, No. 3,
          September, pp. 343–53.

1976*a*   'Comment on Prattis', *Current Anthropology*, Vol. 17, No. 1, March 1976,
          pp. 101–2.

1976*b*   'Comment on Berger', *Current Anthropology*, Vol. 17, No. 2, June, p. 297.

1976*c*   'Reply to Fabian', *American Anthropologist*, Vol. 78, June, p. 345.

1976*d*   Review of Garth Jowett, *Film: The Democratic Art*, in *Journal of Popular
          Film*, Vol. 5, No. 1, pp. 76–8.

1976*e*   'Toulmin and the Rationality of Science', in R. S. Cohen, P. K. Feyerabend and M. W. Wartofsky (eds.), *Essays in Memory of Imre Lakatos*, Dordrecht: Reidel, pp. 311–333.

1976*f* 'On the Limits of Symbolic Interpretation in Anthropology', *Current Anthropology*, Vol. 17, No. 4, December, pp. 687–91, and 700–1.

1976*g* 'Comment on Rosengren', *Current Anthropology*, Vol. 17, No. 4, December, pp. 677–8.

1976*h* 'Nationalism and the Social Sciences', *Canadian Journal of Sociology*, Vol. 1, No. 4, 515–28.

1977*a* 'Understanding and Explaining in Sociology and Social Anthropology', in Fred R. Dallmayr and Thomas A. McCarthy (eds.), *Understanding and Social Inquiry*, University of Notre Dame Press, pp. 189–206 (Cf. 1970*e*).

1977*b* *Window on Hong Kong*: A Sociological Study of the Hong Kong Film Industry and Its Audience, Hong Kong: Centre of Asian Studies, pp. 223.

1977*c* 'Comment on Dutton', *Current Anthropology*, Vol. 18, No. 3, September, pp. 398–9.

1977*d* 'More on Symbolic Interpretation', *Current Anthropology*, Vol. 18, No. 3, September, pp. 546–7.

1977*e* 'The Present Structure of Capitalist Production', in John Tulloch, ed., *Conflict and Control in the Cinema*, Macmillan (Australia), pp. 177–94. (Extract from 1970*c*.)

1977*f* *Una Sociologia del Cinema*, Milan: Franco Angeli Editare, pp. 306 (Italian translation by Vito Messana of 1970*c*).

1978*a* Review of *Nanook of the North, American Anthropologist*, Vol. 80, No. 1, March, pp. 196–7.

1978*b* *Movies as Social Criticism*. Aspects of their Social Psychology. Metuchen, N. J.: Scarecrow Press. Pp. 225.

1978*c* 'Verstehen und Erklären in Soziologie and Sozialanthropologie', in Karl Acham (ed.), *Methodologische Probleme der Sozialwissenschaften*, Darmstadt: Wissenschaftliche Buchgesellschaft, pp. 224–252. (German translation by Wolfram K. Koch of 1970*e*.)

1978*d* (with J. Agassi), 'Das Problem der Rationalität von Magie', in Hans G. Kippenberg and Brigitte Luchesi (eds.), *Magie, Die Sozialwissenschaftliche Kontroverse über das Verstehen fremden Denkens*, Frankfurt: Suhrkamp, 1978, pp. 120–49 (German translation of 1967*b*).

1978*e* 'Seeing Through Movies', *Philosophy of the Social Sciences*, Vol. 8, 1978, No. 4, December, pp. 374–97.

1979*a* Review of *The Explanation of Social Behaviour* by G. Studdert-Kennedy and *Social Theory as Science* by R. Keat and J. Urry, *British Journal for the Philosophy of Science*, Vol. 30, No. 1, March, 100–4.

1979*b* (with J. Agassi), 'The Rationality of Dogmatism', in Th. Geraets, ed., *Rationality Today*, Ottawa University Press, pp. 353–62.

1979*c* Review of Martin Hollis, *Models of Man, Canadian Journal of Sociology*, Vol. 4, No. 3, Summer, 325–8.

1979*d* Review of *Cantonese Cinema Retrospective* (1950–1959), *Journal of Popular Film and Television*, Vol. VII, No. 3, 326–9.

1979*e* 'The Social and Cultural Significance of the Decline of the Cantonese Movie', *Journal of Asian Affairs* (SUNY Buffalo), Vol. III, No. 2, Fall, 40–50.

1979f 'Laudan's Problematic Progress and the Social Sciences', *Philosophy of the Social Sciences*, Vol. 9, No. 4, December, 484–97.

1979g edited (with J. Agassi), *Spectacles and Predicaments*, Essays on Social Theory, by Ernest Gellner, with a preface by the edtors, Cambridge University Press. Pp. 385.

1980a Comment on Eichinger Ferro-Luzzi, *Current Anthropology*, Vol. 21, No. 1, February, p. 56.

1980b 'The Notion of a Social Science', in H. K. Betz (ed.), *Recent Approaches to the Social Sciences*, University of Calgary Press, pp. 76–88, 93–5.

1980c 'The City and the Camera', in Nelson Wiseman (ed.), *The City and the Camera*, Urban Studies Programme, York University, Toronto, pp. 39–41.

1980d Comment on Guthrie, *Current Anthropology*, Vol. 21, No. 2, April, pp. 196–7.

1980e (with J. Agassi), 'The Rationality of Irrationalism', *Metaphilosophy*, Vol. 11, No. 2, April, pp. 127–33.

1980f 'On the History of Science' (review of Thomas Kuhn, *The Essential Tension* and Gerald Holton, *The Scientific Imagination*), *Queen's Quarterly*, Vol. 87, No. 1, Spring, pp. 65–8.

1980g 'Commentary, Can There Be Absolute Values?' in *The Responsibility of the Academic Community in the Search for Absolute Values*, Proceedings of the Eighth International Conference on the Unity of the Sciences, New York: ICF Press, Vol. I, pp. 61–5.

1980h Review of Philip Pettit and Christopher Hookway (eds.), *Action and Interpretation, British Journal for the Philosophy of Science*, Vol. 31, No. 4, December, pp. 396–401.

1980i Review of S. Benn and G. Mortimore, *Rationality in the Social Sciences, International Studies in Philosophy*, Vol. XII, No. 1, pp. 99–101.

1980j Foreword to David Anthony Daly, *A Comparison of Exhibition and Distribution Patterns in Three Recent Motion Pictures*, New York: Arno Press.

1981a 'Multi-Volume History of the American Movies Project Meeting – Carbondale, Illinois, 16–20 November, 1980', *IAMHIST Newsletter*; No. 10, Winter 1980–1, pp. 15–18.

1981b Edited and indexed *Muslim Society*, by Ernest Gellner, Cambridge University Press. Pp. x + 264.

1981c 'Fanning the Flames: Anti-Americanism and *Objective Burma*', *Historical Journal of Film, Radio and Television*, Vol. 1, No. 2, October, 117–37.

1981d 'Die Anthropologen und das Irrationale', in Hans Peter Duerr, (ed.), *Der Wissenschaftler und das Irrationale*, Vol. 1, Frankfurt: Syndikat, pp. 213–44.

1981e 'Social Perception and Social Change', *Journal for the Theory of Social Behaviour*, Vol. 11, No. 3, October, pp. 223–240.

1981f 'The Rationality of Creativity', in Denis Dutton and Michael Krausz (eds.), *The Concept of Creativity in Science and Art*, The Hague: Martinus Nijhoff, pp. 109–28.

1981g Articles on Karl Barth, William Beveridge, Noam Chomsky, Ronald Fisher, F. A. Hayek, J. M. Keynes, C. Levi-Strauss, Bertrand Russell, J-P Sartre, S. and B. Webb, Max Weber and L. Wittgenstein, in Lord Bullock (ed.), *Makers of the Twentieth Century*, London, Weidenfeld.

1982*a* 'Cinema Histories, Cinema Practices at Asilomar', IAMHIST *Newsletter*, No. 12, Winter 1981/82, pp. 14–18.

1982*b* 'The Problem of Ethical Integrity in Participant Observation', in Robert G. Burgess (ed.), *Field Research: A Sourcebook and Field Manual*, London: George Allen and Unwin, pp. 68–72. (Reprint of 1969*g*.)

1982*c* Review of Tino Balio, *United Artists*, IAMHIST *Newsletter*, No. 13, Summer, pp. 45–7.

1982*d* Review of Hilary Putnam, *Meaning and the Moral Sciences, Metaphilosophy*, Vol. 13, No. 2, April, pp. 161–4.

1982*e* Review of David Thomas, *Naturalism and Social Science, American Anthropologist*, Vol, 84, No. 2, June, pp. 418–9.

1982*f* 'The Social Experience of Movies', in Sari Thomas (ed.), *Film/Culture*, Metuchen, N. J.: Scarecrow, July, pp. 247–68.

1982*g* Review of *A Study of the Hong Kong Swordplay Film, Journal of Popular Film and Television*, Vol. 10, No. 2, Summer, pp. 89–90.

1982*h* 'Popper on the Difference Between the Natural and the Social Sciences', in Paul Levinson (ed.), *In Pursuit of Truth*, Atlantic Highlands, N. J.: Humanities, November, pp. 83–107.

1982*i* Comment on Winckelman, 'Magic: A Reassessment', *Current Anthropology*, Vol. 23, pp. 48–9.

1983*a* 'Realism and the Alleged Poverty of Sociological Theory', in R. S. Cohen and M. W. Wartofsky (eds.), *Epistemology, Methodology, and the Social Sciences*, Dordrecht: Reidel, pp. 107–21.

1983*b* Review of L. Wittgenstein, *Remarks on Frazer's* Golden Bough, *Philosophy of the Social Sciences*, Vol. 13, No. 1, pp. 117–18.

1983*c* 'Rationality and Relativism', *British Journal of Sociology*, Vol. 34, No. 1, March, pp. 44–60.

1983*d* Review of J. Krige, *Science, Revolution and Discontinuity, Canadian Philosophical Reviews*, Vol. III, 132–6.

1983*e* 'The Problem of the Ethnographic Real', with Comments and Reply, *Current Anthropology*, Vol. 24, No. 2, June, pp. 313–25.

1983*f* 'International Film Trade: Hollywood and the British Market, 1945', *Historical Journal of Film, Radio and Television*, Vol. 3, No. 2, October, pp. 161–69.

1983*g* *Movies and Society*. Reprint of 1970*c* by Garland Publishing Co.

1983*h* Review of Mark Blaug, *The Methodology of Economics, British Journal for the Philosophy of Science*, Vol. 34, No. 3, September, pp. 289–95.

1984*a* Review of D. B. Jones, *Movies and Memoranda, Historical Journal of Film, Radio and Television*, Vol. 4, No. 1, March, pp. 105–6.

1984*b* 'Freeman on Mead', *Canberra Anthropology, 6*, No. 1, pp. 80–85 (dated 1983, published 1984).

1984*c* *Rationality and Relativism*, In Search of a Philosophy and History of Anthropology, London: Routledge and Kegan Paul, May. Pp. 157.

1984*d* Reply to Paddoch *et al.*, *Current Anthropology*, Vol. 25, June, pp. 356.

1984*e* 'A Plague on Both Your Houses', in J. R. Brown (ed.), *Scientific Rationality: The Sociological Turn*, Dordrecht: Reidel, pp. 165–82.

1984*f* Review of Arnold Hauser, *The Sociology of Art, Historical Journal of Film, Radio and Television*, Vol. 4, No. 2, October, pp. 229–30.

1984g   Review of Bernard Williams, *Obscenity and Film Censorship, Quarterly Review of Film Studies*, Vol. 9, No. 2, Spring, 156–7.
1984h   'Handlungstheorie in der Sicht der Anthropologie und Ethnographie', in Hans Lenk (ed.), *Handlungstheorien interdisziplinär III*, Vol. II, Munich: Wilhelm Fink Verlag, pp. 980–1002.

NAME INDEX

n indicates that a reference is in a note; q a quotation; and t that a term is explained.

Adam 24
Adorno, T. W. 76, 255n
Agassi, Joseph 15, 16, 33, 49n, 67n,
  68n, 86, 91n, 92n, 93n, 107, 125,
  150n, 160n, 181n, 183, 194n, 195,
  199, 207, 209, 210n, 211, 224, 230n,
  231, 272n, 300n, 312n, 316n, 319,
  352n, 365n, 366n, 463n
Agassi, Judith Buber 463n
Alexander, H. G. 273n
Allen, Woody 386
Alloway, Lawrence 300n
Allvine, Glendon 388n
Altman, Robert 386
Anderson, Juliet 410
Andersson, Bibi 440
Andreski, S. 92n
Anonymous 184, 195
Arbuckle, Roscoe ('Fatty') 379
Archibald, G. C. 48n
Arendt, Hannah 460
Aristotle 6, 51, 67n, 95, 293
Aron, Raymond 35, 48n, 97
Asch, Timothy 213, 227
Asimov, Isaac 345 345n
Astaire, Fred 382
Astyr, Bobby 464n
Atkinson, G. A 345n
Attlee, Clement 89
Attwood, Margaret 396, 397, 435
Agustine, St. 6
Austin, J. L 88
Ayer, Sir Alfred 256n, 367n

Bach, C. P. E. 274, 277
Bach, Johann Sebastian 265, 269, 270,
  271, 274, 275, 277, 300n
Bacon, Francis 286, 300n
Bacon, Sir Francis 6, 16, 24, 35, 58,
  68n, 76, 117, 195, 204, 257, 268,
  353, 362

Baigrie, Brian 463n
Barnes, Barry 16, 94n
Barnes, Harry Elmer 96
Barnes, J. A. 160n, 161
Barnett, James H. 213, 231
Baron, Martin 92n
Barry, Kathleen 397, 399q, 401–2
Bart, Pauline 458q, 459
Barth, Frederick 61, 68n
Bartley, III, W. W. 77, 80, 86, 92n, 94n,
  121n, 125, 165, 265, 319n, 366n,
  463n
Bat-Ada, Judith 399q, 412, 428, 436–
  37, 468n
Bateson, Gregory 214, 231
Beattie, J. H. M. 93n, 113q, 116, 117n,
  118n, 125, 194n
Beatty, Warren 441
Becker, Howard 96, 356
Beethoven, Ludwig van 275
Bellarmino, Cardinal 307, 308
Benda, Julian 352, 367n
Bendixson, Terence 334n
Benedict, Ruth 160n, 161, 259
Benjamin, Harry 419
Bentham, Jeremy 98
Berelson, Bernard 49n, 457q
Berger, Peter 34, 46, 188, 195
Bergman, Ingmar 288, 441
Bergman, Ingrid 407
Berkeley, Busby 229
Berkeley, Bishop George 218, 219,
  247, 272n, 286, 293, 307, 308
Berkowitz, Leonard 457
Berkson, William 209, 211
Bernal, J. D. 365n
Bernanos, Georges 270
Bertrand, Daniel 368q, 388n, 389
Beth Anna, 464n
Betz, H. K. 93n

487

SUBJECT INDEX

n indicates that a reference is in a note; q a quotation; and t that a term is explained.

TITLE INDEX

511

BOSTON STUDIES IN THE PHILOSOPHY OF SCIENCE

Editors:
ROBERT S. COHEN and MARX W. WARTOFSKY
(Boston University)

1. Marx W. Wartofsky (ed.), *Proceedings of the Boston Colloquium for the Philosophy of Science 1961-1962.* 1963.
2. Robert S. Cohen and Marx W. Wartofsky (eds.), *In Honor of Philipp Frank.* 1965.
3. Robert S. Cohen and Marx W. Wartofsky (eds.), *Proceedings of the Boston Colloquium for the Philosophy of Science 1964-1966. In Memory of Norwood Russell Hanson.* 1967.
4. Robert S. Cohen and Marx W. Wartofsky (eds.), *Proceedings of the Boston Colloquium for the Philosophy of Science 1966-1968.* 1969.
5. Robert S. Cohen and Marx W. Wartofsky (eds.), *Proceedings of the Boston Colloquium for the Philosophy of Science 1966-1968.* 1969.
6. Robert S. Cohen and Raymond J. Seeger (eds.), *Ernst Mach: Physicist and Philosopher.* 1970.
7. Milic Capek, *Bergson and Modern Physics.* 1971.
8. Roger C. Buck and Robert S. Cohen (eds.), *PSA 1970. In Memory of Rudolf Carnap.* 1971.
9. A. A. Zinov'ev, *Foundations of the Logical Theory of Scientific Knowledge (Complex Logic).* (Revised and enlarged English edition with an appendix by G. A. Smirnov, E. A. Sidorenka, A. M. Fedina, and L. A. Bobrova.) 1973.
10. Ladislav Tondl, *Scientific Procedures.* 1973.
11. R. J. Seeger and Robert S. Cohen (eds.), *Philosophical Foundations of Science.* 1974.
12. Adolf Grünbaum, *Philosophical Problems of Space and Time.* (Second, enlarged edition.) 1973.
13. Robert S. Cohen and Marx W. Wartofsky (eds.), *Logical and Epistemological Studies in Contemporary Physics.* 1973.
14. Robert S. Cohen and Marx W. Wartofsky (eds.), *Methodological and Historical Essays in the Natural and Social Sciences. Proceedings of the Boston Colloquium for the Philosophy of Science 1969-1972.* 1974.
15. Robert S. Cohen, J. J. Stachel and Marx W. Wartofsky (eds.), *For Dirk Struik. Scientific, Historical and Political Essays in Honor of Dirk Struik.* 1974.
16. Norman Geschwind, *Selected Papers on Language and the Brain.* 1974.
17. B. G. Kuznetsov, *Reason and Being: Studies in Classical Rationalism and Non-Classical Science.* (forthcoming).
18. Peter Mittelstaedt, *Philosophical Problems of Modern Physics.* 1976.
19. Henry Mehlberg, *Time, Causality, and the Quantum Theory* (2 vols.). 1980.
20. Kenneth F. Schaffner and Robert S. Cohen (eds.), *Proceedings of the 1972 Biennial Meeting, Philosophy of Science Association.* 1974.
21. R. S. Cohen and J. J. Stachel (eds.), *Selected Papers of Léon Rosenfeld.* 1978.
22. Milic Capek (ed.), *The Concepts of Space and Time. Their Structure and Their Development.* 1976.

23. Marjorie Grene, *The Understanding of Nature. Essays in the Philosophy of Biology.* 1974.
24. Don Ihde, *Technics and Praxis. A Philosophy of Technology.* 1978.
25. Jaakko Hintikka and Unto Remes, *The Method of Analysis. Its Geometrical Origin and Its General Significance.* 1974.
26. John Emery Murdoch and Edith Dudley Sylla, *The Cultural Context of Medieval Learning.* 1975.
27. Marjorie Grene and Everett Mendelsohn (eds.), *Topics in the Philosophy of Biology.* 1976.
28. Joseph Agassi, *Science in Flux.* 1975.
29. Jerzy J. Wiatr (ed.), *Polish Essays in the Methodology of the Social Sciences.* 1979.
30. Peter Janich, *Protophysics of Time.* 1985.
31. Robert S. Cohen and Marx W. Wartofsky (eds.), *Language, Logic, and Method.* 1983.
32. R. S. Cohen, C. A. Hooker, A. C. Michalos, and J. W. van Evra (eds.), *PSA 1974: Proceedings of the 1974 Biennial Meeting of the Philosophy of Science Association.* 1976.
33. Gerald Holton and William Blanpied (eds.), *Science and Its Public: The Changing Relationship.* 1976.
34. Mirko D. Grmek (ed.), *On Scientific Discovery.* 1980.
35. Stefan Amsterdamski, *Between Experience and Metaphysics. Philosophical Problems of the Evolution of Science.* 1975.
36. Mihailo Marković and Gajo Petrović (eds.), *Praxis. Yugoslav Essays in the Philosophy and Methodology of the Social Sciences.* 1979.
37. Hermann von Helmholtz, *Epistemological Writings. The Paul Hertz/Moritz Schlick Centenary Edition of 1921 with Notes and Commentary by the Editors.* (Newly translated by Malcolm F. Lowe. Edited, with an Introduction and Bibliography, by Robert S. Cohen and Yehuda Elkana.) 1977.
38. R. M. Martin, *Pragmatics, Truth, and Language.* 1979.
39. R. S. Cohen, P. K. Feyerabend, and M. W. Wartofsky (eds.), *Essays in Memory of Imre Lakatos.* 1976.
42. Humberto R. Maturana and Francisco J. Varela, *Autopoiesis and Cognition. The Realization of the Living.* 1980.
43. A. Kasher (ed.), *Language in Focus: Foundations, Methods and Systems. Essays Dedicated to Yehoshua Bar-Hillel.* 1976.
44. Trân Duc Thao, *Investigations into the Origin of Language and Consciousness.* (Translated by Daniel J. Herman and Robert L. Armstrong; edited by Carolyn R. Fawcett and Robert S. Cohen.) 1984.
46. Peter L. Kapitza, *Experiment, Theory, Practice.* 1980.
47. Maria L. Dalla Chiara (ed.), *Italian Studies in the Philosophy of Science.* 1980.
48. Marx W. Wartofsky, *Models: Representation and the Scientific Understanding.* 1979.
49. Trân Duc Thao, *Phenomenology and Dialectical Materialism.* 1985.
50. Yehuda Fried and Joseph Agassi, *Paranoia: A Study in Diagnosis.* 1976.
51. Kurt H. Wolff, *Surrender and Catch: Experience and Inquiry Today.* 1976.
52. Karel Kosík, *Dialectics of the Concrete.* 1976.
53. Nelson Goodman, *The Structure of Appearance.* (Third edition.) 1977.

54. Herbert A. Simon, *Models of Discovery and Other Topics in the Methods of Science.* 1977.
55. Morris Lazerowitz, *The Language of Philosophy. Freud and Wittgenstein.* 1977.
56. Thomas Nickles (ed.), *Scientific Discovery, Logic, and Rationality.* 1980.
57. Joseph Margolis, *Persons and Minds. The Prospects of Nonreductive Materialism.* 1977.
59. Gerard Radnitzky and Gunnar Andersson (eds.), *The Structure and Development of Science.* 1979.
60. Thomas Nickles (ed.), *Scientific Discovery: Case Studies.* 1980.
61. Maurice A. Finocchiaro, *Galileo and the Art of Reasoning.* 1980.
62. William A. Wallace, *Prelude to Galileo.* 1981.
63. Friedrich Rapp, *Analytical Philosophy of Technology.* 1981.
64. Robert S. Cohen and Marx W. Wartofsky (eds.), *Hegel and the Sciences.* 1984.
65. Joseph Agassi, *Science and Society.* 1981.
66. Ladislav Tondl, *Problems of Semantics.* 1981.
67. Joseph Agassi and Robert S. Cohen (eds.), *Scientific Philosophy Today.* 1982.
68. Władysław Krajewski (ed.), *Polish Essays in the Philosophy of the Natural Sciences.* 1982.
69. James H. Fetzer, *Scientific Knowledge.* 1981.
70. Stephen Grossberg, *Studies of Mind and Brain.* 1982.
71. Robert S. Cohen and Marx W. Wartofsky (eds.), *Epistemology, Methodology, and the Social Sciences.* 1983.
72. Karel Berka, *Measurement.* 1983.
73. G. L. Pandit, *The Structure and Growth of Scientific Knowledge.* 1983.
74. A. A. Zinov'ev, *Logical Physics.* 1983.
75. Gilles-Gaston Granger, *Formal Thought and the Sciences of Man.* 1983.
76. R. S. Cohen and L. Laudan (eds.), *Physics, Philosophy and Psychoanalysis.* 1983.
77. G. Böhme et al., *Finalization in Science*, ed. by W. Schäfer. 1983.
78. D. Shapere, *Reason and the Search for Knowledge.* 1983.
79. G. Andersson, *Rationality in Science and Politics.* 1984.
80. P. T. Durbin and F. Rapp, *Philosophy and Technology.* 1984.
81. M. Marković, *Dialectical Theory of Meaning.* 1984.
82. R. S. Cohen and M. W. Wartofsky, *Physical Sciences and History of Physics.* 1984.
83. E. Meyerson, *The Relativistic Deduction.* 1985.
84. R. S. Cohen and M. W. Wartofsky, *Methodology, Metaphysics and the History of Sciences.* 1984.
85. György Tamás, *The Logic of Categories.* 1985.
86. Sergio L. de C. Fernandes, *Foundations of Objective Knowledge.* 1985.
87. Robert S. Cohen and Thomas Schnelle (eds.), *Cognition and Fact.* 1985.
88. Gideon Freudenthal, *Atom and Individual in the Age of Newton.* 1985.
89. A. Donagan, A. N. Perovich, Jr., and M. V. Wedin (eds.), *Human Nature and Natural Knowledge.* 1985.
90. C. Mitcham and A. Huning (eds.), *Philosophy and Technology II.* 1986.
91. M. Grene and D. Nails (eds.), *Spinoza and the Sciences.* 1986.
92. S. P. Turner, *The Search for a Methodology of Social Science.* 1986.
93. I. C. Jarvie, *Thinking About Society: Theory and Practice.* 1986.